J. B. PRIESTLEY

# Vincent Brome's Previous Books

*Biography*

H. G. Wells
Freud and His Early Circle
The Way Back
Havelock Ellis
Ernest Jones – Freud's Alter Ego
Frank Harris
Aneurin Bevan
Six Studies in Quarrelling
Confessions of a Writer

*History*

The International Brigades

*Essays*

We Have Come a Long Way
The Problem of Progress

*Novels*

The Last Surrender
Sometimes at Night
Acquaintance With Grief
The Revolution
The Surgeon
The World of Luke Simpson
The Embassy
The Brain Operators
The Happy Hostage
The Day of the Fifth Moon
London Consequences

# J. B. PRIESTLEY

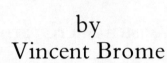

by
Vincent Brome

HAMISH HAMILTON
London

## HAMISH HAMILTON LTD

Published by the Penguin Group
27 Wrights Lane, London W8 5TZ, England
Viking Penguin Inc, 40 West 23rd Street, New York, New York 10010, U.S.A.
Penguin Books Australia Ltd, Ringwood, Victoria, Australia
Penguin Books Canada Ltd, 2801 John Street, Markham, Ontario,
Canada L3R 1B4
Penguin Books (N.Z.) Ltd, 182–190 Wairau Road, Auckland 10, New Zealand

Penguin Books Ltd, Registered Offices: Harmondsworth, Middlesex, England

First published in Great Britain 1988 by
Hamish Hamilton Ltd

British Library Cataloguing in Publication Data

Brome, Vincent
J.B. Priestley.
1. Fiction in English. Priestley, J.B. –
Biographies
I. Title
823'.912

ISBN 0–241–12560–X

Typeset in 11/12pt Bembo by Wyvern Typesetting Ltd, Bristol
Printed in Great Britain by Butler & Tanner Ltd, Frome and London

# Contents

# List of Illustrations

TO ANGELA
WHO MADE IT POSSIBLE

# Acknowledgements

I wish to acknowledge with thanks permission by Wm Heinemann to reproduce copyright material from *Midnight on the Desert, Rain upon Godshill, Margin Released, The Good Companions, Angel Pavement, English Journey, Postscripts, Bright Day, Dragon's Mouth, Journey Down a Rainbow, Literature and Western Man, Lost Empires, Instead of the Trees*. I also wish to acknowledge with thanks permission from the Society of Authors and King's College, Cambridge to quote from E. M. Forster's Commonplace Book; the Society of Authors for the use of a John Galsworthy letter (© 1988 the Estate of John Galsworthy); the Society of Authors on behalf of the Bernard Shaw Estate for two letters from G. B. Shaw; Mrs Mary Merrington for permission to reproduce a letter; Mrs Margot Cory for a letter from Santayana; A. D. Peters for quotations from *The Good Companions*; and Samuel French Ltd on behalf of the J. M. Barrie Estate for a letter by J. M. Barrie. Above all I acknowledge Jacquetta Priestley's permission to use the many collections of Priestley papers, and Tom Priestley for the use of his mother's letters.

# Preface

Surveying the immensity of the task, I hesitated before accepting the responsibility of writing the life of J. B. Priestley. One year later I was so immersed in the work all self-questioning had vanished. It would be tedious to recall the long and tortured journey in detail. Suffice it to say that some of the minutiae can be traced in the footnotes to this biography but they cannot convey the complexity of the evidence or the biographer's perennial struggle to distinguish between reliable and unreliable evidence.

My quest was made possible only by the co-operation of J. B. Priestley's widow, Jacquetta Priestley, who suffered repeated questioning with patience, tolerance and remarkable breadth of mind. Priestley's son Tom Priestley, and his daughters, Lady Wykeham, Sylvia Goaman and Rachel Littlewood, all generously co-operated and certain episodes would have remained unelucidated without their help. Mary Priestley introduced a revealing aspect of her own and her father's life with considerable courage and frankness and her patience under my questioning was remarkable. Nor can I neglect the contribution of Priestley's stepdaughter Angela Wyndham Lewis, who brought an oblique vision to bear on her stepfather, with interesting results. Winifred Scott, Priestley's half-sister, clarified a number of points from the very early days, and Muriel Holland, the sister of Priestley's second wife, unravelled details of his first liaison with her sister Jane Holland.

There are so many witnesses outside the family that any list would become tedious. Major amongst them for reasons which appear in the text are Mary Merrington, who entrusted delicate information to me, some of which I have woven into the text; Diana Collins, who gave me the benefit of her long friendship with Priestley and supplied a number of letters; and Dame Peggy Ashcroft, who was enlightening about her relations with Priestley. Charles Pick, Priestley's closest publishing friend, remained throughout a most helpful collaborator, who spiced his advice with anecdotes. Sir Richard Acland generously provided extensive unpublished manuscript material from his memoirs, as did Maire Lynd, the daughter of Robert and Sylvia Lynd. Mark Le Fanu went to considerable trouble to trace the vicissitudes of the 1941 Committee which Priestley chaired in the war and Martin Gilbert was enlightening about the rivalry between Churchill and Priestley in the same period. Mr and Mrs Lambert supplied invaluable memories, Robert Robinson and John Atkins made available their correspondence with Priestley, and Graham Greene put me right about a threatened libel suit. Terence Kilmartin traced and identified a key review, written by Philip Toynbee; the BBC Archives were very helpful recovering ancient scripts; the headmaster of Belle Vue Boys' School in Bradford, R. Whitaker, and A. C. Wheatley, head teacher of Green Lane First School, supplied invaluable educational facts. I am particularly indebted to Christine Knott, who took considerable trouble to interview local people and supply information about 5 Saltburn Place, where Priestley's writing career began. John St John combed Priestley's correspondence with Heinemann, his publishers, provided invaluable information, and has since written the history of Heinemann.

Among many others I am also grateful for the help of Sir Ralph Richardson, Sir Victor Pritchett, Max Reinhardt, Lord Wilson, Michael Holroyd, Margaret Drabble, Desmond Flower, Sir Rupert Hart-Davis, Peter Cotes, Allan Prior, Rupert Withers, Dr Charles Lack, Joy Pappenheim, Peter Hart, Josephine Pullein-Thompson, Francis Sisson, John Hadbury, Muriel Fullbank, Roger Smith and Petra Lewis. A. H. Robinson made a special contribution which he wishes to remain uncredited. Deirdre Toomey worked wonders among the British marriages and deaths archives and overcame some much more wide-ranging problems.

The dead, in a curious way, contribute to this book from the grave. Over a writing life which spans sixty years I have encountered many famous authors and actors and some like H. G. Wells, Bertrand Russell and Sir Ralph Richardson discussed Priestley, sometimes briefly, sometimes at length with me. Recovered from notes in my diary are a number of these impressions and anecdotes.

The main body of the documentary evidence came from the archives of the Harry Ransom Humanities Research Center in Austin, Texas, where Cathy Henderson, the research librarian, generously co-operated. The archive held Priestley's letters to his father Jonathan Priestley, his second wife Jane, H. G. Wells, Peggy Ashcroft, Compton Mackenzie, Hugh Walpole, G. B. Shaw,

Frank Kendon, Thomas Burke, Cass Canfield, A. D. Peters and many others. The Harry Ransom Humanities Research Center also held letters from A. E. Russell, Hugh Walpole, A. E. Housman, George Santayana, Walter de la Mare, Arnold Bennett, Thomas Hardy, Edmund Gosse, Sir James Barrie, C. G. Jung, Michael Arlen, John Galsworthy, H. G. Wells, T. S. Eliot, G. B. Shaw, H. M. Tomlinson, Rebecca West, Herman Ould, Cass Canfield, Harold Laski, Winston Churchill and many others. There was also a brief exchange of letters between Priestley and Thomas Mann.

Priestley kept no diaries. He also, from time to time, destroyed correspondence with motives which are unclear. He wrote:

> It is a great pity, I realise now, that I have never been a methodical man, carefully preserving what ought to be kept. I have gone marching on, probably towards the sea of oblivion, like Sherman through Georgia, burning and destroying as I went. Apart from some letters, a few pages of notes, an original script here and there, hardly anything has survived . . . any critical biographer who could survive my own discouragement – and several have already failed to do so – would find himself soon more profoundly discouraged by the lack of material.

Priestley overlooked the devotion of some of his close friends who treasured his letters, and universities who scoured the literary byways, sometimes surfacing with splendid collections. It is the biographer's nightmare that having more or less completed his task he suddenly stumbles on just such a collection. This happened through a series of accidents with the valuable collection of Priestley letters to his oldest friend in America, Edward Davison, which are held in Yale University Beinecke Rare Book and Manuscript Library. Due to the original initiative of Peter Davison, Edward Davison's son, and the co-operation of Yale University Library, these letters were eventually made available to me. Despite the fear of Yale University that the shock of new material might be too much for a biographer, after three and a half strenuous months it did manage to reproduce them, and they proved invaluable.

It would have been impossible to write a biography of J. B. Priestley without those fragmented autobiographical volumes: *Midnight on the Desert, Rain upon Godshill, Margin Released* and *Instead of the Trees*. I have drawn extensively on the basic facts they contain. Also indispensable was Jacquetta Priestley's remarkable book, *A Quest of Love*. A whole rich kaleidoscope of memories, values and prejudices emerges in the innumerable essays and articles which continued to pour from Priestley's typewriter far into his seventies. Susan Cooper's and John Braine's two biographical accounts under the same title, *J. B. Priestley*, contained very useful information. David Hughes's reassessment of Priestley's novels and essays and Gareth Lloyd Evans's critical study of his plays were both enlightening. Tribute should also be paid to the comprehensive bibliography of Priestley, compiled by A. E. Day. Without it I might easily have lost my way in the labyrinth. Priestley's contributions to newspapers and periodicals cover 178 pages in Mr Day's bibliography but those relevant to this biography are listed in the footnotes. I have also drawn on a large number of memoirs and biographies which contain scattered references to Priestley and these again can be identified in the bibliography and footnotes.

Priestley's correspondence with his daughter Mary and step-daughter Angela Wyndham Lewis was very useful for documenting the last third of Priestley's life. I must also pay tribute to John Hansman's research in Texas, which successfully isolated some of the most relevant material, and his recurrent trips to the British Library at Colindale where he braved the hazards of newspaper files, which can become so daunting. I myself also underwent that painful pilgrimage.

If for nothing else this biography may be remembered because it publishes for the first time a series of love-letters to the then Jacquetta Hawkes, which reveal an unknown aspect of Priestley's character which will transform his reputation as a human being. After some heart-searching these letters were generously made available by Mrs Jacquetta Priestley for which I am more than grateful. In a sense they are the very kernel of the book and the man. For the rest the North Library of the British Library supplied with unflagging persistence a continuous flow of books over the years, which taken together would constitute a separate library.

This biography does not attempt to be definitive, if such an ambitious adjective might ever be applied to a life of J. B. Priestley. Moreover, it concentrates on the life rather than the work because among many more serious reasons sheer length required that something drastically be cut, since the original ran to a quarter of a million words. People still living put restraint on one or two episodes and some witnesses prefer to remain anonymous. For the rest many more biographies of Priestley will be written. No more fertile literary subject which has not been exhausted by academic investigation is available in the first three-quarters of the twentieth century.

# PART ONE

# Prologue

See him sweeping dramatically into the Savile Club, a burly man with a big black hat set at a slightly rakish angle, an old-fashioned half-cape encompassing the broad shoulders, and the heavy-jowled face full of brooding purpose, and it became clear at once that this was a man to be reckoned with. Follow him inside and watch him pause to lean over the back of a heavy sofa on which sat Compton Mackenzie deeply engrossed in some unspecified task, and the power of Priestley's presence made itself felt to interrupt Mackenzie's concentration.

'You look, Monty,' Priestley said, 'as if you are engaged on the devil's work.'

'I am,' Monty said. 'I'm filling in the pools.'

'How much do you think', Priestley said, 'luck matters in life?'

'Well, you've had your fair share of it.'

'Yes,' Priestley said. 'Ah suppose Ah have.'

In middle-aged maturity Priestley had behind him a record of over fifty books, twenty-five plays, a mass of journalism, innumerable essays, several distinguished forays into public life, a reputation for cantankerous grumbling, and two marriages, with a third imminent – all of which had made his name a household word. He was not only a national but an international figure. Sometimes he deliberately encouraged the pose of the down-to-earth, pipe-smoking Yorkshireman who did not give a damn about literary style and desired nothing more than to entertain average decent people whose tastes resembled his own. Those self-same people would have been surprised to discover what complexities lay hidden behind the image and the mask.

It was Anthony Burgess's belief that 'if he scorned experiment in his novels, he produced in the 1930s a series of plays which brought something wholly original into the theatre'. Philip Toynbee flatly denied such claims and launched an attack on his work which said that Priestley simply lacked the equipment to philosophise about life, either in his plays or his novels.

Nobody could deny that, in his heyday, his novels were more widely read than those of most living novelists. As for his plays, they continued to be performed across five continents and if his critical ratings fluctuated wildly, it was all too much for some critics like Agate who made him the butt of his wit. Priestley developed his own defence against the critics, but even at the height of his fame, when nothing could dislodge his sheer eminence and critics had become a tedious necessity in the creative scene, he still could not quite resist the temptation to take a furtive glance at what his worst detractors said. Heinemann, his publisher, referred to him as the gas-fire Dickens, and at least one of his plays achieved that final accolade – which might not have pleased him – T. S. Eliot's approval.

It was his particular gift that drawing his own life from lower-class roots, he could identify with the moods, values, loves and hates of ordinary people. This enabled those self-same people to transcend everyday experience by mediating it through Priestley's heightened sensibilities, which elevated the commonplace into a different dimension. Accused of writing reportage, it took a different form which echoed round the world and made his mind and personality familiar to millions who had never met him.

Any claim to genius seemed to him absurd, but he admitted that he had 'a hell of a lot of talent'. Tact was not something he cultivated, but he was never afraid of making enemies and had trodden on a number of distinguished feet without considering the effect of his fifteen-stone frame. A moderate socialist vaguely derivative from nonconformist radicalism, he could not abide certain aspects of the Labour Party, and when he contested a parliamentary seat at Cambridge he stood as an independent. He called vociferously for equal shares in public wealth, but considered himself an unsuitable candidate for that mediocre fate. His critics never tired of complaining that he flung words down on paper with indiscriminate haste, but he claimed that inspiration could not wait on fine phrases and what you had to say mattered more than how you said it. This conviction produced invincible readability in his work.

Although he earned royalties which were the envy of other writers and made him rich, he complained that since he paid supertax he really worked for the government, which allowed him a small commission. The picture of a man in a big black hat whose saurian eye scowled at tax inspectors, grumbling that they denied him the proper fruits of his work, was flatly contradicted by his

Elizabethan zest for living and a capacity for good food, drink and laughter which could make him the best of company. Subject undoubtedly to bouts of pessimism, it was no ordinary pessimism. 'I am a life-enhancing pessimist,' he said.

He sometimes converted self-denigration into a cult. 'I am rather given to boasting, as my loved ones have told me more than once. But even they would allow me to declare that my experience has been unusually long, rich and thick.'[1] Referring to his public image as repulsive – disarmingly – he claimed that it was his own creation.

> It has always been my own fault and I wretchedly suspect it has happened hundreds of times. To say that I have been tactless lets me off too easily. I have been a mannerless blundering idiot over and over again. Where a comfortable personal relationship might have flourished, a chance meeting ends in a desert or icy tundra. How conceited! How ill-bred! How bloody rude! Well that's the last time I have anything to say to him! How can such people crying out like that ever be persuaded to believe that my intimate personal relationships survive the closest scrutiny.[2]

The bluff Yorkshireman accused of having the hide of a rhinoceros concealed immense sensitivity within and was capable of depths of emotional awareness which led him into one of the most profound love relationships. Contradictory reactions to those who knew him intimately – love, affection, irritation and occasionally downright rudeness – could be overwhelmed by a personal charm which dissipated all the shortcomings.

According to Priestley's own account there was once a casual stranger who made so bold as to say that he had enjoyed one of Priestley's books. Did Priestley smile gracefully and offer his thanks? No. He scowled, made an 'abrupt impatient gesture' and 'moved away'. Alternatively, Priestley imagined a young woman at a party who was innocent enough to ask him what he was writing now. 'He stares at her, his bristling eyebrows descend ominously, then he looks somewhere else, and finally he growls, "Ah've a roole not to talk about what Ah'm doing!" What a boor.'[3]

Nothing could be more remote from that charming man I first met so many years ago who graciously offered me a chair in the study of his Highgate house and, instead of concentrating on J. B.

1 *Instead of the Trees*, J. B. Priestley, 126.
2 ibid., 129.
3 ibid.

5

Priestley, sensitively enquired into what I was writing and offered to enlighten me about H. G. Wells.

> Half his splenetic eruptions were supposed to be the fruit of a carefully nurtured inferiority complex. He sprang so unnecessarily to defend himself. He was touchy to the point of pathology. People used to say it was all the result of that squeaky voice, that huge pit of inferiority from which he had so articulately climbed. Rubbish. I liked Wells – we got on. He wasn't inferior. He was superior. But he was quite capable of attacking you if you had the temerity to agree with him. And – by the way – unlike Arnold Bennett, he had good taste in women.[4]

Certainly there were many women who appreciated J. B. Priestley. He experienced a range of what Wells referred to as 'passades', three of which led him into deeper relationships and marriage. If he deliberately turned his back on moral ambiguities in his work, retaining the ethical simplicities of eighteenth-century novelists, in his private life he produced a code so relaxed that its exposure could have ruined him. These deviations did not yield unqualified pleasure. The torments were sometimes destructive.

That a man once described as having a potato face, gruff manners and a capacity for brooding withdrawals should be attractive to women seemed impossible, but widespread evidence proves otherwise. Certainly many women involved in his life did not regard him as a graceless boor incapable of understanding their true nature. His gravelly voice – 'it spoke to you out of the forest' – flow of talk and overpowering personality made him a danger to the many women who found him attractive.

Jacquetta Priestley's skills as an archaeologist, employed psychologically, would be more capable than any comparable instrument of excavating the many layers of Priestley's personality which – against the perceived wisdom – went very deep. She certainly revealed evidence which surprised me.[5] Once a member of his family described him as a haunted man. He saw himself in simpler terms. 'The most lasting reputation I have is for an almost ferocious aggressiveness, when in fact I am amiable, indulgent, affectionate, shy and rather timid at heart. Thou hast no enemy but thyself.'[6]

4  Interview, 17 August 1949.
5  Several interviews with Mrs Jacquetta Priestley.
6  *Margin Released*, J. B. Priestley, 231.

The late Ralph Richardson said of him that he 'might be good at making enemies' and 'slaying pompous parasites' but he so easily converted into a 'kind easy-going chap'. His compassion for the human condition was qualified by attacks on the lunacies of mankind's leaders. If the human condition suffered from corruption, malpractice and downright incompetence, his life-enhancing self insisted that it could be improved. He was explosive about bureaucracy and occasionally driven to bouts of benevolent dictatorship. The author as public figure, the representative Englishman who inspired the nation in the Second World War, would have recoiled from such a description. Middlebrow in his thinking and writing, the term was not a sneer in his vocabulary. It described some of the best creative work and he was happy to belong to the genre. He was the last of a tradition which preceded Eliot's *Criterion* and Leavis's *Scrutiny*. If his work like his outlook had certain limitations, it found enthusiastic echoes in millions of minds.

Privately, as a family man, he endured a long-drawn-out tragedy which haunted his life, but there were many among what became a dynasty who loved and admired him. Behind the façade of the family man, three marriages, five children, and several grandchildren, many women came and went. Only one – late in his life – fulfilled his ideal. Not even the initiate knew what it cost him to live a relatively free life and the torments in his letters were unknown to anyone, except himself and his third wife.

Ferocious debate, libel and copyright actions, mad commitments to love, a Niagara of words, family tragedy, a search for – magic – at the heart of commonplace experience and a continuous struggle with the baffling nature of simply being alive were all riven by energies which drove him into fresh experience.

Defeating all the forces which illness brought against him, he survived into his ninetieth year. In those last years he pottered about the beautiful gardens of Kissing Tree, still grappling with vast questions about the nature of human nature. Sometimes he was absent, groping for words which did not come, lost in remembrance of the past, but always there was a presence in the background: a necessary and reassuring presence.

He had lectured from America to Russia, from Iona to Athens, from Stockholm to southern Chile, where students crowded in 'because they thought he was Elvis Presley'.[7] He had been 'bored in Samarkand and amused in Pihshing': he had drunk coffee and

7 *Instead of the Trees*, J. B. Priestley, 127.

whisky in the 'howling dusk of an Aleutian island' and had seen 'a line of great golden kangaroos come leaping out of a wood near Alice Springs'. He had confronted the Taj Mahal, Death Valley, Rainbow Bridge, the temples in Cambodia and Abu Simbel on the Nile. For ten years he ran 'a high-level chamber music festival', for more than ten he produced as well as wrote plays, and even on one heroic occasion became an actor in one of his own productions. He remained a splendid grumbler and frequently, with no particular relevance to the present, he re-encountered in memory episodes of the past. Those early days in Hampstead when he poured words pell-mell on paper to complete *The Good Companions*; the first play, *Dangerous Corner*, doomed to die but saved by his own convictions of its worth; the abuse and delight of the critics; the mounting wealth; the inspired speeches in the middle of the bombing which roused envy in Winston Churchill; the cantankerous image he could not quite escape because he contributed to its reality; his vilification by politicians who misread his views as revolutionary; the cavernous glooms which sometimes absorbed him against all his life-enhancing pessimism; the elaborate series of different personae projected and sustained for long periods to conceal the shy, kind, compassionate man said to be hidden beneath the rubble of so many discarded selves: and the final flowering of a love which carried him through the rest of his days.

All except the last, was done with now. He pottered in the grounds of Kissing Tree House, a sick man. Sometimes he nodded in the half-light of old age. It was all gone, dead, done, and they could measure him as they would. Already measuring Priestley had become a national pastime. It was a difficult task. Donne put it succinctly. This man was not an island: he was a continent.

# I

# The Early Years
## 1894–1912

There, far below, is the knobbly backbone of England, the
Pennine Range. At first, the whole dark length of it, from the
Peak to Cross Fell, is visible. Then the Derbyshire hills and the
Cumberland fells disappear, for you are descending, somewhere
about the middle of the range, where the high moorland thrusts
itself between the woollen mills of Yorkshire and the cotton mills
of Lancashire . . .

We descend further, circling down to a long smudge of smoke,
beneath which the towns of the West Riding lie buried. And then
we are at Bruddersford in *The Good Companions* or Bradford in real
life, the town where John Boynton Priestley was born, at No. 34
Mannheim Road, Toller Lane, on 13 September 1894. At the very
outset one unexpected fact has to be recorded. According to his
birth certificate in Bradford Register Office he was named not John
Boynton but plain John Priestley, and there are at least three
possible explanations. Jacquetta Priestley recalls that he introduced
Boynton to distinguish his name from his father's. There is a village
called Boynton in the East Riding which he visited a number of
times although there is no evidence that it had any special significance in his life. The third explanation – that such a name was more
effective for a writer – is self-evident and Jacquetta Priestley
believes that it contains an element of truth.[1]

His birthplace, Mannheim Road, is a street of small terraced
houses, two up and two down, built for workers a century before in
stone quarried from the moor, which had the indestructible quality
of rock dwellings. Enlivened now by tubs of flowers and freshly
painted new front doors, the area which was once so deeply Yorkshire
is now alive with Asians. No plaque of any kind commemorated
Bradford's most distinguished citizen when I first visited the city in
1985 but many forms of reparation have since been made.

---

1   Jacquetta Priestley to the author, 12 January 1987.

Climbing through what was once a working-class area deeply infiltrated by Irish immigrants, Toller Lane reaches a socially superior area called Saltburn Place. It was to No. 5 Saltburn Place that the growing family moved in 1904 and Priestley's early memories were all centred around that house. He described it in *The Edwardians*. The house had eight rooms, divided between a kitchen where they ate when *en famille*, a front room reserved for more convivial occasions, two bedrooms and two attics with a half-landing and bathroom. The back attic was little more than a lumber room crammed with piles of old magazines over which he browsed far into the night, and the front attic his personal and cherished den.[2]

Externally, the house remains much as it was but the whole character of the neighbourhood has changed. The taxi from Bradford Station was driven by an Asian whose cab exuded the scent of many a rich curry meal. Asked whether he knew Saltburn Place he replied: 'Saltburran Place. Yes – very easy.'

'Have you ever heard of Jack Priestley?'

'Pereestey – no. Saltburran Place, yes – very easy.'

The house was a double-fronted terrace house with steps climbing to a brand-new front door of solid wood painted brown, with shining brass fittings. There were Asian children playing in the street and it was necessary to move between one group after another to reach the door of No. 5. A long pause and then the door opened a slit and there stood a young Asian woman, very pale and pretty, her eyes slightly apprehensive. Her frail body carried the sari with elegance and her face was dominated by a brilliant caste mark.

It is difficult to imagine the reactions of Priestley's father if he came back from the grave to discover that his home No. 5 Saltburn Place was now occupied by the Choudry family. Mr and Mrs Choudry have four daughters and the eldest, aged nine, has grown accustomed to enquiries about the famous man who once lived there. Mr Choudry admitted that he was unaware when he bought the house of its literary antecedents, but they had since become all too familiar.

From the moment of my arrival outside the house, Priestley's presence began to make itself felt and it was difficult to know whether artifice deliberately gave life to his image from steadily deepening research which had left an ineradicable impression . . .

2   *The Edwardians*, J. B. Priestley, 185–6.

until the stairs which Priestley climbed thousands of times nearly a hundred years before were climbed again. There came the highly charged moment of crossing the threshold of the attic only to have the spell – if spell it was – collapse completely because everything had changed implacably. No books, no shelves, no furniture even. The room had been stripped of wallpaper and carpet, and so depersonalised that no hint of Priestley's presence would have survived but for one riveting possible relic. There, within a walk-in cupboard space, was an inscription which read: 'Playhouse A Team', cryptically inexplicable. My co-researcher Christine Nott was told by the daughter, with reverence, 'He wrote that,' but the inscription looked disturbingly fresh, and closer examination destroyed the illusion. The view stretching away from the attic window across the cobbled alleyway had changed too, from Priestley's day, but the new buildings seemed to merge into the old without destroying the dignity of the past. How many a time staring out at the city from this room Priestley had struggled with the beginnings of his writing career.

Winifred Scott, Priestley's half-sister, wrote to me about these very early days:

> The fact is you are enquiring about the only period of my brother's life nobody knows anything about. The first marriage of my father and the birth of Jack are surrounded by mystery. My niece . . . told me the other day that her father told her that never once in his whole life had his mother ever been mentioned.[3]

Barbara Wykeham, Priestley's daughter, clarified the actual dating of the family's development:

| | |
|---|---|
| 4.8.91 | Jonathan Priestley, Priestley's father, married Emma Holt at St John's Baptist Chapel. |
| 13.9.94 | Jack Priestley born. His mother Emma Holt died. Nothing known where or when. |
| 19.8.98 | Jonathan Priestley married Amy Fletcher who worked in a confectioner's shop. |
| 15.11.03 | Winifred Priestley born.[4] |

The received wisdom in the family was that Priestley's mother died shortly after giving birth to him. As John Braine wrote,

3  Winifred Scott to the author, 24 January 1986.
4  Barbara Wykeham to the author, 10 March 1986.

'Priestley's early childhood was not a happy one,' and Priestley told Braine, 'Something was missing that should have been there.'[5] Devotees of Jung or Freud would expect serious consequences from such deprivation but psychoanalytic evaluation is not only premature, but to some extent irrelevant. The death certificate shows that his mother did not, in fact, die until 1896, two years after his birth.

Surrendering to the worst cliché in the psychoanalytic book, his many affairs later in life could be seen as a search for the missing mother figure but that not only invites the charge of gullibility: it ignores the basic facts. As Priestley later wrote: 'When I was very young we had my grandmother living with us and whenever my parents went out for the evening my grandmother fed and entertained me.'[6]

Instead of deprivation, Priestley passed through a chain of three women until he was ten – mother, grandmother and stepmother – each one, according to available evidence, giving him varying degrees of devotion. Certainly he had the luck of the game with his stepmother, who seems to have been an impeccable example of what a stepmother should be.

Priestley did not recall his real mother from the first two years of his life. 'I do not remember my mother at all,' he told John Braine.[7] 'But I was told she was very lively and witty and was once turned out of the theatre for laughing in the wrong place – bless her heart. She was probably a mill girl.'[8] The small years mediated through adult perceptions are frequently romanticised, but there is no special reason for doubting this picture.

Priestley's mother Emma belonged to 'the clogs and shawls back o' t' mill' working class, 'a free and easy, rather raffish' category which lived in 'grim little back-to-back houses', where 'they shouted and screamed, laughed and cried, and sent out a jug for more beer'.[9]

His father was born into 'the superior working class', who believed in the simple, straightforward values, hard work and the preservation of their own kind of respectability. He was a schoolmaster 'and a very good one with an almost ludicrous passion for acquiring and imparting knowledge'. A stocky red-

5  *J. B. Priestley*, John Braine, 9.
6  *Essays of Five Decades*, J. B. Priestley, 308.
7  *J. B. Priestley*, John Braine, 9.
8  ibid., 10.
9  *Margin Released*, J. B. Priestley, 12.

faced man with bright blue eyes, fair hair and a gingerish moustache, he was of mixed West Riding and Scots blood. He 'walked eight miles a day to and from his school, played a useful game of cricket . . . and like so many Bradford people . . . spent much of his time walking in the Dales'.[10]

'I was very fond of my father,' Priestley wrote, 'indeed I loved him. He was unselfish, brave, honourable, public-spirited. He was the man socialists have in mind when they write about socialism . . . among the older citizens up there, I have never really lived up to him, and merely represent a showy falling-off.'[11]

The Bradford of Priestley's youth was a city where men worked long hours for desperately low wages and three generations of one family sometimes lived in the same street. There were older men and women amongst his relatives who had gone out in the 'dark chill of early morning to work in the factories' and continued working all day until they came home once more in the dark. Later in life he remembered all too clearly visiting grandparents, uncles and aunts in the 'wretched little back-to-back houses in the long dark streets behind the mills'.

Among his earliest, indelible memories was a small eating-house which specialised in meat-and-potato pie. 'There was always on view in the window, to tempt the appetite of the passer-by, a giant, almost superhuman, meat-and-potato pie with a magnificently brown, crisp, artfully wrinkled, succulent-looking crust.' That steaming giant pie was to his boyish mind – 'and indeed to my adult mind for we never forget these things – as much an essential part of my native city as the Town Hall and its chimes'.[12] It became a symbol of his past life.

In Bradford you did not become a socialist, you were born one but Jonathan Priestley's socialism derived more from radical nonconformism than from Karl Marx. Priestley senior fought for years to end the 'half-time system' whereby children of twelve or thirteen spent half the day in school and the other half working in a factory.

His socialism was not 'busybody or socially ambitious' but 'public-spirited'. Brisk, humorous, stout-hearted, he was not to be patronised or bullied, but his world lacked glitter. 'I never remember', Priestley wrote in *Midnight on the Desert*, 'seeing him either in

---

10   *The Listener*, 23 July 1959.
11   *Margin Released*, J. B. Priestley, 12.
12   *Postscripts*, J. B. Priestley, 82.

ecstasies nor yet defeated by despair. But he never failed in a duty, left the world better than he found it, was loved by his friends . . . and had a lot of fun . . . Beneath the rather droll surface peculiarities – his love of making acquaintances, of asking questions, of imparting information . . . his distrust of the picturesque, romantic, grandiose things of this life; his odd mixture of impatience and explosive hot temper – he was a living rock of good solid human nature.'[13]

Priestley's early recollections of his father were qualified later by the account he gave to his third wife Jacquetta Priestley. She remembers her husband criticising 'a puritanical streak in him'.[14] This was reinforced by the chapter on his childhood in *Margin Released*.

From the earliest days Priestley was fascinated by all forms of professional entertainment, a reaction which displeased his father who considered the world of the theatre either a waste of time or a dangerous influence on character. Far removed from some of his nonconformist contemporaries, Priestley senior remained a 'conscientious and hard-working member of the Baptist Chapel', a symbol from which his son recoiled.[15]

A passionately devoted Sabbatarian, when Jack broke the rules, Jonathan Priestley refused to listen to reason and tried to win the argument with an explosion of temper. Driven into a corner from which there seemed no escape he would resort to violence and sweep everything off the breakfast table or raise a suitcase above his head and bring it crashing down.[16] Another infallible flashpoint was the time of departure for holidays when anxieties about recalcitrant children and missing trains drove him into bursts of vituperation with an occasional missile emphasising his point. Unrepresentative of his normal moods, these storms disappeared as quickly as they arose and he avoided any final retreat into sulkiness or sarcasm. Ambitious to teach, guide and counsel, he regretted his outbursts and never exploited the power he undoubtedly exercised over the family.

Jonathan Priestley, like his son, was a many-sided man. The austere Sabbatarian could abandon all pretence to dignity when playing games and become 'downright silly, like a boy among boys', a trait reproduced by his son and affectionately remembered by his grandchildren.

13    *Midnight on the Desert*, J. B. Priestley, 133–5.
14    Interview with Mrs Jacquetta Priestley, 15 September 1985.
15    *Margin Released*, J. B. Priestley, 9.
16    ibid.

Priestley recalled that Christmas time became a riot of parties and games-playing which ran on for several consecutive days, threatening to become a milder form of Saturnalia when he sometimes laughed himself into 'a red haze and danger of choking'.[17]

Recollecting the past in a good mood, Priestley could romanticise these very early days with phrases like: 'Until my middle teens . . . I was happy at home.'[18] In his seventies, talking to John Braine, he revised that view: 'Something was missing that should have been there.'[19] Certainly his early days in the infant class at Whetley Lane Primary School put him in the power of a woman teacher who disliked him. 'I remember my own terror and despair, at the age when you don't realise that time may soon change everything, when you feel small, helpless and apparently doomed, arriving day after day with fear curdling your inside.'[20]

These were strong reactions which cannot have failed to affect his development even if his robust Yorkshire constitution was capable throughout his life of throwing off experiences which would have scarred frailer spirits.

As we have seen, two years after the death of his mother, his father married Amy Fletcher who defied all traditional stepmother images, being kind, gentle and loving. Indeed she completely reversed the destructive attitude of Jack's first teacher, overlooked his boyish eccentricities and in no time was declaring – 'with the over-emphasis peculiar to women of the north' – that 'I was a genius and might therefore be excused.' He entered what has inaccurately been called Belle Vue Grammar School at the age of eleven. Strictly, Belle Vue School was a 'selective school' for much of its life and from 1904 became Belle Vue Boys Secondary School, with a two-year preparatory school.[21] Priestley qualified for the 'senior department' when he was thirteen and at last began to find a certain satisfaction, if not pleasure, in his education.

Education – the word rang loud in Priestley's ears because the subject ebbed, flowed and re-echoed throughout a household frequently invaded by teachers, each loudly proclaiming his own educational Utopia. Education to Jonathan Priestley was the touchstone of life which, properly invoked, could open up illimitable prospects.

17  *The World of J. B. Priestley*, ed. Donald MacRae, 4.
18  *Margin Released*, J. B. Priestley, 10.
19  *J. B. Priestley*, John Braine, 10.
20  ibid.
21  Letter from the headmaster to the author, 25 June 1986.

According to Priestley, his grandfather was a mill worker who earned thirty shillings a week in the 1880s and performed miracles of thrift to enable his son to reach a teachers' training college in London. The family celebrated Jonathan's triumphal return to Bradford as a full-blown professionally recognised teacher with a big party and ceaselessly flowing beer. 'Education to him', Priestley wrote, 'was a prize, a jewel, not a modern convenience laid on like hot and cold water.'[22] Jonathan Priestley's civic virtues ranked high but they had another flaw which Priestley junior could not accept. He cared too much about what the neighbours thought. Already practising that kind of endearing self-deception which convinced him that he was a wonderful fellow, Priestley began to act and dress the many roles he saw as possible alternatives – writer, musician, actor – and what the neighbours thought of his performances seemed of little concern. Providing he did not become publicly offensive he felt that he was entitled to dress and behave as he wished, an early crystallisation of character which suffered occasional modification later in life but no basic change.[23]

Jonathan Priestley's sexual codes can be judged by the effect on him of the appearance of H. G. Wells's novel *Ann Veronica*, in which a young woman student elopes with a biology teacher and lives in sin. Sound, Baptist, chapel-going men like Jonathan could not countenance such wickedness, even from the pen of an admired writer and educator like H. G. who cocked such satisfying snooks at the upper classes. Jonathan Priestley's confidence in the great panacea, Education, wavered in such dangerous waters but did not evaporate, and now he applied himself to the task of getting 't'son properly educated'. Simultaneously he taught not only in the day, but at evening classes, and any stranger casually encountered on the train was liable to be 'deluged with enlightenment'.

The local West Riding industrial community in which Priestley was brought up had a free-ranging camaraderie which appeared to undermine the social hierarchy so rigidly enforced in those days in many areas of England. He did not pretend that it created an oasis of classlessness but firmly believed that it came closer to such an ideal than anyone from the south could contemplate.[24]

Priestley lived in a house full of passing visitors, alive with

22  *Margin Released*, J. B. Priestley, 8.
23  *The Listener*, 23 July 1959.
24  *Margin Released*, J. B. Priestley, 7.

conversation and noisy with the claims and counter-claims of the teaching profession. They were 'all the noisier because . . . once they were warm in argument [they] could not help using their classroom voices'. Powerful memories remained far into life of people smoking pipes and drinking hot toddy before glowing coal fires to the accompaniment of torrential talk. 'Giggling and scuffling in the background', young Jack came to regard these over-large adults with their big earnest manner as comic figures displayed for his amusement, and frequently he would sit waiting for 'the great drolls to arrive'. Percy Monkman remembers him from childhood days playing football vigorously and 'keeping his end up however rough the weather', but most if not all his boyhood friends are dead and the evidence is scarce.[25]

The world in which John Boynton Priestley grew up uneasily reconciled many contradictions. The years 1870–98 saw enormous material expansion accompanied by inexplicable economic depression, and the irrepressible movement towards closer integration of the world economy produced a sharp reaction against free trade. The deep divisions between wealth and poverty, worker and employer, individual and union, once hidden beneath a superficial prosperity, showed signs of breaking into the open. The Fabian Society entered the political scene in 1884 and the Independent Labour Party revitalized left-wing politics in 1893. Improved standards of living were qualified by large areas of social degradation and the spread of democracy accompanied the growing powers of government.

The younger Priestley was very much a product of Bradford's culture, which modified the more austere general mores of the day with the robust vitality and immediacy of Yorkshire life. In the wider perspective the Protestant ethic held sway everywhere. Personal integrity and honesty were reinforced by hard work, ambition and the imperative of social as well as personal progress. In the eyes of many poverty was synonymous with idleness, the unemployed were victims of their own fecklessness, criminals were incapable of treatment and the role of women was essentially that of wife and mother of children. Large families were common, contraception practised – if at all – in the crudest forms and regarded by some as a pact with the devil of sensuality. Long skirts encumbered and concealed female legs, the family was sacred and unquestioned, the relations between the sexes sometimes required chaperons for

25  P. Monkman, to the author, 4 December 1985.

the most innocent occasions, religion penetrated all areas of life, prolonged engagement preceded marriage, sex was regarded by some as an unfortunate prerequisite of reproduction, premarital intercourse was frowned upon and the conspiracy of silence about the facts of sexuality was profound. And yet already the early stirrings of a peculiarly English brand of socialism in the Fabian Society and the Labour Party were beginning to make themselves felt.

The development of the novel transferred spiritual and creative energies away from traditional patterns with Robert Louis Stevenson indulging boyish day-dreams, Conrad re-examining the old heroisms, Gissing gloomily expressing his frustrated scholarship and Butler becoming the disillusioned theologian. It was Herbert George Wells rather than Dickens who held Priestley's father's attention from a first excited reading of *The Time Machine* to the relaxed sprawling narrative of *Kipps* and *Mr Polly*. Thirty years separated the birth of H. G. Wells and J. B. Priestley, but the novelist in Priestley had some resemblances to Wells, and the socially conscious world manipulator who wrote the *Outline of History* and *A Modern Utopia* found echoes in the adult Priestley.

We have much harder evidence of Priestley's beginnings as a writer than we do of some other aspects of his life. In 1927 he wrote an article in the *Daily News* which said:

> I began writing when I was a small boy at school. My greatest enterprise was a magazine entirely written (in every sense of the word) by myself. Only one copy of each number was produced and the subscription was one halfpenny for a look at two numbers. As a matter of fact I never got further than the second number, and even that, if I remember rightly, was a rather scrappy affair. I do not think my powers of composition failed me. I was defeated by the labour of copying everything out in a fair round hand. The first number, however, was a prodigious performance, for not only did it contain editorial notes, sporting chat and a competition, but also the first instalments of no less than four serial stories.[26]

Such a spectacular demonstration should have survived all frustrations but when he announced to his father that he wanted to leave school without any immediate plan of earning a living, writing as a career could not have been further from Priestley senior's mind. Looking back, later in life, it surprised Priestley that his father 'was not violently angry' when he broke the news but he

26  'How I Began', *Daily News*, 18 June 1927.

admitted that scenes, which may have taken place, could have been obliterated in memory. Tired of school and all its pettifogging limitations, already one desire dominated all others – to write – but denied a literary career, he was prepared to make concessions to conducting a symphony orchestra or doing 'a little great acting from time to time'.

Realistically there were three possibilities: staying at school to work for a university scholarship, getting a job, or drifting on at school for another year under fierce pressure to face up to adult responsibilities. Having 'done very well at school', especially in his favourite subjects, English and history, he had no fear of failing to win a scholarship. However, he did not see himself 'in courts or quads under dreaming spires'. Unlike his friends, who concentrated on getting to university, he resisted the spell of English traditions and felt 'alienated rather than attracted by everything that had been long established'.

At the age of fourteen Priestley contrived the feat of falling in love simultaneously with 'two very different goddesses'. One was simply the girl next door and the other Miss Mabel Sealby, then playing Principal Girl in Bradford Theatre Royal pantomime. His father's puritanical dislike of all theatrical life allowed Jack just one glimpse in the flesh of Miss Sealby, but the image of her 'saucy black curls' took possession of his imagination and thereafter he so vividly conjured up her long legs and beautiful dresses that he was haunted by her. He did not dare to wait at the stage door or write her letters, but indulged in sumptuous imaginary conversations, which were made more vivid by his already developing creative powers. Worshipping his ideal from afar he never managed to break through his boyish inhibitions and although Miss Sealby had a long career, and Priestley became an inveterate theatre-goer, he never encountered her again and his vision of a young and unattainable goddess slowly faded.[27]

The relationship with the second goddess, the girl who lived next door, was closely similar. Some unexplained hostility between her parents and his meant that they went to different parties and his craving for closer contact had to be satisfied by patient waiting at the bay window of his house to catch a glimpse as she came and went. 'Not a smile, not a look' rewarded him but his vigil persisted over the months, and in that time he searched a number of novels hoping to find her name in print which might grant a vicarious

27  *Outcries and Asides*, J. B. Priestley, 166–7.

intimacy. It was his first love, full of adolescent sadness, dwelling on music in a minor key, lost in sorrowing dusks and sunsets. Thus it was, at the age of fourteen, that he led an almost Jekyll and Hyde existence in which the husky footballer who could, when required, bully his way down the pitch and return home to gobble two helpings of suet pudding laced with syrup, concealed inside himself 'a frail poetic being, a junior Shelley' who lived in a 'high rarified atmosphere of double enchantment, without even a kiss during Postman's Knock coming my way'.[28]

One man stood out from school memories, a schoolmaster named Richard Pendlebury. His physical appearance combined many of the characteristics of a Spanish grandee – 'tall, intensely dark, handsome and commanding'. He lacked the qualities of those finer minds who could write a PhD on 'the use of the semi-colon in the later works of George Eliot', but he was devoted to literature, understood and loved good writing and above all could 'communicate and share that love'. Priestley found it difficult to disentangle his liking and admiration for Pendlebury from his early appreciation of literature. Inexplicably, it seemed to Priestley that because Pendlebury discussed poems, plays and essays with such warmth and insight, his literary sensibilities were the source of his grave courtesy, the cutting edge of his talk and glints of humour.

> I can see and hear him again, quite clearly, across years that changed all human history; and if his influence on me was far greater, as indeed it was, than that of all the professors and lecturers I heard later in Cambridge and the critics I met in London, that was because I sat in a classroom, at the right time, with a teacher who loved good writing.[29]

At this stage Priestley was quite prepared to become prime minister or star in Shakespeare, but the written word lured him for reasons he could not fully explain. In the end he left school, still without any idea of a career.

Jonathan Priestley was a man who regarded Bradford's basic industry, the wool trade, as a necessary but philistine activity constantly threatening the culture created by local teachers, and yet in 1909 he suddenly decided that his son must go into 'the wool business'. Priestley commented later in life: 'It was as if a fanatical teetotaller had told his son to get a job as a barman.'

28   ibid., 167–8.
29   *Margin Released*, J. B. Priestley, 6.

There were 'wool men' amongst Jonathan Priestley's acquaintances but none became his friends. The image which automatically
presented itself to him whenever wool traders were discussed was
of fat, red-faced, loose-lipped, cigar-smoking gentlemen who
spent half their days squandering ill-gotten gains at the races.
Priestley senior knew quite well that this was a libellous distortion
of many people in Bradford's wool trade, and in less vituperative
mood he acknowledged, with respect, the combers, spinners,
weavers and dyers who constituted the backbone of the industry.
Moreover, any boy who had 'something about him' could stand on
his own two feet in the wool trade. The prize waiting at the end of
years of struggle was 'a nice girl, a house of his own, a bedroom
suite, a piano and a pram, with whist drives and chapel high-teas –
and concerts in the winter, and the summer rising to a peak in ten
days at Scarborough or Morecambe'.[30] What more could a man
ask?

Having no alternative plan of his own and unaware of the wool
trade's limitations, the teenage boy raised no objections. The desire
to write was already powerful but he vaguely sensed the need for
more experience and claimed, later in life, that he already knew
journalism was 'no use to him'. What he also knew with certainty,
in the Bradfordian sense, was that he 'hadn't anything about him'
and could be said to be 'crammed full of hanky panky'.

Uncaring whether he entered the 'tops', 'nods', 'pieces' or 'yarns'
department, he duly wrote a letter in copperplate handwriting, and
was invited to attend an interview. Describing himself, at this
stage, as a 'stammering oaf', he survived the interview with
difficulty and won the job as a very junior clerk with Helm & Co.,
Swan Arcade, Bradford.[31]

The office hierarchy ran from office boy to managing director
and Priestley's rung on the ladder was lowly enough for him
sometimes to take over the office boy's role. He sat on a high stool
at one end of a broad counter making book entries, while at the
other end the samplers displayed their wares. From this high
eminence he perceived the workings of an elaborate empire and
slowly pieced together its interlocking connections. Sometimes his
imagination carried him away to countries with which they did
business – India, China, the road to Samarkand and, on one
occasion, the rich cosmopolitan life of pre-war Berlin.

30  ibid., 13.
31  ibid., 14.

The commodity which inspired these visionary journeys was known as wool tops, bundles of wool which had been washed and combed ready to be spun into yarn and sold to continental manufacturers. Sometimes these samples brought the smell of camels and the desert into the dreary, badly lit offices and sometimes even distant China sprang to life when a packet of Chinese pigtails, cut off by state decree, arrived from Shanghai. Enormous parcels of such samples were wrapped and carried off – sometimes on trucks – to the post office. Within a few weeks he began to believe that his 'golden youth was slipping away between those sheets of blue wrapping paper'. Less boring but equally repetitive were the endless formula letters to transport, machinery and shipping companies, sometimes struggling with the French language and sometimes, because of tortured business terminology, the English. The Bag Book, which loomed large in his life, recorded all these transactions and had to be kept up to date, but in many a snatched half hour he was reading poetry hidden in the drawer of his desk. Messrs Helm & Company were relatively advanced in their techniques and actually used typewriters, unlike some rivals who still wrote their letters in longhand, but female staff were unknown. 'Ours was an office without a touch of feminine grace and light: everything there solemn and weighing tons.'[32] Letters were copied, not by carbon paper, but by a device which might have graced a torture chamber, with its two massive steel plates and big cross-handles, the spinning of which could crush anything between the plates. Alternatively, with the intervention of what were known as damp sheets, the device produced blurred copies of letters. Subtle skills were required to create the precise degree of dampness in the sheets, and Priestley's preoccupied mind produced many dubious copies.

Discipline was sharp and anyone arriving after the fixed hour of nine o'clock was subject not only to reprimand by the boss, but to ribald comments about the events of the preceding night from fellow workers. In this all-male company, once the management 'ghouls' were out of earshot, badinage easily became sexual. If the day began at a fixed hour it ended in an unruly vagueness, subject to the whims of the boss whose permission to leave had to be sought in his private office. Here Priestley was out of luck. His boss, whose physical presence was formidable, became one of the few men who generated fear in him and his lack of family life produced a fanatical devotion to wool. Instead of finishing at six, frequently the hour

32   ibid., 15.

extended to six thirty or even seven, and if seven the 'sweetener' of sixpence for tea was granted with 'something approaching a grand air'.

Asking the boss whether 'there was anything more' became an invitation to elaborate unsuspected duties and Priestley – exploiting an already adroit manipulation of words – devised a formula which could only be answered in the negative. Any dim hope that one day this new recruit might be drilled into some semblance of an ambitious wool man was dampened at the outset by Priestley's appearance. For him the life he desired not only began when he left the restrictions, gloom and boredom of the world of wool, but was even allowed to invade the office in the clothes he wore. Flaunting all known trade standards this 'idle, smoking, drinking, girl-chasing, verse-writing' eccentric wore big floppy ties, and 'a voluminous sports jacket in a light chrome green'. Greeted with lifted eyebrows and a grin in the office, the wool sorters were much blunter. 'Na, lad! Ah see tha's gotten that daft bloody coat on again.'[33]

Why, Priestley asked himself later in life, did they tolerate such a lazy, poetry-reading adolescent, whose errands outside the office always extended beyond the understood time limit, and whose vocabulary sometimes revealed words unknown to his mates? One explanation occurred to him. Formidable though the boss might be, he lived an austere life in total contradiction to other wool bosses, never went beyond a muttered curse when a wool sample 'went wrong' and was surprisingly well read.

> I was often sent to a superior lending library to find a good new book for him. This was only five minutes away, but he ought to have known – certainly the cashier could have told him – that I would be out of the office for the better part of an hour, enjoying my pipe – we were not allowed to smoke at work – and observing the town through an almost stupefying haze of Cut Black Cavendish, $3\frac{1}{2}d$ an ounce at Salmon and Gluckstein's.[34]

His attitude to his workplace was later spelt out by the chief warehouseman who said, 'Hey yer wor a cough drop, Jack lad. Yer nivver gave a damn for onnybody.'

The second in command at Messrs Helm quickly realised what a rebellious new staff member had come under his control and

33  ibid., 18.
34  ibid., 17.

disliked him at the outset. Indeed, to add to all his disadvantages, Priestley lacked good looks or even charm and he was driven to explain his survival in the job on one supposition. Some 'vague unspoken sympathy', based on books, developed between 'the boss' and himself, which must have increased his tolerance. Priestley speculated that somewhere far back in his career the boss had 'thought of turning writer', and that now explained his own survival.

Very few references occur in the scattered reminiscences Priestley committed to paper of what he was in fact reading in these years. Deprived of any specific dating and slipping from one decade to another, disentangling any coherent sequence from his reminiscences is very difficult. One author stood out as family reading – H. G. Wells – and Priestley's father, despite the small hiccup of *Ann Veronica*, swore by his world. His son picked up his enthusiasm, which drove him to read *The Time Machine*, *The Island of Dr Moreau*, *When the Sleeper Wakes*, *Love and Mr Lewisham*, *Kipps* and *Tono-Bungay*. H. G. Wells was the logical outcome of the long curve which ran from the Renaissance through the Encyclopaedists to Huxley, a curve sustained by the conviction that man was a rational being, that once enlightened education had become universal and scientific techniques widely accepted, hunger, want and war could be controlled. Like Condorcet, he wanted one world peopled by a race of cosmopolitans, but he suffered some confusion of identity between himself and the average person.

These lofty commotions might have been beyond the range of Priestley junior, but the socialist message, the capacity to bring alive so authentically the miseries and joys of the lower middle classes, brought an immediate response in Jack. Wells published in 1910 *The History of Mr Polly* and Priestley read it avidly. He never openly averred any inspiration from the work of Wells, but *Mr Polly* was a celebration of the excellence of the ordinary and it was just such a quality which eventually illumined many of Priestley's novels. *The History of Mr Polly* was full of good sound British sense and all those clumsy, endearing characteristics which gave its hero, under the alchemy of Wells, moments of immortality and phrases of incomprehensible enchantment: 'sesquipedalian verboojuice'. Again there were resemblances to Priestley's work. For the rest we have the evidence in *Margin Released* that he 'read widely both new books and old, always late in the evening, of course', but with no particular authors mentioned. He also recollected long summer evenings spent in Lister Park reading poetry, and we know that occasionally as the sky darkened and the stars appeared he lay alone counting them to find the lucky one 'which would release him from the hell of a world woven in thick coarse wool'. Sometimes deeper thoughts troubled him. What they were never became clear. His novel *Bright Day* did specifically mention certain poets.

> Yeats, Housman, de la Mare and Ralph Hodgson, such lines used to go buzzing in my mind like golden bees. I pondered on these and other poets in my room, carried their more evocative and magical lines with me through the streets and sometimes shouted them idiotically – startling the sheep – on the windy moorland tracks.[35]

These abandoned bouts usually took place at weekends, only to have the dreary inevitability of returning on Monday morning to the depressing world of wool.

In the morning, 'somewhere around' the required hour of nine o'clock, he re-entered that remarkable relic of another age – Swan Arcade – which absorbed its visitors into a world far removed from Bradford.

> You darted out of Market Street into the shade through one of the unnecessarily magnificent entrances; you moved along the marble floor in the hushed interior, with its hint of assignations among the colonnades: you hurried past the mysterious screened windows of those unimaginable agencies and establishments down every aisle. Then you felt for a moment, just before the cage of the lift closed, you had been in some alien but not unfriendly city, a thousand miles from the West Riding, and that if you made a dash for the nearest exit you might find yourself in a street belonging to an altogether different kind of life.[36]

It was this exciting hint of exotic worlds contained within the ordinary which kept hope alive in a 'bored and inefficient clerk' who was, as Priestley put it, converted into a Swan Arcadian.

One other person stood out in Priestley's memory as a redeeming oasis in what he then saw as an inescapable desert of pettifogging duties, small humiliations and defiant gestures. James A. Mackereth was a colourful figure who brought poetic excitement, enlightenment and congenial companionship into the years 1910–14. A minor poet of some repute, he wore a high-crowned soft hat,

35  *Bright Day*, J. B. Priestley, 23–4.
36  *Margin Released*, J. B. Priestley, 23.

heavy boots and the shaggiest of tweed suits which belonged, Priestley believed, more to the wool merchant than the poet. Mackereth's hollow-cheeked face was dominated by a long nose, with two deep-set eyes blazing under a broad forehead. Once a bank clerk, the luck of the game had endowed him with a small private income and he left the bank for ever to devote his life to cultivating his garden and writing poetry. 'He was, you might say, too determinedly poetical, too *gladsome* and *elfin* in one mood, too weird and *eldritch* in another.'

Mackereth lived in a small house in the country three or four miles beyond the reach of electricity, street lamps or tram-cars, and Priestley walked 'scores of leagues' to or from the tram terminus, calling on Mackereth with a cavalier disregard for his convenience. A rapport sprang up between them which led to long evenings spent first in Mackereth's garden until the dusk came down, and then in his study, where tea and sliced cake were served by his handsome wife, whose presence made Jack uneasy. When she left to go to bed a kind of demi-paradise followed with Mackereth's tragedian's face illuminated by the big oil lamp as he read in a deep chanting voice extracts from something he had just written and the lyrical flow was music in Jack's ears.

About midnight he would set out towards home along the lanes where he met nothing except an occasional creaking survival from another age, a covered wagon, perfectly suited to the American West. The late hour, the fresh air, the words still singing in his ears and the growing sense of the wonder of literature, opened his mind 'to that sense of unlimited possibilities, both in this life and some other, which has been described so often by the romantics'.[37] The poet continued to walk with him under the great arc of the sky and the illimitable stars. They lifted him into

> that blessed mood
> In which the burden of the mystery,
> In which the heavy and the weary weight
> Of all this unintelligible world,
> Is lightened.

37   ibid., 35.

# 2

# Embryo Writer
## 1913–14

The world in which J. B. Priestley grew up was a world where the state hardly intervened at all in the life of law-abiding citizens. Anyone could leave the country without a passport, foreigners could spend a lifetime in Britain without reporting to the police or holding a permit of any kind, currency restrictions did not exist, the economy was resilient, income tax stood at 2s 6d in the £1, and drinking took place at any hour of day or night which suited the premises serving it. Surface appearances were very deceptive. Only those over seventy received a tawdry few shillings to sustain them through old age, the gap between rich and poor was wide, unemployment when it came threatened starvation to some workers, opportunity was wide open to the privileged and in 1911 the first crude attempts at unemployment and sickness benefits were hopelessly inadequate. Nevertheless the buoyancy of an expanding economy produced multiple outlets for would-be writers and a proliferation of magazines and periodicals exceeded in number and variety their equivalents today. Priestley constantly looked back to the year 1913 with nostalgia and regret. In an unpublished manuscript written when he was seventy-seven, he said: 'I had no diaries to remind me what I had done and how I felt then. I would have to depend on memory . . . Yet defying common sense, the idea would not go away . . . Somehow I would have to grapple with the year 1913.'[1]

It was a year to be remembered by Priestley, first because he saw it as the end of an epoch in which Europe's 'innocence' faltered and collapsed and second because it marked the turning-point of his youth in Bradford. 'Not everything was good then,' he wrote, 'but afterwards most things were a great deal worse.'[2] He never dreamt, he said, that 'out of the mud, blood and anguish . . . there would be

---

1 Unpublished, partly dictated manuscript, undated: 'It Was 1913: an essay together with some fugitive recollections', written or dictated when Priestley was seventy-seven; hereafter 'It Was 1913 . . .'
2 ibid.

erected a machinery to curtail the liberty of the subject and harass any man who wanted to live his own life without official interference'.

A sense of alienation from the year 1913 pursued and soured him for many years, reaffirming the later image of the always grumbling, gruff Yorkshireman. He was deeply influenced as a young man of nineteen by the spirit of that year, and it 'lingered on, putting an edge to my criticism . . . encouraging all the grumbling and growling'.[3]

Throughout 1913 Priestley continued to leave No. 5 Saltburn Place every morning at eight thirty to catch the 'Duckworth tram' which carried him to work in the Swan Arcade and the Duckworth trams became a symbol of a way of life.

> They were cheap and dependable, even though they swayed, shuddered and groaned. They not only took us to work but . . . out of the city to the edge of the country where . . . a short walk up a steep road the rolling glory of the moors stretched away before us . . . I never remember waiting in a queue for a tram: it seemed always to be there, waiting patiently at your service. We lived a comfortable and inexpensive tram life in 1913, and these – 'high-built glittering galleons of the street'[4] . . . shine in my more affectionate memories . . . I could cheerfully return to a tram life.[5]

He continued to spend leisure hours walking the moors, attending concerts, playing football, singing and, above all, with whatever energy remained after an overwhelming day, writing. A close friend – known in *Margin Released* only as George – would share slapdash piano-playing with Priestley who occasionally burst into loud 'sin-Ging' as it was pronounced. George's mother, a formidable lady whose wiry form weighed no more than six and a half stones, stood out in his memory. She was always 'blazing-eyed' and 'never downcast', and delighted like her husband in company, noise and family jokes. Priestley later derived a few characteristics from her husband for Jess Oakroyd in *The Good Companions*, but it was the wife who remained most vividly in his memory. Especially she liked singing. Commonly regarded as baritone, what Priestley's voice lacked in quality he made up in volume with the result that sentimental ballads suffered but comic

3  ibid.
4  A. E.'s description.
5  From the unpublished manuscript 'It Was 1913 . . .'

songs flourished. Indeed, so accomplished did George and Jack's double act become that one Saturday night they took part in a variety concert at the Mechanics Institute and earned a whole shiny golden guinea, despite Jack suddenly forgetting crucial words in the middle of the performance. He was billed gloriously as Jack Croly of the leading London and Provincial Halls, but no second engagement followed. Private performances in the front room of George's house, always packed with friends and neighbours, produced better results. The good-humoured enjoyment of simple satisfactions frequently laced with pints of beer, produced an elemental happiness later to be reinvoked when he wrote *The Good Companions*.

The year 1913 was memorable for yet another reason. The harsh necessity of earning a living constantly interrupted these mild Saturnalias. Jack felt vaguely uneasy when George's mother took a job as an office cleaner in order to help pay George's way to Cambridge. It did not deflect him from his deeper desire, already expressing itself in sporadic attacks upon writing. The day finally arrived when George was due to leave for Cambridge in a cloud of optimistic glory, and Jack was called upon to admire the special suit, flannels and dinner jacket which George's mother displayed to all the neighbours. He restrained an impulse to burst into satirical comment and patted George on the back with the words: 'Go to thy destiny George and may the dreaming spires not fall on your head.'[6] All too short a time afterwards Jack re-encountered George's mother leaving an office block early one morning looking shrunken, grey and exhausted. Such was the price working-class families were prepared to pay to the god of Education.

Jack continued to find relief in sing-songs, concerts, reading and writing. The open-air summer concerts in Lister Park were great social occasions which involved much more than listening to some of the best regimental bands which Britain could command. There were tiered seats surrounding the bandstand which, in good weather, were always packed with people who absorbed a flow of light music, followed by active discussion and criticism. Priestley, from the outset, found deep satisfactions in music and understood the technical difficulties of scoring string parts for woodwind instruments when regimental brass bands had nothing more than a double bass. Proud of lower-middle-class culture, his father's friends would discuss the relative merits of the Scots, Irish and

6   ibid.

Coldstream guards' clarinet performances, and Priestley first learnt the elements of musical criticism from military performances.

Very different activities were sometimes masked by this veneer of culture. High above the bandstand was a promenade where girls and youths in their Sunday best clothing packed along the rails looking down through a blue haze of smoke at the scene below. It was a scene where a sluggish stream of laughing, talking youth enabled contact to be made casually, although the girls frequently moved in arm-linked trios. Some males were predatory, older men bent on seduction, romantic men searching for 'the ideal woman'. Behind the giggling, nudging and whispering, sexual desire multiplied and, as Priestley later recalled, the place and hour were propitious for mating:

> a summer evening, trees and grass between youth and the dark narrow streets; the hills above the tree-tops fading into dusk . . . a glitter of instruments, the scarlet flash of a uniform . . . and music coming . . . not attended to, a long way off, but music.[7]

It was a good time for the beginning of love: subject, of course, to the possible intervention of outraged parents who might burst into a group on a street corner and whip a girl away with the then unquestionable authority of mothers and fathers.

Among the eight people who dominated Jack's memories of 1913, three stood out in sharp relief. Two were very close men-friends without any hint of homosexuality, and the third a girl who first introduced him to sex. The trio shared the life of the pubs, the theatre, concert and music halls.[8] Jimmy was 'short, rather ugly but not unattractive in a gnome-like fashion, with a keen wit'. He survived as a youth about town by 'playing the system' and enlivened many a trio evening with his witty irreverence for conventional values. Driven to take a job as an uncertificated teacher, he earned exactly nineteen shillings a week and supplemented this with an erratic form of coaching more calculated to undermine than reaffirm any existing talent. Herbert M., the second member of the trio, was 'tallish, fairly handsome and always very carefully dressed'.[9] Spare, dry, ironical, he was the exact opposite of the exuberant Jimmy. The third member of the trio, Esther, gave Priestley his first deeply felt emotional experience. 'I

7  *Margin Released*, J. B. Priestley, 61–2.
8  The following facts are taken from 'It Was 1913 . . .'
9  ibid.

was half in love then, in an eighteen-year-old fashion.' Three years older than Priestley, she was 'mature enough to manage her own copying office directly opposite the Swan Arcade where I worked . . . I often popped into her office at lunchtime to do a little not too high-powered necking.'[10] She had dark brown eyes, black hair, a saucy nose and generous mouth: 'all very feminine and delicious . . . I can see her now, wearing one of those floppy tweed hats . . . taking shelter with me in the woods from the rain.' Sought after by men who could afford to entertain her lavishly, whatever jealousy Priestley felt for Esther was quelled by the discovery that she preferred his racy well-informed talk to the dull platitudes of the 'rich'. His company in a sixpenny gallery at the theatre was preferable to theirs in the expensive stalls. Special privileges were lavished on him when she kept open her basement office after business hours, not only for stolen kisses but to copy manuscripts which she read without much insight. Why she did this for someone as 'raffish as I was' continually surprised him. Fifty years later the blank in his memory would suddenly be filled by the image of Esther and the first enchantment of adolescent kissing.

I can almost catch the long-lost smell of the rain-pitted dust on the roads . . . I see again the curved pale cheek, the pouting of the dark full lips, the fields and woods that vanished years ago.[11]

What he does not reveal in *Margin Released* comes through clearly in the unpublished manuscript, 'It Was 1913':

All this probably suggests that I was more in love with her than I actually was. Esther was essentially companionable . . . I don't ever remember our being angry with each other. But then it was a relationship based on sexual approval and liking, not love, at least not running at full tide.

When he wrote or dictated these words he had at last realised what was the deepest and most profound love of his life and he spoke from experience when he added: 'But while attraction was there, it was without mystery and magic, the clutch at the heart.'[12]

His interest in girls developed when he took advantage of a privilege available to wool-company employees by which a shipping

10   ibid.
11   *Margin Released*, J. B. Priestley, 26.
12   'It Was 1913 . . .'

company offered free passes to employees on its regular voyages. And one glorious day, all gold and blue air, found him 'at Goole, seeking a berth on a small steamer – the so-called butter boats – that being the chief cargo they sought – on the regular run to Copenhagen'.[13] Coming straight from the smoke-blackened buildings of the West Riding into Copenhagen's 'spotless bright Wonderland', his enjoyment increased when he was given a clean quiet room for eighteen pence a night.

> I took my breakfast out in a courtyard and there, facing me, was a . . . factory . . . where delectable girls, at every window, looked, pointed, giggled. Except when I paid a brief visit to Southern Sweden I went every evening to the Tivoli . . . Any place that offered excellent lager, open sandwiches, a hundred thousand soft coloured lights, fairground nonsense, vaudeville, a symphony orchestra and fireworks, was more than good enough for Jack Priestley.[14]

A young man in his eighteenth year, he was held entranced by the beautiful blonde girls with sunburned faces. They were a totally different species from the pallid, worried girls he had left behind in Bradford and they came swarming over the bridges on their bicycles like 'an invasion of Rhine Maidens'. Still a reserved, shy person in public he did not dare to speak to them, but essentially because of the 'absence of sexual urgings' he enjoyed the magic of their presence more. The image he took back from Copenhagen haunted him for many years. The sheer cleanliness of the streets, the brightness of the paint, the relaxed good humour of the girls inspired him to condemn the urban and industrial squalor he found in English towns when he came to write *English Journey*, many years later. The following summer a walking tour along the Rhine reinforced his growing suspicion that something was wrong with the England which – fundamentally – he so much loved. Outstanding among his recollections remained that golden frieze of beautiful girls in Copenhagen which drove him to use a word he was to overwork later – magic. His unpublished manuscript recognised and repudiated the charge. 'It is the magical that I remember and salute, redeeming as it does all the mere trash and sludge of this life.'[15]

13   ibid.
14   ibid.
15   ibid.

All his life Priestley was destined to be secretly sustained by moments which seemed to him – magical. They were not subject to the dictates of rationality or susceptible to solicitation but 'arrived as and when they chose'.[16]

Back in Bradford once more from his German expedition, Jack resumed the treadmill at the wool merchants but by now his literary instincts were not merely alive and active: they were importunate.

Fifty years later, poring through his papers, he regretted the bohemian casualness with which he treated documentary evidence. Indeed, the inconsequence with which he invaded, and sometimes destroyed, valuable records was dismaying. As we shall see later, however mixed his motives, there were highly personal reasons why some areas of evidence should be expurgated. Any critical biographer, Priestley said, who could survive his discouragement would certainly abandon such a project for lack of evidence. Poring over what did remain in the year 1961, there in front of him was 'a mottled box file, ragged at the edges, and I do not know how and when it arrived. What I do know is that it is a piece of luck I never deserved, for it contains not only many letters I wrote home from the First War, but also some assorted samples of the stuff I wrote up in that attic fifty years ago.'

The attic bedroom was lined with orange boxes converted into book-shelves with a sputtering gas fire installed under the window.

> Between the bed and the gas fire, a fierce little thing that could not begin to warm the room without grilling your shins, there was just enough space for two smallish old armchairs, so that when I was not scribbling and scribbling away, I could entertain friends – male, of course, no girls allowed up there.[17]

The family was not poor and lived reasonably well but Jack paid a contribution to the collective budget and had very little to spare for buying books. Many of those he did buy were at the expense of the eight pence he was allowed for lunch. One shop in the covered market sold stale buns cheaply and another concocted a commodity of mashed dates and coconut which, washed down with multiple draughts of water from chained iron cups at the public drinking fountain, 'murdered appetite, so to speak, with a blunt instrument'. The books he bought included classic poets such as Shelley, Keats, Byron, essays by Lamb and Hazlitt and novels by Dickens,

16   *The Moments*, J. B. Priestley, 3.
17   *Margin Released*, J. B. Priestley, 27.

Trollope, Meredith, Wells. A series called *The World's Best Books* led him into mistaken purchases of volumes selected by literary criteria he subsequently found wanting.

The attic became his refuge and his inspiration. Crouched over the fire reading far into the night or scribbling by incandescent gaslight with his nose close to the paper, he left behind the damnable woollen samples, forgot the labels for Hamburg and Gothenburg and became a 'poet, story-teller, humorist, commentator and social philosopher'. Ambitious attempts at poems and short stories brought the series of rejection slips obligatory in any author's life, but they were the living proof that behind his dormer window he was in communication with the literary life.

In the event, his first published works were in sharp contrast to these literary commotions. The year 1913 'wasn't a month old before I was landed with one of the oddest jobs I have ever had'. The local Labour Party decided to launch a weekly periodical called the *Bradford Pioneer* and there, boldly displayed, began a feature 'Round the Hearth' which carried the initials J.B.P. Retrospectively, Priestley could find no reason why a gangling eighteen-year-old lad who was not a member of the party and had no nepotistic friends should become an omniscient cultural correspondent criticising with 'all the intolerance of a youth in his teens' plays, exhibitions and concerts.[18] In the *Bradford Pioneer* for March 1913, for instance, appeared a long review of no less a masterpiece than *Oedipus Rex* which ended with the firm pronouncement: 'Altogether the production was magnificent and Martin Harvey has given us a taste of what we must expect when we have established a municipal theatre.'[19]

One invaluable perquisite of his critical elevation was a press pass which not only opened a feast of entertainment free of charge but enabled him to invite his many girlfriends to join him with the grand air of an impresario. 'We were always falling more or less in love,' he wrote in *Margin Released*, but his unpublished manuscript 'It Was 1913' seriously qualified that picture. Presentation of his magic pass at the Bradford Empire did not immediately open the desired doors but sent the manager back into his private office to scrutinise the fragment of pasteboard and check what was to him this totally unknown and certainly insignificant weekly. A splendid spectacle of a man wearing a white tie and tails, he always brought

18  'It Was 1913 . . .', 12–13.
19  *Bradford Pioneer*, 7 March 1913.

out his monocle for preliminary examination of the pass and finally emerged from his office to scribble something contemptuous to the girl in the box office, the whole ceremony crumbling Jack's originally fine status in the eyes of his girlfriends.

From cultural correspondent he progressed to Page 6 Philosopher commenting on the passing scene. Alas his demise was as sudden and unexplained as his first appearance and in the autumn of the same year the *Pioneer* published a valedictory paragraph:

> We are sorry to inform our readers that in this issue will cease the contributions of our Page 6 Philosopher. Dame Fortune is ever a fickle jade beyond the powers of human control. Circumstances have arisen which make it imperative that our brother scribe should for a time at any rate, retire from his labours. We are sure that some, at least, of our readers will share our regrets.[20]

The old box file retrieved fifty years later, over which he pored in 1961, preserved many examples of his earliest literary efforts. There were a number of scribbling books which he made himself 'while nobody was looking' during that part of the lunch hour set aside as sacrosanct for this purpose – between one fifteen and one forty-five. Each book consisted of fifty pages bound in the oiled sheets used for the copying press. The pages were flexible enough to accommodate writing by pencil on his knee in an armchair near enough to the gas fire to burn his shins. The darkened pages contained closely knit lines, almost indecipherable but revealing a determination which made Priestley later reflect that the youth of nineteen was certainly more resolute than the man of sixty-eight. Even at the cost of ruining his eyesight, this young man was implacably set on the road of learning to write. Not that the mature man could find any of the classically expected promise in these first writings. 'Possibly there is that famous "promise" somewhere here: it seems to me hard to find.'[21] He did not believe he was possessed by a daemon, genius had no connection with his slogging persistence, and much more quickly satisfying prospects continuously crossed his path. What then, drove him? The adult Priestley could find no answers. 'I marvel at the lad,' he wrote and added with a heavy dash of disillusion – 'What did he think he was doing?'[22]

20 *Bradford Pioneer*, 10 October 1913.
21 *Margin Released*, J. B. Priestley, 40.
22 ibid., 39.

Among the confused drives which insisted on steadily more extensive scribbling, two remained dominant. One was a dream of living in a 'ninepence-a-week cottage on the edge of the moors', earning 'from writing the six, five, even four pounds a month on which, in those days, I could easily keep myself', having access to an accumulation of 'amiable red-cheeked girls' and achieving by this means – 'INDEPENDENCE'. No less powerfully the inspiration for all his lonely hard work came from the desire to force the birth of Jack Priestley as a professional writer.

One collection of material underneath the scribbling books in the box file was a typewritten piece with a covering of brown paper headed *Moorton Sketches*. Subtitled *At the Music Hall*, with his name and address boldly displayed in one corner, the manuscript described the different types he met at the theatre from the Youth with Blue Collar and the Fluffy-Haired Girl to the Lanky Male Companion and the Man in the Tweed Cap. It belonged to the class of descriptive sketch widely published in those days and later efforts earned him many a useful guinea. *At the Music Hall* remained unpublished but now the battered manuscript came to the surface in his box file and re-created those dismaying early days when he first struggled to get into print. The second item in the file was a long narrative poem in blank verse entitled 'Lancelot: After the Burial of Guenevere', which ran to 150 lines, failed to rise to poetic heights and simply became a poetical exercise. Steeped in a wide range of classical poetry, the young Priestley was extending his reading in rhetorical flights which proved nothing more than his unsuitability for that medium. An example of his blank verse reveals its limitations.

> 'Sir Bors,' he said,
> 'This is the end. There is no loveliness
> Left in the light of day. God can throw down
> His baton to the starry floor, and sign
> For the long-dreaded withering of the world.'

The third item in the box file was typed – 'by one of the girls' – on thin crumpled paper and consisted of seven eight-line rhymed stanzas under the title 'Evensong to Atlantis'. At the age of sixty-seven Priestley concluded: 'It is very bad indeed; I can never have done worse.' Haunted in 1913 by the idea of Atlantis, the ruins of whose civilisation remain buried under the sea, his fascination with the legend persisted far into life and even survived the 'affectionate derision of an archaeologist and pre-historian very close to me'. As he sat up there in his attic in 1912–13, Atlantis fired his imagination, but the sole record of his inspiration is one very bad poem.

The fourth item in the box file was again a poem, preserved on stronger paper, once more typewritten and entitled 'The Song of a Mood'. It opens with the words 'Tonight I think the world is dying' and the first stanza ends with 'The Women of all ages sewing a shroud'. What troubled Priestley later in life was why a robust lad of eighteen or nineteen, known as 'a loud emphatic talker' who performed clowning acts at parties and could be very brash and dogmatic, should have this preoccupation with lost civilisations and dying worlds. Surprisingly, in an intuitive novelist, he made no allowance for that period when dreaming under the moon, music in a minor key and lament for lost beauty, cloaks a yearning for something unrealised in many a late adolescence.

It was customary in the literary world before the First World War for aspiring authors to send examples of their work to established writers, always hoping for enthusiastic response. Following the tradition, Priestley sent 'The Song of a Mood', among other poems, to A. E., George Russell the Irish writer, and was delighted with the reply:

> I was greatly interested in your poems. The Song of a Mood is, I think, very beautiful and imaginative and is also better in form than the others. You have obviously imagination and feeling but you have not yet mastered the form . . . I think you have a poetic vision and I hope you will go on writing and try, above all, to cultivate the intensity of will as well as the intensity of vision because the will is the begetter of music and rhythm even as the vision is the begetter of thought. I thank you for your kind letter and for letting me see your verses. I would be glad later on to see more of your work, especially if you have things as fine as the Song of a Mood.[23]

A poet who dealt in fairies, angels, gods, demi-gods and satyrs, perhaps it was not unexpected that A. E. should misjudge Priestley's work. Priestley was no poet. He himself regretted this, accepting the poet's supremacy in the pantheon of literature, but he also believed that third-rate poets should grant pride of place to 'honest writers of prose'. However, as he later acknowledged, even his prose at this stage was 'quite shockingly bad'.[24]

23  Undated; 1912.
24  *Margin Released*, J. B. Priestley, 50.

There were exceptions. At least two early short stories contained within his treasure-trove box file revealed the beginnings of the descriptive novelist who later wrote *The Good Companions*. A story called 'A Nocturne' began:

'You tak' the high road an' I'll tak' the low road,' sang the old man, with trembling fingers adding a feeble obbligato on his violin. He stood underneath a street lamp, and the sickly pale green rays were merciful, for the gloom was thick. Here and there the faint light was reflected in little pools and puddles in the road, and the old man's boots squelched ominously at every movement. Everything was dark and wet. Even the rain seemed to be black and unclean, as if the heavens had long ago tried to sweeten the place and failed miserably.

W. W. Jacobs inspired the second story, 'An Excess of Discipline', which dealt with authority aboard ship. The Priestley family were great readers of W. W. Jacobs whose short story 'The Monkey's Paw' still chills the spine today, and Priestley was heavily derivative in 'An Excess of Discipline'. Later he was to write a critical appreciation of Jacobs for the *London Mercury*. Another story, 'Poor Old Dad', carried the narrative thrust later characteristic of Priestley's novels and anticipated with some accuracy a world he investigated in one of his favourite novels, *The Image Men*.

For the rest there were many examples of Priestley's early journalism which he believed revealed him as a late developer. They show him, in fact, as older than his years, writing with considerable balance about matters worthy of *Times* leaders.

The climax to all this preliminary scribbling came one day late in 1913 when *London Opinion*, a popular national weekly, suddenly reversed the flow of rejection slips and accepted an article called 'Secrets of the Ragtime King'. Inspired by the upsurge of ragtime music, it reproduced an imaginary interview with the Ragtime King, one of three young Americans who had descended on Bradford to invade the music halls and electrify the old relaxed routines. Dynamically alive, their bodies vibrating to the exploding banjos, singing and sweating, the three Americans almost hung over the footlights, hypnotising the amazed youth of Bradford who had never heard anything like it before. Among them Priestley found himself carried away on the flood of snap-happy music and it was almost as if on that first occasion 'he felt literally dragged out of the nineteenth into the twentieth century'.

This was the inspiration of Priestley's first publication in a national magazine and the one guinea he received in payment opened up vistas of cloth-bound books and mountains of tobacco which could not fail to impress a father who until then had remained stolidly indifferent to his success on the *Bradford Pioneer*. There was a celebration. A box of cigars appeared and father and son lit up to talk for the first time as men of the world on equal terms. The festival atmosphere was short-lived.

Already restless under the restrictions of home life which excluded any possibility of entertaining a girl privately in his den, Priestley suggested dividing his income from Swan Arcade on a basis which would make him independent, but his father would have none of it. 'We don' wan' lodgers at 5 Saltburn Place.' The wilder moments of Priestley's youth were then revealed in his father's sour comment: 'Somebody saw you half-carrying a girl down the road the other night.' Parental resistance could not stop a newly confident Priestley becoming a literary man about town who imitated the habits of Central European café habitués, and spent night after night talking and arguing in the limited splendours of the upstairs room of one of Joe Lyons's innumerable tea-shops on Market Street. In one section of the rooms the drearily familiar trio of fiddler, cellist and pianist poured out a sentimental flood of 'Destiny' and the 'Indian Love Lyric' until the literati bullied or browbeat them into more ambitious musical flights. The image remained deeply imprinted far into life:

> I can see again the ghost of a grin haunting the cellist's moustache, the look the violinist flashed in our direction, the large indifferent back of the pianist . . . Perhaps somewhere in their place along the fourth dimension, immortally enduring in the fifth dimension, that trio is still performing at the top of the stairs . . . in Market Street, Bradford.[25]

Whenever he returned home late, he faced the usual complaints from his father, but his stepmother quickly accepted his growing independence. The inevitable frictions sometimes led to 'scenes' but by the age of eighteen he completely disregarded any midnight deadline set by his father. It is not widely known that Priestley was a good 'amateur' painter whose roots went right back to these teenage days when he joined the local Arts Club and mixed with a number of minor painters.

Interlaced with these initiations into art and literature were expeditions on the moors when he deliberately played truant from

25  ibid., 77.

the wool merchants, ignored the allure of the tram and went swinging down the road bent on escaping from streets, people and duty. Friends regarded his ability to walk twenty miles without faltering as the performance of a weakling since the average stalwart Yorkshireman took forty miles in his stride, but mileage played little part in the delight of these expeditions. Memory recalled these stolen days ecstatically. The sun was high in the sky, guilt completely blown away by the softest wind, the fresh air intoxicating, the bird-song music and the memory of all those minions tied to their desks while he was – almost – floating over the moors among the summer clouds, made him burst occasionally into the skip and dance of a really free man. On such occasions he simply ran and sang long quotations from Yeats, Coleridge and Shelley. As he sat writing forty years later, those truant walks were still alive in him and 'perhaps I would not be writing now if it were not for them. I am being nourished through a long winter by forbidden fruit.'[26]

All unaware, these momentary idylls were coming to an abrupt end. As he wrote in his unpublished manuscript,[27] long years after, despite the glitter of his full life, a number of published articles, and growing ambition, an uneasy sense that all was not well with England and its great slumbering neighbour, the Continent, persisted.

He chose June of 1913 to take his precious two weeks' annual leave and another free pass from the company carried him to Holland and Amsterdam. There he stared 'long and hard' at the Rembrandts and Vermeers, before pressing on to Germany. When, on the thirteenth day, he set sail for Hull once more, he watched the lights of Europe sink over the horizon unaware that they were going down, not only for years, but for a whole epoch.

26  ibid., 78.
27  'It Was 1913 . . .', 11.

# 3

# War Intervenes
## 1914–15

The world in which Priestley experienced his teens was a world where the pomp and circumstance of royalty still commanded unqualified respect and his Keir Hardie socialism, deriving more from nonconformism than Marx, had no republican aims. Although Queen Victoria had disappeared in the mists of immortality as far back as 1901, George V still seemed to enjoy power at least equal to hers, and not far removed in some respects from that wielded by Henry VIII. This was demonstrated when at three p.m. on 4 August 1914, His Majesty received in audience a solitary minister of the Crown, and these two men, supported by the graces of two court officials whose knowledge of foreign affairs did not extend beyond Buckingham Palace, committed to a prolonged, savage and slaughterous war not merely the 45 million citizens of Great Britain and the dominions overseas, including Canada, Australia and New Zealand, but 50 million Africans and 200 million Indians. Priestley remarked to Hugh Walpole: 'None of these people was ever consulted, least of all that nineteen-year-old adolescent, Jack Priestley.' One minister and one monarch launched half the world upon an unalterable course of wholesale bloodshed, and it was almost as if we were back in the sixteenth century.

On the day the news broke, Priestley's family was away at the seaside and he sat alone reading in his attic bedroom. We have no record of his exact feelings, but much later, one day in the Savile Club, the author, discussing the First World War, asked him, 'What was your reaction?'

It seemed another blind disaster concocted by the politicians – but remember – in those days – the yellow press had built up a lot of hatred of the Germans – some of it justified – and a lot of people said hooray. I was inclined to use a very rude word which has to do with sexual intercourse.

41

Asked whether the threat to his writing career troubled him he replied:

> It certainly did . . . I had such wonderful plans. But suddenly it all seemed trivial. It broke me out of my Joe Lyons literary life and brought me right up against reality. I remember walking round the house saying – What now? What now? And having absolutely no idea of what I would do.[1]

The account given in *Margin Released* differs widely from this but on one main fact they are identical. Moved by mixed motives which later analysis failed to clarify, in September 1914 John Boynton Priestley enlisted in the British Army. This was not the result of any burst of patriotic feeling, or the fear that Britain was about to be overwhelmed by what newspapers referred to as The Hun. The prospect of war producing heroism in his 'unheroic character' did not rate high and he openly expressed contempt for those who rushed into uniform and 'wanted to be marched about'.

It was something deeper, something non-rational which in later years he related to Jung's unconscious, stirred promptings 'in the dark of [his] mind', and at last in September – 'I went at a signal from the unknown.' It remains unexpected that solid Yorkshire John Boynton Priestley, whose youth was far removed from mystical experience, should, looking back, have endowed the lad with instructions from – the unknown.

Analysed in detail, the account given in *Margin Released* is full of ambiguities. No sooner had the unconscious taken charge than Shakespeare's Feeble, the tailor taunted by Justice Shallow into serving Falstaff, is seen as a parallel to his own experience. He quoted not the 'clattering King Harry stuff' nor the 'baronial banging about' but Feeble's 'I will do my good will sir, you can have no more.' It was all a challenge to what he felt was his untested manhood. If men far less fortunate than Jack Priestley had marched, borne arms and fought for their country fired by nothing other than simple patriotism, 'Then why couldn't I?'

Whatever touch of glamour in the eyes of women illumined the young volunteer in his khaki uniform, it was quickly overwhelmed by the murderous machinery of wholesale slaughter which passed under the cloak of military strategy, but that was not yet.

1  Interview with Priestley, November 1972.

For the moment Priestley arrived one morning – 'like a chump' – at the regimental depot in Halifax of the Duke of Wellington's West Riding Regiment, better known in the locality as the Dirty Dukes, and presented himself for service. He wore a smart sports jacket, flannel trousers and the usual floppy tie. A sergeant in the regular army regarded this sardonically and immediately directed the elegantly clothed lad to the lowest form of army chore, removing congealed fat from immense cooking pots. The horrors of the barracks receded every evening for the first week because he was allowed to go home to sleep, only to set out in the dawn – 'yawning and shivering' – on the great double-decker tram, to face another day of ruthless initiation. He presented an odd figure, his uniform ill-fitting, his army boots 'weighing a ton' and his puttees, tight enough to have the effect of a tourniquet, or loose to the point of slovenliness. As the tram stopped at the barracks entrance in Gibbet Lane he straightened his crumpled jacket, pulled himself together and tried to march instead of walk past the guard with some semblance of smartness. 'From Hull, Hell and Halifax, our great-grandfathers declared, God must defend us. I had sailed to Hull from a Europe I never knew again. I had arrived at Halifax to do my soldiering. Hell, no doubt, was on its way.'[2]

It certainly was, for most of his friends who volunteered for the Bradford Pals Regiment were wiped out in the Battle of the Somme.[3] In his unpublished manuscript ('It Was 1913') Priestley claims that his youthful brashness had been tolerated by the comfortable majority of people in civilian life

> but this was not true of my four and a half years in the Army, when I encountered more than my share of dislike, from those in authority. I think this was because I could never take military life seriously. I was the opposite of the type . . . regimental.[4]

Two weeks commuting between home and the barracks ended abruptly one fine September dawn when at four a.m. he was piled into a troop train and began the long journey down to Frensham to become a private in Number 8 Platoon B Company 10th Duke of Wellington's 69th Brigade, 23rd Division. Immediately the brutishness of army life was brought home by living with eleven other men crowded into a bell tent, each performing the ritual of

2  *Margin Released*, J. B. Priestley, 84.
3  Winifred Scott, to the author, 24 January 1986.
4  'It Was 1913 . . .', 4.

43

pissing in his boots and emptying the contents by lifting the tent flaps. Since pissing in the open was an easily available alternative, some military sadist must have inspired this unnecessary piece of discomfiture. Originally endowed with a badly fitting khaki uniform which sat sadly on his boyish shoulders, he was forced to surrender this at Frensham because uniforms were scarce and some more sophisticated soldier needed to resemble a real member of His Majesty's forces. The whole of Number 8 Platoon was now dressed in all-blue dungarees with tiny blue forage caps and – final bizarre touch – civilian overcoats. Photographs reveal Priestley's round face in which innocence and depression mingled and there was nothing to mark out the man destined to become internationally famous.

There were no rifles, machine-guns or bullets, the rifle ranges remained unused and endless square-bashing constituted the life of Number 8 Platoon for the next three months. One day late in November a great flurry of boots and latrine cleaning preceded the appearance of Kitchener himself, to inspect a group of men whose caps leaked blue dye in the sleet which ran down their foreheads until they resembled a bunch of Indian braves.

Christmas leave arrived on 21 December and Priestley never forgot the exhilaration of returning to a civilised home and everyday life, greeted by his family as if he were already a hero. The local girls were less enthusiastic. He had borrowed an outsize black cap, an all-enveloping coat and a brilliant scarf which combined to produce the image of a bloodthirsty Tartar. The girls stared bewildered at this apparition, tittered and said, 'Ah knew you'd joined up Jack – but – Ah mean to say – what are you in?'

Back once more in the steaming bell tent with the mud threatening to engulf the whole regiment, he came to hate the tents with their stinking interiors, and the men crushed into an indecent intimacy where even friends grew to loathe each other. Sundays brought a brief respite from two until seven when groups of three would hurry to a local farmhouse to relax in normal chairs in front of a blazing fire and drink fresh tea with home-made scones. Some said the temptation to desert after this brief skirmish with civilisation was strong, but it did not trouble Priestley who now saw himself implacably trapped in the war machine.

One month later they were finally 'washed out of Frensham' and piled into army trucks heading for Aldershot where the brick huts and reasonable sanitation seemed like a return to civilisation. The whole town was a ritualised ballet of ruthless saluting, bugle calls

and square-bashing, but exaggerated discipline seemed less offensive under such conditions. Six weeks sleeping in water-tight
quarters on something resembling a bed improved Priestley's
morale and when, towards the end of February 1915, they set out to
march to Folkestone, a hundred miles away, he described it in a
jubilant letter home as 'the great march'. Now fully equipped with
new uniforms, rifles and kitbags they marched in reasonable order
accompanied by brass bands. They made a fine spectacle, with
people waving and cheering along the route and the band-master
extracting enough boom and clash from his instruments to awaken
the dead. The route to Folkestone was roundabout, since each
battalion needed accommodation which only big towns could
provide. Not even blistered feet, an endless diet of bully beef and
sleeping on concrete floors quite undermined the gala spirit of
cheering crowds and fluttering handkerchiefs which a newly inured
Priestley 'hugely enjoyed'.

For a second time, without any warning, in mid career of
marching, Kitchener descended on the 69th Brigade one windy
February day and Priestley had a close-up vision of that 'bloated
purplish face' with its 'glaring but somehow jellied eyes'. Unexpectedly, since he could be said to have summoned millions with his
half-accusing finger into a bloody slaughter which indiscriminately
obliterated a quarter of England's young manhood, Priestley later
spoke up for Lord Kitchener. Priestley retained all his life the image
of an ageing man 'already reeling under the load of responsibility he
refused to share', but it was also, according to Priestley, the image
of a man who had – alone – raised thousands of new soldiers 'out of
the ground'.[5]

Arrived at Folkestone, the 69th Brigade was billeted in private
houses and Priestley's first letter home spoke – gleefully – of having
a holiday at the seaside with accommodation which included actual
beds and food which approached the edible. Concealing the
boredom which by now filled every day with dull military parades,
he made no reference in his letter to a plan to desert, and rejoin some
regiment about to be posted overseas, which he and two comrades
had concocted. In the event something far less dramatic intervened.
He was selected to undertake 'officers' mess fatigue' at a detached
villa where commissioned officers led a life of relative luxury. In the
bizarre contradictions which bedevilled every other episode in the
early days of the First World War, it was characteristic that a

5  *Margin Released*, J. B. Priestley, 93.

commercial catering firm, a French chef, a beautifully dressed ex-valet, and many lesser civilians, mixed with two tough army types to produce food and service for officers who were totally inexperienced in any form of warfare. For his part, Priestley, who later wrote a number of semi-documentary novels, eagerly absorbed the behind-the-scenes detail of the catering world.

A third move next took the battalion to Maidstone in Kent where the men were no sooner billeted in private houses than they began digging trenches for the outer ring of London's defences. Possessed by an obsessional hatred of digging, Priestley was relieved when the award of a stripe accompanied his elevation to Company Billeting Officer, which brought him into touch with a number of housewives all too anxious to offer accommodation. One young daughter, remembered only as Dorothy, introduced him to her actress sister whose 'chain-smoking, drinking and nervous uninhibited talk' seemed to Priestley as exotic as 'a mandarin's concubine'. Equally remote, unattainable and desirable was an actress, Nellie Taylor, who came to entertain the troops and plunged nightly into her singing and dancing with such undisguised enjoyment that she seemed to Priestley the 'quintessential' essence of 'young femininity'.

Among the 'snarling clutter' of clumsy males, full of relatively crude talk which frequently became scatalogical, she was a reminder of the grace and beauty belonging to a lost world outside. She also carried echoes of the luxurious mysteries of Shaftesbury Avenue and the Savoy Grill. 'When she blew us her last kisses, and vanished, the lights went down for weeks and my army boots felt heavier and clumsier than ever.'[6]

Further promotion to Battalion Post Corporal brought new miseries from duties which included sustained enquiries about missing parcels and letters. The arrival of a new colonel with a fantastically lah-di-dah accent lightened the atmosphere. His theatrical drawl so clearly belonged to a comic swell in a play, that anyone could guy him behind his back, and mimicry ran rife.

And then after a last brief leave which seemed an unending round of changing trains, farewells, crumpled smiles and tears, the call came, they assembled in full kit and waited about 'until very late one night' to embark for an unknown destination in France.

6   ibid., 98.

# 4

# The Soldier
## 1915–18

B Company of the 69th Brigade relieved the regular soldiers of the 8th Division who had held the line for four months in a quiet sector between Bois Grenier, Laventie and Fleurbaix. The front lines of the opposing armies in this area were so far apart that listening posts in no man's land multiplied and on his third night in France Priestley was sent out alone to man one such post.[1] Initial apprehension quickly gave place to the illusion, when staring hard into the blackness of the night, that shapes were moving, silhouettes materialising, and only a sharp shutting of the eyes revealed, on reopening, nothing but the blackness of the night again. Looking back at sixty-eight, Priestley regarded the youth on the verge of an exploding maelstrom, crouching alone in the night facing every kind of hazard, as less apprehensive than he sometimes became on the first night of a new play. 'Youth, hard training, a genuine desire to get *into* the war at some point, had turned me temporarily into a brave soldier.'[2]

Words are inadequate to describe the crescendo of massed artillery, machine-guns, hand grenades and ordinary rifle fire which broke loose in the next few days to convince Priestley that sheer sound contributed the first element of terror to battle fronts. Thundering in his ears, echoing in his brain, the ceaseless cannonade dulled his senses, wore him down and made him feel that 'flesh and blood had no place in this factory of destruction'. Beginning as the epitome of the gallant Tommy whose heroism was recklessly exaggerated in the popular press, he began to wonder why he had surrendered himself voluntarily to this nightmare – and 'how the hell he could get out of it'.

The ramshackle nature of the 69th Brigade defences was laughable on the Bois Grenier front with breastworks of sandbags instead of trenches and a number of huge catapults which might have

1 'It Was 1913 . . .'
2 *Margin Released*, J. B. Priestley, 100.

survived from the besieging Roman legions 1,700 years ago.

On 25 September 1915 the mass slaughter of the Battle of Loos began and the failure of a limited manoeuvre by troops on the right flank of the 69th created that element of luck which shadowed him throughout the early days of the war. Overwhelmed by his full equipment he stood one day waiting with his platoon in muddy trenches at the foot of the scaling ladders and listened fatalistically to the continuous hiss and roar of shells and bullets above ground, knowing that his chances of survival were minimal. 'Once up the ladders and out of the trench, I felt a cat would not live five minutes.'

But the luck was with him. The gains made by the right-flank assault were too limited to justify throwing in the 69th and there, apprehensive, cold, soaking wet, he remained at the foot of the ladders, exchanging whispered obscenities until – the relief was overwhelming – the order came to 'stand down'.[3]

Later that month he wrote to his father:

Somewhere in France

Dear Dad,

. . . Things are getting very exciting round this quarter now and in the last four days in the trenches I don't think I'd eight hours sleep altogether. It is frightfully difficult to walk in the trenches owing to the slippery nature of things, the most appalling thing is to see the stretcher bearers trying to get the wounded men up to the Field Dressing station. On Saturday morning we were subjected to a fearful bombardment by the German artillery; they simply rained shells – and our artillery rained them back – and there were we – the poor, long-suffering infantry – crouched in our trenches, expecting each moment to be our last. One shell burst right in our trench – and it was a miracle that so few – only four – were injured. The man next to me had his finger broken but I escaped with a little piece of flesh torn out of my thumb. Nothing serious at all – I bandaged it up myself when I attended to my neighbour. But poor Murphy – your Murphy, you know – got a shrapnel wound in the head – a horrible great hole – and the other two were the same. They were removed soon after and I don't know how they are going on.

I have seen some terrible sights, and endured some hardships, but believe me, I never lost my nerve and strange to say, I felt a strange exultation of the soul at the expense of the body. *Do not be afraid for me; – I am not afraid.*

3 'It Was 1913 . . .'

I have just received your parcel, No. 3. for which many thanks. The biscuits were unfortunately broken but still fit to eat. I do not want any winter comforts just yet, I will let you know later. I suppose I am a man now, and am certainly going through an ordeal. Perhaps it would be as well if everybody went through some test of manhood.

With love to all of you,

JACK[4]

In October he wrote home again:

My dear Dad,

Many thanks for your parcel, which has arrived in good time, probably due to the 'Telegraph'. You have taken my last letter too seriously. I was out of sorts and was indulging in the 'luxury' of a 'grouse'. You must remember that it is supposed to be the privilege of a British soldier. This endless trench-fighting and trench-making is very wearisome – we should very much prefer to jump over the parapet and drive the cowards out with the bayonet. We were just on the left of the great advance, and were expecting to have to charge ourselves, but we were apparently not needed. At the present time we are billeted in a fair-sized town, 3 companies of us in an old and very rickety flour-mill. In order to get to the spot where I sleep I have to go up three flights of rickety stairs, dodge under a quantity of beams and old machinery, then down a slippery ladder – and I'm 'home'. This place is full of all sorts of troops including large numbers of Gurkhas, Sikhs and other Indian troops. It is a grievance with our fellows and the infantry generally, the number of men out here with well paid, soft jobs. These bases are full of them, – tradesmen of the A.S.G., A.O.C. and A.P.C. men, and many of the R.A.M.C. and R.E. men. However we get the 'glory' out here, and these fellows acknowledge their indebtedness to the *Infantry*. We have been digging trenches for the R.E.'s since we have been here; it is very hard work, as the soil is extremely heavy clay, the heaviest clay I have ever dug and I've as much experience in digging as most navvies. You may gather the speed we work when a man has to do a 'task' – 6 ft long, 4 ft broad and 2 ft 6 ins deep in an afternoon. Yesterday afternoon I had got right down to the bottom of the trench, and consequently every blooming shovelful of clay I got I had to throw a height of 12 ft to get it out of the back and over the parapet. You try it and see! By the way, our fellows have not received a thing yet from the town of Bradford, though the fellows

4  Priestley to Jonathan Priestley, 27 September 1915.

from Huddersfield, Keighley and other towns have received things. *It's a shame, you know.* What I was grumbling about last letter was the extra-super-officiousness of most of the officers. I'm not grumbling about the ordinary work of the soldier out here. I take that as it comes, naturally. But when it comes to flagrant acts of injustice, my blood boils! The *Times* are very welcome, if there are any more, send 'em! Hoping that you are all well at home.
                JACKY.[5]

By December sleet and snow whitened the muddy no man's land, which threw into sharp relief the black shape of any figure and increasing the hazards of the slightest movement. Priestley referred with English understatement to these conditions as 'very unpleasant' and recounted with equivalent modesty his part in a night raid. Crawling over the mud and craters in pitch darkness, the raiding party reached the first barbed wire which the CO had said was cut, only to find it still there in all its bristling reality. The star shells were already riding high in the sky and there the patrol lay trapped, a sitting target for the machine-guns. Priestley never knew how he and a handful of men grovelled their way back to their own trenches but he remembered all too well dragging with them a badly wounded man. It was a small act of heroism which he baldly records without comment in *Margin Released*.

The raids into no man's land were perilous, and the days when German heavy artillery found their range murderous, but the underlying horror of the conditions in which they lived wore down nerves and morale just as destructively. Clambering from one muddy foothold to the next in trenches, sometimes deep in water, wearing soaking wet jackets, gumboots and three pairs of socks, crawling into any half-sheltered hole to scratch the lice until sheer exhaustion forced sleep upon a tormented body, was an experience he recalled with the same coolness in *Margin Released*. His main complaint was the relatively comfortable quarters of the French and Germans, and the unheeding luxury of British cavalry captains in their châteaux. They saw themselves as generals fit for high command. He wrote to his father late in 1915: 'I have no hesitation in saying that the French soldiers are better fed and better treated than we are – and the British public can put that in their pipes and smoke it.'[6]

Two letters to his father vividly reconstruct his life at this time.

5  Priestley to Jonathan Priestley, 26 October 1915.
6  Priestley to Jonathan Priestley, 'Tuesday', late 1915.

THE SOLDIER

*Sunday morning*

We have been in the trenches this last five days and shall stop for some few more. These trenches are in quite a different part of the line to the others we have been in and it's a part we don't want to see again. Talk about a hole! The communication trenches are simply canals, up to the waist in some parts, the rest up to the knees (one of our chaps was enquiring about the fishing rights). There are only a few dug-outs and those are full of water or falling in / three killed this week with falling dug-outs / and the parapets are tumbling down. O! it's *some* place, I can assure you. And 'Fritz' (our name for the gentle Hun) keeps things pretty exciting here with snipers, trench-mortars, aerial torpedoes, etc. Good old Fritz, he does relieve the monotony. Dull the jobs they give us here. The other night a crowd of us had to go over the parapet with shovels, crawl through deep water and under barbed wire for about a hundred yards, and then start digging about fifty yards from the German lines. But it's little digging we could do, for they must have heard us, and they shot up six flare-lights right above our heads – we of course being as still as statues. But they spotted us, and the bullets came and we had to get back as best we could. Two were killed outright just near me. And mind you, this isn't a V.C. business, it's just a 'working party' in this part of the line. We're attached to another Division here and tis said that they've brought us down here to do these exciting jobs, as the regiments here are too nervy and won't do 'em. Anyhow the Battn. is getting something of a name. I should say that there are – or were – at the very least 300 Bradford men in our Battalion. Of course since we came out here we have had two drafts from the Reserve Battn. to make up the strength, but we're not at full strength by a long way, owing to continual casualties. I haven't had a wash since we came into these trenches and we're all mud from head to foot. I believe the hazardous nature of this place has bucked me up considerably, for I feel more cheerful than I have done for some time. We're supposed to start leaves on the 26th of this month, but it takes a long time to get everybody through. Love to all.

JACK[7]

*Thursday*

Dear Dad,

Many thanks for your letter. So we are all getting commissions, are we? But I don't want one, thanks, notwithstanding the bright example set by Fisher and others. We are still in the trenches, and it is

7  Priestley to Jonathan Priestley, late 1915.

very miserable. I hope you will continue to spend a Merry Xmas, and don't make yourselves miserable on my account. I should be far happier myself if I thought you were having a jolly time. I should have a good time, if I were at home. The chances of seeing Saltburn Place are very remote for a long while, unless I happen to get a 'blighty'. Send a plum pudding by all means. I enjoyed Miss Routhwait's very much. Things are very quiet here now, and rather monotonous save for an occasional bombardment by the artillery.

Goodbye!

JACK[8]

Experiences mediated through recollection are frequently romanticised and it is hard to believe the evidence of *Margin Released* that having reached some dry warm quarters as a temporary clerk, Priestley so hated the job that he longed to get back to 'the men I knew, trenches and shellfire and all'.

Shortly afterwards he was back in the front line once more, only to have a splinter from a rifle grenade wound him and send him first to hospital and then to a convalescence camp at Le Tréport. In any less robust character his repeated desire to escape from safety and return to the front would have been considered suicidal. The convalescent camp was cut off from money, letters and parcels, overwhelmed with 'fatigue duties' and bug-ridden, but it offered a refuge from death and mutilation. 'I still wanted to be with the men who had gone up Gibbet Lane, Halifax, when I did, even though one friend after another was vanishing.'

In March 1916 the whole division prepared to move to relieve the French 17th Division on the Carency–Souchez front. What was known as the Labyrinth had been relatively quiet before the British arrived but within a few days an inspired local commander decided that the morale of the 69th was slackening and he arranged a side-show which brought the wrath of the German guns down on their heads with deadly accuracy. There was no plan of campaign, no ground won or lost, and even battle honours failed to materialise, but at the end of this reckless exercise the 270 fighting strength of B Company shrank to a grim, bitter remnant of 70. As one name after another was called and nobody answered, the shattering truth came home and the men sank back in their trenches in a worse state of morale than when the battle began. Priestley once more baldly states the facts but it is not difficult to imagine the reaction of a sensitive imaginative young man to useless deaths on such a scale.

8   Priestley to Jonathan Priestley, December 1915.

Formulas for accommodating sudden death were multiple: 'Has it got your number on it' – 'It's no use dodging' – 'Learn to co-operate with the inevitable' – 'Jerry doesn't love me any more.' Priestley refused to take refuge in commonplace fatalism but he knew that his luck could not last. We do not have any reliable evidence of how he faced this growing conviction.

It happened one hot June day with everybody thirsty, chalk dust blowing across the front, and nothing of any consequence disturbing the uneasy lull of a beautiful morning. 'I sent Private O'Neill down the communication trench to bring up some water – and sixteen years went by before we saw each other again.'

It dramatically condensed what has to be spelt out. Priestley was apportioning bread, milk and tea to his troop that day – a process unsatisfactory to everybody – when he heard a deep rushing sound as of a train approaching. It was an old familiar sound, a close friend or enemy according to the consequences, and a hundred times before he had experienced the shrinking terror which now over-took him once more. The same fatalistic sense that his time had come was followed, as always, by a sense of detachment as his mind went into something he described as 'slow time'. Coincidence ceased on this occasion at that point. The *Minenwerfer* crashed into the trench no more than two yards away, the world suddenly split and soared heavenwards and young Jack Priestley ceased to be aware of anything.

Miraculously, all his wounds were superficial. Partial deafness followed but the after-effects of the collapse of the dug-out were not mentioned in *Margin Released*. The earth closed in to bury him, and his comrades had to dig him out, an experience according to one witness which left a permanent scar.[9] Later in life he did not like travelling on the underground, and he was disinclined to talk about details of the events which followed the *Minenwerfer* explosion. No memory remained of how he travelled from the front line in France to a military hospital in Leicester, and his first conscious recollections were blurred by the delirium of a high temperature. Then came the picture of his parents bending over the bed, seen mistily, but for the first time identifiable, and the long awkward moments that ensued. Reunion under such circumstances would obviously be highly charged, but in a throwaway phrase Priestley gave an insight into the inner workings of his family life. 'We are affectionate

9 Interview with Angela Wyndham Lewis, 10 October 1985.

and have plenty to say on general topics, but never have we spoken from heart to heart.'

Such a description of a closely knit Yorkshire family, bred in the intimacies of limited accommodation, comes as a surprise, but an even more remarkable revelation followed. The emotional gap with his father was reproduced, he said, in his relations with his own children, and in their relations with their children. Instead of the robust relationship characteristic of lower-middle-class Yorkshire families, the Priestleys – according to this statement – experienced varying degrees of inhibition. 'With us the Lord our God is an inhibited God, visiting the awkward silences and unspoken endearments of the fathers upon the children unto the third and fourth generation.'[10]

The enforced community of uncongenial spirits in a hospital ward created a form of hell against which Priestley quickly rebelled. The repetitious horror of a gramophone record called 'Sussex By The Sea' and the drivelling lyrics sung by 'wobbly sopranos', he never forgot.

> We don't want to lose you
> But we think you ought to go,
> For your King and your Country
> Both need you so.

At the other extreme, he remembered from the trenches bawdy ballads directed at front-line troops – 'Bollocky Bill The Sailor And The Fair Young Maiden' – which had no greater appeal.

His stay in the North Evington hospital was relatively short and the next move carried him into a totally different atmosphere where an old-world couple lived luxuriously in one quarter of a Georgian country house, the remainder of which was converted into a convalescent home. The ideal setting for a 1920s light comedy, something approximating to its reality greeted Priestley on his arrival. Accused of getting one of the maids pregnant, the young and handsome butler not only admitted his crime but made preparations – judiciously leaked to the staff – to commit suicide. Priestley's arrival coincided with 'beautiful VADs melting in tears', crying 'No – no, Alfred, please!' The combined chorus of cook,

---

10 *Margin Released*, J. B. Priestley, 110. There were other, contradictory accounts.

housekeeper, maids and VADs forced the butler to the point where he generously agreed to stay alive and normal routine now absorbed Priestley into a way of life luxurious beyond anything he had known for eighteen months. Marked out by elegance and Kensington accents the nurses managed to treat the patients as heroic peasantry. There remained one professional nurse who contradicted every stereotype Priestley had known. Middle-aged, plump, warm and motherly, she beamed her way round the wards with a bespectacled smile which better suited a female Father Christmas, dispensing medicines like gifts, taking temperatures erratically and endearing herself to everybody.[11]

Priestley's gift for hammering out on the oldest piano some semblance of any popular song or ballad made him the 'Orpheus of recreation rooms, *estaminets*, convalescent camps and mess rooms'. Discovering his facility, the lady of the house invited him to accompany her daughter in César Franck's sonata for violin and piano, and his attempt to sight read the work merely confirmed the daughter's belief that he was little more than a sweaty oaf. Less ambitious works, requiring mere accompaniment, somewhat redeemed his reputation but the wounded hero was still at a stage of musical development where 'slam-banging away' at music-hall songs or students' ditties brought out a gift rarely encountered in the army. Unlike Siegfried Sassoon, Wilfred Owen and Robert Graves, he was not moved by the beauty of starlit nights on the battle zones to distil Georgian poetry but was forced, under pressure from 'comrades', to organise concert parties. A photograph of these troupes is reproduced in this book and we know from Priestley's *Margin Released* that it showed five men in varying imitations of hunting gear 'doing their hunting song number' which brought the house down. This after all was fox-hunting country.

Priestley left the comic opera world of the Rutland house to enter a depot designed to restore complete physical fitness by rigid discipline and ruthless PT instruction. Men wearing black and red striped jerseys strode around issuing orders in stentorian voices to groups of convalescents whose experience of war went far beyond the limitations of their instructors. Friction sometimes broke into open hostility and twice Priestley was driven to reject the fallacy of the English as basically kind and tolerant in all those situations which reveal the cruelty of the callous foreigner. *Margin Released*

11   ibid., 114.

drew a vivid picture of a number of men in authority just below the top rank who were 'insensitive and brutalised from boyhood', inflicting on regimented men disciplinary systems which had long been abolished by other countries. In those days Britain still sent men to the gallows, shot cowards, inflicted cruel military punishments and agitated for revival of the cat-o'-nine-tails.

When Priestley moved on after 'a few sullen weeks' to a quite different convalescent camp located outside Alnwick, Northumberland, his relief was almost equivalent to leaving the front line. Here he quickly learnt the art of fatigue-dodging and every morning assembled his men under the sergeant major's eye waiting for his final command – 'Fatigue parties dismiss' – with no intention of carrying out any fatigues whatever.

The year 1917 was the only year in which he escaped the front and for six of the twelve months he was in limbo, drifting along with camp routine, drinking heavily in the local pub, his sensations blurred, his intuitions stultified. A well-to-do, earnest and very cultured lady put up some prize money in the convalescent camps for an essay and stirred him momentarily out of his haze. Priestley easily won and easily spent the £20. Deterioration reached a point where the splendid recruit of two years before had become disillusioned with the war and his way of life to such a pitch that he later saw himself as one of the anti-heroes of the 1960s.

Passed as fit at last, he reported to the 3rd Battalion of the 96th Brigade in North Wales for training in the OTC. There he found men so terrified of returning to the front that they would bribe and lie to escape what they regarded as a death sentence. The training course brought him out of his lethargy and he quickly showed that he was capable of understanding military textbooks, handling what he regarded as outdated rifles and eating peas without a knife. Passing the final examination easily, he emerged fully equipped with brand-new tunic, Sam Browne belt, greatcoat and British Warm, a shy and glossily new officer who took his place in the Devonshire Regiment. Six weeks later orders came to embark for France and they sailed in a gloriously old-fashioned American steamship surrounded by thousands of raw, hearty American troops who sang to ragtime bands and gave him his first taste of that American dynamism which he later came to know so well.

A new and freshly horrifying experience at Péronne followed. Located in a narrow railway cutting, one evening, German planes came flying over and the dreaded word went round – Gas! Gas! Swiftly buckling on his mask Priestley ran round the position to check his men who loathed wearing masks. They were due to attack the following morning and Priestley somehow managed to drink 'a good many tots of rum' before leading his men forward. Whether the thick swirling mists, the tots of rum, a whiff of gas leaking through his mask, or sheer carelessness was responsible, he quickly lost direct touch with a battle which he could hear all round him, but not see. Uncertain whether he was advancing or retreating, suddenly out of the white mist loomed a German youth of about sixteen who raised his hands in surrender and gibbered something incomprehensible. Any idea that Priestley could accurately shoot down a man with a pistol had been disproved in the training camp where his gift for missing the target had been guyed mercilessly by fellow trainees. Waving his revolver in what he took to be the direction of his own lines, he was surprised when the German youth meekly trotted in the direction indicated.[12] Whether from gas, drink or fatigue his head began spinning, he took shelter in a shell hole and one hour later was brought back to safety by a stretcher party. Recovering quickly in the Medical Board Base Depot at Rouen, he was appointed temporary letter censor and pay-out officer which meant dealing with a polyglot crowd of clamouring privates whose capacity for starting an argument exceeded the intelligence with which they pursued it. Sustained by endless bottles of Guinness at one franc a bottle, Priestley survived the experience without too much suffering. The remainder of his service lasted a short time but dragged badly. Described by the Medical Board as B2 or unfit for active service, he was sent to work for the Labour Corps Depot where he entered the Entertainers Section. There he had a relatively happy time trying out relays of singers, actors, female impersonators and clowns, very few of which he selected to entertain the troops. 'I began to feel like a variety agent in uniform, or a man dreaming he was one.'[13]

False reports of an armistice now began to circulate and one was taken so seriously that the dapper little colonel in charge of the Labour Corps bought champagne one evening to celebrate. Festivities quickly collapsed as news of a fresh attack came through. Saddest, perhaps, of all the moving vignettes scattered through Priestley's brilliantly evocative account of those days was the occasion, walking through the nearby woods one day, when a hobbling crone, grinning toothlessly, produced her credentials

12   ibid., 126.
13   ibid., 128.

which licensed her to practise prostitution and offered her services. Delicately Priestley indicated that he was not quite in the right mood.[14]

The Labour Corps Depot was a large factory beset by dank air and mists which gave a ghostly appearance to the swarms of men set on endless unnecessary tasks for their martial reassurance. When genuine news of the armistice at last came through, it took the sleep-walking atmosphere of the Labour Corps so much by surprise that they 'had to hurry to get drunk enough to go shouting and reeling round the town'.[15]

Priestley recalled the vain attempts he made to generate the appropriate frenzies for such an occasion, only to have his efforts relapse into a contradictory tide of sadness and regret. He was out of the fighting line but had no ambitions. Life in the army had ordered his existence and he enjoyed his impresario role, selecting star entertainers. Beyond lay mystery and uncertainty in a totally strange civilian world. Any illusion that servicemen would immediately escape military discipline and rapidly return to civilian life disappeared in his case when, three days after the armistice, he was ordered to report to a German prisoner-of-war camp near Calais because he spoke a smattering of German. Characteristically, the Germans in the camp had preserved their military discipline and a number of Iron-Crossed, iron-willed men, imposed such strict order on the camp that it slightly intimidated Priestley. Another of his all-revealing vignettes pictured a group of 'these military monsters' gathered round a Christmas tree, singing a German carol with sentimental throatiness, only to stand to heel-clamping attention when he unexpectedly broke in on them.

For the second time, after four and a half years in the army, Priestley was thoroughly enjoying his job when he experienced a final clash with authority which delighted him in recollection. Ordered to remove his men to a camp site which he discovered was full of water-logged shell holes, he reported back to the remote figure of a red-tabbed CO that there must have been a map misreading. The CO reiterated his order and indicated that he would not tolerate any delay or further excuses. A long hesitating moment and Priestley determined to risk the CO's wrath by pointing out that the water-logged site was inadequate even for fit men and some of his men were not only sick, but running high

14  ibid.
15  ibid.

temperatures. A bevy of red tabs and brass hats next descended on his improvised HQ, full of blazing indignation, demanding to know, in loud voices, what 'the devil he was doing' and 'who the devil he thought he was'. Their amazement when he still refused to surrender was increased when he suggested that by viewing the site they could confirm its total inadequacy. Brushing aside such audacity from a mere subaltern, they demanded the immediate execution of their orders, only to be met by a still more resolute but, by now, wily Priestley, who said approximately: 'My war is over and if the Fifth Army wants to court martial me, I do not object, but I cannot accept responsibility for sending my men to the indicated site.'[16]

Dumbfounded, and full of silent threat, the brass hats piled back into their car and drove away, leaving Priestley astonished at his own audacity. Anticipating serious trouble, he immediately went in search of an alternative site and, finding one, reported to HQ that if they held their fire he would, without any extra expense, have the German prisoners build a new camp at the alternative site. Echoes of earlier threats were repeated but grudgingly his scheme was accepted. As Priestley put it, 'Subaltern wins on points.'[17]

One final episode put fully to the test the 'bewildered and secretly terrified' young subaltern of twenty-four, when he found himself in charge of a night demobilisation train running from Lille to Boulogne, packed tight with drunken, embittered and uproarious men, newly aware of freedom and anxious to revenge themselves on years of disciplinarians. Such a job should have been undertaken by a senior officer and now when discipline was beginning – audibly – to crack in all directions, Priestley saw the whole train becoming a battleground liable to be engulfed in flames. Selecting a few NCOs who seemed sober and responsible, Priestley put it to them that without attempting 'anything fancy' a minimum of discipline would see everybody home in England much more quickly. Several threatening situations arose in the night but none exploded. Then came the final attempt to march a 'no-more-bloody-nonsense mob' to a transit camp. Deliberately allowing a completely relaxed column to follow his lead without any attempt at formation marching, they finally approached the transit camp. A pompous adjutant came storming out, glared at Priestley and roared, 'Left Right, Left Right.' The column came to a ragged halt,

16  ibid., 132.
17  ibid.

stared at this immaculate apparition and then hooted with laughter or presented him with the classic two-finger salute. The war was over. Military bullshit already obsolete.

# 5

# Early Essayist and Marriage
## 1919–24

Lieutenant John Boynton Priestley, twenty-four years old, and seasoned beyond his years, emerged from an unknown town in the Midlands, late in 1919, and began his adjustment to civilian routine. Photographs show him as an undistinguished young man, uncomfortable in his first civilian suit, staring moodily at his pipe, aware that having come through the holocaust he had failed to get from it any future directions. He came 'blinking out at last into civilian daylight' without any great resolutions and simply wondered whether he could interlace walks on the beautiful moors with occasional writing for the *Yorkshire Observer*, listening to string quartets and drinking, all of which so long ago had delighted him in another life. He received no rewards for gallantry, he refused to apply for the regulation medals which were due to him and it was as if the War Office had erased his name from the records. He simply 'shrugged the shoulders of a civvy coat and carried on'.

This is not the complete truth because the slow grinding machinery of rehabilitation offered him an educational grant which eventually took him to Cambridge. Meanwhile, late in 1919 an event occurred, highly significant at the time but passed over with an aside in *Margin Released*. It is known from unpublished sources that at different times Priestley had shared violin and piano duets with the daughter of a neighbour, Pat Tempest, but there was no indication of any courtship. Those who in later years remember her describe a pleasant girl with a Yorkshire accent, whose musical inclinations seldom ventured beyond a limited classical range.[1] It is not difficult to imagine what starved senses men four and a half years with the army brought to women in ordinary civilian life, and certainly one recollection of this hunger was quoted to the author late in 1959:

The sight of any woman was magical. Worse, it was dangerous. The

1  Interview with Sylvia Priestley, 10 October 1985.

itch to communicate – physically – became overpowering and there were times when you had to carefully restrain straying hands. I remember standing outside the Empire one day shortly after I had returned from France, and along came a slim young girl in a yellow frock who suddenly seemed to me to be a floating vision of beauty – until my hands began to tremble and I was overtaken by sheer lust.[2]

One other sidelight on Priestley's pre-marriage relationship with Pat Tempest comes from the daughter of a woman who shared musical evenings with her. Mary Widgery said:

> I only have a little girl's version of one of those evenings, but it seemed to me they were very sweet on each other and sometimes I saw them stealing kisses in the back parlour, which I hated at the time because I wanted him to love my mother not Pat, and it all got mixed up in my mind until I hated him. But he was very kind to me. Bought me sweets and things. I'm sure Pat was a very nice woman but she didn't seem like that to me at the time because of my jealousy and all that. I can't clearly remember what she looked like. Blonde, I think, and short. I'm sorry memory fails.[3]

Something very little known intervenes here. Priestley had already written and published a book. According to J. T. Winterich, Priestley's first book, *The Chapman of Rhymes*, was produced 'while serving as a lieutenant in the Devonshire Regiment during the Great War'.[4] According to Priestley it was a 'collection of dubious verse written in my teens before the First War and sent to be published entirely at my own expense during that war when I felt, foolishly, I ought to leave something behind'. Immediately after the war, 'coming to [his] senses', he destroyed 'every copy [he] could lay hands on' and there is no need to delay the narrative with this 'youthful conceit' which contained the seeds of its own decay.[5]

According to A. H. Robinson who later worked in the same reference library, Emily alias Pat Tempest, was employed in Bradford Central Library and Priestley's extensive reading made it fertile ground for developing their relationship. Certainly the romance moved swiftly and on 29 June 1921 Priestley 'committed one of those reckless plunges into married life' which are often

2 Interview, 7 September 1959.
3 Interview, Mary Widgery.
4 'Et tu Priestley', J. T. Winterich, *Saturday Review of Literature*, 15 November 1933.
5 *Instead of the Trees*, J. B. Priestley, 46.

preceded by total ignorance of the person involved. The ceremony took place 'with as much avoidance of fuss as I could arrange'.

The Priestley who had recoiled from the pretensions of higher education then decided that he would risk the dangers of entering a university. Trinity Hall, Cambridge, in those days was over-whelmed by middle-class students whose accents were totally different from Priestley's, which gave them airs of superiority he found intolerable. Still a relatively gauche young man, after the crude baptism of army life, he suffered from culture shock but occasionally, on the verge of allowing his sense of inferiority to surface, he threw it off with the remark 'The next time you get blown up by a *minenwerfer*, you'll know what life is all about.'

If Priestley never 'took to' Cambridge, and Cambridge certainly reciprocated, it could be seen as mutual incomprehension. He found the actual geographical climate intolerable and, coming as he did 'from the high hills', the Fen country depressed him. With the exceptions of the scientists, dons as a race seemed to him reeking with conceit and he never quite reconciled himself to the flummeries of high table. 'Finally, though not without interest to me, once my name appeared in the London Press as well as in the *Cambridge Review*, Cambridge society regarded me as a North Country lout of no uncertain temper.'[6]

The paradox remained inexplicable because his elevation to authorship in the august journal of the university should have had the reverse effect. Priestley made friends at Cambridge with Edward Davison, a poet whose editorship of the *Cambridge Review* opened its pages to him. Several essays were mere squibs but others were more substantial and his friendship with Davison continued long after he left the university. Writing occasional pieces for the press, coaching and casual lectures at a guinea a time became a necessity to eke out his army grant and support his wife. Already uneasy in what he regarded as the pedantry of academic life, he felt the lure of creative writing and decided to collect 'a little book of his undergraduate odds and ends', hoping to persuade 'some imbecile' to risk his money publishing it. The local booksellers Bowes & Bowes were the selected victims and published *Brief Diversions*, a slender volume of sixty pages which satirised people like Sir Arthur Quiller-Couch, Alfred Noyes, W. B. Yeats and James Stephens. David Hughes described it as a book containing a 'litter of small pieces of varying kinds, for the most part those contrived

6  *Outcries and Asides*, J. B. Priestley, 153.

knick-knacks of artifice and wit which are both as graceful and ubiquitous as the etchings popular at the time'.[7]

To the astonishment of author and publisher this casually thrown-off trifle incited reviewers as distinguished as Edmund Gosse to produce rave reviews. As Priestley colourfully put it: 'One quick tiny shot – and *bang* – the bull's eye! Like a man playing a fruit machine, I cupped my hands for the clanging spill of the jackpot. And nothing happened.' Instead of a flood of requests to write reviews, essays, criticism or even at the wildest stretch of expectation another book, there was a profound silence. Priestley fell into deep depression which was only lightened by the encouragement and meticulous ministrations of his new young wife. More musical than literary, Pat Tempest managed to cope with the disgruntlement of a would-be man of letters who had learnt, with devastating immediacy, the total uncertainty of the writer's life. Later he wrote: 'A writer may think of himself as succeeding or failing with a particular book, but never, unless he is a lost soul, does he think of his life and work in terms of success.'

Paradoxically, his own life became the living contradiction of that belief when not all the criticism of individual books and plays came anywhere near destroying the writer, J. B. Priestley. Moreover, Priestley's recorded reactions have to be seen in the perspective of a letter he wrote to Edward Davison from his old home address, 5 Saltburn Place, late in 1922. Gerald Bullett had written what Priestley regarded as a flattering review of *Brief Diversions* and the review inspired none other than Sir Arthur Methuen of Methuen the publishers, to write to him care of Davison's paper *The Challenge*. The letter asked Priestley to 'let them see any books [he] had in hand . . . Of all the things that have happened to me I believe this letter from a publisher appeals to me most . . . at least as a sign of getting on.'[8]

So many contradictions emerged in his early Cambridge years with a young man who still had not committed himself to a career, but the lure of literature – surprisingly – did suffer a severe setback. Flagrantly abusing his first love, he suddenly switched from English to Modern History and Political Science. His passage through the university then proceeded swiftly and at the end of his second year he took his degree (a 2:1) 'without having exhausted many of my resources'. With another year of his officer's grant still

7  *J. B. Priestley*, David Hughes, 61.
8  Priestley to Edward Davison, 22 December 1922.

to run, he made the decision to stay on at Cambridge 'engaged in postgraduate research of how to make ends meet'. Coaching, writing essays, reviews and reading in depth every available newspaper for jobs, occupied his working hours. Economic pressures were constantly building up and many possible jobs occurred, among them a number of full-blown professorships in outlandish places, with names like Katangaland, the whereabouts of which only the closest scrutiny of the map revealed. 'I could never discover what the salaries were worth in London, for no country whose currency was quoted in the *Times* wanted my services.'[9]

Then came another decision which shaped his ends for the rest of his life. Asked to give a specimen lecture to a bored cleric and ten depressed working men in a village institute, he successfully passed the test and was duly appointed as a university extension lecturer in the North Devon region. Although hard evidence is scarce, it appears that his father thought this a splendid triumph and his wife welcomed the security which a regular income promised. In the event, not even the combined pressure of his family, his wife and Sir Arthur Quiller-Couch, who offered him some lectures in English literature, deflected him from a wild course of action which had gathered unconscious power and now broke into the open. He spoke of it later as if the idea came out of the blue. 'I . . . pleased [Sir Arthur Quiller-Couch] and certainly annoyed the University Extension people, by suddenly deciding I would become a freelance writer in London.'

His capital amounting to £50, his wife threatened with pregnancy and his academic reputation depreciating, he set out for London with 'more apprehension than hope'.

A prolonged and exhausting search discovered a seven-roomed flat on the ground floor of King Edward's Mansions, Walham Green, the rent of which – £75 a year – would have been prohibitive but for Edward Davison's offer to share it with him. Davison, who had come to London to edit an obscure magazine called *The Challenge*, co-operated with the Priestleys to redecorate the flat and all three settled into a relatively bohemian life in this seedy area which lacked the class of Chelsea or the brashness of the Fulham Road. The trio converted daily excursions to second-hand shops into 'outings' where Priestley comically imitated an auctioneer selling a double bed to a newly married couple and Davison produced heroic couplets on the slightest provocation. Coveting a Broadwood

9  Contribution by J. B. Priestley to *Coming to London*, ed. John Lehmann, 59.

grand piano, they found the price beyond their means and Priestley first encountered prospective debt in the form of hire purchase, something he came to regard as no less crippling than retrospective debt. His relationship with Edward Davison deepened over the years and Davison became a natural confidant who was later to receive a stream of revealing letters.

For the moment Priestley began living the ragged uncertain life of the freelance writer, one day scribbling a review of a book, another beginning a short story, a third preparing material for a book on English comic characters and a fourth haunting Fleet Street in the hope of developing reviewing connections. Any writer familiar with these early days scraping a living from semi-literary activities will know the inescapable stresses which usually drive the independent writer into overwork, over-anxiety, and a constant realisation of time's winged chariot. Priestley was no exception. A letter addressed to Davison while he was away on one occasion said:

> The whole damned pack of bills, deadlines, unpaid rent, overdrafts, and publishers demanding the impossible are at my heels convinced that I am a quarry worth pursuing, whereas I fumble around inadequately writing nothing of consequence, but I plough on regardless.[10]

The routine of a wool clerk in Bradford was now replaced by a no less disciplined life in London which sent him hurrying out of King Edward's Mansions in the mornings to catch a No. 11 bus to Fleet Street, 'hoping to find some books to review'. The literary scene produced far more weeklies and journals open to outside contributions than exist today, and he scribbled away at everything 'from reviews to critical articles and Shorter Notices' for the *London Mercury*, the *Saturday Review*, the *Outlook* and *Bookman*. Pittances were paid for work of this calibre and Priestley eked out his meagre income by following a tradition which has not changed to this day – selling review copies at half price to a benign old bookseller who sometimes took a friendly intrest in the fate of his black market dealers. Priestley's patron had 'one touch of genius: he always paid us in new pound notes, deliciously clean and crisp and to be handed seven or eight of these was always an exhilarating experience like being in a fairy-tale for a few minutes'. He would hurry out of the shop as if out of Ali Baba's robbers' cave and 'all Fleet Street' was his.

10  Priestley to Edward Davison, 'Tuesday', June 1923.

Sir John Squire, a patron of a different calibre, lorded it over the *London Mercury* and knew half of literary London. A rugged intransigent littérateur, he was a formidable figure. Priestley's poet friend Davison had first introduced him to Squire in Cambridge and with a reckless brashness which concealed uneasy shyness, in the first ninety seconds of conversation he had dared to contradict Squire, a solecism only permitted to the highest in the literary land. Why such behaviour was tolerated and why Squire proceeded to draw him into his circle of contributors, could only be explained by Squire's belief in what he called the Johnsonian vigour in Priestley's writing. Certainly in order to survive and support a wife who presently developed a serious illness, Priestley found himself driven to write day and night, swiftly turning his exhausted hand from a serious critical essay in the day to a Shorter Notice at night. Squire obviously liked Priestley despite the clash of their different backgrounds and introduced him to literary editors and publishers, finally recommending him to John Lane as a publisher's reader. This thankless task involved going to the office of the Bodley Head one morning a week, swiftly surveying last week's manuscripts, rejecting obvious failures and asking the office boy to send anything deserving longer consideration to Walham Green. Despite its drawbacks, the job provided a steady £6 a week to meet basic expenses and was regarded by Pat as her security in the sea of uncertainty surrounding her husband's life. At the time Priestley saw John Lane as a useful and not too demanding patron, but later in life described him as capable of reconciling immense generosity at the lunch table with publishing terms which any successful author would regard as shocking. 'This combination of parsimony with flair meant that the Bodley Head had probably the best list of good first books in town.'[11]

As a reader Priestley revealed that combination of literary discrimination and commercial judgement which recommended, among others, two authors later to become famous: Graham Greene and C. S. Forester. Another choice of his – an 'Amazonian jungle of a manuscript' – was not so successful. John Lane published it only at Priestley's insistence with an introduction by Walter de la Mare. A complex narrative of childhood recollection, the book had the ring of recorded truth but had been re-created from self-indulgent day-dreams by an author curiously named Sunderland Lewis.

11   Contribution by J. B. Priestley to *Coming to London*, ed. John Lehmann, 64.

The long list of distinguished literary people Priestley met through the intermediary of J. C. Squire included Robert Lynd, then literary editor of the *Daily News* for which Priestley became a regular reviewer. It was at Squire's house that he first encountered Lynd and he always remembered the small gaucheries he committed which his host did his best to ignore, only to increase Priestley's uneasiness. Occasionally he had an overwhelming desire to ride roughshod over all the small niceties upon which Squire insisted, but the survival instinct restrained him. There was a classic occasion in the autumn of 1922 when he returned one Sunday from a long country walk with Davison, only to remember that they had been invited to a party at Lynd's house. Under the illusion that it was a casual gathering with a few friends, they arrived wearing shabby tweeds and muddy walking shoes, to be ushered into a drawing-room full of tremendous literary swells all wearing full evening dress. 'Among the guests, seeming in our fancy to pull themselves away from us a little, were fabulous beings like Shaw, Wells and Bennett, no longer caricatures but living, breathing men, chattering away in easily recognisable accents.'[12]

The complete transformation from this ill-at-ease Yorkshireman with his broad accent and cheap clothing, who could not be reconciled with a gift for perceptive writing, into the powerful personality of the best-selling author at ease in any company, took years to accomplish. For the moment there was strain, excitement, wonderment. He was actually mingling with some of the greatest living writers and after a while they exchanged occasional words with him. Maire Lynd, the daughter of Sylvia and Robert Lynd, remembers those days.

> I met Mr Priestley when I was 10 and he was newly in London to make his name as a writer . . . Jack used to draw me caricatures of himself – the long smiling mouth exactly like him – in just a few strokes . . . Jack . . . pretended not to enjoy parties but he really did.[13]

Cheap restaurants in Soho made it possible for Priestley and Davison to return grand hospitality with bohemian meals costing two shillings (20p) without wine, or ten shillings (50p) with wine, brandy, cigars and coffee. The one-roomed Escargot, with only

12  ibid., 66.
13  Unpublished manuscript by Maire Lynd, in my possession, 1–2.

four tables, did not compete with its grander namesake on the opposite side of Greek Street, but supplied freshly cooked meals very cheaply and many a rollicking evening passed in its confines, with the reckless expenditure of another 50p sometimes leaving the payment of rent in doubt. Alternatively, a pub in Poppins Court underneath the offices of the *London Mercury* became the centre of literary lunch-time gatherings where Hilaire Belloc, Robert Lynd, J. B. Morton and the well-known journalist James Bone talked incessantly for two hours, sometimes with wit, sometimes banality, and just occasionally verbal violence.

Drinking, writing, theatre-going were all inhibited in the years 1922 to 1925 by the birth of two girls, Barbara (4 March 1923) and Sylvia (30 April 1924). Neither birth was easy and Sylvia arrived prematurely which necessitated intensive care. Both children, now married with children of their own, have only dim recollections of their mother or those far-off days in Walham Green. The image of a warm, affectionate, straightforward woman who was a good mother concerned for the welfare of her children remains in their minds, but details of domestic life are few. The strain of supporting a family by writing must have been intense, but Priestley was a past master at playing games with children and many an uproarious evening was spent singing round the piano. Paradoxically, good seats at the theatre were relatively expensive in those days, but whenever editors or friendly critics failed to produce complimentary tickets, they settled for the pit or gallery. Ninepence bought a reasonable seat at the old Alhambra and a wealth of distinguished music-hall stars and ballerinas passed across its creaking stage, but these were outmatched by Nigel Playfair's production of *The Beggar's Opera* at the Lyric, Hammersmith. For sheer entertainment nothing beat the evenings spent at home with friends and family gathered round the piano, roaring out the lyrics of *The Beggar's Opera* – all of which Priestley knew by heart. These were the days when Basil Dean produced a row of much more realistic plays like Galsworthy's *Strife*, and Priestley went to see them, unaware that within a very short time his and Basil Dean's paths would cross in a boldly experimental manner.

By 1923 Priestley's literary journalism had multiplied in many directions and articles and reviews now appeared in the *Spectator*, the *Challenge*, *Nineteenth Century*, the *London Mercury* and the *Daily News*. One lead article in the *Times Literary Supplement*, subsequently developed into a small critical book on Thomas Love Peacock, was written within the literary climate of *belles-lettres* which then dominated criticism.[14] No fewer than four books published between 1922 and 1925 contained essays and criticisms written in the less arduous critical atmosphere of the day which was far more personalised and relaxed. Derivative from a professor whom Priestley had once gently satirised in print, George Saintsbury, they were directed at increasing appreciation of literature, not distilling truth from the text.[15]

A letter to Edward Davison from King Edward's Mansions in June 1923 explained the origins of the *Times Literary Supplement* article. Bruce Richmond, the then editor, had read some of Priestley's essays and asked him to call on him at Printing House Square.

> I went this morning to find a pleasant elderly man more like a gentleman than a journalist. He is giving me a leader on Peacock . . . a favourite of his so my screed should either please him greatly or entirely displease him.[16]

Richmond suggested that Priestley should make regular calls on the *Times Literary Supplement* office and he continued to do so over the next few months.

All articles in the *Times Literary Supplement* were unsigned in those days and only the *cognoscenti* were aware that Jack had taken another step forward with his leading front-page *Times Literary Supplement* article on Peacock. His style by now was much more controlled and it even, on this occasion, came near to satisfying the editorial stylistic straitjacket which made articles in the *Times Literary Supplement* almost interchangeable.

Priestley's piece was interspersed with many shrewd insights:

> We see Peacock apparently setting out to show us the importance of opinion, showing us instead how habitual cast of thought can master a man and make him a puppet . . . When a writer turns satirist and proclaims his readiness to laugh at the world's folly we expect to find that he has ensconced himself in some commanding citadel . . . But when we come to Peacock we find that he is continually leading us astray . . . Although he preferred a manner, the comical, not much preferred in this country, he is after all much too English to be cut all of a piece.

14   *Times Literary Supplement*, 27 November 1924.
15   *Brief Diversions*, J. B. Priestley, 44.
16   Priestley to Edward Davison, 23 June 1924.

In the overwhelming clamour of his later fame Priestley's critical work tends to be downgraded or forgotten. His full-length critical discussion of Peacock's novels was reprinted in 1946 and recognised as very stimulating by the editors of the World Classics edition of *Headlong Hall* and *Gryll Grange*. Priestley's appreciation of Peacock easily survived the contradictions in their values but Peacock the élitist would have found Priestley the democrat intolerable. Priestley's summary of Peacock's life remains evocative and poignant.

The essay, as a literary form, flourished in the early 1920s enabling writers to release interior monologues on paper about ants or the universe with grace and ease. Indeed the essence of the essay was to distil the personality of the writer on the page and the more personal he or she became, the better they fitted the mode. Most essayists from Steele and Addison to Hazlitt and Lamb, from Chesterton and Hilaire Belloc to Robert Lynd and J. B. Priestley were highly egocentric. Hazlitt's opinions were unshakeable and Lamb was so preoccupied with his own words, he sometimes failed to hear what others said. Primarily, essays in those days were written as brief entertainments, frequently about topical subjects, in journals and newspapers. None the less, they could be witty, penetrating and sometimes wise. Longer and more serious examples might be collected and survive in book form, and Priestley did produce two such books, *Papers from Lilliput* (1922) and *I For One* (1923). Among these earliest efforts were essays on 'Talking', 'Audacity in Authorship', 'Those Terrible Novelists', 'First Nights', 'Our Theatre', 'T'Match', 'A Fish in Bayswater' and 'Pyjamas'. Many of them catch a mood on the wing which fixes a small part of the reader's reciprocal experience, as in 'A Fish in Bayswater'. The essay describes a day 'when life had seemed no better than the stirring of withered leaves against the tree' and suddenly there on a fishmonger's slab he confronted a big flat beautiful fish which 'immediately carried [the] mind away to the sea and opened up a sudden flashing vision of something life-enhancing'.

It is possible to trace many of Priestley's movements and moods in the early 1920s from these essays and stylistically they reveal a man gradually simplifying his words, removing literary references, but remaining a very eloquent guide to familiar places. The mood swings violently. One phrase rings out as an affirmation of life, only to be followed by the threat of disillusion. 'There are occasions in a man's existence when he must make something happen, must fling a splash of colour into his life, or some part of him, perhaps the boy in him will perish, flying before the grey armies of age, timidity or boredom.' Within a few pages the Priestley who had been blown up and buried alive suddenly feels the breath of a tiger at his back – the 'gleam of an eye, a whiff of hot rank breath' – but the tiger does not spring and the passage ends 'I am still alive.'

Essentially, the most successful of the four books published between 1922 and 1925 was *The English Comic Characters*, a work of a quite different order. The *Times Literary Supplement* praised it.

> These great and familiar figures are seen through Mr Priestley's eyes in all their original freshness, yet tinged with the warm colours of a singularly sympathetic personality.[17]

*The English Comic Characters* appears in bibliographies as criticism, but strictly it is *belles-lettres*, with Priestley sharing common memories with the reader in a new and very evocative manner. He so obviously enjoyed writing the book and his sallies into critical analysis are overwhelmed by his satisfaction in evoking the characters.

His summing-up is as pleasurable as it is perceptive.

> There is only one thing better than a story and that is – a character. A character is half a hundred stories at once – particularly if it is a comic character. The great comic figures wander out of their books . . . for they are nothing if not children of freedom, and so we find them and their starry folly at large in our minds. Their happy absurdities have added something to the whole flavour of our existence.

Priestley's *English Comic Characters* is a little classic of its kind whose evocation of the comic spirit comes surging across the years.

Another considerable book in his prolific output between 1922 and 1926 was a study of George Meredith (1926) which John Squire commissioned in his *English Men of Letters*, a series whose contributors included T. H. Huxley, Leslie Stephen, Alfred Noyes, Anthony Trollope, Edmund Gosse and Priestley's prime satirical victim, George Saintsbury. Priestley's final assessment of Meredith was penetrating:

> An understandably great but puzzling figure: a genuine poet and philosopher . . . who can dwindle at all times into a mere fop; a rich

17   *Times Literary Supplement*, 30 April 1925.

genius in whom there is some curious streak of the shoddy adven-
turer: a man of Shakespearean mould crossed with the strains of
Beau Brummell: and withal the author of an astonishingly full,
brilliant and varied canon in prose and verse, and of at least one
novel, *The Egoist*, that takes its place among the six best pieces of
fiction in the language.[18]

In contrast to his *English Comic Characters*, Priestley remained in
*Meredith* the objective critic and the book survives today as a good
introduction to a rich and complex writer. Once again the *Times
Literary Supplement* praised *Meredith*.[19]

Priestley sent Thomas Hardy a copy of *George Meredith* and
Hardy wrote to him in August 1926:

> I am not at all a good critic especially of a critic and when the author
> he reviews is a man who was on and off a friend of mine for 40 years,
> but it seems to me that you hold the scales very fairly. Meredith was,
> as you recognised and might have insisted on even more strongly
> and I always felt, in the direct succession of Congreve and the
> artificial comedians of the Restoration, and in getting his brilliance
> we must put up with the fact that he would not, or could not – at any
> rate did not – when aiming to represent the 'Comic Spirit' let himself
> discover the tragedy that always underlies comedy if you only
> scratch it deeply enough.[20]

Priestley sent presentation copies of another critical book, *Figures
in Modern Literature*, to A. E. Housman, George Santayana, Walter
de la Mare and Arnold Bennett. The book was a collection of essays
originally printed in John Squire's *London Mercury*, which included
studies of all the recipients. Their reactions make interesting reading. *Figures in Modern Literature* gave implicitly favourable accounts
of all its subjects – they were, of course, still alive. Priestley
described Santayana as 'a philosophical and literary League of
Nations'. Santayana replied with a shrewd criticism of the book.[21]

> I admire the courage with which in criticising those of us who are
> still living, you have faced the hard choice between truth and
> courtesy. Courtesy has carried the day . . . For instance, in the case
> of A. E. Housman it seems to me that with all you don't say the final,

18  *George Meredith*, J. B. Priestley, 200.
19  *Times Literary Supplement*, 27 May 1926.
20  Thomas Hardy to Priestley, 8 August 1926.
21  George Santayana to Priestley, 15 September 1924.

the crucifying word. I was panting for it expecting it to come on page 83: but it wasn't there . . . I wish to indicate in this and other instances the sort of limitation which there is in your account of myself – extraordinarily generous and intelligent as it is. You do not reach the centre, you do not discover the heart pumping the blood through those devious veins and arteries.

Arnold Bennett's reaction was not unexpected. Of course, he wrote, he never missed an essay on himself and he read Priestley's in the *Mercury* with interest. He thought some of his animadversions very good, but he did not agree with everything Priestley said. Like all authors he felt 'deeply convinced that [he was] not understood as completely as [his] amazing merits deserved'.[22] Housman was more critical. He could easily swallow, he wrote, the flatteries brewed by Priestley and F. L. Lucas but he wished people would get their categorisations right. He was a Cyrenaic, not a Stoic. He had the greatest contempt for the Stoics 'except as systematisers of knowledge in succession to the Peripatetics'.[23]

Still trying to discover the correct formula for his literary talents, Priestley now underwent a struggle between the desire to develop his criticism and the deeper mutterings of creative writing. He could easily have surrendered to academe and emerged as yet another lecturer, regurgitating pre-packaged lectures, but his heart was not in it. Dramatic events had already developed in his personal life which did not make his decision any easier.

22 Arnold Bennett to Priestley, 5 September 1924.
23 A. E. Housman to Priestley, 18 September 1924.

# 6

# Second Marriage
## 1925–6

The years 1924 to 1926 concentrated a change in Priestley's personal life which was to set the pattern for the next twenty-five years. His wife developed cancer, its ravages spread rapidly and she was taken into Guy's Hospital, London, to begin a year of tension, struggle and misery, which they never forgot. What might have been a straightforward situation of illness, death and grief became complicated by the appearance of another woman in Priestley's life – Jane Wyndham Lewis, the wife of Bevan Wyndham Lewis.[1] According to Dr Charles Lack, a friend of Priestley's for fifty years, the Wyndham Lewis household was affluent and Jane and her husband gave parties to one of which Priestley came, all unaware of the consequences of a casual invitation. Fascinated by Priestley's personality, Jane said to a fellow guest, 'That is an extraordinary man – I am going to marry him.' Jane repeated this story personally to Dr Lack who described Jane as of shortish stature with jet-black hair and a face which he considered beautiful. Her marriage was already in serious disarray, and shortly afterwards she moved out of the house to live with her daughter Angela Wyndham Lewis in a Boundary Road flat near Lord's where Priestley presently developed the habit of visiting her to enjoy musical evenings with two friends.[2] These evenings were snatched against intense private and professional pressures, but occasionally Priestley stayed late and Jane's sister Muriel Holland thought he slept on the sofa. Within a few months she realised that something much more intimate was taking place.[3] In her eyes Jane was an unemotional person whose quick Welsh brain dominated everything she did, but a quite different person emerged from the recollections of her daughter and stepdaughter. What began as a physical attraction between Priestley and Jane quickly developed emotional complications.

1  Interview with Mary Priestley, 15 September 1985.
2  Interview with Dr Charles Lack, 26 November 1986.
3  Interview with Muriel Holland, 20 October 1985.

Priestley was living at Chinnor Hill on the far edge of the Chilterns at the time and commuting between Chinnor and Guy's Hospital involved long tiring journeys, but Priestley went to visit Pat two or three times a week. The strains intensified and soon it became clear that this was a terminal illness. He now had two daughters, Barbara and Sylvia, and the combined stress of family responsibilities, a dying wife, his struggles to become a writer and the appearance of Jane Wyndham Lewis in his life brought him close to despair. He described it vividly in *Margin Released*:

> I got back to Chinnor Hill, late one afternoon, so deep in despair I did not know what to do with myself. I was nearly out of my mind . . . Had I been close to a town I might have visited friends, gone to a pub or a cinema, wandered about the streets, but Chinnor Hill was miles from anywhere. Finally, just to pass the time while I was at the bottom of this pit, I decided to write something – anything – a few pages to be torn up after I felt less wretched. On my desk was a rough list of chapters for the Meredith book. I chose one of the chapters, not the first, and slowly, painfully, set to work on it. In an hour I was writing freely and well. It is in fact one of the best chapters in the book. And I wrote myself out of my misery, followed a trail of thought and words into daylight.

The evidence becomes very subtle. Recollection of events sixty years ago has dimmed in the memories of those who as very young children shared his experience.

Priestley found himself in a moral dilemma. Since he knew his wife was dying and might be dead before his relationship with Jane demanded complete frankness, did he allow Jane to remain unenlightened in the hope that painful scenes might be avoided? If we have no hard evidence for this, we certainly have for Jane's sudden discovery in 1924 that he had a wife who – though she was mortally ill – had already borne him two children.[4] Almost simultaneously she realised that she herself was pregnant. Jane already had a beautiful daughter, Angela, and she now simply gathered her up with two suitcases and 'disappeared into the country'. If the 'deception' interpretation is valid, clearly it would have shocked any woman, but Jane was particularly vulnerable because her own marriage to Bevan Wyndham Lewis had collapsed and on 22 April 1925 she was to take proceedings against him for

4  Interview with Mary Priestley, 15 September 1985.

adultery.[5] If she had seen a solution to her own problems in the possibility of remarriage to Priestley, the revelation of his marriage would have shaken her badly. Neither she nor Priestley were cold-blooded, calculating people. There was no plan on either side. Drawn inexorably into the complicated net of emotional involvement, Jane simply decided to cut loose and disappear.

The combination of a dying wife and a mistress who had deserted him was further compounded later in June by the death of his father at the early age of fifty-six. Edward Davison now came to his rescue. He wrote to Jane and explained the combined effect of his father's death and her desertion in compelling terms but Jane did not immediately return.

By October of 1925 Priestley had transferred from Chinnor to a new house at 54 Scarsdale Villas, Kensington and Pat was back from hospital living with him but 'far from settled'. Within a few days she had a relapse and woke in great pain at four in the morning. He called the doctor who diagnosed complications from spreading cancer which quickly necessitated day and night nurses, adding medical expenses to other anxieties. His old friend Davison had by now become involved in problems which made him decide to leave London and emigrate to America. Priestley wrote a long explanatory letter and concluded: 'I shall have to earn a lot of money.'[6] He liked the new home at Scarsdale Villas, he said, his study was congenial and he sustained a trickle of reviews and essays interlaced with letters to Jane, but his depression had returned.[7] 'I haven't seen Jane since she left town,' he wrote in another letter to Davison. 'We've written regularly. We shall have to see one another soon but things being so bad we are trying to put it off as long as possible.'[8] It would not be easy to find a meeting-place.

Pat's condition grew worse and she was forced to return to Guy's Hospital but within two weeks Priestley, dissatisfied with her treatment, removed her once more. Back home she quickly relapsed again. Presently, with Pat in agony, the doctor insisted that she must be returned to hospital. Priestley contacted Peggy Bannerman, a friend who was also a nurse, and she arranged for Pat to enter the Royal Free instead of Guy's. Much later in life Priestley paid tribute to the women doctors of the Royal Free who after some callous and stupid medical treatment in Guy's gave her 'civilised

5  Copy of the decree absolute, made 21 June 1926.
6  Priestley to Edward Davison, 1 October 1925.
7  ibid.
8  ibid.

attention'.[9] For the next three days Pat remained seriously ill and Peggy Bannerman said she might die, but by one of those last-minute surges of spiritual life she improved again. Priestley wrote to Davison: 'I can't help wishing for all our sakes it was done with. Pat is worn out and longs for complete rest. Fate has played with her like a cat with a mouse. Her mother too is almost worn out with the business.'[10] As for himself he felt pretty far gone. He could no longer do any serious work, such money as he had was melting away and so were the best years of his life.

His next letter in October to Davison asked whether Dodd Mead had yet published his book of comic characters and suggested that Davison could review it 'in one or two places'. He complained that Dodd Mead had never attempted to promote him and had done him more harm than good. Americans 'were swollen with war profits' and on the verge of discovering a better world than they would ever contrive to make. He resented the whole nation which was, he admitted, absurd.[11]

An unexpected turn of events now supervened if one interpretation of Priestley's letter in October 1925 to Davison is correct. Throughout all the struggles and crises the question whether he should marry Jane once she had divorced Lewis constantly troubled Priestley. Whether he loved her or not is unclear but one witness says that consideration of marriage depended solely on pregnancy. Whatever the truth, emotion, love, torment, quickly entered their lives. His mother-in-law, Mrs Tempest, was obviously privy to many details of her daughter's troubles and it appears from Priestley's October letter that at some stage she had become aware of Jane's existence even if she was unaware of her pregnancy. 'Mrs Tempest', Priestley wrote, 'knew Pat's feelings about it', which clearly implied that Pat too knew of his relationship with Jane.[12]

The dating now becomes vital. Jane had moved into the flat in Boundary Road, London, near Lord's and there on 4 March 1925, a girl Mary had been born and registered under the name of Wyndham Lewis. Muriel Holland, Jane's younger sister, was living with her and later told me that the baby 'looked just like Jack but I didn't realise that Mary wasn't Bevan's child until later'.[13]

And then at last in the autumn of 1925 Pat died. The death of two

9   *Instead of the Trees*, J. B. Priestley, 22.
10  Priestley to Edward Davison, 15 October 1925.
11  ibid.
12  Priestley to Edward Davison, 16 October 1925.
13  Interview with Muriel Holland, 20 October 1985.

of the most important people in his life, his passionate involvement with Jane, their break and reunion and the birth of an illegitimate child must have strained to the utmost any remaining resources, but against all possibility he continued to write. Perhaps, indeed, as he has indicated, it was the therapy which held him together.

By December of 1925 he was writing to Davison: 'By now you will have heard my bad news . . . I've had a bad time old man and am now going away for a cruise to the West Indies.' He had considered visiting Davison in America but he was concerned for his health and the idea of high-powered crowds in America dismayed him. Pat's death, which had taken place in her sleep following a heavy dose of morphia, 'was a good one and a great release for her and all of us'. She had remained unbelievably brave and unselfish 'right up to the end'. He had already recovered some of his working capacity and the penultimate paragraph of his letter said he was writing a weekly essay for the *Saturday Review* 'at six guineas a time' and very-well-paid reviews for *The Spectator* at the editor's request. 'Keep going old man. We haven't forgotten about you.'[14]

Jane's daughter, Angela Wyndham Lewis, now takes up the story.[15] She recalls her mother as 'someone to be reckoned with', a woman who had been to university and could read Russian, French and Portuguese. Warm, volatile, half Welsh, she was of medium height with black hair and a musical voice. She had 'enormous creative artistry which did not express itself in a career but became evident in the homes she created – houses made beautiful by her skills. She had that indefinable thing – good taste.'[16]

One day in February 1926 Jane said to Angela, 'You will be getting some lovely new sisters coming soon,' and this was followed in March by the appearance of Sylvia and Barbara. Already confronted with what she took to be a new baby sister, Mary, Angela received this news with trepidation. Within a month they all moved into a flat whose limitations quickly made life difficult. The growing family needed more space and Priestley finally found a big house called College House (now The Barn House) at Church Hanborough in Oxfordshire, with a beautiful garden. 'I like the house, am even proud of it on certain fine Saturday mornings when I see its reflection in the eyes of a visitor,' Priestley later wrote in his

14 Priestley to Edward Davison, 3 December 1925.
15 Interview with Angela Wyndham Lewis, 10 October 1985.
16 ibid.

collection of essays *Apes and Angels*. The house was certainly attractive, with twin lawns on either side of the path leading to the front door guarded by gigantic pear trees the foliage of which climbed like ivy to the eaves. The loft of a former two-storey dairy set away from the house became his study.

Jane wrote to Davison drawing a picture of Priestley sitting in the window seat, pipe in mouth, wearing tortoiseshell glasses, looking 'rumpled and rather tousled'.[17] (I have never seen in all my researches a photograph of Priestley wearing glasses.) Jane added that Priestley's children Barbara and Sylvia had now been with her for three months and she believed that they were quite settled.

Bevan Wyndham Lewis was still seeing his wife and came to take Angela out on a number of occasions. Inevitably he paid less attention to Mary, but this was compensated for her by the frequent presence of another inexplicable male called Jack. He divided his attention between Sylvia, Barbara and Mary, but since he was already on intimate terms with his two legitimate children, his relationship with Mary was complicated and the family settled down uneasily to accommodate its diverse parts. From the beginning when Bevan came to collect Angela he paid no attention to Mary and when she asked her mother why, Jane replied, 'You're so little, he wouldn't take out such a little girl.' This comment was not calculated to increase Mary's self-confidence and an accumulation of detailed misunderstandings slowly built up to confuse her. The alternating appearance of two men obviously on intimate terms with her mother made Mary ask herself when Jack took her out – this one isn't my father – but if he isn't – who is? Finally one day she put the question to her mother who replied with irritation, 'Daddy is your real father' – referring of course to Wyndham Lewis.

The flood of words which characterised much of Priestley's life had now renewed itself again and he explained to Davison in March 1926 that he had completed more than 20,000 words of a novel to be called *Adam in Moonshine* 'which your friend Harpers will have to publish . . . Jane and Gerald [Bullett] who have had the stuff read to them pretend a vast enthusiasm and I must say I find it great fun, knocking criticism into a cocked hat.'[18]

In September 1926 Priestley married Jane Wyndham Lewis 'with as much discretion as I could muster' and the family began a new way of life together. As they grew older Mary and Angela were

17   Jane Priestley to Edward Davison, November 1926.
18   Priestley to Edward Davison, 15 March 1926.

aware of tensions in the household and Mary records: 'I never discussed it with my father or mother but I sensed their . . . distress. I felt guilty from the beginning.' Mary remembers her mother as 'charming and vivacious, but whereas Angela was allowed out of the nursery [she] was not'.[19] On one occasion she escaped alone into a field, ran towards a water trough, saw the fascinating ballcock controlling the water flow and, not knowing its magic powers, tore it out, with the result that the water emptied away and surrounding fields were reduced to a state of pre-aridity. Challenged by her father Mary readily admitted, 'I did it,' and what Mary saw as one of the more pleasing sides of her father's complex character came to the surface when instead of greeting her confession with denunciation he simply demanded to know why she had done it. There were many other sides. Priestley could be a jolly, games-playing man whose tremendous memory, knowledge and sense of humour seemed to the children astonishing, but the 'general atmosphere of the house' continued to trouble Mary and Angela.

Angela felt that this atmosphere was directed at the children. Jane could be tense, disapproving and very temperamental and Jack 'critical and unaccepting . . . You always felt you had to be pretty damned good to match up to his expectations and doubted whether you could. I was always wondering what I had to do to get by.'[20]

There was no open quarrelling between her parents, Angela said, because it was all bottled up and the atmosphere would, in her view, have improved if they had brought their resentments into the open.[21] Theoretically all the children had to be treated equally, but Sylvia and Barbara knew that there was something different about Mary and gave her special attention. Mary found herself steadily more bewildered in a world where two men seemed to play the role of father, and children with origins different from her own made a much easier adjustment to new surroundings. The developing years increased the strains for Mary, and she became actively preoccupied with the question 'Who is my real father?' On the surface she tremendously admired Priestley who was obviously a very important man, not only in the family but in the big threatening outside world. Underneath there was an 'area of taboo – an unexploded bomb which sometimes set me trembling and shuddering'.[22]

19  Interview with Mary Priestley, 15 September 1985.
20  Interview with Angela Wyndham Lewis, 10 October 1985.
21  ibid.
22  Interview with Mary Priestley, 15 September 1985.

The children were allowed to have meals with the adults on Sundays but Mary disliked the family gathering because too often she developed 'a sick feeling' as she absorbed the atmosphere at close quarters.

According to Mary her mother was too taken up with survival to play a consistently caring role with the children and despite the cultural background, the distinguished visitors and very intelligent parents there was 'no emotional support, no listening' and nobody ever bothered to say to her, 'How did you get on at school today?'

Beneath the superficialities of everyday living, Angela felt that there was a haunted side to her stepfather contributed not so much by the complications and guilt which had arisen but 'because he had been seriously wounded and buried alive in the war'.[23] His darker side – or in Jungian terms, his shadow – troubled him deeply.

It is the irony of family life and the despair of biographers that each member usually has a different vision of their parents and siblings. Moreover, events mediated through a child's vision and sensibility become exaggerated beyond anything an adult would experience. Other members of Priestley's family found much more harmony and happiness at Church Hanborough. Indeed, many years later in adult life, Sylvia, his second daughter, wrote to her father:[24]

This is a letter I have been meaning to write for a very long time . . . It doesn't require any answer and has been wandering around in the back of my mind not being put down as it should have been, because there is a tradition that parents' generosity, strength and help are accepted as a matter of course by children, and only repaid to the next generation. However, I don't really subscribe to this and I have wanted to tell you – and this is leaving aside your great contribution to humanity (and your children) recorded in your writing . . . just how much your love, patience, sense of fair play, generous investment both with our games and our problems – our shared adventures and travel have meant to me as a child. Over that time there is a great dependence, not only for physical welfare, but for a base which gives out these qualities to be tapped in adult life, helping to bring some judgement of one's own, and to bring up one's own children. This is a small appreciation of that childhood and your importance

23 Interview with Angela Wyndham Lewis, 10 October 1985.
24 Sylvia Goaman to Priestley, 15 August 1947.

to me as a Rock of Gibraltar, not a very flattering description but you know what I mean.

Contrast this with Angela Wyndham Lewis:

Our different houses were always full of the rich and famous . . . Why couldn't I be happy in childhood? He was a man of immense talent – never boring, always entertaining, and for these reasons it was worth putting up with the rest of it . . . but the rest of it . . . Sometimes he could be aggressive, rude – not kindly – you didn't risk arguing with him – you became terrified of his reaction. He was non-accepting, very critical and always grumbling. I remember him saying at some time – I am a better writer than human being.[25]

As for Jane herself, there were those who felt that she had a neurotic streak which produced 'bursts of hysteria', and Angela Wyndham Lewis described other shortcomings. 'She never wanted anything you had given her as a present. What's the good of that to me, she would say. Make a special effort or give her something you wanted yourself and she would say – why have you given me this?'[26]

That she cared about the children, took pains to dress them well and went to immense trouble to give them a good education is not in doubt. It would be easy to conclude from some of the evidence that the family lived in a constant state of neurotic friction, but many conventional families generate similar tension. Certainly, in the very early days, Jack and Jane enjoyed some of the delights which go with a new relationship, interlaced with the inevitable problems of reconciling children from two different backgrounds. Moreover, Sylvia and Barbara made no reference to the atmosphere experienced by Angela and Mary.

Another characteristic which distinguished Priestley's second marriage from conventional equivalents was the relative speed with which J. B. became unfaithful and some members of the family trace the tensions to that basic fact. The children were unaware of its explicit details but the carefully concealed anger of Jane could not check reverberations reaching them.

Meanwhile Mary remained one centre of disturbance, and the climax came at the age of six when her mounting curiosity about her origins burst into the open and was at last satisfied by the nanny.

25   Interview with Angela Wyndham Lewis, 10 October 1985.
26   ibid.

She revealed that Jack Priestley was her father and not Bevan Wyndham Lewis.[27] It is impossible, accurately, to re-create Mary's reaction to this revelation which she had long suspected. Moreover, it was not until much later that Jane finally summoned the courage to confirm what the child already knew. The discovery and confirmation of her parentage were the first factors triggering the disturbances which were to culminate in her breakdown.

27  Interview with Mary Priestley, 15 September 1985.

# 7

# Early Novelist and
## *The Good Companions*
### 1926–9

A number of relatively minor works intervened before finally he took the financial risk of plunging into a 600-page novel which was to transform his life. Early in March 1927 Priestley finished a dramatic version of *Nightmare Abbey* which the producer J. B. Fagan received enthusiastically and then abandoned. A holiday in Bandol-sur-Mer with his wife Jane led to a collaboration on a Victorian domestic comedy which once again failed to materialise in satisfactory form. Both undertakings were important as the first glimmerings of that drive towards the theatre which eventually overwhelmed even the novelist in him. Meanwhile he continued to write essays for a number of periodicals including the *Saturday Review*, and it was not until Christmas 1928 that their number diminished. Then came his first novel, *Adam in Moonshine*, which Priestley described as 'a little coloured trial balloon' and the *Spectator* as no more credible 'than a fairy-tale'. *Adam in Moonshine* opened realistically under the great grey vault of St Pancras Station and quickly took flight with sinister inspectors, melodramatic barons, intrigue by moonlight, 'a whole rich pudding of the commonplace and the preposterous'. A secret society, the Companions of the Rose, mistook Adam Stewart for the true heir to the English throne, and the chase which followed brought the highly coloured cast into hilarious action. The plot moved mechanically for all the vitality of the writing, the literary images were strained and the most convincing character in the book was the Yorkshire dales. The whitewashed farmhouse, the stone bridges and the glittering trout streams were more alive than the ravishing girls who flashed in and out of the novel. Despite its shortcomings, the narrative had enormous pace and if the story never intended to be more than light-hearted entertainment, it succeeded at that level. Published in America 'where it was a complete failure', the book, to Priestley's surprise, ran into three editions in Britain.

In the same year, a second novel followed fast on the heels of the first. *Benighted* told the story of Philip Waverton, Margaret Waverton and Roger Penderel, who were forced to take shelter one stormy night in the sinister house of Horace Femm, somewhere in Wales. Written late at night after a hard day's work with literary journalism, it anticipated a modern genre which attempted to 'transmute the thriller into symbolical fiction with some psychological depth'. The writing shows signs of the pressures he was under but successfully creates the threatening atmosphere of marooned travellers, cut off by floods and forced into confrontation with some very odd people. The Femms are a grotesque half-crazy couple with an imbecile servant, and Penderel is a shell-shocked survivor from the First World War. Straining its symbolic content, it is possible to see the shambling figure of the servant Saul as the war which broke into everyday life to bring violent death to Penderel and disruption to everybody else. One passage was a precursor of Priestley's later writing. Penderel had outfaced and driven away the mad manservant Saul, and his sense of liberation is vividly conveyed.

> There came now a moment of triumph, and his spirits went soaring. It seemed as if the corner were turned at last, and he had a flashing vision of life stretched widely and gloriously before him, the shining happy valley, lost for years and apparently gone for ever, a dream bitterly cast off, until this strange night brought glimpse after glimpse of it through thinning mist and now finally swung it into full view. Now he knew what it was to be alive. He could have cried aloud with happiness.[1]

There followed a brief shambling fight in which Saul and Penderel died. It was the stuff of which horror movies are made and in due course the movie materialised. The Americans promoted *Benighted* as a thriller and under the title *The Old Dark House* it sold 20,000 copies. Then came the Hollywood script and a film which continued to be shown over the years into 1986. It was also one of the earliest talkies.

All these activities still left him relatively impoverished. Writing to Davison, Priestley urged him to review *Adam in Moonshine* 'somewhere' because he was 'desperately anxious for good American sales' and needed money badly.[2]

1 *Benighted*, J. B. Priestley, 32–3.
2 Priestley to Edward Davison, 9 March 1927.

As yet unassimilated into American culture, Davison's letters to Priestley revealed a man anxious to return to his home country but Priestley discouraged him on the grounds that jobs were few and far between. Somewhat insensitively he described two offers he himself had received and rejected. First came a readership with 'a good old firm of publishers' and second an English professorship in Japan initially offered him by the one-time English don, Edmund Blunden. He regarded the first as more attractive because although the professorship carried a salary of over a thousand a year, the job had 'nearly killed Blunden'.[3] Asked to pass on details of the professorship to Dobree, a lecturer in English, Priestley told Blunden that Dobree had 'no real qualifications for it'. However, if Dobree were appointed that would get the 'ass out of the way', a fate he desired for a number of academics whose careers in Tokyo he would monitor on seismographs designed to encourage earthquakes.

Priestley persisted with his criticism (*The English Novel*) and essays (*Open House*) and somehow contrived among overwhelming work to slip in an occasional editing job, one of which brought him into contact with Hugh Walpole. In his biography of Hugh Walpole, Rupert Hart-Davis described the day when a letter arrived 'out of the blue' from a man totally unknown to Walpole, signed J. B. Priestley. It invited him to contribute a small volume to a series called *These Diversions*, the editing of which Priestley had undertaken for the publishers Jarrolds. Walpole's interest was aroused, and he invited Priestley to stay with him at his country house, Brackenburn, in order to talk over the proposed book.

In his diary for 1925, Hugh Walpole recorded: 'Arrived Priestley – a North Country no-nonsense-about-me-I-know-my-mind kind of man. But I think I shall like and respect him.'[4]

The following day he recorded: 'I find Priestley very agreeable. He is cocksure and determined but has a great sense of humour about himself and his views on literature most strangely coincide with mine.'[5]

Two days spent walking the fells together preceded another entry. 'Priestley is certainly a very clever man. Like all of us he is not perhaps as aware of his own lacks as he is of others', but he is young yet and is fighting a battle. He will certainly go very far.'

3  ibid.
4  Hugh Walpole's diaries, 24 September 1925.
5  ibid., 25 September 1925.

Animated discussion explored a variety of possible subjects for Walpole's contribution to the *Diversions* series and on the second day at lunch Priestley jocularly suggested the title – 'The Pleasures of Perversity'. Whether he knew that Walpole was homosexual is uncertain, but if he did it was for him an unusually malicious dart. In the outcome, Walpole chose 'The Pleasures of Reading', which eventually emerged as 'Reading: an Essay'.

In May 1927 Priestley again visited Walpole and the two writers decided that they would collaborate on a novel in the form of letters between friends, which was to be called *Farthing Hall*.[6] The underlying motive for the collaboration now became clear. For many months the idea of a very long picaresque novel had fermented in Priestley's mind but the need to support his family made it impossible to concentrate exclusively on such a risky undertaking. Priestley knew that linking his name with Walpole's would bring a large advance and with his share of the money Priestley could then work exclusively on what became *The Good Companions*.

Priestley arrived at Brackenburn on 19 September 1927 and the following day they began work on *Farthing Hall*. Its progress could be seen in Walpole's diary for September:

'Now the Priestley book is obsessing me. How caught up and excited I get over these books, one after another, and all the time Herries is lying waiting at the back . . . It is delightful having Jack here – a friendship that does me all the good in the world because I respect so immensely his intelligence.'[7]

Walpole had found Henry James too old, Conrad too impetuous and Swinnerton too untrustworthy. Moreover, none of them had 'the sweetness and humour of Jack Priestley' . . . He was an 'enchanting companion' and a 'most lovable man'. A last entry in Walpole's diary said that they were 'now moving with breakneck speed' with the new novel *Farthing Hall*.[8]

Priestley recalled their collaboration in *Margin Released*. The story was told in an exchange of letters between a middle-aged scholar and an enthusiastic young man. Being neither middle-aged nor a scholar Priestley preferred that role to the one of romantic youth which seemed to him more suitable to Walpole. He did not approve of the device as a literary form but it made collaboration easier between two men separated by 200 miles.

6  *Hugh Walpole*, Rupert Hart-Davis, 279–80.
7  Hugh Walpole's diaries, 21 September 1927.
8  ibid., 26 September 1927.

In January of the following year Walpole spent a week with the Priestleys at Church Hanborough in 'a rather cold bare stone house strangely like Conrad's, but how much happier . . . here than there. Jane and Jack suit me exactly, both in character and mind – splendid acquisitions for me. We talked a million to the clock.'[9]

If this differed from what we now know about the family frictions, it was inevitable that they would be concealed in 'public'. Priestley and Walpole thereafter wrote letters to each other, sometimes daily, and every letter became a contribution to the novel until late in 1927 it was finished. Walpole wrote: 'Greatly relieved as now I have nothing ahead of me but Herries.'[10]

Priestley later revealed that he did not reciprocate Walpole's admiration. Walpole and Maugham had much more in common than Walpole and Priestley. Walpole was wildly anxious to please whereas Priestley had a talent 'almost a genius for displeasing all but those near to him'. The irony of this after the last chapter will not be lost on the reader. Walpole, Priestley wrote,

> was fond of making lists, of favourite people, books, experiences and so on, something I never did even as a schoolboy. He really enjoyed lecturing, whereas only an urgent cause or a great deal of money gets me on to a platform. Even more, he enjoyed writing – novels, articles, letters, anything – sitting at some fine desk and watching his pen glide over the paper: and I, pecking away at an old typewriter, detest it . . . He kept an eye on a sort of stock market of literary reputation, where that novelist's shares were going up, this critic's going down. I listened to his reports with interest and amusement but couldn't take them seriously, not caring a rap who was in or out, up or down.[11]

A series of elaborate qualifications followed. Walpole, Priestley said, had far more genuine humility than he did and his 'innocent warm vanity' was better than Priestley's 'cool conceit'. Walpole was altogether more 'considerate, more generous, much kinder than I have ever been'. The list of Walpole's virtues multiplied. Nobody had ever enjoyed being a successful popular novelist more than Hugh Walpole except perhaps Jack Priestley, who when *The Good Companions* shortly afterwards swept across England,

9   *Hugh Walpole*, Rupert Hart-Davis, 285.
10  ibid., 286.
11  *Margin Released*, J. B. Priestley, 174.

admitted – with a necessary touch of reluctance – that it was 'not only exciting but jolly good fun.'

Recollecting those days in *Margin Released*, Priestley revealed a streak of generosity which frequently came to the surface in the man who was now thirty-four and approaching what he regarded as middle age. 'Often I laughed *at* him, but more often still I laughed *with* him.'

Long before the completion of *Farthing Hall*, *The Good Companions* fermented in Priestley's mind until its half-imagined episodes began to haunt him. His illegitimate daughter Mary was six years old when *The Good Companions* transformed Priestley's life. His reasons for writing it were multiple, but one reason stood out amongst many others, recorded in *Margin Released*. Some time after the First World War, 'just as life was opening out, there came a period of anxiety, overwork, constant strain, ending tragically'.[12] He conceived *The Good Companions* in reaction to the tensions and complications of his family life and the growing distress of Mary.

Suddenly seized by the urge to give himself a holiday of the spirit, there seemed to him two alternative therapies. He could 'dredge it all up in autobiography thinly described as fiction', which might prove to be more healing, but he was temperamentally opposed to exploiting personal experience directly in 'so-called creative work'. Alternatively, he could escape the tragic circumstances by 'shaping and colouring a long happy day-dream'.[13] So it came about that he conceived a novel in which the characters set out on a journey of adventure as in *Don Quixote*, the supreme masterpiece of the genre. Discussing the idea with his publishers he was told that such a book would not appeal to the current reading public, but he refused to abandon what had become an obsession. 'I doubt,' he wrote, 'if I have spent half an hour wondering what readers or audiences wanted. I have had some bad ideas and done some rushed, scamped work at times, but never because I was not trying to please myself, but a host of strangers . . . I have seen myself described . . . as a shrewd North Countryman who knew exactly how to tickle the public fancy. This is miles out. I am not shrewd.'[14]

An interview in the *Strand Magazine* probed deeper into the wellsprings of what began as a holiday and became an obsession. The *Strand* interviewer found Priestley 'not a talkative man' and as

12  ibid., 186.
13  ibid.
14  ibid., 184.

they sat before an open fire in the shadow of the great model ship which stood on the novelist's very tidy desk Priestley answered his questions with modesty. 'Why did I write *The Good Companions* . . . well of course I wrote it for applause, for money, for Jane, for all the usual things and the usual reasons. I made up my mind to write a novel that I myself could enjoy even if nobody else did.'[15]

Until *The Good Companions*, Priestley had scorned those novelists who claimed that they were sorry to leave their characters after sharing their lives for 200,000 words. Now in 1930 he said: 'They were right. I came to the end of my huge tale not with a sigh of relief but with a sigh of regret.'[16]

Earlier roots of the novel went right back to his boyhood, when in the earliest years he developed a passion for the stage, but the strict limitations of his own music-hall experience drove him to 'work up some local colour' by steeping himself in the columns of *The Stage*. He also spent two nights in theatrical digs to absorb their atmosphere when he was travelling between Walpole's house and Church Hanborough. 'I broke my journey in the West Riding at an industrial town and stopped in some shabby and depressing digs.' The *Strand* interviewer recorded this totally unexpected conclusion: 'Not a single sentence in my novel comes out of that experience.'[17] Priestley told the interviewer that Oakroyd was a 'composite portrait character of a West Riding working man'.[18]

In the summer of 1928 Priestley took a house on the front at Deal with his family, and there, day after day, while his wife and children played on the beach he 'slogged away' at what was rapidly becoming an unmanageable whale. There followed a long break while they moved back into London, this time to No. 27 Well Walk. 'We perched ourselves here on the heights of Hampstead in what I still believe one of the tallest and ugliest houses in London.'

Writing began again in a turmoil of builders, plasterers and plumbers, with Priestley tucked away in 'a little empty room near the roof'. He wrote the last chapters during the great cold spell of 1929 when Hampstead suddenly decided to become part of the Arctic regions.

Day after day the temperature sank, the streets became like glass, pipes were bursting on every side and plumbers were more

15   *Strand Magazine*, April 1930, 329–30.
16   ibid., 329.
17   ibid., 330.
18   ibid.

important than Prime Ministers: but all this was nothing more to me than a vague fantastic dream. I was writing like mad. I would return to my typewriter after dinner and go on until the small and dreadfully freezing hours. I did not know – and I did not care – whether it was sense or nonsense. Out it came like a flood and down it went. Only my wife saw what I had written and she was pleased, and so I was content.[19]

He sent the first half of the novel to C. S. Evans at Heinemann and a glowing letter swiftly came back.

> My dear Priestley,
>     During the week-end I read the first part of GOOD COM-PANIONS, and the only thing I can say is, bless you! In a desert of aridity which I have been traversing for the last six months, your book stands out as a green and pleasant oasis. There is not a line of it that I could have wished away, and I am certain that if you go on as you have begun, we are going to produce a book that the world has got to reckon with. Appreciation so enthusiastic as this may seem a bit strange to you after my luke-warm reception of your two other books; but this is ever so much bigger than either. It has the true creative spirit in it. It has humour, humanity and exuberance – three of the very rarest qualities in the fiction of our time.
>     May I add one little word of warning? Do not let facility take the place of creation. You are a very facile writer, my dear Priestley, and you can do standing on your head what other writers can only achieve with blood and tears.
>     Yours sincerely,
>     C. S. EVANS[20]

He read the letter aloud to his wife, and it was a moment of mutual happiness.

The year 1929 saw that ill-starred, timid, sadly misunderstood Labour Government take office and set out to reshape the social scene. What might have happened if the financiers and industrialists had not convinced Philip Snowden and Ramsay MacDonald that the country was on the brink of an economic precipice, if the Labour Party had not relied upon the Liberals for their majority in the House and a truculent House of Lords had not interposed difficulties, is idle speculation, but beyond these difficulties a veritable thunderbolt waited in the wings. It was a thunderbolt

19  ibid., 333.
20  C. S. Evans to Priestley, 25 July 1928.

which penetrated even Priestley's 'creative cave' in Well Walk and set him arguing with Walpole 'whose politics were dramatically different from mine'.

The 1929 Wall Street crash hit millions of people in totally diverse countries, and before its force was spent threatened to topple the remote towers of the trusts and cartels on which the whole capitalist system relied. In its wake a tide of disorganisation and despair overran the world and protestations that economics were made to serve, not bedevil, mankind, were lost in lamentations that hidden forces would always erupt and destroy the fruits of even the wisest financial counsels. Launched against this depressing background *The Good Companions*, according to one witness, 'soared out of the gloom like a fairy tale to lift thousands of minds into a world of literary enchantment'.[21] Another witness recoiled in distaste from what he regarded as a torrent of self-indulgent sentimentality.[22] Neither had the power to stop the Niagara once it had burst its banks.

Setting up a book of such inordinate length as *The Good Companions* faced Heinemann the publishers with a great risk but they plunged in to print 10,000 copies and published in July. The response was subdued but by the autumn that mysterious upsurge of public interest which publishers still find inexplicable had become an overwhelming tide which necessitated multiple binders and commandeering delivery vans. Basically, of course, it was the intrinsic nature of the book itself which created the storm and towards Christmas the daily sales covered more in royalties than Priestley's total advance. As yet a relatively shrinking flower, he claimed that he could make no public appearances because he was too busy writing another long novel – *Angel Pavement*.[23]

Overnight the overwhelming success of *The Good Companions* made Priestley a national figure and created a personal myth. It was the myth of the calculating, coarse-grained Yorkshire writer who gave the public exactly what it wanted, with the sole motive of making money. 'A modest run of luck, just beyond the limit of our expectations, would have done me much good and no possible harm. Not so this giant jackpot, this golden gusher, this genie out of the bottle.'[24] He was now a 'sort of Quisling of letters' who had committed the ultimate vulgarity of becoming a best-seller. 'If I had

21  Letter from Frank Kendon to Priestley, dated 1929.
22  Interview with Sir Victor Pritchett, 4 January 1986.
23  *Margin Released*, J. B. Priestley, 186–7.
24  ibid.

written *Anna Karenina*, it would have been assumed, among the élite, that I was still turning out twaddle for the mob.'

Priestley analysed the difference between what he called sales-figures criticism and genuine criticism. One automatically assumed that anything widely popular was necessarily bad, the other ignored sales and judged the work on its own merits.

Priestley's aversion to inbred critical theory which was gathering power in 1929 intensified over the years. English Literature departments were unknown in the middle nineteenth century and Priestley regarded their multiplying minions as parasitic growths on literature proper. The case he made was convincing, but carried him into certain extravagances.

> After the First War, when the embittered introverts took over, affection was banished from literature. The critics . . . were without it. The readers who admired the critics hadn't much of it. Affection was out.

It was much easier, he claimed, to become an academic lecturer regurgitating pre-packaged lectures, following fashionable theories, than to write a popular novel and sustain the arduous life of the novelist. It was a remarkable paradox that his most successful novel *The Good Companions* left him so embittered that much later in life he claimed to have failed to establish himself as a novelist.

Ralph Strauss challenged Priestley's critics in the *Sunday Times*: 'Here indeed is a truly great novel which so far from being dead and forgotten within a season or two, will find more and more friends as the years pass by.'[25] *The Times* almost sneered. 'Jolly is the only epithet for a work that goes as gaily as Inigo's song "Slipping Round the Corner".'[26]

Away for a brief holiday in Devon, Priestley read the *Sunday Times* review and wondered whether the public would support what seemed to him 'a splendidly accurate description of the novel'. Sales reached 7,500 by August and then month by month increased until they were 'roaring away and nothing could stop them'. In October Priestley began work on *Angel Pavement*, and even when another year had passed, *The Good Companions* was still selling between 1,000 and 2,000 copies a week. At its peak by Christmas 1929, 5,000 copies a day were despatched from Heinemann's warehouses.

25  *Sunday Times*, 3 August 1929.
26  *The Times*, 30 July 1929.

Priestley first met the literary agent, A. D. Peters, at a party given by Robert Lynd, the literary editor and essayist, at Keats Grove, a centre of literary London life. Maire Lynd, the daughter of Robert Lynd, recalls that Priestley frequently went to her mother's supper parties. 'That's where he met Douglas Jay (an actor with whom he played a ferocious game of tennis) and Mark Gertler (the painter). It was at our house that Jack became friends with Ivor Brown and Rose Macaulay and a great mixture of writers.'[27]

Harriet Cohen played the piano at their parties, Eleanor Farjeon sang 'Kings and Queens' and Alan Thomas recited 'Young Albert', the whole company enjoying a feast of innocent entertainment. Priestley maintained an air of indifference at these parties but Maire Lynd recorded: 'At the big party when James Joyce was over in London to get married at last to Nora Barnacle, Jack Priestley certainly stayed to the end. We listened to Joyce singing at the piano . . . at about 3 a.m. people were doing turns and I remember Dominic Spring-Rice was doing a recitation – very round and red with his eyes popping out of his wide-rimmed spectacles. Jack said: "He looks like a maddened prawn."'

A. D. Peters became Priestley's agent in 1929. Shortly afterwards he met an American publisher in a pub one day and accepted an advance of £100 for the American rights of *The Good Companions* which infuriated Priestley who suddenly realised the international possibilities of the novel.[28] Harper bought the rights and Priestley's dissatisfaction increased until in the late summer of 1929 he wrote to Peters: 'So far as *The Good Companions* is concerned, I've not had a single word about it directly from the firm since they received the MS.' This account of his dealings with Harper does not correspond with the account given by Saxton representing Harper.

Priestley's letter to Peters, written from Goffies Park near Bude in Cornwall, gave some revealing personal news.

I'm doing no work here beyond my *Evening News* and *Saturday*, both of which I do as quickly as possible. I walk down to the beach two miles away every day, bathe there, play about with the kids and walk back again and then I do nothing but loll on the sofa and smoke my pipe. It's a beautiful life but bad for work. My head has been humming with plans however, especially for my next novel – a short one. I've also turned over and over several good ideas for plays. Do you think it better for someone like me to work with a

27  Unpublished ms, Maire Lynd.
28  Interview with Charles Pick, 6 October 1985.

'play carpenter' or not? I asked Walpole this in a letter and he said NO, we should never get on with the carpenter chaps, who do not see themselves as that but as deep fellows.[29]

If Peters did in fact fail Priestley with the advance on the American edition of *The Good Companions* he had none the less arranged the weekly book feature with the *Evening News*, in rivalry to Bennett's column in the *Standard*, and fixed a price of £20 an article, which Priestley regarded as very good.[30] Moreover, excellent news quickly followed on the heels of bad in a second letter to Peters.[31] 'I have wired to you today accepting Harpers Book of the Month terms . . . the price is cut to blazes but on the other hand there is a good chance of a really enormous sale.'

What began as a British best-seller swept across America, Europe, India and Australia. Nothing it seemed could stop its snowballing inevitability. Before its impetus was spent, twenty-two translations were made, a musical was based on its plot with John Gielgud as Inigo Jollifant, two films retold the story and the book continued to sell over thirty years. *The Times* reviewing the musical in May 1931 said: 'No-one will complain here of a dull and mumbling naturalism. This is the theatre all out and thank heaven for it . . . A whale of a play.'[32]

*The Good Companions* runs to 646 pages embracing scores of minor characters whose occasional appearances at the right moment in the lives of the protagonists reveal the skill with which Priestley weaves the whole into an overwhelming wave of narrative, pouring compulsively from the page. Jess Oakroyd, a Yorkshire joiner from back o' t'mill, is middle-aged, dissatisfied and bursting away from a shrewish wife and spoiled son, because he thinks the police are pursuing him for a theft which is illusory. Inigo Jollifant, a mere twenty-five years old, has joyously engineered his removal from a 'deadly prep school job' and sets out like Oakroyd into the outer world with nothing more than his musical talent and hopeless literary pretensions. Miss Elizabeth Trant, domestically entrapped by an ageing father, eventually escapes when he dies and immediately takes her slim, erect, thirty-seven-year-old self off on holiday, recklessly buying a car and risking the perils of the open road. Each storyline is travelled separately until all three coincide in

29  Priestley to A. D. Peters, 21 August 1929.
30  Priestley to Edward Davison, 6 September 1928.
31  Priestley to A. D. Peters, 30 September 1929.
32  *The Times*, 15 May 1931.

the refreshment rooms of the Midland town of Rawsley one early autumn afternoon in October. Sitting in the same refreshment room, the dispirited remnants of a touring concert party reflect on this moment of truth in their originally ambitious plans, and the two groups merge, talk and re-emerge, converting the Dinky Doos into the Good Companions. Inigo, whose off-the-cuff inspiration can produce racy tunes on the piano, will provide the music, Jess Oakroyd, a carpenter by trade, agrees that he will build the scenery, work the curtain and do odd jobs, and Miss Trant 'with a bounding heart' recklessly invests her inherited money into the company to put them on the road again.

From the outset, Priestley shared the creative experience with the reader. Dropping his omniscient control he addressed the reader and drew him or her into the conjuring trick: '[Oakroyd] has walked this way, home from the match, hundreds of times, but this Saturday in late September is no ordinary day for him – although he does not know it – for it is the very threshold of great events. Chance and Change are preparing an ambush. Only a little way before him there dangles invitingly the end of a thread. *He must be followed and watched*' (my italics).[33] The technique created a cosy conspiracy between author and reader.

The first third of the book, divided into six chapters, draws the reader into a combined fairy-tale and myth. The universal dream of breaking out of dreary everyday life to risk 'the open road' is daringly realised by all the characters. The scene is set for happiness if not bliss. The converted company, full of high spirits, sets out to conquer one music hall after another and the novel vividly conveys their exuberance.

When the great impresario steps down from his Olympus and offers to buy some of Inigo's songs for dazzling promotion in faraway London, he refuses to sell unless the impresario demeans himself by visiting the Gatford Hippodrome to hear Inigo's beloved Susie sing. When he reveals his gallantry to Susie, she says, 'Thank you,' quietly and demurely, and then the dam bursts:

her arms were about his neck and she had kissed him, all in a flash. For a minute or two he held her there. No, not for a minute or two. These were not minutes, to be briskly ticked away by the marble clock on the mantelpiece and then lost for ever; the world of Time was far below, wrecked, a darkening ruin, forgotten; he had burst through into that enchanted upper air where suns and moons rise,

33  *The Good Companions*, J. B. Priestley, 5.

stand still, and fall at the least whisper of the spirit. Let us leave him there. We must remember that he was a romantic and extravagant youth and very much in love – a young ass. Nor must we forget that such asses do have such moments. Isis still appears to them as she once appeared to that Golden Ass of the fable, and they still feed upon her roses and are transfigured.[34]

Mixing sentimentality with scepticism, such passages represent the simple emotions which are consistent in the whole novel. Priestley could unerringly put his finger on the pulse of the average human being and represent it in such a way that even the cynic's mood was softened. His humour was equally simple and robust but it went straight to the heart of that fount of laughter waiting to be released as an anodyne in millions of ordinary people. The impetus of the surface narrative, shot through with comic scenes, rarely surrenders to disillusion, but when it does it is not black with despair but reconciled by the pleasures of sadness.

Throughout his early life Priestley was a representative Englishman who concentrated in his person the experience of millions of Englishmen, heightened and brought to a new pitch of awareness by his sensibility. It was this capacity to step into the mind, spirit and body of everyday people which made his appeal universal. Moreover, he mediated suffering through his sentiment and enabled the reader to experience at one remove events which might be too disturbing in raw reality. The death of Oakroyd's wife, for instance:

He tiptoed forward, feeling horribly clumsy, uncertain . . . 'Eh, lass,' he said huskily. He tried to smile but could only make a grimace. 'Nay, nay.' And there seemed nothing more he could say.

Her face was all bone and sharp wrinkles and seemed as brittle as egg-shell. Her mouth was a short line, dark, bitter. But her eyes, though they wandered with an awful slowness, still gleamed in their hollows, and there looked out from those eyes the soul, stubborn, unflinching, ironic, of Mrs Oakroyd. He himself could feel this, though he had no word for it . . .

Her eyes roamed over him. She stirred a little and there came a sickly sweet smell. A hand travelled slowly over the folded sheet, and as he sat down he grasped it . . .

'Jess – What – what – you doing here?'
'Our Leonard sent.'

34  ibid., 553.

At the mention of Leonard those eyes changed, softened . . .

'I didn't tell him to.' Her voice was clear but slow, a voice speaking out of a dream.

'He thowt he'd better send word. He's been a good lad. I told him he's been a good lad to his mother.'

'Time you thowt so,' she said, with a flash of the old sharp spirit.

'Ay, ay, a good lad our Leonard. Is he coming soon?'

'Soon as he can or whenniver you want him,' he told her.

She nodded, very slowly, so that it hurt him to watch her . . . then she looked away, at nothing it seemed, as if he was no longer there . . . He tried to think of something to say, but there seemed to be nothing he could say and somehow his voice, too, had rusted away.

'I'm bad, Jess,' she said.[35]

Commonly assumed to be a straightforward tale of romanticised music-hall life reeking with sentimentality, *The Good Companions* is something more complex. Even in mid-career of song and dance the novel has undertones of sadness which reveal one ambition after another unrealised in the leading characters. Miss Trant, the most realistic, appreciates that this lucky break into music-hall life may turn out to be nothing more than a *jeu d'esprit* which can lead nowhere. Inigo's gift for creating enchanting melodies on the wing is nothing to him beside his desire to create Literature with a capital L. The pretty soubrette Elsie Longstaff longs to escape from dull audiences, interminable travelling and dingy digs into the arms of a gentleman friend. Oakroyd's most private moments carry him away to Canada and his daughter Lily whose company he misses. Jerry Jerningham regards provincial theatres as dreary slums incapable of appreciating his talents and Susie Dean cannot escape the dream of her first night in the West End of London with the press notices applauding the appearance of a great new star. Old troupers like Morton Mitcham fall back on playing the banjo and reminiscing about long-past triumphs, his capacity for renewed attacks on the future exhausted by past frustrations. What began as a soaring flight into a world where deadly routine dissolved into mounting excitement gradually surrenders to frayed tempers and uncertainty. There follow those anxious hours whenever Susie, Elsie or Jollifant find themselves alone and aware of inescapable isolation even in the midst of the Good Companions.

Priestley's narrative cunning enabled him to threaten the reader with disaster when Monte Mortimer, the West End impresario,

35   ibid., 626–7.

becomes involved in a riot engineered by rivals on the very night he is to hear Susie's performance, and Miss Trant faces the possibility of having to pay for the damage, but the ineradicable streak of 'gloomy optimism' in Priestley's make-up quickly arranged a recovery of fortune. The all-powerful Mr Memsworth replaces Mr Mortimer and at last sets Susie, Jerry and Inigo on the road to fame.

In the end we see Jess Oakroyd again leaving a football match on a Saturday afternoon, but swerving away from his old home to reach the railway station from which he sets out on the long journey to his daughter in Canada. We are back where we began, with all the characters facing the ancient truth. In the final analysis every individual is alone in his life. What might have been a bitter reflection softens under the cosy glow of the epilogue of the novel, but nature in all its ruthless realism remains inviolate.

> There are the Derbyshire hills, and there, away to the north, are the great fells of Cumberland, and now the whole darkening length of it, from the Peak to Cross Fell, is visible, for this is the Pennine Range, sometimes called the backbone of England.

The *Times Literary Supplement* reviewed the novel:

> Mr Priestley's *The Good Companions* is a massive volume of 600 pages, a trifle heavy to hold but the not too sophisticate reader will find no difficulty and a good deal of pleasure in reading it through from cover to cover. It belongs to the old and spacious tradition of the English humorous novel where the complications, the adventures, the encounters and the vicissitudes of external life are considered good enough matter to hold the interest without prying into the still more complicated deeps of the soul. Mr Priestley's aim is clearly to revive the tradition of Fielding, Smollett and Dickens . . . Criticism is hardly called upon to lift her head in such an expansive atmosphere.[36]

Victor Pritchett 'simply had to abandon the novel halfway through'.[37] Conversely, Clement Attlee made Priestley's books family reading, and himself read aloud *The Good Companions* to his children.[38] Whatever the critics said, *The Good Companions* swept the world and is still read today. In the first two years after

36 *Times Literary Supplement*, 1 August 1929.
37 Interview, 5 December 1985.
38 *Clement Attlee*, Roy Jenkins, 42.

publication it made £16,318 14s 1d, which translated by a multiple of 30, today would mean approximately £490,000.[39]

Carried to fame by *The Good Companions*, Priestley was seen by the Book Society as a new and splendid star for their Selection Committee. Priestley duly became a member but his relationship with other members was not very happy. He wrote to Hugh Walpole saying that he was bewildered by his curious outburst at a Savoy literary party. It seemed to Priestley unnecessarily resentful and obviously based on 'an entire misconception' of Priestley's attitude towards the Book Society.[40] What he wanted to do was to try to improve the Book Society standards and 'get some more idealistic material'.

Sir Rupert Hart-Davis, secretary of the Book Society in 1932, recalled his relationship with Priestley and his comments on the society:

> I was very fond of Jack Priestley and he was very good to me . . . On one occasion Jack rang me up and said he would like to give me the low-down on the Committee members. Jack said: 'Hugh [Walpole] wants to choose every book. I want to choose no book. Sylvia Lynd wants to choose books by people she has dinner with. George Gordon [President of Magdalen College, Oxford] hasn't time to read the books but his wife has read them so we get her opinion. As for Clemence Dane she takes a positively pre-Caxton view of books: the sight of print on the page excites her to madness.' All of this I found more or less accurate but unfortunately Jack then left the Committee.[41]

39  A. D. Peters Archive, London. I am told that a multiple of 40 would be more accurate, bringing the figure over £600,000.
40  Priestley to Hugh Walpole, 10 June 1929.
41  Letter to the author, 27 October 1986.

# 8

# Fame and its Consequences
## 1929–30

*The Good Companions* rapidly converted Priestley into a rich man and by 1931 he had bought No. 3 The Grove, a beautiful Georgian house looking out from the heights of Highgate. He was unable to gain immediate possession and the family continued living at 27 Well Walk but Priestley sent Cass Canfield, his American publisher, an ecstatic description of the new house. Beautifully proportioned, the elegant drawing-room had four french windows overlooking a large garden with the rich green slopes of Kenwood beyond. The study also presented a wonderful view uninterrupted by habitation of any kind. It pleased Priestley that in this relatively cramped study none other than Samuel Taylor Coleridge had produced some of the finest works in English literature. Preserved unchanged today, the house is owned by Lady Turner who showed me over No. 3 right down to the cellar where the family was to shelter in the air raids during the war to come.

It was in this house that I first met Priestley more years ago than I care to remember, when the editor of *John O'London's Weekly* asked me to talk to him about his library.[1] My memory of the occasion is full of gaps. Mistily groping for the truth, I recall a man of some five feet ten inches who came forward to greet me warmly with a pipe in one hand as the other reached out to shake mine. He was broad-shouldered and burly with a physical presence which made itself felt immediately. He wore a big yellow floppy tie, the only splash of colour in his dress. We settled in the room lined with books and he at once put me at ease, saying, 'You must be the thirtieth chap who's come here to interview me, but it's all grist to the mill.' There was a Yorkshire accent and a certain directness of manner, but as yet he had not put on weight, his face seemed unlined, almost boyish and he treated me with respect as a fellow writer, which was hardly justified. Against all the briefing I had received he began to interview me: 'What sort of books do you read?' Very young,

1 Interview, September 1931.

painfully shy and hopelessly inexperienced, I stumbled into a recital of Keats, Shelley, Shaw and Wells – as incongruous company as any adolescent could assemble. Pressing home his enquiries he demanded to know which poems and which books had specially impressed me and I found myself totally incapable of giving any satisfactory exposition.

Screwing my courage to sticking-point I managed at last to indicate the wall behind me and asked which poets in the Everyman edition had survived from that tiny den in Saltburn Place, Bradford. 'Oh, most of the romantics,' he said.

He wore a casual sports jacket and flannel trousers, and whenever he gestured, it was made emphatic by the pipe, and his voice, which filled the room, had a reverberant quality. Above all, it was his total relaxation I remember, for all the world as if, as a man of leisure, work never broke into his serenity. We walked round the walls examining and discussing Thackeray, Trollope, Dickens, Meredith, Yeats and Tennyson and suddenly coming to the section containing his own books, he picked out *The Good Companions*. 'There are times,' he said, 'when I wish I had never written the bloody thing . . . They never expect anything else from me. Worse than that. I'm not taken seriously because of *The Good Companions*. A ridiculous state of affairs.'

Frowning, he tapped out his pipe and refilled it in silence. Suddenly his face drooped and it was as if, momentarily, he became a man whose success had turned sour. 'I take it', he said, 'you've read my new novel, *Angel Pavement*?' Fortunately I had and I vaguely remember saying how different, how serious, I found it, somewhat distorting my view of the novel in order to preserve our good relations. Once more he reversed our roles and turned the questions back at me. Did I expect to earn a living from writing? Yes. In that case I should, of course, be certified. 'I like Pope on writers,' he said.

> What and how great the virtue and the art
> To live on little with a cheerful heart.
> A doctrine sage.
> But truly not for me.

Suddenly he changed. His eyes lit up, his features came alive and he roared with laughter. His measured speech, restrained friendliness, pipe and sudden bursts of laughter were part of the stereotypic image but there was something beyond all that: a brooding quality.

A number of invitations stood on the mantelpiece. A newly ascended literary star, Priestley received a flow of invitations and slowly graduated from the gauche young man up from some forgotten Yorkshire town into a person who could mask his lack of confidence in many ways. In the beginning, at evening parties 'wearing dress clothes that were a poor fit' he met 'the bright ironical glances of women' and was 'unable to decide whether to drink little and play safe or to swallow everything offered and let rip'.[2] Usually Priestley 'chose the first' but very quickly 'switched to the second'. Since he was often away from London and frequently worked in the evening, he was not a regular party-goer, but time and time again well-known figures like Wells, Shaw and Arnold Bennett crossed his path.

Priestley saw Shaw as a kind of intellectual marionette who responded like a puppet to strongly held views and strode about the literary scene with such enormous eloquence and energy he almost crackled with electricity.

> The performance was often brilliant, always touched with an intensely personal charm not to be found in print . . . It was well for him that he had brought his voice – and a fine voice it was – from Dublin. If he had had a North Country accent, then probably not later than 1895 he would have been lynched.[3]

It was the voice which enabled Shaw to get away with 'polemical murder' but there were occasions when, with all due respect for age and genius, the young, newly arrived and in many ways still raw Jack Priestley insisted on having his say. Far removed as Priestley was from the sophisticated badinage of cultivated literary circles, there came the day when Shaw told Priestley that Mussolini was a greater man than Napoleon. Present at this party was H. G. Wells who retold the story with that boisterous gusto which he brought to half his life:

> 'You should have seen the expression on J. B.'s face,' he said. 'First it paled – then it glowered – then it went red and suddenly he burst out – "Of all the damned nonsense I ever heard. The man's a fraud, a mountebank, a megaphone. He doesn't amount to anything more than a black-shirted bullfrog croaking away in the mud." With that he took a step back, upset somebody's wine glass and packed off into

2   *Margin Released*, J. B. Priestley, 160.
3   ibid., 164.

the night. Shaw simply played his old unbeatable game. He roared with laughter.'[4]

When told that Mrs Shaw was a good listener Priestley remarked, 'God knows she's had plenty of practice.' Meeting Shaw at the Malvern Drama Festival in 1931 Priestley watched the beard, Norfolk jacket and knickerbockers strutting about surrounded by acolytes, and the impulse to ridicule overrode his genuine admiration. What fun it would be, he decided, to engage a dozen six-foot actors, dress them up in white beards, Norfolk jackets and knickerbockers and let them loose in Malvern so that every street was alive with G. B. Shaws.[5]

Later there was to be an extraordinary encounter with Shaw in the middle of the Grand Canyon, but for the moment Priestley mimicked, with some success, one of Shaw's greatest skills – mockery. None of it qualified his deeper conviction that Shaw was a man who unexpectedly reconciled his undoubted genius – 'which nobody but a fool would deny' – with common sense and kindness. His summing-up was acute.

> There was a tricky element in him – a want of complete intellectual honesty, the result perhaps of his having built up a persona as finished and hard as a carapace. Clamped inside it, speaking through a megaphone, he was tricky about sex, about dictators, about equality, about Russia, where he would not have lasted a month except as a distinguished visitor.[6]

Temperamentally different in many ways, Priestley and H. G. Wells shared a dislike if not a hatred of patronising academe. Wells's story of his attempt to bring together a number of history professors to produce a book edited by himself which would embrace a history of the world in one volume, was a favourite with Priestley. Very few academics wished to suffer guilt by association with a 'journalist like H.G.' but quite undismayed Wells plunged in to write the whole book himself, accomplishing the task in nine months and producing a work which sold over a million copies. When Priestley asked H. G. 'how he regarded the book', he replied: 'I saw it as a hussar ride around the rear of those stuffy dons.' What

4  Interview with H. G. Wells, 5 September 1943.
5  *Margin Released*, J. B. Priestley, 165.
6  ibid., 166.

neither Priestley nor Wells knew was that when this remark filtered down to the senior common room at Pembroke College, one don was said to have commented with a slight stutter, 'Y-yes I can see his point. B-but then it s-seems to me Mr Wells has wr-written rather more history than he has r-read.'[7] The split sensibility between academic novels suitable for analysis by their own critical theory and the broad Dickens tradition of straightforward narrative written by H. G. Wells and Priestley was a theme which sometimes inspired both to eloquent vituperation.

Unlike Shaw, Priestley regarded Wells as a friend and warmed to his mercurial temperament, spontaneity and intolerance of sham. Shaw remained the leading actor carrying on a performance instead of a conversation, but Wells 'was with you' and even came embarrassingly close. Priestley enjoyed the company of this 'gnome of a man' with his inexhaustible vitality, his capacity for 'instant rages', his wildly unconventional relationships with women and, above all, the flood of his totally frank talk delivered in a squeaky voice. Priestley was present on one occasion when Wells overheard a very short literary critic saying to no less a man than Conrad, 'Yes – we know Wells is prolific but then he's nothing more than a journalist.' It was one thing for Wells to proclaim with pride 'I am a journalist first and last' and quite another for 'an upstart critic' to convert that statement into objective truth. Hardly dropping his voice Wells said to Priestley, 'Don't worry, she's so near the ground she's unhygienic.' Carried away as usual by words, Wells seemed unaware that a man who was just five feet five inches high opened himself to devastating retaliation.

Whether Wells and Priestley were close enough to share confidences is not known, but whereas Wells's affairs filtered through to a wide public which tried to crush him, Priestley's remained unknown.

Priestley's analysis of Wells revealed acute perceptions which so many of his critics denied him. Wells 'had never bothered about a persona . . . In any company he thought aloud, and many of his books are simply this excited thinking aloud.' His summing-up went to the heart of H. G.

His genius was entirely literary, not scientific, but his early training, his discovery of a wide rich world through science, gave him permanently the air of a man making some hasty last-minute

---

7   H. G. Wells to Vincent Brome.

experiments in a lab. He was an artist gasping for breath in a scientific climate.[8]

E. M. Forster also floated in and out of Priestley's ken without having too much impact. They met one day at a PEN Club meeting and the portrait of Priestley recorded in Forster's *Commonplace Book* was sour:

> J. B. Priestley's coarse, joyless face, into which he caught me looking. It took on a dreary expression: he knew from experience what I was seeing. That Meredith doesn't sell at all, Mr Conrad only a little and Arnold Bennett no longer well, and Hardy as well as ever.[9]

Now thirty-seven years old, Priestley was at the height of his physical and mental powers, indulging both to the full. Seen through the eyes of his close friend Norman Collins, Priestley was a warm happy family man with a very attractive wife, ceaselessly engaged in getting the best out of life. 'I've never known anyone so active.' His daily routine was highly repetitive. He came down in his dressing-gown at nine o'clock, ate breakfast, glanced at *The Times*, prowled about the house – silent, thoughtful, writing in his head – and then at ten a.m. settled down to start work by turning his back on the view through the window and stuffing twists of cotton wool into his ears. The iron rule was that there must be no noise on that side of the house from the children, and Sylvia, his daughter, said, 'We all silenced each other if we were forced to invade the forbidden area.'[10] At twelve thirty he broke for a pre-lunch drink and lunch itself, followed by talk, walks, and family games which might be anything from ludo to some bizarre game invented by Priestley himself. According to his daughter Rachel,[11] Priestley frequently read long stretches of what he had written to his wife Jane in the evening, and if she approved went to bed satisfied, but there were times now when their relations were severely strained and nothing would persuade Priestley to read a word. According to Mary Priestley they did not live a normal family life with sustained communication between parents and children. 'We had our own existence and saw more of the nanny and the housekeeper than we

8   *Margin Released*, J. B. Priestley, 168.
9   *Commonplace Book*, E. M. Forster, 1930.
10  Interview with Sylvia Priestley, 10 September 1985.
11  Priestley's daughter Rachel, born 16 August 1930.

did of our parents. Eileen Binns was a tall lady with her hair done up in a bun who had a kind of attractive ugliness. She was stern but kind, full of folklore and high principles. She regarded her influence as necessary because everyone tended to spoil the children.'[12] The picture of the successful writer splashing down one successful book after another was heavily qualified by Rachel. 'There were a number of black moods,' she said. 'So black that Jane's only hope of cheering him up was to push two of the children into his room and hope that he could not resist their appeal . . . I think that generally he was a terrific father, we got on very well and we always had good relations, but there were bad times too. Certainly we had to tiptoe around certain parts of the house in his working hours.'[13] It was unwise, Rachel said, 'to cross his path when he was at the bottom of one of his black moods'.

Increasing social life brought Priestley into touch with many attractive women. A deeply sensual man who saw no harm in what H. G. Wells referred to as 'passades', his fame and a quality which one woman referred to as 'animal magnetism' made affairs an inevitable part of his life.

Among the family it was understood that Priestley's deviations were matched by Jane's total faithfulness, in one sense forced on her by the responsibilities of the family, but Priestley was about to embark on a trip to America with his wife which introduced one serious qualification into what otherwise seemed an unblemished record.

That Priestley had a number of affairs is agreed by many key witnesses and if specific instances are not easy to elaborate that is partly explained by the destruction of evidence and the reluctance of some among those involved to allow their stories to be publicised so short a time after Priestley's death. He told his daughter Mary on one occasion that he was 'in and out of bed with half the women in London'. In due course three such affairs will be seen in detail, but for the moment it is sufficient to say that before he left for America, relations with Jane had almost reached breakdown as a result of relationships which he sometimes claimed were innocent and she was convinced were not.

12   Interview with Tom Priestley, 5 October 1985.
13   Interview with Rachel Priestley, 6 February 1986.

# 9

# America and Miss Ashcroft
## 1930-1

Priestley began his long love–hate relationship with America in February 1931 when he sailed for New York in the 'old *Olympic*, a friendly ship for all her creaking', in which a first-class passage with a large private cabin including every luxury, then cost £45. From the ship he wrote a letter to Jane full of the love which his affairs so frequently jeopardised.

> My darling Jane,
> . . . The voyage has been pleasant enough although rather dull. On Tuesday, getting out of the Channel, it was quite rough and many people were sick. I felt nothing then or since . . . After the sort of boats you and I are used to this ship hardly seems to move. She is very steady. The only thing is that she's noisier than a small ship – because you hear her expanding joints creaking and groaning all night. I've slept very poorly though late. The first three days I went up to the gymnasium before breakfast and began to feel very fit, since then I have had a touch of cold. Everybody has had a little. It's the quick changes of the Atlantic.
> There are one or two specimens of the New York 'Four Hundred' aboard and quite a number of pleasant people, but nobody exciting. Women seem to dress as they please during the day – a heavy coat over a dress, or jumper and skirt – however in the evening, for dinner, they dress properly.
> I'm looking forward terribly to seeing you again. Do come out if it's humanly possible. And let me know definitely. I'm assuming, of course, that you are coming. The thought of your not coming out is unbearable. All my love to you, sweetheart, and a kiss for the children.
> Your very loving
> JACK[1]

Throughout the letter he is obviously expecting Jane to join him later, and, as will appear, the whole trip included the hope of

---

1 Priestley to Jane Priestley, 17 February 1931.

reconciliation between them.

The *Olympic* called at Boston before proceeding to New York, and there he had his first taste of unscrupulous American journalists. A young man from a news syndicate interviewed him and Priestley's familiarity with journalistic licence in England made his replies cautious. He admitted complicity in certain writing activities which crossed the borders between novels and plays, and confessed to coming from an unknown town in England called Bradford. According to *Midnight on the Desert*, a few hours later the following press release swept across America.

> J. B. Priestly, English novelist, playwright and critic arrived from England today en route to New York with the observation that 'America has a general case of indigestion' and 'mock culture' . . . He was convinced, he said, that London had stolen from New York the right to be known as the dramatic capital of the civilised world. The vigorous 40 year old Englishman remained on board the vessel during its stay here. He concluded his description of Boston by saying that, like the rest of the United States, 'it is in a bad way with afflictions of silly, childish movies, bad plays and cheap novels.' 'Bah' and 'puerile' were his answers to questions regarding American movies. American people, he asserted, eat too many sweet things and have a 'national case of indigestion.' He added that 'sometimes I think it is caused by the movies over here.'

Priestley commented on this report: 'Not one single remark attributed to me in the above report ever passed my lips during this interview.'

Since Priestley remained on board ship there were insuperable difficulties in giving his reactions to Boston. Fully accepting his assurances that the whole interview was a fake, the opinions expressed were couched in terms stereotypic of certain English reactions, and were not far removed from occasional outbursts in the Priestley vocabulary. However, Priestley's name was wrongly spelt, the word movies was quintessentially American and pomposities like 'Bah' far removed from his rugged Yorkshire speech. Intensive research has failed to unearth the original of this interview, or the name of the newspaper.

Arrived in New York he promptly telephoned the news syndicate which had circulated the fake interview. This brought an invitation to meet its director. Elaborately courteous, the director apologised 'for such flagrant misrepresentation and ordered the interview to be withdrawn at once'. By then, however, the mischief had been done, but Priestley refused to allow the episode to sour his first encounter with a country for which he developed a relationship not entirely explained by the term love–hate.

Priestley later enlarged on his reactions to New York. For the first few days he was a man 'reeling with enchantment. All other cities in retrospect . . . [were] like mere huddles of mud huts.' Here once more were 'Babylon and Nineveh in steel and concrete, the island of shining towers, all the urban poetry of our time'. Radio City might house a glittering feast of trivia and bums on the Bowery deny all civilised values, but the buildings themselves 'soared above my criticism'. He hurried down the canyons and gulfs they called avenues, saw 'one magnificent vista of towers' crowned by another, held his breath at nightfall 'to see the glittering palaces in the sky and wondered how [he] could ever again endure gloomy, stunted London'.[2] The first exhilaration of New York quickly gave place to a second phase when unemployment, the bread queues, prohibition and a terrible sense of economic insecurity among the ordinary people of New York slowly permeated his mood. He wrote once more to Jane:

My darling,
    Apparently this is my last sure chance of catching you before you sail. Yesterday I spent the very longest day I have ever spent. It began before seven in the ship, and never stopped all day – I was either being interviewed or photographed from 8.0 in the morning until 6.30 at night. I have been at it all today, and I have another heavy programme tomorrow, besides a large pile of letters to answer. It's terrific. So is this city – like a vast madhouse, though extraordinarily beautiful at times. The skyscrapers really are incredible – they take your breath away. I am going for a proper tour of the city with Saxton in a day or two. Harpers directors are all very kind and hospitable – and the pity is they're such dull, if worthy, fellows. Mrs Canfield seems very nice – younger and livelier than Mrs Saxton – and I have asked her to show you round when you come. She'd be delighted. We'll compare notes about this place when we meet.
    . . . I do hope you're coming out, darling. I'm looking forward more and more anxiously to seeing you. Cable me through Hamilton if you can't. But you *must*. I'll make all the arrangements.
    A thousand kisses for you and hugs for all the children.
    JACK[3]

2  *Midnight on the Desert*, J. B. Priestley, 22–3.
3  Priestley to Jane Priestley, 19 February 1931.

In the event, Jane did go to America but with unexpected results. There is some evidence to show that their reunion in such an exciting city overwhelmed the underlying difficulties and for a few brief days they revelled in a reconciliation which seemed to include sleeping together. It did not last. Returning to England his movements for the next few months are difficult to pinpoint exactly. Certainly in June and July 1931 he was staying at the Lygon Arms in Broadway, Worcestershire, with Gerald Bullett, an editor and writer, for the ostensible purpose of collaborating in writing a novel[4] and leaving home once more may have been necessary for their joint privacy, but a quite new twist now appeared in his relationship with Jane. First he had plunged dramatically into a new and serious relationship. Secondly one of three letters he wrote to Jane from Broadway qualified the belief that Jack's deviations were matched by Jane's unblemished faithfulness. The first letter was innocent enough.

Darling Jane,
   Will you do something for me? I wrote an essay once on the Alexandra Palace, and there's a copy of it in that blue box near the window in the study. Will you please send the essay down here as we shall want it. I'm having a certain amount of trouble with Gerald and there's a frantic amount of re-writing to do, but I shall peg away at it.
   This hotel is beautifully fitted up and the food is good, but it's a fatuous place with a terrible Arts & Crafts atmosphere.
   With much love,
      JACK[5]
P.S. I've no news of Bubble.[6]

Another letter followed fast on the heels of the last.

Darling Jane,
   Many thanks for letter etc. I'm terribly sorry about poor Bubble. Let's hope it's the beginning of new things for her. If you feel too worried or fussed, do please tell me to come back. I haven't been much of a comforter so far, but it isn't too late to try. We jog along here. I am trying to write about 5,000 words a day of new stuff, and

4   The novel, finally called *I'll Tell You Everything*, Priestley regarded as a frolic for sheer entertainment.
5   Priestley to Jane Priestley, Tuesday, 1932.
6   Jane's younger sister.

of course it's pretty hard going. Gerald is doing his best but his best isn't too good – he works slowly and has few ideas. But he slogs loyally and we laugh at ourselves a lot, and that helps to relieve any possible tension. I am terribly sorry for him. He has forgotten how to work eagerly and hard. There's something frozen in his mind – some psychological knot there. You were quite right about Sylvia Lynd.[7] I wouldn't have gone if I'd been at home. The role of Court Jester at Keats Grove doesn't appeal to me at all.

Love to you, my darling.
Your loving
JACK[8]

Then came the crucial letter.

My dear Jane,
Your postcard about Bubble has just arrived. It's horrible that she should have to suffer so much, but it does look as though – now that the gall-bladder is out – she has a good chance to get back to health and normal life again. Please let me know what happens.

There's a train leaves here at 10.41 on Saturday and arrives – from Stratford – at Paddington at 2, and if you're not using the car about then, perhaps [the chauffeur] could meet us at 2. Unless you hear to the contrary we shall catch that train and Gerald will stay until Monday. We have finished the second half of the book, but have had to re-write, in part, the first.

In reply to your letter, I don't propose to be dishonest or patronising or anything of that sort. I agree that everything's wrong with us. And perhaps I am just as lonely and wretched as you are. It's not really my fault that if we ran away there'd be no fun – as you say – because, you see, I'm no longer the man you can have fun with. I feel it all just as much as you. I'd staked a lot on our trip abroad bringing us together again, but somehow it didn't. The trick is we seem to have lost the capacity for making one another happy but not of making one another unhappy. No doubt, our meeting in America has involved a lot of stupid stuff, but nevertheless it hurts me considerably. You at least have had a glimpse of the sort of relation you've wanted. You found a man – Jimmy – in love with you, and found yourself falling in love with him. I've had nothing as good, nothing at all; and behind all this fuss and palaver of my present life, I'm really as bored and lonely as hell, thinking of work and plans all the time because there's nothing else to do. For a long time now, I've

7   Robert Lynd's wife.
8   Priestley to Jane Priestley, 27 June 1931.

been in your eyes just a heavy stupidish man, capable at times of doing annoying things; and, at the same time, I've been nothing to any other woman. I haven't even had an hour or two's intimate talk with another woman for years. You do, now and then, get a glimpse of that romantic feeling which you have – quite rightly too – but I get nothing.

I'm sorry to bother you with all this when I know you must be sick with anxiety about Bubble, an anxiety I share. And do believe, Jane, that I'm being honest with you, just turning out my mind and not trying to score points. I wish I'd brought some adonal with me here. I can't sleep properly and have tried hot drinks, some bromide stuff from the chemist who doesn't keep adonal, but all to no purpose. The result is, I'm tired out though I stick at the work, and by sheer drive, keep Gerald more or less at it. He's willing enough, but he's not really interested in the book and is not used to slogging away. But I mustn't grumble. Gerald's an angel really, and miserably unhappy. And so am I just now.

JACK[9]

What did all this mean? Were his infidelities purely sexual with no real communication? Above all, had Jane consummated her love affair with Jimmy? I could find no satisfactory evidence, but if hard facts about her own behaviour are scarce, Priestley emerges as a very different person from the casual lover indulging every fancy on the wing and taking swift romantic pleasure in many affairs. Later in life he did have satisfactory affairs which finally culminated in the greatest love of his life, but for the moment he was a torn, tormented person endlessly searching for a solution to a marital tie which he could neither tolerate nor break.

Between 1930 and 1932 Mrs Marjorie Watts, later to become secretary of the PEN Club, met Priestley a number of times and remembers him as the most kind and considerate man. She lost her husband tragically in an air crash, and one foggy day shortly afterwards she was walking in the Hampstead area feeling deeply depressed when she encountered Priestley. Seeing her distress he put his arm round her, walked along with her and was so 'sweet and comforting' she never forgot the episode. Arthur Bliss and his wife were also friends of the Priestleys and Mrs Watts remembers Mrs Bliss saying to her one day, 'Jane, you know, has to put up with a lot from Jack.'[10]

9  Priestley to Jane Priestley, 2 July 1931.
10  Telephone interview with Marjorie Watts, 20 July 1986.

The complicated episode which developed in the summer of 1931 exemplified those words and revealed the romantic in Priestley, overwhelming the solid Yorkshireman to plunge into an emotional episode with unfortunate consequences. The tensions in the household again reached breaking-point when Priestley simply announced to his wife Jane that he had fallen in love with a young actress. His acquaintance with Peggy Ashcroft (now Dame) was superficial but according to her evidence he suddenly arrived on her doorstep, declared his love and asked her to go away with him, only to find that she did not return his love. Twenty-three, very pretty and already successful, Peggy Ashcroft regarded thirty-six-year-old Priestley as a middle-aged man who did not attract her.

Once he had committed himself emotionally, no lover was ever more forceful and the power of his personality could be overwhelming. There followed many weeks in which Priestley remained away from home, moving from place to place, pursuing Ashcroft relentlessly. Alas, according to Ashcroft all his efforts were in vain. Mary Priestley recalls this episode vividly. 'He went away and I missed him, and I asked my mother when is he coming back, and she said, "He won't be long."'

He did come back at intervals, which led to further complications in Mary's already confused state. Precisely how long he was away remains obscure but he did revisit the family and Mary, whose attachment to her father had deepened, remembered saying to him on one visit: 'When are you going to come back and live with us again?' Priestley reassured her but accused Jane of deliberately putting words into the child's mouth, only to receive a vehement denial. Mary believes that her question was not inspired by her mother, but spontaneous.

There exists in the Beinecke Rare Book Library of Yale University a tremendous outpouring of twenty-five pages written by Jane Priestley in the summer of 1931 which gives an anguished and very different account of this episode. This material came into my possession long after my original discussions with Dame Peggy Ashcroft. The letter begins: 'I am as you may guess, terribly unhappy and made far more unhappy by Jack's disloyalty and cruelty to me. I don't blame him for falling in love, but he might at least have made a clean cut.'[11]

Against all the received wisdom Jane claimed on the first page of her letter that everything between Jack and herself had '*always* been

11  Jane Priestley to Edward Davison, undated, probably summer 1931.

all right' (my italics). She knew that he was a very difficult person but any unhappiness she experienced arose because, when he drank, his attitude to women changed. Cutting across his reputation as a trencherman Jane claimed that he could not drink and said that when 'muzzy' he easily drifted into a spirit of 'mischievous lust'.

The opening pages of Jane's letter were full of ambiguities which characterised its whole length. Mischievous lust apart, she said they had been happy together and even his unfaithfulness had only produced half a dozen quarrels. She still loved him as much as she ever did and Jack himself had re-echoed similar sentiments before he left to join Gerald Bullett in Broadway. Ten days later he told her that he had fallen in love with a young actress of twenty-three and simply packed a bag and left home.[12] His whole attitude to Jane changed and became so hostile that it surprised even Bullett who knew about this 'calamity'. The first break was short-lived and he returned gloomily within a week but Jane found his attitude unbearable and suggested that he should go away again and make up his mind. Priestley left home once more and within a few days had asked A. D. Peters to discover what solution most appealed to Jane. She replied that it was up to Priestley to decide but she 'would do nothing but leave him free'. Tormenting ambivalences characteristic of situations of this kind quickly overtook Jane and when she heard that her husband had decided to continue his pursuit of Miss Ashcroft she begged to see him before anything definite occurred. Simultaneously she believed that such a meeting remained impossible while he was 'with this girl'. Jane now collapsed and became what she described as seriously ill. Priestley wrote to her:

> My dear Jane,
>     Dr Harvey [their family doctor] says I oughtn't to see you today, so may I see you tomorrow and come if you wish it for good. I'm terribly sorry about all the distress I seem to have caused you. I am horribly anxious and miserable about you.
>     I think I can promise that I won't let you down in the way you dislike again . . .
>     In spite of having drifted apart like this, I am terribly fond of you Jane, and I should hate to smash up everything we've built up together.
>         Yours,
>         JACK

12   ibid.

Much of the evidence for what follows comes from Jane's letter, and it has to be remembered that some members of her family did not regard her as a very reliable witness. Barbara Wykeham, for instance, states that she 'sometimes wrote things that simply were not true'. Given, as she was, to exaggeration – especially of emotional states – there remained a kind of logic in the way events unfolded in her letter. Certainly a message now reached Priestley which exemplified her histrionics. She told her husband that she was dying, whereupon he returned home and said that he had decided to give up the affair 'even before he heard [that she] was dying'. A letter to that effect did arrive the day following his return home. He remained for several days comforting Jane and repeatedly told her that 'everything was all right'. Whether to distance her from the scene and free himself, or in the hope that a sea voyage would improve her health, he suggested that she should take a trip to America. Over the next few days his solicitude was heavily qualified by irritation and presently he began acting in a manner which was so odd that she suspected the relationship had begun again. Peggy Ashcroft was married at this time to Rupert Hart-Davis and Jane now telephoned him, asked to see him and tried to discover whether he knew what was happening. On the telephone Rupert Hart-Davis said that he certainly knew 'all about it' but there was no need to worry. She duly met Hart-Davis, who admitted that he too was 'terribly unhappy' and disclosed that Priestley and his wife were still meeting.

Full once more of resolution, Jane told Hart-Davis that divorce was the only possible outcome if what appeared to be a mad infatuation turned into a serious love affair. 'Rupert agreed that there must be no shilly-shally and told me he'd tell his wife.' As a result, the following day Peggy Ashcroft telephoned and asked to see Jane. Jane's letter gave no details of their reaction to each other but – according to Jane – Peggy Ashcroft said that although Jack was obviously violently infatuated with her, she did not clearly know 'how she felt about it'. Already a disturbed person, the interview left Jane in a state of near prostration. As she put it: 'Jack saw Peggy that afternoon, came home and accused me of leaving him frozen in a romantic attitude.'[13] Jane felt that she could take no more and when a friend invited her to her Cornish cottage she gladly accepted. Complications now began to multiply. Unwittingly Hugh Walpole was drawn into the imbroglio unaware that

13   ibid.

his dual role of friend and buffer between the parties might prove overpowering. All three next met in a Cornish cottage but Priestley spent much of the first few days in a state of 'black and devastating silence', which Walpole found intolerable and Jane 'awful'. Under the threat that Walpole would leave if the atmosphere continued, Jack and Jane made an effort to enter rational discussion and emerged in a state of armed neutrality. The situation now surrendered to the classic temporary solution when Jack asked Jane to 'resume their normal life' and they slept together with results which were either unforeseen or perhaps unconsciously desired. Nerves on both sides were frayed to the point of breakdown but a momentary compromise offered the chance to convert an emotional problem into a sexual solution. In keeping with the established pattern it did not last.

There followed a turmoil of proposal and counter-proposal. They would part, she would go to New York and he would think things over once more: she would not go to New York, she must have 'safe assurances' but she would leave him free to decide. Throwing everything into fresh confusion on the night before Jane left Cornwall, Jack said that 'he hadn't quite given up the affair *in his mind*' (my italics). Jane appears to have taken this calmly and repeated her offer to go away and leave him free. It was the view of at least one member of the family that Jane could easily convert emotional problems into physical illnesses and now she told Rupert Hart-Davis that she had suffered a 'lot of heart attacks' and would ask her doctor whether she was fit to travel. Her doctor could find nothing seriously wrong and she began her preparations to leave for America when a telegram arrived from Jack. 'Stop all American preparations arriving tonight.'

Their reunion was highly emotional and almost at once Jack claimed that he had definitely finished with Peggy, and there was no longer any reason why she should go away. His mood contradicted his words. He was restless, unhappy, unable to work and constantly falling into glooms. Renewed tensions finally drove Jane to ask Hugh Walpole to invite him to the Malvern Arts Festival to 'get him out of the way' and Jack agreed to go. From the festival Hugh Walpole wrote a confidential letter to Jane saying that he was sure all would be well in the end, but she must not take these dramatic swings in Jack's moods too seriously for the moment.

Priestley next moved on to stay with his publisher Frere and wrote to Jane claiming that he was not seeing Peggy and was desperately trying to get on with his work. Fast on the heels of that letter came another which suggested returning once more, an offer which Jane side-stepped indicating that it might be better to 'keep to his plan' for the time being. Brushing this aside Priestley wrote a very friendly reply which said – plan or no plan – he could only resolve his torment by coming home.

He arrived the following Monday, fell into a heavy brooding mood within hours, and refused to talk to Jane who quickly realised that it was not going to work. Suddenly she confronted him with the short sharp statement: 'You have seen the girl.' He said yes but immediately qualified his reply with the words, 'We've arranged a temporary separation.' Jane realised that all these weeks of emotional upheaval and fluctuating resolution had merely returned him to the situation from which it all began. She now asked him bluntly whether he would like a divorce or separation and he replied neither. 'There seems', Jane wrote, 'to be a hitch . . . I can't understand it.'

Priestley left Jane once more and now she brought her resolution to the sticking-point. He must make up his mind before she saw him again because she could take no more.

Then came the news, dramatic in the circumstances: the recourse to sexual reconciliation on a single occasion had left Jane pregnant and against such a background no choice remained but 'to try to stop it'. When she told Jack that she was seeking an abortion, he at first gave no hint of his reaction. Whether by letter or telephone he now explained to her that their relationship had never been satisfactory from his point of view and even the 'children didn't count for him'. Jane flatly contradicted this in her letter to Davison. 'You know how wrong that is.' Jane's long and moving letter concluded 'Oh Teddie when I think of the studio [at Scarsdale Villas] and our struggling days at Hanborough I am heartbroken.'

Jane's next letter came five months later in November 1931 following a week's visit to Holland. She returned to Well Walk to find that Jack had visited the house, removed all his belongings and instructed the chauffeur to pick him up at Chelsea the next day to take him to Brighton where he had rented a flat for six months. Simultaneously Jane received a letter from Walpole asking to see her at once. She met him and Walpole gently broke the news that the situation was so hopeless she must face up to the fact that Jack had left for ever. Once more distraught, Jane attempted to meet Jack but he refused and wrote a long letter conveyed to her via

Peters. Since there were so many deep and fundamental differences between them, he wrote, the only possible solution was a legal separation or divorce. Under the circumstances he trusted that Jane would go through with the abortion because that would remove the most serious complication. Jane replied via Peters to say that she would only answer his letter by talking to him, hoping that another face-to-face confrontation might facilitate reconciliation.

She next consulted her doctor and a Harley Street specialist, both of whom were prepared to carry out the abortion on the grounds of her July illness, although both were fundamentally against it. They pointed out that it could not in any case be done without Priestley's agreement. Another month went by and slowly she came to hate the idea of an abortion until at last she drifted into the expectation of a quiet, lazy winter preparing for the baby which if it happened to be a son might help to comfort her.

Suddenly one day Jack called on her once more and now they had a short business-like discussion when she told him she was having the baby, but did not want to divorce him. They finally decided on a separation. Jane then relapsed once more and became ill, while Jack went off to Brighton. Slowly Jane recovered, helped by the children who were just starting school.

By now Edward Knoblock's dramatic version of *The Good Companions* had been launched in New York and Priestley's next letter to Jane written early in October said:

19 Royal Crescent, Brighton. Dear Jane,
Thanks for your letter. I am glad the oriental things are genuine. Wylie, who only got back on Wednesday, rang me up yesterday to give me the news. Apparently the play had a bad press – as I already knew – because the American critics said the characters were not like those in the book, and in short the play wasn't like the book. As the production was just as good as the one here, obviously they had formed a different mental picture of the people from that of English people. On the other hand, audiences are enthusiastic. The company is quite good, except that Vera Lennox (Schubert's choice) has been a great flop, though she has worked hard and conscientiously. Wylie says business is shocking in New York. The piece played last week to about 13,500 dollars, which is less than expenses but still comparatively good for this bad season. It is now touch and go whether it develops into a success or fades out. The election is knocking us badly here. The figures at His Majesty's have been dropping. And what is worse, the tour, which opens in Manchester on Monday, looks like being a wash-out until after the election. Wylie is very

gloomy about Manchester. Apparently they have had Communist rows just outside the theatre, which have been preventing people going to it, and our bookings, which ought normally to have been enormous, are consequently very poor. There is no doubt that this general slump and political upset is hitting the play hard and proving very expensive.

I meant to get Miss Burke before she went, a list of stocks etc. I have. A great many of these will have to be sold out during the next six months, though that was only to be expected, as they were never meant to be permanent savings. Most of the money I'm getting now is Good Companion stuff and goes into the Trust.[14] There's practically nothing new outside. Meanwhile, I have just got my income tax assessment, and I have nearly eight hundred pounds to pay at the year end; then there is my insurance premium – about nine hundred pounds; there will be the contractors' bill – about four thousand; and our living expenses, which are probably about two hundred a month. I am clearing my New York account, but that will bring only about five hundred pounds. We've no need to sell anything at this minute unless you want to buy some things. I've now a credit balance of over five hundred, owing to a payment from Heinemanns for *Angel Pavement* up to June, which enabled me to wipe out the overdraft I had . . .

JACK

Every twist in the tortured strategies of two people simultaneously trying to break out of and yet remain in a marriage was now further complicated by Priestley's sudden reversal of his whole position. A friendly letter arrived at Well Walk one morning saying that it might be a good thing if he returned to Jane for a few months 'to be on hand' when the baby was born.[15]

Dear Jane,
. . . Probably the last thing you want at this moment is any discussion of our personal relations. And I agree. But whatever is going to happen to us ultimately, I cannot help wondering whether it would not be a good thing, from every point of view, if I gave this flat up at Christmas, returned home for several months – on the basis of friendly compromise – so that I moved into the Highgate house with you and was on hand when the baby arrived, and so

14  A trust was formed to distribute *The Good Companions* royalties amongst the family.
15  Priestley's son Tom, born 22 April 1932.

forth.[16] During this time we might do what we've never really done yet – talk the whole thing over quietly. I think this arrangement would be better for both of us, but if you don't think so – well and good, there will be no argument about it.

We have, I hope, a common interest in trying to stop gossip. Through various friends, I have made the most careful enquiries, and so far as I can see there is little of it about. There may be a certain amount of chatter about Peggy and me . . . but it is not based on anything, and there's always chatter of this kind. Meanwhile, I am doing my best to have what gossip there is stopped. I am giving out – and Heinemanns are sending a paragraph to the literary gossip people – that following my usual practice, when working hard, I have come down to the seaside. As I've said so much, I might as well say a bit more. Peggy has not stayed with me here and so far it is not our intention that she should. If anybody is very nosy about us, tell them that Peggy and I are great friends and have some business together . . . (This is true. Ask Frere or Peters.) And that's the lot. I was worried when I learned you'd been in bed, but I gather now you were resting. I hope you are better than you were and you haven't too much sickness . . .

    JACK

*I have to give a month's notice, so must settle this in good time.[17]

Initially Jane reacted furiously. She did not want him back for a few months only to lose him again when they quarrelled. This was modified later by the possibility that his letter represented a genuine preliminary to permanent peace and she replied asking him to be more precise about his motives for offering to come back.[18] A last letter from Royal Crescent, Brighton said that *The Good Companions* was flopping badly at His Majesty's Theatre in London and likely to come off soon in New York. He had arranged a midnight performance in aid of the Docklands Settlement run by his friend Edward Knoblock, partly for charity and partly because it would be good publicity for the show.

By November a meeting occurred at the offices of Y.P. & Z. Productions Ltd in Golden Square, which produced a sharp letter to A. D. Peters from the secretary of the company. It said that the enthusiasm generated by those interested in *The Good Companions* at the meeting was considerably dashed by a warning that the danger figure would probably be reached in a week. Priestley was

16    Priestley to Jane Priestley, 22 October 1931.
17    ibid.
18    Jane Priestley to Priestley, 13 November 1931.

present and when he brought up the question of revitalising the advertising programme, the secretary said he would have to consult the backers. A short last sentence invoked a picture of Priestley leaving either in disgust or under genuine pressure. 'Mr Priestley, owing to a previous appointment, had to leave before the meeting terminated.'

This letter had in fact been pre-empted by another from the American Dramatists in New York to A. D. Peters which said that the Schubert Theater Corporation was in the hands of the receiver. The American Dramatists explained that they were taking steps to ensure that Priestley's royalties from *The Good Companions* were properly protected.[19] Since the play had earned $4,279.41 (roughly $60,000 today) he seemed to emerge relatively unscathed.

There followed a series of letters, telephone calls and at least one meeting with Jane which recapitulated every aspect of his double relationship with Ashcroft and Jane, but deliberately on Jack's part referred to his plans with Ashcroft not Jane. However, he insisted that Ashcroft had not lived with him at Brighton and that any plans he envisaged were vague. Within a few days he claimed yet again that he had broken with her – finally – and wanted to reopen discussion about their marriage. Jane wrote asking him to be more specific, only to receive the vaguest replies. Describing this last gesture to Edward Davison, Jane said, 'He makes no reference to the events of this summer but only to what he calls the failure of our marriage . . . He asks me not to write as the aggrieved member but rather as a party to a common failure . . . All this, Teddie, seems to me utter madness.' Desperately she still wanted to believe that she and Jack had 'a jolly good relation' and if the beginning of the summer found them in the trough of the wave, but for the intervention of this dreadful episode they would now have been on the crest.

Immediate practical details made the appearance of Peggy Ashcroft in their lives even more complicated – if that were possible. Having recently bought Coleridge's house in Highgate they had made elaborate plans about a new way of life there, before the Ashcroft episode began.

Distinguishing between love, being in love and infatuation can be made to justify different codes of morality according to the category to which the emotions belong. Priestley was certainly infatuated and probably in love, but to him, as to all people in his

19   Y.P. & Z. Productions Ltd, 3 November 1931.

situation, riding the wave of his feelings to their true destiny seemed imperative at the time, and the knowledge that returning home would simply reactivate misery and frustration was not something that Jane could take into account. Like so many wounded women she now referred to him – patronisingly – as a defiant child whose self-indulgence had made her ill. 'I'd be willing to forgive a mere physical infidelity if I had Jack's fundamental loyalty,' she wrote.

According to Jane, as their tortured separation dragged on he continued talking to people like Gerald Bullett as if he intended marrying Peggy Ashcroft.[20] At such moments her pride broke through, it was all too much and the conclusion was final – she must divorce him. Jane's second letter ended in the same state of agonised ambiguity. She wanted 'things to come right', but it was all unbearable.

The children continued to be her main source of solace and sole external preoccupation, with Edward Davison made godfather to Barbara who was 'doing very well' at Halstead Place School in Sevenoaks and Rachel, who stood alone, understanding a great deal but still making sounds intelligible only to the nurse and herself. This letter she concluded was written at the top of her voice but she was not really as bad as that.

At the height of his infatuation with Peggy Ashcroft, Priestley had dashed off a new play especially suited to her talents and people like Peters, his agent, Frere of Heinemann's, Peggy and her actress friend Diana Wynyard, were all, according to Priestley, enthusiastic. The play was a light comedy called *The Roundabout*, which did not justify that view. Now he decided to abandon the play and refused to allow anyone else to take the part. He wrote to Jane from the Royal Crescent Hotel, Brighton in November:

> My dear Jane,
> I have decided to scrap the play and have told Peters so. I understand your attitude about it and in your place I suppose I should feel as you do. It doesn't matter now, I suppose, but I'd like you to understand one or two things about it. The first is that I came last Sunday to see you and the children and not to [indecipherable] anything. As a matter of fact it wasn't until *after* I fixed to come – in fact late on Saturday night when Peters rang me up, that I knew the situation about the play . . . The play was entirely my own idea. I happened to think of the plot of an amusing light comedy and

20  Jane Priestley to Edward Davison, 13 November 1931.

thought it would be good practice at least to have a shot at it. The theme is a quite impersonal one and nothing in it was inspired by Peggy and when I had done it everybody who read it liked it, so it seemed a shame not to go on with it.

However, it's settled now. So that's that. Sorry I lost my temper this morning.

JACK[21]

Against Jane's conviction that he was still shilly-shallying, Priestley wrote to Davison on the same day from the same address:[22]

I have been down here for the last five or six weeks on my own, working. The domestic situation is not yet settled. I have broken with Peggy but have not returned to Jane though actually I've been to see her once or twice lately. I expect we shall try to patch the thing up if only for the sake of the family – but what sort of a job we shall make of it I don't know and frankly – I'm rather pessimistic.

It is difficult to measure suffering and misery. Disentangling their respective reactions it is reasonable to say that Jane and Jack experienced different degrees of both. As for Jack's lack of concern for Jane, he told Davison in another letter that he was deeply distressed about Jane's illness, he missed the children and they missed him, and work required such an effort of will it ceased to be a pleasure.

And then at last he was back home with Jane who did her best to make domestic life run easily and carefully refrained from making any mention of 'their traumatic summer'.[23] Priestley with two more chapters to write pressed on to finish his new novel, *Wonder Hero*. His book column in the *Evening News* had ceased and he had been offered and rejected Bennett's column in the *Standard*, but now pressurised by the editor he surrendered and became a focal point for popular criticism of the novel. Luckily, he claimed, he was easily the best-paid literary columnist in England, getting £60 an article of 1,200 words. The fragmentation of his life over the relationship with Ashcroft had cost a 'good deal of money' but he continued to receive large sums in royalties and had 'just paid nearly £3,000 in income tax and surtax . . . It's really frightful.'[24]

21  Priestley to Jane Priestley, 16 November 1931.
22  Priestley to Edward Davison, 16 November 1931.
23  Priestley to Edward Davison, 6 January 1932.
24  ibid.

Still complaining about Harper's failure to promote *The Good Companions* he explained away its selection for the Book of the Month Choice as the effort of a friend not connected with the firm. Inexplicably, against this rare distinction which would make him even richer, he insisted that he would never forgive Harpers. As for those American reviews of the book which he had read, they were plain silly. Pushing *The Good Companions* away from consciousness he was deeply into another novel – all about London – of which he had written 40,000 words.

Meanwhile Priestley's social life among the literati continued apace. Norman Collins, interviewed by John Braine, told the following story.[25] He first met Priestley in the offices of the old *Daily News*, which became the *News Chronicle*, and close on the heels of *The Good Companions* went to a party given by its literary editor Robert Lynd. Arriving late for the party they found Bennett surrounded by an admiring group absorbing his every word. As the group became aware of Priestley's presence, their admiration, according to Collins, faltered and slowly, in ones and twos, they drifted away from Bennett and joined Priestley. Finally, 'they absolutely melted away from Bennett', Collins said. 'If I hadn't seen it I wouldn't have believed it . . . and all clustered around Priestley. Mind you – and this is important – I don't think Jack gave a damn.'[26] Arnold Bennett never became, like Wells, a friend of Priestley's, and if Collins's account is not exaggerated, the 'constraint tinged with hostility' which characterised their relationship needs no further explanation. However, as early as 1924 Priestley had praised *Riceyman Steps* in the *London Mercury* as 'undoubtedly Mr Bennett's greatest achievement'.[27]

Priestley described Bennett as a man preoccupied by money who was quite incapable of managing his own finances properly. Paying court to Dorothy Chesterton, when he delivered the obligatory bunch of flowers each morning, he was apparently unaware that the flower salesman had sold him fading blossoms which might signally depress their recipient.

Priestley's relations with Arnold Bennett were full of contradictions, the subtleties of which were clearly apparent to Walpole. In a shrewd passage Walpole described Bennett as a man expecting his friends to play up to the persona he projected, but if anyone 'pierced

25   *J. B. Priestley*, John Braine, 22.
26   ibid., 26.
27   *London Mercury*, February 1924.

that armour or damaged the picture' his kindness and generosity evaporated. The passage concludes with a catalogue of people Bennett never forgave, and Priestley figures prominently on the list.[28]

Priestley's summing-up was once more shrewd:

The very last time we spoke we found ourselves moving out of the Queen's Hall together, after a Toscanini concert. 'Gives you' Bennett jerked out, referring to the music, 'a lift – doesn't it?' There is a lot of him in that brief remark. He had responded eagerly to the music, but was determined not to sound high-flown about it.[29]

Within a year of the publication of *Angel Pavement*, Bennett died unexpectedly. In March 1931 when Priestley was away from London, the news of his death came over the radio and Priestley reflected sadly that perhaps it was as much his fault as Bennett's that they never became friends.

It was early in 1931 that Priestley received a page proof of Graham Greene's novel *Stamboul Train* and immediately identified Mr Quin Savory of *The Great Gay Round* as a thinly disguised J. B. Priestley. According to Graham Greene in a letter to the author, Priestley threatened a libel action and corrections were made. Asked by a journalist to estimate his place in literature, Mr Savory in *Stamboul Train* said: '"I take my stand with sanity as opposed to the morbid introspection of such writers as Lawrence and Joyce. Life is a fine thing for the adventurous with a healthy mind in a healthy body." Mr Savory who dresses quietly and without eccentricity does not believe in the bohemianism of some literary circles . . . Our correspondent pointed out the warm admiration which had been felt by countless readers for Emmy Todd, the little char in *The Great Gay Round* (which incidentally is now in its hundredth thousand).'

In the final version of *Stamboul Train*, Mr Savory was redescribed as 'a slim, bronzed figure', which could hardly be confused with the image of Jack Priestley.

28   *Arnold Bennett*, Margaret Drabble, 350.
29   *Margin Released*, J. B. Priestley, 170.

# 10

# *Angel Pavement*
## 1931–2

*Angel Pavement*, according to the received literary wisdom, is Priestley's finest novel. Certainly a far more serious and less romantic novel than *The Good Companions*, it has to be seen in a different context. No longer driven by economic duress, free to relax and write exactly what he wanted to write, Priestley plunged into a second major novel two months after completing *The Good Companions*. When *Angel Pavement* was in turn published less than a year later, *The Good Companions* still sold at the phenomenal rate of 1,000 copies a week and cheques continued to pour in from multiple sources.

*Angel Pavement* received the usual mixture of reviews including one which Priestley would have found disturbing but for 'the young whipper-snapper who wrote it'. Still flexing his muscles as a radical journalist, George Orwell writing under his real name, E. A. Blair, launched a vituperative attack on the novel which echoed around literary London.[1]

> When one has finished applauding Mr Priestley's effort to make clerks and typists interesting, one must add that the effort does not, even for a single page, come off. It is not that he writes ineptly or is lumpishly dull, or consciously plays for cheap effects; it is simply that his writing does not touch the level at which memorable fiction begins. His work has no damning faults but neither has it a single gleam of beauty, nor any profundity of thought, nor even memorable humour. One would not thus assail a competent and agreeable novel if Mr Priestley had not been so extravagantly praised. He has been likened to Dickens and once this absurd praise is discounted . . .

The destructive phrases mounted and even when Orwell made concessions they were no less scathing.

1   *Adelphi*, October 1930.

We salute Mr Priestley for the qualities he really possesses and take *Angel Pavement* for what it is: an excellent holiday novel genuinely gay and pleasant, which supplies a good bulk of reading matter for ten and sixpence.[2]

Bernard Crick remarked in his biography of Orwell: 'If Priestley had noticed [Blair's] early novels, he could well have thrown the same review . . . back at Orwell.'[3]

There are more convincing answers. In the early 1930s academe had not yet formulated the intentional fallacy but it became very relevant to Orwell's criticism. Critical theory nowadays argues that the author's intention may be irrelevant because literature has a life of its own which manipulates the novelist and unconsciously redirects his avowed aims. In this instance Orwell skilfully reversed the roles of critic and author. It was the critic who suffered from the intentional fallacy not the author. He endowed Priestley with motives which he never entertained and himself succumbed to the influence of other critics who had compared him with Dickens, Thackeray *et al*.

Priestley did not set out to emulate the great nineteenth-century novelists or to explore, in all their profundity, the underlying motives of his characters. Nor did he want to create a candyfloss novel suitable for casual reading on holiday with sleep an easily available antidote. He intended to write a serious middlebrow novel which sufficiently penetrated the motives of his characters to reveal the broken hopes, limitations, potential, resilience and persistent optimism of those cipher-like creatures so easily dismissed because of their ordinariness. Himself a superb example of a 'normal' Englishman elevated by his talents to a different level of awareness, his origins enabled him to share everyday experience which his creative powers transformed. How did he achieve these objectives, which were quite different from those Orwell attacked? Consider the *Times* review of *Angel Pavement*:

Whether the characters in Mr J. B. Priestley's ANGEL PAVE-MENT will make so many friends as did those of *The Good Companions* may, perhaps, be doubted, but they are drawn with the same vivacity, intimate knowledge and sympathy . . . The interiors, the contacts, the conversations, indeed the whole fabric of the few lives, are opened up to us with a warm and generous

2  ibid.
3  *George Orwell*, Bernard Crick, 203.

assiduity that is entirely convincing . . . We have been treated to a magnificent peep-show, whose very richness compensates, in part, for its fragmentariness.[4]

Clearly Orwell and the unnamed *Times* reviewer had read different novels. The *Times Literary Supplement* was also favourable.[5]

Combining his own experience in a Bradford wool merchant's office with a week's swift pilgrimage around the City of London, Priestley wrote the first third of the novel in Highgate and the remaining two thirds in a temporary hide-out on the estuary of the Dart in South Devon at Kingswear.

He opened *Angel Pavement* with a leisured description of Mr Golspie's arrival from a suitably questionable port in the Baltic, to enter and disrupt the lives of the people working for Messrs Twigg & Dersingham in Angel Pavement. The captain bids him farewell, cockney wit greets him on the docks, and a very effective evocation of London follows. Within a page or two Priestley once more takes the reader into his confidence. 'This does not mean that we have now finished with No. 8, Angel Pavement. It is for the sake of No. 8 that we have come to Angel Pavement at all.'

*The Good Companions* carried this indulgence into direct address – dear reader – but once the scene was set in *Angel Pavement*, straightforward action followed. Five people make their way every morning to the offices of Twigg & Dersingham. Mr Dersingham, the ineffective but conceited owner of the business, Mr Smeeth, the colourless cashier who loves his repetitive job, Miss Matfield, a contemptuous middle-class typist, Goath the mournful traveller and Turgis the unprepossessing clerk who craves romance in his lonely life. Breaking into their dreary routine comes this exotic stranger, the tough, vulgar and supremely confident Mr Golspie, who transfigures their expectations with an Arabian Nights vision of prosperity. Priestley gently ridicules the petty snobberies of the Dersinghams through the comic fiasco of the dinner party given to welcome Mr Golspie, traces Turgis leaving his grubby lodgings every Saturday night with renewed hopes of passionate contacts, reveals the trials of Mr Smeeth from the extravagance of his jolly wife, and Miss Matfield's disillusion with the Burpenfield Women's Club.

Expectations aroused by Golspie galvanise the office into remarkable occurrences. Dersingham allows himself to be exploited, Miss

4  *The Times*, 19 August 1930.
5  *Times Literary Supplement*, 21 August 1930.

Matfield is swept half willingly into Mr Golspie's arms, Smeeth realises his ambition of getting a rise and Turgis becomes the plaything of Golspie's predatory daughter Lena. The deliberately contrived characters who enlivened *The Good Companions* have vanished from *Angel Pavement* and become people who might materialise in all reality on any London street. If there is no interior monologue, no deep soul-searching, these characters have more than enough life and diversity to involve the reader in their fate, and individual scenes are brilliantly realised. The passionate scene, for instance, after Turgis's last evening with Golspie's daughter Lena:

> Dazed, still aching, still hot and pricking about the eyes, as he went out into the street, he turned to have a last look at the enchanted window above . . . desire burned and raged in him as it had never done when he had vainly searched the long lighted streets for an answering smile, had stared at red mouths, soft chins, rounded arms and legs . . . The flame of this desire was fed from the heart. He was now in love, terribly in love. The miracle had happened; the one girl had arrived; and with this single magical stroke life was completed . . . Love had only to be kind to him and there was nothing he would not do in return; he was ready to lie, to beg, to steal, to slave day and night, to rise to astounding heights of courage . . .
>
> The conductor of the 31 bus, noticing the young man with the rather large nose, the open mouth and irregular teeth, the drooping chin, whose full brown eyes shone as they stared into vacancy, whose face had a queer glowing pallor, might easily have concluded that there was a chap who was sickening for something. But Turgis was alight with love. He sat there in a dream ecstasy of devotion, in which remembered kisses glittered like stars.[6]

Metempsychosis was not an activity commonly indulged by Priestley, but its half-brother – empathy – frequently enabled him to speak from inside his ordinary characters with an authenticity which made their experience moving.

*Angel Pavement* powerfully evokes the social background of its day, when fear of unemployment and the shattering effects of the breadwinner losing his job were part of the climate in which hundreds of thousands lived. *The Good Companions* finishes on a happy note of mutually acceptable compromise. *Angel Pavement* approaches unallayed tragedy. Mr Golspie carries along the illusion of success for a while and the gullible Mr Dersingham reflects it, but

6   *Angel Pavement*, J. B. Priestley, 376–7.

the brief and exciting enchantment is shot through with doubt and the aftermath turns into blank disaster. When Golspie disappears, Twigg & Dersingham collapses in ruins. Mr Smeeth loses his job, a heartbroken Turgis tries to commit suicide, only to have the shilling's-worth of gas exhaust itself before he dies, and Miss Matfield's surrender to Golspie leaves her in a state of self-contempt.[7]

The world of *Angel Pavement* is the real world where problems have to be solved not romanticised. When Mr Oakroyd loses his job in *The Good Companions*, he sets out on his journey with a touch of bravado, but when Mr Smeeth faces the same experience, he comes close to total pessimism. Finally convincing an incredulous wife that the ultimate blow has fallen, he says:

> 'And if you think I'm going to get another job as good as that, or a job worth having at all, in a hurry, you're mistaken . . . I know what it is, with office jobs; and it'll have to be an office job because that's what I've always done. I'm nearly fifty and look it . . .'
> 'I can work,' cried Mrs Smeeth fiercely . . . 'I'll get something. I'll go out charring first.'   'But I don't want you to go out charring,' Mr Smeeth told her, almost shouting. 'I didn't marry you and I haven't worked all this time . . . to get this home together, so you could go out charring . . . When I think of the way I've worked and planned and gone without things to get us a decent position . . . !' His voice dropped.
> 'We'll manage somehow.' And having said this, Mrs Smeeth . . . suddenly and astonishingly burst into tears.[8]

Priestley answered in *Margin Released* the main thrust of criticism directed at *Angel Pavement*. He could well understand, he wrote, that very fastidious readers might find his novels too coarse-grained and broadly humorous but he was not a very refined person and 'if there is an élite, I don't belong to it'.[9]

Nor did Sir James Barrie:

> *Angel Pavement* is, to my thinking, better than *The Good Companions* and I had not thought it likely that there would be a better in my time. Since reading it I find myself staring at the plan of it in shop

7  ibid.
8  *Angel Pavement*, J. B. Priestley, 602–3.
9  *Margin Released*, J. B. Priestley, 188.

windows till I fear that they may think inside that I am considering buying the book which makes me steal away.[10]

Characteristically, Virginia Woolf commented in her diary: 'I invent this phrase for Bennett and Priestley "the tradesmen of letters".'[11]

Recalling my own first reading of the novel, I remember being impressed by Priestley's skilled interlocking of the destinies of his large cast, his power to evoke the atmosphere of London, his understanding of what it meant for an ordinary worker to be unemployed. The general atmosphere was tragic. I emerged from the 605 pages feeling that the Fates had overtaken me. Re-reading it now, my view of the novel was changed by that last scene of qualified optimism in which Priestley so often specialised. 'It was a world that could play all manner of tricks with Herbert Norman Smeeth, but could never capture, swallow, and digest the whole of him.'[12] It was not a tragic novel after all.

Literary work continued unabated. The novel *Faraway*, published in 1932, was the result of a visit to Papeete which followed his first trip to America. In Tahiti, Priestley had long talks with James Norman Hall, who revived the *Bounty* story and discussed the rough plot of Priestley's new novel *Faraway*. Norman Hall, a great admirer of *Angel Pavement*, did not like *Faraway* when it eventually appeared and wrote a letter to Priestley expressing his disappointment. Later Priestley commented, 'He was quite right to be disappointed. I didn't blame him; I was disappointed too.'[13]

At first sight *Faraway* is a straightforward piece of adventure story-telling which begins when William Dursley, living in a boring Suffolk town, suddenly confronts a drunken uncle who rears out of the night to explain that he has discovered an uncharted South Sea island rich in pitchblende from which radium can be extracted. The whereabouts of the island have been cunningly concealed with one character knowing the longitude and another the latitude. William Dursley sets sail in search of the island only to discover that two sinister rivals have reached it first. What begins as a romance quickly turns into near tragedy with suffering, loss and privation slowly mounting to overwhelm the beautifully drawn pictures of the island set in its sapphire sea. What could have turned

10  Letter from Sir James Barrie, 14 September 1930.
11  *Diaries*, vol. 3, Virginia Woolf; entry of 8 September 1930.
12  *Angel Pavement*, J. B. Priestley, 605.
13  *Margin Released*, J. B. Priestley, 191.

into a treasure-hunt story equivalent to *Treasure Island*, became something very different. As the novel progressed, the landscape began to play an all-pervading part with the weird islands towering out of flawless seas infecting the very thinking of the men observing them. No concessions were made to stereotypes of South Sea living. Dubious night-clubs, natives full of slyness and the invasion of European film-makers all contribute to eventual disillusion. Priestley's animadversions on the decay of natural life slowed up the story, and *Faraway* ceased to be a South Seas romance and became a modern morality tale. Alas, by its very nature it was easy prey for the critics. The *Times Literary Supplement* damned it with faint praise:

> And such is Mr Priestley's gift, he is able to hold our interest . . . without taxing our patience. He is always readable and our one complaint is not against the length of his book but against his too patent effort to avoid the obvious in his conclusion . . . We read throughout with enjoyment but put down the book with a sense of undeserved frustration.[14]

Neither *Faraway* nor *Wonder Hero* which followed it were of major consequence in Priestley's oeuvre. Indeed, despite the length of *Faraway*, it and *Wonder Hero* belonged in Priestley's retrospective view to lesser entertainments. *Wonder Hero* could, in fact, be called a *jeu d'esprit*. Charlie Habble ('Wonder Hero') was a plain, simple man whose like could be found in every football team, especially north of Trent. Deliberately exploited by Mr Hal Kinney of the *Daily Tribune*, he was brought to London for one glorious fortnight of highly coloured life in the metropolis to provide Mr Kinney with an article. He encountered those wonders of modern London that are not revealed to northerners who merely come to London once a year for the Cup Tie.

Plunged into a ceaseless round of luxury hotels, night-clubs and cocktail parties, with one artificially devised sensation following another, the hard-headed Yorkshireman rebels against the razzmatazz, and gives Priestley the opportunity to reveal their meretricious fraudulence. A quick glimpse of Miss Ida Chatwick, a girl promoted by a newspaper as the most beautiful of all beauty queens, convinces him that for once they may be right, but before he even considers taking action on that view he is forced to visit a sick aunt in Yorkshire, which confronts him with the diametrically

14   *Times Literary Supplement*, 30 June 1932.

different scene of an economically ruined town inhabited by grey unemployed people and women and children threatened with starvation. Returning to London he finds that the newspaper has exhausted his possibilities and abandoned him, but miraculously all surrenders in the end to the glamour of true love. Moreover, Charlie Habble has his revenge. The man who was supposed to have saved the town of Utterton and half the Midlands from a vast explosion turns out to be an unaware faker who duped the *Daily Tribune* into giving him not only a wild burst of London life with a £500 cheque but also a highly satisfactory wife. This glib account of the book does not do it justice. Priestley's social concern permeated its pages and the plight of people in one derelict area of the north was thrown into sharp contrast with life in London.

*Wonder Hero* became significant in another sense. It was one of the last incursions into entertainment novels for the time being. The theatre was to become the medium for expressing Priestley's more serious examination of social, moral and creative problems.

# 11

# The Playwright
## 1932–3

It all began in 1932 with *Dangerous Corner*. The play, Priestley later wrote, was simply a 'trick thing' in which two-dimensional time was divided by a musical cigarette box. He wrote it to prove to playwright sceptics that a novelist could write an effective play using the strict economy of the stage. According to Priestley the immediate reaction of the critics realised his worst fears. He invented a phrase to demonstrate their attacks – 'This is Mr Priestley's first play and we don't mind if it's also his last' – but there was no corresponding reality among the critical notices. *The Times* in fact treated the play seriously but reflected the general view that it was a failure.[1]

*Dangerous Corner* assembles a group of people related by blood or marriage in the setting of a middle-class drawing-room, and an unrelated guest, Olwen Peel, recalls the name of Martin Caplan, brother of the host Robert Caplan. Embarrassment supervenes because Martin, suspected of embezzling £500 from the family business, has shot himself. Every characteristic in the conventional drawing-room play is faithfully fulfilled with all the players in evening dress discussing whether it is better to mask or tell the truth. Suddenly Freda Caplan offers the unrelated guest, Olwen, a cigarette box which plays the 'Wedding March' when opened, and Olwen immediately recognises the box as the property of the dead Martin Caplan. All unaware, her words set in train a series of confessions which removes the play from straight entertainment, and reveals the loves and hatreds of the whole company, and the complex nature of their relations with Martin Caplan.

The third act contains one of the most telling scenes in the play when Olwen recapitulates her last meeting with Martin, and admits that she herself accidentally shot him. Under the influence of drugs Martin tried to involve Olwen in a series of obscene pictures and when she recoiled, he taunted her with her puritanism, told her she

1   *The Times*, 18 May 1932.

must take her clothes off, grappled with her and produced a revolver. Trying to leave the room she is stopped by Martin waving the revolver, and in the ensuing struggle he is shot. The third act once again reaches the moment when the musical cigarette box was produced in the first act, but now Olwen keeps her counsel, and the 'Wedding March' is overwhelmed by dance music as Olwen and Robert begin to dance.

The dangerous corner – that moment when cavalier fate invests some unconsidered comment with significance far beyond its formal meaning – has been safely passed. Are we the victims of such moments when immense events follow – inevitably – in the train of a lightly spoken word, or is this the masked contrivance of the dramatist to make the play more effective?

The universality of the theme of the play explained its recurring popularity. Everyone could recollect some vital link between the unimportant and important in which one was entirely dependent on the other and produced an apprehensive awareness that some dangerous corner unmarked by anything significant could lie in wait for anybody. At a deeper level the Greeks spoke of *peripeteia* but Priestley kept to the surfaces, preserving the entertainment value of the play. Moreover, the play underpinned the power to intervene and made it possible to escape the dire consequences of unalloyed fate. 'If I had my time over again, I could change it,' became a possibility which was realised when Olwen, in the second production of the cigarette box, kept her counsel.

Deeper levels of awareness were touched upon but not explored in one interchange which represented the crux of the play. Freda's brother Gordon poses the question what would have happened if we had 'gone on pretending like hell to be happy together?' and Betty, his wife, replies: 'Nothing.'

> Gordon: No, if we'd gone on pretending long enough, I believe we might have been happy together . . . It often works out like that.

Gareth Lloyd-Evans complained that 'each character exists in terms of a formula . . . thus Gordon is a weakling, Stanton a plausible rogue, Betty is not so innocent as she looks, Olwen is in love with Robert and so on . . . at times the shorthand is so basic it ridiculously simplifies the realities of human emotion'.[2] An equally serious criticism was the similarity of the dialogue used by the

2  *J. B. Priestley – The Dramatist*, Gareth Lloyd-Evans, 78.

characters. Individual styles of speaking were almost interchange-able. There remained in the play the irresistible appeal of inner secrets forced into the open by accident, and its universal theme gave it a wide potential audience.

Directed by Tyrone Guthrie, with Flora Robson in the lead, it ran for only five performances and then the backers withdrew their support. Thrown into gloom, Priestley took a cold hard look at the situation, made some swift calculations with his agent, A. D. Peters, and plunged in daringly to rescue it. He was, by now, a relatively rich man and he drew on the accumulation of royalties to keep the play running at a loss. In the end his audacity paid off. The destructive notices in the daily press were followed by favourable reviews from Ivor Brown in the *Observer* and James Agate in the *Sunday Times*. The empty seats began refilling, the play recovered to have 'a comfortable run' and finally became one of the most popular plays he had ever written. 'I doubt if there is any country in the world possessing a playhouse that has not seen *Dangerous Corner*,' he claimed, and certainly *Dangerous Corner* entered the repertoire of European theatre.

The most remarkable part of the whole story is that Priestley wrote the play working ceaselessly in one week, and thus set a habit he then considered vital to play-writing. Dialogue should pour out pell-mell as a continuous process. He was never a man to rewrite and polish. Later in life his wife Jacquetta described how he sat down at his typewriter and allowed the words to flow uncorrected, with the first version accepted as the last. It was this uncritical acceptance of first versions which made him vulnerable to criticism.

*Dangerous Corner* brought interesting letters from two dis-tinguished writers, Michael Arlen and John Galsworthy. John Galsworthy wrote:[3]

> I especially wanted to talk to you about your play. I was greatly interested in it and held all through. 'The knife-edge of accidents that we live on' idea . . . [illustrated] at the end with the turning on of the gramophone leaves one with something serious to think of and the technique is very adroit and complete. I think all that I felt to say adversely was that perhaps you were too possessed by the idea of doing something new; in other words, a faint self-consciousness showed through. Perhaps also, theatrically speaking, your main idea was left too late . . . and the device which develops it took perhaps too long to get to one.

3   John Galsworthy to Priestley, 18 July 1932.

Priestley himself had no illusions about the play. Interviewed by the American *Theater Arts Monthly* he freely admitted: 'It is pretty thin stuff when all is said and done.' Infallible formulas capable of producing successful plays made no sense to him. The majority of British and American playwrights agreed with him that failure or success in the theatre was more dependent on that unpredictable goddess Chance than in most other artistic activities. 'Once through the stage door, you might as well believe in astrology.'

Some plays mysteriously met the current climate of thinking and were predestined to success, but nobody could predict success or failure. Frequently play productions were well launched before it was apparent that they were doom-laden, but by then the backer was surrounded by contracted people and could only 'brace himself to meet the next disaster'. Three prerequisites of success were: that the London theatre best suited to the play should be available; that the actors desired by the director were not already otherwise engaged; and that the opening time was exactly right. 'In the circumstances of production in the English-speaking theatre you are compelled to exist in an over-heated atmosphere of dazzling success and shameful flops, you are a wonder man in October, a pretentious clown in March, you are in, you are out.' This atmosphere made serious work in the theatre very difficult, with one foot in the Stock Exchange and the other in the playhouse. Dramatic writing and production became more sophisticated forms of gambling.

Despite these protestations Priestley was drawn into the world of the theatre and for the next few years wrote play after play, outfacing the worst that the critics could do. He refused to live the life of the fashionable playwright 'rushing from dressing-room to dressing-room, sitting up until two listening to theatre gossip', but there was no place to which he more frequently applied his favourite word – magic – than the theatre. Torn between the attractions of the novel and play-writing, he had many intense discussions with Jane who liked the theatre but not theatrical people. Now that their financial future seemed assured, she was all for experiment, but when he read her the script of his next play *Laburnum Grove*, she did not like the first act. Discussion ended in 'frozen silence'. Despite his distaste for fashionable theatre-going he was now living a rich life which brought him into contact with actors, directors, publishers, novelists, playwrights and women. It was not in his nature to neglect the many attractive women who were pleased to be associated with the now famous and still oncoming author, who surprised everybody by bursting into new fields every few years.

Jane, for her part, continued to play the role of wife, helpmate and critic, and presented a façade of married happiness which rarely broke down in public. Priestley's fragmented reminiscences, conveyed to paper with the same inconsequence which characterised some of his best writing, play havoc with the image of Jolly Jack Priestley and insist – almost obsessionally – on the difficult, surly man. It needed only the slightest switch to produce the other Priestley, a kindly, charming, almost avuncular person whose deep voice delivered admiration for a pretty woman, argument, gossip and philosophic asides, with that measured diction which – in the words of one woman – made him 'so convincing'. Moreover, according to Jacquetta Priestley 'Jolly Jack' was first conceived by the staff of the *New Statesman* at a time when Priestley had fallen into a prolonged gloomy mood.[4] It was satirical.

Men like H. G. Wells frequently brought out the blunt – if not rude – Priestley. This *alter ego* was inspired on one occasion by Wells's astonishing statement that we should sweep away the yellow races and give Western civilisation a better chance to flourish. Not to be outdone, Priestley said: 'Well, look at the Irish. You could say the same about them. If we ever have a full-scale Irish Republic next door, perhaps it might be possible to return her exiled citizens and what a grand clearance that would be.'[5] He repeated closely similar views in *English Journey*.[6]

An encounter with Shaw at the Garrick Club one evening brought out another side of his character, the tough man of action who when challenged would fight to justify the course he pursued. Shaw strongly disapproved of Priestley's incursion into production and told him with a great roar of delight, his Irish brogue thickening to make the point more effective, 'It'll ruin you. It'll ruin you. And don't expect me to pull you out of the mess.' Priestley retaliated, 'I have yet to see the mess I can't pull myself out of.'

Underwriting plays in the 1930s involved relatively modest risks and Priestley's next play, *Laburnum Grove*, was launched for £800, with the weekly running costs roughly the same figure. 'The profits, of course, were never gigantic. Today's dashing characters operating through a network of companies would probably need a

4 Interview with Jacquetta Priestley, 5 October 1985.
5 Interview with H. G. Wells, 12 November 1943.
6 *English Journey*, J. B. Priestley, 235.

reading glass to see our figures.'

Despairing of dealing with theatre managements, in 1933 he formed his own production company, English Plays Ltd, and came to an arrangement with J. P. Mitchelhill, owner of the Duchess Theatre, by which he leased the theatre to Priestley whenever he wanted to launch a play. Given a reasonable run, he estimated that their 'get-out take' or net profit would approximate £800 a week, which with a multiple of thirty would translate into £24,000 today.

Costs of production were minimised by ignoring the high rentals of the hiring agencies and exploiting a huge second-hand shop at the corner of Euston Road, where chairs, wardrobes and beds spilled 'over the pavement like air from a cushion . . . we used to go there to buy whatever we wanted for a set, very cheap'.

There were many happy times with Priestley writing a play, choosing a producer, and sharing the casting, while Peters handled the finances. Priestley recorded – optimistically – that they would take plays off after eighteen months but very few plays survived as long as a year.[7]

Under the new Mitchelhill management, the Duchess followed an innovative policy the influence of which was more prolonged than its own short life. Priestley liked working in the atmosphere created by Mitchelhill.

> Our rehearsals were a kind of perpetual tea party, not unlike the Mad Hatter's. Once inside that glorious little playhouse it was forever your birthday. There, like a kind of rich uncle to all of us, would be Mr Mitchelhill. Now cocking a shrewd eye at the stage, now flitting about planning further generosities.

Priestley completed *Laburnum Grove*, his first Duchess play, with a high temperature while recovering from influenza. Produced on 23 November 1933, the play, relative to *Dangerous Corner*, was a success. Priestley himself believed that the characters in *Dangerous Corner* were stock characters whereas George Radfern, the father in *Laburnum Grove*, was created 'in the round'. He described Radfern as 'a man about fifty with nothing remarkable in his appearance, though even at the first there should be a certain quiet assurance and authority visible beneath his easy manner'. His daughter Elsie is bored by the unromantic respectability of Laburnum Grove, her sleek young fiancé is trying to borrow money from Radfern which will make their marriage possible and Uncle Bernard and Aunt

---

7  *Margin Released*, J. B. Priestley, 201.

Lucy are similarly bent on 'raising a loan'. They consume cold tongue and stewed pears with impeccable suburban manners only to have the embalmed correctness of the scene shattered when Mr Radfern (played by Edmund Gwenn) suddenly reveals his double notoriety as forger and crook. Ruined by a take-over bid, Radfern has happily turned to crime, but it is crime which fits a counterfeit society. He makes his revelation with the same quiet enjoyment as he eats his simple supper. This is no confession. It is a stab at the whole financial system where big business is guilty of sins no less serious than his own. 'You see, the banks don't like it, and what the banks don't like must be a serious crime nowadays, like blasphemy in the middle ages.'

Family and guests at first refuse to believe him, but he spells out his crimes with something approaching gusto. His alleged share in the wholesale newspaper business is a front for his scandalous activities and his money, some portion of which all the characters in the play are only too ready to share, comes from a tainted source. By implication they, like him, want to spend money which they have not earned. It is Priestley the social critic attacking not only big business and the banks, but the self-invited guests, the free-loaders, the would-be parasites. Instead of penalising the big financier who ruined his business, the state gave him a knighthood. Values are so contradictory, what does a little quiet forgery by one innocent victim weigh in the scales of justice. The dialogue makes George sympathetic to the audience but whereas the family believes his story, the audience has reason to be sceptical. When Inspector Stack from Scotland Yard arrives to investigate his activities his relations are quite ready to rat on Radfern, a deliberate reflection on family loyalty. Radfern's wife, absent from the first crucial dinner party, returns to the house and reverses the whole situation when she reveals that Radfern is talking complete nonsense and they are the victims of an elaborate leg-pull. At first unconvinced, they accept her story when she reminds them that the whole of his fabrication can be found in a detective story brazenly exposed on the parlour table. Everyone is happy again, especially Elsie, who may have lost her fiancé but has regained her faith in her father's integrity.

Now the tables are dramatically turned once more. When the inspector first called to interview Mr Radfern he gave similitude to the alleged send-up, but now he returns and in all reality it becomes clear that Mr Radfern was, in fact, telling the truth. He has, for years, been one of a gang of forgers, and the net is clearly closing around him. Radfern, always highly sympathetic to the audience, announces gaily to his wife and daughter that they are all going off at once for a prolonged holiday abroad.

The *Times* critic was frankly bored with the first act and doubtful of the second. Thus, two thirds through the play all was neat entertainment without much depth and the 'audience simmered doubtfully'.[8]

Priestley believed that the most important act in any play was the third, and now the *Times* critic justified that belief. Suddenly, he wrote, the audience was 'fairly bubbling' and he concluded his review:

> Inspector Stack pays another visit: he and Mr Radfern sit down to business at the table, and there they are, Mr David Hawthorne and Mr Gwenn transforming the play. The tone is changed; it becomes true and entrancing; all that has gone before though connected in plot seems irrelevant. The battle fought out between these two men is an extremely skilful piece of story-telling, rooted in character, swift in movement, rich in suspense.

As Susan Cooper has written, 'the fates . . . beamed on [this] production, giving it a very long run', and *Laburnum Grove* remains a favourite in repertory theatre. The financial statement for the first five months was revealing. In today's currency it earned over £340,000.[9]

Fast on the heels of *Laburnum Grove* came another play in the same category, *Eden End*. Ralph Richardson who took the lead recalled working with three different playwrights – Shaw, Anouilh and Priestley. 'The most indulgent' was Priestley, he claimed: 'not only as a friend but because of the peculiar quality in his dialogue'. Much as he liked the dialogue of *Peer Gynt*, 'my favourite is the dialogue of J. B. Priestley: his seemingly simple diction is rich in melody. The best shorter part I have ever had was that in *Eden End*. There I was given wonderful jokes, all set to music – what more could one ask?'[10]

Priestley had thought about and lived with the characters for years and when the time came to commit them to paper he retired into the country and after a period of 'that utterly self-forgetful creative zest which more than pays for all the sick vanity and

8   *The Times*, 29 November 1933.
9   A. D. Peters Archive, London.
10  *Encore: The Sunday Times Book*, 95.

vexation of an author's life' he finished all three acts in 'a week or two'.

It has been argued that Priestley's addiction to Chekhov deeply influenced *Eden End* and produced resemblances between the Yorkshire doctor's family in 1912 and the Russian family in *The Cherry Orchard* in 1904. The sitting-room of Dr Kirby's house is described in the play as 'a comfortable well-worn room furnished in the style of an earlier period'. Dr Kirby, the hard-working GP, has a son Wilfred, represented as a weak character, and two daughters, Stella in her late thirties and Lilian in her late twenties. Kirby, portrayed throughout as a good man, realises that his daughter Lilian is in danger of becoming a family 'appendage' who stays at home unmarried 'to look after father'. Stella, already a glamorous actress, is supposed to be touring abroad when the play opens with the old nurse Sarah analysing her character. The dull routine of *Eden End* is suddenly disrupted by the unexpected return of Stella who says she has come back on impulse. Inexplicably, she was afraid to write and had to come in an unpremeditated rush or not at all. 'Don't you understand?' she says impatiently, but their understanding is impaired by the nine years she has been away without a single visit. Even when her mother fell ill six years before and subsequently died, she still had not returned. Sarah, the old nurse, who loves Stella as a mother might her own child, feels the glamour which Stella brings to *Eden End* and the excitement of the reunion sweeps away her criticism. Stella confronts her separated husband Charles Appleby, a heavy-drinking actor who has lost his grip and is fast joining the huge army of actors whose promise has not been fulfilled. This was the part taken by Ralph Richardson which marked the beginning of his association with Priestley. Richardson told the story of a very guarded Jack Priestley receiving him at the Highgate house to discuss the play, with the opening challenge, 'Do you really want to play an actor on the way out?'

Richardson said, 'Well, it's my impression that actors are in and out with such rapidity that nobody ever really knows where he stands. Anyway it would be nice to have the experience of being a has-been – it might help one to cope later.'[11]

Lilian, in the play, is friendly with Geoffrey Farrant, a one-time admirer if not lover of her sister Stella. Lilian has deliberately invited Stella's separated husband Charles Appleby to the house in order to draw her attention away from Farrant. At first angry, Stella

11   Interview with Ralph Richardson, 4 September 1978.

Jonathan and Emma Priestley, Priestley's father and mother.

In the beginning . . .

Priestley in the First World War.

Convalescing after being wounded in the First World War (Priestley front row, last on right).

Priestley as the drunken photographer in *When We Are Married*. (*Photo Howard Costa*)

(*Right*) Priestley rehearsing the part of the drunken photographer with Patricia Hayes at the St Martin's Theatre in 1938.

'In memory of the Groupe', a concert party to which Priestley belonged when he was convalescing after being wounded in the First World War (Priestley with the toy dog and beard).

Priestley's father, Jonathan Priestley.

Jane Priestley, his second wife.

Priestley with Hugh Walpole during
their collaboration on the novel
*Farthing Hall*.
(*Photo Mayson, Keswick*)

Priestley, John Drinkwater and
Bernard Shaw during the Malvern
Festival.

Priestley in
1925, by
Robert Austen.

(*Below*) Priestley in the
study at Well Walk
where he finished *The
Good Companions*.

quickly adapts to the situation but a scene between Charles and Stella creates a disturbance which disrupts the whole family.

It can be said that there are passages in some Priestley plays which employ sentimentality – emotion for emotion's sake – with a skill which almost justifies its use. There are also pseudo-philosophic passages which do not rise to the occasion.

> Stella: It doesn't matter now who we are or how we stand, or anything like that. Just think of the two of us here, in a cosy little room, lost in the moorland rain. We're lost too. There isn't anybody else. Just us. And time's stopped for us.

Stella and Charles are finally reconciled to the world of cheap lodgings, third-rate repertory in shabby local theatres and the constant drag of insecurity. Before they leave Eden End never to return again, there is a scene between the old nurse and Stella which tested thresholds of emotional response in England and America. England rose to acclaim and New York to deplore the scene from which the following dialogue is an extract:

> Sarah: He's not a bad sort for an actor chap, though I'll bet he takes a bit of watching. But you look after him, love. He's nowt but a big daft lad – like 'em all.
>
> Stella (whispering): Oh Sarah, I don't know what to say. There aren't any words.
>
> Sarah: Nay, love. Nay, little love [fondling her face]. And don't catch cold when you're coming out o' the theatres. [Very softly] I'm an old woman now, a'most past my time. Happen I shan't see you again.
>
> Stella (crying): Yes, you will. You must.
>
> Sarah: Oh, I'll see you sometime. There's a better place than this, love.

In *Midnight on the Desert* Priestley said that *Eden End* was 'simply his best play', a role given to at least three plays at different times.

Taken up and replayed by repertory companies, *Eden End* became an irregular source of income, but there were many dissident voices.

# 12

# Family Life and
# *English Journey*
## 1933–4

In 1933 Priestley's affluence enabled him to buy Billingham, an old manor house on the Isle of Wight surrounded by fifteen acres of land, for the absurd price of £2,000. There, he built on the flat roof what became his famous study, with a 'view sweeping across a quarter of the island'. It had five big windows, three of which wound up and down like the windows of a car, while another curved window at each end gave the illusion of being on the bridge of an ocean-going liner. The spectacular view out over the bay swept away to the tower of the Needles lighthouse, but sometimes that view was swathed in mists. As he wrote one day:

> All my five windows show me the same sullen morning. Not a glimmer of sun. All the high downs are lost in mist: the fields look sodden and away on the left behind the tall elms there are fine curtains of rain sweeping down upon Godshill. The calendar says it is spring. Along the drive the daffodils and narcissus and white violet have returned and the banks of the little ditch by the tennis court are fat with primroses . . . Spring is about somewhere this morning, but winter is putting down its last barrage and covering its retreat. The sea might have crept in another league during the night and now be within a mile of us . . . If I stand looking out of the windows stripped of the landscape, it is unpleasantly cold and there is nothing for it but to draw nearer to the fire.[1]

The history of Billingham was rich in ghosts, duels fought in the gardens, Cromwellian soldiers still roaming the grounds and old ladies haunting the summer-house. Priestley never encountered the materialised reality of any of these, but sometimes spoke as if at least one ghost paid regular visits. There was also the secret passage, obligatory to legends of this kind, which ran from the house to Carisbrooke Castle where King Charles I had been imprisoned.

1  *Rain upon Godshill*, J. B. Priestley, 2.

Generating its own electricity, there were times when the household was reduced to candles, and then the sinister shadow play in the corridors gave greater substance to folklore and occasional terrors to the children.

Over the next ten years, at least five novels and eleven plays were written either in Highgate Grove or Billingham Manor. He was now at the height of his powers, physically and mentally. Physically very strong he had broad shoulders and a heavy build which made him very masculine to women.

> His body alone gave you reassurance. You felt you could rely on him in any situation. Indeed, there was a forcefulness about him which convinced you that he could overcome most things, including your troubles. And there he was wonderful. He did reassure you. He took you to lunch, talked about your problems, bought a glorious common sense to it all. You felt he was a kind of rock in the swirling uncertainties of life.[2]

So many witnesses leave a picture of a man reaffirming the positive pleasures of life, and John Braine believed that he now 'literally rejoiced in his superhuman physical and intellectual energy'.[3]

Norman Collins, a close friend, elaborated that picture.[4] He had never known a man so active. Priestley was one of the last of the pianola players and he took his pianola very seriously. He became a man possessed, extracting drama from every note he struck. Whether it was work or play, he threw himself into it with equal energy. Immediately he rose in the morning he wanted to plunge into work and he hated wasting time on such trivialities as trousers and jackets. 'He had a one-piece zipper suit made, lined with wool,' Collins said. 'Unfortunately it wasn't ventilated so he ended up ankle deep in his own sweat.'[5] Collins's picture of family life was equally romantic. He told friends that the best two smiles in England were Jane Priestley's and the present Queen Mother's. He described Jane as pretty, dark-haired and Welsh with a gift for languages which made her a fluent French speaker. She was a natural hostess and she somehow coped with five children at home, a nanny, a butler and other servants, with every weekend an influx of guests which set the house swirling with life. Fourteen for dinner

2  Interviewee who wishes to remain anonymous.
3  *J. B. Priestley*, John Braine, 40.
4  Quoted by John Braine.
5  ibid., 40.

was commonplace and if the demands of the guests took precedence, the children were certainly not neglected. Jane not only ran 'a large establishment' and its surrounding property 'like clockwork' but organised amusements – including horse-riding – for guests and children alike. Her main relaxation – rarely indulged for lack of time – was bird-watching.[6]

Behind this façade, as we have seen, simmered conflicts and problems completely unknown to the outside world. One area of tension continued to concentrate around Mary. Now nine years old, one day out walking with Jack the question of her parentage arose. He became agitated, suddenly broke off the discussion, and said, 'You must keep the secret. I'll be ruined if it comes out.'

Already familiar with the manipulative powers of social pressures which had driven H. G. Wells to conceal two love affairs from the public, Priestley did not exaggerate. Mary's happiest recollections date from the move to Billingham Manor. There, between the ages of nine and fourteen, she frequently encountered happiness, playing bowls or croquet with a father who could be funny, full of jokes, and capable of converting his bursts of aggression into a music-hall act.[7]

Ironically, against the background of Priestley's infidelities the children cannot recall ever having received any sex instruction. Perhaps it was an inevitable reaction. Mary says: 'I simply remember his sexual life outside the family and feeling very hurt at the time, but we were told nothing about sex.'[8] And Angela Wyndham Lewis: 'Sex instruction in so far as it existed was indirect and due to our own efforts. When the parents were away we invaded the library which had some 10,000 books and went straight for the classical erotic literature. I read the *Arabian Nights* and *The Body's Rapture*.'[9]

Until the 1930s Priestley had driven a car somewhat eccentrically since he found driving 'too easy to demand concentration' which made it 'too difficult to be safe'. The climax came in Newport, Monmouthshire in the summer of 1932, when his preoccupation with 'higher thought' drove him into a lamp standard, which collapsed. An angry crowd came surging round threateningly and Priestley decided that enough was enough. 'I was a bad driver so I gave it up.' There followed an episode which illustrated the dangers

6   ibid., 21.
7   Interview with Mary Priestley, 15 September 1985.
8   ibid.
9   Interview with Angela Wyndham Lewis, 10 October 1985.

of infidelity, the improvidence of inventing alibis even with trusted servants and the pitfalls of hiring cars. Priestley sometimes relied upon a chauffeur-driven Daimler to pick him up on demand and carry him in splendour to any important appointment. It was a small luxury which royalties from his work could easily accommodate. Angela Wyndham Lewis tells the story of her mother, one day when Priestley was out of the house, suddenly deciding to visit her daughter. She rang the Daimler hire company and said to the chauffeur, 'I want to go to my daughter's.' 'Yes,' the man said, 'I know where that is.' When they arrived at an address entirely unknown to Jane she immediately suspected the truth, rang the bell and confronted Priestley's new mistress. Her identity we do not know.[10]

The inescapable focal point of considerable turmoil and distress, Priestley continued to write against the worst odds and refused to convert his personal emotional life into literary currency. Only a select few were taken into his confidence.

He played tennis vigorously in an effort to control his weight, worked with ferocious concentration when he worked, and still did not know whether he had exhausted the immense versatility of his talent. At the height of his powers his apparent relaxed confidence was qualified, when, caught off guard, he allowed the scars of experience to crumple the avuncular image he presented to one young admirer. She was a friend of Priestley's American publisher and she had come with her father, Mr Farrastead, to visit Priestley in London, where he did indeed treat her like an uncle, and presented her with a signed copy of *The Good Companions*. 'Suitable reading for the young,' he said. The *enfant terrible* of her family, Angeline Farrastead was to play another role some years later in New York, but in 1932 an episode occurred which remained imprinted on her memory. She and her father went down to Billingham Manor and arrived half an hour early to be received by Jane, who said Jack was still working and could not be disturbed. It was a beautiful summer day and Jane entertained them in the garden with tea, cakes and vivid conversation.

She had this quick mind which handled words so easily and was a very alive person. Unlike a lot of English people, her welcome was genuine and I felt a quick response. But while we were talking an impish urge overtook me.

10    ibid.

Angeline wanted to see the 'private face' of the Master while he was actually engaged in the creative process and, slipping away from the company, she avoided the maid to make her way to the famous study. Climbing the stairs she suddenly realised that she would have to knock on the door before entering and that would 'break the spell'. The luck was with her. 'For some reason I do not know – possibly the heat – the door was open and I crept close up and looked in. He was sitting with his knees wide apart staring down at his stomach looking so gloomy – I was sorry for him. It was more than gloom. A kind of brooding. His pipe puffed away. He frowned. His hands drooped loosely between his legs. I thought he looked a picture of misery.'[11]

Abruptly, everything changed, he swept out of his chair, paced the full length of 'the bridge' and stopped with his arms akimbo staring out of the window. 'He was right about the ship image. He looked as if he were navigating a great big liner.' A moment later he was slumped back in his chair again staring at the ground between his legs 'stonily'. Angeline Farrastead decided that it was the wrong moment to reveal her presence. 'I was afraid he would explode with anger.' She crept down the stairs again. There is no real evidence of what he was writing at the time but Angeline Farrastead thought it might be his novel *Wonder Hero*.

It was in the autumn of 1933 that Priestley set out on a pilgrimage through England from Southampton to London by way of the Midlands, Yorkshire, Lancashire, the Tyne and Tees and East Anglia. The result was a remarkable book, *English Journey*, which attempted to discover and describe how the economic crisis of the 1930s had affected England and what were the characteristics of our common weal of Englishness. Its subtitle, *A Rambling But Truthful Account of What One Man Saw and Heard and Felt and Thought During a Journey Through England*, indicated the Johnsonian strain running through the book. It received short shrift in the *Times Literary Supplement*, but the *Observer* carried a rave review which ended: 'If I had a thousand pages you should have a thousand quotations.'[12]

'I will begin', Priestley wrote in *English Journey*, 'where a man might well first land [in England] at Southampton. There was a motor coach going to Southampton – there seems to be a motor coach going anywhere in this island – and I caught it.'[13] He travelled

11  Letter to the author, 14 January 1986.
12  *Observer*, 16 September 1934.
13  *English Journey*, J. B. Priestley, 3.

with a few basic clothes, the inevitable portable typewriter and a whole paraphernalia of note. ooks, razor blades, pencils, rubbers and of course pipes which settled in a box like a nest of vipers. Muirhead's *Blue Guide to England* became basic reading on the trip and for relaxation in bed *The Oxford Book of English Prose*.

There followed a 450-page panorama of England and the English which evoked time, place and character with a combination of all the skills he had now mastered. From Southampton he proceeded to Bristol, from Bristol to the Cotswolds, from the Cotswolds to Coventry and Birmingham and thence on to the Midlands, Lancashire, Tyne and Tees, Lincoln, Norfolk and back again to London. Travelling frequently by coach, he made endless notes, writing rough chapters sometimes *en route*. Arriving at Bradford he suddenly felt that perhaps he should never have included it in his itinerary because, inevitably, he brought a special spirit to the city.

It was a very different Bradford from the Bradford he had known. The richly successful wool merchants had vanished. Vivid memories recurred of the 'swarms of genial . . . parasites' who with one room and a solitary clerk or typist had escaped – conveniently – from the curse of Adam. 'Mind you, lad,' said one old merchant on this re-visitation, 'they're beginning to say Bradford's makking money again. It's doing nowt o' t'sort. Whatever money is being made's going to t'banks. It's banks 'ats makking money.'[14]

Unable to resist the call of his roots he searched out some old business colleagues in the wool trade. A. W., once a clerk working beside him in the 1910s, was now running the business and facing entirely new hazards which would have dismayed his predecessor. N. remained a warehouseman who 'looked just the same as he did twenty odd years ago. He is a grand type of North Country working man and I was glad to see him still cheerfully pulling the bales about, though in his sixties.' They talked about their old boss and N. said, 'Nay, Jack lad. Ah don't know what t'owd chap lived for. He got nowt aht o' life, did he? Ah've had more fun i' one night that Ah bet he had i' thirty years.'[15]

The big event which forced Bradford into Priestley's itinerary was the reunion dinner of the 10th Duke of Wellington's in which he served during the First World War. Many friends from the battalion had died and he described his reactions as he climbed the

14   ibid., 163.
15   ibid., 191.

stairs of the tavern. The past was suddenly crowded with people who no longer walked the earth and he began to feel like 'a very old man', haunted by the shadowy but familiar figures which frequently moved casually through his dreams, the 'forgotten children of the sword'.[16]

Surviving the overwhelming conviviality of the main party, Priestley escaped to an ante-room where he met members of his own platoon, and they exchanged memories. One figure after another came looming up from the mists of the past and each recollected person – tragic or comic – made their talk more eager, until they shouted and laughed 'in triumph as one always does when Time seems to be suffering a temporary defeat'.

Once more the soggy mud was sucking at their gumboots, the machine-gun bullets ricocheted off tombstones and dark premonitions were gloomily fulfilled. 'It was little Paddy', Priestley wrote, who 'came close to me, finished his beer and asked me stammeringly as ever, if I remembered sending him from the front line for some water for the platoon . . . "Nay", he stammered, "I wasn't gone more than t-ten minutes and when I c-come back, where you'd been, Jack lad, there was n-nobutt a bloody big hole and I n-never set eyes on you again till tonight."'[17]

Priestley helped to provide free tickets for impoverished survivors of the battalion and the conclusion of his account was moving. They could pay for tickets, celebrate their reunion and drink libations to the dead, but what reaction could adequately accommodate the despair of the living who had fought heroically for a world in which they no longer had a place, exchanging uniforms for unemployment and rags. 'And who shall restore to them the years that the locust hath eaten?'[18]

After Bradford, the Black Country. It reaffirmed for him a picture all too familiar of smoking hollows filled with workshops, rows of identical houses, yards filled with rusty metal. He drew a devastating picture of the industrial storm which had laid waste the countryside, left bleeding gaps in the earth and reduced once bright fields to deserts. Nothing he saw in the Black Country, not even the slums, impressed him more painfully.

Depressed areas like Jarrow produced a different kind of horror and drove him to demand why in God's name nothing was being

16   ibid., 167.
17   ibid., 171–2.
18   ibid., 273.

done to relieve the listless decaying life of a city which had been killed by unemployment.

As for nineteenth-century England, he wrote, it had a lot for which to answer.[19] 'It had found a green and pleasant land and had left a wilderness of dirty bricks. It had blackened fields, poisoned rivers, ravaged the earth and sown filth and ugliness with a lavish hand.' The England he travelled in 1933 had been democratised, health and education had improved but everything suffered from a glib standardisation. 'A large-scale mass production job. You could almost accept Woolworth as its symbol.'

His animadversion on the Irish upset a number of reviewers. The Irishman in Ireland, he wrote, might 'be the best fellow in the world' simply waiting with patience to break away from the hateful empire 'so that free and independent at last, he can astonish the world', but he did not astonish Priestley. Too often he 'cut a very miserable figure'. He settled into the poorest quarters and converted them into a slum.

Huge areas of English countryside and personality were mediated through the perceptions, warmth and language of J. B. Priestley to produce a panoramic book which launched yet another aspect of his talents: the popular sociologist. Supremely readable, its style derived from ordinary speech rhythms and vividly brought alive the essential English quality of people and places. The book became one of his favourites, sold well and the critics were reasonably responsive. Before the curtain came down on the whole enterprise, he admitted:

> I wish I had been born early enough to have been called A Little Englander. It was a term of sneering abuse, but I should be delighted to accept it as a description of myself. That title sounds the right note of affection. It is little England I love.[20]

He was using the term in the sense of small not in the sense of narrow and he hastened to disclaim any delight in the boasting Big Englander.

News of the American edition of *English Journey* drove Priestley into a marathon letter to his American publisher which revealed a sensitivity capable of pouring out its wrath.

19   ibid.
20   ibid., 416.

Oct. 6th 1934

Dear Gene,

Miss Herdman has just sent me a batch of press cuttings about *ENGLISH JOURNEY*. (For which please thank her.) It is, of course, a good friendly press. But one feature of it disturbs me, and that is what I want to discuss now. This feature that disturbed me is the general tone of dislike towards my former work coupled with an obvious ignorance of the real nature of that work. Practically every review contains at least one serious misstatement: e.g. that I edit a magazine; that I broke away from writing tales (inferior ones too) to do this journey; and so forth. But what I really complain about can be found in them all. These fellows say, in effect: 'Here is Priestley, who became popular (undeservedly) by writing a lot of sentimental novels, watery imitations of Dickens; he's a bovine, hearty sort of ass; but about a third of the way through this book he suddenly discovers (and about time too) that all is not well with everything in this world.' I do not think this is much of an exaggeration, though it is compressed, of course. Now I resent this strongly. I do not mind if reviewers know nothing about my other work and never mention it, but they have no right to make these generalisations that are obviously based on sheer ignorance. Not a single one of them mentions the fact that last year I brought out a novel called *WONDER HERO*, in which I described with truth and, I think, vividness, the plight of the people in one of the typical derelict areas – and threw the thing into sharp contrast with life in the East End of London. I did this – so far as I know – for the first time. And then again, there are plenty of sidelights on social conditions in *ANGEL PAVEMENT*, a novel that has not a glimmer of sentimentality.

Now this really won't do, my dear Gene. It is bad enough that they should have stopped buying my work, but at least they might not have the damned impudence to associate me with an imaginary body of work, and then reproach me for it. The titles of my books are there, staring them in the face. You see what a ridiculous position I am in. I am reproached by American readers because I will not give them a whole series of jolly hearty tales like *The Good Companions*. I am reproached by American reviewers because I have never written – according to them – anything else but such jolly hearty tales. It isn't good enough, and you and I have got to do something about it. Do you think some friendly literary journalist – say, Canby – could make a little article out of this topic. Or could I, without rushing to give offence, write a letter to somebody like Canby or Mrs van Doren, putting the case I have been putting in this letter? I do feel that Harpers, as my publishers, have a right to resent these sweeping misstatements about my previous work. It would not, of course, be difficult to quote good opinion here, which would show that my novels (to say nothing of my plays) were serious pieces of work and not sentimental catch-penny tushery. Couldn't you do something yourself, in co-operation with some friendly literary editor?

I hope you are well and happy. Jane has just gone off to Germany for a few weeks' cure, which we hope will make her so fit that she will be able to come to America with me some time this winter. I am all right, a little tired after various theatrical excitements. My new – and easily my best play – *EDEN END* is a complete smash hit so far. We have been turning people away nearly every performance, and this in spite of the fact that even our sympathetic critics (and it is a highbrow success) thought it was very good but not 'Box office'. *Laburnum Grove* is touring in the provinces, and playing to packed houses, before it comes to America, where I believe it opens about Christmas . . .

Yours,

J.B.P.[21]

His private life continued its accustomed pattern. Characteristically, as with so many married couples torn by alternations of strife and reconciliation, sex sometimes became a mediator to redeem quarrels – expressed or unexpressed – and there is some evidence to show that Priestley was no longer sleeping with his wife when a dream occurred which would have delighted that master of dream wish-fulfilment, Sigmund Freud. 'I think it left a deeper impression upon my mind than any experience I had ever known before, awake or in dreams and said more about this life than any book I have ever read.'

The dream followed a visit Jane made to the lighthouse at St Catherine's Point on the Isle of Wight to 'do some bird-ringing'. 'I dreamt I was standing at the top of a very high tower, alone, looking down upon myriads of birds all flying in one direction . . . it was a noble sight, this vast aerial river of birds. But now in some mysterious fashion the gear was changed, and time speeded up, so that I saw generations of birds, watched them break their shells, flutter into life, mate, weaken, falter, and die . . . death struck everywhere at every second.'[22]

What was the meaning of this blind struggle towards eager

21  Priestley to 'Gene' (Eugene Saxton, a member of Priestley's American publishing house), 6 October 1934.
22  *Rain upon Godshill*, J. B. Priestley, 304–5.

mating and inescapable death? Each creature's ignoble little history was revealed to him in a flash and he felt 'sick at heart'. He saw the birds as symbolic of men and it might have been better, he wrote, if not one of them had been born and the whole fruitless struggle had never taken place. 'I stood on my tower, still, alone, desperately unhappy.'[23]

The first part of the dream could be seen as a reflection of the disillusion which ran through several letters at this time and those hostile to psychoanalysis would need no further explanation. Any sexual symbolism in the lighthouse tower would seem laughably irrelevant, but Freudian canon insists that flying dreams are frequently sexual.

Consider the following images in the second part of the dream: 'flickering through the bodies themselves, there now passed a sort of white flame, trembling, dancing, then hurrying on . . . and then it came to me, in a *rocket-burst of ecstasy*, that nothing mattered, nothing could ever matter, because nothing else was real, but this quivering and hurrying lambency of being' (my italics).[24]

The description was a gift to any Freudian. What mattered to Priestley were his own reactions. As the dream died away he experienced a deep sense of happiness such as he had never known before. If that happiness slipped away once more into nothingness and he lost his sense of sanctuary that was because he remained a 'weak and foolish man' who allowed 'the mad world to come trampling in'.

In the spring of 1934 the producer Basil Dean invited Priestley to write the dialogue for a film in which Gracie Fields was to appear. 'His humour and strong characterisation would be well suited to the needs of the Lancashire star,' Basil Dean wrote. 'He consented and quickly produced the outline of a story with excellent possibilities.'[25] Since Gracie Fields had established her right to approve the subjects chosen, Dean and Priestley decided to present the idea to her in person and they set out hopefully one morning to visit her spectacular Villa Patrizi on the isle of Capri. They stayed at the Hotel Quisisana and every morning journeyed along the narrow winding road through olive groves overlooking the burnished sea, to dip down along the rocky shore and finally approach the villa. There, many a morning, Gracie, flamboyant in a bathing costume

23  ibid.
24  ibid.
25  *Mind's Eye*, Basil Dean, 204–6.

as highly coloured as it was scanty, greeted them with the warmest embrace and 'Hallo luv'. She immediately 'hit it off with Jack' and as one successful session followed another they drew 'very close together'. Whether anything came of this short relationship is unknown. Dean especially remembered his involvement in the hard physical exercise which Priestley now regarded as obligatory to health.

> Every afternoon we played tennis on the courts behind the hotel . . .
> Two sets of singles was the daily ration. I was always a poor player.
> Long before my penance was over Jack's cannonball service had so
> exhausted me that I could do little more than raise my racquet in
> feeble protest.[26]

The brilliant blue sea, the air fragrant with flowers, the serenity of the nights and the company of a woman who identified with one aspect of his roots made this short interlude delightful. Even the already growing sense that perhaps the film world was not his natural milieu did not prevent his persuading Gracie that with Basil Dean's help they might produce something better than the run-of-the-mill musicals which had dogged and, to some extent, damned Gracie's career. 'Our daily sessions, work and play ended,' Dean wrote, 'Jack and I returned to London leaving Gracie enchanted with new possibilities.'

Using the current depression in the cotton industry as the framework of his story, Priestley traced the hilarious adventures of an unemployed Gracie, searching for fresh opportunities, as she enters the Big Dipper unreality of Blackpool's famous fairground. Stanley Holloway, cast as a Blackpool policeman, becomes entangled with Gracie and pursuer and pursued exploit the full comic possibilities of the ghost train, roundabout and helter-skelters. It was a quick piece of superficial work which Priestley preferred to forget as soon as it was written, but the final film, *Sing As We Go*, became a financial success. *The Times*'s complaint that he was obsessed with the star simply reflected his deliberate intention.

26   ibid., 204.

# 13

# Second Visit to America
## 1935–6

In the autumn of 1935 the whole Priestley family arranged to leave
for America with Priestley travelling alone because he was to take
part in the American production of *Eden End*. The family were to
follow later, travelling to the Pacific coast by sea through the
Panama Canal. They would head direct for Arizona where Priestley
would join them. Any suspicion that he had deliberately planned to
be 'free' on board the *Aquitania* was not altogether quelled by what
would have been the enormous expense of accommodating eight
people in New York's hotels. In the event he was depressed when
he boarded the *Aquitania*, and the depression persisted throughout
the greater part of the voyage. All the cocktails, caviare, deck tennis
and richly diverse company could not repair the havoc wrought by
a particularly difficult parting from his wife. Jane no longer expected faithfulness but whenever they travelled apart the ghost of other
women came up to haunt her and before they parted the atmosphere became highly charged.

At another level the sea remained for Jack a symbol, and the huge
Atlantic rollers seemed full of menace.

> Lifts, glass-enclosed decks, garden lounges and steel shopping
> centres – there is something almost heroic in the spectacular urban
> idiocies of these shops – cannot make you forget the presence of this
> huge element of the sea, at once so menacing and melancholy.

Priestley was a good sailor untroubled by sea-sickness and the first
day out with the 'world newly washed and sprinkled with salt'
should have lifted his spirits. Instead he remained sunk in the
profoundest melancholy. The news pouring into the ship from
London, Italy and Abyssinia was consistently bad, but his bitter
quarrel with his wife before he left converted the North Atlantic
into 'so many shifting mounds of slate' with a 'dishcloth sky'.
Wandering the long corridors of the *Aquitania*, which was twisting
in heavy seas like a serpent, he drank too many whiskies and

constantly asked his actor companion why they were not enjoying themselves. 'There awoke then a sense of oncoming disaster, impending doom,' he wrote in *Midnight on the Desert*, 'that has never quite left me since.'

Two days later when they entered the Hudson river on a clear, beautiful morning with the river sparkling and the air alive with New York vibrancy, his gloom lifted. As he looked down from the high decks of the *Aquitania* at the customs shed where a group of friends waited for him, he told himself that this time he must take New York – quietly. Within fifteen minutes of his landing, the old excitements were mounting and within two days he was once more, as he put it, 'reeling with enchantment'. Here once again was the 'Babylon and Nineveh in steel and concrete, the island of shining towers, all the urban poetry of our time'. Restless, uneasy, the impossibility of sitting still drove him out to see a show, eat and drink, mix with the crowds, until a kind of childish primitivism arose and he simply wanted to 'make a noise'. The teeming urgency of life in New York meant that every minute must be brimful. Take a river trip, go to the theatre, see the Rockefeller Center, find yourself a woman, hurry through the Museum of Modern Art, have yourself a good time and never face the horror of an unfilled empty space unpressurised by people or appointments. 'Time must not merely be killed but savagely murdered in public. In this mood which has never missed me yet in New York, I feel a strange apprehension unknown to me in any other place.'

The first exhilaration of New York quickly surrendered to another phase which repeated itself with implacable invariance whenever he revisited the city. Walking up Fifth Avenue in the brilliant autumn sunshine, standing at a window fourteen floors up, sipping an old-fashioned as the dusk descended and the lights came up, he felt the cannon pulse of American vitality, electrifying his own. 'What more could a man want?' Alas it did not last. The obligatory third phase broke in. 'I could not sleep properly, began to feel tired, empty, desolated.'

His explanation invoked the image of a community where people were 'packed in layers hundreds of feet thick', which meant that self-contained cities of people intervened between himself and the stars. Civilised life became nothing but a 'vast box of humanity' which interrupted internal rhythms to change them irrevocably.[1]

He would find it impossible to sleep more than two or three

1   *Rain upon Godshill*, J. B. Priestley, 65–6.

hours and even 'the quietest apartment, the most cautious dinner or supper, the most artful preparations for sleep would make no difference. Oh those nights of wakefulness, the mind raced away noisily, uselessly, like the accelerated engine of a stationary motor.'

There remained at the heart of his distress an inner excitement 'like that of a famished lover waiting for his mistress' which persisted against all disillusion.[2]

Consciously or unconsciously Priestley revealed in that last sentence something of the literal truth about his second visit to New York. No sooner had he arrived than he made plans to search out and meet again Miss Farrastead, the young lady who had stolen up the stairs to his study at Billingham Manor and observed him in a state of creative introspection. She was then living on Central Park West and her parents raised no objection to their daughter spending an evening with the distinguished British writer, provided he first came to dinner with the whole family. Etiquette satisfied, Priestley took Miss Farrastead to lunch, spent the afternoon wandering in Central Park and enchanted her with reminiscences of his early days in Bradford.

> He figured out a way to make them funny and roared with laughter at his own jokes. Everything was fine until he made the pass. I was confused, too young, too inexperienced . . . I regret it now. Regret not going through with it. But I didn't . . . and he took it – very classy – like a gentleman.[3]

His reaction against early excitement now became so powerful that some deeply buried psychological self took on the characteristics of a dwarf and insisted on reconstructing the city of New York. He felt 'like a midget . . . moving in an early scene of some immense tragedy as if I had a glimpse in some dream years ago, of the final desolation of this city, of sea-birds mewing and nesting in these ruined avenues. Familiar figures of the streets begin to move in some dance of death.'[4] The barker outside the Broadway burlesque show who once wickedly invited everyone to step inside and see the girls slowly became 'a sad demon croaking in Hell', and even the roar of traffic was converted into a 'March To The Gallows' 'infinitely greater, wilder and more despairing' than anything Berlioz wrote.

2  *Midnight on the Desert*, J. B. Priestley, 23.
3  Letter from Angeline Farrastead to the author, 16 September 1975.
4  *Midnight on the Desert*, J. B. Priestley, 25.

In anyone but the robust, physically fit, down-to-earth Jack
Priestley, these symptoms could indicate psychological disturbance
and the fact has to be faced that there were occasions when his
depressions, his capacity for converting the normal into the abnor-
mal, heavily qualified the accepted image of Jolly Jack Priestley. Or
was it simply the literary man allowing the play of imagination to
take over and reveal under the surface an alternative and horrifying
reality? Priestley himself has rejected this interpretation. 'The
mood behind . . . that feeling of spiritual desolation, that deepening despair are real enough. And nowhere else in America do I catch
a glimpse of this Doomsday Eve. Only New York does that to
me.'[5]

It is tempting to invoke Priestley's predilection for Jungian
interpretation and see all this alternative view of New York City as
the product of his shadow self. Priestley's devotion to Jung varied
over the years but at the height of his commitment he did believe
that there was a shadow self which had to be disinterred from the
depths and faced in the process known to Jung as individuation.
The capacity of repressed guilt to break through and disturb many a
fully rational man is commonplace and despite Priestley's theoretical belief in libertarian values, he could not entirely escape the
penalties of his infidelities. The wilder shores of speculative
psychoanalysis could even see 'the final desolation of this city' and
'the ruined avenues' as symbolic of the distress he might have
caused, but anything is possible with such analogies.

The blunt reality of New York life was in fact totally preoccupied
with the Baer–Louis fight on the first few days of his arrival, and
people could talk of nothing else. On the great day of the fight
restaurants installed enormous loudspeakers to carry the commentary and the waiters at the restaurant where Priestley regularly
dined simply forgot their customers. Priestley's English temperament found the commentary nothing but bad rhetoric in which
information sank out of sight. 'Say, it's terrific – brown thunder-
bolts – black lightning' was characteristic of 'the show'. It simply
deafened and exhausted Priestley. He seemed surprised to find an
underlying cruelty in the audience but all 'big fight audiences' have
a sadistic streak.

Priestley had come to New York with the express purpose of
producing what he then regarded as his best play, *Eden End*. Three
plays already produced in his absence in New York were 'badly

5   ibid.

done' and with that sweep of confidence which some people characterised as arrogance, he outraged theatrical New York by deciding that he, a playwright, could do better – 'much better'. Preliminary interviews with agents led him into their world of cynical disillusion. They had first to form a syndicate to back the play and this led into complications which exploded the myth of American efficiency. Superficially, high-powered secretaries, managers and agents gave the impression of being overworked by barking into telephones short sharp 'Yeps', 'Yehs' and 'Yahs' without taking any corresponding action. Since no commitment was possible by phone, endless meetings were arranged, but reaching inaccessible offices through the porridge of New York traffic made interviewing exhausting.

> Once you had penetrated into their private office they welcomed you as a brother, put you into an easy chair and then sent through the cigar smoke . . . some twenty or thirty thousand words of autobiography.[6]

When Priestley explained that he had come to New York to arrange the production of a play they indicated that perhaps he was unaware of a breach of good manners. Driven at last to take action, the agents ushered him into sumptuous cars and gave him a conducted tour around the surprisingly large number of empty theatres. Remnants from another age, some were in a sad state of repair but redolent of long-forgotten actors whose names immediately set the agents off into fresh theatrical memoirs. Above all, the weather – a clammy Indian summer with temperatures well into the nineties – made crossing and recrossing Fifth, Park and Madison Avenues like living in 'cataracts of warm liquid gold'. Walking by day, his ordinary clothes were drenched in perspiration, and at night under the relentless glare of multiple lights his starched shirts became damp and crumpled. Slowly a sense of frustration combined with the heat and exhaustion to reinforce his darkest mood. New York became a jungle of steel, concrete and gasoline vapour, and even Central Park with its thinly covered volcanic rock made the birds and the grass artificial products of a landscape gardener who had lost his connection with nature. The continual torrent of news, pounded out by newspapers which were available day and night, was consistently depressing. Threats of war, which finally burst into reality one year later in Spain, were constantly headlined, and

6   ibid., 35.

the League of Nations, which had lost its credibility, became an easy target for newspaper chauvinism. The excitement of Roosevelt's New Deal was in the air, new shows were being launched, and old dance bands resurrected. People were full of a brittle excitement but Priestley formed the impression that underneath 'nobody felt secure'. The cataclysm of 1929 still haunted the city and not all Roosevelt's New Deal had yet reassured New Yorkers.

Invited to several first nights, Priestley found them as distasteful as their English equivalents and settled more cheerfully to see the rodeo in Madison Square Garden. He broadcast a talk on England, wrote some articles, was appalled by a film of *A Midsummer Night's Dream*, and lunched and dined with agents and actors. 'I had such a good time that nothing will ever induce me to have another one again.'

One meeting in the famous Algonquin Hotel was memorable for a conversation with H. L. Mencken, roughly recalled by Steve Fanton: 'Your plays simply won't do,' Mencken told Priestley, whereupon Priestley replied, 'They may not do for you. They're all right for approximately 200,000 people.' 'Dupes, Priestley. Pure dupes. You don't play fair. People don't behave like that. They're puppets. You can see the Puppet Master.' Priestley considered this for a moment, puffing his pipe, and then he said, 'Well, Mencken, if your wit had half the spontaneity of my plays people would be laughing straight instead of out of the corners of their mouths.'[7]

Priestley took three weeks to cast *Eden End*, and then rehearsals began in a vast shed on Forty-Fifth Street nicknamed The Theatre because banks of seats filled its gloomy space. The shed was draughty, not entirely waterproof and beset by cockroaches who perfectly timed their appearance to coincide with certain dramatic moments. Rehearsals were swift and short and Priestley found the atmosphere too intense to take an active part for more than brief spells. One week later the whole cast moved up to Yale where the university entertained them with rye and sherry in rooms which were 'vaguely reminiscent of the newer colleges in Oxford'. Saturday was chosen for the first night and in the afternoon Yale played the Navy at football, with Priestley as an honoured guest who found the grand carnival atmosphere enjoyable and the cheerleaders impossible. The audience in the theatre that evening included some from the football match who were bewildered by

7 Letter from Steve Fanton's son Richard, September 1950.

the 'vague posturings of these Americans trying to be Englishmen', but the reception, as the curtain came down, was warm. Later that night Priestley finally resolved a question which had been troubling him for days: should he risk the hazards of the first night in New York? His family were due to land on the west coast in a few days and, whatever the frictions, he was missing the children. He decided the time had come to move west.

Susan Cooper has described what followed.

*Eden End* sank without trace on Broadway, after a few weeks of struggling survival. By the time Priestley read the glum telegrams reporting its poor reception, he was a long way from Broadway: standing on the platform of Albuquerque railway station, New Mexico, a windy place where civilisation seems to have been swallowed up by a great embrace of open sky – as indeed it has in one respect, this being several thousand feet higher than most of the United States. After a brief resentful rage he accepted the bad news with a shrug – a characteristic reaction which must have been even easier than usual in that environment – and went on to join his family on the Arizona ranch.[8]

Priestley's account read: 'It was there with a cold gritty wind stinging me that I read the telegrams from New York about the opening. They were as uncomfortable as the wind. I think I knew then that it was all up.'[9]

His comments about American critics to Edward Davison were scathing.[10] These 'smart alecky, ignorant' New York newspapermen were 'so damned insensitive' that they were ruining the serious theatre both in America and England, but more so in New York because they held despotic sway over the public.

Priestley rejoined his family at San Pedro and in consultation with Jane decided not to go straight to Arizona. Instead they spent two weeks at a guest ranch near Victorville on the Mohave Desert, which gave the children a rest after the long voyage out from England. They found the Mohave Desert ranch disappointing. The southern California desert was very different from its Arizona equivalent and, despite its dramatic transformation from time to time by invading Hollywood stars and crazy extras dressed to resemble the hordes of Genghis Khan, Jane in particular found it

8   *J. B. Priestley*, Susan Cooper, 104.
9   *Midnight on the Desert*, J. B. Priestley, 44.
10  Priestley to Edward Davison, 6 November 1936.

alien. Looking through the window of the ranch she saw a wonderful prospect of desert and mountains brilliant in sunshine, but once outside the door a cruel wind followed her, creating with its persistence a headache.[11]

The Mohave ranch gave Priestley one of his earliest impressions of Hollywood types who came roaring over the mountains in high-powered cars to relax for a few weeks at Victorville. They were not the very rich stars or ace producers who usually went to Palm Springs, but lesser characters with their wives and children. The main ranch-house had a very large sitting-room with adobe walls hung with Indian rugs, a wooden gallery and a roaring fire in a huge brick fireplace. There, a motley crew of actors, directors, writers and drifters gathered every evening to enlighten one another about the famous and the infamous. One amongst them, a tough, thickset assistant director of Italian origin, became a friend who entertained the Priestleys royally with drink and anecdotes drawn from a life rich with disillusion. Occasionally he was forced to break off in the middle of a meal because the Hollywood Monsters had summoned him back and he would embrace his two sparkling children, shout goodbye to everybody and go racing away in a big, black, sinister car. Priestley remembered him vividly because he revealed an aspect of American life with which as yet the Englishman was unfamiliar. Below the frank, easy-going American surface full of genial acquaintances, inexhaustible vitality and almost sadistic hygiene, there was an underworld of gunmen, pimps, molls, racketeers and grafters, elaborately illumined by his Italian friend, with highly coloured anecdotes; he sometimes acted out their more extreme characters in the old Hollywood tradition. Priestley saw unravelled before his eyes policemen who belonged to uniformed gangs, millionaires capable of corruptly pursuing further millions, and crooked lawyers able to frame anybody from a congressman to a senator. Instead of a tropical underworld where hot blood and passion transfigured commonplace events it became a grey fungus world driven by greed, cold sensuality and premeditated violence.

In *Midnight on the Desert* Priestley reconstructed the atmosphere in the manner of Dashiell Hammett. 'I had a few more drinks. Then I kicked the old man in the guts. After that I went upstairs and threw the blonde on the bed.'

Sometimes, as Priestley sat there in front of the roaring fire, listening, he found his imagination tearing away to send him racing

11  *Midnight on the Desert*, J. B. Priestley, 44.

up the stairway to protect the sleeping children, and he had to 'shake [himself] out of a shuddering nightmare'.

On this trip to Hollywood Priestley wrote no film scripts because he was overwhelmed with other work and found the Hollywood hierarchy repellent. Writers were of less consequence than producers, directors or cameramen and the stereotype legend of authors lured out to Hollywood by large sums and 'left to droop in silence for months' rang true. Moreover, it seemed to Priestley that the 'six suburbs of Hollywood in search of a city' were really the product of a cunning art director from Metro Goldwyn Mayer and lacked any authenticity as a genuine community in which people lived. Quickly tiring of life on the Mohave ranch, the Priestley family began the journey down to Arizona in one of those big, glossy, old-fashioned trains where steel had not entirely replaced wood. A large family confined for hours to the restrictions of train life arrived in Arizona, nervy, tired and, on Priestley's part, bad-tempered, but now began a way of life in brilliant sunshine which seemed to suit – for a time at least – everybody. The ranch was a scattering of low-lying wooden buildings surrounded by rocky countryside which offered vast empty spaces where the occasional clanking of a far-distant freight train down the valley echoed enormously on the air and left a silence which almost sang in its intensity. The early mornings in the winter were sparkling but cold. Midday brought burning sunshine alive with bluebirds and red cardinals, flashing among the cottonwoods. The afternoons perfectly combined invigorating air, dazzling sunshine and the heady scent of a thousand plants and flowers. 'At sunset', Priestley wrote, 'the land throws up pink summits and saw-toothed ridges of amethyst and there are miracles of fire in the sky. Night uncovers two million more stars than you have ever seen.'[12]

A new novel had fermented for some time in Priestley's mind and now, far removed from London, he began writing *They Walk in the City*, which required reconstructing, miles from their source, the swarming details of a city with which he had developed a complicated relationship. Early attempts were frustrated by the noise of children who found that the wild life of the desert, the horse-riding and wonderful freedoms created a sense of perpetual holiday. Attempts to instil some discipline into their gypsy behaviour were reinforced by Jane who regularly gave them lessons assisted by sporadic efforts from Jack. His gift for identifying with children's

12   ibid., 2.

games became even more effective when offered the possibilities of immense sand dunes, cacti and a wealth of ponies. What greater excitement in the small years than to go riding with real cowboys, to attend rodeos, to travel on pack trails, sleep in sleeping-bags, and cook over open fires. The children lived in a world so highly coloured after the drabness of London that every morning they ran excitedly into the sunshine. Angela Wyndham Lewis said:

> It was a most beautiful place. Very dry and cold at night and a perfect 80 degrees in the day. We spent two winters there and became besotted with horses. We used to play horse games with blocks of wood on our hands for hooves. There were picnics too but Jack didn't like picnics. In fact he liked to have chairs to sit on at a picnic.[13]

Barbara Wykeham recalled the day when they all took the trail on mules along a hazardous track overlooking the Grand Canyon. Jack, a bulky man whose weight was becoming a problem, slowly drifted into a lop-sided position in the saddle, leaning towards the echoing depths below, until she suddenly saw that the girth straps were slipping and might at any moment send her father hurtling to his death. She let out a yell taken up by the others. Jack came to a halt and the straps were tightened.[14] 'Death by mule was not my idea of heroism', Priestley later remarked.

There were five children on the ranch – Barbara, Sylvia, Rachel, Tom and Angela Wyndham Lewis. They lived like a family of Tartars. Dressed in brightly coloured shirts with sombreros, the older children rode horses with a bravado which excited the admiration of hardened cowboys. They practised for rodeos, they mixed casually with cowboys, they talked horse jargon fluently and ran around the hut barefoot. This was the life for any child shot through with ambitions to become one of those 'primitive males, dressed in tremendous hats, gaudy shirts and high-heeled boots, which converted them into tough nasal peacocks unimpressed by any defeatist urban nonsense about quiet . . . respectable clothes'. The younger children were entranced tomboys living an 'equine idyll', converting themselves into galloping ponies when real ones were not allowed in the bungalow. 'The two babies . . . played solemnly for hours with stick horses, taking logs of wood out for a lope and then coralling them again in a stick-horse ranch.'[15]

13  Interview with Angela Wyndham Lewis, 10 October 1985.
14  Interview with Barbara Wykeham, 15 April 1985.
15  *Midnight on the Desert*, J. B. Priestley, 149.

Not for Priestley the rough-shod life of the range. Occasionally he conceded a ride on an enormous ruminating animal over the hills and back down the dry river bed, but the idea of galloping appalled him. Once a 'young brute of a horse' had dashed off towards miles of waterless desert and convinced Priestley that this particular piece of God's ingenuity was incalculable and terrifying. Nothing for him but the old, sleepy and docile.

The ranch had a central command building surrounded by bungalows occupied by individual families, with the inevitable people coming and going. The children compounded this confusion by shooting about like rockets. The necessity to find a writing sanctuary became paramount and now the Americans justified their capacity to 'run up or tear down buildings overnight', producing out of nowhere Priestley's famous Arizona writing hut, casually and quickly. 'You bet,' they cried and went ahead 'with none of the endless palavers' of their European counterparts. Literally a hut no more than ten feet by twelve, the boards were rough and unpainted, with two small tables, one for odds and ends, the other for his typewriter. His working-chair was upright, his armchair comfortable but far from voluptuous. Indian rugs on the floor, a waste-paper basket, a bin full of firewood and a squat tin stove completed his literary home. The stove, always ready-prepared for the match, would send the woodshaves leaping up in flames to engulf the logs and produce fierce heat in a remarkably short space of time. It became his all-consuming Moloch in which letters, documents, manuscripts and many a piece of evidence disappeared, which later biographers would regret. There are those who claim that he used the stove during two winters to obliterate evidence from the record and it is true that of the enormous correspondence which flowed into his different homes and followed him around the world, he preserved relatively little. The letters, for instance, from Jacquetta Hawkes which recorded the most profound experience of his life are missing. Certainly there were long hours of anguish about what he should keep and what burn. There was the occasion when he set out one midnight to his hut because he had taken the harsh decision to burn 'many thousands of words' of the novel *They Walk in the City*.

I remember a particularly fine glitter of stars with no moon and . . . the desert hills so much starless indigo at the base of the sky . . . As I reached the door of my hut and switched off my torch, I looked up and noticed yet once again, with a shrinking sense of unfamiliarity, how all the constellations had been monstrously misplaced. I was far from home.

Far from home geographically, not mentally. The novel, part of which he was about to destroy, concerned – as we have seen – the city which had long replaced Bradford in his life, London. The stove shaking with intense heat seemed to fix its red eye on his manuscript and the temptation to 'pop the whole lot in' became strong. He thought of three separate publishers waiting for manuscripts to arrive and the chaos which the impulse of the moment would create. The manuscripts were his to dispose of with God-like indifference and two months' work, worth possibly thousands of pounds, could be burnt to ashes in a few minutes. He paused and considered. 'It could wait a little longer. I was not sleepy. I cut down the glare of the stove, settled in the larger chair and lit a pipe.'[16] His mood remained black but embedded in it was an element of self-indulgence which gave the blackness 'a velvety quality . . . a rich man's funeral'. The coyotes no longer howled, the desert was quiet but the 'comfortable-looking man in the armchair . . . was inside a half-starved coyote out there on the dark desert howling to the stars'.

The following morning at ten o'clock wearing a shirt, crumpled flannel trousers and slippers, he made his way through burning sunshine to the hut once more, and there with two windows wide open and a thin curtain to protect him from the heat, he settled down in 'a cloud of American tobacco' to smoke and write. His mood had changed abruptly. The depression had given place to creative excitement as he induced from the pages the highways and byways of London and stepped back into the city he had so short a while ago left.

If by his own description, Jack Priestley had suffered all his life from mild spells of manic depression, this was a short-lived example. Certainly, as his children acclaim, his manic side in Arizona made him very good company and sometimes marvellous fun. It also led to high-speed writing. The novel which now unfolded in the early mornings and late afternoons began once more in Yorkshire with Edward and Rose living in Haliford and meeting by chance, one beautiful afternoon, on those wild moorlands to which Priestley loved to escape in his youth. A sensitive account of prolonged attempts to communicate in greater depth ended with an

16   ibid., 16.

engagement to meet again on a carefully specified occasion. What promised to have characteristics of an assignation was totally frustrated when Edward accidentally locked himself in the bathroom and only escaped when it was too late to keep his appointment with Rose. Impetuously, and somewhat unconvincingly, a deeply disappointed Rose decided to join a girlfriend who was leaving for London. Possessed by something resembling love, Edward sets out in pursuit unaware that Rose has disappeared into the universally anonymous life of the waitress. The bewildering intricacies of London streets leads them into a box-and-cox experience where they continuously search for and never meet each other, but come to know the loneliness and indifference of great cities. And now, baulked at every turn, frightened by the threats of city life, they both independently attend a demonstration in Trafalgar Square and accidentally meet only to have a riot overwhelm their reunion. Rose is injured and the great swelling tide of the crowd drags Edward away from her. Melodrama supervenes when a procuress talks her way into Rose's confidence and hints at the rich customers for whom she arranges innocent assignations.

When Priestley first conceived the novel he set out to bring together two simple young people, typical specimens of the 'exploited and helpless class, part them and bring them together again in the fashion of the oldest love stories'. He also intended to set both characters within a strong framework of social criticism. In so far as social criticism can be extrapolated from the novel, it indicted the mechanisation of human life by the cold indifference of great cities and the ruthless pursuit of self-interest. The moral message resounds throughout the novel and tends to limit the full realisation of its characters, but the romantic in Priestley swept back to have Edward rescue Rose from the procuress and bring them together in a last moving scene. The fact that they emerge from the clutches of city life unbrutalised tends to undermine his message, but the novel exemplified that streak of social concern which had first developed in *Angel Pavement*.

Reviews complained that this was a novel of 'brilliant reporting' which Priestley found ironic when he remembered what enormous creative effort it had cost him to project himself back into the streets of London while sitting in the middle of a desert with the temperature in the nineties. He knew quite well that such criticisms were double-edged. Not only was the novel brilliant reportage but, by implication, the highest level which he could hope to achieve. He wrote:

They may be right when they hint that the higher, grander, subtler forms of imaginative writing are quite beyond me; I have never made any great claims for my fiction beyond protesting once or twice that there might be a little more in it than met the top-speed reviewer's eye, and that because I wrote one jolly, hearty, popular novel it does not follow that everything I have written since is exactly the same.[17]

The *Times Literary Supplement* wrapped its criticism in so many obliquities it was difficult to disentangle any real evaluation.

There are two Mr Priestleys. One is a confidential secretary who is an artist at finding at once and in any quantity the appropriate words for the mind of the other. He is employed for the most part in composing descriptive reports, genial and satirical, of the daily round of wage earners of both sexes, though the signs are not lacking that he could, if required, supply minds that should embody more profound words or emotions. The other Priestley is the man of affairs with less sensibility. His wares are excellent of their kind, and if close scrutiny does not associate them all with the hand-made, all the more credit to the hand that devised the machine.[18]

Once *They Walk in the City* was complete Priestley decided to renew his acquaintance with Hollywood. In *Midnight on the Desert* he brilliantly evokes the atmosphere, spirit and artificiality of Hollywood, a place he had early concluded was not for him. All the attributes of a materialist paradise were framed by its slightly artificial mountains, never-fading sunshine, beautiful women and wealth. Men arrived from England, bronzed, fit and smiling 'and then . . . died quite suddenly'. There was no more cosmopolitan place in the world and yet it 'still seemed an American small town suffering from elephantiasis'. Here was a world of brittle sophistication where visitors were solemnly conducted on sight-seeing tours of 'homes', and yet there was no town in the world where there were fewer genuine homes. 'It is a community of wonderful lovers who have neither the time nor the inclination to make love, a Venusburg that will not admit Venus.'[19]

The fabrications on celluloid of dream worlds full of wealth, drama and adventure were peddled by businessmen pretending to be artists and by artists pretending to be businessmen. Inextricably

17  ibid., 8.
18  *Times Literary Supplement*, 1 April 1936.
19  *Midnight on the Desert*, J. B. Priestley, 191–2.

involved in a double life where the publicly proclaimed desire for privacy was part of the necessary publicity for film stars, thousands of dollars were spent projecting their images and defeated any attempt at normal life.

The astonishing reality of Los Angeles was the final paradox because whatever roots the film colony managed to sink deeper than its artificiality, they encountered citizens crazier than the actors and a way of life no less bizarre.

When he first went to Hollywood characters larger than life 'walked in and out of Spanish castles', rode on elephants, stayed up all night drinking and arrived unshaven in sports shirts the following morning at the studios accompanied by women in full evening dress, glittering with diamonds. Now the golden boom town had changed and Hollywood seemed to 'belong to worried business-men wrestling with tax problems'.

Priestley made several forays from the ranch into Hollywood by car and easily picked up commissions for scripts which he could write back at the ranch and convert – magically – into large sums of money. Such scripts are difficult to trace because, to the gratified surprise of his script-writing colleagues, he insisted that his name be removed from the credits.

The creative world in all its forms is littered with the corpses of projects which involved months of ceaseless talk, but Priestley wasted more days and nights filled with vain discussion in Hollywood than anywhere else in the world. The ideas which he did eventually complete were overwhelmed by a wealth of 'projects' which generated a whole heat of 'creative discussion' only to collapse after months of work. One conference followed another, one cigar-smoking genius was matched by another tough-talking actor, one writer was overwhelmed by producers, directors and technicians. Everyone seemed to believe that the faster they talked and the more excited they became, the better would be the film which in the event never emerged from smoke-laden dens called studios. Frequently long hours of this frenzied activity failed to produce a penny in money, but Priestley was just as liable to be paid – handsomely – for a script which was never made.

On one occasion he wrote a storyline treatment about a famous international string quartet made up of 'four middle-aged bachelors of different nationalities'. The producer who 'acquired it' paid £5,000 (at least £75,000 today) for the treatment, but after endless wrangles, interspersed with hilarious discussions about which character should play which instrument, he decided not to make the

film. Excluding jazz, musical illiteracy was endemic among Hollywood producers and the elevated abstractions of chamber music left
them not merely cold but hostile. Nevertheless producer Number
One realised that in some mysterious way Priestley had produced 'a
hot property' and with the cunning nature of all seasoned producers, he proceeded to sell the treatment to producer Number
Two for £8,000. Producer Number Two was a stereotype Central
European who remained in Hollywood for years without making a
single film, but he now entered negotiations with producer Number Three. Serial exchanges of this kind could extend to the fourth
and fifth producer with the chances of production diminishing in
strict proportion to their increase in number. As Priestley finally
wrote: 'Where that script is now I don't know and can't imagine.
No doubt those four string players are now years out of date, but I
still remember them with regret.'[20]

Early in January 1936 Priestley wrote from the ranch to Edward
Davison rejecting an unspecified commission on the grounds that
he had just finished a treatment for a W. C. Fields film which
Paramount intended to make. He had met Fields and found him
'difficult to handle' but Paramount were worse. He had given them
a week to make a final decision and if they decided to go ahead and
make the film, he would have to take another week off to write the
script. 'I can wire you as soon as I have heard from them but of
course if that is too long . . . I shall understand.'[21] Production with
the Fields film ran into a complicated morass and the film died the
classic death by a thousand discussions.

It was during his visits to Hollywood that Priestley encountered
people like Groucho Marx, Charlie Chaplin, Cecil B. De Mille and
Louis B. Mayer. One classic meeting with Charlie Chaplin took
place in an unnamed Hollywood restaurant full of boisterous
customers who could not make out what alchemy brought together
two such diverse characters in such harmony. Priestley, as a boy,
had seen Chaplin playing in the old slapstick Fred Karno sketches
on the stage and now in the brittle glitter of a Hollywood restaurant
they recalled and re-created the music-hall atmosphere with
Chaplin perfectly mimicking the voice, gesture and grimace of one
famous droll after another. There were continuous bursts of
uproarious laughter. Stepping back into the spirit of those days they
recalled the lyrics of the old music hall and as one capped the other

20 *Margin Released*, J. B. Priestley, 217.
21 Priestley to Edward Davison, 10 January 1936.

reproducing yet another verse from well-known songs, they occasionally merged in a joint performance to the mingled delight and dismay of the customers. One fine Cockney lyric told the story of a day in the country drinking beer and the recurring chorus, 'three pots a shilling', re-echoed round the restaurant.

As I remembered it in the silence of that Arizona midnight months afterwards, I could hear again Chaplin's pleasant Cockney lilt and I remembered then how delighted I had been – and secretly a little moved too – by that foolish popular song of yesterday, by its essentially English innocence and dear charm which stole into that hard noisy Hollywood restaurant like a waft of the scent of hay, and suddenly made me sick to go home again.

Priestley was good on Chaplin's artistry:

The films of that laughable sad little man, that wistful tatterdemalion with the ridiculous feet and the haunted eyes, a symbolic figure, half French, half English, and not at all American, have a finer and truer genius of clowning than any others.

Absurdly, on one occasion, there in the middle of this artificial city, the dumpy figure of H. G. Wells appeared, a person so quintessentially a London Cockney that he stood out in sharp relief. As if to reinforce the unreality, Hugh Walpole also materialised, as 'rosy and certain a piece of England' as Wells. There followed 'a droll evening of dinner and boxing, with the two Marx brothers' but unfortunately we have little record of what they said. H. G. inevitably fired off a short sharp piece of criticism. 'Hollywood is hell and even its money is fake.' According to Dorothy Richardson, Groucho Marx replied, 'So what. So why the big fuss. God's a fake, isn't he?'[22]

There was another episode in Hollywood when Arthur Hornblow, who made *Ruggles of Red Gap*, provided Jack and Jane with a wonderful Christmas in 1935 which she appreciated and 'some very good tennis' which he preferred. Hollywood at Christmas time became the fabulous fairy-tale place of legend with whole streets of elaborately illuminated trees, hospitality spilling over at every street corner and such a wealth of gifts displayed in all-night shops that even the adults became like goggle-eyed children. And there in the middle of this undoubtedly vulgar display Arthur

22  Interview with Dorothy Richardson, 10 September 1952.

Hornblow produced, as if out of the magician's hat, none other than Edmund Gwenn and Nigel Bruce fresh from London and the Garrick Club. They had 'a delightful time' enlivened at one point by a mock battle of wits between Hornblow and Priestley. The following account comes from a young technician who was present at the dinner party.[23]

'I don't quite see you as a serf,' Priestley said.

'I certainly see you as a baron,' Hornblow said. 'You've turned down three ideas in a row and here I am begging at the gates asking you to look at yet another one. So help me God, you will have me on my knees yet.'

'That'll be the day,' Priestley said.

Louis B. Mayer clashed with Priestley in a different mood. They were discussing the possibility of a film based on the First World War when Mayer said: 'You know, Jack, I can't get used to the idea that the British think they won that war.'

'Not the British,' Jack said, sending him up. 'I did, single-handed. They threw everything at me – gas, guns, hand grenades, mortar shells, even half a horse on one occasion, but I beat the lot.'

'Goddamn it, you talk like a hero. I like it. Why don't our boys learn to talk like that?'

'Don't worry,' Jack said. 'They do.'

It was deep in the overpowering magnificence of the Grand Canyon where the Colorado River had thrown up a spectacle which split the imagination as well as the earth, that a bizarre and, in a sad sense, debunking encounter occurred with George Bernard Shaw. There, a world away from sophisticate London, Priestley suddenly observed a slightly familiar figure approaching and, as it drew nearer, the plus fours and Norfolk jacket were unmistakable. How they greeted one another is not recorded but Shaw who had arrived with a world cruise party from the Pacific coast was in a very peevish mood. A mind steeped in satirising human life in all its forms was not going to be impressed by the sheer grandeur of a gigantic split in the earth's surface, capable of entombing a city. With a wry smile Shaw gestured dismissively. Then he spoke instead of the wonders of the Cheddar Gorge.

The truth was, I'm afraid, that he was determinedly resisting the spell of this marvel, at once awe-inspiring and beautiful, the most

23   Letter from Frank D. Fellowbury, December 1950.

ego-shrinking of all earth's spectacles. His mockery was partly
defensive, like the beard he grew, the boxing he learnt, the pose he
adopted of being bored with sex.[24]

When the family sallied forth *en masse* for a picnic, Priestley's
preferred mode of transport was not riding or walking but sitting in
the chuck wagon and sometimes remaining there for comfort to eat
steak and potatoes and drink coffee which seemed more delicious in
that crystalline aromatic air. Settling down in some lost canyon
almost unknown to human desecration with the scarred rocks
glittering at a million jewelled points, the blue jays singing in the
cottonwoods and the smoke of a wood fire making a slow straight
signal on the windless air, it all satisfied some deeper, primal urge in
him beyond superficial appetites. And even the thudding hoofs,
jingling spurs and whoops of the very occasional cowboy cavalcade
equally belonged to a past where peace of mind matched peace of
nature.

Jane, in all this, played many roles as wife, mother, educator,
ornithologist and chauffeur, since her husband no longer drove. It
needed her considerable powers of resolution to stop the children's
complete surrender to nature but some elements of the English
education they were missing were drummed into them. Inevitably
it led to scenes and playing truant was much easier in Arizona, but
discipline occasionally prevailed. Jane's relations with Jack
improved in the desert where all possibilities of infidelity were
removed. One pleasure was always indulged independently. She
loved to take the chuck wagon, arm herself with telescopic lenses
and packs of film to spend an afternoon alone bird-watching. There
were periods in Arizona when something approaching harmony
made them happy, and as in all relationships of long duration, some
third entity, in which both partook from years of shared experience, occasionally enabled them to merge and respond at a deep
level. It was only later in life on the verge of breaking away from
Jane that he came to understand how deeply entwined their natures
had become, despite the friction and hostility.

Towards the end of their stay in Arizona there came a visit to Santa
Barbara which, all unaware, deeply influenced his writing for years
to come. Wandering round a bookshop, he picked up a copy of
P. D. Ouspensky's *A New Model of the Universe*, turned the pages

24  *Margin Released*, J. B. Priestley, 166.

and momentarily stood browsing. Simultaneously, the sunlit panorama of palm and orange trees, snapdragons and brilliant blue skies disappeared in a cataract of rain which looked set to last an eternity. On sudden impulse 'we piled our things and ourselves into the car and went roaring and splashing towards the desert. We arrived at the Furnace Creek in Death Valley just in time for dinner that night.'[25] It was there, appropriately, in Death Valley where time, in some senses, could be said to have stopped, that Priestley read *A New Model of the Universe*. Four hundred square miles of land lying well below sea level, Death Valley had traces of the tracks of dinosaurs and areas of salt beds where the temperatures reached 134°F. 'It must be as near Hell as you can get on this earth,' Priestley wrote, 'but there in Furnace Creek, a miraculous construction of modern architecture embraced cool rooms, swimming pool and tennis courts, in the heart of a fantastic wilderness.' Already an amateur theorist about the nature of time, Priestley read Ouspensky with growing fascination. An odd mixture of scientific rationality and mystical insight, Ouspensky's work made an exciting marriage between European and Asian cultures, producing a mathematical philosopher irradiated by oriental thinking. His theories of time in the rambling pages of *A New Model of the Universe* are confusing, but Priestley managed to disentangle his own interpretation of the master's work. According to this, Ouspensky believed that time, like space, had three dimensions which developed the formal three-dimensional world into six-dimensional space-time. Three of these dimensions were extended in space but time, traditionally called the fourth dimension, was extended into a fifth and a sixth dimension as yet unknown to many. Such preliminary outlines were clear, but Ouspensky required his readers to think geometrically about time. Thus time's fifth dimension was said to be set at right angles to the fourth and ceased to suffer clock-like limitations and became eternity. The fifth dimension was not ordinary time 'extended to infinity, but timelessness, the perpetual existence of every moment along the line of the Fourth Dimension, the eternal New'. The present writer finds this more confusing than enlightening but Priestley proceeded to spell it out.

When we say the past exists it must exist along this dimension. But what then is the sixth dimension – the final dimension of what we

25 *Midnight on the Desert*, J. B. Priestley, 267–8.

call Time? Ouspensky does not give it a name but says it is the line of actualisation of other possibilities contained in any moment but not actualised in our Time.

Priestley himself admits that such a concept is difficult to assimilate 'but not incredible'. Any condensation of Ouspensky's 600-page book must do violence to its subtlety, and Priestley's was a brave attempt to achieve the impossible, but for a man who regarded music as not susceptible to explanation by the salts and electricity theory of life, Ouspensky's model of the universe was naturally sympathetic. Einsteinean space-time, Heisenberg's principle of uncertainty, Bohr's quantum mechanics are presented with a rigour and detailed evidence completely lacking in *A New Model of the Universe*, but Priestley preferred the mathematical mysticism which characterised Ouspensky. 'We might', he wrote, 'be compelled to think along a single track of Time, but intuitively and in imagination we are not so narrowly bound. We experience those "high moments of emotion" when we seem to feel the timelessness, the eternal Now of the fifth dimension, and imaginatively we may have some sense of the sixth dimension, that actualisation of other possibilities.'

Looking out on fossilised remnants of the past in the vista of Death Valley with its miles of crystallised salt twisted into fantastic pinnacles, Priestley read the pages of Ouspensky, his mind already trying to reconstruct its subtleties in situations which could dramatically explore its meaning. How could he represent the fact that if we were free 'to move as we wished along the fourth and fifth dimensions, we could experience the Past'? The phrase invokes a miraculous quality unknown to science and hard scientists scoffed at such notions, but Priestley equally scoffed at hard scientists. Next came an even more daring statement. 'If we were given the freedom of this sixth dimension we could change the Past as an artist may change his work to bring it nearer to perfection.'

Thus a noble-minded philosopher, granted Ouspenskinian powers, would 'reincarnate from the future into our age . . . to prevent the coming of the Great War'. The mind boggles at such a total contradiction of the inevitability of the historical record. Conventional theories of time say that the First World War took place between 1914 and 1918 and nothing ever changes the course it took. Ouspensky would have none of it. He believed that so-called history endlessly rewrote the same event 'over and over again'. Even more daunting complications of Ouspensky's thinking excited Priestley's close attention. Ouspensky invited his readers to distinguish between personal time and eternal time without losing the life-cycle of birth and death. According to this theory when a man died he entered his life once more from the beginning and was born again, in the same house to the same parents, with a recurrence of all the events in his life. One important qualification remained. Those who did not achieve some spiritual distinction would continue to repeat their lives unchanged. Others, an esoteric élite, who learned to evolve to higher states of consciousness, would have the power to convert the recurring circle into a spiral which opened the way of escape to – was it a form of immortality? From the rationalist point of view such thinking belonged to mystical fairy-tales and resembled old-fashioned theories of reincarnation, but Priestley found Ouspensky's book 'enormously stimulating . . . with creative excitement mounting' as he read.

A New Model of the Universe is wrapped in complex phrases which diverge at certain points from Priestley's account. However, it was a tribute to Priestley that unlike any other playwright of the day he kept abreast of such literature and if there were points where his dramatic instincts unconsciously manipulated the evidence, that from a playwright's point of view might be a virtue. It was on the freighter returning from his long sojourn in America that he began his first draft of I Have Been Here Before. The play did not pour unchecked from his typewriter in the manner he believed to be classic to good play-writing. Working intermittently between many other commitments he drafted I Have Been Here Before three times and was still polishing different scenes a year later. It suffered at the outset a defect from which it never entirely recovered. The play was not inspired by plot, character or autobiography but was an attempt to dramatise an idea and, above all, a revolutionary idea at odds with normal thinking. The first draft he put aside as unsatisfactory. Meanwhile he had been working on a major piece of autobiographical writing.

A delightful ramble set in the framework of his American experience, Midnight on the Desert, published in 1937, contained some of his most evocative descriptive writing. The thread of the narrative twists and turns upon itself to the confusion of any developing sequence and dates are conspicuous by their absence, but it is a warm, frank river of a book which carries on its surface anecdotes, satires, recollections and provocative opinions about – everything. The first of three attempts at semi-autobiography, the book obeyed no laws known to literature, but its very disorganisation gave it an immediacy which made so many chapters a pleasure to read. Enlivened throughout with animadversions on the short-comings of upstart critics and startling declarations that men and women should avoid sex until they were twenty-one – perhaps a shade hypocritical remembering his record – this was a sprawling but delightful piece of Priestley reminiscence, which the critics received warmly.

# 14

# Jung, Egypt and J. W. Dunne
## 1936–7

The whole family returned to England in the late spring of 1936 and Priestley plunged into work. Priestley's personality had by now reached that degree of complexity where, he admitted, 'Inside I am somebody quite different, never really feeling secure with myself.'[1] Regarded by some as having the hide of a rhinoceros, he could admit a fine array of warts, weaknesses and shortcomings. It was the measure of his maturity in that harsh country called 'writing' that he could embrace many of the criticisms levelled against him by a simple process of exaggeration. His son Tom believed that this was a defence against them, a technique which Shaw already practised with superb skill. Satirical hyperbole was not character-istic of Priestley but he could wittily convert attacks into entertain-ment. 'Of course I am a third-rate novelist but it's surprising the number of discerning people who like the result.'

According to Tom Priestley his routine remained unchanged from earlier writing days.

> Breakfast at about nine in his dressing-gown was followed by a spell when he prowled about writing in his head. Then he would twist cotton wool into his ears, turn his back to the view from the Manor House – put on his glasses and tap away solidly until 12.30. Lunch cooked by Miss Pudduck – lean, active and efficient – followed – and then came an afternoon walk and games. It could be tennis or ludo or ingenious games which he himself had devised for the children. He was a great walker and I remember as we grew older enjoying many a break for ale mulled with a red-hot poker.

A man who later became a formidable trencherman, Priestley drank in those days a dry Martini before lunch, wine with dinner and a whisky night-cap. Interestingly, Tom Priestley made no reference to family 'atmosphere' or tensions, perhaps out of tact.

1  *Instead of the Trees*, J. B. Priestley, 86–7.

There were now so many Priestleys. The perfect host who received his guests diffidently with a formal handshake and a hint of a bow: the man described by Robert Lynd as 'wonderful company who could pull a quotation out of the air as easily as other men breathe': the seasoned trencherman who given a number of Dog's Noses (a favourite drink) could sit down at the piano and vamp out half a dozen familiar tunes: the concerned family man who made over a large part of the vast income from *The Good Companions* to a trust for the education of his children. All of which did not approach another different person who brooded so heavily on deeper matters that he sometimes fell into profound depression. He claimed now that his hobby was a search for wisdom. 'I look for it as other men look for rare birds.'[2]

Jane complained about his grumbling; Richardson said, 'I love him dearly but watch your neck – he can be rude,' and Michael Denison told the story of one of his guests who came up to Priestley and said, 'I've been told to entertain you,' whereupon Priestley replied, 'All right – try.'[3]

It was this Priestley who in 1936 began reading the works of Jung and attempted to disentangle from the immense forest of his thought some of the major characteristics of his model of the psyche. Any recapitulation of Jung's thought is a hazardous undertaking because no one Jungian theoretician gives the same reading of the Old Testament as another. Immense controversies are generated and it is a brave man who ventures into the battle. As Priestley came to understand Jung, the psyche operated through the four functions of thinking, feeling, sensation and intuition. 'Thus,' Jung wrote, 'thinking is the function which seeks to apprehend the world and adjust to it by way of thought or cognition, i.e. logical inference.' Feeling responded to the world through evaluation of pleasant or unpleasant reactions to experience. Sensation and intuition fell into irrational or non-rational categories since sensation reacted directly to experience without evaluation and intuition invoked the inherent potentiality of what was very loosely referred to as 'things'.

Priestley found some of Jung's writings 'hard going' but once his interest was fully aroused he pressed on to master the basic elements. One of the four functions in Jung's model usually predominated and created the particular 'quality' of a given per-

2  *Rain upon Godshill*, J. B. Priestley, 9.
3  *Double Act*, Michael Denison, 30–3.

sonality. In the neurotic either the expression of the 'natural dominant' function had been blocked or the constitutional position of the second or third function artificially elevated. Thus a person might have achieved success in life by exploiting one function and neglecting the remaining three but the neglected function had to be readjusted to reintegrate harmony and produce a fully adjusted person. There were, Priestley discovered, two personality types, extravert and introvert, which had biological bases and were more clearly determined from birth than the function types. The desired goal of the harmonious person not only related the biological typology to the four functions, but the conscious to the unconscious, in such a way as to achieve individuation or, in demystified language, a fully integrated self. Priestley learnt that the unconscious and its powers were at the very heart of Jung's model and unlike Freud he divided that mysterious no man's land into the personal and the collective.

Priestley became steadily more absorbed over the years in the implications of Jung's model and as a creative writer turned to Jung's unconscious to explain those inexplicable processes which suddenly produced creative ideas without the intervention of logical thought. Any exhaustive analysis of the mystery of creativity would be out of place here but despite the relaxed terminology sometimes used by Jung to explain the psychic complexities which may be beyond the reach of verbal exploration, a brief attempt to disentangle the personal from the collective unconscious is necessary.

As Priestley came to understand it, Jung saw the personal unconscious as the repository of all those aspects of life experience of which the conscious psyche was unaware, but he did not emphasise the Freudian repressive mechanism which held in check their conscious realisation. Within his personal unconscious Jung found all varieties of what he named 'complexes', from lesser neurotic conflicts to fully fledged dual personalities. Conversely the collective unconscious was the 'deposit of mankind's typical reactions since primordial times to universal situations such as fear, danger, the struggle against superior power . . . love, birth or death'. The conscious and the unconscious were interrelated and the dynamic powers of the collective unconscious must be harnessed to constructive purposes.

Above all, from Priestley's point of view, each sex had its counterpart in the other, a man internalising the 'image' of woman (the anima) and the woman that of man (the animus). The anima was an 'hereditary factor of primordial origin' which 'engraved in the living organic system of the man . . . an imprint or "archetype" of all the impressions ever made by women'. Priestley felt that his anima was very active.

Detailed evidence of his growing commitment to Jung is scarce and exact dating difficult but from 1936 to 1937 he occasionally applied the anima theory to his own personal relationships and came to the conclusion that it gave a satisfactory explanation which unfortunately he never spelt out. Not until he came to write *Dragon's Mouth* in collaboration with Jacquetta Hawkes did he make full use of his Jungian reading.

In March 1936 he was offered the presidency of the PEN, in those days a prestigious appointment, and wrote to Herman Ould, the secretary:

My dear Ould,

Thanks for your letter of February 18th. You do not say when the term of office would begin and end, which makes it rather more difficult for me to decide. My chief difficulty is that my wife, who was ordered to spend this winter in a desert climate, may possibly be told to have part of next winter out of England too, although she is much better than she was. That might mean that I would be away from January to March next year. If you are willing to risk that, I am willing to let my name stand as a candidate.

As you probably know, I am very keen on the P.E.N. as a force in international goodwill and as a guard against intolerance aimed at writers. It is this side of its work that attracts me. I am not a great admirer of its dinners, as you also know. But if I did take on the job, I should suggest a really big drive to attract to the P.E.N. a large number of English writers of some distinction who do not belong to it now. Many of these, I suspect, were alienated partly by the dinners and partly by the personality of the late Mrs Dawson Scott, excellent woman though she was, and I think many of them do not realise how valuable the Association could be in times like these. So that I suggest that if I am elected London President, Wells and you and I get together and send out in our joint names various personal letters of appeal to these writers, putting the present situation to them. Perhaps you already have a list of such writers. If not, you might like to make one. I should also like to see the Association getting out a report, combined from reports from its correspondents in various countries, showing exactly what freedom of expression writers have throughout the world, and so on. This would be work of extreme importance. My own political sympathies are Left wing, but I am, like you – I imagine, anxious that the P.E.N. should not be used by communists, who are themselves opposed to freedom of expression simply to oppose the repressive measures of Fascism.

Yours ever,

J. B. PRIESTLEY

Priestley's relationship with Ould during his brief presidency of the PEN varied from the sunny to the stormy. He seems to have stormed out of the 1937 International PEN in Paris leaving a number of official functions unattended by its president, but the threat of the French using PEN as a political pawn was too much for him. He did recruit a number of new and distinguished members, he persuaded the executive to set in motion a survey of writers' freedom and embroiled H. G. Wells in a number of activities.

Herman Ould told the present author that Priestley could be relied upon in certain delicate circumstances to be undiplomatic and yet his jokiness when others were depressed, his enthusiasm for extravagant projects and frankness with foreign visitors made him a valuable asset. Throughout his life 'he always ended up bursting out of any committee he joined and he certainly wasn't made for committees. But I had an affection for him. Underneath he was a lovable man.'

Priestley survived for some eighteen months as president of the PEN and then he wrote another letter to Ould announcing his resignation.

Dear Ould,

Please accept my resignation from both the Presidency and the Executive Committee of the London P.E.N. I have done what I could to help during these last twelve months: the Wells dinner, which was my idea, was an unqualified success; and my letters later did bring in a few more good members. I doubt if I could do any more now, especially as I shall be out of England so long this autumn and winter, and by appointing another President, you should derive new benefits from his name and activities, whoever he may be. Some of your members (perhaps all of you) appear to feel aggrieved because I did not attend the later functions in Paris, though I hope there are not many of them like the woman last night who asked the impertinent question. The thing is not worth discussing in public, but I will take this opportunity of putting my own side. In the first place, I had not the least desire to go as a delegate and told you that from the first. You said I would be invited as a guest of honour (I think I was entitled to that courtesy, unless there was some technical reason against it), and when I wasn't, you begged me to go as a delegate, and I gathered that nobody else wanted to be the second delegate. The whole arrangements seemed to me a dreadful muddle. I have no doubt that the French group was worried, but I could not help feeling right from the first that Romains and his colleagues were – to put it mildly – off-hand. The conference in general seemed to have little interest in the motion I put before it. I was not impressed by the floods of oratory of people like Pierard. I was told several times that the official functions in the second half of the conference would probably not take place, so being exceptionally busy arranging the production of a new play, I returned home on Thursday. My wife and I came up specially from the Isle of Wight in January to entertain the visiting members of the Executive Committee to dinner. (We had to give it in a restaurant because our servants were in the island and, anyhow, our small dining-room here would not have held so many guests.) But nobody in Paris went a yard out of his way to make me feel at home there or extended any special courtesy to my wife. I wouldn't mention these things, except to point out that I too have a case. But of course this is confidential, though you are welcome to say a word or two about it to the committee.

What is more important, however, than these trifling personal feelings is the fact that what I saw in Paris (possibly coloured somewhat by those feelings) did not leave me very hopeful of the future of the P.E.N. if it is to be run – as I fear it may be – by Romains and his friends. Sooner or later it will be used as a minor pawn in the political game by the French. And as I felt that the conference regarded me as a not very interesting newcomer, I did not feel confident that I could, by making a fight of it in the near future, check this bad tendency. In short, I do not feel I can be of any more real use, so it would be in the best interests of the P.E.N. to resign and make way for somebody else.

Yours sincerely,
J. B. PRIESTLEY[4]

As he prepared to set out on yet another of his innumerable travels Priestley admitted to being 'a nervous and apprehensive' traveller. This did not mean that he was fearful of the journey itself. He always insisted on arriving early because he not only dreaded a last-minute rush but was apprehensive about missing the train.[5] If

4  Priestley to Herman Ould, 7 July 1937.
5  *Instead of the Trees*, J. B. Priestley, 124.

these fears could be traced to deep psychological roots there were far more compelling practical reasons why he became so obsessionally over-punctual when travelling. He had on one occasion missed the Barcelona–Paris express and condemned himself to 'catching local trains all over France, paying more and more first for frustration and then for increasing boredom'.[6]

Jane's delicate health made it necessary early in January 1937 to escape the worst of the English winter once more and they booked a passage for Egypt on a ship which they quickly came to dislike. The bad weather pursued them, a sunless voyage exacerbated colds and they were confined for long hours to an uncomfortable cabin reading second-rate books. Priestley later commented to Ralph Richardson: 'Tell Jonathan that anyone who has been married for ten years should never take a holiday with his wife, and certainly not on a ship with a double cabin.'[7] They had set out, it seemed, on the rising tide of another reconciliation which threatened to collapse in the first few days.

Determined to do no work for the next two months, Priestley found himself restless and hypercritical, which explained in part the sour account he gave of this first attempt for some years to take a prolonged holiday. Winter relentlessly followed the ship to Algiers and Genoa and the remnants of a chilly wind reduced the temperature even in Cairo. A succinct phrase in *Rain upon Godshill* caught the atmosphere of that city. 'At first sight Cairo was a French provincial city in which a Near Eastern carnival had been let loose.'[8]

Initially, the glare of the narrow streets repelled them but when they retreated into the mosques and museums their mood changed. The glittering vulgarities from Tutankhamun's tomb surrounded by mobs of tourists held them only briefly, and they turned away to the subtler attractions of Ikhnaton's reign with Priestley ordering a copy of Nefertiti, 'one of the loveliest faces I have ever seen'. Steeped in Breasted's history of Egypt they set out on a long trip by car, donkey, camel and boat to see everything from pyramids and tombs to the last elaborate temples in the far south. Priestley had developed a considerable preoccupation with money and now he complained that the 'expense seemed . . . fabulous. I have never before paid out so much and here and now I announce that never again shall it happen.'

6 ibid.
7 Priestley to Ralph Richardson, 10 August 1979; 'Jonathan' has not been identified.
8 *Rain upon Godshill*, J. B. Priestley, 11.

Priestley saw the average Egyptian hotel proprietor or bazaar salesman as a professional extortionist inheriting his skills from thousands of years' practice until 'their outstretched palms are between you and all you . . . wish to enjoy'.

Neither the lure of ancient Egypt nor the mysteries of the Sphinx drew him into communion with the past, and the present was constantly overwhelmed by the sheer expensive worry of being a tourist there. Staring at the pyramids he tried in vain to induce those powerfully mystical responses experienced by Ouspensky and remained unmoved, even when a ghostly presence materialised one night out of the dusk, murmured abracadabra in his ears and slipped away into nothingness without explanation. Americanised-English elements forced him to admit that he was unreceptive to oriental mysticism, but had an immediate response to the majesty of the Grand Canyon. Even the story of the young Amenophis the Fourth, Pharoah of Egypt, changing his name to Ikhnaton to revolutionise religion, art and social values, he mediated through a modern vision which compared him with 'one of the nicer products of Balliol and Bloomsbury, a sort of youthful Aldous Huxley . . . shot back four thousand years'.

If his reaction to Egyptian mythology remained firmly rational-istic and he refused to be taken in by talk of 'mysteries', he found Egyptian history 'staggering'. One moment the Egyptians were neolithic creatures squatting among their flints and the next they produced the greatest sculpture and drawings, carved the Sphinx and built the pyramids.[9] His final summing-up qualified his early scepticism.

A beautiful piece of descriptive prose in *Rain upon Godshill* (1939) captured his mood:

> Luxor works miracles; there at last is the silver Nile, the old enchantress: the valley of the Kings, beyond the river, is a landscape conjured out of pearl and gossamer: and the avenue of the sphinxes at Karnak runs clean out of this world. It is late at night when the last dragoman or pedlar has vanished, when Cook's office is shuttered . . . and the dynasties are all one and the moon begins to throw her pale bridge across the millenniums, it is then that Egypt becomes again the magical old Kingdom of our boyhood fancy worthy at last, during this brief hour, of Rider Haggard.[10]

9   ibid., 16–17.
10  ibid., 21.

One episode had remarkable repercussions when they returned to England. Jane surrendered herself one day to an Egyptian fortune-teller, and among the usual tide of nonsense, one prediction stood out starkly. Someone very dear to Jane would shortly be in great danger and she would have to hurry half across Europe to succour her . . . They both shrugged their shoulders but Jane referred twice to the prediction the following day, and Priestley said, 'For God's sake don't take that stuff seriously.'[11]

The two months in Egypt slipped away and at last as they moved northward to return home the intense heat subsided and Priestley's personal temperature rose. A man intolerant of the normal inconveniences of travel, he found that the elaborate hassle surrounding every attempt to move from one part of Egypt to another drove him into furies. These explosions must have increased the tensions with Jane, but there is no record of their reactions. They made the last stage of the journey in an overcrowded 'suffocating train which chugged its way from one unadvertised stop to another' until they arrived in Port Said with Priestley feeling 'like a homicidal bankrupt'. It was an interesting combination of images – murder and money – and certainly throughout this holiday it was frequently the expense which drove him into the attack. Aroused – unnecessarily – before the dawn to board the home-going boat, Priestley 'stamped and stormed about until a large British breakfast was set before him'. It was these outbursts which made Jane sometimes wish that she had married a man like John Galsworthy who consistently played the role of the dignified author.[12] Two days later, back on board a British ship Priestley became an ordinary sensible man again.[13]

11  Interview with Barbara Wykeham, 16 September 1985.
12  Interview with Rachel Goaman, 10 April 1986.
13  *Rain upon Godshill*, J. B. Priestley, 29.

# 15

# The Time Plays
## 1937–8

He returned to an England where the conservatives had recently overwhelmed the socialists in the elections, a result which inspired Priestley to comment 'When will they learn?' Ramsay MacDonald soared into the empyrean with his famous speech, part of which Priestley memorised and sometimes reproduced for the entertainment of his family: 'Society goes on and on. It is the same with ideas. Society must keep in touch not only with progressive but also with retrograding movements in our advance!' Any confusion in these statements was redeemed – as the applause indicated – by the golden voice in which MacDonald delivered them.

Within a few days Priestley travelled to Liverpool Playhouse where yet another of his lesser plays – how often they were written and quickly forgotten – *The Bad Samaritan* was in rehearsal. Disastrously he had followed the textbook play-writing theory and first prepared a detailed synopsis, clothing each scene in dialogue separately. What might have suited more ordered writers was anathema to Priestley and he claimed that his imagination completely failed to get to grips with characters who lived in the straitjacket of their preconception. Ironically, this play which most dissatisfied him and never came to London was the only play which ever stirred an outside financier to offer to back its London production. A firm of solicitors connected with the theatre wrote one day saying that a well-to-do woman client was anxious to put up several thousand pounds without conditions for a West End production. More amused than flattered Priestley replied that he could not accept because the play simply did not meet his required standards.

Now followed a dramatic realisation of the Egyptian fortune-teller's prediction which came uncannily close to the truth. Priestley's daughter Angela had gone to Florence on a cheap student trip. She was taken ill with what at first seemed a minor complaint, but rapidly developed serious symptoms. Jane hurried out to Italy as predicted, and found Angela with a temperature of 103–4 which remained obstinately at that level for days. Urgent messages sent

Priestley hurrying to Harley Street to collect 'serums' which were not available in Italy before setting off for Florence. 'It was a journey like a bad dream,' he wrote, 'when your very eyelids are stiff with anxiety and every mile and every minute seem agonisingly elongated.'[1]

In the event all his efforts were unnecessary. Angela had suffered a simple attack of measles, the natural recuperative powers of a fifteen-year-old overwhelmed the infection and by the time he arrived she was beginning to recover. They moved her from the hospital and all three settled into a convalescent home in Fiesole, run – a surprising choice for Priestley – by nuns. Suddenly, Priestley himself managed to 'work up' a little illness of his own. No sooner was he forced to take to his bed than – compulsively – he began writing. Smoking heavily, coughing, exchanging badinage with the elderly sister, he re-read the draft of *I Have Been Here Before* and began to rewrite the first act. He recovered as quickly as he had fallen ill and very soon 'one by one we crept out into the garden to look down upon the Arno and the shining city of Florence'.

Walking the 'enchanted streets' the happy trio relaxed in the sunshine and there occurred one of those interludes when family stress disappeared in the sheer exuberance of the occasion. Thrown into deep reflection about the marvellous efflorescence of art which made Florence the flower of Renaissance culture, he resorted to Jung's collective unconscious.

Returning to London they found that two good friends had died and the streets of London suddenly seemed 'narrower and chillier'. Lamb's famous passage about the shrinking of individual lives from succeeding deaths came back to him and he reflected that already in early middle age he knew intimately more dead than living people. A brief melancholic spell was quickly invaded by the meteoric appearance of a brilliant New York producer, Jed Harris, whose successful productions had made his name in New York. Arriving unheralded one morning at No. 3 The Grove, Highgate, he simply announced that he had heard on the bush telegraph of a new play which Mr Priestley had just completed. A caricature of the bustling New York theatrical entrepreneur, his talk was torrential and his response to the play, which he read immediately, totally contradictory.[2] It was 'the best and the worst play ever written' and he could see its splendid virtues shot through with flaws. Instant criticism

---

1  *Rain upon Godshill*, J. B. Priestley,
2  The play was *I Have Been Here Before*.

was followed by instant advice and there followed a bombardment of suggested cuts and improvements which, according to the account later given to James Agate, ran on for two hours and left Priestley for once in his life 'totally bemused'.[3] It was high tribute to the now legendary Jed Harris that the rugged resistance which too much advice always generated in Priestley did not occur and he found himself adopting several major revisions. Multiple rewritings had left him so deeply enmeshed in detail that he could not stand back and evaluate the play afresh. He also regarded Harris as a ruthless editor of plays with a 'touch of real theatrical genius' who would have no truck with Priestley's attempt to modify Harris's suggestions.

The final version of the play owed much to Harris and Priestley had every expectation that he would produce it in New York. A series of bizarre events followed which Priestley's familiarity with the New York theatrical scene should have anticipated. Harris returned to America and letters flowed between them with Harris sustaining his excitement and Priestley explaining how he proposed producing the play in England. A last letter came saying that Harris was sailing shortly for England to make final American arrangements. A cable from the *Berengaria* followed. He would be arriving in two days. Priestley deliberately spent as much time as possible at Highgate fully expecting a repetition of Harris's meteoric arrival. Several days passed and there was no sign of Harris, but friends informed Priestley that he was in fact in London. Priestley set moving a whole network of agents to trace him, with A. D. Peters, his own secretary and even Harris's secretary pressed into service. It was of no avail. Then came the news that Harris had returned to the United States without bothering even to telephone Priestley. Knowing the highly developed capacity of New York producers for blowing hot and cold and the adolescent excitement they could generate for plays, Priestley's mystification was surprising.

> Why he suddenly changed his mind after coming three thousand miles, and why he did not grant me the elementary courtesy of hearing from him that he had altered his plans, and why after behaving so discourteously and mysteriously, he should imagine he had been badly treated, these are things I shall never know.[4]

In the end Priestley regarded him without rancour but saw him as

3  Priestley to James Agate, July 1937.
4  *Rain upon Godshill*, J. B. Priestley, 37.

the 'Great Broadway Enigma – the whole sign picked out in flashing lights'.[5]

London had recently witnessed the pageantry of royal carriages proceeding down the Mall which celebrated the coronation of a new king of England. Priestley's views on royalty varied over the years. At one time he wrote against it on the ground that it underpinned the worst kind of English snobbery and reaffirmed a class-ridden society. However, he rejected the view that the coronation was part of a campaign launched to distract people from the limitations of their lives, and understood the point of view of those who saw royal personages as symbols of the unity of empire 'riding about like fairy-tale characters in glass coaches'.

A few weeks later he was full of disillusion. On the night preceding the coronation, watching thousands of young people milling around, he asked himself what did they have that was worthwhile in such a dismal and depressing world? They had lost the natural world of woods and fields but had failed to achieve a civilised way of urban life. Their dwindling belief in religion was not yet matched by any assimilation of music, drama and art. This seemed a gloomy enough view of the potential of ordinary people but now came a more devastating criticism. 'Most probably they did not know how to make love or even to eat and drink properly. They were not even the old happy-go-lucky mob living with a certain fine carelessness in picturesque squalor.'

As if aware of overplaying his hand Priestley concluded: 'The game has been heavily rigged against them, but they hunger for beauty and joy.' In the event, his gift for cryptically summing up celebratory occasions came through vividly. 'The whole English-speaking race began cheering together. Off they went – flags, banners, beacons, bands, processions – Long Live the King and God Bless Him!'[6]

Interested, momentarily, in royal pageantry, he asked the question – where would the money, energy and *nobility* come to build a happier, more beautiful Britain for ordinary people? The creative writer eventually converted into the political man of action, but fine words did nothing to expunge his melancholy. Turning to the once infallible palliative – work – he struggled to finish at last the play *I Have Been Here Before,* and simultaneously wrote a quick piece for amateurs. Neither relieved his gloom.

---

5   ibid.
6   *Rain upon Godshill,* J. B. Priestley, 40.

His lifelong correspondence with Edward Davison continued. In July 1937 he was busy setting up a new lecture tour in America and wrote to Davison saying that he had just cabled Stephenson of the Emerson Lecture Bureau authorising him to accept any engagements of which Davison approved.[7] Priestley's lecturing divided between popular clubs and culture organisations with a scattering of what the Americans regarded as second-rank universities like Iowa and Utah, and it constantly irked Priestley that Harvard and Yale showed no interest. Another letter to Davison said that as yet he had only a tentative schedule with two dates in the east (New York and Pittsburg) and the remainder between Ohio, Iowa and Nebraska. The lectures were due to begin on 1 November and finish on 22 November. He would like to go straight to the ranch after his last lecture because he would not have seen Jane and the family for some time. They were due to leave England on 10 September on the *Pacific Reliance*.[8]

As if to demonstrate his reckless fertility, August 1937 saw the production of *Time and the Conways* at the Duchess Theatre, and one month later came *I Have Been Here Before* at the Royalty. Priestley was by now steeped in time theory, both that of Ouspensky and, as described below, that of Dunne. His dialogue at the Royalty re-echoed what could be heard at the Duchess. Ralph Richardson remarked: 'Audaciously exploring such heady stuff as time is bad enough, but to repeat the offence twice in the same year invited the gallows. Instead of getting hung he has received a reprieve, and damn me if some people didn't praise him for writing the plays. Bully for them.'[9]

It was the initial conception of *Time and the Conways* which generated sufficient creative excitement to lift Priestley at last out of his bout of gloom. His half-sister Winnie, who rarely appears in his writings, was lunching with the family at Highgate one day when she recalled among old acquaintances one special family.

Suddenly Priestley realised that the life of a typical middle-class provincial family could be interlocked with Ouspensky's theory of time and produce some highly dramatic moments. This was not a routine idea justifying a brief account in his notebook: 'It excited me at once, and I had to begin sketching out the general action of the play.'

7   Priestley to Edward Davison, 31 July 1937.
8   Priestley to Edward Davison, 29 June 1937.
9   Interview with Ralph Richardson, September 1963.

He hurried away to Billingham in the Isle of Wight and quickly roughed out a cast of characters, distilling the personality of each in his mind but putting nothing on paper. Deliberately plotting place and people had proved unfortunate with *The Bad Samaritan* and now it was to be spontaneity or nothing. It quickly became apparent that he needed some period background for the first and third acts which were set in 1919, but he could not wait to carry out the necessary research in London and plunged boldly into the contemporary second act.

> With almost no preparation, without any of the usual brooding and note-taking, I wrote this Act Two of *Time and the Conways* at full speed. It seemed to cost me no more thought or trouble than if I were dashing off a letter to an old friend. Page after page, scene after scene, went off effortlessly with hardly a correction on my typescript.

Moreover, this torrential outpouring did not keep him working far into the night with 'wet towels on his head'. Instead he followed 'a bank clerk's hours and almost behaved like one; and yet within two days I had finished this long and complicated act'. The final flourish of professional creativity was the minimal correction needed – 'only two or three line alterations'. Later, he wrote that the second act of *Time and the Conways* 'has been said to be one of the most brilliant second acts of our time'.[10] Searching for an explanation of instant inspiration he settled once more for a somewhat simplistic version of the unconscious. The technical problems were dangerous enough to involve walking a tightrope, but he had simply run along it unconsciously. Brooding over the characters and their situations he had saturated his unconscious with symbolic representations which effortlessly 'shot up' solutions to his problems 'as fast as they were needed'. Finding this explanation not altogether satisfactory he fell back on that 'old fairy godmother Inspiration'. Still dissatisfied, he next pressed into service a semi-Jungian interpretation which enabled him to tap a buried reservoir of creative energy deriving its force in turn from 'a much greater mind'. Closely resembling Jung's collective unconscious, this mind could invade if not take over the individual mind and the result of such a temporary union was 'the sudden arrival of what seem to us "wonderful ideas"'. Coleridge had struggled without much success to disentangle the difference between Fancy and Imagination,

---

10  *Rain upon Godshill*, J. B. Priestley, 43.

and now Priestley converted the same problem into psychological terms without advancing our understanding beyond its more elaborate restatement.

We have already seen the derivation of *I Have Been Here Before* from Ouspensky rather than Dunne and it was characteristic of Priestley that his dramatised version cleverly domesticates the high-flown nature of Ouspensky's philosophy in the totally mundane atmosphere of an inn. The Black Bull is a moorland farmhouse inn of notable mediocrity and the play opens in the sitting-room. Sam Shipley, the landlord of the inn, is an elderly Yorkshireman whose daughter, Sally Pratt, lost her husband in the First World War, and came to settle at the Black Bull with her parents. Their contented way of life is about to be disturbed by the arrival of four guests. Dominating the opening scene is the German professor of mathematics, Dr Görtler, whose unexpected arrival enquiring about other guests creates at once a mysterious tension. When he tries to book a room, he is informed that they have only four bedrooms, one of which is already taken and the others booked for three ladies. Taken aback at this information, Dr Görtler says: 'Two of them perhaps are married people – the man older than his wife – he might be rich – and then perhaps – a younger man?'[11] Sally insists that they are three lady teachers from Manchester. Görtler wonders whether he has come to the right inn and is redirected to a farmhouse nearby. Before he goes he says, 'This must be the wrong year,' and the landlord says sharply, 'Don't you know what *year* your friends are coming?' No sooner has Dr Görtler left than one of the three ladies from Manchester telephones to say that her friend has been taken ill and all three must cancel their reservation. Oliver Farrant, the young public school headmaster already staying at the inn, comes strolling back tired from a long walk and within a few minutes the unexpected arrival of a businessman, Walter Ormund, and his young wife Janet is heralded by yet another telephone call. Dr Görtler's excursion to the farmhouse is fruitless and he returns to find that the pattern of guests he anticipated has been realised. Breaking momentarily into German – Priestley's method of authenticating his origins – he says, '*So! So! Ich bin glücklich,*' with a touch of triumphant wonder.

Sam:        What language is that, sir? German?
Dr Görtler:  Yes. It means – I am fortunate.

11   *I Have Been Here Before*, J. B. Priestley.

They exit as Sam shows Görtler his room and the stage is empty while the light begins to fade, preparing the way for a moment charged with significance. Returning, Dr Görtler asks Sam, 'You have been happy here?'

Sam:        Yes, I can't grumble at all. I've never made much out o' this place, but I've had all I want. I'd ask for naught better – if I had my time over again.

Dr Görtler: Do you often say that?

Sam:        Say what?

Dr Görtler (slowly): If you had your time over again.[12]

When Farrant first meets Dr Görtler they are mutually puzzled by a sense of recognition and Janet Ormund immediately feels a familiarity in her surroundings which is totally unexpected. Listening to Görtler she is overtaken with an uncanny awareness that he has said 'all this' before, and even Farrant cannot escape echoes from the past when he originally met the Ormunds. The first act successfully achieves a sinister atmosphere reinforced by an old theatrical trick which Priestley used with new effect. Hitchcock could build up an increasing tension with the use of a clock ticking and steadily increasing in power, but Priestley was more subtle. Although the clock is destined to fulfil an important role throughout the play – indeed it becomes another character – its presence is not immediately emphasised. Only when Dr Görtler appears does its chiming coincide with his entrance. The stage direction for Janet's entrance says: 'The clock chimes *at* her.' A self-evident symbol of time, the clock is rich in undertones, hinting that time is running out, and belonging to a world of ticking mystery. The first act establishes a hidden relationship between Ormund burdened with business cares, Sally trying to cope with her husband's death, and Farrant the uneasy victim of troubles as yet unexplained.

The two dominant characters, the professor and Ormund, represent the opposing themes of fate and man struggling to force their will on an unwilling universe. The play dramatically reinterprets Ouspensky's theory with considerable artistic licence. The professor's attempted interference with fate will involve Ormund, his wife and her lover, Farrant and Sam. Granted prescience, the professor knows that Ormund is implacably set on the road to

12  ibid.

suicide and his wife to infidelity. Already familiar with the disastrous consequences of Mrs Ormund's adultery, Görtler desires to enter the predestined circle – which according to Ouspensky has to be repeated innumerable times – and redirect events to a more satisfying conclusion. Ormund's personal choice will be made because he cares about human beings but Görtler is a detached figure more concerned to prove his theory than save anyone from destruction.

Originally, Priestley, in his first draft, had conceived Görtler as almost a visitor from another planet but in the final stage version he has become a mystic whose only love is the love of knowledge, partially redeemed by faith and hope. Farrant and Ormund's wife Janet find themselves inexplicably in love and as they are about to elope, Dr Görtler intervenes.

> Görtler: In this notebook are some records of very unusual states of mind and feats of memory. Some of them came to me like clear dreams . . . In this memory – this dream, if you prefer it – I found myself a year or two older . . . but situated as I am now, an exile living in London . . . The rooms above mine . . . were occupied by two people, a man and his wife, still quite young, but very shabby, very poor and very unhappy . . . She had been the wife of a rich man, older than herself . . . But they had gone on a little holiday together . . . to a small inn . . . there she had instantly fallen in love with a younger man – the one now her husband – and they had run away.
>
> *He pauses again. Janet draws a sharp breath again and looks at Farrant. He shakes his head impatiently.*
>
> Görtler: Then there came out of this, as they now realised, the ruin of many innocent lives.

Farrant and Janet are incredulous but Görtler produces such irrefutable evidence that he is clearly talking about a future part of their own lives. When Janet protests that this is ridiculous and they can shape their own lives as they will, Görtler retaliates: 'Once [you] know, yes,' but knowledge alone gives them such freedom. The unfolding pattern of life could be deeply influenced – if not created – by imagination and will, but something akin to foreknowledge was necessary first. Make the effort at the right moment in the right circumstances and the predetermined circle might be broken. Janet bluntly puts her question in a monosyllable: 'How?' Ormund is meant to be an Everyman figure in the play and Görtler now addresses him:

> Something new may happen. You may have brought your wife here for this holiday over and over again. She may have met Farrant here over and over again. But you and I have not talked here before. That is new. This may be one of the great moments of our lives.

Indeed it is, because Görtler's intervention stops Ormund from shooting himself, checks Janet as she is about to leave her husband and makes Farrant hesitate before foolishly committing himself to a sudden fever of love.

Some of the dialogue in the play dates. However, on re-reading *I Have Been Here Before*, it does not lose its grip even if the very last scene is full of dubious peasant philosophy expressed in dialogue embarrassing to the modern ear.

In the final analysis the play can be seen as a novel examination of the age-old free will problem, but the logical Western mind boggles at the idea of the same couple taking the same holiday at the same inn in perpetuity. Pressed into dramatic service, the theory – clumsily propounded by Dr Görtler – diminishes the complexity of human life and emotions so sensitively created by the remainder of the dialogue. Priestley struggled long and painfully to fuse intellectual theory with human experience and if in the end he failed, the play remained satisfying to some surprising people. Beatrice Webb wrote in her diary:

> went to Priestley's play *I Have Been Here Before* based on Dunne's hypothesis that you can, if you have the gift, see forward as well as backward in time and (this seems self-contradictory) by knowledge alter the happening. The metaphysics of the play as expounded by the German philosopher were absurd but he and four other characters were cleverly conceived and admirably acted . . . altogether the play excited never bored us.[13]

When Priestley came to write the preface for the printed version of the play he found its primary theme represented in Ormund. He was 'a kind of Everyman of my own generation who passed through the deep distrust of life felt by so many moderns' and discovered a universe 'not hostile or indifferent to his deepest needs'.

13  *Diaries*, Vol. 4, Beatrice Webb; entry for 27 October 1937.

James Agate wrote an entertaining but highly sceptical review of the play:

> Our author likes to play at the Game of Recurrence and Intervention because it gives people a second chance and in the theatre, people who are given second chances invariably lead better lives. But hold on a bit. The Game is only half of Mr Priestley's theme. The other half is pattern. All the people in the new play are as closely inter-related as the threads in a piece of cloth: you cannot alter one without a corresponding change in the lives of others. Now let us see where this leads. I am a naughty little boy. My schoolmaster is a brutal fellow who likes using the rod. It makes me grow up into a good man and I die a millionaire at the age of ninety. This happens thousands of times. Then one fine day my schoolmaster stops being a sadist, conceives a positive distaste for the rod and so spoils me that I take to drink and die in the workhouse. And that, dear Mr Priestley, or dear Mr Ouspensky, just won't do.[14]

Obsessionally preoccupied with the interlocking theories of time, from *Dangerous Corner* onwards, Priestley never sought the reassurance offered by Freud's repetition compulsion, and the analyst's ability to change the past in analytic recollection. Fast on the heels of *I Have Been Here Before* came *Time and the Conways*, the second play deriving from J. W. Dunne, not Ouspensky. Indeed Dunne himself was invited to see *Time and the Conways* and gave the cast what he intended to be a preliminary talk. This expanded into a sparkling fifty-minute lecture, with Dunne drawing incomprehensible diagrams on the blackboard and delivering a running commentary about Minowski, Einstein and the Miller effect. No scene in the play quite matched this absurdly significant picture with the deepest implications of the 'earnest original thinker' bewildering the painted players still in their costumes and make-up ready to go on and give the performance of their lives.

Far back in 1927 Priestley had reviewed *An Experiment with Time*, which first aroused his interest in the subject, and *The Serial Universe*, published in 1934, inspired *Time and the Conways*. Dabbling in intellectual matters was one of Priestley's hobbies but he could never be described as a rigorous intellectual. Speculation about serial observers came naturally to him and sometimes a sleepless night was made less painful by reflecting on the self *experiencing* a dream, the self *in* the dream and the waking self

14 *Sunday Times*, James Agate, September 1937.

*recalling* the dream. Time, similarly, had multiple dimensions and Dunne's book *The Serial Universe* illuminated the whole subject in a new and to him exciting manner. It was characteristic of Priestley that reading a semi-philosophical text he could not exclude personal interpretations. Dunne believed that each person was really a series of observers moving through a series of Times, in which Observer One, the fully awake self, existed in a three-dimensional world with the fourth dimension represented by ordinary linear Time.

'To Observer Two, which is the self we know in dreams, when Observer One no longer functions', Time would appear as a fifth dimension. 'This second observer has a four-dimensional outlook' which explains 'the fantastic scenery and action characteristic of dreams in which everything seems to be so fluid, incidents have no proper beginning or ending'.

Dunne kept a careful record of his dreams over a number of years and came to the conclusion that they were in touch with the future as well as the past. They could in fact predict. Both Dunne and Priestley ignored the classic criticism of such dream interpretation which said that for every serial explanation of futuristic dreams there was a straightforward rational explanation which had nothing to do with predicting the future. Priestley was not unaware of alternative explanations, but 'Dunne's theory had always seemed to [him] not only the most fascinating but also the most satisfying'. There was another reason why Dunne had a special appeal. Priestley had discussed problems of death with H. G. Wells on one occasion, and Wells who scoffed at immortality declared that man was immortal not as an individual but in the life of the race. Correct, Priestley said, if the individual preferred to live in the relative poverty of Time One, which marked the dates on the calendar. Dunne offered a new and arresting form of immortality which even if it required such logical contortions that complete conviction faltered, still seemed very plausible to Priestley. He wrote: 'As a series of observers with our attention for ever moving across new fields of Time that are really added dimensions we must, in Dunne's view, be immortal, or at least the ultimate observer in us must be immortal.' He developed his exposition: 'As the three-dimensional Observer One in Time One, we use the physical brain which must perish when our Time One comes to an end. But that brain with its sharp focus has been teaching the mind to think.'

Philosophers had long struggled with the mind-brain problem and the idea of the brain teaching something called the mind to think did not make sense because nobody could satisfactorily determine whether the mind had any independence of the brain. Priestley and Dunne firmly related the two and claimed that the immortal mind needed 'more instruction' than the brain. On this view Priestley said the flesh-and-blood existence in Time One served as a kind of apprenticeship to richer and more complicated 'existences in unknown times and dimensions'. There was no conventional passing from one life to another 'because we exist from the first as a series of observers in a series of times'.

These assertions were advanced with the confidence which customarily accompanies statements for which the evidence is strong, but all Dunne's attempts at documentation seemed strained. Priestley himself finally admitted 'that there have always seemed to me many baffling complications in the machinery of this progress'.

Steeping himself in Dunne's second book *The Serial Universe*, Priestley was pleased to find that he attacked and answered the wave and particle view of modern physics, which involved a quite different interpretation of time. Dunne claimed that the self-created dilemmas of modern physicists were the result of misunderstanding the nature of time, a charge which they felt should be directed at him.

Priestley emerged from his total absorption in this view of the universe with the belief that Dunne's theory of time 'must be somewhere near the truth'. He plunged into writing *Time and the Conways* and it is high tribute to his intellectual receptivity that having struggled heroically to marry time theories to drama in *I Have Been Here Before*, he did not hesitate to risk another engagement. In the event, as we have seen, the play 'practically wrote itself'.

What first distinguished *Time and the Conways* from *I Have Been Here Before* was the absence of any strained attempt to explain time theory. Theorising was more successfully married to character and Görtler had no real equivalent in *Time and the Conways*. Set in 1919, Priestley's first act showed Mrs Conway with her daughters Madge, Carol, Hazel and Kay and two sons, Robin and Alan, celebrating a birthday party. One daughter, Hazel, expects to marry wealth, Kay to become a novelist and Madge to persuade the world to accept her political ideals. Each is skilfully evoked with contrasting effect, not least the uninspired son Alan, a municipal clerk who does not share the excited expectations of the remainder of the family.

Act One moved smoothly from sharp reality into the dream-like quality of Act Two, and the text opens with a careful stage direction: 'When the curtain rises, for a moment we think nothing has happened since it came down . . . It is the same room, but it has a different wallpaper, the furniture has been changed round . . . the general effect is harder . . . and we guess at once that this is the present day [1937]. Kay and Alan are not quite the same, after nearly twenty years.'

Understatement could go no further. Kay, the would-be novelist, has become a popular journalist, Madge the socialist daughter has surrendered to the demands of work as a bourgeois schoolmistress, Hazel is unhappily married and Carol died before she could even taste the bitter fruits of disappointment. The unambitious Alan is the sole member of the family, despite his shabby appearance, who has 'about him a certain poise, an inward certainty and serenity'. The second act is full of bitterness and disillusion with an angry quality enlivening some of the dialogue as the characters force themselves to continue living among the ruins of their expectations.

Alan, the nearest equivalent of Dr Görtler in *I Have Been Here Before*, now links the dialogue with Dunne's theories but less explicitly.

> Kay: Remember what we once were and what we thought we'd be. And now this. And it's all we have, Alan, it's *us* . . . If this is all life is, what's the use? Better to die, like Carol . . . before Time gets to work on you.
>
> Alan: No – Time's only a kind of dream, Kay. If it wasn't, it would have to destroy everything – the whole universe – and then remake it again every tenth of a second. But Time doesn't destroy anything. It merely moves us on.
>
> Kay: Alan, we can't be anything but what we are *now*.[15]

Alan offers to lend Kay one of Dunne's books, an artificially intrusive moment, followed by this piece of exposition:

> What we *really* are is the whole stretch of ourselves, all our time, and when we come to the end of this life, all those selves, all our time, will be *us* – the real you, the real me. And then perhaps we'll find ourselves in another time, which is only another kind of dream.[16]

15 *Time and the Conways*, J. B. Priestley, Act 2.
16 ibid.

The opening of Act Three shows Kay sitting just as she was at the end of Act One, having apparently fallen asleep and dreamt like Dunne about the future. Looking about her, slowly, Kay says, 'No – I wasn't asleep. But quite suddenly I thought I saw . . . we were . . . Anyhow you came into it, I think, Alan.'[17]
The audience has been granted the vision which Dunne gave to Observer Two and has, in fact, become Observer Two endowed with omniscience. It is very much part of the play. Kay sums up the situation:

Mrs Conway: This is just like old times, isn't it? And we seem to have waited so long. I ought to tell fortunes again tonight.

Kay (sharply): No.

Act Three is full of the irony that the audience is aware of what will happen, but the characters are not, with the result that they pour out hopes, expectations, intentions which sound completely hollow. Carol, a source of innocent *joie de vivre* in Act One, is used in Act Three to underpin the irony with a long speech in which she excitedly enumerates the wonderful things she is going to achieve. 'I'm going to live,' she says, not knowing that she is going to die.

Two themes which interlock in *Time and the Conways* pervade the last two acts of the play with a qualified pessimism. The world was dragging reluctantly towards the Second World War and Priestley was deeply nostalgic about the expectations of 1919 which had disappeared by 1937. Full of hope about the new order, younger members of the family want their own world to remain inviolate but Priestley realises that the Conways' values and way of life will have to surrender one bastion after another. Unaware of their fate the Conways are even less conscious of the other dimensions in time and life represented by Dunne, and Alan's attempts to mediate meet strong resistance.

There was no doubting the grip of the play even for such remote intellectuals as Beatrice Webb's husband Sidney and the poignancy did not fall over into sentimentality, but Dunne's theories were perilously simple in the eyes of modern philosophers. The *Times* critic was prepared to give Priestley the benefit of the doubt.

It is a tribute to the *Times* critics that throughout Priestley's career they never ignored his works, and, caught off their guard, just

17  ibid., Act 3.

occasionally revealed something resembling enthusiasm.[18] As for Priestley's favourite journal, the *New Statesman*, it sent what Priestley regarded as 'some silly little youth from Mayfair and the South Kensington Museum to do my Conways play' with 'ridiculous results'. Priestley then broke all the rules, rang up Kingsley Martin, told him that 'he'd had enough' of that sort of treatment and persuaded Martin to have a second review written by Desmond MacCarthy who, according to Priestley, 'did it properly'.[19]

It can be argued that Priestley loaded the dice so heavily against the Conway family in the second act that the whole play became unconvincing. They lost their money, their charm, and their expectations. Madge's ideals were crushed, Robin took to drink, Kay's ivory tower suffered the invasion of a Fleet Street journalist, Conway's wife became depressed, and Carol, whose modest ambition it was to live, achieved nothing more than to die. None the less one critic, Peter Fleming in that short-lived journal *Night and Day*, remained very positive. 'In *Time and the Conways* (excellently produced by Miss Irene Hentschel) J. B. Priestley has written a play of brilliant dramatic quality . . . As theatre it gets full marks. Its philosophic content seems to me jejune, arbitrary and unoriginal, but you can't have everything.'[20]

18  *The Times*, 27 August 1937.
19  Priestley to Edward Davison, 3 November 1937.
20  *Night and Day*, Peter Fleming, 2 September 1937.

# 16

# A Lecture Tour and
## *Johnson Over Jordan*
### 1938–9

The autumn of 1937 was overwhelmed by work which attempted to reconcile two plays already in production with writing yet another, *People at Sea*, a series of articles for the *Sunday Express*, preparing for a lecture tour in the States, and a flood of letters surrounding these activities. The demands of his family became clamorous at the prospect of crossing the Atlantic again. In the event, his wife and children sailed before he did, not to New York but once more to the west coast via the Panama Canal.

The third play, *People at Sea*, was really a pot-boiler where the characters became ventriloquist puppets combining to express the cliché that a common danger demanded co-operative effort. Set aboard a ship in danger of foundering as the result of a fire, the situation had considerable dramatic possibilities which were inhibited by the author's message. Pressured by his commitments, Priestley rushed up to Bradford where the Civic Theatre tried out *People at Sea* before the London production. In the mornings he concentrated on journalism, in the afternoons rewrote and recast *People at Sea* and in the evenings made exhausted attempts to 'knock together some lecture notes'. Most plays, he claimed, do not require the author's presence at rehearsals, but *People at Sea* failed in large part to be successful because he was 3,000 miles away when the final rehearsal took place.

Due to leave London at the beginning of October, he found himself trying to do five men's work. 'For several weeks I lived the life of a madman . . . I have known dramatists and producers who felt that they had to have a good holiday after doing one play. They should try doing three. And then on top of that all this other work!'[1] He had never before or since, he wrote, led such an existence.

Too nervously exhausted and excited to sleep properly, I would

1   *Rain upon Godshill*, J. B. Priestley, 53.

wake early in the morning, crawl out and do an hour or two's work, then start dictating replies to letters immediately after breakfast, see the morning's rehearsal at one theatre, argue with agents, managers, publicity men all through the lunch interval, attend the afternoon's rehearsal at another theatre, then look at contracts, bills, programme material, continue all the arguments after lunchtime, absent-mindedly eat dinner, that would make me aware of itself, perhaps see more rehearsals or go home and do some work, finally with my eyes heavy and hot and a mind rattling like an old Ford engine, retire to bed only to remember fifteen important things that ought to have been done that day and would certainly have to be done in the morning.[2]

When, finally, he left London in the middle of October aboard the *Queen Mary* he was 'like a wet rag', and after a rough crossing arrived in New York which immediately produced another bout of sleeplessness. The familiar routine repeated itself. In reaction against New York's irresistible stimulation, lack of sleep induced a feeling of tiredness, emptiness and even desolation. Accustomed now to this rhythm he was glad that he had arranged to spend a few days with his wife in New Orleans, equidistant between Arizona and New York, before launching into a lecture tour of daunting dimensions. The train journey from New York to New Orleans became an ordeal. Leaving late on Saturday afternoon, in the early evening, as if by conspiracy, everybody began coughing, and as he retreated from the Pullman to the club car and from the club to the diner, the coughing like a harsh Greek chorus followed him, until his own throat began to itch and he was coughing too. There followed one of the longest and dreariest Sundays he could remember, which reminded him vividly of the yawning Sabbaths of childhood when inertia took the life out of the very air he breathed.

> We ran through Georgia under a low blanket of cloud and then through Alabama in rain. If there was anything to see, I missed it. The men's room was filled with men even fatter than myself: the books I had with me had no more savour than the train's food: even dozing was hard work . . . When at last we crept into New Orleans it was not merely raining, it was pouring.[3]

We have very little evidence about the state of his relations with Jane in 1937, but reconciliation could go no further than suffering

2   ibid., 54.
3   ibid., 68–9.

such a journey in order to meet her so briefly. The following morning the rain stopped, the sun came out and 'there came to my nose from all over the city . . . the glorious smell of roasting coffee'. Priestley's reference to his wife throughout all his writings is minimal and once again he described the delicious smell of coffee and made no reference to his reunion with Jane. His fame had preceded him and on the first day the telephone began ringing and a wave of hospitality engulfed them. Organised by an old Orleans family, the Roark Bradfords, the Priestleys were escorted to every 'sight worth seeing', drank innumerable Suzerac cocktails and ate lavish dinners which centred around the most delicious seafood they had ever tasted. The best restaurants – Arnaud's, Galatoire's and Antoine's – served specialities like *pompano en papillote* and *huîtres en coquille à la Rockefeller* which combined the old and new worlds in mysterious dishes unobtainable in Paris because the ingredients were American and the cuisine French.

Sightseeing began in the old French quarter with its tiny crumbling mansions and patios with their exquisite wrought-iron traceries. The past did not move Priestley to nostalgic admiration, but created a feeling of fusty desolation with sinister undertones. Perhaps it was his visit to the famous Girod Street cemetery – his wife refused to go – which soured his vision of New Orleans. In the cemetery, built upon swampland, the dead were buried above ground in brick vaults and the whole area was literally rotting away as if the land had putrefied with dead bodies. Some of the vaults were broken open, others cracking at the seams and as the contents became visible, a skeletal frame gave the impression of a 'grisly resurrection' taking place. 'If a rotten hand had made feeble motions at me I would not have been much surprised.' It was no exaggeration to say that the cemetery produced loathing and horror in Priestley as if he 'might have been murdered or buried alive in some previous existence'. As we know, he had once been buried alive. Dunne's serial universe with its implication of several possible lives was fresh in his mind and must have reinforced vague ideas of reincarnation, clothing them in horror. 'A solitary night visit to that graveyard would be a test beyond my nerves.'

All the charm and grace of his hostesses could not reconcile him to the hothouse climate which brought everything to 'quick maturity' only to condemn it to 'a shabby, sad and lingering death'. His hostile reaction to the south came from varied sources. He had read many accounts of the old days when the wharfs of New Orleans were thick with steamers, prosperity was abounding, and slave labour created a temporary aristocracy, but he could not share their nostalgia. On closer acquaintance the 'famous old life of the south' did not impress him. What, he enquired, had it produced? Where was the great painting, music or writing? Gone with the wind? Yes – the title was apt.

There were many accounts of hot-blooded young men challenging each other to duels over superficial women with a flair for provocative sex, and flashily dressed gentlemen seemed to swagger endlessly in and out of gambling dens or brothels.

> These fortunate people in the great white plantation houses, surrounded by slaves with wealth pouring in for several decades, seemed to have created nothing but a doubtful legend of romantic gestures and lazy living.[4]

He ploughed his way through the diary of one such gentleman and found it little more than a social round of 'tip-top beaux' and 'sweet and charming belles'. 'How could such foolish, hothouse personages produce anything of value?' What they did produce was the Civil War without which the southern way of life would have drifted to a lingering and unedifying death. It was the war which created the legend of a lost golden age, a 'glorious ghost of the past'.

Within a week Priestley had snapped out of his cynical mood and returned to sophisticated New York where he was due to give a lecture at Columbia University and introduce a programme of documentary films. This arose from a meeting with the Englishman John Grierson, the doyen of British documentary films. Grierson had read an interview given by Priestley in which he suggested that the traditional method of converting a narrative into moving pictures could be reversed by making a narrative out of a series of photographs. Grierson offered Priestley a residue of shots from a film he had made about the Swiss Post Office and suggested converting them into 'a lecture film'. Nothing if not versatile, Priestley accepted the invitation. Already familiar with a very different film world where producers lunched at the Savoy Grill with bankers who poured wealth into the laps of Central European characters inspired by the Hans Andersen's story of 'The Emperor's New Clothes', he found the straitened circumstances of documentary film and the austerity of its dedicated disciples stimulating. Grierson's films – *Voice of Britain*, *Night Mail*, *Drifters* – have since become classics and Priestley's contribution, *We Live in Two*

4   ibid., 75.

*Worlds*, did not aspire to their distinction. *We Live in Two Worlds* analysed the new internationalism of communication and transport which was transforming the world. 'Anybody who would like to meet in a film, a gigantic and apoplectic frog talking with a broad Yorkshire accent should have a look at me in *We Live in Two Worlds*.'[5]

> It looked as if somebody had been trying to map the adventures of a crazy giant in seven-league boots reeling around the Middle West. There was, for example, that nice little jump from Battle Creek, Michigan to Tulsa, Oklahoma, which was pretty much like being told that after Danzig, your next lecture would be Avignon.

Now came one of the most demanding periods of his life which exceeded the stresses of even those preliminary crowded months before America. Caught off his guard one morning during his Egyptian trip, he had surrendered to the lure of a cable saying that this was his last chance to accept a richly rewarding American lecture tour. Attempting to foreshorten what might turn out to be an ordeal, Priestley arranged with the agent to condense his twenty lectures into four weeks, but when he examined the itinerary and measured the distances, a sense of nightmare overtook him.

The first lecture took place in the harsh city of Pittsburg where Priestley was very aware of his agent in the front row concentrating the scepticism of twenty years in the lecture business. Afterwards his comments were wry and dominated by anxiety about Priestley's physical stamina. For his part, the agent said, he slept better on trains than he did at home and he hoped Priestley had a similar facility. Priestley replied that he slept badly at home, worse in trains, and frequently did not sleep at all. The essence of austerity in his own way of life, the agent hastily hurried away to buy a bottle of the best Scotch whisky which he pressed on Priestley with the admonition 'Try this'. There followed four weeks when he lived and slept in Pullman coaches, a travelling prisoner, released at intervals to be greeted by his gaolers whose innumerable hands he shook before addressing them from platforms where they fired at him questions which invariably mixed the unexpected and idiotic.

Physically, Priestley was undoubtedly tough but it needed all his resilience to continue facing the whirlwind rush from one rendezvous to another, where the lesser the place the greater the expectation. The universities demanded no more than the delivery

5   ibid., 79.

of his lecture and a cocktail party followed by dinner, but lesser towns tended to fête him from the moment of his arrival. Following lunch, cocktails and dinner they would listen spellbound to the 'tired old man' mouthing phrases whose familiarity made them meaningless in his ears, and ply him far into the evening with questions about God, the Universe and the American Way of Life. On one occasion he changed trains twice in the course of the night and emerged before his overwhelmingly friendly audience a haggard, hoarse spectre who had not slept at all.

Underneath his nerves and exhaustion this dashing across thousands of miles to be disgorged at mysterious railway junctions at dawn, in towns which differed as much as countries, secretly appealed to some adventurous streak which gave him 'idiotic satisfactions'. He also enjoyed lecturing in wooden shacks to sixty backwoodsmen who gaped with admiration at his flowing sentences and shared their pork and beans out of a can, washed down with firewater whisky.

And then suddenly in the middle of his tour, his raw nerves and exhausted body rebelled and he slumped behind the green Pullman curtains in the deepest depression. The sense of schoolboy fun was overwhelmed with a sense of futility, and he heard his 'own voice going on and on . . . like a big, fat . . . parrot'. Stimulating America became flat and sterile, the men who hawked and spat in the train, uncivilised, the women preoccupied with disguising signs of age, hard and brittle. Indiscriminate applause met anyone who lectured, from the bogus Hindu mystic to the Russian ex-princess who had known Rasputin. Lecturers were all performing animals and the ringmaster was money. Why did he do it? Why was he there? The answer came ringing back in the middle of the night – Because I am a fool.

As the four-week rodeo came to a close he paused one night in Kansas City Union Station to take stock of his situation. He had launched two plays in New York, arranged the production of a third and survived an itinerary calculated to kill. What would happen next?

The Kansas City he confronted was a station of magnificent proportions which a booklet proudly pronounced cost $50 million to build. In a moment of self-mockery and swelling pride he said to himself – 'They designed all this for me! Looking back with a glance that has more irony than regret in it, I can see myself there, a balloon filled out with the gas of vain accomplishment.' One mistake in the station's construction converted what might have been a touchstone into a disaster in that they forgot to display prominently in the grand lobby 'a little bit of wood for me to touch'. Normally a rational man Priestley was occasionally overtaken by bursts of superstition which nobody working in the theatre could escape, but now he saw very clearly that it was the sudden shrinking of the ego's self-approval compelling him to 'perform this ancient rite'. Some visceral belief that internal psychological events could influence external reality, temporarily convinced him that if his swollen ego had surrendered to the superstitious ritual it might have deflected the disasters which followed. Instead, his run of good luck suddenly changed, and everything began to go wrong. Can we legislate for luck? he was later to ask, but of all the fair goddesses attendant on human affairs, she was the least likely to answer.

The next few months produced sudden losses and disappointments which reminded him of those deeply disturbing days when his first wife and his father died close on the heels of one another. Expectations of large sums from London and New York dramatic royalties did not materialise, the sale of film rights collapsed, his novels experienced a slump and there were hints in his letters of a very bad patch in his relations with Jane who clamoured for his return to Arizona.

Everything changed once more as he stepped back on to the tiny platform at Wickenburg in Arizona with its amethyst mountains, wine-like air, and eternal sunshine. His family received him tumultuously and there, waiting for him, was the small isolated hut with its tin stove where creation could take place with no regard for commercial rewards. Picturesque old-timers were not so numerous, a new filling station had men in smart uniforms and most of the guests were newcomers, but a quick visit to the hut with its simple table and chair drew him magnetically back to work again. Most writers come to the blank sheets of paper with loathing but Priestley, the old professional, knew how to overcome that initial repulsion and now, in no time, he plunged into the opening scene of a play which had haunted him throughout his lecture tour. Preliminary consultation with his small, shiny notebook full of play jottings, revealed the following entry anticipating the three acts of the play, *Johnson Over Jordan*.

### Smith

(1) The Office
(2) The Night Club
(3) The Inn at the World's End

His whole approach to writing the play was conditioned by reading Dr Evans-Wentz's *Tibetan Book of the Dead* in which the intermediate state which follows death was compared to 'a prolonged dream-like' condition 'in what might be called the fourth dimension of space filled with hallucinatory visions'. According to this account the dead man no longer knew that his body had died and translated 'characteristic thought forms' into 'objective entities', such as we employ in dreams.

Day after day Priestley made his way between the cabins which surrounded the ranch house and settled down in his hut. There, with a mixture of pleasure and apprehension among the litter of books, tins of tobacco, pipes and letters, he slowly relaxed and wrote. The rough painted boards, the Indian rugs, simple desk, battered waste-paper basket and typewriter constituted a place equivalent to sanctuary, like a monk's cell in his monastery, but Priestley's thoughts were sometimes anything but monastic. It was late one night under the glare of the two naked electric light-bulbs, for instance, that he conceived the famous brothel scene in *Johnson Over Jordan*. Thinking his way deeper into the play Priestley decided that Johnson, in the first act, would be symbolic of the anxieties which were characteristic of such a man. Conception of the second act proved intractable and as he brooded over the possibility of Johnson surrendering to murderous sensual tendencies, he decided that such experiences should be handled with restraint. Unable, as in all his work, to allow evil to emerge triumphant, the third act would purge the second through terror and remorse, which recalled those experiences that had 'quickened his mind and touched hs heart'. Protestations that his best plays were written in continuous bursts of inspiration are qualified by plays like *I Have Been Here Before* and *Johnson Over Jordan* with which he struggled over long periods. For the moment, restored to his family, no longer a prey to agents and managers, eating regular meals and relaxing in the wonderful Arizona sunlight, he 'felt a noble human being and tried to write like one'. The dialogue did not come painlessly but in intermittent bursts and he was glad to relieve the struggle with long sessions of tennis-playing and occasional picnics. As we have seen, he was a very bad picnicker and preferred, if possible, to have a chair to sit on but one excursion enabled him to climb a neighbouring peak even if he emerged puffing and blowing at the top. Weight was to remain a problem for the rest of his life and as fast as he reduced it by tennis-playing, he replaced it by eating and drinking. Long sessions of ping-pong produced a sweaty and sometimes furious Priestley who disliked losing. Conceding victory to Barbara on one occasion, he said, 'You don't have to carry so much fat about.' Dinner became a hilarious send-up of dieting, with Priestley demanding a second helping because he could not remember the first. After dinner, by special request from the children, he was always prepared to bang out on an old piano worthy of a honky-tonk, 'The Lady Is A Tramp'.

Originally it was not their intention to spend the whole winter in America but several events intervened to persuade them to stay. *Time and the Conways* was due to be produced in New York, his elder daughter Barbara did not want to miss another term at school, and an old friend was coming to join them from England. Jane, Jack and the children boarded the local train from Wickenburg to Ash Fork on – of all days – Christmas Day, with the result that the attendants provided their solitary passengers with a Christmas dinner of Babylonian proportions. The famous Chief Train then carried them to Chicago and the equally renowned 20th Century to New York. The journey covered three days, but for once these 'steel coffins on wheels' did not roast or freeze Priestley and he came close to enjoying the journey. Waiting to receive them was Frank Case, the proprietor of the Algonquin Hotel, but the thoroughly British reception he had arranged was broken into by the simultaneous arrival of a bunch of actresses all embracing one another to the much-repeated exclamation 'Darling!' After the culturally deprived Arizona desert, New York was one long indulgence, from a few hours among the Frick Collection to Thornton Wilder's play *Our Town*, which Priestley described as 'produced with a touch of genius'. Slowly the whirl of agents, publishers, writers and producers drew him once more into its vortex, but one of the men who most impressed him did not belong to this jungle. Tom Wolfe became for Priestley 'a symbolic figure of the American character and genius, a young Titan out of the New World with great bleeding hands . . . with eyes like a child's, hewing and battering his way towards the summit of another Olympus'.[6] How Priestley could write when someone moved or deeply impressed him. He drew a vivid picture of Tom Wolfe labouring day and night, building great mountains of prose-poetry from which occasionally a huge chunk was torn off with hammer

6   ibid., 118.

and chisel to appear in the likeness of a rogue boulder liable to overwhelm the reader.

For the following weeks Priestley immersed himself in the New York production of *Time and the Conways*. Since the London production was still running successfully, a new cast had to be selected and this involved him in the choking web of trade union rules. Auditions at last produced a number of actors who were joined by Sybil Thorndike and Jessica Tandy from London, but this hybrid mixture may have doomed the production from the outset. In Priestley's view Jessica Tandy as Kay did not quite match the flashing bitterness of Jean Forbes-Robertson in the original production, but she 'made up for this by bringing to the Third Act an exquisite heartbreaking quality'. Unfortunately American audiences failed to respond to this and once again the different emotional climates in New York and London converted what were intended to be moving moments into sentimentality. The *New York Times* critic met Priestley at the Algonquin one night and told him bluntly that he 'wrote down to his audience'.[7] Priestley admitted 'writing down' in some of his novels but claimed that in the drama he was 'at once boldly experimental and extremely conscientious'.

The Broadway production of *Time and the Conways* was an unhappy experience. Priestley found himself enmeshed in a jungle of parasitic financiers all stalking one another like lions in search of a share of the kill. Stagehands were paid 'a small fortune' to remove a cup and saucer and remained idle for three-quarters of the play because craft restrictions crippled their activities. The reaction of the critics was equally dampening. It was to be expected that the rugged four-square Priestley, a highly successful man, should ride their attacks like an old trouper, but his reaction was full of pique.

> With each of the Time plays both in London and New York many dramatic critics with an air of vast intellectual superiority produced observations that were childish. [He could not think] why any man who spends most of his evenings looking at bad plays should think he is going to set me right in a trashily written column.[8]

These were depressing days in New York with the play earning no money, the weather appalling and his wife bedridden with a

7   Jean Nathan.
8   *Rain upon Godshill*, J. B. Priestley.

severe chill. The warmth and sunshine of Arizona beckoned powerfully but their friend Dorothy Brook had been delayed and they lingered on in New York waiting for her arrival with growing distaste for the whole city. Occasionally they sallied forth from the civilised sanctuary of the Algonquin and on one occasion witnessed the remarkable spectacle of a packed audience of hard-boiled film representatives literally melting before the mush of the first night of Disney's *Snow White and the Seven Dwarfs*. They unexpectedly encountered old friends, they found good restaurants, they watched Toscanini conducting Radio City's vast orchestra, but at heart they both remained tired and dispirited.

Newspapermen continued to misrepresent Priestley's views, financial juggling to sustain the play became a torment, and an unusually prolonged state of indecision found him turning the pages of his little black notebook desperately trying to determine what he should write next. Normally indecision finally concentrated his attention on one idea which surfaced in crystallised form but now 'half a dozen ideas' made more or less equal . . . attempts to gain my attention'.[9] Badgered, weary, earning no money and distressed about the state of the world with the first thunders of war beginning to re-echo from Germany, he at last retreated to Arizona. He arrived to find the sun banished, the rain pouring down, and a flow of cables and telegrams converting the ranch into a post office. Should *Time and the Conways* be taken off, was it worth risking a New York production of *I Have Been Here Before* and could he afford to reject renewed offers from Hollywood? The first rudimentary form of *Johnson Over Jordan* needed close revision, but another idea had already germinated and steadily came to dominate his mind. Brushing aside the detritus of plays and films, he suddenly struck out boldly to write the first act of a play to be called *The Linden Tree*. He conceived the chief character of the play, Linden, as an engineer of genius recently returned from a long sojourn in the east to chair a meeting of his board of directors, bringing with him an oriental philosopher. The pursuit of wisdom now interested Mr Linden more than the manufacture of car engines and his address to the board left them wondering whether their founder had gone out of his mind. The first act flowed easily and some parts of the second act came spontaneously alive until the whole play seemed set to complete itself. Then, suddenly and unexpectedly, he had to break off. Baffled, he decided to show the

9   ibid., 131.

unfinished manuscript to his wife, confident in the belief that she would either like it or suggest minor modifications. Instead, she strongly resisted the play, said it was completely uncharacteristic of him and might have been written by another author. Re-reading the play he came to the conclusion that she was quite right and looked in vain for an explanation. Later he wrote: 'So I put the manuscript on one side; and though I know it came home with me . . . I do not know where it is and do not care.'

As will emerge, these beginnings of *The Linden Tree* were finally shaped into a play which had its first production nearly ten years later in 1947. Whether to escape his problems or solve them in the midst of this impasse, Priestley decided to take to the trail and re-explore 'the blazing miracle of the South-West'.

His friend Dorothy Brook had arrived from London, another old friend Fig Newton joined them, and together with Pont the *Punch* artist, also staying at the ranch, the whole cavalcade including seven children set out in the station wagon equipped with duffle bags.

The Priestley family were already familiar with the spectacular sights of the south-west and now they escorted Dorothy and Pont through Death Valley to the Boulder Dam and Grand Canyon. They cooked over open fires, ate out of tins, slept in auto-camps or sleeping bags.

> Sometimes the car was unpleasantly hot and dusty and at other times it was skidding on snow. We ranged from five hundred feet below sea level to seven thousand feet above it. We enjoyed everything, deserts and mountains and miraculous blue air; solemnly and happily absorbed in it all, refreshing and rejoicing the spirit.

The hilarious high spot of the whole trip occurred in Scotty's Castle, Death Valley, when a mechanical organ suddenly burst into Liszt's 'Hungarian Rhapsody' and all exploded with laughter. Death Valley, a phoney prefabricated castle, a mechanical organ and Liszt made bizarre bedfellows, but the castle turned out to be an inspiration.

Bounced about among the duffle bags, Priestley thought through yet another story and if, in perspective, *The Doomsday Men* written in 1937 was not to become an important work, it turned into a highly entertaining novel. Derivative from that far-off novel *Benighted*, it was crazily romantic and moved with tremendous pace. Throwing literature to the winds Priestley brought together three madmen – a fanatic, a millionaire and a scientist – to build a huge folly of a castle in the middle of the Arizona desert for the express purpose of destroying the world. All the ingredients of the romantic thriller were included, from the beautiful girl steeped in feminine allure to the handsome young men about to rescue her. Hollywood did not offer to convert the novel into a film, the reviewers treated it as a *jeu d'esprit* and he himself concluded, 'I suppose *The Doomsday Men* was a mistake.' Certainly the excitement of writing it, when he returned to the ranch, dissipated his restlessness and made him forget the Hassayampa river, swollen by torrential rains and roaring past his shack in a 300-foot-wide torrent.

He continued a limited correspondence from Arizona and one letter went to Edward Davison analysing the threat of war. He believed that Britain should put up a bold front with madmen like Hitler who were lost in some vast Teutonic dream of Siegfried victory and conquest. He was weary of endless American press attacks which sneered at Britain for making war by re-arming and simultaneously condemned the English for not fighting at 'the drop of a hat'. When all was said and done, if those same critics had not ratted on Wilson when he went to Versailles, the League of Nations with America a member would be a reality and Hitler would never have arisen.[10]

The time drew close to pull out of Arizona once more and most members of the family underwent the now familiar withdrawal symptoms. A temporary reprieve came in the form of a trip to the famous Rainbow Bridge. The Indian reservation in northern Arizona covers an area roughly equivalent to England with Rainbow Bridge in its northern area overlapping Utah. Normally the tracks were snowbound in the spring, but now came word from the Nelsons, who ran Rainbow Lodge, that they were open and immediately preparations were made to leave. Once more Jane, Jack, their children and a young handyman borrowed from the ranch piled into the station wagon with the children in tears and Jack looking back with regret as the driver 'hurtled them up the corkscrew road towards Prescott in the North'.

Rainbow Bridge spanned the Little Colorado Canyon, a lesser equivalent of the Grand Canyon, having implicit in its 'abrupt, sheer, black-shadowed' appearance, something menacing. Priestley found it no less strange than the Grand Canyon and even 'more terrifying'. The Painted Desert belonged to a distant past vividly recaptured by dinosaur tracks, the huge three-toed imprints

10   Priestley to Edward Davison, 17 March 1937.

surviving from millions of years ago and suddenly creating images of those monsters struggling hopelessly in their death throes. The atmosphere of the Painted Desert was dominated by a silence so profound that it had a physical presence which seemed to stop ordinary conversation as if it were an undignified triviality in the profundity of the past. Setting out for a walk from a trading post they found that their talk dwindled away and when all efforts to rekindle it failed, they decided that you 'could not talk against it . . . there was something intimidating about its very completeness'. The Indians were as silent as the countryside and whenever an occasional solitary figure materialised out of the earth, he stood immobile, staring for a few minutes, without uttering a sound and then was suddenly absorbed back into the Painted Desert. The inanimate momentarily became animate but without the gift of speech. Later, that first evening, back at the trading post they joined an old Indian trader, a woman from Los Angeles and a trader's wife who brought sacrilege to the Painted Desert by banging out on a honky-tonk piano, old vaudeville songs. Strolling outside for a moment, the vast amphitheatre of marble silence seemed to Priestley to absorb and obliterate this small blemish of life on its beautiful surface.

They remained at Rainbow Lodge for a few more days and Priestley recaptured the atmosphere not in his own words, but in those of his daughter Barbara aged thirteen, who frequently strained her eyes around a camp fire at night to keep her diary up to date.

> Mummy and Mr Wilson and me went to the hogan of Red Shirt and family . . . Inside was Red Shirt's mother-in-law one of the three squaws of the chief, at least they didn't have a chief but he was an adviser. She wore a green-grey faded velvet shirt and an old tattered dirty red skirt, very torn with a green stripe at the bottom. She had lovely moccassins and a beautiful bracelet. The hogan was filled with about 20 dirty sheepskins they slept on, a fire that smoked because of the wind. There were broken saucepans, bowls of dirty water, a beautiful bow with arrows, a saddle, a blanket and bridle etc. Mummy gave her some collops and she thanked us and giggled like a little girl. She told us with signs and Navaho language her eyes hurt her because of the wind and she was cold and showed her ragged skirt. Her husband and son-in-law etc. were away in the hills and her daughter was herding sheep . . .
>
> In the morning we made our beds then there was a lot of talk and we decided to see the cliff dwellings in the Navaho mountains . . .

We went quite a long way to an old fort, then further up several other ruins all covered with chips of pottery. It was bitterly cold, there were only a few clouds but in the wind it was biting. Mummy and Mr Wilson stayed down and built a fire and all us went up.

We went up quite a long way and found just one or two quite nice ruins on a ledge . . . We all climbed up to the top and there were about 6 well-preserved houses and some walls. We found caves with figures in and old corncobs and I found wads of pottery pieces. When we went home all my pockets rattled and I had to hold them.

Shortly afterwards six people, once more laden with duffle bags and provisions, piled back into the wagon, and buffeted their way through a 'wilderness of boulders, grey sage and twisted juniper', with the engine frequently boiling, until at last they came within sight of Rainbow Bridge.

It was no disappointment. This was indeed one of the wonders of the world. Nature had flung a great arc of stone several hundred feet high in almost perfect symmetry, which combined noble grace with delicacy.

The day was perfect. The sky seen through the vast arch was an indescribably brilliant turquoise, several shades darker than the shining stone of the Bridge itself. The view through the arch with a patch of bright green vegetation below, brilliant sky above and between them the burnished coppery cliffs and bastions of the canyon sharply framed, was an enchantment. You felt you had only to walk through that noble arch to find yourself in another and better world. [11]

Regarded by the Indians as a sacred shrine, it inspired their famous prayer which invoked the four winds and ended with the words: 'that it may be peaceful before me, that it may be peaceful behind me. All is peace, all is peace.'

It was time to think of the east again, but as they moved along a tiny ghost road into Marble Canyon they were lost once more in the magical scenery, wildly different from anywhere else in the world. Great ramparts of salmon pink, vermilion and bright red towered over the trail and suggested to Priestley a Martian landscape where some new and startling interplanetary adventure was about to begin.

The final act of this great trek was bizarre comedy which kept them laughing for days. There in the middle of New Mexico they

11  *Rain upon Godshill*, J. B. Priestley, 155.

stumbled on a family of Navaho traders who came from Lancashire and had preserved their local character, accent and gritty determination in the face of every effort to assimilate them into the way of life of southern America. Priestley understood their grim provincial outlook and North Country humour which led into long hours of hilarious exchanges as if they were all staying at the same boarding-house in Blackpool.

And then at last, a somewhat tattered group of weary travellers with no more luggage than their duffle bags arrived at Lamy and there was a modern locomotive ready to carry them back to the amenities and horrors of raucous Chicago. Melancholy, nostalgic and vaguely excited at the prospect of city life once again they knew that they 'were leaving the West for a long time, perhaps for ever . . . Now we had turned again towards the crowded streets and the anxious eyes and the evil harvest of news.'

# PART TWO

# 17

# When We Are Married
## 1939

In a superficial interview given to the *Daily Express*, Jane Priestley
drew a portrait of family life in the mid-1930s which romanticised it
out of all recognition.

> As my husband's work is done at home, the children see more of
> their father than most children do. We have six of them – five girls
> and then Thomas the youngest . . . and they all adore him. I always
> love to see how they all rush to him the moment he appears . . . He is
> just as devoted to them too and sees as much as possible of them. The
> children lead their own separate nursery life in the charge of a
> Yorkshire Nanny. In spite of a very full day, my husband spends
> quite an appreciable time with the children. Always after breakfast
> they come to my room – only the youngest, four and two, of course
> because the others are at school. They come in for about ten minutes
> . . . and then daddy is there . . . After tea, when the ten and nine
> year old are home from school is the best time . . . there never was
> anyone better with children.[1]

It was interesting that she referred to 'my room' but the supposition
that they had separate bedrooms was not confirmed in another piece
of chatty journalism in *Homes and Gardens*.[2]

A highly intelligent, cultured and sensitive person, Jane
Priestley, as we know, was as alive to historical echoes in the
Highgate house as her husband, but she concentrated for the *Daily
Express* readers on relative trivia. 'If he is busy on a play or a book
then nobody interrupts, however important the business . . . and
the telephone is cut off.'[3]

His correspondence, she said, was enormous and letters with the
vaguest addresses successfully reached him. It all read like the
perfect bourgeois family where happiness flowed unchecked, but

1   *Daily Express*, 19 October 1934.
2   *Homes and Gardens*, October 1935.
3   *Daily Express*, 19 October 1934.

clearly Jane was reaffirming the public image created by the media. There remained elements of truth in the picture. He could be 'wonderful with children'; he could sometimes play the role of the 'perfect father' and the charm uncovered by another interviewer, Daphne Clare, was always available for those he liked. If the grumbling, sometimes cantankerous, occasionally rude Priestley could easily materialise behind the pleasant family man, there were many times when all these characteristics were swept away. There were others when depression returned and his work and the world about him seemed overwhelmingly meaningless. Loneliness was an obligatory part of the writer's life and now he wrote: 'I do not much mind being alone . . . a great part of nearly every day I spend isolated from my kind.'

Travelling for professional purposes, he preferred to be alone because he became more sensitive to experience, but a few days of isolation produced a 'mood of boredom mixed with melancholy' and such a mood generated some of his best work. Company made him either cheerful or aggressive, acting upon him instantly as drink did upon certain people. When alone his habitual mood was sombre and brooding, more inclined to pessimism than optimism.

Newspapers did not arrive at Billingham until lunchtime and on the particular day when he recorded these reflections he picked up *The Times* after lunch and read the news with disgust. A long interview with Aneurin Bevan which summed up the international situation drew his attention. Bevan did not believe that the civil war in Spain between Franco and the republicans would remain confined to the Iberian Peninsula. He believed it involved the very fundamentals of the historical process which would never stop short at Spain, Germany or Italy, but would overrun half the world before its force was spent, and he did his best to press this view on the Labour Party, against a wall of indifference. Priestley, who always voted Labour, did not agree with Bevan's analysis of the Popular Front. According to Bevan the world had recovered from Manchukuo and Abyssinia, France had outfaced the Stavisky scandals and Hitler entering the German Rhineland, but the emasculated policy known as non-intervention in Spain left Blum visibly weeping and deeply disturbed the 'real left' in Britain. Bevan felt that Spain and its democratically elected government were about to be sacrificed to a medieval Catholic hierarchy, aided and abetted by fascist governments ready to test their new equipment in another land. Huge armies were rising in Germany and Italy, a vast war potential steadily absorbing more men and materials, and in Bevan's words 'the fever of Fascism' was beginning to run high.

The pessimistic view of the future in *Time and the Conways* reflected the view Priestley shared with Bevan that another war was threatening. Since the last one had trampled his early world into the mud, he was doubly sensitive. Disillusion temporarily overtook him, professionally, emotionally and sexually. Professionally he scoffed at the legend of the successful writer becoming the talk of the town with famous hostesses courting him and publishers haunting his doorstep. 'If any literary aspirant is being lured on by this nonsense he had better stop now. Not only will all this not happen after one successful novel or play, it will not happen after ten.'

A newspaper had recently suggested that he was making a four-figure weekly income from his plays, whereas with several plays running 'his weekly budget was showing a loss of a hundred or two and a little more of that astounding success would have left (him) broke'. Emotionally, relations with his wife were once more at a low ebb and the word love between them had lost its meaning. Constantly cropping up in explosive moments, threats of divorce never materialised. As for sex, a brief passage in *Music at Night* – which he wrote under ferocious pressures in 1937 – seemed highly relevant:

> Sir J.: It's a feeling I have there's a catch in this love-making business. It's like a lot of other things – it's a let-down. There's something about a good-looking woman that makes you feel, if she'll treat you right, that at last you'll get clean out of yourself, like a door suddenly opening into another sort of life. But – afterwards – you see that it hasn't worked. It's just another let-down. Nearly everything's a let-down.[4]

Priestley had committed himself – 'recklessly I fear' – to providing two producers, H. K. Ayliff and Roy Limbert, with a new play for the Malvern Festival. Never at a loss for ideas he remembered one which had occurred to him thousands of miles away in Rainbow Lodge as he listened to the Navaho Indians singing their prayers to invoke the Black, Blue, Yellow and Iridescent Winds. Its conception was simple, its execution difficult. The play would attempt to dramatise 'the mental adventures of a group of people listening to the first performance of a piece of music' and would

4   *Music at Night*, J. B. Priestley, Act 2.

reverberate from surface moods to 'deeper and deeper levels of consciousness'.

Time was so short that *Music at Night* had to be cast before he had finished assembling the characters and he found himself 'fairly sweating at the piece'. Two thirds through the play with the deadline closing in, he suddenly decided that he could not finish in time for the Malvern Festival. Ayliff received the news with alarm since the festival authors had been announced and no one could take over at such a late stage. Two days of idleness were followed by a fresh and ferocious attack on 'the tortuous thing'. It was like 'wrestling eight hours a day with a gigantic eel'. Intending to penetrate the deepest level of consciousness in the last scene, Priestley suddenly switched from prose to verse which would be chanted in chorus, only to find that whatever gifts he might once have had in that form were very rusty. Actors and producer were now looking over his shoulder with no more than a week to go, but still he chopped and changed, breaking his routine and working far into the night.

The brochure for the Malvern Festival in 1938 contained a short essay – 'A Note from the Workshop' written by Priestley. A dramatic festival, he said, should be a laboratory in which playwrights experimented and here was the result of one such experiment. 'I shall be most happily surprised – to find more than half the audience liking the play.' *Music at Night* brought together a cabinet minister, a businessman, a society woman and a gossip writer, revealing through their reactions to music equivocations of thought in the cabinet minister, relaxed morals in the society woman and the search for sensations which corrupts the gossip writer. A microcosm of society, the characters enabled Priestley to penetrate their personas and bring them together in an underlying pattern which freed them from pollution. Unfortunately his verse did not carry the necessary authority and the play fell between the two stools of naturalism and experiment.

The years 1937–9 absorbed him in a bewildering array of play-writing, rewriting, production and acting and even, on occasion, philanthropy. Despite the pressures he still found time to defend the claims of indigent authors in his new role as a member of the Royal Literary Fund. The young Dylan Thomas had applied for a grant to enable him to continue writing poetry but the internal machinery of the fund threatened to distort and reject his claim. Writing to Philip Guedalla, a member of the Fund Committee, Priestley said that he had moved the acceptance of Thomas's claim not because he knew him personally or had read his work closely, but on the basis of de la Mare's very careful and considered judgement. It was easy for Mr Courtauld, another committee member, to glance cursorily at the poems as they were presented to him and proceed to read 'a rather obscure verse in the unsympathetic manner one instinctively adopts at such times',[5] but that simply was not good enough. Applying a similar technique he would guarantee to show that the late Yeats or T. S. Eliot, to say nothing of poets like Auden and Spender, were equally unacceptable on grounds of literary merit. 'I do not even know that [Thomas's] circumstances warrant our assisting him but I am very disturbed at this slap-dash method of passing judgement.' Priestley sent copies of his letter to several younger members of the committee, but it was all of no avail. Thomas appealed against their verdict, again supported by Priestley, only to be told that since he was not an established writer he could not expect a grant. As he pointed out to Priestley, if he had been an established writer he might not have required assistance.[6]

Before *Music at Night* was in its second rehearsal Priestley had plunged into a quite different and far more sympathetic undertaking, writing at high speed the first and almost final version of *When We Are Married*. This was a comedy full of northern drollery in which three solid Yorkshire couples share their silver wedding day only to discover that none has been legally married.

> Often I laughed while I was writing, not because I thought I was being very witty, but because memories of favourite words of that period, such as 'flabbergasted', came back to me, and it was such fun introducing them into the text.[7]

Simultaneously he negotiated with Amner Hall, Michael MacOwan and Thane Parker to underwrite productions at the Westminster Theatre, shared rehearsals of *Troilus and Cressida*, nursed rehearsals of *When We Are Married*, rewrote dialogue on the spot and took part in a new production of *I Have Been Here Before* which was preparing to face New York audiences. What might have overwhelmed a lesser person, Priestley claimed brought him fully alive. Originally converted from a chapel, the Westminster Theatre had launched several successful productions before Amner Hall decided to take a world cruise and suggested that Michael

5 Priestley to Philip Guedalla, 14 October 1938.
6 *The Life of Dylan Thomas*, Constantine Fitzgibbon, 252.
7 *Rain upon Godshill*, J. B. Priestley, 184.

MacOwan and Thane Parker should 'find another silly old man to put up money'.[8] Priestley went irregularly to the Westminster and formed the habit of climbing the stairs to Amner's office to sit there smoking and talking late into the night. Amner's imminent abdication led to a telephone call to Priestley suggesting that perhaps such a sophisticated man of the theatre might be interested to clinch their dealings and invest money in new productions. Priestley agreed to put up £3,000 provided an equal sum was contributed from another source. That source proved to be the playwright Ronald Jeans.

This took Priestley into the thick of theatrical work and for the following three years he found pleasure and satisfaction collaborating with Irene Hentschel, Basil Dean and Michael MacOwan in productions, and A. D. Peters, J. P. Mitchelhill and Thane Parker in management. It was very tricky working with people in the theatre, he said, because despite the authority of being the author, there on the stage, 'away from daylight and common sense', everybody knew best.

Basil Dean later commented:

Jack brought a breath of fresh air into the whole business – he was rugged, forthright and sometimes downright rude but his enthusiasm and readiness to adjust his script endeared him to most of us.[9]

Dean cast Frank Pettingell in the role of the drunken press photographer for *When We Are Married*, with Raymond Huntley as the meanest husband in all the world and Patricia Hayes as the Yorkshire 'skivvy' who bounced in and out of the play brashly displaying her own enjoyment of the laughter she created.

The rehearsals went swimmingly . . . Priestley seemed to thoroughly enjoy his own characters much as I imagine Dickens must have done . . . The certainty of success which he trumpeted loudly added to the happy atmosphere which in sum was in extraordinary contrast to the anxieties in the street outside.[10]

*When We Are Married* opened at the Opera House, Manchester, on 19 September 1938 and played to packed houses, with, according

8 Interview with Elspeth Parker, 2 November 1985.
9 Interview with Basil Dean, 2 December 1975.
10 *Mind's Eye*, Basil Dean, 261.

to Dean, 'the laughter growing louder every week'. He believed what later events reinforced, that in this time of international crisis with Hitler threatening the peace of Europe and Chamberlain little more than a foil to his demagoguery, people wanted to hear the clarion call of good English humour: 'confident . . . strong . . . native' and 'untarnished by any alien influence'. The Manchester critics were enthusiastic, with the *Guardian* commenting 'This is not only a night out for Priestley, the serious dramatist, but for all of us who want to forget Europe for two and a half hours.'[11] After a week in Manchester the play moved to the Grand Theatre, Blackpool and received another warm reception, but by now the threat of war dominated everything and Dean became gloomy about a possible London production. Carried away with the success of the play Priestley sat outside the Imperial Hotel beside Basil Dean and 'roundly declared that there would be no war'. In the immediate event he proved correct because, before the Saturday matinee, the news broke that Chamberlain had succeeded and there he was waving his 'little piece of paper' which enshrined the peace of the world.

Following the matinee Priestley and Dean joined Julian Wylie, 'reigning monarch of the London Hippodrome', to discuss a London production. Tough, hard-headed with a wry sense of humour, Wylie chain-smoked continuously with cigarette ash coating his lapels, but it quickly became clear that he was impressed. As Dean wrote, he prophesied certain success in London. 'You've got a hit, Basil!'[12]

If Priestley was delighted with the reactions to *When We Are Married* he was totally disillusioned by the people he met at Blackpool. The play coincided with the famous illuminations week and Blackpool was overwhelmed not by residents but by people from the Midlands and Scotland. He described them ruthlessly. They were 'mostly small, rather mis-shapen, toothless men and women, harmless enough but very unattractive in the mass'. The Blackpool of his childhood with its free and easy atmosphere was now overwhelmed by 'a kind of weary, mindless quality, an empty idiocy exploited with ruthless efficiency by large-scale commercial interests'.[13] If such exploitation had been endemic to Blackpool for half a century it still left Priestley alarmed and depressed.

11   ibid.
12   ibid., 262.
13   *Rain upon Godshill*, J. B. Priestley, 192.

From the Hotel Metropole, Blackpool he wrote a letter to Jane:

Dear Jane,

Although I was very very disappointed when you couldn't come here and I miss you very much, I must admit that – on second thoughts – I don't think you'd have enjoyed it. The town is crowded with people – mostly unpleasant – and this hotel is full too and the service very slow and inefficient. The illuminations are very gorgeous but not very pleasing. Even the air doesn't seem its usual self, because the days are windless, both damp, muggy – curiously unhealthy. The result is that nearly everybody in the company feels seedy. Pixie has been very queer and keeps ringing up her London doctor and spends all her free time in bed. Muriel George had a touch of flu – the little servant girl has a cold, etc., etc. The play went wonderfully last night and we had a good audience, and now we are rehearsing all the new stuff I wrote last week – really two new acts. It should be incredibly funny by the time it's finished . . .

We don't know what is to happen to theatres if there is war. The people will want entertaining – more than ever – but I can't believe they'll allow people – especially in London – to congregate in non-bomb-proof buildings like theatres. I still feel, in spite of all the precautions, that the chances are that Hitler won't plunge Europe into a war – once he clearly realises it means a war. If things ease up and you can get away, your best plan would be to come up here by car on Saturday and then stay for the first night at New Brighton. If that goes well I can finish with the company then. What I'd better do, if war comes, I don't know, because it's no good going to London unless I've something to do there, and it doesn't look as if there'll be room for me at Billingham, even if I can come over. But I must see you soon my love, and I'm thinking of you all the time, and admiring you more than ever for the way you're helping those children. If you want me in the mornings, please ring Blackpool (Grand Theatre) or this hotel 2–2.30 or 6–8.

With much love, my darling.
 Your
 Jack[14]

Another letter followed fast on the heels of the last. Jane was to run a hostel for child evacuees during the war and Priestley referred to what seemed to be a preliminary experiment with a number of children at Sevenoaks.

14 Priestley to Jane Priestley, 27 September 1938.

Dear love,

Many thanks for your card. You must have been frantically busy, not a bad thing just now. No news here except that the play goes well and should make some profit this week. It is hard rehearsing the new stuff during the day because – with all these rumours flying about – it is hard to concentrate – and so everything seems more difficult than usual. This morning there is a wind blowing – at last – and the air is fresher. I feel much better than I did in Manchester, where I felt half dead.

I'm dropping a note to Miss Woollens this morning asking her to have the cellar at 3 The Grove looked at as a possible bomb-proof shelter. I'll go back to London next Tuesday or Wednesday – according to the way the play goes.

Had a nice comical letter from Mary this morning, in reply to mine. Incidentally, I don't consider Sevenoaks at all safe and think that children ought to be removed.

I'd like to see you with your new houseful. I can't imagine where you put them all. There can't be a spare inch anywhere.

I'm tired of this place and all the people in it and I wish us to be together again, anywhere.

With very much love,

JACK[15]

*When We Are Married* opened in London and completely fulfilled Wylie's predictions. The crowded audiences at St Martin's Theatre responded 'rapturously' and even the critics were generous. Then came a setback. Involved in an accident, Frank Pettingell who played the drunken photographer was put out of action for several days and Dean searched frantically for a substitute with no more than twenty-four hours to spare. As if to demonstrate yet another dimension in his continuously developing versatility Priestley offered to take over the part. The publicity value was obvious and the press officer sent out a release which brought the photographers flocking to St Martin's. Nobody, not even Basil Dean, knew what it cost Priestley to become one of the characters in his play, fully exposed to public scrutiny. He found the near-clowning character acting required for the drunken photographer a natural extension of some of his performances for the children in the family, but there were problems. It was a sustained part requiring precise timing, occasional bursts into pure 'comic business' and in the third act some close interacting with the remainder of the company. Irony

15   Priestley to Jane Priestley, 29 September 1938.

ran high. Having spent hours interpreting lines and characters to the actors, he was now expected to give a demonstration in front of an unpredictable and completely unknown audience.

He went to bed on the Sunday preceding the Monday performance and for several hours lay sleepless, repeating his lines, discovering with horror wide gaps where memory simply broke down.

> I came down in the morning with a little hollow place in my stomach and feeling as one always does at such times . . . that nothing could be properly touched or tasted, that I had wandered awake into a menacing dream.[16]

Photographers swarmed over his first attempts at rehearsal and reduced his comic lines to outrageous farce, but by the afternoon he 'dried less frequently' and experienced the first glimmerings of an uneasy confidence. He returned home to rest and his confidence immediately faded. He felt like 'a man condemned to an early execution, a feeling obviously shared by the members of my household who regarded me with tender solicitude'. Already a seasoned lecturer, he knew that preliminary nerves which threatened to paralyse him frequently disappeared when he actually confronted an audience and now the tired, uneasy Priestley whose 'butterfly stomach' troubled him like a true professional, uneasily answered his call. Immediately he felt a response from the audience he regained his confidence. It was not a brilliant performance and he stumbled on the occasional line, but the press – which he had so often criticised – treated him with 'chaffing approval' and that night he slept soundly. It was a tribute either to his lack of vanity or scorn for critics that he never kept press cuttings books, but he made an exception on this occasion and treasured for years a little album which might have qualified him to earn a few pounds as a comedian if all else failed.

On 20 November in the same year Priestley's play *When We Are Married* made television history and became the first play to be televised during an actual performance. It led to chaotic reorganisation in the theatre with seats removed to accommodate cameras, floodlights destroying the subtler aspects of Dean's production, and cables festooning the theatre to trap the unwary audience. Seat prices were reduced to 5s or 3s 6d, but that turned out to be unnecessary since they were playing to full houses. Following the London success the play went on a short suburban tour and then

16 *Rain upon Godshill*, J. B. Priestley, 195.

returned to London for a season at the Princes Theatre, but by now the audiences were dwindling and Dean wrote, 'I fear the experiment brought my partner little profit.'

Successful because it was not experimental, the dialogue in *When We Are Married* remained totally authentic for the three solid Yorkshire couples who dominated the play. Alive with homespun humour and compassion it touched a chord in a wide variety of people. Experimentation with Priestley never involved the use of language or verbal innovation. His dialogue has a similarity throughout but he frequently devised new settings or dramatised new 'intellectual' concepts. *When We Are Married* comically exploits human failings from snobbery and self-deception to expediency and pomposity, until the tide of self-revelation reaches the explosive point where one short speech silences everyone. They have just discovered that they are not married and have been living in sin for years. Allegedly there was a technical flaw in the marriage services. 'Joe, Herbert, they mustn't know. Nobody must know. Why – we'd be laughed right out of town. What – Alderman Helliwell – Councillor Albert Parker – Herbert Soppitt – all big men at chapel too! I tell you, if this leaks out – we're done.'

*When We Are Married* carries no particular moral message but guilt riddles the play. Joe says: 'I won't tell you a lie, love. I can't help it, but ever since I've known I'm not married I've felt *most peculiar.*'

Frank for its day, the play unravelled the darker side of marriage, spilling out one shocking secret after another, anticipating the black humour which characterises Alan Ayckbourn's work.

Patricia Hayes played the termagant maid with bristling counter-attack, ready for explosion before the slightest provocation, and each new military entrance through the sitting-room door was brought to an abrupt halt by some fresh outrage of conventional behaviour.

Henry Ormonroyd, the photographer bent on conveying his story to the press, staggered drunkenly from one misunderstanding to another with comic encounters at every turn. A Falstaffian figure he echoed Falstaff: 'Let's 'ave a bit o' life' (Falstaff: 'Give me life I say'). And life he certainly added to the play.

The first act was leisurely, the third dangerously near slapstick farce, but the second rose to the superb comic scene between Ormonroyd and Ruby the maid, one of the most original Priestley ever wrote. This was not an experimental play, but Priestley's dialogue throughout was sharper and snappier than any in previous comedies.

Servants like Ruby in *When We Are Married* were no longer funny characters but a means of mocking hypocrisy and deception. They and the tart Lottie Grady were given a dignity which the other characters lacked. Priestley takes his revenge on the Parkers, the Soppitts and the Helliwells, on the greedy wool merchants who became aldermen, councillors basking in boozy hypocrisy and a whole cast of Edwardian *nouveaux riches*. He also exposes the awful fate of so many women at that time who were doomed to underpin their husbands' ego trips and serve as reflecting mirrors for their vanity. Seeing the 1986 production at the Whitehall Theatre, the present writer was impressed by the sheer theatricality of the play, the clockwork precision of the exits and entrances and the comic impetus which carried the play along at enormous pace.

Only one of the three marriages faced the central issue raised by the news of their disreputable liaisons. After twenty-five years of sin Councillor Albert Parker, played by Timothy West, was determined to make an honest woman of his wife. Mousy Annie, suddenly lit up with the possibilities of escape into a world of travel, liveliness and people who were amusing, astonished him by demanding 'What for?' The fat cigar almost exploded in Timothy West's mouth and his eyebrows flashed up and down signalling total outrage, a performance of overwhelming virtuosity.

The *Guardian* commented: 'Ronald Eyre's delectable Priestley revival shoots lines of pleasure right across the drab face of the West End Theatre. It will surely induce in respectable audiences what an evening of cocaine and champagne achieves for illicit sybarity.'[17] Notwithstanding a patronising review in *The Times*, the play seems to have a kind of immortality, it has been revived so many times.[18]

Close on the heels of *When We Are Married* came *Johnson Over Jordan*, a play in a different category which ranked high in Priestley's canon. Since their earliest collaboration in the theatre, Priestley had constantly talked of a play he was writing especially for his friend Ralph Richardson, and Basil Dean takes up the story.

> One day he handed me the script of *Johnson Over Jordan*, a modern morality play in which the outstanding events in a man's life flit through the middle years of temptation, thence to unsullied youth – a life history in reverse order as it were. I realised that it would afford rare opportunities not only for the display of Ralph's gifts but also

17   *Guardian*, 7 March 1986.
18   *The Times*, 8 March 1986.

give me a chance to resume my experiments in new production methods.[19]

Brief bursts of journalism, and a visit to his daughter Barbara who had gone to Switzerland to recover from an illness, were interspersed with polishing *Johnson Over Jordan*. In its finished form he considered the play his best work for the theatre and spent long hours 'nursing it', especially because the actual production was to be experimental. Dean, who had met Benjamin Britten in Maynard Keynes's circle, invited him to compose the music for the play and that was Britten's first contribution to English theatre. Selected as the designer, Edward Craig foreshadowed the almost empty stage of some modern productions with two cycloramas, one back stage painted and hung in accordance with Max Husait's technique and the other of fine silk set in mid-stage. Each was to be lighted as if the other did not exist. Conventional scenery had no place in the production.

*Johnson Over Jordan* was presented at the New Theatre on 22 February 1939 and according to Dean – a view not accepted by Priestley – received an ovation.

> Edna Best played Johnson's wife Jill, appearing in the first scene at the time of her widowhood . . . brave, common-sensical and touchy . . . But first and last thoughts must go to Ralph Richardson. His performance of Johnson remains one of his greatest achievements.[20]

Towards the end of the first week it became clear that the play was not going to reach the minimum audience required by the contract. Bronson Albery gave the usual two weeks' closure notice which, when it reached the press, brought people crowding into the theatre, but at the end of the third week – inexorably – the play closed.

In a burst of anger Priestley wrote an article for the *Sunday Pictorial* which said: 'What's the use of my wasting my time writing plays like this? For two pins I'll never write another play in my life.'

Later, in *Rain upon Godshill*, Priestley said that the fashionable play-going people who could be relied upon to fill the more expensive seats stayed away as if afraid of the plague. Friends who avoided mentioning 'this lapse from dramatic sanity' would not

19   *Mind's Eye*, Basil Dean, 264.
20   ibid.

have been surprised to know that the play failed to achieve one hundred performances and lost 'several thousand pounds'. There remained a handful of younger critics who thought that it was 'the best thing' he had 'ever done'.

Remembering his success in backing *Dangerous Corner* after its threatened closure, Priestley once more relaunched the play ten days later at the Savile Theatre, reducing prices and boosting publicity. His determination to *create* an audience where it seemed not to exist was matched by his audacity in backing a play without popular appeal. No amount of apparent failure dismayed him.

In his preface to the printed version of *Johnson Over Jordan* Priestley said that here for the first time he tried to make use of all the resources of the theatre, including music and ballet.

The play explores that final experience in life – dying – not death, when the body surrenders, the heart ceases to beat but some inexplicable element remains to reflect on the person's whole life before he crosses into the unknown. There were many dimensions. The play concerns not only life after death, but the new life which Johnson's mediation of his old one enables him, with great pain and struggle, to choose. Implicit in so many Priestley plays is the theory that we can qualify to live our lives again if we have the moral courage and resource to examine the past with ruthless integrity. *I Have Been Here Before*, *Time and the Conways*, *Johnson Over Jordan*, all deal in this philosophical currency. Johnson walking into the blue immensity of Basil Dean's decor is not heading for Heaven or Hell, but for the possibility that some essence of whatever he had experienced in life may survive and live a different and better life. There were echoes of Gurdjieff whose preparation for death consisted in a gradual detachment from the ego in all its difficult aspects and an extension of non-identification in favour of essence.

The first act confronted Johnson with the Examiners and treated deep anxieties from recollections of his past. The second act, which cost Priestley considerable writing torment, was dominated by 'sensual, bestial and murderous tendencies' presented in highly symbolic form. In the night-club scene Johnson lusts after a young girl, stabs her young man, tears the veil from the girl's face and there – most dramatically – is his daughter. There are touches of autobiography running through the play but the play became something much more ambitious than a re-examination of his own life. Johnson was to be a man of our time, an emblematic figure of an ordinary citizen of the suburbs faced with the ultimate experience. Purged by remorse in the third act, Johnson realises what

Priestley calls 'his best self' to wander 'in and out of his own past' until the four-dimensional Johnson sets off on a 'new dimension of living'.[21]

Each scene was lit differently and a large cast interweaved music and dancing as an integral part of the action. Ambitious in its theme, the production flouted all the cost-benefit principles of commercial theatre and replaced the single sets and limited casts of earlier plays with twenty-three actors and many scenes.

Priestley took his greatest risk by writing Johnson's last speech in blank verse. If it lacked the authentic ring of nobility, Ralph Richardson delivered the speech with a grandiloquence which carried his audience away.

> Johnson: I have been a foolish, greedy and ignorant man;
> Yet I have had my time beneath the sun and stars:
> I have known the returning strength and sweetness of the
> seasons,
> Blossom on the branch and the ripening of fruit,
> The deep rest of the grass, the salt of the sea,
> The frozen ecstasy of mountains . . .
> But what have I done that I should have a better world,
> Even though there is in me something that will not rest
> Until it sees paradise . . .
>
> The Figure (gravely): Robert Johnson, it is time now . . .
>
> *He puts on his hat and is now ready to go. He looks up at The Figure doubtfully.*
>
> Johnson (hesitantly): Is it – a long way?
>
> The Figure (suddenly smiling like an angel): I don't know, Robert.
>
> Johnson (awkwardly): No . . . well . . . goodbye.

The Figure disappeared, the staircase vanished and there alone against the empty immensity of the brilliantly lit background, Johnson, diminished and forlorn, was carried away by the great surge of Britten's music as one instrument after another combined to overwhelm everything. The last scene never failed to bring a wave of applause as the curtain descended.

Basil Dean standing at the back of the pit on the first night was deeply moved: 'I found myself gulping down involuntary tears . . . In his curtain speech Jack made generous reference to my work.

---

21   *Johnson Over Jordan*, J. B. Priestley, epilogue, 129.

Coming on top of that emotional climax and all the cheering, it quite overwhelmed me. I ran away and hid myself in my office.'[22]

If expressionism can be described as emphasising emotion at the cost of intellectuality, realising doubt in place of faith, exploiting masks and special effects in the process, then *Johnson Over Jordan* is expressionistic, but the implacable streak of qualified optimism in Priestley gave a different note to the finale.

Press coverage was enormous and opinions chaotically contradictory. The *Times* critic summed up: 'a deeply conscious, impassioned and charitable attack upon a great subject and that in the theatre is more than half the world'.[23]

The *Observer* claimed that the play was Priestley's first failure.[24]

Already embattled with the critics, *Johnson Over Jordan* brought the argument into the open and even those who appreciated his work, like Ashley Dukes, were disappointed. According to David Hughes, Priestley too readily assumed 'that they had turned reactionary and were now too much enfeebled by bad plays to hold up the flag of progress and novelty in the theatre. But they were not hostile, merely disappointed.'[25]

H. G. Wells was ambivalent, voicing a number of objections in a letter written shortly after the play was produced. He concluded: 'Forgive these suggestions. I am the sort of man who would edit *Hamlet*.'[26]

Priestley commented in *Margin Released*: 'Apart from the fact that I often look and sound like a man ready to quarrel with anybody, I cannot understand why I was thought to dislike the critics so much. I did less wrangling with them in public than many other playwrights.'

Later gladiatorial exchanges were to put that statement in question. Meanwhile Bob Benchley, criticising *Johnson Over Jordan* in the *New Yorker*, concluded his notice: 'Now shoot me, Mr Priestley.'

22   *Mind's Eye*, Basil Dean, 269.
23   *The Times*, 23 February 1939.
24   *Observer*, 26 February 1939.
25   *J. B. Priestley*, David Hughes, 155.
26   H. G. Wells to Priestley, 23 February 1939.

# 18

# Broadcaster in the Second World War
## 1940–1

On that fateful Sunday, 3 September 1939, Priestley's wife was driving him from the Isle of Wight to London. He carried with him the manuscript of a popular novel, *Let the People Sing*,[1] deliberately designed to be read over the radio, and now they were hurrying to Broadcasting House to deliver the first instalment. It was a serene beautiful morning with sunshine reflected from the dazzling road, but the road seemed very quiet even for a Sunday morning. Approaching London, down the long hill from Bagshot they became aware of heavily loaded cars passing them at speed, but nothing happened until they entered the long narrow streets of Staines.

> It was then, clean out of a quiet blue, that all the sirens screamed at us. Beneath the astonished noonday sun, people in steel helmets came hurrying, shouting and gesticulating. It was then I learned we had been at war for the last hour.[2]

Taken by surprise, trapped in a traffic jam, 'I must confess', Priestley wrote, 'to having a moment of very real fear.' There was no parallel with the gangling young soldier in the First World War who had volunteered for service. A civilian fulfilling his round in the cheerful muddle of ordinary life, he could not envisage the immediate consequences, but he was 'for a moment terrified by the thought that it might be the worst I'd ever imagined, or, indeed, something unimaginable; a mumbling horror'.

No bombs fell that morning. The London they entered was already a strange new city of shelters, sandbags and first-aid posts, and the sudden conviction overtook him that the London he had left some seven weeks before 'had vanished for ever'. Arrived at the Highgate house, he packed a few belongings and began the short drive down 'through the long vacant roads of Kentish Town and

1 *Postscripts*, J. B. Priestley, 60–1.
2 ibid., 61.

Camden Town, which were as empty of life as old cities of the plague'.[3] Broadcasting House with its sandbags, checking points and studios deep in the bowels of the earth did revive First World War memories and the cup of putrid tea consumed in a canteen reminded him of the 'frowsty Brigade Headquarters in the reserve line'. There, settled at last before the microphone, wheezing a little from the long journey, he read the first instalment of *Let the People Sing*.

The novel uncannily anticipated the mood of the people and provided an inspiring catch-phrase which re-echoed when the attack on London finally began. It was a pot-boiling novel and watered down ingredients from *The Good Companions* which evoked the romance of a concert party in conflict with big business. Inspired, like H. G. Wells's novel *Mr Britling Sees It Through*, by a nation closing its ranks against the threat of the war, the emotional climate of the book fitted the mood of the moment.

In the ninth month of war Winston Churchill became Prime Minister and quickly formed a coalition government with Labour and Liberal leaders in the Cabinet. The collapse of France followed with the shock of an amputation. Then came Dunkirk and the story of the little ships crammed to sinking point bringing a whole army safely back home and accomplishing the undertaking with some slight dislocation of the service from the irritating attacks of German planes swarming across the Channel. These were the golden summer days when the thunder of battle in France could be heard in England and Priestley read one officer's report with astonishment. Approaching Dunkirk, the officer wrote, he saw 'what seemed to be vast black shadows on the pale sands' and could not momentarily determine their identity. As it grew lighter he saw that the blacknesses were enormous formations of men standing waiting. He saw them thus 'whenever he entered', 'coming or going. They did not seem to change; they did not seem to sit nor to lie down; they stood with the patience of their race waiting their turn.'

There followed the famous postscripts which were to reinforce Priestley's reputation in a quite different manner and convert him into an oracular figure whose gifts for stirring people's emotions in language intelligible to everybody was reinforced by his rugged personality and rich baritone voice. Replaying the postscripts, the Yorkshire accent does not seem pronounced, but his diction had a

3 ibid., 62.

rolling certainty which carried the conviction that he at least would remain undisturbed, whatever was brought against him.

In the earliest days of the war Jane remained with her husband at No. 3 The Grove and sent the children off to a remote cottage in Criccieth, Wales, where there were no threats of air raids. In September of 1940 she wrote a letter to Edward Davison which gave a vivid picture of their harassed life.[4] 'If you could see us this minute, I think you'd have to laugh. I am sitting on a mattress in the basement of my house in Highgate, and opposite on their mattresses are the cook and parlourmaid and on her left the housemaid with the Master of the House on my right.' There was just room for five mattresses, she said. Shored up by ten heavy wooden beams covered with fireproof paint, the basement was vaguely claustrophobic and reassuring. The windows which gave on to pantries and thence on to the basement area were covered with double wire netting. Every window was blacked out with thick curtains but in the shelter itself there were naked electric lights. 'It is now 10.30 p.m. The air raid sirens went just as we were finishing an early dinner . . . and ever since the anti-aircraft guns have been banging away like huge muffled drums.' They were, she wrote, all quite cheerful with the maids flushed with excitement, chatting and laughing among themselves. Jack had installed a typewriter in the next room and dodged in and out trying to finish an article but every time he settled down, the gunfire intensified. 'At the moment he has given it up and is back on his mattress.'[5]

Since the children were then all settled in schools in Wales they were considering shutting up the Highgate house for a few weeks because Jack found it difficult to get to and from the BBC. As we shall see, there were other reasons why Priestley needed to escape from family life and he easily accepted Jane's plan to take the maids and retire to the country.

Norman Collins has described how Priestley came into Broadcasting House late one Saturday night

> with his suitcase and typewriter, and on Sunday at 7.30 p.m. sat down at his typewriter with cotton wool in his ears to bash out yet another Sunday Home Service typescript. He'd put the pages of the script together then bash out another of similar length for North America. He'd finish the Home Service script for about 4.30 p.m. and the North American script for about 6.30. It was almost

4  Jane Priestley to Edward Davison, 11 September 1940.
5  ibid.

uncanny to watch . . . then he'd have a drink and broadcast the Home Service piece. Then at 2.30 a.m. he'd do the other. I can't remember that there was ever any need to revise the scripts. His attitude towards the finished piece was 'Why should I read through what I have written? I've written it.'[6]

Play-writing had familiarised him with the spoken word, he knew the actors' tricks for timing his phrases with just the right pauses between, and voice modulation came naturally to him. He was a born broadcaster, as one producer said. His first talk delivered on Wednesday 5 June 1940 opened:

I wonder how many of you feel as I do about this great Battle and evacuation of Dunkirk. The news of it came as a series of surprises and shocks, followed by equally astonishing new waves of hope . . . What strikes me about it is how typically English it is. Nothing, I feel, could be more English . . . both in its beginning and its end, its folly and its grandeur . . . We have gone sadly wrong like this before, and here and now we must resolve never, never to do it again . . . What began as a miserable blunder, a catalogue of misfortunes . . . ended as an epic of gallantry. We have a queer habit – and you can see it running through our history – of conjuring up such transformations . . .
      And to my mind what was most characteristically English about it . . . was the part played . . . not by the warships . . . but by the little pleasure-steamers. We've known them and laughed at them, these fussy little steamers, all our lives . . . These 'Brighton Belles' and 'Brighton Queens' left that innocent foolish world of theirs to sail into the inferno, to defy bombs, shells, magnetic mines, torpedoes, machine-gun fire – to rescue our soldiers.

An unpublished manuscript left by Jane claims that it was she who persuaded her husband to 'go to the BBC who were very glad to give him a programme'.[7] A woman with considerable drive, she then sought around for some direct wartime contribution which she herself could make and suddenly remembered her friend Lady Reading. She made contact with her and two days later Lady Reading telephoned and said, 'What we want most is someone who will start a hostel for [evacuated] children with their mothers.' The search for a suitable house began with no less splendid a possibility than Blenheim, but within forty-eight hours the implacably

6  *J. B. Priestley*, John Braine, 109.
7  Unpublished ms held by Tom Priestley.

powerful army had stepped in, taken over the palace and thwarted her plan. A furious Jane telephoned the War Office and in one long sentence spiced with suitable barbs re-told the story of the army's intervention in her private and public life. A month later came a telegram from the War Office saying that Broxwood Court in Hertfordshire had also fallen a victim to their relentless expansion but had proved incapable of coping with a whole regiment, with the result that they were now offering her the accommodation. So it came about that Jane began to organise a highly successful evacuee home, which was eventually to occupy all her energies.

Essayist, novelist, playwright, Priestley had now discovered yet another of the nine lives he eventually achieved – broadcasting. Only one person could match him – Churchill, but Churchill spoke with the aggressive personality of a war leader, using the accent and mannerisms of his class. Priestley, as rugged as Churchill was aggressive, seemed to speak from inside the ranks of the people themselves, using a voice with which they could identify. Vilifying Germans was obligatory in the war climate and he referred to them as thinking in terms only of Force and Fear, making great play with the differences between the English and German temperaments. His second talk on Sunday 9 June ended: 'what they don't understand, because there's nothing in their nature or experience to tell them, is that men also have their hour of greatness, when weakness suddenly towers into strength; when ordinary easy-going tolerant men rise in their anger and strike down evil like the angels of the wrath of God'.[8]

The appeal throughout was unashamedly patriotic, each aspect illustrated by telling vignettes crystallised around a single person. The third talk included this:

> going home the other night, there came the recollection of a tiny paragraph I'd seen in the papers that morning. It said that a German woman – like so many thousands of others, the hopelessly mentally distressed victim of Nazi persecution – had been found drowned in the Thames, and had left the following message: 'I have had much kindness in England, but I decided to leave this world. May England be victorious.' And I asked myself earnestly if really there was anything more to be said at this supreme hour than that.[9]

The *Daily Mail* commented that Mr Priestley's broadcasts were a

8  *Postscript*, J. B. Priestley, 18.
9  ibid., 5.

privilege. As the hours grew darker and longer his common sense and Yorkshire stoicism 'reflected the real and everlasting spirit of our race'.[10]

In nineteen broadcasts between 5 June and 20 October immediately after the peak period of the nine o'clock news, he built up an immense following which ranged between 30 per cent and 40 per cent of the adult population. The *Yorkshire Post* echoed the explanation given by the *Daily Mail*. It was the warm and reassuring voice of Mr Priestley which gave him a following almost equal to Mr Churchill's.[11]

Unaware as yet of the fate which was to overtake his Highgate house and Billingham Manor, Priestley moved into the Langham Hotel opposite Broadcasting House, which might have killed him but for one of those perverse twists of fortune which enlivened several of his plays. In September 1940 he had finished two broadcasts on the Sunday and was due to give another on the Tuesday, which made him think of having an early night. An urgent message came from Canada House asking for a special talk to the Canadians on the Blitz. 'Growling and cursing' he agreed, and left the Langham for Broadcasting House. He told the story in another postscript broadcast on 18 September.

> Good evening. I don't know if you're interested but last night I had a very lucky escape. You might as well hear about it because after all it's part of the war, and in any case until I've got this story off my chest I'm quite incapable of talking about anything else. The night's air raid began and the bombs sounded loud and near. They seemed to be concentrating on our part of London. Then rumours of what was happening outside began to circulate as usual, and soon I heard that an hotel had been hit. A little later I heard that *my* hotel had been hit, not all of it, apparently, but one wing. I spent some odd moments then wondering *which* wing had been hit . . .

After a not very comfortable night he interrupted some intermittent dozing by getting up in the 'weird small hours' from time to time. Then, when it was fully daylight, he went out into shattered streets and made his way to the Langham only to discover that his own room had been destroyed by one of the bombs. He would not have missed the sight of the hotel entrance that morning 'for anything'. Everybody had been evacuated and when Priestley

10  *Daily Mail*, 2 July 1930.
11  *Yorkshire Post*, 16 July 1940.

arrived they were drifting back in groups conveying the successful conclusion of a 'landing on a well-watered tropical island after a recent shipwreck'. If the guests were somewhat dishevelled, there, standing at the entrance hall, welcoming everybody was the little manager, an unruffled figure immaculately dressed in morning coat and striped trousers with an impeccable manner. He spoke with a creamy smoothness in his voice – 'Good morning, sir, good morning, madam. Ah yes . . . Your room is number . . . I'm afraid you won't be able to return there. Well, no, sir, there's no breakfast but we hope to be able to arrange some lunch . . . Certainly, sir, the barber's shop is open . . . '

Priestley commented: 'I hope you discover in all this, as I certainly do, a kind of heroism just as much to be admired in its smooth morning coat and striped trousers style as the cheerful dauntless heroism of so many of our East End folk.'[12]

Dashing from one appointment to another Priestley frequently slept in his clothes and his family life became completely disrupted. Two days after he escaped the bomb, feeling tired, sweaty and dispirited he encountered Edward Hulton, the publisher of *Picture Post*, who invited him to relax in the comparative luxury of the shelter beneath his Mayfair home. A steamy bath was followed by a quick retreat to the basement where he prepared to sleep between fresh clean sheets, only to hear the fire alarm ringing. An incendiary had dropped and the house was on fire.

The bright eye of danger 'never fascinated' Priestley. 'If I am not quite a coward, I am much closer to being one than I am to being any sort of hero.' Yet those disturbed nights with death distributed indiscriminately became enjoyable and he liked living in the West End where 'we were all an improvement on our unendangered selves'. This Puritan streak of self-improvement ran through more episodes in his plays than it did in his early life, but it was something after which he constantly sought.

In *Margin Released* he satirised this characteristic. More than half the English confronted with sacrifice, insecurity, direct danger or disaster could survive reasonably well, but boredom produced fear and detestation. 'They should be offered crises, not guarantees of prosperity and security.'[13] They were now offered anger, insecurity and impoverishment in unequal proportions and following his dictum a large part of the nation rose to the occasion. Before an

12   *Postscripts*, 18 September 1940.
13   *Margin Released*, J. B. Priestley, 220.

official storm of protest developed about his broadcasts he wrote to Jane.

Darling Jane,
They say you hadn't a comfortable night. I do hope it wasn't too bad. Anyhow it won't last long. No news here. I've done my B.B.C. talk and lunched with Barnes who read it and liked it very much. I sent off all the postcards and Angela rang up last night and I gave her the news. Dorothy rang up. She's waiting for news of you. Barbara has had to go to Barnet today. You are in my thoughts – nice tender thoughts – all the time, my love, and I am hoping this first difficult period will be soon over for you.
With much love,
JACK[14]

Jane had by now been evacuated with the youngest children to the country. Another letter followed in August.

My dear love,
Forgive my typing, but there's a lot to say and I feel my handwriting would be more than usually weird this morning . . . I wired you this morning because there was a little air raid early this morning – about 3 a.m. it started, just as I was getting off to sleep after my late broadcast, and I believe a few bombs were dropped in N.E. London. I had heard the planes and some crashes, fairly distant, some time before the alarm went. When it did go, we all trooped down to the basement and sat there, yawning, on kitchen chairs. It lasted about three-quarters of an hour. Everybody here quite cool.
Getting back to the strain of this job, I feel more than ever that we must get a little place for me – Albany or somewhere – not too far from the B.B.C. And our country place, if possible, should be away from air raid sirens, so there's at least a chance of a few quiet nights every week or so. I'd a terrific long day yesterday, working steadily from nine in the morning without a break until seven at night, then I dined with Frere and another man from the Min. of Labour, then went to the B.B.C. So you can imagine that by the time I got to sleep this morning, almost daylight, I was pretty weary. But I've a slacker day today, am going down to the Westminster to see a rehearsal this afternoon, then seeing Peters about various things, then I trust home very early to bed . . .
A great mass of correspondence of all sorts here, but no really important news. The *Sunday Express* want me to do a series of six

14 Priestley to Jane Priestley, dated 'Thursday' (1940).

articles for them at seventy-five pounds each, very good pay for wartime. I suppose we really oughtn't to bother too much about these bits of rents, so long as we can settle ourselves properly. What I don't want to do, of course, is to be landed with a long lease . . . Not much of you and me in this letter, my love, but I think about you all the time, and am longing for you to be settled in a place you like so that we can at least have two quiet days a week together, in a little bit of sanity in this vast madhouse. My love to you and to all the children.

Your loving JACK[15]


As we shall see, within a year Priestley's Keir Hardie socialism was to harden into much more systematic form, but by late 1940 the establishment already suspected the motives behind his broadcasts. Colonel Scorgie of the Ministry of Information and Lord Davidson ex-chairman of the Conservative Party both complained about their content and tone. Priestley's first response was to write to the Director General, F. W. Ogilvie, stating that by far the greater majority of the 1,600 letters he had received between June and October were enthusiastic.[16] By September occasional critical sallies had hardened into 'deep concern' about his 'left-wing views'. Sir Richard Maconachie, head of talks, echoed comments made by Norman Birkett who pointed to a form of left-wing bias in the postscripts. Priestley, Maconachie wrote to Ryan, the Home adviser, had 'definite social and political views which he puts over in his broadcasts and through these broadcasts is, I think, exercising an important influence on what people are thinking. These views may be admirable or otherwise, but the question which I wish to raise is whether any single person should be given the opportunity of acquiring such an influence to the exclusion of others who differ from him merely on the grounds of his merits as a broadcaster, which are, of course, very great.'[17]

George Barnes, director of the Third Programme, replied that 'soft soap will not raise home morale'. 'Complacency in a regular weekly speaker', he said, 'is the attitude best calculated to irritate the public and create distrust in the Government and the B.B.C.'[18]

Any idea that his first series of postscripts was arbitrarily stopped

15  Priestley to Jane Priestley, 23 August 1940.
16  Priestley to Ogilvie, 2 August 1930; quoted in *The History of Broadcasting in the United Kingdom*, Asa Briggs, 211.
17  Maconachie to Ryan, 6 September 1940.
18  Barnes to Maconachie, 10 July 1940.

by the BBC because Priestley laced patriotism with socialism was contradicted by the opening of his final talk:

> This is my last Sunday postscript for some time, perhaps the last I shall ever do. The decision was mine and was in no way forced upon me by the BBC . . . I had some good reasons for wanting to stop; in the first place people get tired of hearing the same voice at exactly the same time each week.

In the second place the whole situation in the country and people's reaction to it had changed:

> As many of you will remember, I began these postscripts just after Dunkirk . . . when France collapsed and we were threatened with immediate invasion, and world opinion began to think we were doomed. We knew very well that we weren't doomed, and our people began to show the world what stuff they're made of.[19]

Another aspect of the broadcasts which alarmed the establishment was his inability to suppress the truth about the war situation which included some harsh facts not calculated, in Ogilvie's eyes, to improve morale. There followed a letter from Priestley to talks organiser Marjorie Wace in October 1940 which gave another interpretation of the sudden cessation of the talks. Admitting that he was feeling the strain of irregular hours and snatched meals, Priestley said he had decided to stop broadcasting for a while because he was 'more and more disappointed with a Government which does not make the big imaginative gesture needed at this juncture'.[20]

Official hostility built up powerfully when Priestley proposed a second series of broadcasts in November 1941. Six fortnightly feature programmes were to be launched under the title *The Long Road Home* with subtitles 'Freedom'; 'Security'; 'Money'; 'The Enemies'; 'Two Types of Great Men'; 'The Kingdom of Heaven'. Asa Briggs in his history of the BBC stated that: 'The Minister of Information had given his approval subject to the clear understanding that Priestley would not be allowed greater liberty in this setting than in the others.'[21]

Ogilvie immediately objected on the grounds that the proposal 'strayed so undeniably into politics that the whole idea should be

19  *Postscripts*, J. B. Priestley, 97.
20  Priestley to Marjorie Wace, 9 October 1940.
21  Quoted by Briggs from the Home Board Minutes, 29 November 1940.

rejected'.[22] Priestley then suggested substituting a series of talks to replace the feature programmes but insisted on having the Sunday night nine o'clock spot. A deputation from the 1922 Committee at once protested to Duff Cooper and Churchill himself 'complained that the first [talk] expressed war aims which were in conflict with those of the Prime Minister'.[23] Whether Priestley's war aims differed from the Prime Minister's was irrelevant to his audience and the first broadcast in the new series brought over 1,000 appreciative letters with some 200 which were critical.

One passage in the 21 July broadcast typified the material which upset the establishment:

We cannot go forward and build up this new world order, and this is our war aim, unless we begin to think differently . . . one must stop thinking in terms of property and power and begin thinking in terms of community and creation. Take the change from property to community. Property is the old-fashioned way of thinking of a country as a thing, and a collection of things in that thing, all owned by certain people and constituting property; instead of thinking of a country as the home of a living society with the community itself as the first test.

The establishment retaliated with a talk by Sir Archibald Southby which did little else than criticise Priestley and a Listener Research report was initiated to discover the public's real reaction. Taking one highly controversial contribution called 'Meditations in a Railway Train' they found that seventeen listeners out of twenty approved of Priestley without qualification. Surprisingly, Duff Cooper as Minister of Information defended Priestley's right to broadcast but wanted the series to stop at six, and later proposed varying the speakers.

A minute from Ryan to Walter Monckton, on 18 March 1941, said: 'Priestley series stopping . . . on instructions of Minister.'[24] Whether Churchill brought his personal influence to bear remains unclear. The real truth still cannot be told. The crucial Ministry of Information files – the Prime Minister's personal minutes to the minister – remain offically closed for many more years. Even Martin Gilbert, Churchill's official biographer, could find no hard

22  Ogilvie to Duff Cooper, 11 December 1940.
23  *The History of Broadcasting in the United Kingdom*, Asa Briggs, 321.
24  Home Board Minutes, 21 March 1941.

evidence.[25] The result of Ryan's minute was swift. A. P. Herbert, a pleasant, liberally minded writer, took over the Sunday Night postscripts. Priestley bluntly told the BBC that they had abandoned their most successful talk feature and refused to contribute any more talks 'to any service whatsoever'.

Whenever the question of fees arose Priestley's internal relations with BBC officials became combative. Paid for six half-hour broadcasts as much as an ordinary worker received in a year, he still expressed dissatisfaction since newspapers were prepared to treble these fees. Moreover, one regional security officer wondered why he was paid at all because his views – he claimed – could not be distinguished fundamentally from those of his rival Lord Haw-Haw on German radio. National Socialism attacked straightforward capitalism and believed in revolution, a combination of views which – the regional officer imagined – were shared by Priestley. Political naïvety, prejudice, vindictiveness all at different times characterised attacks on Priestley, but the secret Monitoring Intelligence Unit had more factual complaints. Occasionally they claimed Priestley's words were quoted by German radio for propaganda purposes. The unit reported this fact to the Minister of Information and he informed Churchill.

Priestley's summing up of the whole situation occurs in *Margin Released*.

> I received two letters – I kept them for years but may have lost them now – one was from the Ministry of Information, telling me that the BBC was responsible for the decision to take me off the air, and the other was from the BBC, saying that a directive had come from the Ministry of Information to end my broadcasts.[26]

In later years he regarded the reputation built up by the broadcasts as inflated but in the middle of the war whenever he entered a shop or bar, immediately he spoke his voice was recognised. People were driven not only to talk to him but, if they could achieve it without too much intrusion, touch him, as if by the laying on of hands they could prove that he was more than a disembodied voice. Literally thousands of times, hands were discreetly and sometimes indiscreetly disposed about his person.

Priestley's correspondence continued apace. A letter to Gene

25  Letter to the author, 12 March 1986.
26  *Margin Released*, J. B. Priestley, 221.

Saxton, a member of his American publishers Harper & Row said:

Dear Gene,

. . . I have just begun the actor novel, which I have titled *THESE OUR ACTORS* – the familiar phrase from Prospero's speech of course. This title can be changed for America, if necessary. I am aware of the bookseller's prejudice against theatrical novels. (It was rubbed into me hard when I was writing *The Good Companions*.) There has not, so far as I know, ever been a serious intelligent novel about an actor. It is not my intention in this novel to make the mistake made by most theatrical people – namely, to assume that the reader is equally interested in the Theatre. The values will be different from those in ordinary theatrical writing. This actor of mine is a real artist, always haunted by a vision of what the Theatre – or life itself, for that matter – might be, and never able to realise it. He is a very intelligent fellow (modelled to some extent on my friend, Ralph Richardson). I am writing this novel to get a lot of stuff out of my own system, just as I wrote the autobiographical books – and *not* as I have written novels these last few years – and my attitude is *LIKE IT OR LUMP IT*. But I believe you will like it very much because I shall put a lot of myself into it and you don't dislike me. (I am not sure of this reasoning, though.) By the way, my reputation seems to be changing here. A few years ago I was that despised thing, the popular novelist, the best-seller, the rich mountebank, fair game for any young highbrow. But now they are all turning round, perhaps led by Desmond MacCarthy, and I receive solemn tributes from the solemn young. I think the autobiographical books and the experimental plays have done this. I believe it might pay you to change your note about me a little, dropping the references to *The Good Companions* period successes, and rather concentrating on the work of the last three years, linking it up perhaps – as is sometimes done here – with the Huxley-Heard critical attitude towards modern life etc. (Not that I entirely agree with them, but on the other hand my own explorations in some respects – such as those on the Time problem – have gone much further than theirs.) Or put it like this – rather more emphasis on the philosophical side and less on the pure entertainment side . . .

I don't think your explanation – that my work is outside the present New York pattern – really penetrated the mystery. It might possibly explain why the N.Y. critics all say they dislike my plays for *different reasons*. But what is so strange is that no people have been more enthusiastic about them in London than Americans who have said to me over and over again: 'Wait till they see this in New York!' Also, my serious and experimental plays arouse more enthusiasm abroad than they do in London, so it is not that they are too English. My own feeling is that the plays are not easy for N.Y. critics to like – even if one of their pet Irishmen wrote them, they would still have to make an effort – and that as they have made up their minds that I am an obstreperous Englishman of the most irritating type, they are not even going to try to make the effort – the hell with him! It's very important because I feel at the moment that it's no use offering New York any more plays until the critics are prepared to give them a little intelligent consideration, and there are several good ones, *JOHNSON, MUSIC AT NIGHT*, and two new ones, that America hasn't seen. Will one of you please do this?

Yours ever,

J.B.P.

P.S. You haven't all the big figures over there. Foyle's Book Club here have chosen *LET THE PEOPLE SING* (which is, by the way, the name of a song now in Cochran's revue) for next Christmas, and have ordered a modest 175,000 copies. Let's hope the paper holds out. (I take this to be a confidential matter, so don't use it yet.)[27]

Another letter to the Editorial Director of his American publisher in April 1940 said:

Dear Cass,

After doing 30,000 words (and good words too, some of 'em) of the actor novel, I have decided to abandon it. My reasons are as follows: this was to have been a serious novel about the Theatre, and I have come to the conclusion that such a novel must necessarily be too narrow and technical for the great majority even of intelligent readers; and again the Theatre is such a small world that it would be difficult to persuade people you were not taking everybody from life. So it's off. And you can imagine that after doing 30,000 words in blood and sweat and tears at a time like this, I don't abandon them lightly.

I want to do a novel as soon as I can find a subject that lends itself to big serious treatment (unless it's a definite advance on my previous novels it's not worth doing), but as you can imagine at a time like this the choice of subject is very difficult – not the background or the people but the *period* is the snag. I should like something that covers a great many years but not in a straightforward 'Milestones' fashion, but obliquely, like Proust, whom I'm re-reading with great joy.

Meanwhile I have enough material for a sequel to *MIDNIGHT* and *GODSHILL*, very good material too – descriptive and reflec-

27 Priestley to Gene Saxton, 27 March 1940.

254

tive – and am thinking of setting to work on it and calling the book *SLOW TRAIN THROUGH THE BLACKOUT*, that being the setting I would choose, as my shack was the setting of *Midnight* and a day in my study here was the setting of *Rain upon Godshill*. Perhaps I had better add that my plan roughly is that there should be four of these books altogether, under one covering title, making I think a noble piece of work. I have always seen the fourth book set in a forest of great redwoods in California, but God knows now if I'll ever find my way there.

It takes me most of my morning to recover from the effects of my morning's mail, for nearly every morning the Poles send me fresh news of Nazi horrors (this morning it was details of Polish girls sent off by the thousand to military brothels), pacifists ask me why we can't come to a nice gentlemanly agreement with Hitler, economic theorists tell me it's all the fault of the bankers or the landlords, there are urgent requests to help this person or that cause, and one seems to be living in a vast madhouse. If I hadn't so many people dependent upon me and so many decent irons in the fire, I'd gladly do some simple clear-cut job in one of the fighting services; but I have a profound conviction that this time I must keep clear of that and try to do what I can on the civilian side. With best wishes to you all,

Yours ever,

J.B.P.[28]

If a by-election had opened the way for Priestley as a candidate for the House of Commons at this time he might have won a large majority and changed his career for a number of years. Indeed two Labour organisers tried to persuade him to speak at a series of public meetings and, although he refused, very early in 1941 he became chairman of the 1941 Committee. This was a body described as 'a sort of Leftist Brains Trust with progressive' political views. Asa Briggs found a terse comment from a BBC official written across a press cutting from the *Evening Standard* describing the formation of the committee. 'This looks bad.'[29]

It was in March 1941 that Beatrice Webb wrote in her diary:

Priestley is the dominant literary personality of the England of today; he has outdistanced the aged H. G. Wells and G. B. S. owing to his superlative gift for broadcasting.

28  Priestley to Cass Canfield, 29 April 1940.
29  *Evening Standard*, 16 January 1941, quoted in *The History of Broadcasting in the United Kingdom*, Asa Briggs, 322.

Then came this garbled interpretation of Priestley's political views:

> He is revolutionary left and exhorts the Labour leaders to leave off kow-towing to reactionary groups of big capitalists and aristo-cratic landlords led by Winston Churchill and the puppet King and Queen. He comes out boldly for complete Socialism. He never mentions the U.S.S.R. or Soviet Communism. I doubt whether he has any notion of what should be the manifest structure of a Socialist state.[30]

As we shall see, echoes of these remarks were shortly to be picked up and reinforced in Priestley's relationship with Sir Richard Acland.

Very much under Priestley's influence, the 1941 Committee produced a preliminary statement called 'We Must Win' which called for a declaration of national 'ideas and objectives after the war'. This brought him into direct conflict with Churchill who refused to commit himself to any precise post-war aims. As Priestley himself admitted in *Out of the People*, severe criticism of his views did arise from ordinary people.[31] Moreover, he was at odds with two Labour members of the coalition government, Sir Stafford Cripps and Ernest Bevin, both believing that 'loyalty and restraint' should be exercised until the war was won. This early clash with Labour Party leaders was to rumble on into the 1945 election.

Meanwhile Priestley became involved in organising writers for the war effort. His Writers' Committee was the logical outcome of the Authors' Planning Committee set up on 28 July 1939 six weeks before the invasion of Poland. Under the chairmanship of Raymond Needham KC, it included Priestley's agent, A. D. Peters, R. H. S. Crossman, A. P. Herbert, Dorothy Sayers and Kilham Roberts. Possibly as a result of the prolonged phoney war nothing positive emerged from the Authors' Planning Com-mittee and in May 1940 it was dissolved. Initiative then passed into the hands of Priestley, and a new group was formed called the Authors' National Committee with a very impressive array of names.[32]

Two very distinguished writers refused to join and George Bernard Shaw wrote:

30 *Diaries*, Vol. 4, Beatrice Webb, entry for 11 March 1941.
31 *Out of the People*, J. B. Priestley.
32 *Authors by Profession*, Vol. II, Victor Bonham Carter, 60–2.

My dear Priestley,

Evidently you have never been on a Committee of Authors. I had ten years of it in the Society of Authors. In their books they are more or less delightful creatures according to taste. In committee, to call them hogs would be an insult to a comparatively co-operative animal.

Outside literature I have no special abilities which you could conscientiously advise the Government to employ. There are quite enough duffers in the national service already; and I am the prince of duffers except when I am doing what terrifies the Government and confirms its 'strange prejudice' (surely a very natural one) against an ungovernable profession.

So don't put my name down.

It is an author's business to find out and decide for himself what he can best do in a national emergency. Official direction is of no use to him: if he needs it or will submit to it he had better go into the barrack yard and form fours threes (?) until somebody shoots him. I am not that sort; and neither are you. For the moment there is nothing to do but fight, because until we make up what we have lost in the first round we cannot negotiate from a strong position; but when that phase is over and we have to state our terms, then we shall have some fun, you and I.

The broadcasts are a fearful waste of your time; but they are very enjoyable.

Always yours,

G.B.S.[33]

Max Beerbohm's response was very different. Of course, he wrote, he sympathised with the idea that Whitehall should no longer look askance at the possibilities of harnessing authors' talents in the war. Alas, his own talents were ill suited to such purposes. They were too delicate, personal and ironic, easily to accommodate great issues. Unexpected were the limitations of a style deeply ingrained from early youth.[34]

The committee attempted to persuade the Ministry of Information to attach authors to various services as if they were war correspondents or artists, with the intention of recording events in greater depth. Walter Monckton rejected this and the committee then asked 'William Collins if he and a group of publishers would undertake the publication of a series of short books dealing with the problems of reconstruction after the war'.[35] Collins embraced the

33  G. B. Shaw to Priestley, 1 August 1940.
34  Max Beerbohm to Priestley, 2 August 1940.
35  *Authors by Profession*, Vol. II, Victor Bonham Carter, 60–2.

idea enthusiastically and at once commissioned Priestley to write the first title, *Out of the People*. He produced this with alarming facility and met such a ready audience that by 1942, 41,000 copies of a print order of 50,000 had been sold. Further titles in the series were crippled by the growing shortage of paper and disagreement in the committee. Priestley made it quite clear that he believed in reforming society on socialist lines and at least three members of the committee – Margaret Storm Jameson, Professor John MacMurray and Denys Kilham Roberts – strongly resisted these aims. Priestley fought back but by now his grossly overcrowded programme of writing, broadcasting, lecturing and travelling gradually overwhelmed his work for the committee and the committee died a natural death.

The Common Wealth episode in Priestley's career is one which he preferred to forget, but Sir Richard Acland made available some fascinating unpublished material. He wrote:

> At this time (1941) another figure well known for his books and plays emerged as a powerful factor on the political stage . . . J. B. Priestley . . . Second only to Churchill and not far behind him, Priestley was responsible for sustaining the morale of the people through the worst months of the war . . . [His] thinking, though not identical to mine, was often parallel to it.

Acland then quoted the postscript of 21 July 1941 which was at the centre of the storm Priestley aroused.

In his unpublished reminiscences Acland wrote: 'In the very moment of hearing such a broadcast I knew that Priestley and I together could gather an enormously powerful political and social team.'[36]

A romantic figure driven by the highest ideals, Acland had conceived a new political party to be known as Common Wealth whose aims were crystallised in its title. He spelt out his programme in *The Forward March*, audaciously published in the middle of the war. Common ownership was desirable not for its own sake nor because of alleged greater efficiency, but because it was the essential prerequisite of a new society.[37]

As early as 1940 he had already invited Priestley and Wells to join him but Wells regarded his thinking as extravagant and 'hated his

36  From an unpublished account of his political life written by Richard Acland to his son, 1977–8.
37  *The Forward March*, Richard Acland.

guts'. As Acland wrote: 'He exploded in anger saying I should flounder like an imitation Hitler' and then 'I suppose we should hear less of you'.

Priestley's response was friendly but he disagreed with Acland's tactics. Acland suggested that Priestley should speak at a series of meetings sponsored by no particular organisation but having loose associations with the left. Priestley expressed dislike for meetings but 'offered to work on a short forcible memorandum to the War Cabinet with representative signatures'. The memorandum would be 'accompanied by the threat of launching a new party'.[38] Acland claimed that this was Priestley's 'conventional response to people who turned to him to take a lead'. One letter written by Priestley soon after he had settled on the name of the 1941 Committee deserved, in Acland's view, to be set out in full.

> In your demand for first, a changed attitude and second, an immediate proof of a changed attitude I am actually more in sympathy with your standpoint than with that of most of the members of the 1941 Committee. (But don't forget that my primary job is still to hold the thing together.) Even if it only ticks over or flounders about until the war is over, its very existence will then be of immense value. Unfortunately it is a tough job for a very busy man just keeping everybody more or less together and not flying off at tangents, and it shouldn't be necessary for me to inject life into the thing.[39]

Since Priestley was not considering any fundamental change in society during the war he presented no programme to the 1941 Committee, but he pointed to a central weakness in Acland's position.

> There are two questions that you should be prepared to answer. It is certain that many people in this country will oppose Common Ownership. All right – what do you do with them? Obviously you can't have secret police, summary arrests, concentration camps and the rest. So what do you do with these determined obstructionists? The second question is this – can this country which is overcrowded and far from self-supporting afford to make a clean break with international capitalism – I mean even allowing for a lower standard of living for a few years? I don't know. I'm not an economist. But I always feel we are so highly industrialised and by temperament such

38  From an unpublished account of his political life written by Richard Acland to his son, 1977–8.
39  ibid.

a wasteful careless people that our position is always precarious. We are like an elaborate machine which could so easily go wrong.[40]

On 26 July 1941 Acland took two rooms in the St Ermin's Hotel near St James's Park and representatives of Forward March and the 1941 Committee met to form Common Wealth. There followed a short honeymoon period quickly broken into when Common Wealth began to sympathise more with Forward March than the 1941 Committee, and Priestley wrote again to Acland:

Do not imagine that I regard you as the villain of the piece. You have done nothing that I did not think you would do. But it was to my mind extremely important that Common Wealth should seem quite different from Forward March because I felt it very important we should attract political figures who might have joined the 1941 Committee but never the Forward March. Thus I felt that if one of the old strains should have to take predominance, it was much better for sound political reasons that it should be 1941. But it has gone the other way.

The crunch came on 28 September and Acland wrote to his wife Anne:

Priestley has finally resigned and I must say I find his behaviour incredible . . . At midnight I was rung up from Bristol saying Priestley unable to speak as he has resigned . . . My only conclusion is that he wanted us to be on the phone begging him to stay on as chairman. I do not need to say that a gloomy company gathered at Gower Street on September 30th in response to frantic telephone calls.

Two dinner meetings with Labour representatives discussing a possible compromise led nowhere and Priestley left the first meeting with the comment, 'Well, goodnight. I must go. It's like being the poor relation of a silly old rich lady.' At the second meeting Priestley once more spoke forcefully in a manner which pleased Acland.

The tortured negotiations which followed become boring in detail. Suffice it to say that at the most important meeting, Acland called upon Priestley to speak. He rose and said:

I have been silent for half an hour as you may have noticed. But I can only say that I see it this way. This country cannot now maintain its

40   ibid.

greatness on any compromise with capitalism whatever. You've got three elements. The Tories – well we all know about them. They're over there and they are not the most dangerous. The most dangerous are those who pretend that in some painless way you can put together a little bit of this and a little bit of something else (manoeuvring two brandy glasses with a ferocious glare) and get a lovely solution to please everyone. You can't. This country is up against a chasm. Either you cross it or you go right down there. And you have got to do it in one. There may have been days for gradualism but those days are not now.[41]

Acland wrote in his diary how much further forward they would have been if Priestley had made such a speech when the 1941 Committee was considering by-elections two years before.

Late in September Priestley called a conference of the 1941 Committee and Acland wrote to his wife:

The . . . Committee was breathtaking. We've never had such a triumph at any time . . . Morning session a terribly dull American bored everyone to tears with talk of Anglo-American-Soviet world co-operation. Thunderous and unnecessarily prolonged applause. In the afternoon Hulton – meandering – and an awful little man called Balogh, terribly conceited and laying down the law on utterly non-moral economic trivialities. Then I had ten minutes – and I was utterly amazed. The same thunderous applause . . . The after-tea sub-committee on economics where Balogh again held forth almost uninterrupted for an hour. He's an awful man. He's bedevilled the 1941 Committee.

In the end the 1941 Committee also bedevilled Priestley. He emerged from continuous meetings and entanglements with nothing resolved. The whole Common Wealth episode left Priestley uneasy since the role of revolutionary sat uncomfortably on his so English shoulders.

41   ibid.

# 19

# Another Love Affair
## 1942–4

Two events broke into Priestley's already confused private life in 1941 to complete its disruption. An agitated telephone call came through to Highgate from the gardener's wife at Billingham. The Black Watch, she said, had commandeered Billingham and refused to let her enter the house. They were, she said 'wrecking things', a warning all too accurate in the light of subsequent events. Behaving with near barbarity they stole and looted, gave Jane's clothes away and 'lost' an Augustus John painting. Shortly afterwards a land mine dropped on the church near the house at Highgate, damaged the roof and made that, too, uninhabitable. No one was resident at the time.

Barbara Wykeham, Priestley's eldest daughter, spelt out what happened to the family.

> We were at boarding-school at the beginning of the war, except for Angela who went to the Oxford Playhouse (ENSA). I went from school to the Anti-Aircraft in 1941 . . . Sylvia went to Slade in Oxford, then joined the Wrens . . . Mary left school at sixteen and went to the Royal College of Music. We were completely homeless during the war which was very bad for Tom and Rachel and their parents. They lodged at one of Mummy's hostels for bombed-out babies. She took furnished cottages for holidays.[1]

Overwhelmed with family problems, telephone calls, battles with the establishment, political activities, writing and broadcasting, Priestley moved between the Langham Hotel, a flat in Whitehall Court and Herefordshire, but London remained the centre of his life. Parted from his wife and children, his freedom facilitated infidelity which expressed itself in something much more serious than a passing affair. Thrown into close contact with one of his BBC producers – Mary Hope Allen (now Mary Merrington) – it was inevitable that he would develop a relationship with someone

---

1 Barbara Wykeham to the author, 15 August 1986.

so vivacious and attractive. Mary Hope Allen had been evacuated with part of the BBC staff to Manchester where she occupied a depressing billet with a rich grocer. After lunch one day at the BBC she entered the lift and just as the gates were closing Priestley slipped in. Since he was the last in he was the first out, but he waited as Mary Allen walked past him towards her office. Following her he accosted her and said, 'I know you.' Mary Allen replied, 'I don't think you do.' 'Yes I do – nearly twenty years ago you were at every theatre first night with people like Herbert Farjeon and Hubert Griffiths and I remember in the intervals – seeing you – your face blazing like a lighthouse.'[2]

An invitation to dinner at the Midland Hotel followed and a sense of rapport brought them closer. There followed another dinner at the Midland with Sir Basil Cameron sitting at the next table looking enviously across at two people full of vital talk and laughter. At last Cameron said, 'Can I come over and sit at your table?' They agreed, he joined them and immediately he explained: 'I've got my first violin and his pianist and he will talk about nothing but pianistic hygiene.'

The trio enjoyed the remainder of an hilarious evening. Mary Hope Allen recalls that Jack was completely without the sense of the great man of letters. Since his postscripts had made him so famous that people stopped him in the street, and just to touch him was a thrill, it became an unusual exercise in modesty.[3]

Writing to the present author, Mary Hope Allen described her early reaction to Priestley. Thank goodness he was not the 'cross-patch' she had expected and she need not dread producing the series of talks. He escorted her back to a house which she shared with a friend in Platt's Lane where he gave her 'a rather lingering hug which . . . by that time did not surprise' her.[4]

Her next memory concerned the first night of his series which she had been sent back to London to produce.

> I remember walking down a sort of plank path from Broadcasting House above Portland Place . . . before rehearsal and talking and laughing and getting on so well . . . Nicholls . . . a high up Director of Programmes had lent me his grand office from 8 to 11.50 p.m. to receive my daily set of 'Famous People' . . . I remember that summer evening standing in front of Nicholls' desk with the sun

2  Interview with Mary Hope Allen, now Mary Merrington, 26 February 1986.
3  ibid.
4  Mary Hope Allen to the author, June 1985.

pouring through the window as Jack put his arm round me and said 'This is custom-made – you fit just over my heart.'[5]

Gladys Young, the actress, had lent Mary her Thurloe Place house while she was in the rep at Manchester and Jack came to visit her there. Unaware that anyone was in residence, the air raid warden noticed a light in the house, repeatedly rang the bell and demanded entrance. Mary Hope Allen did not identify Priestley but simply said she had a visitor and – tactfully – the air raid warden retreated. During the whole of her relationship with Priestley there was no mention of or any discussion about his wife. 'I didn't and don't even now know her Christian name.' Priestley did disclose that he had a delightful stepdaughter and told a story about his son Tom, once again without naming him. The boy had opened the drawing-room door one night and finding a party in progress stood silent in the doorway. Cooing noises were made by the guests and the child said: 'Not speakin'. Jack said to Mary Hope Allen, 'I've often felt like that.'[6]

They became lovers and their relationship ran on for five years. In those years Priestley wrote letter after letter, sometimes on railway stations in the black-out, sometimes in cafés and hotels. The letters poured out on a tide of love. On one occasion he wrote to her, 'When you are depressed or miserable remember what I wrote to you in these letters from the oddest places. That may lift your spirits.' Mary Allen said: 'In that dark depressing world of black-outs and bombs and rationing – as you can imagine – it was bliss.'

She conveyed the impression that she had undergone an experience which remained imprinted indelibly in her memory. Not even the inconvenient rendezvous they were forced to use to avoid publicity diminished their relationship.

Some of Priestley's letters to Mary Allen were written from Broxwood Court where Jane ran her hostel for evacuated children.

I'm wrestling with the third Act of my play and liking neither it nor myself doing it.[7] I suppose the trouble really is there isn't sufficient incentive, and I don't care enough. It brings me not one glimmer of creative joy. (Though oddly enough that doesn't always mean a thing's bad, just as the presence of live joy doesn't

5  ibid.
6  ibid.
7  *They Came to a City.*

always mean a thing's good. Indeed, sadly enough, some of the worst writers and artists are those who enjoy working the most.)

Did I tell you I had a most unsatisfactory letter from Ogilvie?[8] I wrote a long and sharp reply, but then tore it up. It's a strange position I'm in – On record I'm the best propagandist in the country, both for here and overseas – and here I am, doing nothing – (I believe there was a Cabinet Meeting today to come to some decision about the Min. of Inform.)

Returned to London he continued to write letters to his wife. Late in December he wrote from the Mount Royal Hotel, Marble Arch:

Darling Jane,

This is chiefly to say that I shall be coming home by the 9.45 on Saturday, as I have to record my American talks for Dec. 25th and Jan. 1st on Friday afternoon. This week will be a terrible rush – with the Oakroyd programme to be rehearsed tomorrow and recorded Tuesday, then my last Notebook on Thursday – also a meeting with the Co-op people about the possible play and in addition must still write my third American talk and an article for Reynolds for Friday – and I've written two talks and an article this weekend. Last Tuesday was a terrific day, as I had to rehearse in the morning, finish my Oakroyd script in the afternoon, rehearse and go on the air till nine, then sit down and do an entirely different American talk (because of their declaration of war) and do it at 2.30. I'll try to get a few odds and ends of presents for the older children this week. The play is going well in Bradford but I have decided to do a certain amount of re-writing and re-casting before it opens in London, probably at the New early in February. I shan't have time, I don't think, to have a word with Fuller and Muggeridge, but my feeling is that America's entry into the war will dry up the funds for the hostels. I am hoping to be at Broxwood (at Mrs Exley's) for at least a fortnight and am looking forward to the rest and being with you and the children. I shall be very tired by Saturday.

Much love, JACK[9]

Despite her special relationship, Priestley grumbled – as usual – to Mary Hope Allen about the war, its leaders, the BBC, its producers, the food, the black-out, the bombs and, above all, the unbelievable ingenuity with which the whole vast war effort concentrated on creating his inconvenience.

8   Director General of the BBC.
9   Priestley to Jane Priestley, December 1941.

Later in life he claimed to be an inveterate grumbler. The record of his life going back to early childhood established the fact indisputably. He envisaged himself as some programmed malcontent convinced that he had been sent to the wrong planet. His sagging face, saurian eye, weighty underlip and deep rumbling voice all contributed to that image. Money could not buy a better grumbling outfit, but he was to claim much later in life that he 'always sounded much worse' than he felt. 'When I am displeased – but not when I am pleased . . . for some reason . . . I tend to overact my part. Often when I am merely annoyed, a little put out, I appear to be blazingly angry or lost in the deepest sulks.'[10]

Family life became more difficult as the war advanced. Jane remained at Broxwood while Tom and Rachel divided their time between Broxwood, boarding-school and Joyce Cary's cottage.[11] According to all available evidence Jane never took advantage of her freedom, which remained relative because of her work and the children, but she was still an attractive woman.

The complex pressures surrounding Priestley's life might easily have crushed out his writing in the war. Instead he wrote no less than four plays and seven books, and if the books were unimportant in the sweep of his work, one, at least, of the plays reinforced the language of the postscripts and came as an inspiration to thousands of young people trapped in a war to which they saw no end.

*They Came to a City* represented Priestley's dream of a socialist society where justice, wealth and truth were equally distributed. Such high aims were difficult to realise dramatically, and any condensation of *They Came to a City* must violate its nature, but put at its simplest the play opens outside the dream city with a group of people waiting to enter. The nine characters, a rough cross-section of English society, have all arrived by mysterious means to coincide and they speculate about the nature of the city whose gates are closed against them.

The bright sunlight turns to purple night, night to a soft dawn and there the gates are slowly rolling back and the nine characters enter. In the second act they emerge once more from the city having spent a day among its just, harmonious, sunlit brotherhood. Lofty commotions about ideal cities alive with enlightenment are fraught with dangers of embarrassment. Priestley kept the embarrassment at a low pitch and the inspiration – for some – high. Numbers of

10   *Delight*, J. B. Priestley, 1.
11   Priestley and Joyce Cary became friends in 1939.

young people who were to vote Labour in the 1945 election came away from the play with a touch of something resembling inspiration and others felt sufficiently disturbed to question for the first time, in the fierce perspective of wartime living, where this gigantic eruption in human affairs would eventually lead. In the play the charwoman and her daughter are prepared to throw in their lot with the city, but the small-time financier and the bank clerk's selfish wife are not. Underlying motives are dramatically explored but the heart of the play centres around Joe, the one-time stoker, who wants to carry the message of the city to the world beyond, and Alice who desires nothing more than to escape from harsh reality into the warm serenity of this dream world. Joe has fallen in love with Alice and their disparate reactions threaten to split them apart. As the gates are closing for the last time Alice joins Joe to plead with him, and he insists that somebody must return to the outer world to carry the message – a new Jerusalem has arrived.

The present author remembers seeing a production of the play in which he found himself drawn into the brilliant patch of sunlight which moved around the stage sucking the spectators back into the orbit of the city. Against all scepticism a glow remained as if one had actually visited a more enlightened place.

Many years afterwards Priestley remembered the determined professionalism of the cast of *They Came to a City* during some of London's worst bombing. Irene Hentschel produced the play and never failed to arrive punctually. Three other members of the cast were over seventy but not the worst of the bombing kept them away. It was during one rehearsal of *They Came to a City* that Priestley underwent the treatment later described good-humouredly in *Delight*: 'When rehearsals are going badly I am often rushed out of the theatre, given drinks, flattered, cajoled, simply to keep me out of the sight of the players, those pampered creatures.'[12]

Tried out at Bradford Civic Theatre in 1943, *They Came to a City* was transferred to the Globe Theatre in London and had a relatively long run for a wartime play. James Agate reviewed it in the *Daily Express*.

One judged from the warmth of the applause that the audience en masse endorsed Mr Priestley's views en bloc. Were there dissenters? One thought very few. Did one or two people coming to the theatre for pure entertainment (oh dear) find themselves let in for a good talking to? If there were any such let us hope 'sitting under' Mr

12  *Delight*, J. B. Priestley, 4.

Priestley did them good . . . If anybody asks me whether I thought *They Came to a City* was good theatre I shall be forced to say no. And proceed to say very quickly that it isn't bad theatre either. That, in my view, it is magnificent sermonising.[13]

Gearing his work more and more to the war effort, in 1942 Priestley arranged to visit a number of aircraft factories to prepare the ground for the semi-documentary novel *Daylight on Saturday*. He talked to scores of men and women in the factory and for once planned the novel in considerable detail. Because of the long hours worked in the factory the employees saw the daylight during the winter only on Saturday, which gave him the title of the novel. His description of the throng at last breaking off work at midday on Saturday was vivid.

And out they came into the daylight, blinking, chattering, grum-bling, laughing, sniffing and tasting the cool air. It was a misty afternoon in early November. The sunlight was weak and watery, no more than a little pale silver in that green hollow. The blue and gold Saturdays of summer were a long way off. There were sodden, dead leaves plastered like handbills on all the walls. The western sky was sagging under a load of rain. There was no wind, and the long line of buses rumbling up began to pollute the air. But the sun was there and so was the honest daylight, and this was Saturday.

Edwin Muir suggested in *The Listener* that this was Priestley's best novel, a surprising judgement for a work not intended to qualify as in any way major. The novel realistically explored the impact of war on ordinary lives and the atmosphere in the sharper, harder line of the prose. One man's wife has been killed by a stray bomb and he is deeply embittered; the superintendent cannot escape lusting after women since his wife died in childbirth; and the welfare officer's affair with a married schoolmaster is full of dissatisfactions. Stereotypic characters and situations were represented with some delicacy and if *Daylight on Saturday* does not compare with *Angel Pavement*, it is more than a hastily put together topical novel.

Throughout the production of *They Came to a City* Priestley continued to write to Jane from various addresses and she seems to have been unaware of his affair with Mary Hope Allen.

Tired of the nomadic life moving from one address to another, in 1943 Priestley rented an apartment in Albany, that classic oasis at

13   *Daily Express*, James Agate, 14 September 1943.

the very heart of Piccadilly. It lies behind a shuttered entrance protected in those days by a splendid liveried giant who resembled the
archetypal image of all regimental sergeant majors. Built for Lord
Melbourne as one self-contained house, when the Ropewalk was
added in 1804 the surrounding bachelor chambers accommodated
in their time Lord Byron, Lord Lytton and Canning. From the
famous Ropewalk – a long canopy-protected passageway – stair-
cases led at intervals to exclusive flats and it was to No. B4 – the
same address as John Worthington in *The Importance of Being Earnest*
– that Priestley came in the summer of 1943 for a preliminary
examination.

Characteristically in the middle of yet another emotional crisis,
literary work continued, but *Manpower*, published in 1944, was
prepared for the Ministry of Labour and National Service,
published anonymously, and told the story of Britain's mobilisation for war. A letter to Jane at this time said:

Dearest Jane,
    Thank you for your letter. I am sorry mine disappointed you. It
certainly wasn't as good a letter as yours, but it oughtn't to have
been disappointing. I think we ought to decide when and where to
do our talking after we have had a day or two together in Bradford.
What I would like best after Blackpool is to have about a month in
some quiet place with you where we can get together and I can finish
my novel, which ought to be finished as soon as possible. I can't
work on a big job like that anywhere where I'm liable to be
interrupted. I don't want to attempt an elaborate London move
before finishing the novel. But we can talk about all that next week.
The rest of Friday night after I rang you was mostly air raids – very
noisy and quite impossible to sleep through. Then on top of
practically no sleep yesterday I had a rehearsal in the morning, a
Book Society meeting at lunchtime, took the Chair at a British
Drama League meeting in the afternoon, then another rehearsal
from 5–8 in the evening, ending in another air raid alert.[14] I have to
finish off these rehearsals, prepare three American broadcasts, write
an article for America ('Harpers Bazaar'), do five Book Society
letters, and do some hard work on my Man-Power booklet, all
between now and Sunday morning. And if there are more raids,
there'll not be much sleep, as the barrage is now continuous and
heavy. I'll try to see Angela tomorrow . . .
    I must get off to rehearsal now so must close, hoping that you are

14  Rehearsing *They Came to a City*.

feeling better in every way. Please accept my deep devotion and give my love to Tom and Rachel.

Your loving
JACK[15]

The confusions of their box-and-cox wartime lives brought Priestley's next letter to Jane from Broxwood Court and it appeared from the letter that Jane had gone to London to prepare the new Albany flat while Priestley retired to Broxwood Court.

Dearest Jane,

Thank you for your note. I was just going to write. I'm terribly sorry for the [indecipherable]. It just would happen like that. I'm sorry about Monday too. It was a chapter of accidents and so far as I have made it worse for you, I humbly beg your forgiveness. I will work really hard to help with the Albany flat. Not much news here. I saw Beaumont yesterday and talked to him about the . . . play and left a copy with him. I spent the evening with Ralph R. who had another brush-up with his girl and isn't doing much work, and is feeling very miserable. I saw MacOwan this afternoon about the Army play, arrangements for which are now progressing very smoothly.

. . . I'm going down on Sat. evening to visit an Air Force station commanded by Walter Pickarel – Pixie's brother, to give a talk to the lads in the mess. It's a chance to discover what these R.A.F. lads are thinking . . .

With much love, JACK[16]

Whether by now Jane suspected or knew about his relationship with Mary is unclear, but his next letter to Jane once again expressed his love for her.

Darling Jane,

Thank you for your very good letter which was full of love and steadiness and good sense. In a few weeks we'll try to get a real solid basis of understanding. I have a very deep real feeling for you which operates all the time – and not only when we've quarrelled and I see you unhappy – and though you may not believe this – it is a fact that I always put you first. Ten years ago, of course, I was in a psychological tangle (Jung would say I was the victim of 'anima projection') but I have not returned to such a tangle and am free of it or anything like it. But we'd best talk of that later . . .

15  Priestley to Jane Priestley, 19 January 1943.
16  Priestley to Jane Priestley, 'Thursday', probably 1943.

With much love, my darling, and I hope you find your father better.
Your loving
JACK[17]

Two events come through clearly in three letters written between January and February of 1943. First a new pitch of intensity entered their emotional struggles, with Priestley subjecting himself to ruthless self-examination. Second, Jane fell ill with what appears to have been inflammation of the gall bladder and that reinforced a strong bout of guilt in Priestley. His self-laceration expressed itself eloquently, but was he driven by guilt or did he rely so much on Jane that he had to blame himself for fear of losing her? Certainly his clandestine affair with Mary justified conventional guilt.

Dearest Jane,
Just had your telegram. I'm glad it's not jaundice but disappointed – for you and myself – that you can't manage Bradford . . . I agree about the 'job' – you have certainly had some wretched luck lately. And like Job you certainly don't deserve it. I've hurt you and you'd done nothing to hurt me, though I certainly didn't want to hurt you, and was feeling very close to you. It's true I'm sometimes afraid of you – I suppose it's my conscience – but I do know that when I'm with you and you're happy, then I'm happy and when I know you are suffering then I suffer too. And that seems to me genuine love. I am always thinking about you and talking about and am proud of you. I think you are a magnificent person – very brave, very intelligent and fundamentally nice and generous. And I hate thinking of you in any other terms than those. If you could look into my mind or heart you would see an image of yourself which would please and comfort you. It is I who am the unsatisfactory partner, though I do honestly try to do the best with myself. Sometimes I think I am perhaps complicated by the largely unconscious relationship between myself and the public. If this seems fanciful, please ignore it. As for talking, I really am ready to try it. I'm not afraid of talk, but of emotional scenes that could easily do much damage! I hope you are getting something out of Jung. Sometimes he seems to me too elaborate and Teutonic but he has certainly flashes of great wisdom and insight.
I do hope you are better and with much love,
JACK[18]

17 Priestley to Jane Priestley, 'Friday', 1943.
18 Priestley to Jane Priestley, January 1943.

Darling Jane,

Harvey gave me the news this morning, and then the hospital rang up this afternoon. Hurray! Harvey said there was definite inflammation and that the operation was certainly necessary. Thank you for your letter which I've just had. I'm sure that place is all right. It had the right kind of look about it. Barbara and I are having salmon kedgeree and peas tonight and wishing very much you were with us. I shall write the messages tonight and post them too. Mary rang up to enquire. So did Dorothy . . .

I'm so glad the worst of this is all over for you, and I'm sure you're going to be well repaid for your sense and courage in having the thing out . . .

Bless you, my love, and get well soon.

Your loving

JACK[19]

Darling Jane,

I hope you are feeling better with not too much pain and discomfort as you start moving more. I've no particular news except that I'm making a start again on my novel and see the way to draw the ends together – also that so far I've slept rather badly because I've suffered from continuous WIND . . .

There followed an indecipherable reference to some work which had brought him

nearly another £3,000, so we are not short of money. I've also just received about £550 from the serial in America of *Black-out in Gretley*[20] and the play brings me about £150 a week – so we are not hard up and if you want to stay in London comfortably, don't hesitate to make the necessary arrangement.

I think of you continually, hope you are thinking of me not unkindly and believe too that with some patience and essential tenderness we can make something better than we've had for a long, long time. I'm sorry that so often I make such a poor visitor to the nursing home but I did frequently feel very tired and worried and

19   ibid., January 1943.
20   *Black-out in Gretley* was the first of three novels which drew on the war for their subject.

it wasn't until Harvey explained first what was wrong that I felt better . . .

Bless you,
Your loving
JACK[21]

Some time late in 1943 Priestley moved into not one but two flats in Albany, the duplication possibly the result of marital problems. Occasional accommodation of family or visitors, complicated by Priestley's insomnia, could be an alternative explanation.

A number of incendiary bombs fell near Albany but Priestley remained undisturbed. Indeed, recollecting those days later in life, he said that even when he was driven to firewatch almost every night and sleep sometimes dwindled to two hours, he still enjoyed aspects of the situation. A West End of London which suddenly emptied of life appealed to him and those people he did encounter seemed an improvement on their old selves: 'No longer suspicious of quiet' they 'almost sparkled'.[22]

Given a rush of words to the paper there were times when Priestley became a professional hyperbolist but no amount of exaggeration could dim the satisfactions he found in the war years. Well into 1943 he sallied forth sometimes in the middle of a raid to give yet another talk which caused further trouble, and for him deeper satisfactions.

In 1944 the BBC discussed an alternative series – 'Questions for Tomorrow' – and various speakers were proposed with Priestley's name mentioned and hastily withdrawn.[23] Regarded by the cynical as a magnificent piece of Allied bluff, talk about a Second Front was widespread and in February 1943 Priestley proposed a series of 'six talks to strengthen public morale at an hour of great tension'. His success as a broadcaster on the North American Service was unquestioned and his impact on American opinion widespread. The BBC agreed that he should give the talks but felt that the invasion of Europe was much too doubtful a topical peg. Before they reached a final decision, hostile Conservatives went into action. Commander Bower, Captain Alan Graham and Lees Jones gave notice of a parliamentary motion 'that in the opinion of this House the continuing practice of the BBC in giving excessive

21   Priestley to Jane Priestley, 20 February 1943.
22   *Margin Released*, J. B. Priestley, 220.
23   Board of Governors' Minutes, 18 November 1943.

preference to Left Wing speakers such as Mr Priestley calls for censure'.[24]

The BBC, surprisingly tough-minded, briefed the minister in reply that 'Broadcasters of all schools of thought' were given full consideration, and support for the BBC came from the Tory Reform Committee. Labour MP John Silkin pressed home the motion congratulating the BBC 'upon the revival of broadcasts by Mr J. B. Priestley'.[25]

A book, *How It Can Be Done*, now appeared (1943) written by Sir Richard Acland with a preface by Priestley which confirmed some Conservatives' worst fears. Priestley lived under the illusion that every political party believed in planning, but now asked the question – 'planning by whom and for what purpose?'

> As for Public Control of Private Enterprise, it seems to me just three words too long. Why not have Public Enterprise and be done with it? And notice the artful use of words here. 'Control' immediately suggested something rigid, negative, uncreative and sterile; and Enterprise all elastic, positive, creative, fruitful, hinting at big businessmen sitting up all night to plan something cheap and delicious for us. Why not switch the terms round? Private Control of Public Enterprise? . . . I believe the big, hard boys would still have the real power in their hands just because they still owned the resources. It would still be their country not ours. And it would end in Private Control of Private Enterprise with the public left clean out.[26]

These were inflammatory words. Fortunately Priestley had completed his new series of broadcasts which echoed similar sentiments in far less challenging form.

Still he met Mary Hope Allen and their affair continued. Still he kept in touch with Jane and wrote letters to both.

Darling Mary,

Excuse typewriting but I've no paper to write on. I'm at Brighton this week as I was last, because my daughter who is in the WRENS had an accident just before Christmas, then was given sick leave, so I brought her down here. I had a bad cold too that wouldn't go and the doctor thought it a good idea I should come down too. All this changing of plans and messing about has made it impossible to let

24  *A History of Broadcasting in the United Kingdom*, Vol. III, Asa Briggs, 619.
25  ibid.
26  *How It Can Be Done*, Richard Acland, preface by J. B. Priestley, 10.

you know anything, as I don't know what I'm doing a day or two ahead, but I'll ring you when I can. Not much news. I'm not doing any work at the moment, though the Old Vic has asked me to do an experimental play for them, but at the moment I haven't an idea for it, and find it rather difficult to fulfil their particular conditions. My play about the Inspector[27] is coming on fairly soon, I hope, probably when Hardwick returns from France, for he is to play the chief part. The other play, about the little ex-air raid warden who crashes the conference, we are leaving until the war is nearer finishing, and at the moment God knows when that will be.[28]

Everything was now geared to the overwhelming need to launch the Second Front, which Priestley felt had been delayed far too long. Tom Harrisson of Mass Observation, who was about to be dropped behind the lines in Borneo, gave a tremendous farewell party alive with distinguished people from all walks of life. Present was Woodrow Wyatt, then a major in the army, and he left a savage picture of what took place.

J. B. Priestley was loudly and ever more drunkenly explaining that some broadcasts he had made were the reason why we were winning the war; the government did not understand the nature of the British people; only he, the blunt Yorkshireman, did. 'Utter balls. You're just a wind-bag,' I shouted at him. That was not my complete view when sober, but it did well for a party, rousing Priestley into furious volubility to the general pleasure.

As midnight dragged by Wyatt turned to Harrisson and said, 'I must be getting back to Portsmouth' and Harrisson immediately replied, 'Yes – but you must drop Priestley first. He's absolutely out.'

William Empson offered his services and between them Wyatt and Empson managed to manipulate a 'reluctant and staggering Priestley into my army jeep'. Priestley, Wyatt wrote, said he lived in Albany. 'The three of us set off. Dreadfully drunk I couldn't remember where Albany was . . . For a quarter of an hour I drove round and round Eros in Piccadilly Circus at 30 m.p.h. on the wrong side of the road.' Another approach towards Jermyn Street proved equally fruitless. Priestley had several times been prevented by William Empson from jumping out into the road. Once in Jermyn Street, almost at Albany, he managed it. 'We'd better get

27  *An Inspector Calls.*
28  Priestley to Mary Hope Allen, 10 January 1945.

him back into the jeep. You can't leave a distinguished man like that,' Empson said. Wyatt prodded him with his foot. 'He's only a silly old dramatist,' he said. In his book, *Confessions of an Optimist*, he commented: 'We left him there. He must have got home. He went on writing, talking and complaining for years afterwards.'[29]

29    *Confessions of an Optimist*, Woodrow Wyatt, 96.

# 20

# The Independent Candidate
## 1945–6

When at last the Second Front was launched, the expectation that
such an overwhelming armada of ships, planes and men could not
fail to crush the enemy in a few months quickly evaporated.
Priestley experienced a powerful sense of anticlimax. He followed
the news with increasing impatience and sometimes dismay that
these great turning-points in history refused to be manipulated in
their entirety by mere human beings. A vast distribution of men
and arms throughout half the world were locked in such complicated battle that gains in one area accelerated losses in others, and
even the gigantic wave which swept across the coast of France lost
its impetus all too quickly.

Priestley continued to live a semi-bachelor life centred on his
Albany oasis. We have no hard evidence to what degree he took
advantage of his relative freedom, but his marriage was moving
into a new phase.

Turning through his papers one day he came upon a letter which
H. M. Tomlinson had written him.[1]

I've noticed the way you have been speaking out and I'm fully in
accord. It's the old tradition and an English one – not Marx but
Morris. . . you've been putting the case for us in a manner that tells.
My son, now a gunner, has written to us . . . in high approval of
your . . . *News Chronicle* articles; and he is a sticky critic: and he has
always hated Fascists and Nazis with a white passion. So there you
are. The young men hear and understand you.

It stirred Priestley to deeper examination of the possibilities of the
actual political scene. Late in 1944 he roughed out a 'Letter to a
Returning Serviceman', which became a useful pamphlet in the
1945 election. The final version was addressed to an imaginary
person called 'My dear Robert'.

1    H. M. Tomlinson to Priestley, 20 June 1941.

No doubt it is very hard for you to imagine me as anything . . . but a plump middle-aged author, sitting in a cosy huddle of books, pictures and pipes in my Albany study where we last met. But I want you to remember that I was once a returning serviceman too . . . I think you celebrated your twenty-first birthday in the desert: I know I celebrated mine in the water-logged trenches of 1915.

Priestley rambled on in that colloquial style he had perfected in his postscripts which gave the impression of a friend at your elbow talking exclusively to you. After the last war, he said, those who emerged clamouring for a new way of life were quickly over-whelmed by conservative resumption of traditional values. Here and now in 1944 history was threatening to repeat itself. 'The reformer, the revolutionary, the one who says there must be no more of this murderous nonsense, is being told in a hundred different ways, not to be an ass and a bore.' Stripped of a great deal of verbiage, the letter said do not sink back in the comfort of victory but take an active part in politics and insist on asserting your rights. Only thus could the country be saved from once again surrendering to the old muddle, exploitation and injustice. 'Letter to a Returning Serviceman' was widely read and brought a multitude of replies. Their number became an embarrassment and Priestley quailed before the inevitable consequence of political appeal. He turned, in reaction, to matters theatrical. Driven by the irrelevance of so many dramatic reviews in Sunday newspapers, he launched an attack on theatre critics in the *Observer*.

It has been my experience that the older dramatic critics have, on the whole, been hostile to experimental work. Often they grumble (as well they might) when given the same old stuff. But too often they grumble still harder when shown something that is not the same old stuff. They are too apt to think that dramatic technique arrived at final perfection about the time when they were young and that any further refinements . . . are merely so much arty pretentiousness.

James Agate wrote immediately to Priestley: 'I have been looking into my records and I give you a few out of the hundreds of encouraging things I have written concerning plays which were in some way or degree experimental.'[2] He then enumerated plays by Strindberg (*The Dance of Death*), Andreyev (*The Seven Who Were Hanged*), Jean-Jacques Bernard (*The Unquiet Spirit*) and came at last

2  James Agate to Priestley, 9 April 1945.

to J. B. Priestley. 'Priestley's *Time and the Conways* . . . This is the place and time and both together and one as much as the other to say that Mr Priestley has made a play which is magnificent drama if you grasp what it is essentially about, and first-class entertainment if you don't.' Agate concluded:

> I need hardly tell you that just as I would insist upon the modernity of such young critics as Alan Dent, J. C. Trewin and Philip Hope-Wallace, so I will admit the conservatism of some of the older ones. I have been moved to write this letter because what I maintain about my own work I maintain about the work of men like Ivor Brown, Desmond MacCarthy and Anthony Cookman, loyal servants of the theatre honourably bearing the brunt of a battle that never ends, critics who have never shut their minds to novelty justifying itself or containing the seeds of justification. Isn't it time, my dear Jack, that you learned to discriminate?[3]

Priestley replied within three days.

> Dear Jimmie,
> Certainly you have sometimes praised experimental work, though some of the plays you mention do not seem to come into that category. And I cannot help wondering what you would have said of *The Dance of Death* if I had written it and not Strindberg. Just as when I saw *Peer Gynt* at the New and remembered *Johnson Over Jordan* (which held and moved the audience far more and brought a far better performance out of Richardson) I could not help wondering what some of you would have said if I had written it . . .

A curiously immature pique characterised much of the remainder of the letter. He did not complain, Priestley wrote, that Agate had failed to praise such plays as *Johnson Over Jordan*, *Music at Night* and *They Came to a City*, which had given stimulating and memorable evenings to people at least as sensitive and intelligent as Agate. It was his failure to give them careful critical attention which was lamentable. He, Priestley, had an international reputation as a dramatist and when a senior critic like Agate simply amused himself being witty at Priestley's expense it had not only injured Priestley, he struck a blow at the 'poor struggling English Theatre'.

Elspeth Parker who knew Priestley well and worked closely with him at the time said that the exterior toughness concealed an

---

3   *Ego*, James Agate, 8.

over-sensitive artist. Certainly when he rounded on his critics it was sometimes self-destructive, and such an old trouper should have left retaliation to others. An array of flattering reviews of his plays was easily available as uncontaminated ammunition.

The picture of Agate 'honourably bearing the brunt of a battle that never ends' seemed to Priestley derisory.

> You have not borne the brunt of any battle. When Ronald Jeans and I, neither of us rich men, subsidised the Westminster Theatre before the war, just to give London some intelligent productions at easy prices, your whole attitude was grudging and querulous. You have never . . . at any time carefully examined the theatrical situation in London . . .
>
> Forgive this hurried stuff; I'm tired and very busy. If it sounds unfriendly forgive that too. Remember that there was many a time when I could have hit you back and never did.[4]

Whereupon Agate countered with a marathon letter which recapitulated his reviews of *Johnson Over Jordan*, *Music at Night* and *They Came to a City*, showing just how seriously he had taken all three. The charge that he amused himself by airing his prejudices at the expense of Priestley was false.

> You are at perfect liberty to say that the line I took about them was wrong: I don't pretend that my judgements are necessarily right. What I do say is that right or wrong, those judgements were the result of the utmost attention and that they were based on principles of criticism which I have in part taken from my predecessor and in part evolved for myself during the last thirty-eight years . . . You are entitled to say that my judgements are insensitive, unintelligent and stupid if you like. You are not entitled to say that they are not the result of careful critical attention.

Agate concluded his letter with a piece of prescience which did not redeem it in Priestley's eyes. Why didn't he have another think about the theatre? Why must he believe that he had to continue writing plays about the Beveridge Plan? If dear Jack wanted to go into the House of Commons why not change gear and do so, whereupon he, Agate, would immediately vote for him. 'But for heaven's sake don't drag the House of Commons into Shaftesbury Avenue!'

4 Priestley to James Agate, 12 April 1945.

Perhaps wisely, Priestley did not reply. Within a few months he was in fact stamping the country speaking on behalf of the Labour Party, which reminded him of his whistle-stop lecture tours in America. He travelled through the Midlands to the north-east and took in the slums of Glasgow, reiterating the message which had grown from the postscripts.

Out of the ruins left by the war one dominating task remained: to reconstruct a society driven by the scramble for personal gain, the profit motive and privilege into a society where wealth and income were redistributed, co-operation modified competition, and men could claim that social as well as legal justice was freed from class manipulation. The powers granted by a wartime economy had generated a new community spirit which forced on us some aspects of this idealistic vision. It was the unfortunate paradox of war that it brought about something resembling a revolution at the cost of regimentation.[5]

Later he drew a romantic picture of his pilgrimage: 'Candidate after candidate drawn from very different backgrounds' he wrote, responded to him with an enthusiasm and eagerness which 'seemed to light up their committee rooms'. Having given so readily and received much in return, life was a richer, more meaningful adventure.

The image of a man committed to the writing life, essentially a literary person, had undergone severe modification. He was prepared to step out of his study into the glare of the hustings but he stood for a university seat and did no campaigning.

Alas, his *alter ego* was unsuccessful. What persuaded him to choose such a hidebound Conservative seat to contest as an Independent candidate is not clear, but no socialist in his senses would have accepted Cambridge as a launching pad for a political career.

The result was declared on 31 July 1945. K. Pickthorn the Conservative candidate won 73,641 votes, H. Wilson Harris, Independent, 6,536, and Priestley came third with 5,745. Priestley did not sleep that night. He had expected defeat but not quite so decisively.

The next morning he read the *Daily Herald* streamer headline 'Labour In Power' with mixed feelings. According to the *Herald*, bonfires were set burning in the old bomb sites of the East End, dancing broke out on the streets of Bethnal Green and thousands of

---

5 'Letter to a Returning Serviceman', J. B. Priestley, 29.

people crowded around the People's Palace demanding a glimpse of their triumphant candidate and new prime minister – Clement Attlee. There followed a procession up the Mall to Buckingham Palace, a procession not unlike scores which had preceded it, but said to be impelled by a very different motive. 'We want the Prime Minister,' it chanted, aware – as Priestley was – that something very remarkable had happened in British political history.

The composition of Labour MPs in the new government especially interested him. The final count gave the Labour Party 394 seats against the Tories 197 and the Liberals 12. For the first time in its brief history – only forty-five years before, it was a persecuted minority – the Labour Party had gained indisputable power and a complete reorientation had taken place. As Priestley realised, this was not the upsurge of one class challenging and overpowering another. There were large numbers of middle-class voters among the Labour majority and the composition of Labour's 394 MPs reflected the new alignment. On one side stood 44 lawyers, 49 university and school teachers, 26 journalists, 15 doctors and dentists, 16 managers and technicians: on the other 150 manual workers, 8 working housewives and 39 miners. This breakdown of Labour's composition arrived in Priestley's post one morning in an official Labour Party document, and he read it with fascination. Perhaps this crystallised Churchill's greatest mistake. Romantically, he still saw insurmountable division between one class and another and considered the mass of working people with a benevolent paternalism at least a century out of date. There remained for Priestley a deep personal sense of frustration and disappointment.

It could be said that at this stage a familiar struggle renewed itself in Priestley's psyche. It was a struggle between the journalist, writer, novelist, playwright, social commentator and politician. It was as if first one and then another incarnation detached itself from the parent body to dominate and suppress the others, only in turn to be subdued by the gathering power of fresh embodiments. However interlocked in the struggle, slowly, implacably the literary man always emerged the final victor. It was so now. The year 1944 had produced two plays, *Desert Highway* and *How Are They at Home?* The year 1945 saw a novel, *Three Men in New Suits*, and another play, *The Long Mirror*, completed, but none of these was of great significance.

The affair with Mary Merrington diminished in 1945–6 and after the war Priestley and Jane resumed their intermittent life between Albany and Billingham with Jane mainly centred on Billingham.

The year 1946 began badly with a serious illness. *The Times* recorded that Priestley had been taken ill on 12 January with influenza but was responding well to treatment.[6] His eminence was now underpinned by a series of bulletins; on 17 January he was said to be 'a little better' and then on 18 January Jane, who had nursed him devotedly, herself became infected and retired to bed. When even the servants showed signs of succumbing, the whole household was threatened with paralysis. By 18 January *The Times* recorded: 'Mr Priestley who has influenzal pneumonia is improving, but will be confined to bed for two or three weeks yet.'[7]

In the first of those three weeks Priestley lay inert and against all precedent did not write a line. Half recovered in the second week, he plunged back into work and that was the beginning of yet another outpouring. In 1946 *The Secret Dream*, an essay on Britain, America and Russia, *Bright Day*, a novel, *Russian Journey*, six articles collected from the *Sunday Express*, and *The Arts Under Socialism*, an essay, were published but the novel *Bright Day* and the play, *An Inspector Calls*, remained paramount in 1944–6.

*An Inspector Calls* was, in fact, written in the autumn of 1944 partly as the result of a lecture Priestley gave at the request of Michael MacOwan, the theatrical director, to a group of ATS officers. 'At the end of the lecture,' Priestley wrote in a letter to MacOwan, 'you asked me why I had never done anything with an idea about a mysterious inspector visiting a family that I had mentioned casually to you before the war.' This set Priestley searching his 'little black notebook' and there he found the details of the inspector and the Birling family and quickly began 'writing the play at great speed, blinding on past all manner of obstacles and pitfalls and only realising afterwards how dangerous they might have proved'.

Critics later claimed that the play was rejected by various London managements but Priestley stated that it was simply a matter of the unavailability of a suitable theatre which persuaded him to send a copy of the script to Moscow. This was in May 1945. 'Ten weeks later, two famous companies, Tairov's Kamerny and the Leningrad Theatre Company, were presenting the play simultaneously in Moscow where it was an immediate success.' After the Russian debut the play went on European tour to various state theatres and

6   *The Times*, 14 January 1946.
7   ibid., 18 January 1946.

at last reached London to be produced as part of a new repertory scheme at the Old Vic.

*An Inspector Calls* re-echoed back to *Dangerous Corner* using a similar duplication of events brought to a crucial turning-point when the central suicide of the play is anticipated before it actually happens, exploiting once more Dunne's theory of movement through past and present. Consonant with the well-made play of the day, *An Inspector Calls* rose above the mechanical limitations of the genre and reached beyond the conventional thrill of the detective plot. The opening scene showed the comfortable – indeed, complacent – Birling family whose celebration of an engagement is suddenly broken into by the arrival of an inspector. A shrewd determined figure, the inspector places his questions with such skill that the family becomes uneasy under his interrogation. A girl, Eva Smith, has committed suicide and the inspector's relentless questioning implicates the whole Birling family. Eva Smith was a ringleader in the strike at Birling's factory and Birling sacked her for having the audacity to ask for half a crown a week rise. Miss Birling, the daughter, complained to Eva's next employer and had her dismissed, the mother influenced a charitable committee against helping the girl when she became pregnant and Birling's son is none other than the child's father. It quickly becomes evident that Priestley has overloaded the family with such unrelenting complicity that verisimilitude is threatened and only the dramatic pace of the play sweeps aside doubt as the family uneasily examines its history. Some are frightened by what they find, but father and son confront each other in mutual recrimination. The inspector's authenticity dwindles when his alleged photograph of Eva Smith comes under suspicion, but such a flood of moral questioning has broken loose that everyone is driven to self-justification. Even when a telephone call to the hospital reveals no trace of the dead girl and the local police station denies all knowledge of the inspector, moral recrimination continues apace. Only the son and daughter admit their guilt without qualification. As the air clears, the inspector becomes an imposter in their eyes and complacency returns to modify guilt. Suddenly the telephone rings and the actors freeze in a tableau. An inspector is again about to call because a girl who poisoned herself is dying in hospital in all reality.

*An Inspector Calls* had considerable dramatic impact when produced at the Old Vic, but the play received a cool, almost hostile, reception. Constructed as a thriller, it maintained suspense but there were depths beyond those of a thriller which reduced its pure entertainment value. The inspector was more than an inspector. He carried an air of omniscience behind his questions and his character ebbed and flowed between the straightforward police inspector and some emblematic figure who could personify universal conscience. If it seems unlikely that all the characters without exception could have contributed to the death of the same girl, that factitious element was necessary to drive home the play's main theme – that we all have to share something and 'if there's nothing else, we must share our guilt'. Partly derivative from Ouspensky, most of the family when they return to relive the events before the inspector's revelations easily laugh off their complicity and fail to comply with Ouspensky's prerequisite for changing and improving the spiral of their lives. They have learned nothing.

Priestley complained bitterly about the play's reception in England and reinforced the view that Europeans responded much more positively to his work. The first production in Germany alone ran to 1,600 performances, for which by some monstrous juggling with currencies known only to the Foreign Office, Priestley received exactly ten pounds. Since then, of course, the play has had many revivals and is one of the most popular in repertory.

The once fashionable theories of Dunne and Ouspensky are no longer taken seriously today and a recent production of *An Inspector Calls* (1987) revealed the critics in disarray. *The Times* averred that Priestley knew exactly how to put together a play with a message,[8] but the *Independent* referred to J. B. Priestley as an engaging old war horse and complained that a 'creaky moral mystery' sought to 'instruct and edify in the most overtly pious way'.[9]

According to *Margin Released*, *Bright Day* was written towards the end of the war, and became Priestley's favourite novel. Disclaiming autobiographical roots, the story is none the less resonant with his early youth and coincided with Priestley's recoil from the commercial film world – which matches the revulsion of his narrator Dawson. *Bright Day* was the only serious novel which Priestley wrote in the first person, and Dawson represents an interplay between the real, middle-aged, pipe-smoking Priestley and his narrator. Middle-aged and pipe-smoking himself, Dawson recreates Priestley's youth, but the mature man interlaces the narrative with ironic comment about Priestley, the author of the novel. None of this is explicit. As David Hughes has commented:

8   *The Times*, 16 May 1987.
9   *Independent*, 16 May 1987.

The book is written as though Dawson had met Priestley and liked him, finding that they had certain attitudes in common, but quickly discovering that certain aspects of his temperament needed to be watched. Priestley and his hero are too close to be parted but they are not the same man.[10]

Gregory Dawson, a middle-aged film-script writer, has retired to Cornwall – Priestley sometimes did just that – to complete under pressure *The Lady Hits Back* in which the peerless Elizabeth Earl will star. Dimly recognising a family group in the hotel, he at last identifies Lord and Lady Harndean as the Malcolm and Eleanor Nixey he knew when he worked as a clerk in a Bruddersford wool firm. They represent the beginning of the break-up of the bright day which had preceded the year 1914. As we know, Priestley left a long unpublished manuscript full of nostalgia about this watershed which became a constantly recurring theme mulled over as if to reconcile the dissatisfactions of the present. *Bright Day* encapsulates that mood. Struggling with his script, modern life and values, the present constantly surrenders to the past and those enchanted days before 1914 when John Alington, his employer, and his three daughters created a different world of youth, poetry and music.

Once again manipulating time – past, present and future – Priestley moves so skilfully from one to the other that the reader is almost unaware of transition. Overlapping past and present relations with Elizabeth he examines old and new values with ironic emphasis on that flamboyant new flower of modern culture – the film industry.

The past mediated through the present adds another dimension because Dawson knows now what happened when those wonderful 1914 days surrendered to the tragedy which overwhelmed the Alington family. One daughter fell to her death with reverberations which remained in the background as an ever-present threat. After the war, Gregory Dawson – like Priestley – left Bruddersford to become involved in Hollywood script-writing, sucked into a fundamentally superficial way of life where survival meant unscrupulous manipulation. Finally driven back to his Cornish hotel to write under pressure a script he despises, the whole of his preceding life begins again in recapitulation. And then a private group of film amateurs who have decided to set up their own film company invite him to join them and he recklessly abandons a big Hollywood offer, to recover his integrity.

10   *J. B. Priestley*, David Hughes, 177.

I was growing old in a tragic world, and if I had anything to say, I wanted to be able to say it even if most of the customers run screaming from the Box Office. I'd done my share of administering the anaesthetic . . . so the script and I between us at that late and lonely hour had to play a farewell scene. 'Exquisitely glamorous lady,' I murmured, 'who couldn't draw two breaths in the real, thick, sweating, suffering world, go forth and show them in ten thousand darkened halls how you hit back and yet found your way to happiness. And . . . for all our sakes, I hope you won't do it for less than a gross of a quarter of a million sterling. Be a Big Success, Darling. And goodbye for ever.'[11]

Notwithstanding Priestley's protestations, there were too many points of coincidence to deny autobiographical roots. The *Times Literary Supplement* reviewed it:

As a writer of fiction, Mr Priestley has always been inclined to draw over much upon the resources of the discursive essayist. Shrewdly and pleasantly put together though they are, most of his novels have made only the lightest kind of impression because they lacked imaginative substance. It is such substance that gives distinction to *Bright Day*, which in one respect at least is a better novel than any Mr Priestley has written and more genuinely of a creative stamp.[12]

The whole review had an avuncular ring and was full of vague phrases, but there was no doubting the insignia of approval from an august journal which had seldom raved about his work.

*Bright Day* is one of Priestley's two most important and successful novels, the other being *Angel Pavement*. The theme expressed much more than Priestley's dissatisfaction with the film world. He was now fifty-two and into the midlife crisis about which Jung had written so elaborately. Tired of script-writing, uncertain about his powers as a novelist, questioning his many undoubted successes in the theatre, he underwent a period when he wondered where the quintessential Priestley talent could best be applied without this haunting sense of disillusion. This was a rare moment of decision-making. In general it was Priestley's habit to take H. G. Wells's advice when he said, 'I care not whether I am crowned King or drunk or dying in the gutter. I follow my leading.' In *Midnight on the Desert* he wrote:

11   *Bright Day*, J. B. Priestley, 325–6.
12   *Times Literary Supplement*, 22 June 1946.

I have a restless nature, easily bored, and so I flit from one kind of work to another, partly sustained by a very genuine interest in the technical problems of all forms of writing. I have always wanted vaguely to be an all-round man of letters on the eighteenth-century plan, which allowed or commanded a man to write an essay or poem, novel, or play just as he pleased.[13]

Much later in life he told Susan Cooper: 'I've never in any sense planned a career – just gone from one thing to another. In that sense I've never really had a career . . . My muse goes to bed with whoever she likes.'

Priestley's visit to Carl Gustav Jung in the summer of 1946 made a deep impression and reinforced his reading of the psychologist's work. We have no details of their meeting but Jung's son Franz said that they found one another sympathetic and talked far into the evening.[14] Priestley gave a BBC talk about Jung's work and Jung wrote to Priestley in August 1946:

Thank you very much for the copy of your talk and for the book. I have read both in the mean time. I cannot say how much I enjoyed your luminous and comprehensive talk. It is really remarkable how you succeeded in getting your vast subject together and making a whole of it. I must say I have never seen a better summary of my ideas in such a concise form.

Neither the letter nor the translation served to sustain and certainly not to increase Jung's reputation.[15] It was a farrago of generalities extracted from the simplest skeleton of his model, but Priestley was pleased to get the letter. Shortly afterwards he heard the news that H. G. Wells had died and for the remainder of the day he was invaded by a melancholy which recurred at intervals. Priestley felt that something bigger than H. G. Wells died that August day in 1946, something ceased to stir in the bloodstream of the modern mentality.

The actual day of the funeral became one of the most remarkable in Priestley's experience. In the midst of a full dress rehearsal of a 'little box of experimental tricks' called *Ever Since Paradise* at the Scala Theatre he was asked by the Wells family to deliver the address at the service in Golders Green Crematorium. No sooner

13    *Midnight on the Desert*, J. B. Priestley, 9/10.
14    Interview with Franz Jung, 24 September 1976.
15    C. G. Jung to Priestley, 9 August 1944.

had he finished rehearsing the first act than he rushed up to Golders
Green to deliver the address and then, with no break but a car
journey, rushed back to the second act of what was a comedy. In
recollection Priestley reflected how H. G. would have grinned and
chuckled. 'I can hear that high-pitched croak of his beginning,
"Yers – yers – Priestley – busy man – pretending to be a parson one
minute – then, next minute, messing about with the silly old stage –
yers –".'

At the time of the actual cremation his reactions were very
different. A handful of distinguished people went to Golders Green
Crematorium. No one wore mourning. Priestley wrote and read
the address which moved many in the audience.

We have come together today to say goodbye to our friend Herbert
George Wells . . . This was a man whose word was light in a
thousand dark places . . . When he was angry it was because he
knew far better than we did that life need not be a sordid greedy
scramble, and when he was impatient it was because he knew there
were glorious gifts of body, mind and spirit only just beyond our
present reach.

# 21

# Plays, Opera and a Visit to Russia
## 1945-7

Many of the old landmarks in his life were either decaying or vanishing and certain people among them like Shaw and Wells had seemed indestructible, but now Wells was gone and many lesser lights. His antidote to gloom when his wife Pat was dying had been to plunge into work – his study of Meredith – and now he surrendered himself to the theatre once more.

Michael MacOwan, one of the leading play directors of his day, recalled the reopening of the London Mask Theatre in collaboration with Priestley after the war. 'I went into the Arts Council . . . I did about a year or eighteen months there. Then I resigned. Soon after, in 1947, Thane Parker, Jack and I met and Jack said, "Let's get going again at the Mask Theatre . . ." I think it was he who suggested Mitchelhill. He'd been connected with him at the Duchess in the thirties.'[1]

Elspeth Parker, Thane Parker's widow, vividly recalls those days when she played an important role in the reopening. Her husband told Priestley that there was very little money and no play. Priestley promptly put up some capital (£3,000) and said a play would follow shortly. The Parkers were living in a £6 per week furnished house in Notting Hill and one day shortly afterwards a messenger arrived with a parcel which would not go through the letter box. It was a copy of the script for *The Linden Tree*, with a note which said, 'Don't lose it. I've only got one other copy.'[2] Within a few weeks Michael MacOwan had selected a cast which included Sir Lewis Casson, John Gielgud and Sybil Thorndike.

Priestley has described the long gestation of the play from the days in 1938 when he was still rewriting *Johnson Over Jordan*. He abandoned the first version of *The Linden Tree* when his wife said it was completely uncharacteristic of him, and the second version had no connection with its predecessor.

1  *J. P. The Man Called Mitch*, Peter Cotes, 48.
2  Interview with Elspeth Parker, 1 January 1986.

Trapped in Billingham by the heaviest snowfall the Isle of Wight had known for a hundred years, Priestley found the household short of fuel and very hard to warm. Besieged by 'this cruellest of Februarys' he ate, slept and wrote in one small room and for nearly a fortnight had little company beyond the Lindens.

The published play was dedicated to J. P. Mitchelhill. 'So far as the play itself has any virtue,' Priestley wrote, 'it was a virtue plucked out of necessity . . . And then – what luck! – I was back with you, back with the others, back at the Duchess, and all went miraculously well.'[3]

Sybil Thorndike has left an account of how she became involved in *The Linden Tree*. In the summer of 1947 she was playing in Clemence Dane's play *Call Home the Heart* when Jack Priestley came to her dressing-room with a manuscript. 'There's nothing in it for you,' he said, 'but I want you to read it because of Lewis.'[4]

That night she read *The Linden Tree* in bed and was enthusiastic because Professor Linden brought alive her husband Lewis on the typed page in living reality. 'Here he was as the Professor with all his integrity and his devotion – his complete dedication to work . . . And here too was his philanthropy and his gentleness and his understanding in spite of the fierceness of his nature.'[5]

Sybil Thorndike decided at once that she must play the Professor's wife – 'that poor empty-minded woman so tired of poverty and unable to live up to her husband'. Who else, she said, 'since she was already married to the Professor and knew his every mood?' Her husband shared her enthusiasm for the play and was 'thrilled . . . it was a long time since he had played such a star part'.

Elizabeth Sprigge in her biography of Sybil Thorndike Casson records Sybil's reaction to the first reading of the play given by Priestley himself.

'We were all simply struck dumb. Then Jack said, "That's a bloody good play" and we all laughed and wholeheartedly agreed. He came to many of the rehearsals and we all worked happily together.'[6]

The play opens when Linden, professor of history at a provincial university, confronts clear evidence that if he does not resign he will be forcibly retired. His refusal to surrender is based not on personal motives but a conviction that new appointments to the university

3   *The Linden Tree*, Preface, J. B. Priestley.
4   *Sybil Thorndike Casson*, Elizabeth Sprigge, 259–60.
5   ibid., 260.
6   ibid., 261.

will lead to what he regards as uncivilised policies. Simultaneously, his daughter returns from a rich marriage in France, another daughter arrives from her London hospital alive with progressive ideas, and his son revels in his somewhat dubious success. Only his youngest daughter Dinah sympathises with his desire to remain at university. His wife and family think he should retire, go away into the sun and enjoy himself. At sixty-five, they argue, he is entitled to retirement and all his high-flown talk about individual freedoms and non-utilitarian values is misplaced. They try to persuade him in vain. He is going to fight back.

'I was telling my family who don't give a damn,' he says to his friend Lockhart, 'that we're trying to do a wonderful thing here . . . But somehow not in a wonderful way . . . Sometimes our great common enterprise seems only a noble skeleton, as if the machines had already sucked the blood and marrow out of it. My wife and family tell me to go away and enjoy myself. Doing what? Watching the fire die out of the heart and never even stooping to blow? Here is Burmanley – with Dinah and her kind – and a few friends and allies – I can still blow a little – brighten an ember or two.'

Lofty commotions of this kind are, by their nature, insubstantial but in so far as Linden's true aim can be distilled from the dialogue, he desired to infuse the idealism of the young with the wisdom of older civilisations.

'The whole lot of you,' Linden says to his family, 'except young Dinah, are now busy turning away from life, giving it up. The Lindens are leaving the mucky old high road. And somebody's got to stay.'

The professor attempts to elevate his nostalgia into philosophic insight and becomes the omniscient eye observing his children who are the guinea pigs of society, each one representing a different reaction to the post-war world. It is a world where disillusionment with the Labour Government and all its works has begun, food and fuel are still rationed, power cuts part of everyday life and the hopes of a new society instinct with high purposes, crumbling under the austerities of material living.

The professor's wife leaves him, his son and two of his daughters pursue what he regards as unsatisfactory lives and he is left alone with Dinah. She comes down in her dressing-gown late at night and asks her father to read to her from his book on history. The extract has to be sufficient for his daughter to have time to fall asleep. The danger is that boredom will also send the audience to sleep. Priestley timed it perfectly. Smiling at his now sleeping daughter, Linden turns to correct a word in his manuscript as the curtain falls.

Elspeth Parker recalls: 'We rehearsed in the spring of 1946 with no light, no heat, and went on tour for twelve weeks. We opened in London to an enthusiastic reception . . . It ran from July until the end of the year and made £35,000.'[7] This would probably translate into at least £400,000 today.

According to Sybil Thorndike, the play was a 'smash hit', a verdict with which the *Times Literary Supplement* agreed in very different language.

*The Linden Tree* was Priestley's last successful production in the West End for sixteen years. Not until he collaborated with Iris Murdoch to dramatise her novel *A Severed Head* did he repeat that success.

Fast on the heels of *The Linden Tree* came *Home is Tomorrow*, a play which Priestley regarded as being as 'sound and strong a piece of dramatic writing as *The Linden Tree*', but this drama of a United Nations special agency on a tropical island does not justify that claim. Priestley remained convinced that with a 'certain amount of nursing' *Home is Tomorrow* would have survived as *Dangerous Corner* did under similar treatment, but inflation defeated him. 'By 1948 the economics were too steep. If it had cost as much in 1932 to keep *Dangerous Corner* running past itself, that play also would have vanished, never to be heard of again.'[8]

Priestley had three dominating themes in his serious plays, time, family life and social commentary. Curiously, in the *Collected Plays*, *The Linden Tree* is included under the time plays, but it is clearly sociological.

Priestley's delight in music drove him in the summer of 1945 to realise yet another incarnation of his many selves. Sir Arthur Bliss has written:

The seed of my opera later to be known as *The Olympians* was sown during a talk I had with Priestley at the Cheltenham Festival of 1945. I could not have chosen a better collaborator. He is a quick thinker, prolific of ideas, and with an enviable experience of the theatre.[9]

Early in August, Priestley wrote to Arthur Bliss:

7   Interview with Elspeth Parker, 1 January 1986.
8   *Margin Released*, J. B. Priestley, 205.
9   *As I Remember*, Sir Arthur Bliss, 170.

I enclose a very rough synopsis of the opera plot . . . It is important that you should feel its chief characters musically as I do dramatically. For instance, a character like the half-barmy old beggar woman Margot, who doesn't give a damn for anybody and has a kind of second sight, is useful for me dramatically but she may be for all I know a mere headache musically. If so, then we can if necessary scrap her. And so on.[10]

Bliss replied:

Here are some thoughts about the sequence of events. Act I – I feel the players must be more important in this than they appear in your first synopsis.[11]

Another letter from Priestley followed two weeks later.

We must be careful . . . with so many characters, not to disperse the interest. In my view which I am certain is dramatically sound, the emphasis must be on the ordinary human beings first and the actor-gods no matter how tremendous they are in Act II, must be subsidiary. We must get this straight. Either the piece is about what happens to gods when they find themselves actors among human beings or it must be about what happens to human beings when actor-gods come amongst them.[12]

The plot in its final form was not altogether unexpected coming from Priestley. The old legend that classical gods and goddesses lived on after the advent of Christianity, in humble disguises, Priestley converted into a troupe of strolling players in the reign of Louis Philippe. Called the Olympians they were to travel the roads of Europe century after century, and every hundred years, on Midsummer Night, they suddenly recovered their divine powers. Set in a Provençal village, the opera was conceived on the grand scale and Bliss and Priestley struggled to reconcile words, music and theme for two and a half years.[13]

Priestley's cantankerous, grumbling image dissolved into that of the perfect collaborator described by Bliss as 'generous and sensitive'. Nine months were to elapse before music and libretto began to fuse into the first act, and in that interval Priestley visited Russia. It was a journey he never forgot. Jane went with him, and they

10  J. B. Priestley to Arthur Bliss, 1 August 1945.
11  Arthur Bliss to Priestley, 18 August 1945.
12  Priestley to Arthur Bliss, 20 August 1945.
13  *As I Remember*, Arthur Bliss, 170.

travelled in a Red Dakota, not without apprehension because it was piloted by a woman. Everybody smoked, accordions were played, passengers sang, bottles were circulated. In other circumstances Priestley would have enjoyed it all but not on this plane. He arrived safely in Moscow to find himself one of the most popular authors in Russia 'which was to say the least most gratifying'.[14]

Against the received wisdom Priestley and Jane strolled around Moscow freely, making last-minute changes to visit unexpected places. 'Nobody objected,' Priestley wrote. 'Moscow looked gloomy when we first saw it but later, when the snow came, it had a strange beauty of its own.'

Muscovites were vigorous but 'withdrawn' and eternally battling with their transport system, food was – euphemistically – 'less plentiful than in other cities'. His written record of the trip frequently anticipated and explained away criticisms, sometimes with facts which were difficult to believe. 'Moscow citizens on higher scales of rationing do better than London.'

The state worked on the principle that 'the more valuable you are to society the more food you received.' This left unanswered the question why you were more valuable, but a popular newspaper series imposed severe limitations. According to Priestley differential rationing did not create a class system but was the result of a 'policy improvised to meet a crisis'.

They were surprised to find that luxury shops existed selling goods off the ration at high prices and Priestley claimed that 'most citizens could afford an occasional blow-out'. There followed a splendid piece of English understatement: 'Housing conditions are still very difficult.' No doubt the Muscovites looked shabby, made the best of inadequate transport and lived in crowded discomfort, but they had fought a prolonged and vicious war and were in the process of building a new economy. Under all the philistine pressure to survive, it was still possible to buy a theatre ticket in Moscow for the price of an ice-cream.

The audience for his first lecture overflowed into the streets and their enthusiasm matched that of a football crowd in England. There followed a series of gargantuan meals and drinking sessions which would have felled any lesser man. 'Here [in England] I am considered a hearty man at the table but among those Soviet men of the soil, I am a mere weakling.'[15]

14  *Sunday Express*, 18 November 1945.
15  ibid.

Jane had spent four months learning Russian before they went and she put it to good use by demanding to see Tolstoy's house on her own without a guide. She poured back a long correspondence to the children which gave an account of the Russian trip as graphically subjective as Priestley's was generalised.

Dearest all of you,
    Here we are on a warm sunny morning after 36 hours on the train, but I'll go back to the Friday evening party and it was quite pleasant. Ayonov, editor who is coming to London soon, asked me to dance with him and then said he wished I was his mother . . . Tolstoy's Moscow home which is now a museum is kept by his grand-daughter. The museum was touching. Everything as it was – the family rooms, the children's rooms. Tatiana the eldest was a painter and quite good. Masha followed her father's ideas and everything in her room was most simple, a Spartan truckle bed. Tolstoy's dressing room had a camp wash-stand and by it were his dumb bells. The simple study was just as it used to be.[16]

There was no mention of Priestley visiting the Tolstoy home. 'I get so bored with fellow authors,' he once said. Jane's letters ran to several single-spaced pages full of gossipy description but they were unenlightening about her husband.

Priestley insisted on visiting collective farms and became friendly with a number of chairmen, each with his small office in the village. 'I soon came to have an affection for these places.' They consisted of a 'simple colour-washed room with its portrait of Lenin or Stalin and rather lurid war pictures'. They smelt of 'grain or apples or grapes with the inevitable middle-aged woman who did the accounts with the help of an abacus' and an 'earnest chairman bursting with pride and figures'. At one such collective Jane grappled with her limited Russian to slip away and talk to the women. She did not record what she discovered.

The high-powered itinerary was ruthlessly pursued by their Russian hosts. The journey from Moscow to Kiev became pain-fully slow because the train track had been continuously fought over and was 'nothing but a gigantic battlefield'. Packed with every kind of person, the train carried troops on the roof, between the carriages and sometimes in the lavatories. The rich, fat, smiling Ukraine produced a 'livelier and free-er atmosphere' in Kiev than Moscow, but the fine buildings at the centre of the city lay in ruins

16   Jane Priestley to her children, 23 September 1949.

and the devastation everywhere reminded Priestley of Berlin. Optimistically he felt that Kiev was 'rapidly' returning to its old vigorous and relatively prosperous self. 'They gave us a roaring, if exhausting, good time which included everything: theatre, ballet, opera, parties in town . . . except to us frailer mortals, an adequate amount of quiet and repose.'[17]

They flew over the steppes, the Black Sea and on between snow-capped mountains to the Volga. Following the Volga they bounced along a road to Stalingrad, and there encountered a vast wilderness of shattered tanks and planes. An assistant commissar escorted them and pointed with pride as they approached the city: 'Stalingrad,' he said, but all they could see was 'miles and miles of ruins'. Dwellings had been hammered together from flattened petrol cans and the cave dwellers 'came out to grin at us'.[18] The tattered remnants of the Wehrmacht were working all over Russia and thousands concentrated at Stalingrad, a 'cigarette-smoking, shambling, mournful lot'. Priestley believed that the Russians were tough with Wehrmacht survivors but not vindictive. Leningrad followed with its noble sweep of waterfront, Italian palaces, innumerable canals and bridges, one beautiful vista overtaken by another.

They left Leningrad cloaked in snow and he later wrote:

> The last we saw of Russia was the sight of . . . friendly, smiling faces whose image remained with us as the lights vanished and there was only a vague blur of snow in the darkness. They welcomed us as friends, we said goodbye as friends.[19]

Priestley summed up his Russian experience in his last *Sunday Express* article. A direct, warm-hearted and generous people, the Russians enjoyed similar pleasures to Priestley which created a ready-made rapport. The outside world put a sinister interpretation on much apparently Machiavellian manoeuvring in Russia which was really the result of bureaucratic stupidity or inefficiency. It would be recognised as such if it happened anywhere else than Russia. Marxism might have some validity as a political and economic creed but as a philosophy of life, its pedantic dialectic was too narrow for the 'brooding Russian soul'. Russian interpretation of Marxism had concentrated too much on materialism – 'producing

17   *Sunday Express*, 25 November 1945.
18   ibid., 9 December 1945.
19   ibid., 23 December 1945.

so many tractors an hour' – and said too little about psychological and spiritual matters, 'on which they could issue a formidable challenge to capitalist countries'.

Priestley admitted the political police, sudden arrests, labour camps and 'all the grim tactics of suppression' but tried to reconcile the writer's life under such a regime.

> They cannot publicly produce work that violently disagrees with Soviet policy but they instinctively work parallel with the general party line, living as they do in the same atmosphere and desiring the same end.

An element of rationalisation ran through so much of what he wrote about this trip in 1946 and many years later he realised that he was not altogether free from the charge of gullibility. Conservative MPs accused him of something worse: seriously distorting the facts.

Retrospectively, Priestley's articles must be read in the perspective of the political climate immediately after the war when heroic Russia had suffered more than any other of the Allies, and won international respect. No one wished to cause gratuitous offence to the mutilated bear and Priestley went out of his way to avoid doing so. It was a common practice.

Back in London by April of the following year, Priestley was writing once more to Arthur Bliss about their opera. 'Thanks for your letter. I am delighted you have made such an enthusiastic start and are finding the words easy to work with. Where any scene or aria refuses to come to life musically in your mind because my treatment and rhythm do not help you, then don't hesitate to say so – and we'll go over the passage and we'll find different words.'[20]

By August of 1946 Bliss wrote:

> I think after the rapid sequence of events in Act I and the exciting balletic scenes later in Act II, that the opening of this second act should be in the nature of a quiet intermezzo, a link between two ground swells . . . Lavette will break the moonlight quiet with his outburst but Madeleine will recapture this meditative nocturne mood with her song, and the love scene with Hector will also be a meditating one. I think that the mood of this human scene before the gods appear should be affected by the light. We all talk, sing, think a

20  Priestley to Arthur Bliss, 24 April 1946.

bit differently under a full moon, and except for Lavette's jagged and irritable intrusion, I feel the first quarter of an hour or so could well be labelled 'Nocturne in F Minor'!

When Diana addresses the moon it is a very different thing. It is hers.[21]

By April Priestley was worried about the title of the opera:

The Gods Grow Old has much to recommend it as a title, particularly in sound and shape and neatness. But as one or two people (notably Peters) have pointed out, it has a rather melancholy ring that in fact does not suit our piece. I have spent a good part of this morning with dictionaries of synonyms and the like, trying to improve on it. Gods in Exile (this was the name of Heine's piece and is an exact description of our plot). The Gods Go By, Passing Gods, Banished Gods, but I am not satisfied yet with any of these alternatives. I have spent so much time – an unusual thing with me, by the way – on this title that I seem to have gone stale on it, and perhaps we need some fresh minds on the problem.[22]

Accepted by Covent Garden in 1947, The Olympians did not go into production until 1949, and there were ominous signs at the outset. Bliss received a cable from Benjamin Britten and Peter Pears in America wishing him good luck but its wording implied that he would certainly need it. Within a few days the very different temperaments of the conductor Karl Rankl and the producer Peter Brook clashed and tension mounted to the point where they avoided speaking to each other. Bliss described other difficulties. He did not get his principal tenor until ten days before the opening night and he made the mistake of inviting critics to the dress rehearsal, apparently unaware of the dangers involved.

Bliss retreated into the Garrick Club on the first night convinced that all was lost. His final comment became a masterpiece of understatement: 'The Olympians was understandably greeted with very mixed criticism.'

Priestley's later account of the birth and death of an opera should have been torn and traversed by personal complications in the years 1947–9 which led him into the most profound love relationship in

21  Arthur Bliss to Priestley, 29 August 1946.
22  Priestley to Arthur Bliss, 8 April 1947.

his life. It was remarkable that against such a background in 1946–9 he produced no less than six other plays, independently of essays, journalism and lectures.[23]

23   *The Arts Under Socialism* (lecture); *Theatre Outlook* (criticism); *Ever Since Paradise, The Linden Tree, The Rose & Crown, Home Is Tomorrow, The Golden Fleece* (plays); *The Olympians* (opera libretto); *Summer Day's Dream* (play).

# 22

# Jacquetta Hawkes and Jack Priestley
## 1947–9

A tall, gravely beautiful woman with a touch of austerity in her features, Jacquetta Priestley today could easily qualify as the high priestess of some modern archaeological cult which combined creative life with intellectuality. Underlying this image is the warmth of someone very much a woman. As a young girl she treasured two pictures on her nursery wall which enshrined attitudes later to become part of her credo: 'The Cat That Walked By Itself', taken from Kipling's story, and a Rackham painting of Puck from *A Midsummer Night's Dream*, inscribed: 'Lord What Fools These Mortals Be'. Her upper middle-class family automatically stressed the value of self-discipline and tended to frown upon almost any form of demonstrative behaviour. Such restraints left something unsatisfied in Jacquetta and in reaction she dared to revel in the noise and excitement of a midsummer fair although the exhilaration of the merry-go-round was qualified quickly by sickness. Fireworks at any time were exciting and Guy Fawkes Night was an occasion which she loved passionately. 'I was the founder president of a trespassing society with marks awarded according to the dangers of capture.'[1]

Searching for the origins of her early passion for archaeology, she admitted deeply unconscious influences but refused to believe that Freud's theory of a desire to return to the womb had any personal validity. There remained a possible connection with her total lack of interest in any sexual matters. 'I was not fascinated by my faeces or nipples. I had absolutely no knowledge of masturbation, or desire for such manipulation of myself or anyone else. Although I did learn the facts of life from an excited small girl at my dame-school, I was so little concerned by them that I quite forgot the information and had to rediscover it by logical questioning at the time of my sister's marriage.'[2]

1   *A Quest of Love*, Jacquetta Hawkes, 208.
2   ibid.

Roman and Anglo-Saxon antiquities scattered in the family garden also influenced her but they were not the prime cause of her passion – 'interest would be too cool a word' – for nature and the past.

'Born to the scientific heart of Cambridge, I was able to benefit early and fully from the struggle for the higher education of women that had begun in earnest some half a century before.'[3] Jacquetta Priestley vividly recalled the historic occasion when undergraduates stormed Newnham College overwhelming the heavy bronze gates to join the college dance. 'It was an act as symbolic of revolution as the storming of the Bastille.' Elaborate restrictions designed to prevent women from sharing not only the men's lecture rooms but their beds and even their sofas were still rigidly enforced.

By the time she went up to Newnham the tide of liberation had so far risen that chaperons were no longer necessary and many of the more austere college rules relaxed. Her attitude to women's liberation today acknowledges the value of the advances made, but dislikes those 'militant female persons who seek to mutilate our language and destroy all useful, mutually pleasing, civilised little conventions that help to express the true nature of sexual relationships.'[4]

Throughout her undergraduate years she remained unaroused and did not expect any of her men friends to desire her. Two early proposals came from men who shared her interest in archaeology, one a large, blond Etonian, who invited her to a May Ball week. He chose to entertain her to dinner at a farmhouse in the Fens and comedy supervened. 'When, towards the end of a frightful meal, he asked me to marry him, the bench tipped up, as one leg sank into the mud. We still went to the ball but passed the night in miserable embarrassment.'[5]

According to her own account it was Jacquetta Hawkes's upbringing, total lack of understanding of either sex or love, and – in her own words – stupidity, which next led her into serious involvement 'long before [she] was ready'.[6]

Reading for the Archaeological Tripos in her second year at Newnham, some actual experience of excavation became a prerequisite of further development. The initiation site chosen was

3   ibid., 206.
4   ibid., 207.
5   ibid., 209.
6   ibid., 195.

Camulodunum, the pre-Roman capital of Cunobelin at Colchester, and there she met a clever young man, Christopher Hawkes, whose double first at Oxford had led to an already brilliant career, accompanied by a private reputation as a lady-killer. The air was thick with rumours that Christopher successfully reconciled the roles of distinguished archaeologist and Don Juan.

His family and upbringing in London had been very different from hers in the country and he moved on the edge of 'society', where Ascot and presentations at court were part of the natural order. His girlfriends appeared to Jacquetta 'alarmingly smart and sophisticated', but since she did not regard men as sexual objects that did not especially disturb her. Newnham friends who spoke of his success with glamorous young women indicated that if she did possibly have an interest in him she would not stand a chance against such competition. Challenged by the gossip, Jacquetta set out for Colchester with 'a keen interest in my Director of Excavations'.

Expecting to meet the dashingly handsome grandson of a Spanish grandmother she was deeply disappointed by Hawkes's lack of inches and short-sightedness. Her evaluation of men changed dramatically over the years from those first adolescent expectations, but for the moment she felt badly 'let down'.

Archaeological digs are fertile grounds for affairs with the camaraderie of a mixed group, sharing mutual interests, the open-air life and the tension of being on the verge of exciting discoveries. There were many suitors attracted to Jacquetta and they cultivated her company but none could compare with Christopher Hawkes, a 'lively, clever, immensely energetic master of my beloved subject'. He courted her continuously but – surprisingly – she cannot remember when or how he first declared his love. Back in London, he escorted her through a social round, displaying immense confidence, encyclopaedic knowledge of worldly behaviour and unmistakable devotion to her.

Astonished by being placed in the first class of the final tripos, Jacquetta was awarded a travelling scholarship which carried her away to excavate in the Mount Carmel caves, and with her went a framed photograph of Christopher, at which she gazed every evening, debating whether she should marry him.

By the spring of that year they were 'officially engaged', but there was a lack of total commitment on her part which constantly troubled her. She and Hawkes shared an 'earnest involvement in their subject', she was moved by his devotion and admired and liked him, but an element of doubt persisted. 'Did I "love" him? How could I tell? I knew that I felt little pleasure in such kissing and embracing as we had practised – but might not bliss arrive without consummation?'[7] Against all her hopes she remembered a feeling of betrayal when she 'discovered that for all his reputation my fiancé, too, was virgin'.[8]

Their first serious clash arose because Christopher, a devout high Anglican, insisted that they must be married in church, and she, who had never been baptised, felt the fraudulence implicit in such a celebration. 'There was a day at Winchester College when he marched me weeping round and round the cloisters until I surrendered and agreed to be wed in my father's college chapel.'[9]

Once committed to a conventional wedding she was – as she put it – helpless before her masterful mother-in-law. Christopher's mother took over the arrangements, a satin and gold gown was specially designed, a smart theatrical couturière fitted out the bridesmaids and every detail of the wedding was planned.

A sense of unreality pervaded these proceedings and in between writing endless thank-you letters for unwelcome wedding presents she tried to preserve remnants of individuality and self-respect by writing her very first scholarly article.

Sensing that her daughter had considerable reservations about her choice of husband, her mother asked at intervals whether she really wanted to marry Christopher. Jacquetta suspected that her questionings were not based upon compatibility or its lack in Christopher, but on a fear that he might prove to be too lustful (Spanish blood) which would lead to extravagant demands classifiable in her dictionary of sexuality as nasty.

'I recall a sense of bewildered incredulity as I went up the chapel on my father's arm . . . I saw through my veil that Christopher was wearing spats . . . I floated through it all lost in unreality.'

A last remark of Jacquetta's as the best man, Count Orloff, was seeing them off from Cambridge station, crystallised her fears. She leant out of the train window and said, 'I wish you were coming with us.' Her words did not then strike her as ill-timed.

The honeymoon on Majorca moved between pleasure and disappointment with Christopher insisting that a vast *letto matrimoniale* should replace the twin beds and the resultant uproar from

7   ibid., 210.
8   ibid., 211.
9   ibid.

manipulating the monster into the bedroom, shaking the small hotel to the roots. There was no tumult of sexuality but straight-forward occasional indulgence. 'While I came nowhere near to passion, it would not be just to say that I proved frigid or altogether indifferent. I wanted to please my husband and even gained some little pleasure in the attempt.'[10]

Whether Christopher Hawkes's instinctive reactions to life had been crushed by a domineering mother whose impact was rein-forced by the austerities of Winchester, while Jacquetta as a late developer suffered emotional arrestation, are questions to which she found no complete answer.

As Jacquetta wrote: 'If we had ever known real passion together, everything else might have been well – but why had we not attained it? I now understand that all delight and intensity of passion in love-making depend upon the mood, upon imagination.'

True though that was, it really begged the question which she proceeded to answer: 'For the imagination to be kindled some profound psychological polarity between the individual man and the individual woman is evidently necessary.'[11]

In her prolonged search for an explanation of sexual attraction, Jacquetta Hawkes came to the conclusion that 'the magnetism of polarity' was the basis of what later became the most satisfying relationship in her life. For the rest any attempt to spell out the meaning of magnetic polarity was 'a mystery and I hope it will be allowed to remain so'.

A son was born in the fourth year of her marriage which compensated in part for the growing sense that the marriage was not working. Christopher disappeared into the book he was writ-ing, working far into the night with a fanaticism which needed more than inspiration for its full explanation. Their meetings in leisure hours diminished, their social life dwindled away and without open quarrelling a vague sense of unhappiness steadily became obtrusive.

The Second World War broke into their married life to disrupt it decisively. It was decided that for their son's sake Jacquetta should move out of London to the illusory security of Dorset and before she had time to settle into the new routine a disturbing and quite new emotional experience broke into her life. 'It meant a sudden undamming of feelings of an intensity I did not know I possessed,

10   ibid., 212.
11   ibid., 212.

and I shall never lose the beauties of spring in the Dorset countryside that came to me while my love was at its height.'

It is necessary to indicate a merging of fact and fiction in Jacquetta Priestley's account in *A Quest of Love* of the relationship which followed with 'Amelia', the details of which as reproduced in her book have certain analogies with reality. As told in *A Quest of Love*, 'Amelia' – which was not her name – had always strongly attracted Jacquetta against her better judgement. When she confided in her, 'Amelia' laughingly remarked that women who cultivated their brains risked the danger of destroying their instincts. Events moved swiftly after that encounter. Jacquetta's attraction to 'Amelia' deepened, she told her she was about to move to London to write a book and visiting Amelia one day as she played in the music room, 'the simple fondness with which I watched the woman at the piano . . . was turned instantly into a wild love'.

There came the evening when 'anatomising' various acquaintances and laughing together over their findings, the great silent house, the candlelight and the intensity of their communication enraptured her, but when 'Amelia' invited physical fulfilment Jacquetta had no inclination whatever to respond.

Shortly afterwards she determined to return to London and rejoin her husband to face the second half of the blitz, which had by now produced a stoical resignation in most of the population. For the first time Jacquetta faced and overcame extreme physical fear and shared with Christopher the hardships of a blacked-out, beleaguered city. Later, the two experiences combined to 'make a small compensation for the deceits that were to follow'.[12]

Immediately she became an administrative civil servant in the War Cabinet offices and saw, from within, the workings of the higher bureaucracy with interest, insight and amusement. The disruptions of private life produced a new form of social life and in the midst of the turmoil she tried 'two foolish experiments', which proved as unsatisfactory as her marriage. She remembers that she was first unfaithful to the sound of Mozart. It is still not possible to name the man involved but he had recently exchanged a cut-and-thrust correspondence in the *New Statesman* with – and here we reconnect with the main subject of this biography – J. B. Priestley.

This coincidence of names did not at the time have any special meaning for Jacquetta. All unaware of what was to follow she read the correspondence with enjoyment, discussing the pros and cons

12   ibid., 203.

with her new lover. A 'fascinating man' who was also a 'well-known womaniser', he developed a relationship with Jacquetta which reconciled love-making with intellectual friendship. So intense did this become that on one occasion, meeting him unexpectedly at an art exhibition, Jacquetta 'all but fainted'. If the springs of her emotions had been released by her swift relationship with Amelia, that had prepared her for this her first satisfactory realisation of heterosexuality. Overwhelmed by the torrential release, she found herself subject to 'visions akin to those of godhead' and poured out poetry some of which was later regarded as good.

This affair was one of two or three 'experiments', all clandestine and carried out with increasing difficulty, because her family life was now complicated by a son. Her relationship with her new lover continued undetected for several years and then suddenly he died of a brain haemorrhage and she was overwhelmed with grief. Out of the ashes of that affair there was now to grow an entirely new and much more profound relationship which justifies the exploration of her previous life in some detail. Simultaneously with J. B. Priestley's selection as a delegate to the UNESCO conference in Mexico City for 1947, Jacquetta became UK secretary for UNESCO, which meant that she constantly sent him endless preliminary documents signed J. J. Hawkes. Priestley later declared that months before he met her he was already unaccountably fascinated 'by the name at the foot of these documents' and his secretary took to referring to her as 'Your Mrs Hawkes'.

There followed a UNESCO briefing session in Belgrave Square at which Priestley sat shoulder to shoulder with Rab Butler and across the table from Sir John Maud, a seasoned civil servant with whom, it was said, one 'always had to take the smooth with the smooth'. As Jacquetta came into the room Priestley noticed her and her attention was immediately drawn to him, but it was not until the meeting broke up and a reception followed that they actually met. A 'gooey, pink confection – probably jelly' was served and Jacquetta went up to Priestley with hers and offered it to him 'in such a way as to suggest mutual, amused distaste'.[13] Their words were few, their communication brief, but some indefinable response – the magnetism of polarity – made them feel that 'all was decided from that moment'.

Before he left for Mexico dramatic new developments in Mary's life nearly threw his plans into confusion with the result that he

13  Interview with Mrs Jacquetta Priestley, 1 September 1985.

almost missed making the trip necessary to the development of the most important experience in his life. As a musical student Mary intended to study in Paris but when no suitable 'digs' were available she went to Geneva where she met another student, Sigvald Michelsen, and fell in love with him. They returned to London in the holidays full of the glow of youthful romance but their enthusiasm was quickly dashed by their reception in the Priestley household. Although Priestley was so musical he strongly disapproved of this her first love and as Mary put it succinctly 'they all hated him'. Indeed, her mother, she said, disapproved of all her boyfriends.

Clearly Michelsen's working-class origins were not objectionable to a man with Priestley's ancestry but he worried about a disturbed person like Mary becoming involved with a penniless student. Against her father's advice Mary became engaged to Michelsen and that built up stronger resistance from her parents who presently insisted that they must part for six months and 'think things over'. She began living alone in one room in the flat of her sister Sylvia, subsisting on casual violin work eked out by money from her father. A prey to nightmares, Mary was already under analytic treatment from Dr Gerhard Adler and when he suddenly took a holiday she felt completely unsupported and broke down.

In the beginning Priestley did not appreciate the nature of her illness, and wrote Mary a letter on 20 February 1947, the contents of which he later regretted. Within a very short time it became apparent that he had badly misjudged Mary's condition. A psychiatrist recommended that she should be parted from her parents for a time and she entered St Andrew's Clinic in Northamptonshire. Conventional treatment with pills, relaxation and therapy had no result and the doctors decided that there was nothing for it but ECT (electric convulsion therapy). Mary claimed that she was supposed to be dying from dehydration but 'my father went off to a UNESCO meeting leaving Mother dreadfully unsupported'.

Mary described occasions when her mother suddenly fell ill for no apparent reason and was suspected of having heart trouble. Sometimes she had beside her bed a glass containing 'heart drops' or digitalis tablets but it gradually became clear that there were strong psychosomatic elements in many of her apparent illnesses. There were even occasional surgical solutions to problems which might have yielded to psychiatric treatment. Her sudden 'flops' were liable to take place at highly inconvenient moments and some could be seen as manipulative conversions intended to concentrate Jack's attention exclusively on her. These were the occasions when according to his daughter 'she drove him bonkers'. However, there was every reason now for Jane to experience 'breakdown'.

It is fashionable nowadays to assume that schizophrenia is not psychological but has a predisposing chemical basis. This ignores the fact that disentangling the genetic from the environmental with any certainty is very difficult. There are cases where the psychological disturbance is so powerful that it may predominate, and frequently psychological stress contributes the triggering factor. If Mary's disturbance was not psychological, stress remained a very strong component. However, according to Mary, the original suspicion that she had suffered a schizophrenic breakdown turned out to be qualified and the final diagnosis was manic depressive, a much more encouraging report since unlike schizophrenia there need be no mental deterioration.

The cruder forms of shock treatment were still practised and the effects on the patient could be shattering. Certainly, with Mary, the results were reasonably good, but as so frequently happened, not lasting. In recollection her happiest years were between nine and fourteen when the family was living at Billingham Manor with croquet and bowls occupying the afternoons, and Jack playing one game after another with a theatrical aggressiveness which could be very funny. For the moment her mood was far removed from happiness.

Seen from Priestley's point of view Mary's picture of events changes perspective. Before he left for Mexico in the middle of Mary's breakdown Priestley had written to J. J. Hawkes, secretary of UNESCO, cancelling his proposed attendance at the conference but his family intervened and finally persuaded him to go because 'they felt he was getting too much distressed'. Inevitably Jane came under great strain from her daughter's breakdown and fell ill but the precise nature of her illness was not clear.

Mrs J. J. Hawkes and Priestley sailed for the conference in Mexico on the *Queen Mary* and when her usual seasickness overtook Jacquetta she failed to appear at a meeting of delegates. Priestley was deeply disappointed. Characteristically, whenever he travelled by sea, he would select a woman he hoped to sleep with before the voyage ended and the frequency with which his expectations were realised made Jacquetta in recollection refer to him as a 'hunter'.[14]

14   ibid.

It was not until they were installed in the modest Mexico City Hotel where the plumbing flooded on the slightest provocation, that seasickness developed for Jacquetta into enteritis. Her first visitor was Priestley who brought with him a medicine bottle full of brandy and announced that everybody had enteritis. Big, burly, confident, he was now a man of fifty-three, with a deep voice, which resonated in the room. Jacquetta claims that this was the first time she had a genuine sense of being looked after, a sense which she further claims she never lost in their relationship.[15]

A dinner invitation inevitably followed. The first sparkling response between them was qualified when she told him that she did not much like his writings, and Priestley became cross, pointing out that she had read only a select few of his works. Conversation quickly recovered its pace, communication deepened and for Priestley something which he could only describe with his special word – magic – marked out this first real encounter. Writing about it later, Jacquetta said, 'When we went back to our hotel along the noble and now quietening Paseo de la Reforma there seemed to be just the two of us walking as one beneath the stars.'[16]

What at first had characteristics of romance quickly revealed for Jacquetta, a woman in her late thirties, 'the pleasures and spiritual transformations of total love'.[17] She was, in her own words, 'created anew'. A special delight for Priestley was to discover that her 'excessive' external coolness was 'no more than a deception'.

Despite the sense of total commitment to something more than a conference affair, as the six weeks of the conference drew to a close they tried to reconcile themselves to the inevitability of parting. Appointments in New York forced Jack to leave earlier than other delegates and as his train drew away flooded by a sunset which might have been specially created for the occasion, he was already writing her an urgent passionate letter.[18]

Tuesday night

My Darling,
  I know I shouldn't be doing this – it's against everything I meant or even said – but I can't help it. I must write one letter to you – if

15  ibid.
16  *A Quest of Love*, Jacquetta Hawkes, 216.
17  ibid.
18  Priestley to Jacquetta Hawkes, from Mexico, 'Tuesday night', November 1947.

only, selfishly, to try and relieve myself of this terrible weight of sadness and loss. (I'm trying to write very slowly, on a train that is not only swaying but bouncing.) You were right of course not to come to the station – it would have been a messy anti-climax. I was looked after by Godfrey-Williams and George, and all went well until about six o'clock, when the whole landscape took on an unearthly beauty. I had opened my bottle of Scotch and was sipping and staring and brooding when you came flooding back to me in full terrible force and then ever since it's been hell. Missing and missing and missing you. I'll get over the worst of it soon, I suppose, but just now I feel older and emptier and sadder than I ever remember feeling before. I seem to have walked straight into the emotional trap. Would I really have it different – remembering how miserable I was on my way to Mexico City? I don't know – honestly, I don't know, my darling. In any case, I suppose, I've feasted – on beauty and strangeness and comradeship and fun – and now here comes the bill. Hell, that's my affair and at least I can thank you, which I do most humbly and tenderly, for all you gave and all you meant – all the enchantment that I thought had gone for ever. (Ah – but the exile now, my darling! The blank staring face of the world!) Hell, I have known all this last week, with every deepening moment, that we had gone further than we told ourselves we would. Already we began staring at each other out of sadness and loss – homeless lovers. How strange it has been – as strange as your curious changing beauty, which does not really belong to my world. (But I knew it deep down, from the first – recognised, before my heart was involved, the priestess of the archaic cult – said so in what I thought was fun. 'J. J. Hawkes' my God!) Take this miserable letter, kiss it once, and then burn it. If you can get a letter to me at New York that will be wonderful, but no letter will be possible, to me, in England, as all go through secretaries; but I'll get hold of you some-time, soon too, unless my family crisis develops. I sit here in the damned train, holding your lovely image in my arms. I can hardly see for tears. If it will make you happier to forget me, then do so – and God bless you!

    J.

This was the beginning of a flow of love-letters which revealed a Jack Priestley different from any public or family image. To all intents and purposes a fully mature man of fifty-three he was still emotionally so unrealised that for the first time in his life he was caught up in an overwhelming love which brought semi-poetic passion into his writing. Jacquetta's response was equally ecstatic

but coolly recollected in tranquillity: 'I remember wandering joy-
fully through the streets of the old city, hunting for a post office
from which to send him a telegraphic message of accord.'[19]

A second letter followed fast on the heels of the first:[20]

My darling,

There was a taxi just along the road and the driver was having a
pee, so I had one too, and claimed him to drive me home. I got there
in no time, got myself a whisky, and then discovered this remaining
bit of notepaper, and felt that I must write something on it to you.
After all, my dear, we are writers and after a wonderful evening it is
our job to try to understand what is happening.

I know that you feel it is all very simple, but to the simple soul – to
me – it is all very complicated. I try to break it down into bits, but of
course I can't. First there is the curious and fascinating mixture,
impossible to convey to you, of strength – the power and thrust and
passion of that wiry body – and fragility – the delicate ghost body –
the epitome of everything romantic and feminine – who vanished
into the shadows of the garden that night at Cuernavaca. Then there
is a kind of honesty and non-feminine (there is a schoolboy grin with
it) gallantry, the useful admission of mistakes, idiocies, that catches
at my heart. (Here I pass by though you won't want me to, the
absolutely feminine and straightforward appeal of the lovely strong
legs, the fine breasts, the hair that induces a wonderful tenderness in
me.) Then there is, at another level, a side of us as two chaps
belonging to opposing camps, a Greek and Trojan sentry meeting,
who find, perhaps reluctantly, much value in each other. Then,
below that, is the sense of a great welcome strangeness that is yet a
coming home. You explore the last continent, the forgotten city,
and find in the heart of it, behind the god in the great temple, your
favourite books, the chair you always wanted, and somebody
playing the lost lovely tune. (Darling, a reproach. You are an egocentric lover, though a self-less friend, hurrying towards your own
sensations. Let's talk about this.) I am absolutely certain that we
need each other in a very special way – and only pride will prevent
our admitting this – and that we are able to bridge a colossal gap, not
just because you are exquisitely lovely and desirable (though you are
– bless you –) but because, though we differ in so many things, each
of us has a very personal vision of mankind as a whole, you through
the long vista of pre-history, and I through drama and politics. We
turn into poets though different kinds, more or less at the same

19  *A Quest of Love*, Jacquetta Hawkes, 217.
20  Priestley to Jacquetta Hawkes, 'midnight Monday', November 1947.

moment. This is the last bit of Maria Cristina so I use it to say I love
you.

     J.

Unfortunately Jacquetta's replies to these letters were either
destroyed by Priestley or have simply disappeared. We know that
occasionally he had his own private holocaust of papers in his
famous incinerator, sometimes in Arizona, sometimes elsewhere,
and invaluable documentary evidence was destroyed. His motives
are unknown. There were episodes which he wished to conceal,
although the current moral climate today would make his caution
unnecessary. A third letter, without an address, probably written in
December of the same year, complained that Jacquetta's written
response was too guarded.[21]

> I had hoped to be able to write a long letter to you, but I have to do
> everything – packing etc. – in a great hurry – against time.
>
> First, business – there is nothing dutiable in my suitcase, which
> contains nothing but clothes brought out from England. Secondly:
> we must have a meeting of our UNESCO Publicity Sub-Commit-
> tee before Christmas. Please get in touch with me about this.
>
> Ritchie Calder has just rung up. If you had given him a letter for
> me – a fine, long, frank letter, not a cool and cagey one – I'd have had
> it now. This relationship has to pass two tests. One: ordeal by
> glamour girls – it has already passed here, for while beautiful young
> actresses look at me with such adoring eyes, I think of you. Test
> two: Home again – will be stiffer but it will survive that too.
>
> I'm sorry about this wretched scrawl but it just can't be helped.
>
> I feel closer even than I did in Mexico City – and that guarded little
> letter of yours made no difference.
>
>     Your loving J.

It was Ouspensky who inspired another letter to Davison at this
time which said that he proposed to change his work and dig deeper
to the unconscious level in the hope of releasing the poetic stuff –
'unless it is too late'. This would correspond with Davison's
criticisms and those of a brilliant new woman friend, Jacquetta
Hawkes.[22]

Meanwhile Jane had written an anguished letter to her husband
giving an account of Mary's progress. Jane said she was very tired
and worried, first because of Mary's breakdown but second because

21   Priestley to Jacquetta Hawkes, 2 December 1947.
22   Priestley to Edward Davison, December 1947.

their marriage seemed to have run dry yet again. She could understand why he had to go to the UNESCO conference but there were times when she wondered whether his new political activities would not multiply the strains of his writing and reflect badly on their home life. It was difficult enough already. Two people (unnamed) had asked her why he had gone off and left her to cope with Mary on her own. She did not listen to them because she knew he cared about Mary and was faced with a *fait accompli* but she hoped he would not be away much longer. This letter was followed by a number of cables, one of which said that Mary's condition had improved and the signs were hopeful.

Coincidentally with his letters to Jacquetta and Davison Priestley continued writing to his wife. While he was still at the Hotel Maria Cristina in Mexico, his first letter to Jane read:

Dear love,

This will be a short letter. I sent a longish one to you a few days ago, but am worried about it because they seem very vague about airmail here. Have had only one letter from you so far but the good new cables have lifted a great load from me. So far I don't like it much here. The altitude plus the doubtful food, the noise and the Conference fuss leaves us all feeling exhausted and everybody has tummy troubles. (Like Egypt.) The eczema on my hands is gone but I am putting Harvey's ointment on them all the time. We are not making much progress so far in the Conference, but I am hoping to be home earlier than was first planned, though this will probably mean flying from here to N.Y. and then from there to England. But I'll let you know as soon as I have definite news. Because of airmail difficulty, I must keep this to one sheet.

I think of you, my love, and of our dear Mary, constantly and with great love and tenderness. Bless you!

Your loving JACK[23]

Another letter followed nine days later.

Dear Jane,

Your letter of the 14th has just arrived. It seems slow going and I'm hoping you have received the letter from me enclosing the little silver things for Mary. I got your two cables, the disappointing one and then the better one (thank God) on one of my busiest days here, when I was preparing to put through the large Programme and Budget Commission a great half-million dollar production which I

23 Priestley to Jane Priestley, 12 November 1947.

initiated. I've now done this – to much applause, because it's the boldest thing UNESCO has attempted and now I have only a sub-committee on this scheme, to work out details for my International Theatre Institute. I am hoping to leave here by train on Tuesday, arriving in New York on Saturday morning. How I get from New York home I don't know yet, as there are no British boats sailing until the Q.Mary on the 11th, and I'm not going to wait so long, even if I have to fly. I'm not flying from here to N.Y. because I'm very tired and rather seedy from the altitude and queer food and so I must have a few days' rest on the train. I shan't stay in New York a day longer than I have to, because I don't like it – and anyhow I want to get back to you. One day I hope, we'll come and explore this strange country together – outside this city, which I detest, it becomes fascinating though, a strange and arid landscape. I long for you, my dear love, for this sad business with Mary puts a great strain on me too, and I've found it impossible to join in most of the parties here etc., though I tried hard not to brood and to do my part as best I can. But my heart's not in it. I'll be with you, my love, as soon as I possibly can.

    Yours,
    JACK.[24]

In the multifarious forms of love which make it possible to love two people simultaneously but differently, it was clear that Priestley had by no means detached himself from Jane but how far guilt influenced what he wrote is difficult to determine. Inescapably he was disturbed about leaving Jane to cope with Mary but his love for Jacquetta now overwhelmed everything. The situation was further complicated by the account he gave to Jacquetta of the fierce atmosphere perpetually threatening his marriage, due in part he claimed to Jane's bursts of hysteria, which, according to her, were inevitable given what she modestly described as her husband's 'unreliability'. Back in England matters became very complicated. Still living with Jane in a state of armed neutrality his meetings with Jacquetta had to be fitted into their mutual commitments as married people. Despairing of his home life Priestley found himself torn between a desire to break away completely and a deep-rooted instinct against deserting his family. His writing commitments, his clandestine life with Jacquetta, his unexpressed quarrels with Jane and his responsibilities to Mary led him into a labyrinth through which one single thread always led powerfully back towards

24  Priestley to Jane Priestley, 21 November 1947.

Jacquetta. Living in the cross-current of so many tensions, Priestley remembered the days far back in 1925 when his first wife was dying and his affair with Jane had just begun. Much greater strains now tested his resilience because Mary remained an entirely new worry and his inability to divide his attention between all his responsibilities led to sleepless nights, and writer's block. The Good Companions Trust Fund supplied some of the finance for Mary's treatment, but private analysis had to be paid for by her father.[25] She remained an inescapable part of his life and there were times when he felt weighed down by her 'as if by a huge, entangling anchor'.

Priestley's letters to Jacquetta reflected the fragmented assignations snatched in odd places at uncertain times which characterised the relationship over the next two years. Christopher Hawkes remained ignorant of his wife's infidelity, and Jane might have known but was unaware whether this new affair had any more significance than those which had gone before.

It seems unexpected that Jacquetta Priestley with her background should have assimilated their mutual unfaithfulness as inevitable but it has to be remembered that she was brought up in the heart of the Cambridge scientific milieu. She realised that the conventional values of the day would not only damn her relationship with Priestley but in their existing circumstances regard it as 'deplorable'. Nevertheless, its ever deepening power swept all such scruples away. 'Knowing how full of wonders it was' even at this time, she could not accept society's censure.

Early in 1948 Priestley continued his correspondence with Jacquetta.[26] His first letter said that he was coming up to London but Jane intended to accompany him which would make meeting Jacquetta difficult. He must find some reason for staying a few extra days but he would not know whether that was possible until he arrived in London. If Jacquetta had already made arrangements he would understand and they would certainly have more time later. He was wrestling with hay fever which had not been as bad as usual and he had managed to continue working. 'Last week seemed to me one of our very best evenings, and I loved every minute of it. This is a wretched little note but I'm very busy, have a headache, and woke up far too early. Behind it, however, is a deeply devoted type.'

25  The money earned by *The Good Companions* was placed in a trust fund to be distributed among the children.
26  Priestley to Jacquetta Hawkes, early 1948.

They met whenever and wherever they could and each of these meetings, 'delicious in themselves', always had one among many other ends in view: 'We made love indoors and out, by day and by night, in borrowed offices and flats, in the box of a provincial theatre or the garden of the Institute of Archaeology.'[27] Completely surrendered to the relationship, Jacquetta revelled in its wild, clandestine nature, telling herself that it was a finer thing to be a mistress than a conventional wife. Later in life she saw an 'element of display' in this behaviour but it was directed not to the external world but to her inner self, which made it, in her eyes, forgivable. 'Having lived for so long without knowing what it was to love a man and be loved, in a union of body, heart and mind, and then to attain it so suddenly and mightily with a man who moved in so exciting a world – surely I can forgive myself if I gloried in it, indulged in a kind of foolish pride in this long delayed fulfilment?'[28]

Priestley's next letter written in January 1948 was in response to a letter of Jacquetta's which objected to his reading too many detective stories and criticised his writing habits. It was a tribute to the overwhelming nature of their love that Jacquetta, born into a classically correct background with values inherited from a different upbringing, should have merged so profoundly with a man drawn from opposite roots. Her writing was clear, lucid, flowing with an element of classical detachment; his colourful, direct, and highly subjective. The contradictions multiplied. Instead of Jacquetta referring to their relationship in spiritual terms, Priestley saw her love expressing itself through her body but such simplified extrapolations could not encompass its complicated richness.

The long letter in January 1948 expressed the view that he had been 'ambushed' by love and revealed the devices to which they were driven even in correspondence.[29]

My Darling,
    Have started my work again, but must write to you, rather under difficulties, if only to stop thinking about what I shall write to you. First, my reception of your letter may easily, I fancy, confirm a view of me as an irritably vain man, too used to easy praise and flattery. What you have to remember is that I have got you tied up in my mind, not as a person when I meet you but when I read such a letter, with a type and generation whose attitude I am tired of – its

27   *A Quest of Love*, Jacquetta Hawkes, 217.
28   ibid.
29   Priestley to Jacquetta Hawkes, 19 January 1948.

intolerance of work it does not happen to be interested in, work that may be immensely difficult to accomplish. (If it isn't, sit down and try it.) Hence the irritability, which is not personal. Thus I am tired of the assumption that a (to me) clearly bad play in second-rate verse is somehow altogether superior to an extremely involved and successful play worked out in terms of prose and realism (really symbolic). Also, you take certain playful references of my own to my habits too seriously. My reading is not confined to detective stories (actually I read very few now) but is probably about as wide as that of any man you know, as a glance at my books here and in London would prove. Like most men I drink heartily when meeting lots of other people away from home, but here I drink very sparingly, live very quietly, and work regularly and hard. I give an enormous amount of thought and preliminary attention to a really creative job of writing, which I rarely begin until after long preparation. I do not write carelessly, although I am often able to write quickly now, just because I went through a long course of self-discipline in writing in my twenties. It is one of my grumbles that prose writing is now so shockingly bad, chiefly because of the absence of this self-discipline, and a lack of initial humility fostered by this conceit and intolerance, which in their turn have made contemporary criticism so poor. With much of this you would probably agree, but nevertheless I do feel that you are much influenced by the attitudes of your particular generation and background. I like the little I have seen of your own writing, but believe it needs better focusing for the reader – that in it the writer-object relation is first class but that the writer-reader relation is still not right. But I look forward to seeing the poems.

You are to me a most curious and fascinating woman: hence all this. It is as if some woman of a very remote and strange race, with whom one had had once the most glorious intimacy, suddenly appeared on this scene pretending to be a highbrow female of the '07 vintage, with all the attitudes, prejudices, nonsense of a fairly familiar type. This one writes a letter (under provocation, I admit) and all is nearly lost. But the bodies move; the eyes meet (almost out of a lost world); and then all is wonderfully well. Over and above that I found you right from the first (at Mexico City) a good chap to be around with, a satisfying sort of companion – and this is a pretty good test. Just that teatime talk the other day, with all the overtones of course, was immensely satisfying, if tantalising, to me. But alas we need more time – to talk at ease – to explore – and that is the snag at the moment. My dear love, I can't go on now. You have my heart, please take care of it.

(I've opened this to add some more. Oh – the damn complications! It looks all easy to you, but you should please imagine Christopher – turned into a suspicious character – trying to deceive you under your nose.)

Don't expect another letter very soon. I must concentrate on the job, and try hard to dismiss you from my mind and not let that inner attention, which is the basis of good work, drain away in your direction. You have so much – a glorious honesty (which I deeply admire), passion; a kind of frosty fun, like the Snow Queen on her birthday; a folded-in sort of handsomeness that turns into amazing beauty at the right moment (but I haven't seen that face yet in 1948); lovely intelligence, especially when you speak straight out of yourself and do not 'take a line'; and somewhere – somewhere – I will swear – though I haven't reached it yet, and perhaps it isn't for me – an exquisite tenderness. It is odd how everything is reversed for us. I, the easy sensualist, regard you most un-sensually, except when immediately excited by you; whereas you find love for me in your body (which doesn't really even need me) but little or none – alas – in your mind. But this mind-body dichotomy won't work, of course. It's really personality – and there, I fancy, we meet on equal terms, with our particular odd mixtures of masculine and feminine curiously balancing. But remember this, whenever you find me lacking, that, unlike you, I don't want to be in love. The cancelling of one evening in Mexico City would have prevented it, but I'm damned if I know which – I was stealthily ambushed, though certainly not consciously by you.

All this talk! I wish I was holding you.

J.

P.S. In case you're tempted – don't try the scheme of the letter in the official stuff . . . But try answering me and keeping the letter.

Jacquetta's deception of a husband fanatically lost in writing produced strains no less disturbing than Priestley's large family, jealous wife and pressurised professional life.

As if afraid that his letters might fall into indiscreet hands, in the first part of another letter he created the fictional character Elizabeth Heron, who was in fact Jacquetta Hawkes, and they frequently spoke of themselves at one remove through this imagined person.

The letter opened formally, 'Dear Jacquetta', and ended 'Yours ever', but managed through Elizabeth Heron to convey intimate feelings within a friendly framework. The first part read:

Billingham, Friday/Saturday

Dear Jacquetta,

I feel I must write to you, at the end of a longish day, which, though I have been feeling tired, was full of good things. First, early this morning, out of the blue our friend Elizabeth Heron rang me, so unexpectedly, so delightfully, that I, who usually dislike telephone calls and am bad at them, was enchanted, and felt that E. was with me all the rest of the day. Then this morning we had an early preliminary reading, ten days before rehearsals start, of *Home Is Tomorrow* and I was extraordinarily pleased and excited by the cast we have chosen, much larger and more varied (because of the international theme) than I generally have. I work very much through the ear in the Theatre, and it was like listening to a fine small orchestra tuning up, knowing you could do grand things with it later. Everybody is feeling excited by the play, which is very rich, harder and more brilliant in tone, more contemporary in feeling, than anything I have done lately. It should make people sit up. Then after a late lunch in town, discussing theatre business, I came down here, feeling suddenly depressed in the train, probably because I was tired. There was nobody here but the servants – MacOwan comes tomorrow so that we can work together on the production of *Home Is Tomorrow* – but I found a letter from Elizabeth waiting for me, a gem of a letter that has warmed my heart all evening. You were quite right about her. She has a wonderful capacity for a relationship of this kind – and is at once adorably foolish and wise.

The film story is now developing in my mind . . .[30]

He knew, he wrote, that he could extract enormous fun from the film and if he was allowed to co-produce – he intended to insist upon it – then he hoped to create the kind of 'film wit' characteristic of Clair and Lubitsch.[31] Certainly he was going to try because it gave him the perfect excuse not to persevere with a novel whose form – not subject – now came close to boring him. He certainly hoped to see Elizabeth, if only for a glimpse, while in London, but he had no time to visit the Savile and it would be better to write to 'one Michael MacOwan' at the London Mask Theatre, 25 Catherine Street, WC2. He was, he said, glad he had resisted the many pressing invitations to the Breslau [writers] Conference, which Kingsley Martin described with such ironic insight in the *New Statesman*.

30  Priestley to Jacquetta Hawkes, 'Friday/Saturday', 1948.
31  The film was never made and the script has vanished.

The last letter in this group began 'Darling Jacquetta' and ended 'Your Loving Jack'.

. . . Sorry I couldn't get a private note to you before. No trouble at the weekend, and your name never came up. This suggests that Maud[32] either knows (or rather guesses) a lot or imagines nothing; but if the latter – why does he sometimes talk to you as if he knew you were more in touch with me than he is? He was in pretty good form – piling on the charm, little jokes etc. – and we had some useful talk about UNESCO, during which he gave me the impression he was being as frank as he could be. He agreed that Laves was a bad administrator and didn't know how to handle people – and had no objection to his going – but defended him against some charges, and clearly thought more blame attached to Huxley.[33] He obviously dislikes Grierson[34] and proposed to leave him out – if he decided to hold a meeting. He thinks Grierson cannot keep his mouth shut and is altogether too indiscreet. We had much talk on my suggestions for reorganising UNESCO both on the programme and administrative side – more or less on the lines we have discussed . . .

Good news (for me) about your not going to York. Also, the new premises. If you are actually moving there next week, will you see that I have the telephone number either here before Thursday morning or waiting for me in Albany on Thursday afternoon. Please keep Thursday evening for me. I'm enormously looking forward to it. So far this time there have been no mysterious surges of antagonism coming up from the depths, and all is calm, clear and tender. But I've been having (plus hay fever) a hell of a time with the last little scene of my play, where I wanted a real verbal heightening into poetry of a sort. The trouble is, my mind won't function like that now. I've worked too long on this prose level, so that I can't fetch actual writing up from a deeper level. I fetch up the dramatic stuff – characters, situations, effects – from there, no doubt about that, for now I rarely consciously invent, and there *is* poetry – strictly dramatic poetry for the Theatre – in these richly symbolic situations and effects; but verbally – as yet – I can't do it and find myself working on a thin conscious level. It's maddening of course, but there it is. But please don't underrate the other thing, this hauling up of dramatic material from the unconscious, because actually it's rarer than unconscious verbal power and felicity . . .

Lost as I am in my hay fever (very bad today with this high wind

32  Sir John Maud, an important member of the UNESCO committee.
33  Julian Huxley, the biologist.
34  John Grierson, the documentary film-maker.

blowing) and my frustration with the very end of my play, I am yet gloriously devoted to you; and spend much time pointing out to myself and enjoying, though not without being much tantalised, all your rich magnificence of character and person.

Your loving,

J.[35]

The telling phrase 'So far this time there have been no mysterious surges of antagonism coming up from the depths' indicated a conflict about Jack's meetings with Jacquetta.

As Jacquetta wrote: 'We did occasionally contrive to get away just long enough to experience the satisfaction of whole days and nights of one another's company, but always the end was in sight; they were escapades.'

35  Priestley to Jacquetta Hawkes, undated.

# 23

# The Love Affair Develops
## 1949–51

From the outset they had agreed not to break up their marriages but as their bond deepened this resolve became less realistic. Each leave-taking was painful, each reunion intense, and behind the strains the submerged desire to live together steadily grew. It reactivated in Jacquetta's mind a scene far back when she was staying with her parents and her frail old father needed some small service which her mother immediately performed. 'I shall never forget how, quite suddenly, their eyes met and a look of indescribably tender fondness ran between them.' The whole meaning of the phrase – 'till death us do part' – was concentrated in that look.

The incident came back to her when she and Jack were bowling up Regent Street in a taxi one soft summer's day and the world seemed full of the delight of simply being together. She recalled the scene to Jack and remarked how it revealed the poverty of her relationship with Christopher. Jack immediately replied that she and Christopher still had their shared interests, not least in archaeology. Jacquetta rejected this, claiming that since the war even that side of their marriage had seriously diminished. Whereupon Jack exclaimed – 'in that voice of his that could be so heartbreaking' – '"Then you have nothing? Nothing?" The lights of Regent Street flickered through the taxi windows as that dire "nothing" seemed to echo round me.'[1]

By 1948 Jane and Jack had decided to leave Billingham Manor and move into Brookhill, a large house on a hill overlooking the sea with a stately hall capable of accommodating the orchestras he occasionally hired. A letter written in late September said:

Darling J.,
   As far as I can see now I ought with any luck to be up in town next Tuesday, 28th, and free in the evening. If I know definitely I'm not going to be, I'll let you know: otherwise I'll telephone during the day. As I said before, I'll be up the whole of the week beginning the

1   *A Quest of Love*, Jacquetta Hawkes, 218.

4th, but don't know yet whether I'll be alone, and anyhow there will be rehearsals on some evenings. It would be a great help to have somewhere to meet if I am not free in the evenings but could manage late afternoon, somewhere central and convenient for both of us, but unfortunately I don't know anybody with the right sort of place. You might give this a little thought on your side – I fancy it's something more easily arranged among women than among men.

I'm not doing much work and am not being sensibly lazy – messing about rather in an unsatisfactory way. We may be changing house here quite soon, and there is much planning. But plans for travel later in the autumn are still not settled, and this adds to the messing-about-and-waiting feeling. Just lately I've acquired the miserable habit – the one I dislike most of all – of waking quite early and not being able to get off to sleep again, except perhaps for a light doze. This gives me plenty of time to think – though not always very cheerfully – but I do think about you a lot – and remember delightfully so many things – e.g. that long mannish stride of yours – a queer little *timid* peep at me you give sometimes – a sudden wide schoolboy-girl-grin – the choky little voice when specially moved – the whole rich mixture of donnishness, witchcraft, impudence, timidity, absurdity, wisdom. I am feeling intensely devoted to you. But I must get this off to you . . .

Written after lunch by a pear-shaped man (who has just eaten a magnificent pear too.)[2]

In September Priestley's normal routine was further disturbed by the move from Billingham to Brookhill with all the 'endless taking down, sorting out, unpacking and re-sorting'. Odds and ends of journalism apart, he was free of any sustained work, but he directed a series of animadversions against furniture movers, 'a race of morons', and inanimate furniture which had 'its own malignancy'. Stress invades every family in the middle of a move but it multiplied in a household where the head of the family worked at home and the tensions normal to everyday living were already exaggerated.

. . . In the muddle I think of you constantly and with delight. Friday was very special for me too – there is no accounting for these queer ebbs and flows of feeling and pleasure and sense of rightness – the whole story seems to take place below the conscious level, which hasn't had much of a go with us, who rather tend to disapprove of one another on that level and have to be prodded from below – or is it above? But that seems to be the place to deal with – if one wants

2 Priestley to Jacquetta Hawkes, 21 September 1948.

large and lasting satisfactions and all sorts of queer magics. Probably on the conscious level we don't operate very much because it happens that both of us are more or less nicely fixed up on that level, got just the people we ought to have etc. etc., so that leaves us free for all the other impulses. Along these lines I've known nothing like it before and certainly don't expect to know anything like it again. You're different – and may get up to all manner of relationships before you're through, if ever. I can't help feeling that just lately I've been very uncharming (but I feel like that about the world too these days) and you must have had to be patient. But I'm not good at these short times together, crowded in between a lot of business engagements, and I need room in which to expand and relax and take a really good look at you. I was thinking the other night you are twice as good-looking as you were when we first met, though you were pretty good, and I insist· on taking a bit of credit. But if in these rushed meetings I seem sometimes offhand, be patient – and hope for longer times. The sun is bright – and I adore you, my sweet girl . . .[3]

One upheaval followed another to disrupt his meetings with Jacquetta and Jane still seemed unaware that something very different from one of his affairs had entered his life. Another letter to Jacquetta said he would be in London the week after next but once again did not know whether he would be alone. Clearly his meetings were fitted into his arrangements with his wife and concealment required prior commitment to any appointment with her.

The Priestley family slowly settled down in the new house, Brookhill, and the impetus of old friends and relations prolonged their habitual way of life so convincingly that it gave the impression to visitors that nothing had changed. A great stone house built in Edwardian style, Brookhill stood atop a steep slope of gorse and bracken which swept down to the sea, with a magnificent view along the chalk cliffs. This was Tennyson country with a wealth of ruins, ancient trees planted for prehistoric rituals, 'strange swales and lanes and heights and views and winds'. This description was given by Peter Davison, the son of Priestley's old friend Edward Davison, who went to stay in Brookhill and described the baronial establishment as 'teeming with family and friends'. Davison could not get used to the English country-house atmosphere with its firmly fixed rituals. 'Breakfast was sumptuous, brisk, with hot

3   Priestley to Jacquetta Hawkes, September 1948.

dishes of kidneys and kippers on the sideboard at a stated hour.' Both Priestley and Mrs Priestley, Davison wrote in his book *Half Remembered*, disappeared early in the morning, one to write, the other to check the accounts of 'their vast farm'. Much of Jane's time was spent supervising not only the housekeeping, the tenants, and bailiffs, but the herds of Galway and Guernsey cattle. The whole family including the children seemed to disappear early in the morning leaving Davison to read *Faust* in his room. The house came alive again in the afternoons with 'fierce tennis on the private court', tea on the terrace, cocktails and late lavish dinners. Davison simply did not know what to do with himself or for that matter what to say in this very English company. Everything he did say seemed to 'bristle with gaucherie'. Left alone, he wandered up and down the empty halls, along the lanes and garden paths, wondering if he might meet a gardener and if so whether to talk to him or hide behind a tree. Clearly, amidst all his troubles Priestley remained a wealthy man leading the treble life of famous author, self-appointed member of the landed gentry and clandestine lover.

A letter to Jacquetta written in September gave an assessment of her poetry:

> Just a word first about the poems, though of course I don't really know them yet. It is genuine original poetry, beaten out of life and not out of other poetry. It is very like you, ranging from something awkward, bony, thin to something flashing and crying with beauty. The greatest weakness, from my point of view, is obscurity, not, as with so many poets, an obscurity from the telescoping or maladroit use of images, but an obscurity of thought – or perhaps, more accurately, an obscurity in the transitions of thought. The first half of the book seems to me considerably better than the second. I like best the poems where thought and image are completely wedded and the whole thing finely beaten out – e.g. 'Death and Life' – and least, one like 'Intimations', which is to me not a poem but notes out of which a poem might be made – but this, I know, is the fashion now. Incidentally, I don't think your publishers have served you very well – many of the poems are not well placed on the page and a bit more paper could have been used with advantage. But I am very glad to have them – they bring you very close.
>
> I don't think next week is going to be very good – because I shall be knee-deep in family matters and have a good many odds and ends of things to do in addition. Rather than snatch an hour in a baddish atmosphere I'd prefer to leave it a bit, for we're at our best when we have time and a bit of space of our own. I say this because it's

possible you might like to get away for a time that would include those three days – 12th to 15th. We shall, I hope, have far more time a little later; and it would certainly be a much better time for me, not having to concentrate so much on family affairs. I hate not seeing you but I hate still more snatching at you in the wrong atmosphere. I'm rather tired and dispirited now too and would rather see you when I have more zest. I have a feeling too – purely intuitive – that we'd be wise to go easy for a few weeks – I'm referring now to security and secrecy and not to our own feelings; so don't let's rush this. I'm most deeply devoted to you – it's a real thing among much unreality – but I must make a special family effort this month. I know you will understand what I mean, my love.[4]

By the time he wrote the next letter Jacquetta had taken a short holiday in Paris and while she was away he had an X-ray for some urethral trouble. The doctor who carried out the examination was 'one of those boring, humming and hawing mystery-mongers' who said he might have a stone in his urethra which meant a trip to London for a day to see a specialist. Personally he did not think it was anything serious and should easily be treatable but it might explain his irritability and occasional sudden tiredness. He was busy planning a trip to the north – Nottingham first, followed by Harrogate – with the Griller Quartet and he saw no reason why his urethral trouble should stop him going or seeing Jacquetta. Referring to Jacquetta's Parisian holiday he wrote:

Thursday, aft.

Dearest Jacquetta,

Are you enjoying yourself? I hope so. And now the weather is better Paris should be looking bright as a new pin. I like the wonderful light, the odd corners, the pictures and the food there, but I have never felt at home in the place, perhaps because I don't really like the people . . . I hope to see you on the Tuesday evening first, of course. Last night, for the first time to my knowledge, I dreamt of you – nothing complicated and symbolic – nice and ordinary – we were trying to see each other – and succeeding, though I don't think we managed even any dalliance. It was just a pleasant wish dream. There you were! I'm pottering rather in my work this week – the N.S. articles (two now) – some alterations in the last scene of *Home is Tomorrow* – and now I am meditating re-doing the first scene of *The Flowering Thorn*, making it rather richer. (This play is very tricky indeed – comedy of ideas merging into a

4 Priestley to Jacquetta Hawkes, September 1948.

poetic romantic piece – and I'm determined to make it as good as I can.) I can't work very hard, either because of the time of year or because I'm not very fit. I've been reading, in proof, the first instalment of Winston's war memoirs, mostly dealing with before the war. Readable and often likeable, but monstrous as history and with the bitterest bias against Labour, which he now seems to dislike more than he does Nazism. He's at his best dealing purely with war as war, which of course he loves, like a boy with a fort and lead soldiers.

A nice note from Norman Collins this afternoon saying he saw my *Inspector Calls* on television last night and found 'the authentic magic was there'.

In bed this morning I thought about making love to you, and it seemed a wonderful thing to do, which indeed it is. I want to start all over again . . . as if Mexico City never existed. (Perhaps it doesn't.) You are my own wonderful, delicious woman. I want you. I love you.

JACK[5]

In the same month, September, he was writing an article for the *New Statesman* called 'More Cantankery' which would, he hoped, contain some 'bits of real new thinking'. He reflected that if he could not qualify as a thinker in the sense that Whitehead was, he had intuitive flashes which classified him – humbly – 'among the myth-making types'. This might explain his odd reputation which bulked surprisingly large if the world was taken as a whole and continued – he claimed – to puzzle Jacquetta who tended to estimate him according to familiar categories. Since the hierarchy of literary significance gave pride of place to the myth-makers his humility was really an example of those occasional bursts of boasting which sometimes lost their theatricality.

Another letter in September to Jacquetta opened:

My darling Jacquetta,

(and what a lovely thing to begin a letter with! Worth falling in love just for that) I wish I had read your letter before you telephoned on Monday morning because I could have told you then that there was nothing I wanted to argue about, that I found the letter or letters deeply satisfying and moving, and that anyhow all the resentment has vanished. (You were right in adding that you made too much of it.) There was none of it on Sunday, when I found you very sweet and only wished I was in a better condition to be companionable. (I

5  Priestley to Jacquetta Hawkes, September 1948.

really was feeling wretched with the M. & B. and am much better now.) You must remember that when we first talked in Mexico you were inclined to take a rather tough detached masculine 'line' . . . and this made me treat you as if you were almost another man instead of being a deeply feminine creature, as I now realise you are. Thus I have hurt you when no hurt was intended. Same probably applies to your treatment of me now and again, because I tend to seem far more conceited and self-confident than in fact I am. (I have deliberately built up a persona on these lines, have had to, in fact, and I imagine you are beginning to realise this.) Anyhow, now I feel towards you a deep tenderness and much warm friendship, the rarest thing in an exciting love affair, I often think. I wish I was in Paris with you. Please keep some of me with you, sharing the best bits. Thank you very much for the notes on the farce. All are admirable but some more useful than others. I have not checked them with the text, as this is away, being copied. But there is no hurry as we cannot do this piece now before *Home is Tomorrow*, which as you know is being most maddeningly delayed . . . Yesterday's award business was very fatuous . . . Peggy Ashcroft was the actress of the year and I found myself sitting next to her at lunch, regarding her amiably and thinking of you all the time. I feel now – what I ought to have felt before, I suppose – that you are giving me something, not only when we are together (I always felt it then) but when we are apart, the thought of you being refreshing, heartening, creative. I am deeply devoted to you my darling. Enjoy yourself – for my sake as well as your own.

Yours,

JACK[6]

Early in 1949 Priestley regarded himself one morning in the bathroom mirror and decided – ironically – that he had lost too much of those sylph-like lines which might have made him a ballet star. The recurring problem of weight became so pressing that he decided to take a rigorous course of dieting and massage in an expensive clinic. Simultaneously trouble with his teeth reached a point where the dentist said there was nothing for it but to remove the remaining four of the top set, leaving the lower teeth more or less intact. The dieting and massage did temporarily reduce his weight by fourteen pounds, followed by surreptitious concessions which threatened to replace them. Meanwhile adjustment to his dental plates became a further reminder of the penalties of artificially replacing the erosion of nature.

6   Priestley to Jacquetta Hawkes, September 1948.

Professionally the long-drawn-out saga of his collaboration with Bliss in the opera *The Olympians* approached the climax of actual production, the details of which are already familiar. Priestley quickly became involved in the friction which developed between Karl Rankl, Peter Brook and Bliss. A letter to Jacquetta written in March 1949 said:

> Darling J.,
> Just to welcome you back, my first chance of doing so. I had a day up in town last week, just out of my diet clinic and there was urgent opera business to attend to, and rang up to ask when you were returning.

He might, he said, be up in town in a fortnight.

> and may possibly have no chance of letting you know in advance. As I shall definitely have longer periods in town later, with productions going forward, I would rather take it easy now and not risk spoiling the better time afterwards; though this does not mean I am not terribly anxious to see you – bless your heart! . . .
> The little essays on delight are about finished, and there is much enthusiasm among various types about them.[7] I read you on Emblems in the *N.S.* and though you worked hard at it, it sounded as dull as hell. I start the Letters for them this next month.[8] No other news. It's been a poor sort of place without you – a terrible lack of exquisite long eyes, ditto legs, and astringent talk in a queer mumbling voice that is an acquired taste and develops a kind of beauty.
> J.[9]

7  *Delight*, J. B. Priestley.
8  On 9 April 1949 he began a series of articles in the *New Statesman* called 'Letters from Two Islands'.
9  Priestley to Jacquetta Hawkes, 24 March 1949.

## 24

# Things Fall Apart
### 1951–2

When Mary was about to leave St Andrew's Hospital in 1948, the psychiatrist said to her, 'Is there any question you want answered?' and she immediately replied, 'Yes – who is my real father?' When Priestley arrived in his chauffeur-driven car to collect his daughter the question was repeated and Priestley replied, 'I am of course. We have been through all this before.'[1]

Mary's prolonged illness led to three main attacks in 1947, 1958 and 1964, with varying degrees of severity. None the less she recovered sufficiently from her first breakdown to marry the Danish student Sigvald Michelsen and went to live in Denmark with him, against strong resistance from her parents.

Priestley began a desultory correspondence with Mary in 1947, which ran on over the years until his eighties. It was as if he wanted to maintain a lifeline to ensure that he did not repeat an experience which had created deep distress.

Some of his letters to Mary were certainly caring letters. In May 1949 she had treatment for a gynaecological ailment in hospital and he wrote to her:

Darling Mary,
   I was sorry not to see you after you had gone to hospital but was glad to know everything had gone off well. Of course it is disappointing for you, but you can well afford to wait a bit until you are more settled down and Sig. has found a steady job, which I think he ought to do until he gets better known as a soloist. I can understand your not liking life in Denmark very much so far but I do think this is largely due to being so hard up and unsettled. If Sig. were earning about £700 a year, it would be very different. (And don't forget this is what he *promised* to do, in fact, told me he could get a job any time with the Royal Chapel at £900 a year.) In my opinion it would be a mistake to come back to England, because it is running away from Denmark just when something might turn up, and it is absolutely

1   Interview with Mary Priestley, 10 October 1986.

impossible for Sig. to get work at once here. And anyhow it's a mistake to make these sudden retreats just because everything is not wonderful. Take a hard crack at one place at a time, I say.

I rely on you in all this business because I think you've lots of courage and common sense and it's your job to take hold of the situation. A year somewhere like Aarhus might be a good idea – I'm sorry, I couldn't take Mrs Jenssen, whom I liked very much, but the Czech actress is far more like the kind of Russian girl we want to suggest and she has a British passport too, which makes it simpler.

Let me know if there is anything I can get for you here. I don't know why the Spanish music hasn't turned up yet – it was ordered weeks and weeks ago.

It was nice seeing you but would have been much better if you'd been up and seen me smashing plates at Tivoli.

Much love from DADDY.[2]

Correspondence and creative work were interlocked with multiple activities which brought him back into many public places. In 1947 he was presented to the Russian Ambassador, Mr Maisky, and was appointed a member of the Royal Commission on the Press. In 1948 he became chairman of the British Theatre Conference, chairman of the London Philharmonic Advisory Council, and chairman of the National Theatre Institute Congress at Prague. As chairman of the British Theatre Conference he invited George Bernard Shaw to join them and received the following reply:

Dear J.B.P.,                                              16th January 1948
I am glad to know that you have not forgotten this old crock; but as to the conference I have nothing to contribute but a hollow laugh. I dare say the young ones will enjoy it and I think they are doing something important; though nothing can or will be done except spend your far too generous gift. There is not even an agenda, much less a program. If there was they wouldn't agree on a single item.

For ten years I was on the executive of the Society of Authors and did all I could for them; and they hated me for it. At 91½ I have too little time left to waste any more of it on them.

I was in at the birth of the Authors' League of America. It was a great effort, boiling with high hopes; and all they did was to give away right after right to the managers and publishers, including their new and enormously valuable film rights. You are too young to grasp their ignorance in law, and incompetence in business,

2  Priestley to Mary Priestley, 30 May 1949.

which makes them unemployable in any other occupation than sitting alone in a study and indulging their imaginations. They dread and detest anyone who has discovered that 2 plus 2 equals 4, and has heard of the Copyright Act of 1911.

However, you have let yourself in for it, and will get plenty of comedy for your money so I send you my blessing, which is all I can spare for this folly.

G. BERNARD SHAW[3]

A spectacular exchange with Michael Foot took place early in 1949, fired off by Priestley's provocative article written for the *Sunday Pictorial*.[4] Throughout his career Priestley never entirely abandoned writing for popular newspapers and was indeed proud to continue. Priestley in his *Sunday Pictorial* article professed 'to tell the truth about democracy which meant that the quarrel over that dog-eared object of perennial worship between the great powers had become unreal and irrelevant'. Americans, Russians and the British people all 'claimed to espouse their own peculiar forms of "Democracy" but the quarrel is ridiculous because all the powers are moving away from democracy as fast as they can go'. Foot commented: 'It is Mr Priestley's belief that if we had a Tory government instead of a Labour one, or imported American big business men or Russian commissars to Whitehall the result would be the same.'[5]

I checked these quotations and found them to be true. In full flood of invective Priestley rose to further heights. The rich were the untrammelled masters of the United States and Britain. 'Politicians and senior civil servants are beginning to decide how the rest of us shall live. The National Health Service may or may not be a good scheme but it is in my opinion fundamentally undemocratic, just because it turns the private relationship between doctor and patient into official business.'

Foot commented: 'The general conclusion seems to be that most of the world is travelling towards a new form of tyranny, that one had better make the best of it and not worry our heads about words which have lost their meaning.'

Gross exaggeration could go no further but Foot concluded: 'All this we believe to be wicked and dangerous nonsense. It is none-the-less wicked and dangerous because it contains one grain of

3  G. B. Shaw to Priestley, 16 January 1948.
4  'J. B. Priestley Replies to His Critics', *Sunday Pictorial*, 6 February 1949.
5  'The Futility of Mr Priestley', *Tribune*, 16 January 1949.

truth.' It was true, for instance, that 'bigness' was certainly our enemy. For the rest Priestley talked a specially nauseating brand of nonsense.

Britain was riddled with all kinds of institutes, debates and discussions about government policy which had no equivalent in Russia. Mr Priestley claimed that a commissar in Whitehall would produce the same result. 'Rubbish!' As for the lack of democracy in America it was self-evident everywhere. The Health Service demonstrated forcibly that democracy flourished in Britain because the cash relationship with the doctor had been so revolutionised that anyone could now afford to go to his doctor for treatment. 'When the nation advances towards a new society and fulfils the ambition of many hardworking democrats over the years, [Priestley] greets the idea of sharing more fairly the medical skills . . . which Britain possesses with all the alarm of a Bournemouth hypochondriac.'

It was the inevitable paradox of polemical argument that an opponent could be attacked for views which he did not hold. Foot made full play with this strategy:

> It is possible for ordinary men and women while retaining their freedom and their democracy to change society to remove injustice, to share fairly the fruits of their labour. But Mr Priestley objects. He sets out to make that faith appear sour, senseless and utterly insignificant. Such is the pessimism of the intellectual who will not deign to join the striving of the common people.[6]

It marked a new watershed in Priestley's political convictions but fundamentally they were very different from those with which Foot endowed him. The *Sunday Pictorial* piece was a momentary blaze of rhetorical anger and Priestley's later summing-up put the argument in perspective. The Labour dream of a New Jerusalem had failed, but dimly in the background the lineaments of a new semi-socialist way of life still persisted. The Labour Party had lost its way and was only concerned with getting back into office but that could not destroy the groundswell towards a socialistic Britain where private and public enterprise would marry morganatically.

Driven by such multiple activities, Priestley – the undismayed professional – continued to write books and struggled in 1949–50 with another monster novel, *Festival at Farbridge*, the longest he

6   ibid.

ever wrote, which ran to 250,000 words. It made ferocious demands on a writer in his late fifties.

He described its inspiration in *Margin Released*: 'I wanted to write a large-scale comic novel about post-war England . . . and, stupidly as I see now, I chose the 1951 Festival of Britain, which I welcomed and never sneered at, as a peg on which to hang the tale. Its reception disappointed me as that of no other novel of mine has done.'[7]

Politically prejudiced against the festival some critics were automatically hostile and what Priestley referred to as 'the intellectual reviewers' did not like his uninhibited high spirits. Their comments were sour.

The central figure of the novel was Commodore Horace Tribe, 'a bulky, oldish fellow' with a 'piratical nose, and tiny bright eyes as busy and wicked as mice'. A deep, rich voice made somewhat husky by thousands of whiskies, drunk in exotic places, completed his portrait. Part benevolent idealist, part splendid con man, the commodore gives an account of himself from the outset which is dubious. 'After serving for some years in the Royal Navy I – er – was attached, chiefly in an advisory capacity, to the navy of one of the South American republics and had the honorary rank of Commodore.'

These rugged individuals – big, burly men with strong personalities and a delight in performing – recur frequently enough in Priestley's novels to make their autobiographical roots a strong possibility. Priestley, after all, was supremely the con man in his novels, convincing people that his fantasies were real, his puppetry alive with flesh and blood, but if *The Good Companions* frequently lost touch with reality that elusive condition permeated *Festival at Farbridge*. The actual Festival of Britain was part of the Labour Party's attempt to introduce some high spirits into the five years of post-war austerity. Emerging from years of organisational muddle and farcical argument, the pavilions on the South Bank of the Thames were hammered into place at the last moment and ridiculed by the *Daily Express* as Morrison's Folly, but the fever spread throughout the country and miniature reproductions of South Bank festivities enhanced many a small town and village. It was in one such town, Farbridge, that the commodore met the handsome Theodore Jenks, whose Malaysian background gave him a striking bronzed head with queerly set eyes from his Chinese grandmother.

7  *Margin Released*, J. B. Priestley, 194.

Both men coincided in a tea-shop, cosily named The Old Oak Nook, and there, almost waiting to receive them from the pages of *The Good Companions*, was Laura Casey, a young and independently minded secretary who had just lost her job. Repeating the technique of *The Good Companions* each character was introduced separately until the different threads merged in the tea-shop meeting.

Impeccably crafted, the complicated narrative never lost its way and interweaved major and minor incidents around what – in Susan Cooper's view – was the major character in the book – English society. A much more mature and skilful novel than *The Good Companions*, any resemblances between the two disappeared after the initial chapters. The lesser characters in *The Good Companions* were sheer incidentals who quickly vanished from the scene, but *Festival at Farbridge* delicately wove such characters into the main action of the book. Tightly organised, *Festival at Farbridge* revealed Priestley as a professionally sophisticated novelist at the height of his powers, but the coincidence of fact and fiction, the appearance of real people like Robert Boothby, tended to undermine the verisimilitude of the remainder of the characters. They were vividly drawn, the incidents funny, the narrative pace sustained but they failed to cohere into a completely successful novel.

Bluff, hearty and plausible, the commodore brings his roguish eye to bear on the possibilities of setting alight the drab town of Farbridge with a festival which will remain in its memory for many a year. The three protagonists charm, flatter, manipulate and sometimes shout their way through a series of comic situations which successfully parody English local life until the town breaks into a fountain of high spirits. Commodore Tribe comes completely alive, bustling from chapter to chapter, but Theodore Jenks, representing the observing eye of the ex-colonial, quickly loses his initial force and Laura's relationship with Theodore has no depths of awareness. In one sense the novel is a fictional reaffirmation of Herbert Morrison's official policy and in another it is a comic social portrait of the time which no other writer attempted.

The *Times Literary Supplement* said:

> There has always been the suggestion of a note of underlying sadness in Mr J. B. Priestley's work; and notwithstanding the buoyant treatment of up-to-date subject matter in *Festival at Farbridge*, its emphasis on contemporary vexations . . . on persecutions at the hands of the votaries of Kierkegaard or Kafka gives this nostalgic

hint of days gone by and of the vanity of human life, in somewhat increased measure . . . His keen dramatic sense supplies unexpected climaxes and illuminates back-stage scenes – some of the best in the book . . . At times, however, he seems to have been tempted to partake of the heady wine of Mr Evelyn Waugh's style . . . A shorter book would have given more scope to the occasional almost poetic descriptions such as 'A little round man who looked like a child that has been allowed to stay up late for about 45 years'.[8]

It is difficult to find the wholesale condemnation implied by Priestley among the reviewers. His friend Norman Collins wrote in the *Sunday Times*:

It is all set down with the most tremendous gusto and above all with a sort of geniality that for the most part has entirely vanished from the contemporary novel.

The novel was a Book Society Choice for the month of May and Herbert Morrison read it with 'unconcealed delight'. In America its reception was good and the *New York Times* described it as 'light, gay, hearty . . . Priestley at his best', which was perhaps ambiguous.

Correspondence remained a curse from which he could not escape, and constantly interfered with the writing of *Festival at Farbridge*. The famous, eccentric, besotted and abusive continued to interlace letters concerning everyday business and personal affairs. To some he replied and others he ignored.

A series of letters to his stepdaughter Angela Wyndham Lewis, which began in 1947, produced a revealing letter in 1950.[9] Angela, already a successful actress, had by then married.

My dear Angela,
    I have just opened your letter to Mummy as she is still away. She went motoring down to the Camargue with Miss Frey and Dr Bannerman and another chap and is not expected back here until Sunday. I am very glad to learn that you are coming to Pitt Place in July. I am under the impression that Ba's baby is not expected until towards the end of July but she will be here this weekend and I will ask her to drop you a line. By the way, I am hoping to run a little Chamber Music Festival here for three days at the beginning of

8  *Times Literary Supplement*, 11 May 1951.
9  Priestley to Angela Wyndham Lewis, 14 June 1950.

September and I hope you will be still here then as it should be very good.
    Love,
    DADDY

Here for the first time the name Bannerman occurs. Dr Bannerman shared Jane's enthusiasm for ornithology and clearly Priestley was happy enough for his wife to go on holiday with him. Indeed he told Diana Collins, an old friend, that Bannerman's admiration for Jane pleased him. Did he want her to find a lover? Some members of the family believe that their mother's morality was now far too austere to countenance adultery even though this holiday marked the beginning of a relationship which was to end in marriage.
Another letter to Angela Wyndham Lewis said:

My dear Angela,
    . . . I really didn't expect a present – it's too difficult between countries – but of course if one turns up it will be very nice. I sail on the *Mauretania* on the 9th, will stay a week or so with the Davisons in New York and then head for Arizona, the Pacific Coast, West Mexico. I really need this break as I have done a prodigious year's work, including the comic novel, nearly 270,000 words long, and a play for the Festival, which Binkie asked me to do (I hope to get Ralph for it). It is called *The Golden Door*, and is about a bankrupt art gallery in the same provincial town that the Lindens lived in; and it is a very powerful and exciting play, with a terrific climax. Binkie and Peters are very enthusiastic, but I have not had Ralph's reaction yet as he is filming in Ceylon for Carol Reed. Binkie is trying to get Edith Evans too, and she and Ralph would be a nice bit of modest casting.

Priestley continued to write letters to Jacquetta between 1950 and 1952, some restless, many irradiated with undiminished love, and occasionally shadowed by anxiety. Running through them was a concern to preserve the confidentiality of their relationship, and the privacy of their letters.
Any writer knows how destructive emotional upheavals can be to productivity and only an old professional could have written against the turmoil of his life between 1947 and 1952 a novel, *Festival at Farbridge*, *The Arts Under Socialism*, *Theatre Outlook*, *Delight*, a film script, *Last Holiday*, and no fewer than nine plays including *Dragon's Mouth*, a play written in collaboration with

338

Jacquetta Hawkes. The turmoil had intensified by 1951–2 as the repressed desire to live together broke surface, and shifted their aims away from accommodation to open avowal. They analysed all possible strategies but Jacquetta insisted that since she had committed adultery and Christopher remained faithful she must suffer what was then the ignominy of a woman being sued for divorce. Her motives were mixed. In part she was subserving her view of 'equal honour among the sexes' and later she regretted this proud gesture because it led into Jack's humiliation. The machinery of the law ground its way slowly to the final disintegration of two marriages but in the prolonged interval between, Jack continued, devotedly, to write to Jacquetta.

One letter referred to her remarkable book *A Land*, published in 1951.[10]

Thank you for your letter – coolish but matey. I don't like this time of year either and know what you mean by saying you feel plain, though you don't look it. Easier to be a man and go weeks without wondering how you look or indeed knowing you have any outward appearance. I have always dodged discussions on the air just because they are either messy or involve one in too much work. Perhaps ours would be wrong – not good enough to include in the book and too hard work to be specially done for what money they'd pay us. Also, broadcasting is too public – and you have the feeling that all kinds of chumps are listening to you and about to complain, whereas a book collects its own audience. However, we'll see. Listening to the recording may tell you something. If you've time, you might as well achieve a manner that pleases them, just for your own talks. I always felt one was talked over at BBC meetings etc. I am certain their attitude towards me is that I am very difficult, though effective. (I deny that I am difficult. This is one of those popular illusions.) I remember once, on TV, having seen the producer through the programme, which had to be made up at the last moment (it was the Shaw memorial programme, I think), he had a few quick drinks and said what he wouldn't have done in other circumstances, and I gather then that he and his chums thought I was almost insufferable, but a tremendous chap for seeing the thing through and bringing it off. So I am, but why insufferable? . . . Incidentally I'd like to clear out to NY if possible before the General Election. I find myself very impatient now with routine Socialist arguments that have no reference to any actuality . . . Good

10  Priestley to Jacquetta Hawkes, 30 July 1951.

advertisement of *A Land* in one of the two Sunday papers. I doubt if you're missing many sales at the moment, during the slump, and the great thing – as Heinemanns say – is to see that the book is prominent at the beginning of the autumn season.

The second part of Priestley's letter half fulfilled Jung's prediction that his original enthusiasm for Jung's model would, in time, be modified.

. . . Not much likelihood of my being up before about the 12th, I fancy. It depends when [Jane] goes to Copenhagen . . . I find myself wanting to read and think about Jung again. This all-knowing, highly selective Unconscious worries me. How can an Unconscious, without an ego, carefully appraise an elaborate situation, select the right symbols, etc. etc.? This is God – or one of His lieutenants – and not the primordial rudimentary mind. It is the Jungians, in their analyses, rather than Jung himself, that worry me here. Late last night I re-read that analysis of me based on *Rain upon Godshill*. It seemed to me rather better than it seemed the first time, probably because I began last night by accepting its faults. You might probably agree with its conclusion that I am kind, generous, gifted, etc. etc. but over-extraverted, demanding from the outside world something it can't give and so on, and probably with Shadow and Anima trouble . . . Even 'on his shadow side he remains honest and candid, and there are few people of whom so much could be said' and. . . . my Shadow 'is neither repulsive nor evil but not unlike one of those genies or spirits in the fairy tales which accompany the wanderers in secret' – not too bad. There can be no doubt you are one of the Anima girls – hence the trouble you cause in literary and scholarly circles, where the boys are busy projecting Animas. But I like to think I see you as a woman, and an exceptionally fine woman, a marvellous mixture of a rare gifted creature, all very grand, and a honey of a girl – an entrancing combination.

# 25

# Divorce and Remarriage
## 1951–2

The book *A Land* published in 1951 revealed Jacquetta Hawkes as a writer who could reconcile geology and archaeology to create an image of the land of Britain – 'in which past and present, nature, man and art appear all in one piece'. Any attempt to describe *A Land* must fail because 'the nature of this unity cannot be stated and it remains always just beyond the threshold of intellectual comprehension'.[1]

Beautifully written, skilfully constructed, the book from the first page created a pantheistic atmosphere freed from the worst abuses of that persuasion. It carried the reader into communion with the spirit of the past which found a response in thousands of readers.

> This hard ground presses my flesh against my bones and makes me agreeably conscious of my body. In bed I can sleep, here I can rest awake. My eyes stray among the stars or are netted by fine silhouettes of leaves immediately overhead and from them passed on to the black lines of neighbouring chimney pots, misshapen and stolid, yet always inexplicably poignant . . . By night I have something of the same feeling about cats that I have always and far more strongly about birds; that perfectly formed while men were still brutal, they now represent the continued presence of the past.[2]

The book traced the shaping of Britain and its people from the first lifeless pre-Cambrian rocks to the days of the ice-cream carton and the hydrogen bomb. Wells, in *The World Set Free*, foresaw men leaving the earth to set out on a breathtaking adventure of exploring outer space and other worlds. Jacquetta Hawkes's prophetic vision was different. Consciousness itself must now explore its beginnings and rediscover its kinship with 'earth, air, fire and water, past and future, lobsters, butterflies, meteors and man'.

1   *A Land*, Jacquetta Hawkes, Preface.
2   ibid., 8.

The mediation of archaeology through the sensibilities of the author transformed it and produced a book which 'made her name'. The *Times Literary Supplement* review concluded: 'What matters is that she has written with vision, with passion and with style and that her book helps us to understand both the land on which we live and the life we live on it.'[3]

The book brought into sharp relief the differences between Jacquetta Hawkes and Jack Priestley, one converting her training into classically written literature, the other subjectively exploring his imaginary worlds from which science was excluded. One major identity remained. They were both writers and that was mutually satisfying.

Despite the growing conviction that they must find some new solution to their *modus vivendi* they were still denied the relaxed pleasure of a shared holiday and in another letter Priestley wrote:[4]

No news here . . . I've had a lot of odds and ends to attend to since I came back and have just made a start, a slow uncertain wobbling start, on my South Sea Island piece, called at the moment (after Milton) 'Close By The Moon', which does express the piece to some extent. I shall work at it slowly except when it insists upon issuing at full speed from the depths. (Not much evidence of that yet.) Just read a review of you by Grigson in *Country Life*. Respectful to the book but not to you. A silly fellow. He grumbles because you introduce your feelings into the book, and then proceeds to introduce his feelings into his review. I dreamt last night (when the wind was howling here) that I was on a very large ship and the Griller Quartet were aboard, but the place of the viola player had been taken by a tall young negress with whom I became very friendly. (It was not an erotic dream. I very rarely have erotic dreams.) The ship was too large and confused, with a good deal of losing one's way in it, but otherwise a cosy pleasant dream. We had two grand evenings, didn't we? I have the happiest – though shortly to be tantalising – memories of the new blue and white Prudence dress. You looked very beautiful in it, as I told you at the time. Though now into your forties, my dear Mrs H., you are much better looking than you were when we first met in '47 – no comparison at all. I wonder how you went on with your BBC cousin? I don't feel inclined myself to make any arrangements with those people. We'll do our duets in a book as soon as we can get round to it, but not over the air. I wonder if you know what I mean

3  *Times Literary Supplement*, 23 June 1951.
4  Priestley to Jacquetta Hawkes, 'Sunday', July 1951.

when I say that just now I've hardly any opinions and views on anything, that, strictly speaking, I don't *know anything*; but that at the same time I feel on the edge of knowing a lot I never knew before – I get glimpses of new opinions and views at odd times, chiefly in the night, but couldn't express them yet . . . Don't imagine you have any decisions to make. There are no problems – except whether to take lunch with you or risk finding some at a pub. There's probably a lot to be said for our not writing at all while you are away. I hold clear a beautiful smiling image of you that will – alas – shortly disappear. It is then the thought becomes tormenting. Better – much cleverer – not to bother about one another for three or four weeks, perhaps clean forget, then start discovering all over again. But no, it wouldn't. Everything that's happened is part of it.

A relatively cool letter followed.[5] He was planning, he said, to auction off the dairy part of the estate to realise some capital, keeping the remainder, about 1,000 acres, for arable, beef cattle and pigs. This would suit him perfectly because he would rather have money in land and stock than in anything else.

I seem to have run into a patch of belated hay fever pollen, waking me early and giving me headache and sniffles – a great nuisance . . . Had another look at the last chapter of *A Land* . . . While I agree about bad use of land, disappearance of traditions and crafts, I think there is more to be said for the townsman (my own type) than you say, and I should like to defend him. Have always been prejudiced myself against farmers and peasants, wherever found. I keep finding myself talking to you, which is a sad nuisance and a situation to be avoided; yet I need somebody with that relationship, somebody I deeply respect as a person as well as have lovely fun with, and you seem to be that one, even if you don't see it that way yourself – as I often think you don't. I must catch the post with this or you won't get it tomorrow but Monday. Bless you!

    J.

It was in the summer of 1951 that Priestley wrote to Davison revealing a dramatic change in his political views which he discussed at length with Jacquetta. The revolt of the left-wing group of the Labour Party led by Aneurin Bevan had gathered fresh disciples and Priestley believed that it might precipitate a general election. He was dismayed at the thought of a Tory victory, he said, but equally worried that an opposition led by Bevan could swing the

5   Priestley to Jacquetta Hawkes, 27 July 1951.

Labour Party too far to the Left. He proclaimed vociferously his hostility to the Conservative Party but expressed serious doubts about 'the psychological aspect of much of what Labour does'.[6] They were putting too much emphasis upon drab security and a dreary kind of equality with too few incentives for people to work hard and plan their future. The victims were the poor old middle classes – 'the most useful people we have in and out of working hours'. They were ignored by both parties since the Tories were preoccupied with the rich and Labour with trade union workers. What we needed was a strong revival of the Liberal Party. It all led to intense discussion with Jacquetta. She had gone to Ireland with her son before another letter ruefully remarked with a touch of seriousness: 'You have only to fall in love with some bloody Irish poet to complete the sombre picture.'[7] The letter said:

I feel this is an evil time. Any news I get is bad news. (Have just received this morning a very adverse report – from John van Druten, a very knowledgeable judge of the New York Theatre – on the prospects of *The High Blue Door*[8] for New York. Actually he doesn't much care for the play at all – thinks it lacks sympathy, like several other people. All depends on whether you like chief character, Harkfast. You and Thane do, apparently, as I do, but most others, actors included, I'm afraid, don't. And the Theatre depends chiefly on this damned sympathy. Heigh ho! I am going through one of my depressive phases and when awake at night (all too frequent) see myself as useless and despised and surrounded by powerful enemies. An interesting point about the people who dislike my work and me, strongly noticeable in print – it isn't that they think I have a few small virtues much overpraised by the stupid – but they allow me *no merit at all*, not a glimmer of anything. Now there are lots of writers I don't like and might be ready to attack, but I can see that they have considerable abilities and virtues of their own – e.g. the overpraised Graham Greene, Elizabeth Bowen, Compton-Burnett, Chris Fry, Jean Anouilh, Sartre, Tennessee Wlliams, etc. But I'm not allowed any, which is absurd and suggests that the dislike is temperamental and irrational rather than strictly critical – I'm a Dr Fell. And, by God, feel like one. But I am working away, slowly but not badly, at my South Sea Island piece, letting the people say what they please and not crowding them too much. I'm writing it in slightly

6  Priestley to Edward Davison, July 1951.
7  Priestley to Jacquetta Hawkes, 23 August 1951.
8  A minor play written in 1951.

heightened naturalistic dialogue, which I think is working out not too badly. Not a word of it written this morning, though . . .

I am doing what I can about my contours – not drinking much (it's booze that does it), not eating much fatty stuff, etc., etc. My bill at the Savoy from Monday afternoon until Friday morning was sixty-five pounds odd, not including some odd tips I handed out. Although, sitting in that miserable little sitting-room, I actually earned well over three hundred pounds, when you deduct tax I am well out of pocket. I really am tired of all this nonsense – punitive taxes, monstrous prices, etc. Some good articles by Graham Hutton in the *News Chronicle*, attacking the Unions for restrictive practices and the Government for not freeing but limiting energy.

Odd how we felt alike about not expressing feelings at the beginning of this absence. I shall go up to town on Tuesday very heavily, knowing there's really *nobody there*. You are better off in Ireland – all new and peculiar, holiday spirit, nice son to have larks with. I feel a grumpy old charlatan – a nasty combination. You have only to fall in love with some bloody Irish poet to complete the sombre picture. I'll probably write early next week. You can risk one letter to me at Albany next week, though I'll understand (but grieve) if you simply don't feel like it. Have a good holiday and don't worry about me. I grumble and growl but can look after myself at a pinch. Bless you!

Another letter showed Priestley's constant anxiety that their correspondence might get into the wrong hands or their relationship risk discovery. Since Jane was long familiar with his infidelities, expectations of faithfulness had vanished but if she felt that 'a woman always lurks somewhere in the background' she had no idea at this stage of her identity. Jacquetta's carefully cloaked *alter ego*, Elizabeth Heron, figured large in the letter which analysed his doubts and commitment. There were times when he was overtaken by bursts of resentment that he, a man of fifty-seven, should be so inescapably entangled by love but now, four years after it had all begun, a deep calm sense of security gave him a new reassurance.

Your letter arrived by the post this afternoon after I had begun to worry about it, but if you didn't post it until Monday morning, that is not too bad. All the same please don't write again after Wednesday as it's not worth risking. I may just miss getting it until Friday night as I have to go up to London (how dull without you!) on Thursday evening . . . I shan't be up on the 13th but will be up on the 14th for a day or two, though I can't here and now guarantee I shall be alone. I

345

shall be up a good deal in October of course and may with any luck
have a stretch alone like last week. (I agree with all you said in your
letter – your delightful letter – about last week, the same occasions
standing out for me.) It's still hot here . . . This is not the sort of
letter I want to write to you – something quite different and
altogether more intimate – but I feel horribly self-conscious when I
think of you opening this and trying to read it at the Hawkes family
breakfast or lunch table at the guest house. Let me say this, though,
that later on Sunday, several hours after I had written to you, I felt a
strong desire to write to Elizabeth Heron (that delicious girl) to tell
her that not since I had known her had I felt such a calm sweet
certainty of being deeply in love with her, that all the hostility that
used to come rushing up was entirely absent, that in place of the
feverish magic, often resented, was something quieter and deeper,
with passion there still but touched with great tenderness. You
know Elizabeth better than I do (or do you?) so you will know
whether she cares about this kind of feeling – I have often thought
she didn't want tenderness – or didn't want it from me, who, in my
sentimental old bearish way, have much to give – and I can only
hope I am wrong – and that she understands and enjoys it.
Sometimes I felt about her that all she really wanted was a sort of
passionate excitement, almost an impersonal sexuality, that any
virile male could supply, and that therefore if she couldn't see me for
a few weeks she would then switch on to some other man, concentrating upon him to secure the same excitement. But now I no
longer feel that – and at last believe her when she says that the kind of
feeling she has developed is not something to be switched on and off
easily – and I know too that now good and true things are being
given and are being received by each of us. And nothing – except
sheer wicked idiocy, probably on my part – can take that away now:
it has been experienced, the roots have gone down. Give her my
dearest and most devoted love – I think of her constantly.[9]

By 1952 Priestley was working steadily on *Treasure on Pelican*
which seemed to shape well 'though perhaps closer to the ground'
than he had hoped. *Festival at Farbridge* was having disappointng
sales and Priestley reflected that the old snowball into giant sales of
twenty years before was no longer possible. He hoped that *Festival*
might pick up again in the autumn but he temporarily resigned
himself to what might prove to be a bad financial patch. He wrote
again to Jacquetta complaining once more of missing the in-
between areas of communication:

9   Priestley to Jacquetta Hawkes, 31 August 1951.

Here's something a woman would understand, I fancy, better than any other man – that what one misses most are not the two extremes of earnest talk and making love but all that lies in between – talk that is half making love and making love that is a kind of talk – for all of which one person is essential and no substitutes can be found . . .

Plans still rather unsettled. I may get back to the Island next Tuesday or Wednesday but because of uncertainty you'd better not write, after you receive this, until you hear from me again . . . But careful with those legs.[10]

By now Priestley and Jane had tried every permutation including living separate lives under the same roof to salvage their marriage but nothing worked and presently they sold their two dairy farms, a move which had the symbolic effect of an erosion in shared property. Jane had always managed the family's finances and she it was who originally decided, against all Jack's inclinations, to buy and run not one farm but two on the Isle of Wight. She went to great trouble to learn farming techniques from expert advisers but the two farms were not a success, partly because the 'locals' on the island organised a boycott and would not buy their produce. Jane had a different attitude towards money from Jack who was sometimes accused of meanness, and could swing from one pole to the other. Returning from America he usually brought the children lavish and expensive presents but painting with Tom, he sometimes watched him squeeze the paint on to his palette with the words 'Don't use so much paint.' The borderline between thrift and meanness was sometimes narrow.

A letter to Jacquetta indicated that Jane had known about Priestley's relationship with her for some time and then came the announcement that she was thinking of buying a farm of her own in Scotland. This had the double effect of resolving a long-standing difference between Jack and herself while simultaneously adding another small step towards her independence.

A number of letters written by Jane to Dr Charles Lack were preserved by Tom Priestley and revealed the struggles and torments she underwent in this period, one moment determined to end it all summarily and the next containing herself with a supreme effort. A long talk with Charles Lack produced a special letter intended for Priestley which was never posted. Writing to Lack, Jane said, 'I went to see my solicitor who said "Yes it's a good letter but why not try and get a friend to approach him . . . or wait till

10   Priestley to Jacquetta Hawkes, 'Thursday', August 1951.

there's a crisis which we think will come from his side." So I didn't send the letter and am going to possess my soul in more patience.'[11]

Another letter from Jane to Dr Lack said that Jack was staying in London 'and Barbara and I are trying to find a small house where Miss Pudduck and Gertrude will keep house for him'. It was remarkable in the midst of the worst crisis in a long series of crises that she was still deeply concerned for his welfare. The letter disclosed that no 'bulletin had been issued to friends but it is hoped that they will infer gradually that our interests have grown apart'.[12] It was a masterpiece of understatement. During this period he sometimes turned for solace to re-reading Ouspensky and tried to follow his precept of disengaging himself from angry moods.

Ouspensky's thinking, which had influenced Priestley over the years from the first reading in America, entered and conditioned family life and behaviour at this time with considerable power. As Diana Collins, the wife of Canon Collins, wrote to me: 'At one stage he [Priestley] told me that he used to read a bit of Maurice Nicoll's Commentaries [on Ouspensky] every night and . . . found them most helpful, particularly the idea of non-identification.'

During the most difficult stages with Jane he often felt very angry but his refusal to identify with his angry self made it, according to him, 'so much easier to cope'. Diana Collins said, 'I think the example of his father made him determined not . . . to give way to violent anger.' He also said to his son Tom, apropos some TV discussion, 'The secret is never to let anger come into your voice.' Diana Collins believed that this produced a 'happy and harmonious atmosphere in his home' but this was not the view of some of the children during the break with Jane. Diana Collins clearly saw that repression of anger might have been responsible for the famous grumbling, a sublimated response to instinctual urges.[13] The received wisdom today believes with Freud that anger if not aggression should be given free range and some members of the family would have preferred this alternative.

Late in 1951 his private life finally fell apart. A trivial incident about some wine led to another highly charged moment with Jane which threatened to erupt in full aggression but Jane developed what was said to be 'flu and took to her bed. From then on they

11  Jane Priestley to Charles Lack, April 1951.
12  ibid.
13  Diana Collins to the author, July 1986.

stopped speaking to each other and Tom Priestley had the unhappy role of go-between, carrying messages from one to the other. Jane professed to have clung to the marriage and kept up appearances for the sake of the children, waiting until the last child left home. Tom Priestley said he spent his happy adolescence at Bryanston School and his suffering adolescence at home. Then came the day, early in 1951, when Jane said she had something to tell him, took him for a long walk and revealed that she was divorcing Jack.[14]

She wrote to Edward Davison saying that it was quite impossible for 'either of us to see the truth, we are each too involved', but she felt that their relationship had been steadily undermined by Jack's continued infidelities. They had been together twenty-five years but ever since the success of *The Good Companions* 'a procession of ladies' had haunted her. This, however, was not the real explanation, because throughout twenty of those years there remained a worthwhile element in their relationship. It was only in the last five years that something had gone wrong – 'I don't know what it is' – and since then their marriage had been 'empty'. She had become merely a business manager, a housekeeper, someone to receive his grumbles with no affection and not even friendship. The tensions had mounted unbearably and coming back from a trip to France with Jack one weekend she suddenly realised that she had finished one part of her job since the children had now grown up. She then saw that it was all finished for her. Jane claimed in her letter that when Jack saw her solicitor he told him that he wanted 'a wife in name' to deter people from attempting to marry him. 'I hope he will go ahead now and let me be free.'[15] She would marry again and hope to find peace and affection.

In the autumn of 1951 Priestley left for New York where he met Sir Cedric Hardwicke who was playing in Shaw's *Don Juan in Hell* with Charles Laughton producing. Hardwicke asked Priestley to dine with him at the Algonquin and persuaded him against his better judgement to 'enjoy Sir Cedric's minuscule talents'. 'I felt no desire to renew acquaintance with his particular chunk of Shaw and I imagined that Charles Laughton's production was a stunt affair, designed to exploit filmstars . . . I finally agreed to . . . and out of this decision *Dragon's Mouth* may be said to have been born.'[16]

14  Interview with Tom Priestley, 30 July 1986.
15  Jane Priestley to Edward Davison, undated, probably early 1952.
16  *Dragon's Mouth*, Jacquetta Hawkes and J. B. Priestley, VII.

This play was to recur in Priestley's correspondence over the next few years and became an interesting part of his professional relationship with Jacquetta. Laughton's production of *Don Juan in Hell* in a small Brooklyn theatre certainly qualified as a highly experimental play. There was no scenery, costumes, make-up or stage lighting; the actors wore evening clothes and pretended to read their parts.

According to Priestley it 'created a feeling of freshness, zest, attack to which the audience immediately responded'. Still considered by the uninitiate as a hidebound, traditional playwright, Priestley's enthusiasm for Laughton's production revealed an open mind at the age of fifty-seven which did him credit. 'Here was something new and exciting' which brought 'both the dramatist and the actors much closer to the audience'.[17] Hurrying backstage after the performance, Priestley talked enthusiastically to Charles Laughton, 'who gave me one of his huge, knowing grins, in which the extreme of innocence and sophistication seemed blended'.

Mr Shaw's play moved to the Century Theatre a week or two later and since it was 'round the corner from my hotel', Priestley haunted the Century discussing with Laughton themes in which Laughton felt he could exploit the new techniques.

Nobody in the New York milieu knew of his involvement with Jacquetta and even as late as 1952 he innocently referred to finding 'a most valuable and distinguished collaborator'. It was after one of the performances at the Century that 'I ran into Mrs Jacquetta Hawkes, then returning from visits to Harvard and Yale', where she had been lecturing. Enthusiastically discussing Laughton's production they agreed to collaborate on a play to be called *Dragon's Mouth*. Priestley would adapt the play to Laughton's techniques, and Jacquetta contribute those gifts so 'intelligent and deeply poetic that had shone in *A Land*'. Realising how difficult it would be to convert Jacquetta's lapidary sentences into dramatic dialogue, Priestley had grave doubts about the co-operation but once launched into the work, his qualifications disappeared. Before they left New York there was no time to do more than sketch the dramatic frame which derived from the work of Jung and crystallised his fundamental concept that all human beings conformed to four characteristic functions: thinking, feeling, sensation and intuition. The imposition of this psychological pattern gave coherence

17   ibid., VIII.

to the play and its characters, since the interplaying between the functions was itself dramatic.

Back in London, during snatched intervals, the collaborators arranged the long speeches of the four characters between them. According to Priestley 'we did not divide these characters according to our own sex but each took a man and a woman.' Most of the linking dialogue was originally Jack's and each one criticised the work of the other. Subsequently some critics were trapped by this mutuality into ascribing to Jacquetta certain scenes belonging to Jack. This account, given in Priestley's preface to the printed version of *Dragon's Mouth*, is elaborated by Jacquetta. She states that she 'wrote the parts played by the Denisons – Nina and Stuart – with Jack adding small linking speeches which were part of his plotting.' Thus the plotting of the whole play was his together with the dialogue for Matthew and Harriet.

Priestley was at this stage a 'hugely impatient' man who once ideas had crystallised had to rush pell-mell into their realisation. An incurable optimist at the conception of an exciting new idea, he 'could not bear waiting long for anything good to happen. I have never been able, as superior beings are able, to plan far ahead, to settle today what I shall be doing in two or three years' time. I rush at everything – even work.'[18]

Work now gave him an excuse to enjoy Jacquetta's company and distracted his mind from problems which steadily multiplied in their relationship. Laughing, arguing, criticising, sometimes fiercely defensive, the two lovers merged creative work with their love life and realised those depths of mutuality which belong to the deepest relationships.

The script sent pell-mell to New York was received enthusiastically by Charles Laughton and even his hard-headed business partner, Paul Gregory, agreed that it had 'possibilities'. Unable to find a theatre immediately in New York, Priestley plunged in to cast and produce it in England. He was 'longing to make the experiment not merely on paper but in actual halls'.

Michael Denison has left an account of what followed. Already a good friend, Priestley invited Denison to his flat in Albany and 'solemnly handed [him] two yellow scripts inscribed *Dragon's Mouth, A Platform Drama in Two Parts*. 'It's the best thing I have done,' Priestley said, 'but I can tell you I've been lucky with my collaborator, Mrs Hawkes.' He went on to explain in that sombre

18   ibid.

West Riding manner of his which had so often overlaid an intense inner excitement that the idea had been born the previous autumn.[19]

Denison saw Nina in the play as a part portrait of Jacquetta, 'the relaxed acceptor and lover of the physical world'. He had met her only once before at the Caprice restaurant where she made a striking figure wearing a cloak and sombrero, smoking a long cheroot. He felt an immediate rapport between them.

The play unfolded the drama of four people aboard ship waiting for results of blood tests to discover whether anyone had been infected by a violent tropical disease which was already responsible for the death of a member of the crew. Each character revealed a confident superiority in his or her attitude to life but the threat of death gave an edge to what they said. Each person represented one of Jung's four functions: thinking, feeling, sensation and intuition, but any derivation was not mentioned in the dialogue. In the second act the characters discover that one person has in fact been infected but the radio breaks down before the victim's identity is revealed. The self-confidence bordering on arrogance revealed in the first act becomes a deeper soul-searching in the second. Nina emerges as the spokeswoman, reaffirming the Jungian theme that a balance or fusion between their dominant characteristics is the desired end. The audience never knows who is to die.

*Dragon's Mouth* now went into rehearsal and it was on 30 March 1952 that the actor Michael Denison suddenly found himself in a role different from any in which he had been cast before. He became chaperon to Jacquetta during a visit she paid to Brookhill with Jack and assumed the mantle with ironic charm. He gave a vivid account of the visit. Priestley warned Denison that he had told his wife to take whatever furniture she wanted 'but she won't have done it yet'. When they arrived Priestley flung open the door to the beautifully proportioned hall only to discover – according to Denison – that it was completely empty except for the famous pianola and billiard table. This description Jacquetta disputes. According to her the 'table and the pianola were in a quite small so-called music room'.

It was after this visit that Priestley wrote another letter, early in April, analysing 'dangerous and important ground' which ended with a new and promising collaboration. The word was flatly contradicted by the passion of the last sentence:[20]

19  *Double Act*, Michael Denison, 30.
20  Priestley to Jacquetta Hawkes, 'Wednesday night late', March 1952.

Dear love,

I have been trying to do a bit of work after dinner, in a sleepy sort of way, and now I've packed it up to write to you. I looked in your bathroom and saw one or even two nail brushes I don't remember there before – are they (or is it) yours? This house very quiet, empty and rather sad (it is, you know) after you'd all gone this morning. I thought I'd tear into work but didn't, though in the end I didn't do too badly, by dint of sticking at it. Two things I want to say. First, some doubts I had (not entirely my fault, I think) melted away during these last few days. Secondly, I had last night, as you moved grave and slender through the dusk of the garden, an extraordinarily romantic feeling about you, a link with and back to certain impressions I had when we walked together in Mexico City, to and from some restaurant, but stronger than that, because so much had been added. Sometimes you dress (when you are feeling close to me) with peculiar genius, creating the very part I want you to play. All this is wonderful, that you should bother to do it, that I at my age and so battered and weary, should feel it so freshly. Somehow, without trying, we covered a lot of important (and dangerous) ground together these last few days, and my mind (I hope yours too) is easier. What sort of ground? Oh – our relationship, a new and promising xxxxxxxxxx (I'm too tired to spell) collaboration, other things. I long now for a night, preferably warm, of talk-plus-love, of talk when we are empty of desire and we can raise our voices if we want to, smoke and eat and drink and kiss and talk and behave as if time and other people didn't exist. Perhaps, following your habit, you have drawn away from me now, and are hurriedly lunching and dining with 'gardeners', but I feel very close, and that is why I write at once, to say what there was not time to say last night or this morning. You are Jacquetta – beautiful, wise and kind – and you are Woman; and I am in love with both. My darling –

JACK

Preparations for the final production of *Dragon's Mouth* were far advanced and the launching of their first big collaboration in the theatre generated the usual mixture of apprehension and excitement. A second letter following their joint visit to Brookhill revealed the strain which their mutual presence in Brookhill generated to modify the pleasure of sharing a deeply embedded part of his way of life.[21]

21   Priestley to Jacquetta Hawkes, March 1952.

Dearest Jacquetta,

It's very warm up here in my study, though the day is rather cloudy. I hope you had a comfortable journey and that all is well. I came down yesterday afternoon to an empty house – still tired but fairly cheerful . . . The little quarrel with MacOwan is a nuisance, particularly with the new piece looming up, and I have just written him a long, frank letter. This last week was grand, particularly as it gave you at least a glimpse of the kind of atmosphere in which I have to spend much time; but on the other hand the queer nervous strain (which is far greater than the actual demands of the work) did mean that I was always rather exhausted and preoccupied: but I felt you understood that, with beautiful sensitiveness and tact, and made the necessary allowances. It is up to me now to look on at some archaeological conference or dispute, or to hang on to the fringe of some group of raging poets, to share your kind of experience. This sharing of experience is very valuable, and it is a weakness of clandestine relationships that they have so little of it. It's all very fine the two people staring at each other and probably they soon want to be alone anyhow, but it's fun to see the other person in relation to people in general, work, different environments, and anyhow the shared experience enriches the saga. I know two people who have pretended to be tough characters, swigging brandy, in a hot little hotel room in Mexico City, who have walked hand in hand in a tropical night in Cuernavaca, who have nagged and wept and argued in Claridges, Savoy, Mayfair, etc. etc. to say nothing of the television studio, who have walked Yorkshire moors, embraced in Government offices, kissed and laughed in Central Europe – and so on and so forth. He is a fat, conceited chump, bumptious and aggressive and tactless, though now and again he does something thoughtful and charming – I mean, in relation to her. She is extraordinary, at once exquisite and delicate and yet earthy and fruity, a lovely ardent woman who is at the same time a rich character, as if Dr Johnson and Diane de Poitiers had somehow got mixed up together in one person. Even this fat chump realises that she is adorable and has the sense to know how lucky he is . . . I will write again in a day or two.

Bless you my love.

Throughout his collaboration with Jacquetta on *Dragon's Mouth*, it was necessary for Jacquetta to avoid staying simultaneously at the same hotel as Priestley, and his letter of 6 May was explicit:[22]

22   Priestley to Jacquetta Hawkes, 6 May 1952.

Darling J.,

. . . I don't know what you mean about my instructions and the Mitre. I said you had better *not* stay there, as I was staying there. I suppose it doesn't matter as it's so obviously the best hotel that it's natural for both of us to be there. Still – I'll either be at the Mitre (lunch time or early afternoon) or at the Town Hall, so look for me there. Can't tell now what time we'll rehearse. Molecey seems to think it would be difficult for the coach to return from Cambridge late on Sunday, so that means staying. On Monday I shall be lighting the piece in the afternoon and then having a dress rehearsal at seven – which I imagine you will want to attend. We could eat together some time but not dinner. By the way, if you want to avoid an agonising experience, I advise you not to sit in the audience on Tuesday but to lurk and skulk and peep and drink with me.

But possibly you won't mind. Oddly enough you mind more as you get older. I remember how I sat proudly in a box through my first play – I couldn't do it now.

I am doing no work, beyond making a few notes. Not laziness now, for I should like to be at it, but the feeling I'm not ready. Please remember I've always had such a contempt for the laziness and sloppiness of my profession that I've probably made too much of 'the man getting on with his job' idea, and marched to my desk too often, too soon.

Love,

JACK

P.S. It's pouring with rain – and I'm just off to the dentist's – hooray!


Heavily derivative from Laughton's production, the final stage version of *Dragon's Mouth* did in fact abandon one of its main innovations, the insistence on characters reading their parts. Discreet arrangements of white ropes suggested the deck of a yacht, noises off created the chattering of a motorboat and the hooting of a distant steamer added touches of reality to the stark formality of Laughton's effects, but all the characters, as with Laughton, wore evening dress.

*Dragon's Mouth* went on tour late in March 1952 and romantically the company intended to hire a private bus in which they would all travel, accompanied by Priestley who planned the itinerary. They expected to cover fifty-two one-night stands, beginning in Malvern and reaching far north to Newcastle, playing mostly in city halls. Priestley had the nostalgic notion of realising the actuality of *The Good Companions* but this quickly turned sour. Dulcie Denison (Nina) announced that her lifelong addiction to travel sickness would result in innumerable unplanned stops while she was sick in the ditch. She foresaw a pale and stricken wraith trying to cope with her part on the first night, still suffering from sickness-hangover. Priestley 'capitulated with ill grace' and Dulcie travelled alone with Michael Denison in his car. The bus driver proved to be a bad map reader and the journeys became so prolonged that Priestley 'withdrew to Brookhill in high dudgeon to console himself by entertaining a string quartet'.[23] He subsequently rejoined the tour at Bournemouth, accompanied by Jacquetta.

Arriving late for the first night they almost collided with a 'Colonel and his lady beating a premature retreat'. 'Ah sensible fellah,' said the colonel. 'I see you are leaving too.' As Denison commented, 'It was Jack who told us the story.'[24]

The play finished its tour at the Winter Garden Theatre, Drury Lane, London. A mixed reception ranged from rave reviews about Dulcie's performance as Nina to Kenneth Tynan who hated the play but admitted that it contained 'several flights of the best rhetorical prose I have ever heard on the stage'.

The high point in the play which brought a burst of spontaneous applause was Nina's description of a woman lying alone on a South of France beach lost in sensual surrender to her surroundings. Suddenly a seagull makes a lethal dive at her.

Nina: Its eyes were pale and fierce and utterly without thought: its bill was wide open – screaming. I felt as though I had been assaulted, as though a steel dart had been thrown into the very centre of all my nerves and senses. In a way it was agonising. My tongue knew what it was to be the tongue in that bird's hard and narrow bill and my muscles shared in the pull on its wings and yellow legs. Of course it only lasted an instant leaving me in a bathing dress lying under a green and white umbrella . . .

The speech which lasted five minutes invariably left dead silence afterwards to be followed by thunderous applause. However, something remained seriously wrong with the play and a later production proved a complete failure.

A letter to 'Darling Angela' detailed professional activities. He had been away on tour with *Dragon's Mouth*, he said, and although attendances were small, all 'went wonderfully, the audience loving every minute'. Optimistically he believed that whatever the

23   *Double Act*, Michael Denison, 30.
24   ibid.

financial results there was no doubt that the experiment had succeeded and a new form of drama had been born. Carried away with self-generated enthusiasm, he said that the American contract had been signed and Laughton 'should be doing it'. The letter ended 'love – Daddy'.

Correspondence with Jacquetta continued unabated.

Darling J.,

I don't want any more domestic ties, but the fact remains that I miss you, just as you probably do me, and it's damned silly we have to be away from each other when we both might be quietly working down here, and walking and talking our heads off as well. Spent a long solitary evening reading Rupert Hart-Davis's life of Hugh Walpole, which he'd sent me. Rather well done on the whole, though I doubt if the reader not particularly interested in Walpole would want it all, and of course there is much that Hart-Davis can't say. I keep popping up in the later chapters of it, and I suggest that if you come across the book you glance at the index and then look at some of these entries about me, as you might find Walpole's opinion not too different from your own . . . Not within sight of my Edwardian Comedy yet;[25] I have the atmosphere, the setting, most of the people, have had them for some time; but I need a cunning plot, productive of amusing situations. 'Damn your lines,' cried the old Regency actor. 'What's your situation?' And he was right. Especially if, as I intend, you want to write a comedy in the classical tradition. And these things can't be forced. Once the general situation is there, I can work out the developments in cold blood, but the main idea must come of itself. I'll take a walk this afternoon and perhaps something might happen. I don't know how it is with you but I cannot achieve a good idea by thinking all round it. I have to think about something else, after telling my unconscious to start worrying, and then suddenly it arrives. Just like trying to remember a name. How wildly different Friday night, all Saturday, and yesterday lunchtime were! And yet how satisfying and right! Bless you!

JACK[26]

The die was cast by the time another letter arrived and all the horrors of divorce in 1952 further complicated the difficulties of their relationship. These were the days of faked adultery when a

25  A play he never completed.
26  Priestley to Jacquetta Hawkes, 4 March 1952.

paid conspirator was discovered in bed with the litigant at some dubious hotel where the staff corroborated in what became a farce.

For the moment he was more preoccupied with what he described as the 'frenzied behaviour of Jane'. According to Priestley's daughter Rachel, throughout this period the atmosphere in the house was like being in a refrigerator.[27]

Next came the unfortunate episode of the letter from Priestley to Christopher Hawkes which the judge later exploited to decry Priestley's behaviour. The letter said that his planned trip to Japan with Jacquetta was platonic and professional. What the judge did not know was that Hawkes had insisted on Priestley writing the letter which Priestley did with the greatest reluctance. His next letter to Jacquetta said:

Sunday night late

(after the piano playing
for eight hands)
Darling J.,

Here is a letter that I am sending like this so that you may decide whether you think C. should have it or not. I wish we'd kept off this subject on Thursday night as it spoilt – or nearly spoilt – a very happy useful time together, during which I forgot all the complications of our lives . . .[28]

Having enjoyed their collaboration with *Dragon's Mouth*, Jacquetta and Jack now completed an early version of *The White Countess*, another joint venture destined to undergo a very mixed reception.

I don't know what you feel but I think our actual collaboration, while being more difficult technically, was much happier in the *Countess* than in *D's Mouth*. This is an important conclusion because *D's M.* might easily have been a *tour de force* and we might have had hellish rows with our next. But, to my mind, we were closer and easier than before; and I think I worked better because I was doing it with you . . . I'm glad to be leaving Brookhill because it's got all tangled up with you now, so I feel lonelier here than I would elsewhere. I've done two short articles since you left but have not got on with my stories as I felt too bored and tired. There were things in that Thursday night talk that left me worried, rather

27 Interview with Rachel Priestley, 6 February 1986.
28 Priestley to Jacquetta Hawkes, September 1952.

unhappy. I'll let you know if I get any reaction from Peters to the
*White Countess* . . .
Much love,
J.[29]

Talking on the telephone to Jacquetta at this juncture Priestley
almost persuaded her to go down to Brookhill to stay with him but
at the last moment Jane decided to make a return visit and a serious
confrontation was narrowly missed.

My darling,
Not a good day, except for weather – very hot. Jane rang up
Parkin (farm manager) to tell him she was descending upon the
island tomorrow evening, against all good sense and good advice.
What a stupid frenzied woman she is becoming! It is this that worries
me – and I'll confess I am worried and what with this, that and the
other, divorce, money, solicitors, accountants, farming, the future
of *Dragon's Mouth*, the need to do more writing, am drawing near
the end of my tether. Even Parkin, who came up tonight, and who is
no sensitive plant, wondered openly how much more I could take
and said he was surprised I didn't want to leave the country.
Anyhow it spoilt today, as you can imagine. I did some work on the
story but it went slowly in a stiff fashion, as it does when not enough
of the mind is being given to the job. You are probably right in
thinking that it would be wrong to do a reminiscence book in these
circumstances. I may sound gruff and off-hand when you offer
advice – but I take such advice very seriously, though I do believe I
have more intuition than you have. On the other hand I am not even
mildly clever about myself – never was. Being a going-out sort of
person I never get a clear view of myself in the picture – tend to
exaggerate or minimise my size, etc. But I have a clear and lovely
image of you at the moment, which I treasure, especially as we were
both just a trifle cross about our prologues and epilogues. At these
times, fewer and fewer, you think I'm arrogant and insensitive with
you, and I *know* you're arrogant with me. To hell with John
Hayward! I was writing good prose when he was a schoolboy.
Which doesn't mean I can't take correction from you – so long as
you'll take some from me – but please don't drag in your pre-
Mexico highbrow pundits, who mean not a sausage to me. But all
this is nothing, not beside the clear lovely image, very strongly held
and regarded with enormous tenderness. I don't think you're a
goddess at all. But I know you're an immensely desirable woman,

29  Priestley to Jacquetta Hawkes, 1952.

with a strange beauty of her own; an excitingly original personality, belonging to yourself, standing on your own ground more and more; my own comic girl with a rather stiff choky voice and a sudden wide grin; my wisest and dearest friend; my devouring female monster and my little love, all rolled into one. That's a lot, like falling in love with Hatchards, Fortnum & Mason and the pub round the corner, and having them all. There are some sticky bits I don't like, just as I have some great fatty pieces, all boasting and vulgarity, you don't like. What a good thing I didn't persuade you, last night on the telephone, to come down! I nearly tried. It might have been a nasty mess. Darling, soon I must bring you into my life more or turn some of you out of my heart and mind. This present balance doesn't suit me, though God knows I couldn't offer myself with confidence as a house partner. Perhaps if we did settle down, we'd start deceiving each other and lying like mad. But our minds do seem to work better together than they did or do with our respective marriage choices. We're honester people than those two – not so good in the narrow sense, more disreputable, but decent types of toughs, we are. Goodnight, my love – it's 1.25 a.m.

JACK

P.S. I'm attending to the weight.[30]

A letter simply dated 'late on Monday evening' evoked the strains suffered by Jacquetta and explored new aspects of his differences with his wife. Jane's moods continued to fluctuate wildly from hysterical outbursts to sudden illnesses from which she quickly recovered. This letter, addressed to Derbyshire where Jacquetta was away on holiday, re-examined their relationship through Ouspensky theory.

Monday evening

Dear love,

Thank you for the fine little letter that arrived this morning. I thought you might like a love letter to greet you in Derbyshire. (I hope the weather changes for you – cold here and probably colder there.) I am sorry there was even more fuss at home than you let me know about; I'm afraid C. is really in a rather poor way – the reaction of the various people at my party suggests that. You don't know what to do for the best, my poor darling, and I can only help by holding your hand and telling you I'll do whatever's best for you. It may be though that this absence in Japan may push things along

30  Priestley to Jacquetta Hawkes, 'Wednesday, very late', 1952.

someway or other: he may console himself elsewhere (but where's he going to find a good exchange for you?), or alternatively make demands on you (e.g. to see no more of me) that will change the present situation sharply. Meanwhile I'm game to go on as we are if we can stick it (which I doubt) or to set up in sin and shame (lots of drawbacks, though) or to marry, which also brings its drawbacks too . . . I've just made a sort of start on my Jap lecture but find it a dreary grind. The truth is, I hate trying to think – or giving the appearance of thinking – in a logical consecutive way, because my mind doesn't work like that – but only in quick intuitive flashes – and one can't lecture like that. Also, I don't really want to tell anybody anything – I'm just not ready. However, I must earn our airplane passages . . .

I agree about the sweetness of Thursday – though I feel that too often I blur the edge a bit on these occasions as I don't, for instance, when you're here. I damn the Essenes with you. Re-reading Ouspensky expounding Gurdjieff at the weekend – some interesting stuff about personality (almost the persona) and essence; and it occurred to me that right from the first, while our personalities were almost antagonistic, our essences felt the rightness of one another. With Jane, I think, it was the opposite, as I think it probably is with you and C. Your personalities fit in all right – similar background, interests, friends, etc. – but your essences are all wrong. But perhaps this is all too easy. Some fascinating stuff, mixed with nonsense, in the Gurdjieff–Ouspensky theories, about which more when we meet . . .

I have been told that I am VERY THICK with a fascinating creature who still looks (and always will, I believe) like a high priestess from some strange race but is also the sweetest, kindest, most companionable being on earth – what an astonishing mixture! And what do you get – merely a fat man from Yorkshire – though of course perhaps among members of that strange race there have always been wonderful legends about fat men from Yorkshire – and you have been sent on a mission to enthral one of them. Have a nice holiday, my love – bless you.

JACK[31]

In September 1952 Priestley set off with Jacquetta to lecture in Japan, all unaware of what was to follow. The trip to Tokyo involved touching down at Iceland, Honolulu and Wake Island. Writing to Angela Wyndham Lewis he said that the Japanese trip was 'enormous' fun, including a few days in Hollywood to check

31  Priestley to Jacquetta Hawkes, 'Monday evening', 1952.

the casting of *Dragon's Mouth* which he found stalemated by some 'pansy quarrel' between Laughton and the actor Paul Gregory. There followed ten days at Remuda, the perfect place to rest after incessant travel, followed by a flight to New York to find the right female star for *The White Countess*. It was no longer possible to cast a play quickly in New York or London but he was hoping for a production of the *Countess* in one city or the other and considered the play highly original. As usual he was busy with work, reflection and consideration of the next piece of writing. ABC had asked him to do a successor to his film *Last Holiday* and he was planning a new play which would attack the mechanisation and depersonalisation of the modern world. The letter concluded:

> *In strict confidence*, I think it likely that Jacquetta Hawkes may soon be divorced by her husband, which will make a great difference to me. I am certain you would like her very much, because not only is she beautiful and brilliant, but, what is rare among beautiful brilliant women, she is essentially kind and sweet-natured too. This is not the verdict of hasty infatuation but comes from a knowledge of her, which includes much work together, going back years. She is an unusual mixture of the scholar and the poet, as you can see from her book *A Land*, which is one of the few books of our time that will certainly become a classic . . .
> DADDY[32]

The climax in Jacquetta's life came at Christmas 1952 when she returned from New York to find that her housekeeper had been carried off to hospital and against a background of domestic chaos she prepared to tell her husband that she wanted to marry Priestley. She waited until Boxing Day and suddenly found herself telling him in a completely unpremeditated manner. 'He was very sweet about it, most of the agonies having been assimilated in the summer when I went to Japan.' Inevitably the whole day was charged with emotion 'funnily and justly enough mainly in me, for with the end in sight I felt most horribly sad and kept weeping'.[33]

Jacquetta also suffered qualifications to her self-esteem. It was never against her principles to be unfaithful to her husband but 'letting him down' and 'breaking up' his home were another matter. She was forced to face the fact that she could do something she 'more than half condemned', a truth which she had never accepted before on any large issue. Re-examining her motives she

32  Priestley to Angela Wyndham Lewis, 28 December 1952.
33  Jacquetta Hawkes to Edward Davison, 1 February 1953.

realised that one side of her would have liked to continue with the 'half and half arrangement' to avoid wounding her self-esteem, but since her love for Jack was the deepest part of her personal life 'for heaven's sake let me have the guts to behave badly in order to fulfil it'.[34]

As we have seen, it was customary in those days to provide evidence for divorce with a sham mistress but they both thought 'what a waste', when Jacquetta could openly fulfil the role herself since she no longer worried about social censure. A touch of hilarity entered with the policeman's otherwise painful intrusion.

Darling J.,

Thanks for your two letters, though I enjoyed them much less than usual. They seemed off-hand and busy; notes to any gardener.

Thursday proved a false alarm. Jane never left Ryde, after learning various people she wanted to see down here were away; and Parkin put her on the next boat. He said she seemed dazed and miserable, and hearing this, after feeling angrier than I had ever done before, I felt sorry for her. If she would only take it easy.

A sort of retired police inspector man arrived yesterday from Exeter and took down a statement I made about my stay at the Hotel Scribe. The idea is to pass this to the judge in place of the Scribe evidence. It was all solemn humbug, except when he said 'Can I say you acted like man and wife?' and I replied 'We acted better than most men and wives,' and at this sally he went purple with mirth. The name of the lady was not divulged, of course; and indeed he never expected it to be. He says this ought to go through quickly about 29th July at Exeter, with the decree absolute following about mid-September . . .

I'm not making good progress with my story. All this talk about a new way of writing is merely making me feel self-conscious, stilted and constipated. I've lost my old not ungraceful ease but have not acquired anything better. It's hell being a writer, particularly of fiction etc., when things won't go properly, because you can't force this sort of writing, can't will it into existence.

Figures down at the Winter Garden. Nobody asks me to do anything or go anywhere (true I'd refuse, but I like to be asked). I'm disgruntled. Lunch on Thursday wouldn't work out – come to Albany for a drink and sandwich before the theatre, then supper afterwards.

JACK[35]

34   ibid.
35   Priestley to Jacquetta Hawkes, 14 June 1952.

Late one Saturday night in July 1952 at Albany Priestley sat down and gave Jacquetta an account of his current professional life, which was full of contradictions. More revealing were his comments about Jane since they had finally parted.

Darling Jacquetta,
. . . I have left my copy of our *Countess* with Ralph, who had only read the first act when I parted from him. He seemed to feel that our Sophia was taking herself a bit heavily but said the criticism meant nothing in view of his ignorance of the other two acts . . . I enjoyed my stay with Ralph, who has rented a pleasant country house, about 8 miles from Stratford. I saw *Macbeth* (not too good from any point of view), *Volpone* (good all round) and *The Tempest*. Contrary to the press reports, Ralph seemed to be very good as Prospero, making him more human and sympathetic . . . Every night, having eaten a large meal at 11.30, Ralph and I sat up for hours and hours drinking whisky and talking about everything, so that I feel sadly short of sleep.
(After Caprice)
We had a pleasant dinner, with the place mostly filled with Americans . . . Saw Jane's sister (who lives near Woodstock) en route here today, and she told me Jane will be marrying again shortly after the divorce is through, that she seems happier than she has seemed since 18, and that old Bannerman orders her about and she apparently likes it . . .
This is just a gossipy idle letter, so I'll only say I miss you and am most grateful for the kind, wise letter you wrote me last Monday. Bless you!
JACK[36]

The scene was now set for the final break-up of two marriages, and divorce proceedings. In February 1953 a letter to Angela Wyndham Lewis gave interesting news about his work and he was now predicting the date of his marriage to Jacquetta. Various members of the family had visited Brookhill to recover from 'flu while Priestley went to London, only to find himself running a temperature which threatened to put him to bed. He recovered rapidly except for a cough which persisted and made him sound remarkably like J. M. Barrie aged seventy. He gave Angela detailed family news with Tom, his son, flourishing 'majestically' at Cambridge and Mary in reasonably good shape.

36   Priestley to Jacquetta Hawkes, 'Albany, Saturday night', 1952.

He had just finished a new play, *Take the Fool Away*, which was already loathed by Peters and never likely to be a favourite with Keith Prowse. Some years before he had written for television a civil service farce called *Whitehall Wonders* which made the Royal 'family' laugh so much that Princess Margaret personally told him so. Converting the play into a film he reflected that it was too mad and highbrow for ABC but since they were paying him handsomely for a treatment, its ultimate fate was a matter of indifference. He was more concerned to know whether the American agent had yet succeeded in casting *The White Countess* and *Dragon's Mouth*. As the coronation approached he hoped to let Albany for three weeks, including the services of Miss Pudduck and Gertrude, through his lifelong friend Davison, which would enable him to roam abroad on the dollars. He then disclosed, in strict confidence, that the Hawkes divorce would take place late in May, 'which if it goes properly will leave me free to marry Jacquetta sometime in July. I hope you will meet soon.' It was typical of Jacquetta 'that night a year ago when you were due to meet, she quietly melted away because you were feeling disturbed . . . Let me hear from you soon. Lots of love, Daddy.'[37]

On 6 June 1953 *The Times* reported the divorce.

Judge Tudor Rees sitting as a special commissioner in the Divorce Court granted a decree nisi to Professor Charles Francis Christopher Hawkes, aged 47, a professor of European Archaeology at Oxford University, on the ground of adultery by his wife Mrs Jessie Jacquetta Hawkes.[38]

Determined to make Priestley an example His Lordship said that he was a writer of fiction, a capacity which he had demonstrated in letters to Professor Hawkes when the professor became suspicious about the relationship between his wife and Mr Priestley. Turning the knife His Lordship continued: 'In my view he wrote these letters in a deliberate and cunning attempt to deceive Professor Hawkes as to his conduct. Mr Priestley and Mrs Hawkes collaborated in writing and producing plays in Japan and elsewhere and it is quite clear that it was not only a literary collaboration but an adulterous one. I think Mr Priestley's conduct mean and contemptible.'

Such comment from a divorce court judge in proceedings today would be regarded as totally out of place. He held forth in ignorance

37  Priestley to Angela Wyndham Lewis, 20 February 1953.
38  *The Times*, 6 June 1953.

of the truth that Professor Hawkes had himself insisted that Jack should write the 'deceitful' letter. When in July 1953 Jacquetta and Jack married in Caxton Hall they hoped to avoid publicity but had to face about thirty press cameras. A sumptuous buffet lunch for some fifty people followed in Albany in an atmosphere of goodwill which Priestley regarded as public as well as private.

Almost simultaneously Jane Priestley married Dr Bannerman, the distinguished ornithologist, and it was as if the gods had decided to compensate both for years of torment. Their marriages ran on successfully for over twenty-five years with periods where that impossible state 'married bliss' came close to realisation.

# 26

# Interlude
## 1952–4

The recurring references in correspondence to *The White Countess* involve immensely complex personal and professional interactions. At Christmas 1952 Priestley was staying with his daughter Barbara, at Gayford House, Wattisham, near Ipswich. They were living under threat from the dramatic east coast floods which had inundated large areas and caused great destruction.

A letter from Barbara Wykeham said that after her father left she was 'fairly ill and in fact bedridden', until her son William Philip Priestley was born in March 1953. She commented: 'It must have been a rather dull time for him' (Priestley).[1] Part of that time he spent writing letters, one of which went to Jacquetta.[2]

His disillusion with the theatre had temporarily reached a pitch where he felt that forces were at work trying to drive him out.

Darling J.,
 Thank you for your letter, which has just arrived – middle of the morning . . . Yes, I know what you feel about the *Countess* – and I am determined that this play shall not be shelved. I must see for myself how it plays. (I believe in it.) But just as you are superstitious about this, I am correspondingly superstitious – and so depressed – about all my theatre work. Let me put it this way, from the non-rational part of my mind – I feel SOMETHING is determined to drive me out of the theatre – therefore, as this is a powerful SOMETHING, everything that can go wrong does go wrong – and everybody feels the influence of this SOMETHING – even old and admiring friends like Peters and Thane. With Peters I must have a definite showdown. Either he puts in some hard work for me or I must find somebody else who will. I've not heard from Ralph of course as I'm not getting mail forwarded here. But I wouldn't take Maggie Leighton's reaction too seriously – she really is very young and naive for her age. Actually, although I'm always interested in

1  Letter to the author, 4 April 1986.
2  Priestley to Jacquetta Hawkes, December 1952.

what actors and actresses have to say about an unproduced piece, I never consider them sound judges; they love conventional situations and mental attitudes; which is why the real Theatre never flourishes under actor-managers . . .

Much love,

JACK[3]

When he wrote *The White Countess* in collaboration with Jacquetta, according to Elspeth Parker he 'conceived the idea of getting Greta Garbo out of retirement to play the lead'.[4] Priestley divided his comedies into three types: High, Light and Broad. High comedy included relatively sophisticated works like *Ever Since Paradise, The White Countess* and years later *A Severed Head*. It differed from light or broad comedy in having an intellectual content. This was certainly true of *The White Countess*. Light comedies he regarded as 'admirable vehicles for popular and highly skilled star performers without whom these flimsy pieces are apt to look very thin indeed'.[5] Broad comedy – *When We Are Married* – had the strong character and situations lacking in alternative categories and skilfully reconciled social criticism.

Very occasionally criticism of class distinction, pomposity, social climbing and cupidity approached black humour but he never pressed the dagger home. The dramatic impetus of broad comedy was towards serious complications but before they developed too far, Priestley converted them back into 'straight' laughter. He was most at home with broad comedy and *The White Countess* did not fall into that class. Whatever the cause he could not rouse enthusiasm for the play and the visit of Thane and Elspeth Parker in February of 1953 did nothing to help.

Elspeth Parker, the wife of Thane Parker the theatrical director, recalled the event with a mixture of dismay and affection. The express purpose of the Parker invitation to Brookhill appears to have been to extract from Thane and Elspeth their joint opinion of *The White Countess*. Friday evening and Saturday passed without any direct reference to the play but by Sunday they knew that the terrible moment had come.

When Jack directly asked the question we both hesitated to prepare him for the shock and then we said: 'We are terribly sorry, we don't

3   Priestley to Jacquetta Hawkes, 'Wednesday', December 1952.
4   Interview with Elspeth Parker, 1 January 1986.
5   *Collected Plays*, J. B. Priestley, preface.

think it works.' There was an awkward silence while he glowered – broodily. Then he said to Thane: 'When have you ever written a play?' It was such a bloody stupid reaction we did not at first know what to do. Then Thane said: 'All right, get somebody else to read it. We may be wrong.'

The next morning we were on the point of leaving when Jack came down in his dressing-gown with a long grey face and said that he'd had a terrible night. He hadn't slept. Thane said: 'I'm sorry if you're hurt but we had to tell you – genuinely – what we think.'[6]

A. D. Peters disliked the play too. He had become so tired of the whole 'theatrical circus' that he burst out one day: 'I've had enough. I'm not going to handle any more plays for anybody.' A. D. Peters was 'a flat-faced Dane' without much imagination, who, like Priestley, had left his wife some years before and now lived with Margot Graham, an actress, whose 'hair was red, her personality forceful and her cleavage that of a barmaid'. She had won an Oscar in *The Informer* and now compensated Peters for two cold and unhappy marriages.[7] Until their impasse over experimental plays Priestley and Peters had a relationship which combined warmth and understanding. No great talker, Peters would sit opposite Priestley, while both smoked obsessively and for long periods neither said a word, but something more than money had created a semi-silent bond between them. Moreover, their relations varied according to circumstance. The mood of mutual contemplation could – in the sand pit of the Savile Club – break into four-letter word exchanges when each hurled bugger at the other indiscriminately. When Peters closed his play department Priestley promptly went to another distinguished play agent, Peggy Ramsay. Alas the results were no better. Elspeth Parker summed up: 'I was very fond of him – we had a good relationship – he could be marvellous company – but underneath he was marshmallow.'

In the event *The White Countess* was produced in Dublin and Bradford before it came to London. The anguish of rewriting the play continued over several months as was evident in Jack's letter to Jacquetta headed simply, 'Albany, Thursday Night'.[8]

Dear Love,
    . . . The situation is this: even when Act 3 opens less farcically and

6  Interview with Elspeth Parker, 1 January 1986.
7  Interview with Michael Sissons, 9 February 1986.
8  Priestley to Jacquetta Hawkes, 'Albany, Thursday Night', 1952.

Viveca plays her defence scene sympathetically (which she did on
Wednesday after we rehearsed her) and everybody plays better,
there is a definite drop in interest after Varennes says he must bring
himself to his senses and even though it has its moments, the play
never properly picks up again. I am absolutely certain of this . . .
Your beautifully written scene for the Countess and Klaren goes for
very little because the dramatic situation is not supporting. Either
they know already Klaren will get her or they don't care. Our
problem is to pick it up at that point and make it better than ever,
while keeping the main ideas, e.g. her relationship with Klaren, his
notion of relationships, etc. . . . Remember we are only dealing
roughly with the last ten pages of the script – it is not a big job of
rewriting, only of clever revising. Anything can happen so long as
Varennes and the Count are rejected and Klaren is accepted . . . If we
could make this part of the play as theatrically brilliant as the best of
the supper scene and yet keep in your wisdom and good writing, we
could bring off the play, triumphantly. But as it is, even with
improved playing, it will always limp with any audience. It just isn't
good theatre. (My fault.) The situation just isn't strong enough to
support the talk. The audience, fatigued by this time, need some
movement, some visual change, as well as the good talk . . .

Running through his correspondence at this period were a
number of references to the *New Statesman*. These concerned a
series of articles which began as a result of John Freeman looking for
a writer who would enliven that periodical. Freeman asked Tom
Baistow, the assistant editor, one day in 1952, to recommend a left-
wing writer and Baistow mentioned Priestley. Freeman took
Priestley to lunch and commissioned him to write a number of
articles, as a result of which, as Tom Baistow put it: 'Ever after I had
to deal with his moans and groans. His complaints were of two
kinds: one about money – "I don't think it's worth doing for that
much – I don't know why I do it!" Second, whatever article he was
trying to write he always argued ferociously about length. "I write
to a natural length," he said. "You can't remove that para" which
meant *any* para.'[9] His articles ranged from 'Eros and Logos', 'The
Newest Novels' and 'Grey Eminences', to 'Another Revolution',
'The New Drolls' and a 'Note on Billy Graham'. These highly
controversial articles were to lead into an eloquent outburst against
the threat of nuclear war which launched the massive campaign
known as CND.

9 Interview with Tom Baistow, 4 October 1985.

A letter at this time to Edward Davison revealed another revolution in his political thinking which made it paradoxical that he should continue writing for the *New Statesman*. He now believed that the socialist-capitalist duel was hopelessly out of date and considered the whole social situation called for fresh thinking instead of 'wrangling about dead issues'.[10] Because they mistakenly believed in his blind adherence to socialist thinking, the Beaverbrook press according to Priestley had persistently criticised his personality and work, and it would be interesting to know how they would react when they discovered the change. Simply, he reflected, by accusing him of political chicanery.

10   Priestley to Edward Davison, 26 April 1952.

# PART THREE

# 27

# A Writing Honeymoon
## 1954–5

The fate of *The White Countess* continued to echo into the first few months of Priestley's marriage to Jacquetta, but the very first week of living together at Brookhill produced a complication of a quite different order. As Jacquetta put it, Priestley fell into 'a queer mood and missed some meals'. She said to herself: 'Oh God, what have I done?'[1] The inescapable strains of two unique individuals at last adapting to actually living together dissolved almost as quickly as they arose and there now began a new way of life which was relaxed, unhurried, capable of yielding the deepest satisfactions and quickly enlivened by what was in effect a long honeymoon trip to South America. In England they divided their time between Albany and Brookhill, and Priestley later recalled that 'all my happiest memories clustered round that house'.[2]

> To watch the entrancing view emerge from the golden mists; then to pick mushrooms all afternoon; then in the evening to listen to the Brahms Clarinet Quintet: we were half-way to heaven. We also had a little terrace within easy reach of the kitchen and dining-room, and there when the day was all sunlight and blue air we would enjoy our drinks and lunch on sea-bass, freshly caught. I remember Neville Cardus among others staying with us on a bright summer weekend and after a few hours of it saying slowly to me 'It's like a dream . . .'[3]

There were inescapable drawbacks. The house could easily be engulfed in mist for days, a thick winter fog would cut off the whole island and a south-western gale produce prolonged banshee howls.

In the summer of 1953 minor complications were quickly overwhelmed by the full realisation of the most important love

---

1  Interview with Jacquetta Priestley, 1 September 1985.
2  *Instead of the Trees*, J. B. Priestley, 142.
3  ibid.

relationship in both their lives. 'We are both absurdly happy',[4] Jacquetta wrote to Edward Davison. 'So much so that we fear it will encourage us to fleet the time carelessly until we are both ruined.'[5]

The early autumn brought a spell of perfect weather and the New London String Quartet arrived with Leon Goossens for the festival which Priestley had arranged every autumn over a number of years. Brookhill was 'packed tight' with people and everything soft and movable was requisitioned to accommodate the audience. The performance Jacquetta described as 'powerful'.

Bounded to the north by Newport, that 'fine old county town in miniature', the West Wight remained, in their time, unspoilt, and on Sunday mornings they marched their guests over heath and downland to Freshwater Bay. There, sitting outside the pub they were given one of Priestley's favourite drinks, a Dog's Nose, a mixture of gin and draught ale – 'not intended for the sedentary'.

The remainder of the island was highly picturesque but something beyond the great cliffs, coloured bays and sweeping downs created an atmosphere which Priestley could only describe with his favourite word – magic. 'It began to make you feel after a time that you were entranced in a waking dream.' Perhaps the poets helped here. There was Keats beginning *Endymion* at Carisbrooke, 'Tennyson, composing his favourite (and mine) *Maud* at Farringford, and where did Swinburne write *Atlanta in Calydon*? – why at Shorwell, halfway between us and St Catherine's'.[6]

Life in London lacked the pleasures of the Isle of Wight, but replaced them with all the riches of a London that Priestley still, at different periods, loved. There was no gearing up of social life but occasional dinner parties could now openly be conducted with Jacquetta as hostess.

On either side of the first-floor landing in 'B' Block Albany were two sets of chambers which the Priestleys shared. The larger apartment, B4, consisted of a drawing-room, dining-room and kitchen, with two Sickerts and a painting of Eugene Goossens conducting at Covent Garden on the walls of the drawing-room. Across the landing in a separate second flat was the study, 'a fine, tall room' with 'a large and extremely tidy desk',[7] but they rarely worked seriously in Albany. The walls of Jacquetta's bedroom were decorated with a Frances Hodgson over the fireplace and on

4 Jacquetta Priestley to Edward Davison, 1 February 1953.
5 ibid.
6 *Instead of the Trees*, J. B. Priestley, 143.
7 *Homes & Gardens*, July 1970.

other walls a head by Turner and a Gwen John nude. Priestley had a separate slip of a bedroom which bore out their belief that separate bedrooms were better for 'sleeping and sex'.[8]

Both were seasoned travellers and now they planned a trip to America, the first expedition untroubled by risk of discovery or moral scruples. Both believed in travelling purposefully and they set out to Texas and New Mexico (USA) intent on 'comparing some of the earliest men with some of the latest' for which the American south-west offered opportunities not to be found elsewhere. Some of the earliest inhabitants of America made their home in New Mexico and just across the state line men lived in the richest and most rapidly expanding cities in the western world – Dallas and Houston. Emblematic of modern life Houston proudly displayed its crimson and gilt Woolworth store as the largest such store in the world and mechanised man drove about the city in luxurious motor-cars built to exceed unnecessarily high speeds.

In New Mexico the Pueblos never moved from their ancestral lands and still preserved their ancient culture, and the cliff dwellings of prehistoric Pueblos were 'some of the most remarkable remains of any primitive people in the world'.[9]

Jacquetta's archaeological training and temperament automatically selected the old world as her province and Jack, who knew his modern America so well, could not escape the new. They set out together in a state of happy anticipation. Arrived in America they began the long train journey through the middle west heading towards Kansas City. From diaries, letters and notes they later created a remarkable joint account of their explorations, moods and reactions. This was no ordinary honeymoon trip.

'I lay back comfortably in my seat,' Jacquetta wrote. '. . . I was in that state of railway drowsiness when one isn't asleep yet cannot control one's thoughts . . . My will had one success, however, and that was in a mental exercise I have often practised before. First I imagined the interior view – four long lines of passengers supported semi-prostrate in this steel tube with its dim, deep-sea light, each one aware of himself as an individual . . . Then leaping in imagination to some nearby eminence I saw the gigantic train, nearly half a mile of it like a thick snake or blind worm moving through the night and the vast fields of the Middle West.'[10]

8  Interview with Jacquetta Priestley, 15 September 1985.
9  *Journey Down a Rainbow*, J. B. Priestley and Jacquetta Hawkes, preface.
10  ibid., 2.

Rousing herself from drowsiness around one o'clock that night as they approached Kansas City, she prepared to part company from a sound-asleep Jack. He had arranged to change trains at Kansas City en route for modern man. Her diary recorded their parting straightforwardly: 'He climbed down onto the platform (and it really is a climb from these towering American coaches) and said goodbye. I remember the heavy smell of oil and steel which seemed to make separation on the dark platform all the more forlorn.'

Back in her seat, trying 'to settle down again', a scene followed which was all the more distressing because of her parting. A male American voice kept repeating 'We have the inside seat' with such insistence that she realised it must be directed at her. 'I looked up to where the wide curled brim of a man's felt hat was just visible in the gloom and protested that this was impossible. I had come from Chicago and was going on to Albuquerque. I made no attempt to move.'[11]

'Let my daughter have her seat. The inside seat is hers.' The man's manner was flat, unpersuasive to Jacquetta, who indeed felt almost insulted. She summoned the attendant, who simply confirmed what the man said and indicated that she would have to take Jack's vacant place. 'It was quite reasonable and I should suffer very little discomfort, yet my protests went on – it was disgraceful I should be disturbed in the middle of a long journey; it was a piece of abominable mismanagement and so forth.' Jacquetta's final comment in her diary was curt: 'I made an ass of myself.'

She stepped gladly out of the dead overheated train in the middle of an afternoon, which was brilliant with sunshine and yet preserved a coolness in the air. She had received a flowery telegram from her hotel, which said that her train would be met, but there was no one at the station. She found a porter and they were soon advancing on the 'exaggeratedly Spanish precincts'. Passing the Hispano Indian Museum she paused to peer through its windows and was surprised to find that it obviously contained first-rate materials.

'Here within a few minutes of arrival I was being introduced to the two points of attraction in the cultural life of New Mexico – the Indian and the Spanish.' Deeply infiltrated by the oil industry, ranching and even atomic fission, the Pueblos had reacted on the invaders and sent back a creative wave which the Americans found

11   ibid.

irresistible. Their culture had grown 'from the land and the imagination' which produced shapes and combinations of colours which were exclusively theirs. The Americans could throw bridges across impossible chasms and railways over continents but they failed to produce, she believed, something which remained exclusively American. Hence the attraction towards the arts and traditions of a poor and relatively powerless people like the Pueblos.

When the porter shut the door on the modern bedroom which had no connection with traditional Spain, she suddenly realised that she was committed to an expedition whose precise objectives were sufficiently vague to qualify for the word half-baked. Her sense of inadequacy drove her to find a modern solution. She telephoned the owner of a bookshop who knew she was arriving and shortly afterwards confronted a totally unexpected person.

'I saw a large untidy woman pleasantly ample in hip and breast, with humorous rolling eyes set in those full lids which often go with the most naturally feminine kind of sexual attractiveness.' Her house repeated certain aspects of her personality: 'wonderfully rich, warm and careless'. Far removed from the western image idealised in glossy women's magazines, it lacked the 'false elegance of gracious living and overflowed with cats, cosmetics and under-clothes. But for me though I myself lack the confidence to be half so untidy, the Hacienda del Lago was a delight and a happy reversal of all my earlier expectations.'[12]

Jacquetta's first few hours introduced her to lingering traces of Mexico, and the jagged mountain ranges dominating the rolling desert, but these were far removed from the prehistoric sites she sought.

Priestley's parting from Jacquetta had been hurried because the connection with the train leaving for Texas was casual. American efficiency insisted that if one were late the other would leave without waiting. 'I might not have a moment to waste,' Jack wrote. 'So our midnight goodbye was a brief exchange outside the dim-lit hot steel coach.' Lost in the immensity of the cathedral-like station with a roof soaring out of sight into the night, Priestley had recourse to whisky instead of the telephone and since it was forbidden in the state of Kansas, it tasted twice as good. His porter had warned him that the connecting train was in fact an hour late and he drifted 'down long, mysterious corridors, up incredible

12    ibid., 6–8.

stairways into vast meaningless halls with lights burning everywhere, but no people about as if we had arrived in a city of the dead'.[13] It was two o'clock before the porter returned to escort him to the train and he found himself in his 'little steel bedroom, a cube of hot metal', as they rumbled out towards Texas. Many hours later he arrived at Dallas and the Local Enthusiast was waiting to meet him with the news that the hotel could not take him because it was conference time. 'So the Local Enthusiast proposed to take me to his house which he added with the quick generosity that is one of the most endearing American traits, was mine to command.'[14]

The city of Dallas in total contradiction to Albuquerque towered over him and left him breathless with its continual insistence on skyscraper glory. 'It's a Place in the Sun.' 'Gets Bigger All The Time.' 'A Sky-line Ever More Imposing.' 'Impressive, Restless, Changing, Climbing Silhouettes.' The superlatives flowed unceasingly and Priestley was reminded of 'the children of giants playing with Meccano sets'. His introduction to his quest had been no less stimulating than Jacquetta's, but he was missing Jacquetta as much as she was missing him.

Jacquetta wrote to Jack: 'Considering how vague my working plans are, I've launched them in an incongruously well-ordered way.' She drove out to the Sandia Cave, which had given its name to the earliest known culture. 'The cave is a fine one as caves go, tunnelling far into the rock but unless one is a child or a speleomaniac there isn't a great deal to be said for caves once they have been excavated.' Excavations in the 1930s revealed an archaeologist's dream unfolded in stratified layers as neat as a cake. First the recent remains of Indian pottery with the bones of a ground sloth and below that remnants of an old Stone Age people – the Folsum – thought to be the world's oldest inhabitants. Dates reached back 25,000 years corresponding to aspects of the palaeolithic, the age of cave paintings and the last glaciation.[15] Her letter concluded: 'I'm glad I went. I like visiting shrines whether Dove Cottage or the Sandia Cave.' Jack wrote back:

> I thought you ought to know about this as soon as possible . . . I have coined some new names and from now on I shall use them . . .
> First then, Admass. This is my name for the whole system of an increasing productivity, plus inflation, plus a rising standard of

13  ibid., 18–19.
14  ibid., 25.
15  ibid., 48.

material living, plus high-pressure advertising and salesmanship, plus mass communication, plus the creation of the mass mind, the mass man.

The Admass empire consisted of many kingdoms. Nomadmass recognised the sovereignty of the internal combustion engine, and insisted that if you want to enjoy life 'you must never get out of your car'. There were other divisions like Hashadmass and Luxad, in which life was converted into Gracious Living of the type dreamt up by advertising copy-writers.

His letter concluded:

> So here they are – Admass, the great empire itself, and the satellites: Nomadmass, Hashadmass, Luxad. They have almost a biblical ring, these names, but those raging old intuitives, the Hebrew prophets, would have made short work of them – Woe! – Woe! – Woe! And to you if I don't hear from you soon.

Jacquetta replied rapidly that she was beginning to understand how the different parts of Indian history fitted together with the Bandalier Monument at the bottom of one of the deepest canyons where they arrived one evening. They were the only people in a ruined city which sprawled for miles along the cliffs. 'The light was failing but I was determined to reach the ceremonial cave which lies high up, just below the canyon lip. The way up was by means of rough ladders of the sort the Indians use . . . Mrs A. and her friend dropped out of the climb. (Let me not deny that I was pleased.)'

Jacquetta was the first to step into the cave and she moved softly not wanting to disturb the silence or spoil her expectations. Then she saw it. Dark against the sky the ancient Kiva, the same circular wall and pair of poles sloping upwards from the hidden chambers which she had just seen among the living Pueblos. A very visually minded person, this sudden joining of hands between past and present made a deep impact on her.[16] Squatting there in the thick dust she induced images of the Pueblos coming through the hole in the Kiva roof to dress themselves in masks, horns and skins before plunging into dancing.[17]

It was a long fascinating letter, full of details of rituals, practices, and dwellings, which ended: 'I've gone on much too long. You won't want to read all this stuff in your millionaire world. But please keep the letter – it will be my chief record.'

16  ibid., 60.
17  ibid.

Priestley followed this with a brilliant account of a football match at Fort Worth, where, it seemed to him, that even at play Admass was at work. Remembering the learned senators and aristocratic ladies who had accepted without protest the elaborate cruelties practised in the Roman circus he had a terrifying vision: 'if the future should prolong the lives of the present, if civilisation should mean organisation and not values, if sensation should become more and more blunted and some release had to be found for the dumb, dulled mob, then blood-stained games might once more affront the sun – and this time be relayed on coloured television for invalids, stay-at-homes and children'.

The time had come to rejoin one another and Priestley underwent a series of air journeys culminating in a small plane which 'bounced over the jagged hills to the North . . . As soon as the little brute came to rest I shot out of it terrified that it might take off again and bounce me for months about the savage peaks of New Mexico.'

The account of their reunion was painfully formal. 'I greeted my wife in my favourite weather.' They shared a ramshackle car to Santa Fé and there talked and talked, prepared dinner, ate it and talked on far into the night. Afterwards they went out into the icy breath of the night air, 'to see the huge glitter of stars from the familiar blaze of constellations to the . . . vista of illimitable worlds . . . I forbore for once to make my speech about higher levels of being. It was a night when a man could believe there was a good life up there, a good life down here and perhaps some possible connection between them, without saying too much about it.'

In Santa Fé, scrutinising Pueblo artefacts in clay, metal and weaving, Jacquetta paused before the mystery of the aesthetic impulse. She gave a grave and beautiful account of ritual dancing, with the earth-stamping passion of the participants matched by the colour and demeanour of the spectators. The whole spectacle was charged for her professional eye with special meaning.

Priestley conjured up a world encompassed by cars where people hurtled in tin boxes 3,000 miles to get nowhere: Jacquetta a world where with no more effort than a casual stroll, inhabitants found a continuously renewed meaning in the simplest way of life.

When admonished that the wages of sin was death and the gift of God eternal life, Priestley attacked that account with a lay sermon to Admass. Sin consisted in ignoring 'being', to concentrate exclusively on 'becoming', to reduce the meaning of life here and now by concentrating on the hereafter. 'Nor is it necessary that we should be saints, mystics, the profoundest of philosophers to know something of that experience. All moments of noble living, the ecstasy of love, the compassion and understanding that enter into every genuine personal relationship, the creative and rapt appreciation of great art, the adventures of the mind among significant ideas, even an amazed wondering about ourselves all demand this unknown dimension, this timeless being.' Rhetorically expressed, some doubts about the applicability of these lofty sentiments to Admass remained. It was none the less a splendidly rousing statement of one man's credo.

As if in reply Jacquetta wrote that the Indians lived by an 'intuitive psychological wisdom', which Americans and Europeans had lost. The handicap of our greater consciousness made it difficult for us to incorporate psychic factors 'fully and generously into the life of the mind'.

Did Jacquetta have the last word? The *Times Literary Supplement* said: 'Their book is an adroit and brilliant entertainment, but it is aimed to hit much harder than that. We are meant to feel the mantle of the seer and hear the rumble of his prophecy.'[18]

The afterglow of such a wonderful excursion was momentarily clouded by an episode which briefly preoccupied Priestley. He published in 1945 an unusual novel, *The Magicians*, which brings three Wise Men into a country house alive with financial talk, cigar smoke, and city corruption to carry out an 'experiment' and vanish into thin air by means which can only be described as occult. The novel centres around the exploitation of a new drug, 'Sepman Eighteen', which is capable of removing anxiety, feelings of guilt or inadequacy and 'acts as a buffer between the brain and reality in its less pleasant aspects', without causing addiction. Who would not buy such an elixir?

The ubiquitous theory of time returns to permeate the novel when Ravenstreet, one of the characters, is taken back to scenes in his youth where success, vitality and happiness made life worthwhile. Now mature but embittered he is shown the error of his ways and determines to benefit from the experience. His readjustment is rewarded and the novel ends on a glowing note. Derivative in one sense from Jungian theory it could be seen as a fictional exploration of Jung's individuation.

Simple enough material with no possibility of inviting volcanic eruption, it did just that for one powerful critic. Philip Toynbee no sooner read the novel than he launched a vitriolic attack on the book

18   *Times Literary Supplement*, 14 October 1955.

and the author.[19] His chosen medium was the *Observer*; his method ridicule; his impact serious. First he quoted from Priestley's comments about new writers: 'These either did something rather badly that older writers had done well or they tried to do something that didn't seem worth doing . . . Trivial, small-minded, cliquish, fancy boys and girls, they were not writing for solid men of the world.' Some of the most highly praised new writers seemed to Priestley 'like neurotic curates', Toynbee wrote: 'And that, I suppose, marks the end of Jolly Jack Priestley, the "Good Companion".' Everybody said of him (Priestley) that he was 'a pretty good chap when you got to know him' but not any longer. 'Writing as a round-about-forty bounder and a neurotic curate', Toynbee said, the double role was hard to assimilate, 'but I begin to see what's meant – it is natural for me to regret a change which is so much to my disadvantage.' Toynbee continued: 'This book might have been good entertainment if it had not been ruined by the constant intrusion of Mr Priestley's private but by no means unique or illuminating prejudices.' As for the frustration of the evil men who sought to exploit the new drug for their own profit, this was brought about by a thinly disguised Mr Priestley and three 'rather long-winded' angels who intend to save people from another epidemic of intoxication. 'It is easy to see why Mr Priestley sells so many copies of his books. He has a narrative skill which is unusual, a genuine technical ability in putting a book together. He knows how to end a chapter in such a way that a reader will quickly turn over to the beginning of the next.' Then came the twist: 'And it must be said again that the book does not purvey a single difficult new or unpalatable idea.'

Following an erotic scene in *The Magicians* Priestley remarked that men and women made the mistake of believing that making love was a purely physical act, whereas it quickly became psychological with two personalities at play.

Where Mr Priestley makes his mistake, Toynbee continued, is in believing that he has the philosophic equipment to write a 'modern morality of this kind'.[20] He tried to give the impression of a lonely thinker, heroically out of touch with a debased age. Instead he simply replaced one set of *idées reçues* with another.

Then came the clinching phrases: 'He has left the army of the social optimists and joined the much less amiable but scarcely

19   *Observer*, 21 February 1954.
20   ibid.

smaller army of the embittered malcontents, the decriers of the age who hope by decrying it to elevate themselves above it.'

It remains to be said that as with so many of Priestley's more extreme critics, Toynbee attacked a number of straw figures. Priestley did not pretend to be a philosopher or moralist, he would not claim that he was a great writer, he saw no self-elevation in criticising the shortcomings of his time, and any confusion between himself and original thinkers seemed to him absurd. He was an immensely popular writer with unusual creative skills whose animadversions on the contemporary scene sprang naturally from a disillusioned man with his own insights. Moreover, the novel was written with pace and verve.

# 28

# Canadian Expedition
## 1955–6

Priestley was now a man of sixty, who had survived two wars, two marriages and such a gamut of experience, nothing short of three volumes could contain it. 'About my experience,' he wrote, 'I am rather given to boasting, as my loved ones have told me more than once. But even they would allow me to declare that my experience has been unusually long, rich and thick.'[1] Battling continuously against overweight, his plumpness threatened to get out of control, his jowls were heavier, the streaks of grey in his hair multiplying. He could be rude, aggressive, enchanting, loving and such good company visitors stayed with him far into the night, talking and drinking. There were so many selves: the literary gladiator shortly to do battle with Evelyn Waugh, the politician ready to launch yet another movement which would sweep the country, the rollicking anecdotalist with an Elizabethan zest for living, the life-enhancing pessimist with a penchant for gloomy philosophising, and the richly self-indulgent dreamer. He did not have erotic dreams and for a very simple reason. 'No eager, shapely girls come smiling out of the dark to reveal their charms, to open arms and legs. Is this because I am prudish, severely chaste?' No. It was because he had been lusty and given to lechery with no inclination to conceal his desires from himself. Never a 'sexy inclination' had been hurried 'out of consciousness'. He had, in short, come to terms with Eros.[2]

Insomnia which had pursued him from the age of forty-five seldom relented.

> This last week I have had a succession of bad nights. It is not merely that I cannot easily find sleep. No, it was waking in the middle of the night, expecting to welcome the daylight, breakfast and the morning post only to discover that it was pitch dark with the clock registering three and sometimes four o'clock.

1   *Instead of the Trees*, J. B. Priestley, 126.
2   ibid., 105.

There stretched ahead an eternity of time in which sleep maliciously evaded him, one moment pretending a preliminary drowsiness and the next the sharpest detail of attention. 'You roll over, turn back, then over again, curl your legs up, stretch them out, push your hands under the pillow, then take them out, all to no purpose: sleep will not come.'

These dark hours generated a special brand of thinking in which no tangible danger threatened but 'you are alone, completely alone, really feeling for once that you are imprisoned in your consciousness'.[3] This immutable self-consciousness of the night was a 'truly horrible glimpse of hell'. Inside you there was 'something alive, sensitive, shuddering, a bird beating its wings against the bars'.

At lunch one day with Jack Lambert in the Garrick Club, they discussed insomnia and dreams for two hours and Priestley concluded: 'Unfortunately Shakespeare got it wrong . . . we are not such stuff as dreams are made on . . .' It was at the Bath Festival in 1954 that Jack Lambert first met Priestley coming out of a performance of *Susanna's Secret*, and asked him whether he enjoyed the performance. 'It goes on too long,' Priestley said. 'Everything goes on too long nowadays.'[4] For a man who had recently written the 250,000 words of *Festival at Farbridge* the remark should be read ironically. Shortly afterwards there was a big luncheon given by Heinemann to celebrate the opening of The Windmill Press with Somerset Maugham, Jacquetta and Priestley among the honoured guests. It was Jacquetta and Jack's first joint appearance at a public function since their marriage. Priestley subsequently gave a good but quite non-malicious imitation of Maugham stuttering the words 'I now de-de-clare this Win-Win-Windmill Pr-Pr-Press . . .' When he came to the word 'open' he stalled completely and Priestley ever after declared 'that they had to force the damn thing open'.

Mrs Jack Lambert gave an analysis of Priestley's attraction for women. He managed, she said, to combine the hint of a 'come hither' look in his eyes with vibrations which made you feel very feminine, and his 'sexy voice' put into words 'what you thought you could have thought but failed to do so without his help'.[5] He could, she said, 'speak of the feelings inside me,' and he did it all with language which was 'as fresh as the dew caught on the rose'.

---

3   *Essays of Five Decades*, J. B. Priestley, 108–9.
4   Interview with Mr and Mrs J. W. Lambert, 3 July 1986.
5   ibid.

Both Mr and Mrs Lambert agreed that Priestley could be a consummate showman who knew exactly what effect he wanted to give and his talk would build up to that effect with tidal inevitability interlaced by wonderfully engaging chuckles. 'He worked very hard at it,' and made a marvellous shape out of words. It seemed impossible that such a sensitively responsive person could be capable of suddenly 'putting a heavy foot down on something fragile'.

Mr and Mrs Lambert both drew a picture of Priestley turning to his wife with an expression on his face which made it a 'joy to see him looking at her'. Moreover, he never failed with Jacquetta to pay impeccable attention to small courtesies which were observed not as polite rituals but as part of a tribute to their relationship. As we have seen, he could be surly with people who irritated him, he could be unexpectedly difficult with anybody and occasionally downright rude, but never with Jacquetta. Right down to the small detail of rising to hold the chair in position for her he was the ever-attentive – how to find the right word – lover, husband, devotee – perhaps according to Mrs Lambert he combined elements of all three.

It remained in his sixties one of Priestley's most endearing characteristics that he could marry bursts of boasting to incisive self-criticism. He had, he said, a wide and greedy appetite, but not for the lotus. For over sixty years he had tried to use his imagination 'but always in a positive outgoing manner, never to saunter through or loll in sagas that glorified J. B. Priestley'. 'I can't attribute this to modesty, having always had a good opinion of myself.' It was the day-dreamer he suspected, 'busy with his foolish fantasies, awarding himself prizes conjured out of the air . . .' Day-dreamers suffered from slackness and lethargy, 'a reluctance to face the glare and din of the arena'.

Priestley never failed to face that glare and din. He had plunged into one incarnation after another – clerk, soldier, essayist, novelist, playwright, polemicist, and now, in his early sixties, battle-scarred and unrepentant, he had become an international figure who emerged in his own way still uneasily triumphant. He might be less confident of his powers as a novelist and on the verge of abandoning play-writing but neither would be given up without a struggle. Meanwhile one incarnation – the lecturer – continued to travel the world with a ferocious disregard for the penalties exacted, and at sixty-one yet another incarnation was about to emerge.

It was the lecturer who set off for Canada in 1956 to fulfil a gruelling schedule which led into unexpected battles. Priestley hated airports but had no secret dread of flying. 'True on flights of any length I have always travelled first class. This is not for social grandeur, smoked salmon and champagne (I don't even enjoy it) but because I am a bulky man and the space allotted to tourist passengers becomes unendurable.'[6]

That such a seasoned traveller should be 'always nervous and apprehensive about missing the plane or train' seemed unexpected but Priestley insisted upon 'arriving early, dreading any last-minute rush'. Waiting in an airport lounge he always felt less than half his usual self 'and the people all round you . . . look at least as bad as you feel, many of them so drooping and mournful. Even the brassy drinking type – another for the road old boy – are clearly overdoing character parts.' That last bus or walk across the tarmac to the plane was not warmed by laughter or even smiles. 'We might be on our way to some kind of concentration camp. We are in the grip of the machine.'[7] This was all consistent with his later view that he never undertook an important journey without a vague sense of foreboding.[8]

His various accounts omitted one vital episode. He never forgot an occasion when he and Jacquetta were entertaining Dr Richard Sandiford and his wife to dinner at Brookhill and looking out of the window they became aware that a big seaplane taking off from the nearby air-base was in difficulties. The plane tried desperately to rise, failed and then just two miles away crashed on an adjacent hillside. In his imagination there was an appalling picture of living people struggling from the wreckage, some injured, some burning, which engraved itself indelibly on his memory. Dr Sandiford and Priestley had both hurried from the house to help, Sandiford regretting that he did not have his 'black bag' with him. Later Priestley expressed astonishment that when the ambulance arrived it had no morphine to cope with multiple agony but he gave no further account of the disaster and it was almost as if it remained too painful and had to be repressed in his unconscious. Remarkably it did not create fear of flying but every plane trip must have strained the mechanism which kept the episode either repressed or under control.

His Canadian lecture tour can best be followed in his letters to

6  *Instead of the Trees*, J. B. Priestley, 123.
7  ibid., 124–5.
8  *Outcries and Asides*, J. B. Priestley, 176.

Jacquetta. No sooner had he left London than he was missing her. He arrived in Canada towards the end of February, and wrote:

Darling love,
No letter from you yet . . . Woke very early this morning, so started working (debate with Dr Gallup on Friday – they want a summary of my argument in advance) before nine . . . Please note, in case of any urgent message, that I am away from here, in Ottawa, Sunday and Monday nights, then next Thursday and Friday nights, 28th and March 1st, in London, Ontario – this includes the travelling too of course. There seems more interest in the play [*The White Countess*] in New York at present than in London, but I would much rather do it in London first – for various good theatrical reasons. I must see that the piece is as good as we can make it if only because it's the best chance at present of making some real money and giving me an opportunity of laying off little jobs. I see in this morning's paper that . . . the stupid Tories have played into the hands of Labour by increasing price of children's milk and meals etc.
The damned telephone keeps ringing. All my love, sweet puss.
JACK[9]

Another letter followed fast on the heels of the first:

Darling love,
Thank you for your letter. Last night I debated (more or less) with Gallup, for this Public Affairs Conference and also partly on TV, and he turned out to be an extremely nice man, about my age, and he and his wife are tremendous admirers of *Journey Down a Rainbow*, which they've read aloud etc., etc. There's something really unexpected. I was on TV twice yesterday, and have a heavy day tomorrow, going straight from my lecture in the afternoon to a discussion TV programme called *Fighting Words* and then taking the night train to Ottawa, where I give my lecture on Monday night, flying back here on Tuesday afternoon . . . No news from anybody . . . I am still having trouble with my bowels – a kind of half-looseness and suddenness, not like Chile but far from normality. The result of all the medicines taken in Chile and Peru. The frequent suddenness is a great nuisance. Did I tell you Ralph Richardson wrote, to ask for your address and telephone number, which I gave him. He more or less apologised for his reception of us after the matinee but said he really felt ill.

9  Priestley to Jacquetta Priestley, 20 February 1956.

I shall be glad when all this is over and we are back at Brook, working hard and walking among the primroses. I believe they had a mild winter, this time. Much love to you, my precious one.[10]

The lecture tour ran hectically across the Canadian continent from Toronto to Vancouver, from Edmonton to Ottawa, with many stops between.

Vancouver

Darling love,
    We had our first Discussion here last night, and in spite of the subject – the Individual v. Industry etc. – which was the one I liked least, it was a great success from every point of view. About a thousand in the audience, and they seemed to enjoy it, and although I had to sit, as we all did, at a small table with a mike in front of me, because of the recording by the CBC of the proceedings, and I detest not being able to move about when I speak and always feel this method is like broadcasting without a script, I managed pretty well and everybody congratulated me. I was tremendously relieved and feel the worst hurdle is over now . . . Today I take part in a discussion TV programme, my fourth TV programme so far and the other three were much liked, and as I collect cash for each of them as I go along, it is not working badly at all. . . . I am appalled by the Americanisation of Canada, especially in all the silly little things – I've just had a call to say a man has arrived to claim the typewriter – I'll write from Edmonton.
    Bless you, my sweet love. I hope the work goes well.
        Your loving JACK[11]

By April he was tiring of the whole undertaking, longing to be back, badly missing Jacquetta.
    Taking the night boat from Vancouver to Victoria on 22 April he selected the best stateroom he could find and slept soundly – 'for a change' – going ashore at 7.30. A Canadian journalist, Bruce Hutchinson, joined him and took him to his camp overlooking a lake where they ate a very good picnic lunch in company with a pleasant surgeon. Priestley regretted having to hurry on to Victoria but as always there was a plane to catch, a schedule to fulfil, and from Victoria he flew straight back to Vancouver. Almost immediately they took off again for Edmonton, arriving very late at night. At sixty-two he was still very strong, with large reserves of energy

10  Priestley to Jacquetta Priestley, 23 February 1956.
11  Priestley to Jacquetta Priestley, 21 April 1956.

on which he could call to keep him going but he no longer had the resilience of the earlier American tours. Arriving at Edmonton a disillusioned Priestley wrote to Jacquetta:

Darling love,
. . . This is the town that has grown enormously in the last few years – it is the town for the new oil wells – and it seems to me a horrible place. A stag dinner tonight at a club with a lot of business and similar types doesn't promise any delights. I've spent most of this morning talking to newspapermen, and dodging into the lav as I've suddenly got a touch of something like dysentery, probably due to the sudden changes of water and temperature. I slipped out to a chemist's, tried to explain to a middle-aged woman assistant what I wanted, and she blushingly handed me over to an elderly man, who dished me out with the usual white mixture. There's no drinking here (which is probably as well, in my present state inside) and not much of anything else except six radio stations all churning out programmes indistinguishable from the usual idiotic American radio. (I know because there's a radio with a lot of knobs in my room and I tried them all early this morning trying to get some news and all I got was advertising and rubbish. I don't perform here until tomorrow night – worse luck – and then on Wednesday we have a hell of a rush to get from here to Winnipeg (about five hours flying) to perform that night. Oh well – I would do it . . . I've also got into a great row because I heatedly refused at the W. H. Smith lunch in Toronto to autograph books, after the chairman blandly announced, without anybody asking me, that I would. It really was intolerable, and now I'm being abused by these bloody columnists, who of course thrive on these events. Looking at this town, I'm more glad than ever that we didn't decide on your coming, though God knows I miss you – and look at your photograph fifty times a day, longing and longing to be back . . .
Your loving,
JACK[12]

His description of Canada and Canadians was highly critical but when he met Robertson Davies, who subsequently became an internationally known novelist, he spoke warmly of him to Jaquetta.

Nevertheless he believed that some enthusiastic young people could transform Canada and even he was half tempted to try to make 'something out of this huge sad place' which had lost the

12   Priestley to Jacquetta Priestley, 23 April 1956.

secret 'that the laughing Eskimos' knew. Then followed the astonishing comment that he suspected no real sex occurred in Canada, an opinion qualified by Gordon Hawkins, his travelling companion, who believed Canadian women to be incredibly naïve about such matters. Priestley quickly added that he had never found himself wanting to put this to the test. [13]

At last the gruelling experience was over and he returned to England tired, haggard and disillusioned with Canada. Almost immediately he plunged into a limited working schedule, interlaced with occasional letters to his family. Caring family man though Priestley could be and a willing recipient of his children's complaints, his claim in a letter to Angela that he was 'a man you can tell anything to' did not correspond to her experience.

He complained that although he had specifically asked Mary to let him know as soon as possible how things were in Denmark, he remained without news. £380 had accumulated in The Good Companions Trust but he did not want to encourage Mary to 'take some wild step' such as bringing all three of her children over to England by disclosing its existence. Angela probably knew her state of mind better than he did and he would appreciate any news she could give him.

Then came a paragraph which excited a smile in its recipient. 'Tom comes down this weekend. If there is anything you can tell me about him I ought to know and he probably won't tell me – I wish my children would realise that I am a man you can tell anything to – please pass it on.'

He was going up to Glasgow to unveil a memorial to Bridie, and the following day intended to hear the first reading of the Citizens' Theatre cast of a new play, *These Our Actors*, which they were trying out for him. It was a play nobody liked and perhaps he would not when he heard it but he regarded the play with the enthusiasm he always brought to the initial stages of any work. 'Jacquetta is well and happy, and Nicholas, [14] now an officer stationed at Winchester, is at present at home on leave. Our love to you all. Daddy.' [15]

13  Priestley to Jacquetta Priestley, 28 April 1956.
14  Jacquetta Priestley's son.
15  Priestley to Angela Wyndham Lewis.

# 29

# The CND Campaign
## 1956–7

In November of 1956 Priestley wrote a short, semi-comic, deliberately formal letter to Jacquetta addressing her by her married name recovered from the days when entirely unknown to one another he was intrigued by the signature J. J. Hawkes on UNESCO memos:

> My dear J. J. Hawkes,
> I have now known you for over nine years and after careful consideration I must say – I love you.
> Yours truly,
> J. BOYNTON PRIESTLEY[1]

Literary work diminished in 1956–7 but combined a swingeing exchange with Evelyn Waugh, an attack upon Dr Leavis and – biggest event of the period – launching CND.

Priestley's attack upon Dr Leavis appeared in the *New Statesman* for November 1956 and developed the full flood of his invective. Dr Leavis had given his famous lecture at Nottingham University – 'Literature in My Time' – in which he declared that there had been no literature in his time. 'He knocked hell out of everybody,' Priestley wrote, 'and no doubt had all the Lucky Jims rolling down the aisles . . . Virginia Woolf was "a slender talent", Lytton Strachey "irresponsible and unscrupulous", W. H. Auden "the type career" fixed at the "undergraduate stage", Spender "no talent whatsoever" . . . the whole age "dismal", the outlook "poor".'[2]

Priestley lacked the pleasure of Dr Leavis's acquaintance but he had a 'vague and impressive vision of him, pale and glittering eyed, shining with integrity, marching out of Downing College to close whole libraries, to snatch books out of people's hands, to proclaim the bitter truth that nobody writes anything worth reading. There is Lawrence; there is Leavis on Lawrence; perhaps a disciple Jones is

1   Priestley to Jacquetta Priestley, 21 November 1956.
2   *New Statesman*, 10 November 1956.

writing something – let us say Jones on Leavis on Lawrence; after that nothing.' And if by unfortunate accident anyone encountered Priestley, well clearly no time need be wasted on him.[3]

With a quick turn of the wrist Dr Leavis dropped another array of eighteenth-century authors – Smollett, Sterne, Goldsmith and Fielding – 'into the ashcan'. Priestley claimed to be 'as vain, touchy and aggressive as the next man – in fact it is ten to one I am vainer, touchier, and more aggressive', but when confronted with a massive original talent – 'probably the most precious thing in the world' – he became humble. Not so the Almighty Leavis. 'Literature is not well served when its giants are mutilated and slaughtered to fit a critical theory here today and gone tomorrow.'

Subjected to Dr Leavis's icily severe standards, Virginia Woolf might be a slender talent but Dr Leavis did not exist at all, and his claim to have written even one sentence worth reading collapsed in confusion. 'This is where the arrogantly dogmatic, absolutist critic, behaving more like the Grand Inquisitor or Calvin than a sensible man of letters walks into a trap.' If time was too valuable to be wasted on people like Fielding it was profligate squandering to read Dr Leavis. Dr Leavis might claim to be a good teacher but he was not really a serious critic of any *gravitas*. He was 'a sort of Calvinist theologian of contemporary culture. To be an author in his view was to invite damnation', for only a few – 'D. H. Lawrence, himself and a favourite pupil or two – would be saved.' His brutal severity did not derive from a native fastidiousness but was probably the result of a neurosis triggered off by an Alsatian who frightened him as a child. He was an unusual man 'with genuine gifts, hard and passionately at work on the wrong job'.

The summing-up was in keeping with the style of the whole article. 'Although I enjoy my vision of little Doc Leavis slugging away, with the lecture-hall a red ruin of literary reputations, truth compels me to add that I think he and his kind in universities both here and in America . . . have done much mischief to the art they are boarded and lodged to serve.'[4]

A young student devotee of Dr Leavis's brought the article hot-foot to the Senior Common Room of Downing College and was about to retreat into safe obscurity before the storm broke when the

3  Leavis wrote in *The Great Tradition* (1948): 'Fielding . . . is important not because he leads to J. B. Priestley but because he leads to J. Austen to appreciate whose distinction is to feel that life isn't long enough to permit of one's giving much time to Fielding or any to Mr Priestley.'
4  *New Statesman*, 10 November 1956.

doctor insisted that he must wait. He read the article with an expressionless face, turned to the student and said: 'Will you take this back to wherever you got it from. I don't deal in gutter verbiage.'[5]

Priestley's review of Waugh's novel *The Ordeal of Gilbert Pinfold* (1957) identified the middle-aged character who lived in an old house in the country, dividing his time between Catholicism, snobbery and Bellamy's Club, as none other than an author called Evelyn Waugh.[6] The boozy half-doped Pinfold of the novel arranges a three-week cruise to the Middle East but from the moment he enters his cabin voices, belonging to persecutors who have no existence, begin to talk inside his head: 'For the benefit of both the Shadow and the Anima . . . busily engaged in their spectral intrigues,' Priestley wrote. Pinfold finds himself in a waking nightmare from which he does not emerge until he returns home. His doctor informs him that he has been victimised by the chloral and bromides he has swallowed indiscriminately but he arrives back from the cruise safe and sound to settle cosily into his study and begin work on a new novel, *The Ordeal of Gilbert Pinfold*. Priestley commented: 'But if Pinfold imagines his troubles are over he is a fool. Because the voices talked a lot of rubbish, making the most ridiculous accusations, he is ignoring the underlying truth.' Waugh was not a Catholic landed gentleman, pretending to be an author, but an author pretending to be a Catholic landed gentleman. The question immediately arose – why should he not be both? 'Because,' Priestley magisterially proclaimed, 'these two identities are not compatible'. Waugh's voices had told him that he was an alien who had changed his name, a traitor, a homosexual, even a would-be murderer but this was all rubbish. If they would stop their clowning and speak plainly they would say: 'Pinfold, you are a professional writer, a novelist, an artist, so stop pretending you represent some obscure but arrogant landed family that never had an idea in its head.'

'Pinfolding', an artist pretending to be something other than himself, was a well-known device in literature, elaborately practised by no less a writer than Congreve. When Voltaire deigned to visit Congreve he heard, with astonishment, that Congreve regarded himself as a gentleman of leisure not a playwright whereupon Voltaire riposted: 'I would not have wasted my time

5   Author's conversation with Dr Kettle.
6   *New Statesman*, 31 August 1957.

calling upon a gentleman.'

'Let Pinfold take warning,' Priestley concluded. Whatever Mrs Pinfold and the neighbours might think, 'Pinfold must step out of his role as the Cotswold gentleman,' and accept the role of English-man of letters or the consequences would be dire. 'He must be at all times the man of ideas, the intellectual, the artist, even if he is asked to resign from Bellamy's Club.'

Disdaining to reply in a 'dubious rag' like the *New Statesman*, Evelyn Waugh filled a whole page of the *Spectator* with counter-attack.[7]

'What gets Mr Priestley's goat . . . is my attempt to behave like a gentleman. Mr Priestley has often hinted at a distaste for the upper classes but having early adopted the persona of a generous hearted, genial fellow he has only once, I think, attempted to portray them.'

Naturally Waugh said he hungered for the good opinion of Mr Priestley, but he was 'an old dog to learn new tricks'. What really troubled Priestley was the bad example Mr Waugh set by his behaviour which meant that he abdicated his responsibility to the team. 'If authors and artists in this country,' Priestley had written, 'are not only officially regarded without favour but even singled out for unjust treatment . . . then the Pinfolds are partly to blame. They not only do not support their profession: they go over to the enemy.'

Priestley was an older, richer and more popular author than Waugh, but Waugh could not forbear to reciprocate Priestley's words. 'Let him take warning. He has had some sharp disappoint-ments in the last twelve years; perhaps he would call them "traumas". The voices he hears, like Pinfold's may be those of a wildly distorted conscience.'

Twenty years before, Waugh said, there occurred a memorable *trahison des clercs* which left the literary world much discredited. Many astute and distinguished writers foresaw the social revolution and went to great lengths to suck up to the lower classes, or as they called it 'to identify themselves with the workers'. There followed a clever reinterpretation of *Black-out in Gretley*, the wartime novel written by Priestley. Launched, Waugh said, at a very dark time when national unity was vital, 'its simple theme was that the English upper classes were in conspiracy to keep the workers in subjection even at the cost of national defeat'. Tarlington in the novel concentrated every vice behind his virtuous exterior. 'A man

7   *Spectator*, 13 September 1957.

of good family and of smart appearance, a Conservative, the director of an engineering works, a courageous officer in 1916 – and of course a German spy.' Among the workers only two reveal moral delinquency, the first as a German officer in disguise and the second 'and more wicked . . . a Roman Catholic'.

Waugh then quoted a telling passage from the novel: 'This country has the choice during the next two years of coming fully to life and beginning all over again or of rapidly decaying and dying on the same old feet. It can only accomplish the first by taking a firm grip on about fifty thousand important and influential gentlemanly persons and telling them firmly to shut up and do nothing if they don't want to be put to doing some unpleasant work.'

Waugh commented: 'Came the dawn, Mr Priestley was disappointed. No concentration camp was made for the upper classes.' As for the triumphant workers, they expressed their aesthetic impulse by piling into charabancs 'and tramping round the nearest collection of heirlooms . . . quite enough to inflame the naked artist with an itch of persecution mania'. If there was some confusion of targets it all read splendidly and Waugh retired with the conviction that the laurels were his.

These skirmishes preceded the biggest event of 1957, the launching of the CND campaign. Once more Priestley's chosen platform was the *New Statesman*. John Freeman frequently became acting editor when Kingsley Martin was away on one of his many trips abroad and it was to Freeman that Priestley suggested a long, signed article 'calculated not to raise the rabble but the people against the bomb'.[8]

Christopher Driver's account of the campaign's initiation traced it to four sources: Aneurin Bevan's speech at the Labour Party Conference of 1957; the launching of the first Russian sputnik; the Reith Lectures by Professor George F. Kennan, United States Ambassador 1952–3, entitled 'Russia, the Atom and the West'; and J. B. Priestley's articles in the *New Statesman*.[9]

Canon L. John Collins gave a different account. 'Whether other events may have contributed to the emergence of CND, J. B. Priestley's article exposing the utter folly and wickedness of the whole nuclear strategy was the real catalyst.'[10] Priestley's article opened with an attack on Aneurin Bevan who had asked delegates

8  *The Life, Letters and Diaries of Kingsley Martin*, ed. C. H. Rolph, 323.
9  *The Disarmers*, Christopher Driver.
10  *Faith Under Fire*, Canon L. John Collins, 302.

not to confuse 'emotional spasms' with 'statesmanship'. So-called statesmanship, Priestley said, had for the last ten years produced 'little else but emotional spasms'.

Priestley argued that deterrence became a meaningless phrase when one ultimate deterrent succeeded another. After the bombs the intercontinental rockets, and after the rockets, according to the First Lord of the Admiralty, the guided-missile submarine which will 'carry a . . . missile with a nuclear warhead and appear off the coast of any country in the world with a capability of penetrating to the centre of any continent'.[11]

We are told, Priestley wrote, that all this 'is to the good' because no statesman in his right mind would let loose such powers of destruction. Any criticism of that attitude was regarded as woolly-minded idealism but idealism saturated anybody who believed that men would always act reasonably in their best interests.

Tell me, Priestley said, when and where have these preparations for nuclear warfare ever been subjected to the test of public opinion? The whole mad conspiracy had been conducted in the 'stifling secrecy of an expensive lunatic asylum'. Moreover, the prolifer-ation of these evil weapons was haunted by another and quite different danger because the more elaborately involved and hair-triggered the machinery became the greater was the chance of pure accident exploding the whole gigantic volcano. 'Three glasses too many of vodka or bourbon-on-the-rocks and the wrong button may be pushed.'

The case could, he continued, convincingly be argued that our civi-lisation was bent on self-destruction and 'hurriedly planning its own doomsday'. How otherwise explain the 'wearisome recital of plot and counter-plot in terms of world power, the curious and sinister air of somnambulism there is about our major international affairs'.

The Soviet Union survived the last war because its rolling continent was vast and its population able to absorb colossal losses. The same factors gave it enormous advantages over a tightly organised, overcrowded island like Britain which would succumb as a whole to the onslaught of a mere handful of bombs.

'If there is one country that should never have gambled in this game it is Britain . . . we may have been fooling ourselves, we have not been fooling anybody else.'

Now came the crux of his polemic: 'In plain words: now that Britain has told the world that she has the H-Bomb she should

11   *New Statesman*, 2 November 1957.

announce as early as possible that she has done with it, that she proposes to reject in all circumstances nuclear warfare.'

The idea of a third force which would mediate between communism and capitalism modifying the extreme expression of both had been popular amongst some members of the Labour Party since the end of the war. The author remembers discussing this strategy with Priestley and Thomas Mann. Both agreed that democratic socialism represented by growing numbers of European countries could build a buffer between Russia and America introducing refinements in political thinking which might diminish 'bigotry' in both blocs. Priestley put it differently. 'We ended the war high in the world's regard. We could have taken over its moral leadership, spoken and acted for what remained of its conscience, but we chose to act otherwise. The melancholy consequences were that abroad we cut a shabby figure in power politics and at home we shrug it all away or go to the theatre to applaud the latest jeers and sneers at Britannia.'

With his gift for concentrating criticism in a small vignette, Priestley added, 'That is why we are so happy and excited when we can send abroad a good-looking young woman in a pretty, new dress to represent us, playing the only card we feel can take a trick – the Queen.'

The article mounted to a splendid concluding paragraph which sent a surge of inspiration through the readers of the *New Statesman*:

> Alone we defied Hitler: and alone we can defy this nuclear madness . . . there may be other chain-reactions besides those leading to destruction: and we might start one. The British of these times, so frequently hiding their decent kind faces behind masks of sullen apathy or some cheap cynicism, often seem to be waiting for something better than party squabbles and appeals to their narrowest self-interest, something great and noble in its intention that would make them feel good again. And this might well be a declaration to the world that after a certain date one power able to engage in nuclear warfare will reject the evil thing for ever.[12]

The results of the article were immediate. It brought an overwhelming tide of correspondence into the *New Statesman*'s office. Standing amidst the unopened piles one morning, Kingsley Martin ruefully surveyed the mass and said: 'Jack, what have you done to us? How in hell are we going to cope with this lot?' Priestley said: 'That's your job, not mine.'

12   ibid.

'Why not ring up Diana Collins?' Martin said. 'They've got the NCANWT lot behind them with an office and some staff.'[13]

The NCANWT – clumsily named from ferocious committee differences – had been organised in 1956 to launch a National Campaign Against Nuclear Weapon Tests under the chairmanship of Arthur Goss, a leading member of the Society of Friends. Canon Collins had become involved in its activities, which centred on a Fleet Street office, made available by the National Peace Council. Collins left an evocative picture of Kingsley Martin and the conversations which followed. 'With his hooded eyes, he sometimes looks like a brooding eagle and appears to be carrying all the troubles of the world on his shoulders, weighed down by a guilt too great to be borne but a glimpse of the real Kingsley seen in the sparkle of an eye wll soon dispel any idea of a man of doom and gloom and may prepare you for those stabs of wit and humour, of which, if you are wise, you will try to avoid being the butt.'

Since NCANWT had a one-roomed office, three paid staff and a bank balance of £450, it was not the ideal organisation for coping with a CND campaign, but Peggy Duff approached Arthur Goss to collaborate. At this point Kingsley Martin disclosed that there had already been discussions with Priestley about a nation-wide campaign not only against the testing of nuclear weapons but for banning the weapons themselves. What Martin and Priestley had in mind was a non-pacifist campaign intended to do what pacifism had so far failed to achieve: deflect British foreign policy away from developing further nuclear strategies. A letter from Priestley to Kingsley Martin said: 'I have just written to Pat Blackett – as a test case so to speak – to see if he would join a sort of arts/science etc. non-political group to denounce nuclear warfare. Let us see how this develops. I am not strong on generals. I have exchanged letters with Horrocks who seems a nice civilised chap, but his position as Black Rod would probably prevent him joining anything.'[14]

There followed a meeting at Kingsley Martin's flat at No. 1 Roberts Street with Jacquetta Hawkes, J. B. Priestley, Bertrand Russell, Lord Blackett, Denis Healey and Professor George Kennan present.

'The next I heard', Canon Collins wrote, 'was a telephone call early in December, I think from Peggy Duff who was then

13  Interview with Kingsley Martin, 10 September 1961.
14  Priestley to P. M. S. Blackett, 3 December 1957. Blackett wrote several books about atomic energy.

organising secretary of NCANWT. She invited me to attend a meeting of the sponsors of that organisation and asked whether the meeting could take place at my home in Amen Court.' According to Christopher Driver the NCANWT thought it could press its own view of the new campaign on the meeting, but despite their efforts to place Ritchie Calder, a less political figure than Kingsley Martin, in the chair, it was Martin who conducted proceedings.

Between fifty and sixty people took part in a second meeting at Canon Collins's house on 16 January, including Dr Sheila Jones of the Anti-Testing Committee, Peggy Duff, Kingsley Martin, Bertrand Russell, J. B. and Jacquetta Priestley. They met again on the 27th when the NCANWT agreed to amalgamate with the new organisation accepting Canon Collins as chairman and Bertrand Russell as president. Christopher Driver has written of Canon Collins: 'Dedication and diplomacy, quick footwork on committee and plain speaking in the pulpit were neatly balanced in his character.'[15] He irritated Priestley on occasion but they became close friends and Priestley's inability to accept the Christian faith did nothing to disturb a warm and lasting relationship.[16]

Christopher Driver states: 'There is little doubt that the composition of the new executive had been effectively decided beforehand among the Martin–Priestley group and when it was all over Canon Collins was Chairman of CND.'

During the first year Professor Rotblat and Mrs Jones resigned and new members were co-opted: Jacquetta Priestley, Benn Levy, A. J. P. Taylor, Lord Wilmot, Sir Richard Acland and Frank Beswick MP. Many meetings at interlocking levels followed and Jacquetta remembers some highly diverting moments after the split caused by the foundation of the Committee of One Hundred. Canon Collins would visit Bertrand Russell, 'have a successful talk of conciliation with him and he would then go upstairs to consult his wife . . . only to return to say all reconciliation was off'. Russell himself gave a vivid vignette of Priestley's activities to James Cameron: 'Jack brought a moral indignation and a grand common sense to bear on the problem. On one occasion he exploded, while being interviewed, like the H-bomb we wanted to jettison. Fall-out was felt all over London.'[17]

The inaugural meeting of the Campaign for Nuclear Disarma-

---

15  *The Disarmers*, C. Driver, 43.
16  *The Life, Letters and Diaries of Kingsley Martin*, ed. C. H. Rolph, 394.
17  Interview with James Cameron, 22 December 1979.

ment packed the Central Hall, Westminster, to overflowing and thousands of people were swept away by speeches from the Executive Committee. The launch was dynamically successful but two men stood out in Canon Collins's memory: J. B. Priestley and A. J. P. Taylor. According to Collins each spoke with his own inimitable wit and intellectual vigour. Both were quite uncompromising in their demand that 'Britain on moral as well as expedient grounds should, regardless of what others might do, give up her own nuclear weapons altogether, and these were the speeches most applauded.'[18] Mrs Collins and Jacquetta Priestley organised an equivalent women's meeting which excluded men but created a no less enthusiastic response.

When Canon Collins announced future plans at the end of the meeting there was a call to march from the Central Hall to Downing Street which Collins resisted. Breakaway groups did march and were met by police with dogs which led to scuffles and arrests. This created the kind of publicity which the Executive wanted to avoid at all costs. Displaying an exemplary sense of balance *The Times* reported the Downing Street scuffles and arrests but not the Central Hall meeting. Nor did *The Times* print Canon Collins's statement that the Executive had agreed to back the Direct Action Committee's proposal of a mass march converging on Aldermaston for the Easter weekend of 1958.

Later the Direct Action Committee's leaflet said: 'Walk for a weekend, a day or an hour, all who are opposed on any ground to nuclear weapons whether possessed by British, American or Russian governments.' In the event it was the coldest Good Friday for forty-one years and the initial number of demonstrators, small but between 5,000 and 10,000, eventually marched the last mile to Falcon Field, Aldermaston in total silence. There was something moving and deeply impressive about this unending procession of people drawn from all walks of life, converging on the symbolic centre of world disaster in an ordered silence which made itself heard throughout Britain, if not the world.

Much later in life Priestley told C. H. Rolph, who edited the *Life, Letters and Diaries of Kingsley Martin*, 'Kingsley always seemed to me to be dodging in and out of this . . . I don't merely mean that he didn't often join the marches . . . he wasn't wholly with us . . . John Freeman of course was against us but editorially he behaved superbly.'[19]

18   *Faith Under Fire*, Canon L. John Collins, 108.
19   Martin Papers, University of Sussex.

The second Aldermaston March organised by CND in the spring of 1959 reversed its direction at the suggestion of Jacquetta. She had proposed that the march would carry much more weight if its ultimate rendezvous was the final seat of political power – not Aldermaston, but London, where many of those employed in the establishment strongly resisted the whole campaign. Jacquetta and Canon Collins drove out to Falcon Field that morning, not knowing what to expect. 'When we arrived there were already some six or seven thousand people on the field. Many of the younger ones had slept out the night before in order to be there on time.' Slowly the disorganised mass fell into a rough and ready column and moved off untidily towards the capital. As fast as people dropped out exhausted, new recruits joined, as soon as one group looked weary and depressed, another sang campaign songs which re-echoed down the column. 'As we approached Whitehall and Trafalgar Square the crowds thickened until the pavements were packed and it looked as though we would hardly be able to get the march into the Square.'[20] Among the marchers was Jacquetta, who walked 'every inch of the way on every Aldermaston March from 1959' and Michael Foot. There were times, during the later stages of the march, when Michael Foot looked 'as if he were going to die by the roadside, and his blisters became so bad that he was reduced to hobbling'. His condition did not prevent him from delivering the final speech from the platform, a scathing attack on the folly of nuclear war and an appeal in a rising tide of passionate eloquence for Britain to abandon the bomb. The whole of the mass media rose to the occasion on the following day and a tide of publicity resounded throughout Britain and half of Europe.

All this was triggered off by a vivid piece of journalism amounting to not more than 2,000 words written in the quiet of his study – by Jack Priestley. If it was not a repetition of the postscripts, it certainly swept him back into international headlines.

One leading member of CND is an invaluable witness to the life and character of J. B. Priestley: Diana Collins, wife of Canon Collins. A friendship which began in the heat of political battle ran on until his death, and Canon and Mrs Collins and Mr and Mrs Priestley became a quartet, sometimes taking holidays together, always mutually sympathetic. Diana Collins understood contradictory elements in the bond between Jack and Jacquetta better than most people, partly because Priestley took her into his confidence,

20  *Faith Under Fire*, Canon L. John Collins, 313.

partly because she was a very perceptive person. 'Jacquetta', Jack told her, 'is all ice outside and fire inside. The streak of masculinity in her responds to the streak of the feminine in me. She tends to be more introvert and I more extravert. We react on each other.'[21]

'He was a lovely man,' Diana said. 'He believed and practised some of the best virtues: integrity; honesty; loyalty to his old friends. He was kind, generous, immensely understanding and I never heard him flatter anybody. He was a wonderful giver but not a good receiver because he didn't want to be beholden to anybody. Behind the big public figure he was really a shy man who believed in old-fashioned courtesy. And what a lovely father figure he made. Deeply aware? Of course he was deeply aware. Sometimes in the afternoons I noticed a great melancholy overtaking him. He would talk then of the individual being a bubble on the stream of life which quietly burst when its day was done and disappeared downstream, but he stopped short of the idea of complete annihilation.' When Priestley said to her, 'I prefer the company of women to men,' Diana Collins replied, 'But I wouldn't mind being a man in another life.'

'You wouldn't like being a man,' he replied. 'You'd find it very boring.' He did except certain women from his recklessly admired *galère* and described one particularly political example to Diana Collins as 'having an orgasm every time a resolution was passed'.[22]

Diana Collins and Jacquetta Priestley continued to take part in the CND campaign and marches. Among the thousands who joined the march year after year were deeply religious Christians, young people who believed that Britain's security would be strengthened rather than weakened by nuclear disarmament, Communist Party members convinced that their ends justified any means, congenital protesters, intellectual moralists, professional people and the inevitable sprinklng of political manipulators who saw in this spontaneous movement a wonderful new weapon to be converted to their own ends.

It was this last group, the Marxists, which drove Priestley in the final analysis into disillusionment. As Jacquetta records: 'He said to me one day: "I don't like this any more. We're not going the right way. We're going the wrong way." Towards the end he felt that

21 Interview with Diana Collins, 26 June 1986.
22 ibid.

power-hungry propagandists had taken over a good movement simply for the sake of getting power.'[23]

The campaign continues to re-echo today but the voice is very different from Priestley's. One myth remains to explode. Priestley – a man of sixty-four – did not actually take part in any of the marches, but it was not because of his age. As Jacquetta Priestley put it: 'He had a strong and very positive objection to marches generally and he seemed to foresee what would develop.'

23   Interview with Jacquetta Priestley, 5 September 1986.

# 30

# *Literature and Western Man*
## 1958–61

Between the years 1952 and 1958 Priestley continued his correspondence with Angela Wyndham Lewis, Mary Priestley, and Jacquetta interlaced with letters from a galaxy of famous people. In March 1953 Charles Chaplin wrote, returning the script of the play *Treasure on Pelican*, which Priestley thought would make a film. Chaplin was very blunt. He did not like the subject-matter and his one desire, he said, was to escape from the current milieu into a world where individualism played a bigger role and common human decency permeated society. Personally he was fed up with the twentieth century, the future and all their many manifestations. He happily consigned the twentieth century to hell.[1]

Priestley had written to Rebecca West saying, 'I disagree with your defence of McCarthy,' and she sent a swift and vigorous rebuttal. She had never said a single word in defence of McCarthy and regarded him from the beginning as a stupid and violent demagogue. It was no use Priestley trying to get round the fact that he had made ill-informed accusations which implied that her articles defended the creed if not the person of Senator McCarthy. Priestley replied that she had exaggerated his mild protest: 'Words had run away with her.'

In the summer of 1959 T. S. Eliot wrote thanking Priestley and his colleagues at the Masque Theatre for accepting a play (*The Family Reunion*) which 'had such obvious theatrical defects'. It was very sporting of Priestley. It gave Eliot great pleasure to write the letter because Priestley was one of the very few contemporary dramatists whose plays he respected.[2]

The papers of A. D. Peters, Priestley's agent, include an account of his earnings from plays for the years 1955–7. The whole breakdown is given in the Appendix. For the moment, taking a minimal multiple of ten, it is clear that he earned from English plays

1  Charles Chaplin to Priestley, 25 March 1953.
2  T. S. Eliot to Priestley, 3 May 1959.

alone in 1955–6 £70,000 and from 1956–7 roughly the same. This excluded foreign royalties and journalism. Clearly he remained a relatively rich man.

The old adage that money could not buy happiness was re-affirmed in 1958, when Mary had another major breakdown. Jacquetta had become Archaeological Correspondent to the *Sunday Times* and went away on an excavation in Mosul where she received this disturbing letter from her husband:

Dearest love,

The luck's out here. Sylvia rang up this morning to say she'd found Mary obviously in a breakdown – things smashed, no food for at least a day, rambling talk, so I told her to get hold of Harvey, who was too tied up to go but sent a doctor along, and finally this afternoon Mary was taken to the Holloway Sanatorium at Virginia Water. It may have been taken in time, and Sylvia said she was more sensible on the way out to the hospital, and perhaps quick treatment may save her. Ashmore[3] obviously comes into it – but he told Sylvia he hadn't had a row with her or anything, but Sylvia said she was talking about him all the time. As she is now under observation and treatment weeks earlier than she was in '47, perhaps it won't go as far . . .

Hayles[4] was pretty bad last night, and having transfusions, but he has picked up a bit today but they've gone and told the poor chap he'll now have to have a second operation on the other kidney. This looks like being a long job, I'm afraid. Miss Pudduck goes in on Sunday so she'll be all right for when you come back. Winnie[5] arrives tomorrow and I'll do what I can to cheer her up, which I'm afraid I can't be doing to you. I hesitated about telling you all this sad stuff but thought then you'd want to know . . .

Though I miss you already like mad, I'm not sorry YET you've got away because this is one of those dreary times that are bound to happen, and you've just finished your story, which I genuinely enjoyed and think with a bit of tidying up, cutting, it might have a modest success, and ought to be away a bit, new scenes, new people. It'll all look better here when you come back – it's still looking sullen yet and you've seen enough of it. I'm annoyed with myself because I seem to have a lot of good half-formed thoughts that I can't find the right words for – they change into something more obvious when I

3  A friend of Mary's.
4  The gardener.
5  Priestley's half-sister.

try to express them . . . which is maddening. It may mean I'm beginning to think or that I'm starting to fail in expression.

Bless your dear heart, which I miss every moment, my dear sweet love,

JACK[6]

Another letter followed five days later:

Dearest love,

No word from you yet. I hope all is well and that you are enjoying the trip . . .

Tomorrow afternoon I go out to Mary's sanatorium, chiefly to see the chief doctor. Harvey was pessimistic about her on the telephone the other night, though he hadn't seen her himself – he doesn't like mental cases. But Ba and Tom saw her on Sunday and thought she seemed very calm and sensible, better, Tom said, than she had seemed the week before. The sanatorium is nothing like as dear as I'd expected, thank God! . . .

No other news except that I miss you the whole damned time – and somehow much more now the sun is out – is no news. Hurry back, my love, our place is beginning to look nice again, and I miss like hell all our little pleasures and joys and comforts together, morning, noon, and night . . .

And now it's time I heard from you. Bless you, my love –

JACK[7]

P.S. Short, because must catch post.

The last of a group of three letters said:

Dearest love,

. . . I have now seen Mary twice in the sanatorium. It is not a bad place, fortunately, and she didn't seem to mind it – and said she liked the people. Both times she was obviously unbalanced but the second time not deranged but more like a child of about eight in a rather excitable silly mood. I find it terribly distressing myself, but luckily her sisters seem to mind much less and are visiting her regularly – at least Ba and Angela are. And Tom goes at the weekend and is very sweet with her. She's certainly not as bad as she was eleven years ago – not violent and badly schizophrenic. But I can get no proper information from them yet about her and I have arranged with Angela to obtain and keep the rest of us posted. Apparently she had a bad day yesterday and could not have visitors . . ..

6   Priestley to Jacquetta Priestley, 18 April 1958.
7   Priestley to Jacquetta Priestley, 23 April 1958.

I've just arrived and it's a warm sunny day, which makes me wish harder than ever you were here . . .

Only six days now, I hope. If more than seven, I find another woman, for whom so far I've not been at all in the mood.

Bless you; my greetings to the Ames.

JACK[8]

It was in this unhappy period that yet another incarnation – Priestley the painter – became more active. Increasing age did not diminish his travelling but he needed a new hobby to occupy him when they were away on holiday and he plunged in to become 'a bumbling old amateur dauber . . . amusing myself'.[9] His one hope was that he would not be 'shockingly bad, making my wife and friends wince and turn away in embarrassment'. He avoided oils because the necessary equipment was far too clumsy to transport. Water-colours also had inbuilt complications. Brought up among the water-colourists who explored the Yorkshire Dales, he filled his house with the works of painters like Cotman, Varley and Girtin but as Priestley put it, only a fool imagined he could match such men. He did make brief attempts at water-colours but failed from the start. 'I have tried again on occasion, dreaming of some sudden miraculous gift descending on me but I have never been any good at my favourite medium.'

There remained the intervening world of gouache, opaque water-colours usually requiring tinted paper. Dashed off in odd half-hours, some of his landscapes – *Death Valley in California*, *A Yorkshire Dale*, *The New England Coastline*, *Lake Sevan in Soviet Armenia* – were very effective. Defensively he would say to friends: 'Some of them have even been noticed amiably – by one of our greatest artists.' These paintings were swift indulgences for the personal pleasure they gave him and some of his friends. The 'happiness came from the concentration, the deep absorption and the result if I felt I had caught something essential (to me) memorable in the landscape'.[10] Thus yet another Jack Priestley emerged in a carefully generated cloud of modesty to surprise his literary friends. There seemed no end to the multiple births.

From August 1958 Priestley exchanged a series of letters with his ex-wife Jane and his son Tom about Mary which reveal a man at a loss what to do next despite the accumulated advice of a number of

8  Priestley to Jacquetta Priestley, 29 April 1958.
9  *Instead of the Trees*, J. B. Priestley, 54.
10 ibid., 56.11, Priestley to Jane Bannerman, 8 August 1958.

psychiatric luminaries. Mary herself, now in St Andrew's Hospital, did not want to prolong her stay, and one letter early in August[11] to Jane said:

> Mary was here yesterday – quite rational but obviously making an effort . . . On Wednesday I spent the evening with Harvey and we had a long talk about Mary and her [son] David . . . I think you got on better in the end with Sigvald than I did and I am wondering if you would care to write to him an exploratory letter with the object of discovering if David would be welcome there . . .
>
> Now about Mary herself. Her chief concern . . . is some plan for the future because she [does not want] to spend years in that place . . . I am baffled just now as to what ought to be done . . . I am working desperately hard [on *Literature and Western Man*].

Later in August Priestley wrote again saying that he had received a worrying letter from Mary who was staying with Barbara because the hospital had finished its course of treatment.[12] By October Mary was much better and wrote a lively and amusing letter, explaining that she would none the less like to see a psychiatrist. Priestley wrote to Jane pointing out that he was sceptical of 'these experts and their tests', and thought it all too easy to waste 'a lot of money on them', but he would make the necessary arrangements.[13] Priestley continued a desultory correspondence with Jane between 1958 and 1959, and considerable friction developed about money. The divorce settlement made on his wife was severe for him in contemporary terms since according to Priestley, Jane received 'more than half my capital and continued to receive a fifth of [my] income'. 'You ask me', he wrote to her in May 1959, 'why I bother about money when we may have so few years to live? I bother about it because I have to sit down and earn it. Why do you insist upon dragging this fifth of my income out of me? It is completely inequitable . . . You are married again. Why should I have to go on and on contributing to your income? This is my final appeal to you to make a decent gesture remembering that in all this business I have paid for everything and taken all the mud that has been flung, to drop this ridiculous claim on my income.'[14] At this stage Jane made no response to his appeal. It is clear from another letter that she was

11 *New Statesman*, 2 November 1957.
12 Priestley to Jane Bannerman, 15 August 1958.
13 Priestley to Jane Bannerman, 19 May 1959.
14 ibid.

still sending him bills. 'I am frankly bewildered by this account', he wrote, 'and I do not understand why I am supposed to pay by myself a bill of this kind which seems to work out at a rate of over £20 a week . . . I must point out that when the farm is sold up in the autumn because it was over-valued originally I shall *not* get three-fifths of what I originally owned but will be lucky if I get half. And now a bill for nearly £300 about which I have no say whatever is suddenly thrown at me. This really is not good enough.'[15]

Throughout 1958 plans were made to move at last from Brookhill and in 1959 Jack and Jacquetta first took possession of Kissing Tree House in Warwickshire which remained their main home until Priestley's death. They now divided their time between Albany and Kissing Tree House, a beautiful white mansion standing in its own grounds with a great lawn stretching away almost it seemed to the horizon. In the summer they lived behind sun-warmed English walls where peaches and nectarines grew and squat doors looked as if they might open, as Susan Cooper said, on an enchanted world in one of those other dimensions of time. Thirty-five acres of quintessentially English countryside protected the house from encroachment with an almost idealised English meadow grazed by a neighbouring farmer, noble trees whose roots were deep in the past and flowers scattered along a fence distilling the scent of roses and honeysuckle. Spring at Kissing Tree House revealed 'everything that made Browning glare with such homesick distaste at his gaudy melon flowers; a great yellow sweep of daffodils flows away from the house and into the distance, as far as you can see; owls call at night among the trees, and every morning early the world is still and misted and new-green, and the grass hazed white with frost'. The only sign of twentieth-century England beyond the meadow was an occasional red double-decker bus which slid past, half hidden by a hedge.[16]

Inside the house a long, marble-floored hall-way led to the lofty library on the right with books from floor to ceiling, an open fire, and tucked away facing a wall a functional desk which had been specially constructed for Priestley. It made an effective combination: an unremarkable desk, an ordinary weather-beaten typewriter facing a wall, with a twisted mass of pipes, 'like a nest of snakes', and on the wall exactly in the typist's vision a painting of Jacquetta by Mary Potter.

15   Priestley to Jane Bannerman, 6 April 1958.
16   *J. B. Priestley*, Susan Cooper, 157.

Michael Denison came to visit Kissing Tree and described entering the front door to encounter the long stretch of marble-floored corridor which ran right through the house to another window at its end. Denison drew a picture of Priestley emerging from his library to stand silhouetted against the window, greeting his guests with 'a little half bow'. According to Denison it was a somewhat self-conscious performance, but Denison regarded Priestley as a very good host and a poor guest.

It was in this period that he corresponded with his son Tom, discussing the moneys accruing from The Good Companions Trust, the running of which was taken over by Tom some years later. Tom emerges as a focal point in the family, always there to give advice, distribute funds and keep a watching brief on Mary.

Priestley's relationship with his son Tom reproduced the family pattern where affection but not intimacy conditioned everyday exchanges. They would occasionally meet to discuss the Trust and sometimes world affairs intruded but there was no serious analysis. In earlier years they played games together but with Tom the full-blown man everything became neutral. From the very beginning he had said to his son, 'I will pay for your education and after that your life is your own.' Tom Priestley saw him infrequently at Christmas and on bank holidays, and he would perhaps say – 'Are you happy?' but there was no enquiry into his way of life, little if any discussion of values and certainly no quarrelling. One of their more intimate meeting-points frequently concerned Mary.[17]

Anxieties about Mary recur in Priestley's letters to Tom and he is constantly investigating new means of helping her.[18] Mary's condition varied widely in 1958 and there was a period when instead of living in a totally imaginary world she was fully aware of her condition which gave her a distressing double vision. Momentarily she even turned against the very world in which she had been trained – music.

In 1960 a major resurrection of one of Priestley's old selves, the literary historian, produced yet another 500-page volume under the all-embracing title *Literature and Western Man*. In *Margin Released*, published in 1962, Priestley remarked, 'Not long ago I published a large book that half killed me – *Literature and Western Man*.' Priestley wrote the book in under eighteen months 'and sunk back into white exhaustion when I at last escaped its clutches'.

17  Priestley to Tom Priestley, 11 April 1958.
18  ibid.

John Braine described *Literature and Western Man* as the 'result of a lifetime's voracious and intensive reading, an almost inhumanly retentive memory, a capacity for organisation of the highest order and above all the strength to carry a workload that would break many a younger man'.[19]

Books of this kind usually divide into three categories: works of reference through which the reader can browse and make personal selections; works following a predetermined theme which conditions the literature selected; and works which are deliberately personal, parading the author's individual preferences and prejudices. It was the remarkable feat of Priestley that *Literature and Western Man* attempted to marry all three and came close to achieving the impossible.

The frame of the book was an anti-snobbish, common-sense appreciation of literature which followed Tolstoy's dictum that any great work ought to be assimilable by the average man. Writers and even poets must make themselves widely understood. Thus Priestley preferred the 'first and . . . most ambitious of our realistic modern novelists', Balzac, to the 'grey, thin' work of Henry James. Balzac was the planner and architect of the 'Human Comedy, the novelist of society itself, in Paris or the provinces . . . high life, low life, finance, politics, fashionable intrigues, occult researches, everybody and everything'. Priestley saw clearly that behind Balzac's 'impressive apparatus of realism' there was a 'wild-eyed and passionate romantic'.[20]

Suspecting the subtleties of James as something slightly sinister, he saw the current reverence for him as rejecting 'the richness and fullness in life and art'. It was, of course, precisely these subtle qualities which devotees of James admired in his writing. As for poetry, T. S. Eliot was too much the conforming poet and any major poet in bad times should make powerful enemies. Poetry was not intended to be private and esoteric but a direct, because intimate, form of communication.

Priestley's approach was consistent throughout. The idea that psychopathological literature was somehow superior to straightforward, tough, optimistic writing was to him anathema and realism had no necessary preoccupation with a cynical, jaundiced view of the slums of the mind or streets. Such a point of view he claimed was not 'fundamentally realistic' – it was 'sentimental-romantic'.

19  *J. B. Priestley*, John Braine, 141.
20  *Literature and Western Man*, J. B. Priestley, 167.

In drama his analysis of Ibsen clearly admitted the influence of Jung, who remained a ghost looking over Priestley's shoulder throughout the book: 'it is this terrific pressure from within finding some relief in his art that compelled Ibsen to reveal more than other nineteenth-century dramatists . . . to suggest to his audiences the misty and often sinister borderland between consciousness and the unconscious, turning himself into a prophet in the Theatre of the depth psychology that was to invade the clinics . . . A Jungian before Jung.'[21]

Priestley was driven into the whole undertaking of *Literature and Western Man*, he said in the preface, because, like Jung, he felt that ours was an age of supreme crisis. 'Some account of Western man in terms of the literature he had created and engaged might help us to understand ourselves and to realise where we are and how we have arrived here.' It was Jung who appreciated the 'perilously one-sided' nature of modern man which had made him so certain of 'conscious control of himself and events that his mind, no longer fortified by the symbols of religion, was almost entirely at the mercy of his unconscious drives and fantasies'. It was Jung who foretold from analysis of his German patients that sooner or later Germany would explode into a barbaric fury of violence and destruction.[22]

Academic criticism did not trouble Priestley throughout his book. Extravagances of critical theory which were placing critics above writers in the hierarchy of literature he dismissed with a flick of the wrist. What he regarded as one of his supreme advantages over academic critics they would consider his greatest weakness. He had read just as widely as any professor of English literature, not for dissection and analysis but for the pure enjoyment which permeated wide areas of his book.

The author remained firmly in place as the creator of the work and the interface between author and reader produced a reality which had its own validity. He did not push the author off the top of the Eiffel Tower (like Barthes), cut part of the text from a novel, semiotically measure each word and show that linguistic structures programmed its writer's work beyond his individual control. Rubbish, Priestley said. Literature was there to be enjoyed before anyone dared to vivisect it. Part celebration part criticism, the book reassessed eighteenth- and nineteenth-century writers like Fielding

21  ibid., 288.
22  ibid., 323.

and Dickens, and admirably illumined writers like Ruskin, Melville and Valéry. It conveyed the pleasure of reading Svevo, remained balanced about Wells and modified first thoughts on Henry James. Many stock literary assumptions were examined and found wanting.

A balanced review in the *Times Literary Supplement* remained puzzled. 'He seems to be denying the most hopeful elements in the pre-war literature and artistic scene and just those which a man of his outlook might have been expected to approve.' The review put a final question: 'Has he given up because his real interests ceased with Thomas Wolfe and Thomas Mann? If so we must regret it because he is going against his own nature.'[23] Certainly there was a pessimism in his attitude to the current literary scene which was difficult to justify, but his reassessment of James Joyce was shrewd. Perennially critics repeated that Joyce was the master of the modern novel who opened completely new avenues of expression for young writers. Where, Priestley asked, could one find the multiplication of novelists who had succumbed to his influence? Joyce, the lonely arrogant giant of modern literature, had done no more than follow the pattern of the Odyssey in *Ulysses*, a feat which strained nobody's talent beyond the imitative. Joyce, the great artist, had taken seventeen years to write *Finnegans Wake*, 'a length of time that suggests an elaborate hobby rather than a passionate desire to create something'.[24] Priestley could find no single younger novelist of any importance who derived from Joyce. Certainly he did not invent – though he possibly enriched – narrative techniques like interior monologue, free association and stream of consciousness. Greatness could not be denied him but he created his own magnificent cul-de-sac and did not 'open new avenues for the novel'.[25] 'Not having, like Joyce, a love–hate relationship with Dublin, do we need for the purposes of the novel as much of Dublin as he gives us? Is Bloom as solidly and convincingly created as he is thought to be?' What began as criticism slowly developed characteristics of a diatribe but it was splendidly done and re-echoed in the minds of many a non-academic reader with conviction.

Re-reading the 500 pages drew the present author into a prolonged and fascinating pilgrimage but the last note in the book remained pessimistic: 'literature itself now becomes one-sided,

23 *Times Literary Supplement*, 26 February 1960.
24 *Literature and Western Man*, J. B. Priestley, 416.
25 ibid.

inevitably because it is over-introverted, often so deeply concerned with the inner world, with the most mysterious recesses of personality and so little concerned with the outer world. It now becomes a literature largely for specialists themselves nearly always equally introverted; and people in general for whom it is really intended find it either too "difficult" or "too neurotic" and unhealthy.'[26]

The awkward question arose: was such literature intended for people in general? If not, were the 'new novelists' creating an inbred audience limited to intellectuals and academics which represented a split in the culture far more subtle than Snow's art and science hybrid? Or were they justified in introducing new refinements of literature in novels which were never expected to have a wide audience? Some believed in Milton and hoped to find 'fit audience . . . though few'.

Priestley, for his part, believed that the authors of this 'inbred' literature had obeyed their own daemon but 'it meant little or nothing to the mass of the people, in danger of losing . . . individuality and personality to the collectives of our time'.

There is of course no entry under 'Priestley' in this book but some reference is inevitable. He was driven sometimes to anger by glib associations between his own novels and those of Dickens; there are certain resemblances, but he believed himself to be more derivative from the ironic Fielding although any precise analogies would be difficult to elaborate.

*Literature and Western Man* became a Book of the Month in America and led to a sharp exchange of letters with his American publishers, Harper. He had given his agent two copies of his next book, *Saturn Over the Water*, for the American market and Matson offered them simultaneously to Harper and Doubleday. Canfield of Harper returned his copy at once saying – rather petulantly in Priestley's view – that he refused to make a competitive bid, whereas Doubleday immediately offered a large advance. Since he did not instruct his agent to make simultaneous submissions – perhaps disingenuously – Priestley said that he was not responsible for Harper losing the book. 'If Harpers had lost money on *Literature and Western Man*,' he wrote to Davison, 'I might have felt under an obligation but they didn't, taking as they did half of the Book of the Month money.'[27]

Raymond Mortimer wrote of *Literature and Western Man* in the

---

26    ibid., 443.
27    Priestley to Edward Davison, 26 December 1960.

*Sunday Times*: 'Mr Priestley's triumph . . . a survey in some 500 pages of over 700 European writers beginning with Machiavelli and ending with Thomas Wolfe . . . I can think of nobody else except Mr Aldous Huxley qualified for a task requiring such breadth of reading and such liveliness of mind.'[28] Michael Foot gave the book a rave review in *Tribune*.

Early 1960 brought another excursion into polemic about colonialism which left a bad impression in the minds of many Australians. Priestley and his wife had visited Australia as the guests of the Melbourne Peace Congress, a hybrid organisation seen by some as a front for communist manipulation and by others as a genuine international peace forum. The monthly magazine *Encounter*, commenting on Priestley's visit, said: 'Recently at a Peace Congress in Melbourne Mr J. B. Priestley argued vainly for a resolution claiming freedom for every true artist to express and communicate his vision.' *Encounter* appreciated the irony that Priestley found himself in a minority of one. According to Jacquetta when 'we reached New York en route for the conference we heard that the Foreign Secretary, Casey, had written to all the Australians telling them that it was a communist front and that they had better withdraw or else . . . It was disgraceful . . . A number of Academic and Church adherents withdrew thus . . . giving the communists dominance. Inevitably, after this, we were attacked unscrupulously by the press from the left and right . . .'

According to Mr Krygier, Priestley's conduct in Australia had been an exemplary display of silliness and his written comments no less absurd. Why, for instance, should he condemn those who warned him that the Peace Congress was communist-dominated as McCarthyite? The truth shone through his animadversions. Fully aware that the congress *was* communist-dominated Mr Priestley could not care less. Facing a communist front in England he would have shunned any connection but 'that sort of thing was good enough for Australia'. The editor of the *Sydney Observer* also wrote, concluding his letter with the words: 'Australians are beginning to fear that the last traces of English colonist prejudice are now found to be in London radicals.'

Priestley replied in the same issue of *Encounter* that Mr Krygier was quite justified in his correction.[29] He, Mr Priestley, and his wife Jacquetta were guests at, not delegates to, the conference and

28 *Sunday Times*, 14 February 1960.
29 *Encounter*, June 1960.

therefore took no part in the 'official proceedings'. However, they did associate themselves with the protesting minority in the Writers' Section. For the rest, Mr Krygier's letter was grossly inaccurate and ill-natured. Priestley had fulfilled a heavy schedule of public meetings, radio and television interviews, which bore no resemblance to the 'silly conduct' of which Mr Krygier spoke. Among those who warned him that the congress was 'communist-dominated' had been certain members of the Melbourne University faculty who 'did not write to me until I arrived'. Even if they had written to him before his arrival he would still have ignored their warnings because the congress offered him an opportunity to press home his campaign for nuclear disarmament. He concluded his letter: 'Australia – big, generous, friendly . . . must cope herself with sour types [like Mr Krygier].'

Another crisis blew up with his London publishers Heinemann early in 1961, which revealed Priestley as a devotee to old-fashioned loyalties. According to one account Heinemann encountered 'difficulties' which led to their new owners Tillings proposing a merger with the Bodley Head.[30]

Charles Pick, Heinemann's one-time managing director and a lifelong friend of Priestley, described a meeting at Priestley's Albany flat where A. S. Frere, then managing director of Heinemann, gave warning of the crisis. Present were Priestley (who had become a director of the Bodley Head in 1957) and authors like Graham Greene, Georgette Heyer and Eric Ambler.[31] According to Pick, Frere proposed that they should leave Heinemann and join the Bodley Head but Priestley immediately protested that he would never abandon the company which had launched him and seen him through so many vicissitudes. In the event Tillings withdrew from their agreement to merge the two companies and Graham Greene departed from Heinemann quickly followed by Georgette Heyer, Eric Ambler, George Millar and several others. Priestley was not among them. Greene, in a letter to the author, states that the crisis had nothing to do with Heinemann's financial difficulties but concerned the attempt by Tillings to kick his old friend A. S. Frere upstairs to president.[32]

Priestley the inveterate traveller set off on a second visit to Russia late in 1961 which led him to revive his favourite word –

30  Max Reinhardt to the author, 16 April 1986.
31  Greene and Reinhardt were also Bodley Head directors.
32  Greene to the author, February 1986.

magic – with romantic efflorescence. His first visit to Russia in the autumn of 1945 was state-organised but now he and Jacquetta travelled as tourists paying their way with royalties accumulated on the Russian translation of his books. The account he wrote for the *Sunday Times* was disappointing. A travelogue brilliantly describing scene and place, it lacked any deep penetration into political or literary developments. If the multiplication of new building in Moscow made a first impression of an almost unrecognisable city, that impression was enhanced by a new atmosphere of comparative freedom with 'no more lowering of the voice or looking over the shoulder'. Politically sophisticated though Priestley was, he too easily assumed that the inbred talk of privileged writers matched the general relaxation in censorship rules.

Unconvincingly he complained that the Russians built a tremendous new opera house only to leave the paving stones unfinished outside, whereas the British paved the approaches and the 'street does not arrive at anything likely to lift the heart of man'. He seemed genuinely to believe that their top priority was our lowest and looked forward to the day when we made a frank assessment of what was best in both systems. Freed at last from social realism, the Russian artists were really beginning to paint and he himself made several swift forays into gouache to record scenes he would never forget. The obligatory entertainment from the Writers' Union he found exhausting but his speeches were received enthusiastically and he was not a man to complain if an Elizabethan zest for living produced gargantuan drinking and eating.

Never a man to make literary pilgrimages, Priestley could not resist an offer to see the house in Yalta where Chekhov wrote *The Cherry Orchard* and they left Moscow within a few days to fly there. 'We stayed at the Writers' Rest House beautifully situated and nicely run but perhaps rather too much on girls' boarding-school lines for our depraved Western tastes.' He saw the writer not as the state's literary performer but 'as somebody brooding apart' owing allegiance to nobody. Yalta offered a variety of contradictory experiences and they travelled on to Armenia where what he described as 'the stupendous and the divine began'. Staggering mountain scenery crossed and divided a country where climbing a vast gorge reminiscent of Kublai Khan they found a cave monastery which had an unbroken ancestry going back a thousand years and there on the roadside, untroubled by Marx or the five-year plan, some peasants were busy sacrificing a sheep. Another day they went up to Lake Sevan where they enjoyed a meal of salmon trout fresh from the water, laced with endless toasts in Armenian cognac and Priestley and Jacquetta watched with trepidation as their chauffeur religiously drank one after another.

Returned – perilously – once more to civilisation they visited the splendid new opera house in Erevan but found Armenian opera 'excruciatingly tedious'. Among all the kaleidoscope of life in Erevan one woman stood out in Priestley's memory – the head of the Tourist and Information Department. She was an 'extraordinarily handsome brunette, all dark, flashing glances, fluttering eyelashes, smiles and dimples', who reminded Priestley of a princess stepped straight out of the *Arabian Nights*. The old flirtatious Priestley ready to respond to a pretty woman came to life in his description of a person whose red lips poured out a flood of statistics about the birth rate, the electric current per head of population and the latest industrial developments while continuing to look as if 'she were in some moonlit rose garden'. As they were about to depart the woman 'looked at us and laughed, squeezed my wife's hand and gave my shoulder an almost caressing rub as if to tell us that Logos had not utterly defeated Eros'.[33]

Next came Tiflis which had somehow preserved its narrow romantic streets among a wild proliferation of new building. The rumbustious Georgians struck a sympathetic chord in Priestley but even he could not keep pace with one toast after another accompanied by unending adulatory speeches. The toasts were frequently drunk from magnificent horns which must have been frowned upon 'about the time of Ethelred the Unready'. Since he preferred vodka to wine and his glass was ceaselessly refilled, many a literary evening ended very mistily. The poet Shalva Apkhaidze, born in the same year as Priestley, gave a literary-cum-family party and Priestley remembered reciting Hamlet's dying speech very late at night without, as he put it, 'the slightest provocation'.

En route towards a collective vineyard at Tsinandali, they encountered a group of peasants packed around a fire eating skewered mutton, real shashlik, roasted chickens, raw onions and great hunks of flat Georgian bread. The invariable rule repeated itself and endless toasts were given by a leather-faced spokesman who suddenly burst into serious declamation about the evils of war. 'Packed . . . between the sun and the fire we were hot and the onion

33  *The Moments*, J. B. Priestley, 153.

reek was very powerful, but the curious friendly eyes and the crinkling smiles were irresistible.'[34]

An old man produced an ancient stringed instrument, plangent notes broke through the vineyard improvising a song of welcome; a teenage boy began to dance only to be joined by an old lady with 'a face like a walnut shell'; and wine was continuously poured from skins into bowls or even directly down throats. It could all have happened at any time in the last thousand years.

Tiflis had its amusing moment. Dutifully, as a literary man, he made the acquaintance of English language and literature teachers at the University and Institute of Foreign Literature. The *Magazine of Foreign Literature* had – tactfully – just published a short story of Priestley's called 'The Thirty-First of June'. Solemn discussion of its significance brought the question – why did he write it? Priestley replied that in the Soviet Union and especially in a university he hesitated to explain. The simple truth was that he had written it 'for fun', whereupon as if releasing a repressed load, everyone roared with laughter and applause. It was, as he said, a supreme example of the luck of the writer's game. A forgotten short story simultaneously brought a handsome option offer for its translation into a musical and set 'half a million Soviet citizens pondering over its little jokes'.[35]

Spending only a short time in Tashkent, shortly afterwards a plane dropped them early one morning on Samarkand's makeshift airport and disillusion broke in. The secret dream of narrow twisted streets, caravanserais of camels, courtyards alive with fountains and highly coloured robes and turbans, collapsed into a featureless town, with lorries grinding along half-finished boulevards.

The ferocious Tamburlaine, half emperor half brigand, brought 150,000 merchants, artisans, architects and craftsmen to fashion out of its rudimentary elements the splendid capital city of Samarkand. All that remained were the scattered blue-tiled domes and minarets, and its family mosques and mausoleuems.

Throughout his article in the *Sunday Times* and its expanded version in *The Moments*, there is little political discussion, no encounters with any of the masters in the Kremlin and little criticism, but Priestley evokes scene and place and relives many Russian encounters vividly: the moment, for instance, when he lost his hat in Samarkand, with philosophic resonance. Priestley's big

34  ibid., 157.
35  ibid., 159.

black hats were made for him by Scott's, but they required 'a year or two's training before the crown was low enough or the brims take on strange curves'.[36] Conveying the impression of something between 'a decayed bandit' and a folk philosopher they missed the image of ruffianly intellectuality at which he was aiming. No sooner were they approaching just that degree of seedy perfection than – woof – some mysterious wind from another dimension carried them away to be lost, obliterated or simply stolen. One left him in California, another in Australia and now in Samarkand a third simply vanished. Samarkand should have revived his belief in magic but sadly failed to do so. Jacquetta qualifies this impression. The old city still had its splendours which redeemed their early reactions.

A giant jet took Jack and Jacquetta back from Tashkent to Moscow accompanied by peasants carrying babies, bundles, pomegranates and water melons in string bags. Stepping off a cart after a five-mile trip into town the peasants were completely blasé about vast air journeys of 2,000 miles, and since roubles were more available than goods Priestley imagined peasants 'popping off at nine miles a minute to let Grandma . . . take a look at the baby'.[37]

In Moscow he met the editors of literary magazines and publishing houses, writers like Leonid Leonov, Konstantin Simonov and Korneli Zeliusky, and British correspondents who agreed that the atmosphere was now much freer. Finally he pleased a large Russian press conference by a number of witty asides which were somehow translated into Russian. It has to be remembered that Priestley's three-month visit took place in the liberalising atmosphere of Khrushchev's reign. When Khrushchev fell and the literary trials began, they resolved not to go again although they had £8,000 royalties due to them.

He was glad to get back home; he always was: because this was the country where he could live. There remained moments coming back from places like the American south-west or Russia when he felt that he 'had left a high and wide adventure to drop into a church bazaar, crowded with too many people quarrelling in too many different accents'. Characteristically they did not last. England was like nothing else in the world.

36   ibid., 149.
37   ibid., 159.

# 31

# Iris Murdoch and
## *Lost Empires*
### 1962–4

If there was some diminution in the creative flow which characterises most writers at the age of sixty-seven Priestley's novels
between 1961 and 1962 were mainly thrillers like *Saturn Over the
Water* and *The Shapes of Sleep*. His notebooks for the years 1960–5
revealed an extensive travel schedule: 1960 America; 1961 Jan.,
Feb., Luxor then Paris; July, France, probably the Dordogne;
Sept., Stockholm followed by Hamburg and Frankfurt. In Germany he collected local colour for *The Shapes of Sleep*, a novel
written with all the pace and excitement of *Benighted*, but brought
up to date in method and content. The Mayfair News Agency gives
Steindale, a local reporter, a piece of investigative journalism which
leads him into kaleidoscopic adventures with guns, mugging and
violence as the natural background of his quest. It was Priestley
once again the master of suspense, rushing straight through a lesser
novel only to be greeted by a consensus of rave reviews which
surprised him. He mournfully reflected that in his view they would
better have suited some of his more serious work.

*The Shapes of Sleep* (1962) marked a new explicitness about sex:

> She came out and without saying a word, moved straight into his
> arms again, straining against him, putting his hand on her breast,
> keeping her mouth open against his as if the break had heightened
> her excitement . . . when Steindale began to feel like a stallion in
> April she pulled away and looked at him.
>
> 'Take me, Ben,' she whispered. 'Okay, it's still lust, curiosity and
> vanity – but take me. I know – and you know – I'm frightened still –
> but perhaps that's what you like.'[1]

The words threaten to become comic in today's sexual climate.

1   *The Shapes of Sleep*, J. B. Priestley, 100.

*Saturn Over the Water* (1961) was another thriller which received the kind of review in the *Observer* which writers dream about:

> Mr Priestley's new novel is immensely entertaining and the fun and excitement give point to the seriousness of his conclusion. *Saturn Over the Water* has the pace of the best Buchan, together with some of the SF qualities of Professors Hoyle and Lewis; and above all the moral – or rather spiritual – values of the late Charles Williams . . . Mr Priestley . . . has added a secret something of his own and created a potent and exhilarating punch.

In the same period came a short illustrated celebration of Dickens which revealed the sheer professionalism of Priestley. Tom Rosenthal, then at Thames & Hudson, rang up Priestley and made an offer of £1,500 advance for 20,000 words on Dickens to be delivered by the following 13 September. Precisely to the day an impeccable manuscript ready for the printer arrived with a short business-like note from the author.

More important was an elaborate piece of autobiography, *Margin Released*, which became an indispensable source book and colourfully recapitulated scattered episodes in his life covering the years 1910–60. Compulsively readable it was written in a relaxed style which comfortably accommodated his prejudices and vividly recovered one experience after another.

A film company took an option on *The Shapes of Sleep* in 1962 for £1,000 covering fifteen months with an eventual purchase price of £10,000.[2] The world motion picture rights were also sold by Harold Matson, Priestley's New York agent, for $30,000.[3] A. D. Peters's London files revealed a continual flow of moneys large and small from English, American and European sources but Priestley complained of a diminishing income. Certainly compared to his heyday it had fallen away.

The big dramatic event of 1962–3 was the adaptation of Iris Murdoch's novel *A Severed Head*. 'I enjoyed that,' he told Susan Cooper. 'It was a challenge,' but his face drooped in recollection. 'It was a year before we got it on the stage and after that we couldn't get it off, it ran for two and a half years.'[4]

Iris Murdoch told the author: 'I first wrote a play version of the novel and showed it to Jack. He pointed out that it wouldn't do. He

2   A. D. Peters Archive, 19 May 1962.
3   ibid., 4 March 1977.
4   *J. B. Priestley*, Susan Cooper, 153.

then, with me, replanned the structure of the play and altered some dialogue and cut large parts . . . I learnt a lot about dramatic structure. . . It was marvellous watching him.'[5] Her reaction to the first night was ecstatic. She wrote to Priestley: 'Darling Jack, after my experiences on Tuesday night in Bristol I feel fairly certain about one thing. I think WE HAVE WRITTEN A TERRIFIC PLAY. I found it dramatic, funny, moving, all we hoped and evidently the audience did too. I was very excited by this impression which I got now for the first time seeing the thing whole and new. Hooray for us! I embrace you.'[6]

The dialogue of *A Severed Head* is different from any straight Priestley play. It is snappy, sophisticated and the opening scene immediately plunges into the aftermath of sex. Georgie Hands and Martin Lynch-Gibbon lie half undressed and half embraced in front of a fire. Georgie Hands says: 'Are you sure she doesn't know?' Lynch-Gibbon replies: 'About us? Certain.' Priestley was of course personally very familiar with this category of dialogue. Essentially this was a southern play, a 'high-level' comedy with dialogue from polished and sophisticated people, and Priestley handled the transformation superbly.

Iris Murdoch described her reactions to Priestley and Jacquetta to John Braine:[7]

> I adored him – at once. What a man, what a character, what an appetite for life! And I adore Jacquetta too – I'd never before met anyone so beautiful and regal. They really are King and Queen figures! Yet Jack also is Falstaff – I always think of him as expressed by his own essay on Sir John . . . He is . . . not just a humane man but a powerfully benevolent one while being a bonny fighter too. Apart from all this, what a wonderfully shrewd political critic he has been over such a long time. He is not only a vastly talented and exceptionally versatile and wise writer. He is such a remarkable human being. And such an Englishman. I love him very much.

Late in 1963, Priestley nearly surrendered to a quite new theme for a play which would have been considered daring in those days and involved erotic scenes unmatched in his work. An old friend, a research pathologist, stayed with the Priestleys for the weekend and retold a story of incest which his sister had encountered as head of a

5  Iris Murdoch to the author, March 1986.
6  Iris Murdoch to Priestley, undated (1963).
7  Quoted in *J. B. Priestley*, John Braine, 143.

large girls' grammar school. Priestley described the incident in a letter to Diana Collins.

A sixth-form girl of great promise suddenly performed very badly in class and when the headmistress pressed home her enquiries she discovered that the girl had surrendered to repeated sexual intercourse with her father, a distinguished civil servant. His wife, past the menopause, had refused sex with her husband, which she had never liked. The father's relationship with his daughter created a burden of guilt under which both broke down and she found herself unable to work. The headmistress refused to call in the police because, as Priestley put it, they 'would . . . finish the poor devil for ever'. Priestley brooded for weeks over this 'wretched triangle' which was so determined to preserve its privacy intact and wondered whether he could dramatise it effectively. It would be half a black comedy without stressing the prurience and clearly had intense dramatic possibilities. In the end the play was never written.[8]

*A Severed Head* was Priestley's last serious – and highly successful – venture into the theatre and immediately afterwards in January 1964 he and Jacquetta left for Morocco. It was another year of intensive travel, recorded in his notebook: May–June, Moscow and Leningrad; October, New York; December, Singapore etc.

Work continued throughout the year and produced *Lost Empires*, one of the few remaining important novels written after 1960, which has since turned up in so many guises – film options, paperback, television – that its life seems perennial. Priestley himself wrote a real-life prologue and epilogue to the novel which describes his visit to Richard Herncastle, a water-colour painter living in Askrigg, who 'like a good Yorkshireman – shouts a bit to cover his shyness'. Herncastle – now ARA, CBE – recalls the days when he was assistant to a small-time illusionist on the variety stage and claims that he has transferred his conjuring skills to painting. The Lost Empires are not conquered British territories but the network of music halls throughout the country which are rapidly falling into decay and Herncastle's story is the story of their downfall. 'My belief is', Priestley wrote, 'that by 1913 when it was organised like big business the variety stage was already well in decline. The talent was going into films with people like Chaplin and Stan Laurel.'

The novel opens with a scene set in those pre-war days. An

8  Priestley to Diana Collins, 30 July 1962.

orchestra plays the 'Ballet Egyptian' as the curtain goes up to reveal a glittering Indian temple, designed by Uncle Nick who makes his entrance dressed in flowing robes as a tall, authoritative Indian magician. A Hindu maiden hands him empty bowls and vases from which a cascade of flowers, silks, gold coins and plants are conjured to thunderous applause from the audience. The applause rises in crescendo when the Hindu girl climbs into a box on the stage to have three shots fired into it only to reveal, when the box is opened, nothing inside. Every innocent trick in the game was played but somewhere in the background boredom threatened to swell up and engulf the whole performance. Initial sympathies for Uncle Nick are quickly overwhelmed by his chauvinism which reduces Cissie to a sexual object slavishly obeying his commands. Priestley succeeded all too well in his attempt to make Nick an outsize character, half monster, half lovable showman.

All the characters in *Lost Empires* are very different people from those inhabiting the pages of *The Good Companions* and the author of *Lost Empires* has a totally different vision from his *alter ego*. *The Good Companions* romantically dressed up life in a travelling troupe while *Lost Empires* realistically revealed the desperate, the lecherous, the suicidal. Two of the company are gay, a dwarf is overwhelmed by a swarm of midgets, one at least of the company is going mad, two are voyeuristic, some of the women are ravenously sexual and everybody is desperately vulnerable. Harry G. Burrard, the collapsing comic, is laughed at by the audience for all the wrong reasons and pelted off stage. Tommy Beamish, as tough and successful as Burrard is weak and a failure, hears the audience laughing at Burrard as if they wielded a death rattle. 'It's the cruellest bloody sound in the world . . . People laughing like that give me the creeps.'

Pessimistic moments notwithstanding, the novel has a rumbustious quality running through it, comic invention enlivens one scene after another and together they redeem the gloom and convert the novel into a successful entertainment.

Disliked by the whole company, a recurrent failure desperately buoyed up by false hopes, Burrard at last shoots himself in the dressing-room and what might have become melodramatically sentimental is handled with restraint.

'And perhaps we made him,' Cissie comments, '. . . but even now I can't help feeling he was so awful. I stopped speaking to him weeks and weeks ago. And somehow that makes it worse.'

Her final comment, 'And perhaps now it will never be the same again,' is tersely re-echoed by Priestley, 'And perhaps it wasn't.'

*Lost Empires* is a wonderfully old-fashioned novel which might have been a documentary but escaped the limitations imposed by the prologue and epilogue. The pages between are pure fiction and when the epilogue deliberately traces the later lives of the characters in all reality, fact and fiction skilfully merge. The last scene where Meg, the young daughter, capers in front of a gramophone to shattering pop music, reflects the eternal urge of the young to dance and the quite new forms which will overwhelm the Lost Empires.

*The Times* commented: 'Certainly one of his best . . . exhibits all his virtues and talents to the full.'

Priestley sold the film rights of *Lost Empires* to Victor Savile for $50,000 with an up-front payment of $10,000, 'but Savile was never able to get the film made'.[9] Ironically Priestley felt he had driven too hard a bargain and decided to return part of the money to Savile. In 1986 *Lost Empires* was televised in eight parts, the paperback brought an English advance of £41,000 and *Lost Empires* together with another minor novel, *Sir Michael and Sir George*, commanded an American advance of $21,000.[10] After the publication of *Lost Empires* Priestley abandoned his American publishers Harper on the grounds that they had allowed so many of his novels to go out of print, a fate common nowadays to most novels within a short period. Peter Davison, the son of his old friend Edward Davison, published him from then on under the imprint of Little, Brown or Atlantic Monthly.

9   Interview with Mrs Jacquetta Priestley, 1 September 1985.
10   A. D. Peters Archive.

# 32

# Seventy Years Old
## 1964–8

He was now seventy years old. Heavily built with a considerable stomach, his saurian eye regarded a world in which his old gods were sadly eroded. Insomnia sat on his shoulder 'like a silent owl far into the night'.[1] Success with Iris Murdoch's adaptation did not reconcile him to the world of the theatre and there were to be no more plays of consequence: Jung no longer had irrefutable access to the truth about human nature and his skills in reconciling the conscious and unconscious had revealed certain flaws: the possibility of an afterlife, once regarded agnostically, was now converted into survival of an individuated self in Dunne's Time Two. The Labour Party had become a party prepared to manipulate truth in order to stay in power and if his socialism survived it was a highly individual variety which found no echoes in Transport House. 'We who are growing old', he wrote, 'must face a sharp challenge. In the later afternoon of life going down the other side of the hill we look towards death . . . There is a pretence that we are all on the morning side of the hill and might soon with the help of goats' blood or sheep's glands stay there longer and longer. But if we who are growing old are wise we shall reject this pretence and go unprotesting down the other side of the hill.'[2] He had been married three times, had five children and several grandchildren, he had written innumerable books, over thirty plays and committed himself passionately to experience in myriad forms, but 'the truth is that although I have known tragedy, and also have my share of grievances, I have been on the whole a very lucky man'. His work had penetrated to the far corners of the earth and he had miraculously combined writing what he wanted to write with handsome rewards. 'Perhaps if I had to do it all over again I would not have written so much and so many different things.'[3] Some habits had

1 Priestley to Ralph Richardson, 3 June 1964.
2 *Essays of Five Decades*, J. B. Priestley, 311.
3 *Instead of the Trees*, J. B. Priestley, 151.

changed, some remained inviolable. Still he smoked, drank, and grumbled. His growing horror of stag parties whether pompous or drunken had given him a sharp preference for feminine company. Reading in bed no longer consisted of literature but old-fashioned detective stories. Shaggy young men playing electric guitars, belting out banalities in endless repetition, produced signs of nausea. He regretted no longer playing tennis and once remarked that at seventy his ideal form of exercise was a strenuous sit-down. A pretty woman could still stir him to flirtatious conversation, but his relationship with Jacquetta had deepened, and if his eye roved it always came back to her.

The mature Priestley who remained a close friend of Diana Collins looked back on his younger self and told her: 'I was so boorish and bad-mannered.' Priestley, in his sixty-eighth year, was, Diana Collins believed, 'the result of quite a lot of – not just experience but – to use a modern jargon phrase he would have hated – of work on himself'.

She recorded of the fully mature Priestley, 'I found him deeply intuitive, understanding and wise as well as consistently sweet-tempered.'

The first time she visited Yorkshire with him they went round the pubs and it was 'almost like a royal progress. So many people wanted to come and shake Jack's hand and say admiring things to him . . . I used to tease him because he did not like not to be praised but after a bit of it he would set off smartly in the opposite direction.'[4]

The preparation for death, Diana Collins recorded, 'consisted in a gradual detachment from the ego in all its aspects . . . an extension of non-identification in favour of Essence (Gurdjieff) or the Self (Jung)'.

The boundaries between these states and mysticism became blurred, but Priestley strongly resisted any suggestion that he was a mystic. He frequently said to Diana Collins: 'What is this meditation that we hear so much about?' He vehemently denied to her that he was sensitive but he was, she said, 'profoundly intuitive and alert to atmosphere'. He denied being any kind of an idealist – 'I'm a realist.' The final test of happiness, he said, was 'to be prepared to have it all over again exactly as it was'. Most people were prepared for a replay with certain highly significant changes but that was loading the dice. Diana Collins said to Jack, 'Yes. I'd have it all over

4   Diana Collins to the author, July 1986.

again exactly the same,' and he thought for a moment and replied, 'No. I wouldn't want it.'[5]

A shower of celebrations burst around his seventieth birthday with media interviews, articles, and a host of reassessments. Telegrams, letters, telephone calls poured in. Iris Murdoch, Sir Ralph Richardson, C. P. Snow, Malcolm Muggeridge, Michael Foot, Michael Denison, Peggy Ashcroft, Canon and Diana Collins, Raymond Mortimer . . . the list was endless – sent congratulations. He wrote to Angela Wyndham Lewis: 'I hope you will be around about the middle of September. My 70th birthday falls on Sunday so a grand Savoy party will be arranged for Monday, 14th.'[6] The crowning moment came with a leader in *The Times* entitled 'The Disappearing All-Rounder':

> the most cursory contemplation of Mr Priestley's career impresses upon one what an all-rounder he is – critic, novelist, dramatist, essayist, journeying philosopher, commentator, broadcaster – he has shone at them all. He is a man of letters in the good old sense of the phrase. We rejoice in him all the more because so few of his kind are left.[7]

Kingsley Martin wrote him a birthday letter:

> We have both had a good run since we first met in your rooms in Trinity Hall . . . In spite of Cambridge you have kept up a Red Brick personality ever since. You stand in the public mind as a Yorkshire stalwart, a good trencherman, a Falstaffian character who smokes a pipe and won't stand any nonsense . . . By and large you have been wonderfully successful. Countless people read your novels and some of your plays will be acted for many a long day.

Martin said that some of the attacks on Priestley were due to his political unorthodoxy since the establishment usually got 'its own back one way or another'. The reaction of the establishment combined with Priestley's 'exaggerated desire for praise accounted for much heart-burning'.[8]

Priestley's obsessional interest in the nature of time drove him to produce in his seventieth year yet another volume, which re-examined his various incursions into the subject. 'I would say', he

5   ibid.
6   Priestley to Angela Wyndham Lewis, 1 May 1964.
7   *The Times*, 14 September 1964.
8   *New Statesman*, 11 September 1964.

Priestley off on a lecture tour of the USA.

Dinner at the Bradford Arts Club while collecting material for *English Journey*, in 1933 (Priestley in the middle).

Priestley at the microphone during one of his Second World War broadcasts.

(*Left*)
Priestley,
Ronald
Colman and
Mrs Jane
Priestley.

Priestley at
work in his
study.

Priestley's Isle of Wight home, Brookhill. (*Photo Skyfotos, Lympne Airport, Kent*)

Priestley's last home, Kissing Tree House. (*Photo Rosalind Pulvertaft*)

Priestley gave up driving after a minor accident in 1931.

Mr and Mrs Priestley at the height of their successful marriage.

Mr and Mrs Priestley in Moscow in 1962.

Mrs Diana Collins, Canon Collins and Priestley at the time of the CND campaign. (*Photo Tomas Jaski Ltd*)

Priestley with Iris Murdoch during their collaboration on *A Severed Head*. (*Photo Horst Tappe*)

Priestley in philosophic mood. (*Photo Mark Gerson*)

wrote, 'that *Man and Time* has been the hardest task I have ever set myself.' Rejecting the professional historian's impersonal approach he mixed personal experience and dreams with a mass of evidence drawn from multiple sources.

The answer to the question – why was Priestley so preoccupied with time? – seems too simplistic to be satisfactory. Many contributory factors converged for him on the commonplace awareness that every moment – however treasured – slipped away even as we savoured it. 'The moving finger writes and having writ moves on . . .' In his seventy-fourth year Priestley was busy trying to outwit time and Omar Khayyam.

Appearing on BBC's television programme *Monitor*, he appealed for experiences of precognitive dreams and telepathic communications. Letters came pouring in to Kissing Tree in such numbers that his secretary was overwhelmed and a picture of Priestley shows him standing undismayed before a flood of correspondence which threatened to swamp his billiard table. Eventually the letters were reduced to five categories, three of which he considered important. 'The B pile consisted of clearly stated and what seemed to me trustworthy accounts of precognitive dreams.' Priestley had a predisposition to believe in dreams which anticipated real-life events, but in *Man and Time* he was much more sceptical than usual and elaborated psychological and even semi-scientific objections. 'Some depth-psychologists tell us that a strong emotion of a certain kind experienced in a dream linking up with a similar emotion felt in our waking life can persuade us that the dream and the later event are alike.'[9]

*Man and Time* made Priestley's first concessions to science, with relativity jostling cheek by jowl with space-time continuums and Dunne's theories. Relativity saw time as a fourth dimension and made no reference to fifth and sixth dimensions with the interesting possibilities characteristic of Dunne. The relativity chapter in the book outlined modern theory crisply and clearly, despite the violation of detail inevitable in such a condensation. Einstein's special theory states that time is not absolute but relative to the position of the observer. Common sense says that the time interval between two events should be invariant whatever the position of those experiencing such events. The special theory of relativity showed that if two observers in different positions were moving in relation to those events then the time interval differed. Thus there

9 *Man and Time*, J. B. Priestley, 195.

was no simultaneity of events. For one new school of thought this gave a degree of academic if not scientific respectability to the possibility of travelling forward in time and hence to prediction.

What had all this to do with ESP, telepathy and dream prediction? Heisenberg's principle of uncertainty had removed the possibility on the microscopic scale of knowing simultaneously all the co-ordinates of an atomic particle which, for some physicists, implied a break in the chain of causation. This, from the physicist's point of view, made prediction on such a scale impossible. Within a macroscopic scale prediction became a statistical probability which could be manipulated to link in with Priestley's theme. Suddenly a full-blown empiricist, suppressing temperamental hostility, Priestley took the revolutionary step of consulting a number of physicists. One replied: 'I do not think the development of quantum mechanics has engendered a different attitude towards the future and its predictability.' Wrestling with obscurities in his analysis Priestley attempted an analogy with remembrance of things past to illustrate the possibility of simultaneously experiencing two if not three time levels. If we recall our schooldays vividly enough, he argued, we are back reliving them and yet our brains and bodies are still in the present. Thus for a brief period we are inside and outside the past while simultaneously experiencing the consciousness which the intervening years have 'enlarged and sharpened'. Like all analogues this one is inexact. The brain can retrieve impressions made years ago on its memory cells which can be reactivated to recall a particular incident but it does not enter a different time structure: it recollects an event imprinted on the brain with the consciousness of the present. Pushed to its extreme this line of thinking led into solipsism.

*Man and Time* has been neglected in Priestley's oeuvre. It is beautifully written, lucid and shot through with his personality. If it sometimes breaks the rules of rigorous conceptualisation it introduces the reader to one of the most complex and difficult subjects and, for once, allows the scientists to speak. Not, of course, that you would expect their interpretation to undermine Priestley's.

Allegiance to the prophet – Gurdjieff – produced an important chapter in the book. Anyone who has entered the quagmire of Beelzebub's thinking in Gurdjieff's work will be lucky not to be engulfed and suffocated but Priestley survived the experience with the shining conviction that here was a new form of an old message which he had long accepted. Put at its simplest Gurdjieff believed that men must make an effort to escape the waking sleep in which they lived to become fully conscious of the central 'I' in place of the contradictory 'I's whose multiplication confused everyday living. Negative emotions must be jettisoned to enable essence to take the place of false personality. According to Gurdjieff the glib assumption of possessing an immortal soul was false but with unremitting effort men might create in themselves such an indestructible entity. The Gurdjieff chapter reaffirmed a philosophy similar to that of Ouspensky. Priestley embraced it warmly but saw its inconsistencies.

Throughout the book the strain of being objective mounted until it proved too much for Priestley. His conclusion reiterated his old faith, with Jung resurrected: 'I believe that his "individuation" and achievement of "Self" are a preparation for existence outside Time One in Times Two and Three. Probably in Time Two we move from personality to the essential self, never realised in Time One; and that now in Time Two the Self must take on as it were its final shape and colouring.'[10] By implication some vague equivalent of a human being prepared itself for entry into a dubious hereafter. The analysis left an uneasy feeling that he had not thought through the detailed consequences of such a theory, some of which converted immortality into a very odd experience.

In his seventieth year a trip with Jacquetta to Ceylon proved something of a disaster. For two whole weeks after their arrival 'it rained in blanketing torrents, so nothing could be seen except the colony of little black ants that shared our rooms'. When they held a mass meeting under his pillow with delayed delegates hurrying over his face Priestley and Jacquetta felt that 'enough was enough'.

People had exclaimed when they heard that the Priestleys were going to Ceylon: 'Oh, Ceylon! You are lucky! We were there once and adored it.' Priestley commented: 'Well, from first to last, side trips and all I hated it.'[11]

Barbarism reached unexpected refinement when a gang of sullen boys watched him painting one day and systematically stoned him until he had to retreat to his hotel. Something much deeper and more pervasive spoilt the whole expedition. It was almost 'as if the abominable cruelties once practised in Kandy' were still on the air

10  ibid., 308.
11  *Instead of the Trees*, J. B. Priestley, 7.

poisoning the very atmosphere. 'Certainly as we moved around there came moments of tranquillity and beauty when for the time being one's heart and mind were at peace. But these were set against what seemed to me this darkly brooding atmosphere into which a great deal of hate, both racial and social, had been spilled.'[12]

Redeeming features were few but among them Arthur C. Clarke who lived in Ceylon brought his self-confidence into the scene to dissipate the sinister atmosphere in a wave of English common sense. Snugly at home by the sea not far from Colombo, Mr Clarke seemed to Priestley the happiest writer he had ever met, but that was because he had the 'heart and outlook of an enthusiastic boy about sixteen'.

Another encounter which remained in his memory was the day they hired a car and drove up the corkscrew road to what had once been the Imperial Hill Station of Nuwara Eliya. They entered a stately club where white-garbed servants provided an excellent English meal with great solemnity and slowly they slipped back into the year 1910 drinking tea in circumstances redolent of Rudyard Kipling.

Saluting the fallen grandeur of the British Empire, Priestley reflected on the consequences of that collapse. Remote from anything resembling an imperialist he was not convinced that the new freedoms created a way of life any better than their imperialist past. 'Indeed, I think, large numbers of them are worse off being poorly governed and heavily taxed to support their independence.'[13] Wide experience in the colonies had too often brought from the lips of former colonials, 'Wish the British were back.' In Priestley's view independence was stained by more blood than the occasional horrors of empire had ever let loose.

In the year following the Ceylon trip he was offered a peerage by the then prime minister, Harold Wilson, and invited to join the board of the National Theatre. Wilson asked him to call at Number Ten, Downing Street in April 1965 and suggested that he would make a first-class spokesman for the Labour Party in the House of Lords, an offer which Priestley found it relatively easy to refuse.[14] Such honours seemed to him meretricious, and he did not see himself robed and restrained, conforming to a role which ill suited his spontaneous nature. He spent forty minutes with Wilson and

12 ibid.
13 ibid., 8.
14 Letter from Harold Wilson (Lord Wilson of Rievaulx), 27 February 1986.

found his energy undiminished and his general grasp of affairs impressive.[15]

He wrote to the BBC compere Robert Robinson about his seat on the board of the National Theatre:[16]

Dear Bob,

. . . You seemed to us much easier in the last two Saturday programmes. But the attempts at serious discussion still don't work. And everybody was so busy being for or against Tynan and his word that nobody remarked that the actual discussion was one of the feeblest on record. Incidentally, I have just joined the board of the National Theatre – about which I have many grave doubts – and if I should propose, as I might in the fairly near future, that Tynan should go, probably I'll be told this is because he says 'fuck' in public. This didn't shock me except that I thought it bad manners and, if he didn't warn you, unfair to you and Sherrin. The trouble about Tynan, who is a clever chap who can write, is that he doesn't really care about the Theatre, which he uses as a trampoline for his ego . . .

Yours ever,

J.B.

Robinson became a good friend and they joined forces in producing three excellent television programmes, celebrating various Priestley occasions.

Another letter went to Robinson and his wife in January 1966.[17]

My dear Jo and Bob,

A hasty note to say how sorry I was to spoil a fine friendly occasion and a good lunch by my masochistic hurry to reach the dentist. The truth is – I had a great hole in a wisdom tooth, and I saw myself exposing the nerve somewhere in Guatemala. But the dentist, though he scraped away and filled the tooth, had taken an X-ray and then told me I needn't have worried because the nerve had gone – 'withered away' he said. That's me – *nerve gone, withered away*.

. . . will keep in touch, love

JACQUETTA, JACK

Priestley and his wife took a long two-months' holiday in Ireland in April–May of 1967, partly from Jack's point of view to paint. He

---

15  Priestley to Edward Davison, 16 May 1965.
16  Priestley to Robert Robinson, 24 November 1965.
17  Priestley to Robert Robinson, 4 January 1966.

revelled in the wild, rich, many-coloured landscapes and painted almost recklessly 'morning and afternoon'.

Between the years 1964–7 the life of Priestley's daughter Mary had undergone dramatic changes. She had divorced her husband Sigvald and he remarried but by 1964 his second wife was leaving him for another man and he went into a psychiatric hospital to be treated for complicated illnesses. Mary took legal action against him to recover custody and care of her twin children and won the case but by 1967 Sigvald made it quite clear that he wanted the children back again and in May of that year Priestley wrote to Mary:

We had a really wonderful holiday. Western Ireland at least out of the high season . . . is all that it is cracked up to be. Marvellous scenery, nice friendly people, empty roads and quite good food . . .

I'm very sorry you haven't felt well. There is no doubt in my mind that this is due to worry about Sig and the boys. I want to do everything I can to help here. Sig is obviously hopelessly unreliable. He hasn't contributed a penny to their upkeep and I can't help suspecting that his wish to have them back is partly based on the hope of being subsidised from this end . . . You may rest assured I am absolutely on your side in this matter. I have had a letter from your mother, who clearly feels as I do. The twins must stay with you.[18]

On the 27th of the same month Priestley returned to Kissing Tree, as he put it, victorious from one of the toughest jobs he had ever undertaken: giving the Memorial Lecture on Arnold Bennett at Stoke-on-Trent. The lecture delivered to a packed hall was simultaneously broadcast direct on the BBC Third Programme. He spoke spontaneously for fifty-five minutes without a script or note of any kind and for a man in his seventy-third year 'that's a feat of concentration and memory' he wrote to Edward Davison. 'Hurray for me! (This is what my kids used to call the braggies.)'[19]

In July and August of the same year Priestley and his wife launched into an extravagant journey to Daytona Beach via New York. Their presence in Daytona was occasioned by a madcap expedition of the London Symphony Orchestra, the origins of which were so bizarre that Priestley felt compelled to follow the

18  Priestley to Mary Priestley, 6 May 1967.
19  Priestley to Edward Davison, 22 May 1967.

trail to record the event in 1967. As *Time* magazine commented: 'It is so mad, so utterly wild a scheme that we can't resist it.' The LSO management were forced to cancel twenty recording sessions, five concerts, and refuse an invitation to the Athens Festival in order to bundle the orchestra off to that big sandbox in the sun – Daytona. They were to be the main attraction at the First Florida International Music Festival and the first European orchestra to settle in a US city for a whole month. As *Time* magazine put it, ninety-six musicians, forty-three wives, and thirty-six children swept across the Atlantic and dropped out of the skies to be met by a caravan of forty cars which carried them to a network of expensive hotels. Priestley's record of their first encounter with Daytona was depressing: 'Early on the evening of Sunday, 9th July (the year being 1967), I arrived at a most disturbing conclusion; I had made a fool of myself and on a large and expensive scale too.'[20]

He was sitting in the furnished house he had rented, in the upstairs room because the air-conditioning in the rest of the house had failed. The air-conditioning expert who called next day remarked with a cheerful casualness which approached the infuriating that 'he always expected to take out between sixty and seventy gallons of water (caused by humidity) in the first two days – "Yes, simply out of the curtains, clothes, carpets, and walls!"' What crazy inspiration had persuaded Priestley – against Jacquetta's advice – to fly out their complete household from Kissing Tree, he could no longer imagine. Nothing less than a 'rising tide of male grandeur and folly' could have swept aside Jacquetta's objections and 'landed him in a soaking furnace'.

One minor disaster followed another. Turning on the shower upstairs the water malevolently poured through a hole in the dining-room ceiling; opening what should have been an empty cupboard released an avalanche of broken toys and old clothes; drawers were packed to bursting point; locked doors refused to stay closed; open doors were jammed beyond any possibility of release. Any apparent exaggeration in this account was rejected by Priestley who wrote: 'the gags get cornier and staler, it belongs to the world of *Punch* and slapstick films . . . I even found myself hammering on a bathroom door because I couldn't get out.'[21] Even the man who came to plaster the hole in the ceiling was clad in the kind of white overalls which had a custard-pie ancestry. 'Men came and went all

20  *Trumpets Over the Sea,* J. B. Priestley, 1.
21  ibid., 2–3.

day, chiefly to stare at the failed air-conditioning with an air of total competence.' Bursting with technological talk and energy they quickly surrendered to an all-pervading vagueness, replaced brisk-ness with evasions and simply faded away again. As for the typewriter he hired the following Saturday morning, it turned out to have a glittering array of newfangled gadgets, none of which he understood. At any moment it seemed Buster Keaton might materialise out of the floor. Not all this hilarious accumulation of malignant interventions killed the excitement of their arrival but one question constantly recurred: 'What the devil did he think he was doing?'

Broadly speaking Priestley now saw himself as 'a rather indolent and self-indulgent man, deficient in willpower and any determina-tion to succeed . . . to make the very best of himself'.

'In one matter alone do I show – and have long shown – a certain obstinancy and independence of mind and spirit. I decide for myself what I shall do and I hang on to the chosen task like a bulldog.'[22]

From the very first day at Daytona Beach that precept was poisoned by moods which blew hot and cold with impetuous frequency and the question kept recurring, 'Was I or wasn't I making a gigantic and expensive fool of myself?' In the event his worst fears were not realised.

Priestley wrote a short but exhilarating book which was as much a celebration of his love of music as an account of the LSO's triumph over disaster. The *New York Times* complained that the opening programme – Handel's Water Music, Beethoven's Fourth Piano Concerto, Brahms's First Symphony in C Minor – could hardly have been more hackneyed but Priestley was carried away into philosophic reflections about the nature of music. 'I thought how music doesn't interpret history but the eternal myths that are at once above and below history.' Under the spell of Handel's Water Music, George I's brutal age became 'for a moment a fabled Avalon' where 'I seemed to catch a glimpse of the unfading apple blossom'.

There were many experiences: an over-zealous general manager shut Jack's hand in the car door but he refused to see a doctor because the American Medical Association fees were too high; they escaped from a party including André Previn and Perlman to sit hand in hand watching the molten silver of a lazy sea come rolling in soundlessly; they parted company to have Jacquetta go off to the

22   ibid., 4.

Everglades National Park and return with such a vivid account of bird life there he ever afterwards spoke of it as if it was his personal experience; and they returned many a night from a concert silenced by the music which re-echoed subtly in their minds to the exclusion of physical reality.

The year 1966–7 brought complaints from Priestley to his American publisher Peter Davison about literary agents. In June he said that Peters 'sat on' all the American rights, draining off his 10 per cent on all sales without doing a 'damn thing' to promote them.[23] By October he was 'going through a crisis' with both Matson his American and Peters his London agent. They were not active literary agents, he wrote to Peter Davison, but passive collectors of commission. He claimed that Peters was seriously understaffed and had lost Priestley a number of film and television rights but he gave no details of the losses.[24] It was characteristic of most author-agent relationships that disillusion set in at some stage and consistent with many authors Priestley easily forgot those years when Peters did promote him on a big scale. In the same month, October, Priestley complained that before the war he drew a 25 per cent flat rate from Heinemann for new books and was never offered less than 10 per cent on cheap editions, whereas 'the other day a biggish mail order deal' proposed a 4 per cent royalty.[25]

Disillusion with his American publishers multiplied in that year. In February of 1967 he was depressed to learn that not only had his American sales fallen away but his reputation too.[26] Peter Davison sent him a review of *Lost Empires* which more or less described him as 'an entertaining and cheerful old codger' instead of a 'serious and important modern novelist'. He was prepared to bet that the reviewers would not have written in a similar vein about Graham Greene's *The Comedians*. The trouble with American reviewers, he said, was that they simply 'didn't know enough'. There was now a hopeless confusion in print and on the stage between shock tactics – with shit, cunt and fuck liberally distributed – and those who wrote from 'an excess of energy, observation and genuine creativity'.[27] It was a wonderful exercise in rationalisation.

The American lecture circuit presented a similarly depressing picture. No first-class American university such as Harvard or

23  Priestley to Peter Davison, 29 June 1966.
24  Priestley to Peter Davison, 10 October 1966.
25  Priestley to Peter Davison, 22 October 1966.
26  Priestley to Peter Davison, 5 April 1967.
27  Priestley to Peter Davison, 6 February 1967.

Princeton had ever asked him to deliver a single lecture. Apparently unaware that it constituted no argument, he claimed that he was 'more experienced' than most of the writers they did invite.[28]

Peter Davison brought up the question of publicity appearances on television and radio in September 1968 and Priestley described a whole week of intensive interviewing for one book which failed to sell a single copy. His reward was blood, sweat and tears he said, whereas a single filmed interview for BBC television brought him a fee of £275.[29]

In the same month he received another depressing piece of American news. The advance sales of *Lost Empires* totalled 14,505, and three months later these had increased to 17,046, but after eighteen months, taking 'returns' into account, the figure fell to 11,770.[30]

Meanwhile the first volume of *The Image Men*, entitled *Out of Town*, was due for publication in February and the second volume, already nearing completion, would be published in the late autumn under the title *London End*. All three books had involved a constant drain on his dwindling energy and were only completed by refusing offers of journalism and television. 'This is probably the last time I shall work at this pace.'[31]

A rolling monster of a novel – 300,000 words – the longest he ever wrote, *The Image Men* quickly took the place of *Bright Day* as his favourite novel. Summarising 300,000 words in a few paragraphs must violate its contents. Put at its simplest *The Image Men* tells the story of rangy, ambitious Cosmo Saltana, and Dr Owen Tuby, a fat Welshman who has a power over words and shares with Saltana a resourceful and magnetically persuasive personality. Despite their gifts they are both penniless in a shabby Bayswater Hotel soon to become the setting for their meeting with a rich widow called Mrs Elfreda Drake and their invention of 'Social Imagistics'. A cloud of talk and double whiskies gives birth to the Institute of Social Imagistics which is prepared to re-create the image of any person, product or institution.

First conceived as a sociological department in a state university, Saltana and Tuby manage to con the university into believing that

---

28  Priestley to Peter Davison, 14 November 1968.
29  Priestley to Peter Davison, 12 September 1968.
30  Priestley to Peter Davison, 20 September 1968.
31  Priestley to Angela Wyndham Lewis, 11 January 1968.

the institute has a serious scholarly purpose but in no time the lure of public relations takes them into the glittering world of Admass where richer prizes await the image projectors. Springing to fame with suspicious alacrity the institute mounts from one success to another, exploiting a degree of gullibility in its clients which would be hard to find in the real commercial world today. Conquests varying from love to lust are skilfully interlaced between an enormous *dramatis personae* of over 100 characters, and the outcome is never in doubt but few jocular rogues are more engaging than Saltana and Tuby.

A splendid send-up of sociological jargon occurs when Saltana addresses the vice-chancellor: 'Ignoring not only the complicating factors of Sex, Age, Class, Income but also group functional and dysfunctional aspects and without any consideration of Pattern Maintenance, Adaptation, Goal Attainment and Integration . . .'

There was a penetrating and perhaps reminiscent description of the life of a mistress: 'She seems to me exactly the kind of girl who had one of those long-tormenting messy affairs with a married man, one with several children and a haunting conscience, years of hasty notes, waiting at the telephone, uneasy nights after falsifying the register in the back bedrooms of country pubs, catching sight on the wall while undressing in the cold damp: "Thou God Seest Me".'

Comic love scenes in which terms of endearment interlock with technology and psycho-dynamics overwhelm beautiful breasts, are sometimes hilarious. However, the overpowering charm of Tuby and Saltana is exaggerated, the insistence that people over forty can experience wild sexuality a cliché, and no amount of conceited cross-chat between Tuby and Saltana quite elevates their conversation to the philosophic levels which Priestley clearly intends. The novel remains one long romp capable of simple enjoyment in chapters where unnecessary diversions do not clog the narrative.

The final section as the two old comrades split up and deliberately provide the leaders of the Labour and Conservative parties with almost identical images, drives home the idiocies of public – if not human – relations.

Priestley described how he enjoyed writing the novel to Susan Cooper: '"*Image Men* – well, that just flowed out. I loved those two characters, Tuby and Saltana; I'd gone on for three hundred thousand words and yet it was a wrench to leave them. I could have written a novel of two million words about those two. But I had to say goodbye to them, and I've been a little sadder since . . ." He grinned, like an oversized imp, and rubbed his hands.'[32]

There was a much more personal reason for his pleasure which he did not disclose. Saltana was Priestley, the Falstaffian professor, fulfilling a role which might once have been his and rollicking through a long-drawn-out send-up of academic gullibility. Split into two volumes, *Out of Town* and *London End*, partly because of bifurcation *The Image Men* was not a success.

The *Times Literary Supplement* treated it severely:

> The novel falls far below Priestley's usual standards and it would be patronising to pretend otherwise . . . The story-telling is extremely weak and disbelief never suspended . . . Cut to a third of the length these two novels would have made a lively little comic novel.[33]

Priestley wrote to Diana Collins about *The Image Men*:

> Delighted you are enjoying the novel so much . . . What I ought to have said the other night is this: my work fails to appeal on the one hand because I am not a popular or fashionable personality; on the other hand because it is either dismissed or completely ignored by the English Literature lecturers and the like quite shockingly in fact, so that students won't be encouraged to buy or read me. For example Angus Wilson and Iris Murdoch will be solemnly considered, lectured upon, recommended by academics who will be completely silent about me.[34]

The letter enlarged on the difficulties which would arise for his wife and children if his books no longer continued to sell and adimtted that there might be hurt vanity concealed behind his complaints. Many people still read him but they were not those opinion-makers who could be widely influential. Was it because he had been denounced – 'with monstrous unfairness' as he put it – or that he had lived to preserve a 'certain professional dignity and integrity'?

His correspondence with Mary and with Angela Wyndham Lewis continued throughout the years 1967–9. By April of 1968 he was describing a trip to Israel:

> Darling Mary,
> . . . I suppose we saw most of Israel in one way and another, though of course without the newly acquired territories it is only

32  *J. B. Priestley*, Susan Cooper, 211.
33  *Times Literary Supplement*, 22 February 1968.
34  Priestley to Diana Collins, 16 February 1968.

about the size of Wales. We stayed for some days first at Tiberias on the Sea of Galilee, then we went down to Bathsheba and looked at the desert and Masada . . . and from the point of view of painting this was the best part of the whole trip . . . I was disappointed in Jerusalem and would not want to visit it again.

Mary's ex-husband's case against her to recover custody of the children had by now failed, and Priestley commented: 'I am glad . . . that Sig has lost . . . though I doubt if you will get very much out of him. I am out of touch with Tom and must remedy this . . . I have no plans except to stay here and work hard.'[35] Tom Priestley had now become a distinguished film editor. Priestley's letters to Mary always began 'Darling Mary' and ended with 'much love' continuing to show throughout concern for her welfare.

In August of 1968 he complained that he heard little and saw less of the other members of the family because, as a passionately nomadic race, they were always travelling. He never liked August except when a new play produced rehearsals and mounting excitement interspersed with depression until the September openings. He had undertaken to write a social history of the Regency for Heinemann and spoke of the agonies it cost him despite the collaboration of research workers. Disingenuously he claimed that he had never worried about money until now, with 'income tax, surtax, SET insurances, and the price of everything going up and up'. It was all quite daunting.

In the same month he became concerned about the activities of his grandson John who bore the name of Priestley. As we have seen, Mary was originally registered under the name Mary Wyndham Lewis but she wanted to change her name by deed poll to Priestley. Priestley now wrote:

Reading about John working in an hotel reminded me of something I wanted to say to you earlier: these boys bear my name and are my grandsons and there is always a chance that some journalist may get hold of them so I do want them to be *very* careful how they behave and what they say. Journalists in search of a juicy 'story' can be unscrupulous and as I frequently refuse to give interviews they might like to get back at me.

Anticipating one of the most successful science fiction films of recent years, the ever-resourceful Priestley concluded that he was

35  Priestley to Mary Priestley, April 1968.

445

trying to finish a book called *Snoggle* intended for adults as well as older children. It concerned a lovable creature out of a spaceship who became a kind of pet from another planet which three teenagers and their grandfather were forced to hide.[36] Very much aware of the danger of stolen ideas, he said all this information was highly confidential.

By September of the same year a letter to Angela Wyndham Lewis thanked her for a birthday telegram and said that he had abandoned the idea of a family birthday party since everyone seemed to be away. A forty-five minute *Omnibus* interview with Robert Robinson was being transmitted on the 22nd followed by a play he had written for BBC Television's Wednesday 'slot'. The letter seemed anxious to build up the impression of a fountain of activities. Irene Worth was to appear in one of his short-story melodramas and Ralph Richardson might do a 'repertory season of two or three historic pieces of Priestliana', but knowing the capricious nature of the theatre world he preferred to consider the possibility 'vague'. 'I'm not counting on it.' In fact he did not count on anything any more. 'I believe in what the Chinese call Wu Wei, just being passive and letting things happen, not pushing anything.'[37]

As we have seen, Priestley was still in touch with Jane and now he wrote a contentious letter about the children which made a poor case in his own defence.[38] Combining his shareholdings with a life insurance policy he had bought a relatively handsome annuity – a guaranteed income for the rest of his life. Because he lived so long it became a good investment, the annuity mounting as the capital increased. The annuity was never great but the capital became really substantial and valuable to Jacquetta on his death.

Dear Jane,

Thank you for your letter of the 19th. I would have replied before but I had to go to Frankfurt, for the Book Fair, where I had to speak at a banquet.

The Trust, which would acquire all my copyrights up to the end of 1965, is urgently necessary now because of death duties. If the Estate Office put a high value on these copyrights – as they very well might – then the death duties would be so high that my estate might be 'frozen' for some years until the duties were paid. And as my

36 Priestley to Mary Priestley, 20 August 1968.
37 Priestley to Angela Wyndham Lewis, 13 September 1968.
38 Priestley to Jane Bannerman, 23 September 1968.

children are the chief beneficiaries of my copyrights, then it is they who would suffer. And as I eat, drink, smoke and work too much, I don't see myself living many more years: I am, I suspect, the 'sudden death' type. Therefore, if you agree with this scheme, I hope you and your solicitors will try not to hold it up.

When you say the children have received no other help, apart from yours, you are mistaken. Mary, with Tom in charge of the fund, has received several thousand pounds from me. I helped Rachel, giving her first all the dollar currency I had, on her trips with poor little Lucy, and when she told me she was going by train to Spain, I insisted upon paying her air fare. I have not helped the others because they don't need it, but each Christmas costs me several hundred pounds, and I do what I can with concerts, dinners, books, various other treats. All this comes out of the only savings I now possess, based on non-taxed money on the purchase by the University of Texas of manuscripts etc. [1968]. All my shares went on the purchase of an annuity, which I combined with a life insurance, a scheme I regret now because the values of shares go up and up and the value of money goes down and down. Moreover, Jenkins's new legislation, increasing the area of death duties, affects me badly. Labour still think they are 'soaking the rich', whereas the really rich always escape and it is self-employed successful professional men like me who really take a hiding.

But I have not the least wish to be driven to the Channel Isles, Malta, Switzerland, the Bahamas. If the taxman can decide where you live, then that is his final victory. But we writers do take a terrible caning now: we are allowed no entertaining expenses; we cannot regard, in spite of our frequent protests, any of our copyrights as capital assets; we are not supposed to spread our earnings to avoid appalling surtax; and so on and so forth. Our summer has been as bad as yours seems to have been good . . .[39]

As for the children he had of course given them expensive boarding-school educations and paid Mary's fees at the privately run and expensive St Andrew's Hospital in Northamptonshire.

A letter to Angela followed in December discussing her father Bevan Wyndham Lewis's financial situation. Wyndham Lewis had recently completed a large and very successful book on Goya but he suddenly developed eye trouble which threatened his sight. Angela's mother, now Mrs Bannerman, enjoyed a relationship with her third husband no less successful than that between

39  Priestley gave his children £5,000 each – enough in those days to buy a house.

447

Jacquetta and Jack, and was no longer directly responsible for the welfare of her former husband Bevan Wyndham Lewis.[40] The psychosomatic nature of many of the illnesses which had bedevilled her over the years was clearly revealed one day when a doctor examined her and said that physically she was as sound as a bell.

Writing to Angela, Priestley explained that he had written to the secretary of the Royal Literary Fund giving him a brief account of Bevan Wyndham Lewis's case and asking for advice. He did not believe that there was any immediate problem about money because Bevan's wife had some income and he knew that Rainbird had paid Wyndham Lewis £2,000 for his Goya book. A postscript said that Angela's mother was well off, though she pretended not to be, and she might well have given a thought to poor Bevan.

Priestley wrote again to Mary:

> To give Miss Pudduck and Gertrude a needed break so they could go home we spent a few days covering a weekend in London dining with Marghanita Laski, her husband and Diana and John Collins, whom we hadn't seen for some time and Ba, who wanted me to meet [her husband's] new boss . . .
> Here the central heating is not working properly and I have just returned from the downstairs lav, shivering as if I'd been sitting with a bare bum in Greenland. I've just had a cheerful postcard from Tom who has now returned to California as you probably know after cutting miles of Vanessa's Isadora.[41]

All the money he earned, Priestley wrote, was being eaten away by taxes and maintenance of Kissing Tree House, 'the latest being dry rot in the billiard room cum office'.

In the following spring Jack and Jacquetta spent a brief holiday in Marghanita Laski's Corbières house, where she found him very sympathetic but quite capable of telling her that she was stupid if she disagreed with his commitment to – say – Dunne–Ouspensky thinking. She described him as an intuitive man, delighting in naughtiness, capable of performing simple conjuring tricks and a clever entertainer but in the world of the theatre there remained the disappointment that he was never asked to join the administration at Stratford.[42]

So deep was Priestley's commitment to Dunne, Ouspensky and

40  Priestley to Angela Wyndham Lewis, 8 December 1968.
41  Priestley to Mary Priestley, February 1969.
42  Interview with Marghanita Laski, 1 October 1986.

Gurdjieff that Marghanita Laski thought it became a substitute for religion. Certainly all three writers offered a form of semi-spirituality and even immortality which enabled the non-Christian to find reassurance in its terminology without the need for a deity or the acceptance of religious doctrine. Ouspensky's series of repetitive lives also opened up the possibility of a moral universe in which good behaviour would be measured by some unspecified means and rewarded, if the exact nature of the reward remained vague. Parallels with Christian religion were everywhere without abandoning secular terms, and the need to concentrate upon improving the individual's moral, emotional and intellectual sensibilities satisfied the demand for self-improvement. Reason, science, technology and above all religion no longer offered strategies for coping with life which could satisfy sceptical modern man but a semi-mystical creed made respectable by a semi-scientific appeal to mathematics found many disciples, among them Priestley. In the final analysis all this cohered into a philosophy of life for Priestley rather than a religion.

In 1968 when *The Image Men* appeared he was working hard on another book, *The Prince of Pleasure and his Regency*, with research collaborators, and told Mary that she would receive 'a copy of [a] large and handsome book' in the following summer. The Regency book brought a related commission for *The Edwardians* and now his troubles with research workers reached a peak. 'Unfortunately I had to sack [Miss X], a friend of Angela's as she really could not pick up the knack of the job.'[43] Both books were relatively lesser works but they revealed once more Priestley's versatility, giving accounts of the period which combined simple exposition, a high degree of accuracy and vivid evocation. Once again in the role of popular historian he proved very effective although the pressures of his by now formidable personality could not be excluded from either book. Evidence tended to be mediated through his own values which unkind critics sometimes claimed were prejudices.

Writing to Peter Davison in April 1969 he said he was a kind of Edwardian himself since he placed the period between 1901 and 1914 and, as no one any longer took him seriously as a commentator on contemporary affairs, he enjoyed retrospective history.[44] In July of the same year he learnt from Peter Davison that expectations of selling 15,000–20,000 copies of *The Image Men* had collapsed and

43 Priestley to Mary Priestley, February 1969.
44 Priestley to Peter Davison, 1 April 1969.

only 9,641 copies had been sold.[45] Accustomed by now to the decline in the sales of his fiction, his mood of depression quickly passed.

By 1969 everything was building towards the great event of his seventy-fifth birthday and he wrote to both Angela and Mary, sending £35 cheques expressly intended to buy dresses for the Savoy party already arranged for 15 September.[46] Another £150 from The Good Companions Trust also went to Mary. Giving her advice about her children he said: 'There is of course always a pulling away from the parents at their ages. They have to be given time. You may remember that Tom never looked like doing anything very much until he found what he wanted – films and then went straight ahead.'[47] This was a little disingenuous because one member of the family – not Tom himself – claimed that Priestley's belief in people standing on their own feet prevented him from introducing his son to influential people who could have helped him because that would smack of nepotism.[48]

45  Priestley to Peter Davison, 2 July 1969.
46  Priestley to Mary Priestley and Angela Wyndham Lewis, 7 June 1969.
47  Priestley to Mary Priestley, 3 August 1969.
48  Witness who wishes to remain anonymous.

# 33

## *Over the Long High Wall*
### 1969–73

There gathered in the rococo splendour of the Savoy Hotel on 13 September 1969 a glittering assembly of people to celebrate Priestley's seventy-fifth birthday. They converged from all over the world and among them were so many household names that their recital might be considered pretentious. For fifty years Priestley had remained a star on Heinemann's list and now they spent lavishly under the direction of his old friend Charles Pick to make this a great occasion. Susan Cooper has described the scene:

> It was like a gigantic family party, and on all hands people who had never met before in their lives found themselves, with no astonishment, talking energetically away to one another with the casual assurance of those who have been close friends for years. Through Priestley, they all spoke a common language; he, and his writing, had played a part in all their lives.[1]

Canon Collins, Sir Kenneth Clark, Iris Murdoch, Norman Collins and Robert Robinson all in their individual styles paid tribute to Priestley, the man and his work. Robert Robinson echoed the common sentiments in an uneven speech.

Pausing to glance across at the stocky figure with its plum-coloured velvet jacket and air of resignation Robinson told the following story:

> I remember going out to dinner with Priestley and . . . the waiter asked him: have you a reservation? And I remember thinking in a moment, as the mundaneness of the situation seemed just for a second to be transcended, that – No, he has no reservation. But in the roll-call of Time he will turn out to have something rather better: he will turn out to have been among the founders of the feast.[2]

1   *J. B. Priestley*, Susan Cooper, 235.
2   ibid., 236.

Robert Robinson had compiled a long colourful programme celebrating in television a life so full of friends and events it seemed on the small screen grossly overcrowded. Jack and Jacquetta watched it in Canon Collins's house in the shadow of St Paul's, which Priestley had immortalised as a symbol of Britain's survival in his wartime postscript. There were anecdotes, recollections, readings from his books as everything mounted to the carefully designed climax: a shortened version of the last act of *Johnson Over Jordan*. According to Susan Cooper: 'Again there was an awkwardness, for this more than any of his plays translates badly to the medium of television, needing the depths of a craftily lit stage to suggest the immensities of spaceless time.'

It was of course Ralph Richardson who transcended the limitations of television to give a brilliant and moving performance. 'Time had made one of those curious spiralling turns, for Richardson had grown older to meet the play, and fitted easily now into the role for which he had once had to draw in an extra couple of decades on his face.'[3]

Bowler-hatted, carrying briefcase and umbrella, once again Richardson turned to walk slowly into all-engulfing infinity and the now famous words came from his lips with just the right halting flow:

The Figure: Robert Johnson, it is time now . . .
Johnson:     Is it – a long way?
The Figure: I don't know . . .
Johnson:     No – well – goodbye.

Many in the watching group were moved. Susan Cooper turned to glance across at Priestley: 'I don't know what I expected him to offer us: a non-committal snort, perhaps; a rumble of technical criticism; at the most, a bit of knowledgeable praise for Richardson. But Priestley sat silent for a moment, gazing into space, looking unusually small in a very large armchair; and then he rubbed his eyes. "I shed tears," he said, rather gruff and low, "not for what I have seen, but for what I have been remembering." Then he hoisted himself up; and was his proper height again.'[4]

Anne Chisholm interviewed Priestley in the *Radio Times* and described him as a big, rumpled man with a face which resembled 'a

3   ibid., 237.
4   ibid.

glowering pudding'.[5] His manner was gruff and in repose he seemed truculent but suddenly he tried a joke on his listener and getting the right response 'grinned with pleasure'. Behind the gruff manner a self-mocking streak frequently intervened and with it a 'certain aura of melancholy'. He was growing old, he said, and his efforts to adapt to modern technology were constantly frustrated. All his attempts to use a silent typewriter were useless because it was like typing on a steak and kidney pudding. As a youngster he had been told to shut up because he was young and now the same admonition came his way because he was old. One good thing emerged from the multiple erosions of age: 'You don't give a damn what impression you make.'[6]

One big regret ran through the celebrations. He expressed it in a letter to Diana Collins:[7]

> It is a fact that apart from a wire from Tony Greenwood and his wife nobody in the Government or the official Establishment generally has thought fit to offer me a single word of congratulation.

Meanwhile Mary rebuked him for not keeping in touch with her and he replied saying that when she understood the circumstances which surrounded his momentary neglect of her, she would probably agree that her criticism was misplaced. After the long slog of finishing *The Edwardians* he was about to relax when all the pre-birthday brouhaha rose up to overwhelm him and he plunged into recordings, interviews, photographs, parties, correspondence – 'day after day of it'. When he finally came back from London he expected to take a complete rest – but no, there was a mass of cables, telegrams, letters, messages to answer and he spent days writing or dictating thank-you letters. Hence his – temporary – lapse.[8]

Within a few weeks the celebrations were marred by what seemed a deliberately delivered snub from the council of his own city, Bradford. Priestley's name was one among several put forward to the informal subcommittee which accorded 'freedoms' and of its eight members only one voted in favour of Priestley. Two new freemen were appointed at the meeting – Henry Hamilton Stewart, a neurologist and J. H. Shaw, a businessman – with no representation of the arts or letters. Philistinism could go no

---

5 Interview, *Radio Times*, 11 September 1969.
6 ibid.
7 Priestley to Diana Collins, 20 September 1969.
8 Priestley to Mary Priestley, 3 November 1969.

further. Asked by *The Times* to comment, Priestley said, 'I don't think that if it had been offered I would have accepted. I have refused other things in the past you know.'[9] This was a reference to the offer of a peerage and the C. H. – twice – which he declined on both occasions convinced that Lord Priestley would ill become a socialist with roots reaching far back into the past.

A brief holiday in central Wales with Jacquetta followed and he wrote to Mary:

> The holiday in Wales was pretty good. Apart from morning mist the weather was dry and fine and I did a good deal of painting. . . . I don't want to start another book just yet. Ever since I was told at my birthday how young I looked and what a fine fellow I was I have felt aged, decrepit and rather miserable.

Early in 1970 he commented to Mary:

> I keep reading what a marvel for his age Harold Macmillan is and then I remember I am the same age but nobody tells me what a marvel I am.[10]

The correspondence with Mary continued to flow over the years revealing states of mind and writing activities, and never failing to reassure his daughter that whatever happened she had his support. His son Tom emerges as the unflagging Good Samaritan who as a trustee of The Good Companions Fund kept a watchful eye on what was happening. Letter after letter dispensed advice to Mary, the would-be writer who eventually had considerable success. In the end she found a new *modus vivendi* when she became a fully trained musical therapist and published three books.[11]

In March of 1970 Jacquetta and Jack were entertaining Peter Davison and his wife Jane, a sad occasion because Edward Davison, Jack's oldest friend, had died a few weeks before in America. 'There were four of us, all beginning to write, who were great friends at Cambridge – 1919–22. Frank Kendon, Gerald Bullett, Teddie Davison and now I am the only one left.'

Almost simultaneously a small but perceptive book of eighty-seven pages on Chekhov was published by the International Text-book Company. Priestley wrote the book at great speed and began

---

9  ibid.
10  Priestley to Mary Priestley, 12 February 1970.
11  *Going Abroad, Music Therapy in Action* and *Analytische Musiktherapie.*

by exploding the myth that writers, by reason of their profession, were nice people. Chekhov was a rare exeption. Priestley saw him as the model for a new kind of man who successfully reconciled literary sensibility, scientific knowledge and a commitment to practical work which remained uncontaminated by ideological passion. Alas, the mould, he said, 'was broken before our blind mad century was five years old . . . There has only been one Anton Chekhov.'

By June he was 'working pretty hard trying to finish the introductory chapter – probably the most difficult – of my 1850s book which I now call *Victoria's Heyday*. All this stuff involves an enormous amount of reading with my desk and study cluttered up with books. Even so I'm glad to be doing it.'[12]

*When We Are Married* was to undergo one of its almost perennial revivals at the Guildford Repertory Theatre in 1970 and Priestley sat for hours at the end of a telephone suggesting possible actors and actresses.

The revival of *When We Are Married* exemplified a streak in Priestley's business integrity rare amongst playwrights, many of whom – quite rightly – were forced into opportunism. Having committed himself to a company called Duncan C. Weldon Productions with the play going on tour first from Guildford, he received persistent approaches from Laurence Olivier who was very anxious to produce the play at the National Theatre. Priestley said no to Olivier, refusing to go back on his word, and as if to reconcile himself he commented: 'I think we shall get a very good cast for *When We Are Married*, better in fact than the National Theatre (who wanted to do it) could offer me.' He added: 'I can enjoy an occasional return to the Theatre, I think, though I would hate to be mixed up in it all the time – too fussy and demanding for an old codger.'[13]

In the same month he received an honorary doctorate from Bradford University. 'We had quite a pleasant time – quite good food for once – and I got tremendous applause from the assembled graduates and parents, and then to my astonishment appeared briefly in the BBC television news that night.'[14]

His astonishment was revealing. Did he no longer expect the media to be interested in J. B. Priestley or the honours which were,

12  Priestley to Mary Priestley, 18 June 1970.
13  Priestley to Mary Priestley, 5 July 1970.
14  Priestley to Mary Priestley, 13 July 1970.

as he put it, 'coming thick and fast'? He was now MA, Litt.D, LL.D and an Honorary Fellow of Trinity Hall.

*When We Are Married* played to capacity the whole of the three-week run at Guildford and proceeded to Hull and Bournemouth with a transfer to the West End a constant possibility. Tempted to follow the play round, Priestley was dissuaded by age and 'a really stinking cold' which put him to bed for several days. Jacquetta as always nursed him devotedly and promptly caught the cold. Matters were not improved by an attempt to turn from heavy to light oil for their central heating system. 'A series of daft disasters, due to the sheer clownishness of so many workmen, left hundreds of gallons of oil floating around in the engine, for days. No hot water nor central heating and the whole house smelling like a ship's engine room. About six different firms have been involved in this mess and not one of them will get one penny from me. And as Jacquetta and I are so involved with our respective books that we cancelled a holiday we hoped to take in the West of Ireland, at the end of September, you can imagine our disgust – what with colds, oil and all.'[15]

Friction arose with his daughter Mary by January of the following year.

Two letters arrived one morning from Mary which he classified as No. 1 General, and No. 2 Angry. Exercising his considerable powers of controlling immediate reactions he read, he said, No. 1 with interest and No. 2 without himself getting angry. Admitting that in some senses he might have been a negligent father he explained that he dreaded interfering too much with his children and above all did not want to make them fit into some mould or pattern of his own devising. He was very aware that the children of well-known fathers experienced special difficulties and he did not want to aggravate them. This was his second letter as a contrite father.[16]

All the agonies of the past with Jane had long disappeared and he was now on friendly if sometimes bickering terms with her. By June of 1971 Priestley insisted on some resolution of his long-drawn-out financial tangles with her and wrote a letter which at first had no result:

Dear Jane,
. . . I must tell you frankly that I expect my income to go down

15 Priestley to Mary Priestley, October 1970.
16 Priestley to Mary Priestley, 6 January 1971.

rapidly in the near future. I had hoped to make some return to the theatre but I doubt now if this will be possible on any lucrative scale. I have done the last of the three social histories I arranged to do – and these are rewarding financially – and do not see myself doing any more. Money from plays and books abroad is dwindling rapidly. And of course the cost of living is shooting up and will be worse still if we go into the Common Market where we shall be subsidising inefficient French peasants. Surtax has been so brutal that at the end of every year lately I have been borrowing from my publishers to carry on and I can no longer do this if I have no really promising book on hand. Now the arrangements for your 20 per cent allowance on earned income worked well enough when (a) I earned a large income and (b) taxation was so high. It was better you should have the allowance than that the Inland Revenue should sweep it away. But if my income drops – as it certainly will – and direct taxation is lower (but inevitably with a great deal of indirect taxation) the solution is very different indeed and I want you to give this some serious consideration.

In the event Jane did, as a result of which she agreed to take 20 per cent of his income *after* he had deducted his expenses instead of before, a refined concession which was only significant because his income remained relatively high.[17]

In the spring he was working on another book, *The Carfitt Crisis*, rewriting another play begun years before and collaborating on a semi-autobiographical documentary. This was to be a 'presentation' by Leslie Sands with his wife and two younger players who would 'perform' extracts from Priestley's novels, plays and essays. In the background scrappy notes began to accumulate for a very personal book eventually published under the title *Over the Long High Wall*.

Another birthday – his seventy-seventh – loomed in August 1971. 'On Monday, 13th September (with luck) I celebrate my 77th birthday, so we are giving an evening party in Albany (starting at 9 and delicious buffet supper) for family (but adults only this time) and some of our friends.'[18]

Still vaguely Jungian he recorded an example of synchronicity when Jacquetta took an enormous coloured lithograph of a grass-hopper by Graham Sutherland which she hung on her bedroom wall only to find a moment later the living equivalent in her bed.

17  Priestley to Jane Bannerman, 28 June 1971.
18  Priestley to Mary Priestley, 19 August 1971.

'Never before had a grasshopper been in her bed, in her room, even in the house. Indeed I've never seen one even in the garden.'[19]

By March of 1972 a series of domestic upheavals sent a minor ripple through what had become the Indian summer of their marriage. Gertrude, the maid, now sixty-four, felt that she ought to go home 'and live with her folks', the rent of the two Albany flats, £2,400 a year, had become 'murderous' and they were forced to give up B4 and move exclusively into B3. Above all Priestley complained that money was steadily becoming 'tighter'.

He was, he said, trying to keep out of London because fares were so high and any break of more than a few hours interfered with work on his new book – *The English* – which had become 'difficult'.

An enforced break intervened when the Poles invited him to give some lectures in Warsaw and he spoke to them of liberty, equality, paternity. Peter Lloyd, then British Council representative in Warsaw, recalled the occasion. In his lectures Priestley said that he was 'against equality because we are all different, disliked fraternity when enforced because it led into difficulties, which left only liberty, and he was all for liberty'. This raised a cheer from his Polish audience, Peter Lloyd said, 'which was very much in the mood for liberation. Afterwards, I invited him to a folklore festival.' Asked to explain the nature of the folklore, Peter Lloyd said that it meant stylised dances in national costumes. 'I don't think that's for me,' Priestley said. At the farewell luncheon given by the British Ambassador, John Fretwell, Priestley looked 'very pale and haggard'.[20]

Two stories illustrated the theatrical braggart in 1972. Priestley was on the committee which awarded Michael Meyer the Whitbread prize for his brilliant three-volume biography of Henrik Ibsen. Introduced to Meyer after the award Priestley said, 'I did more for the theatre than Ibsen.' Those who knew him well believed that it was meant to be theatrically shocking but Meyer felt he believed it.

In the Savile Club later the same year Priestley again discovered Monty Mackenzie filling in the pools and asked him why he persisted in such an exhausting and foolhardy task. 'I might win £50,000,' Mackenzie said. 'Ah've got £50,000,' Priestley replied. 'Supposing it was £100,000,' Monty persisted. 'Ah've got £100,000.' The sum steadily mounted with Priestley constantly

19  Priestley to Mary Priestley, 5 December 1971.
20  Interview with Peter Lloyd, 4 January 1972.

claiming possession of its equivalent until it reached half a million. Priestley once more repeated his claim, to be met by a swift request, 'Could you lend me a trifling £1,000?' 'Ah need notice of that question,' Priestley said. Throughout he was joking.

Late in August, suddenly, out of the blue, he 'became the victim' of prolapsed strangulated haemorrhoids which were very painful and forced him to retire to bed for several weeks. By the end of the same month he developed a cold which complicated his recovery. 'Hope to see you,' he wrote to Mary, 'when I am fit to be seen . . . I want you to do something for me.' *The World of J. B. Priestley* led by the actor Leslie Sands had toured the north of England with 'very good press notices' but business so far had been 'terrible'. It was opening at the Theatre Royal, Windsor for three weeks and Priestley asked Mary for her support 'not only by going yourself (get a lift from somebody) but by pressing other people to go'.[21]

*Over the Long High Wall* was about to appear but he didn't care what the reviewers said because he no longer even looked at reviews. He described *Over the Long High Wall* as an 'impatient book written by an impatient old man'. It examined the possibilities of immortality, ESP, reincarnation and all those supernatural areas of human experience which imply a dimension beyond the physical. Under the guise of objective investigation it was Priestley, now seventy-eight years old, exploring his own reactions to the approach of death. Distancing his emotional responses in philosophic reflection he could not conceal a need to believe that there was something beyond.

'What happens after death?' he asked, and answered, 'I don't know. Neither do you . . . I . . . feel I can be allowed to do some guessing. Nor I believe will it be altogether wild guessing because I already have some bits of evidence.'[22]

Priestley belonged to the school predisposed to accept the evidence of people like J. B. Rhine, Maurice Nicoll, Jung, and Dunne, whose justifications for spiritual survival were implicit in telepathy, many-dimensioned time, and psychokinesis. These were not theologians pleading the cause of Christian immortality but highly intelligent men using quite different methods to test other forms of survival. Hard scientists regarded their activities with scepticism and saw their work as an attempt to reassure themselves about a future life. Priestley wore the mantle of the

21  Priestley to Mary Priestley, 10 November 1972.
22  *Over the Long High Wall*, J. B. Priestley, 115.

enquiring but highly intelligent layman sifting the evidence with a self-generated hope of finding reassuring answers. Sometimes his statements had no hard core of logic; sometimes he retreated into semi-mystical language. There remained a sense that if anyone qualified for the hereafter by reason of the rich life he had led, the sheer power of his personality and the efforts he had made to 'improve' that personality, that man was Priestley. Verification of many of his statements remained impossible. For instance, 'consciousness survives the death of body and brain because while they inform it they don't own it'. The conviction with which he announced such beliefs carried a highly personal authenticity. Aware of certain limitations in his logic he spelt out the point: 'We can put it another way and declare that part of the self or psyche is able to escape from the limitations temporal and spatial to which body and brain are strictly subject.'[23]

Like all such statements it begged the question: what part of the self or psyche? And immediately the interlocutor was into the classic recessive argument of self-multiplying questions with no end in sight. Priestley did not believe in a soul. He forswore any prolongation of *bodily* life in the beyond and sensibly assumed that whatever undefined 'presence' had survival potential was not subject to the laws of time and space. 'This does not mean, as no doubt many people still believe, that we are launched into immortality. I for one make no such claim; it is far too large and grand for me or anybody I know.'

None the less a few pages later he does commit himself to a form of Dunnian immortality: 'If, as I believe, consciousness survives the death of the body and brain to exist in the remaining Time orders of Time . . .'

Priestley was very frank. Why, he asked, have some of the finest brains conceived on this earth – Plato, Aristotle, Shakespeare, Bacon – passed over into the void without sending back a single signal or enlightening us about the nature of the beyond? Without entirely dismissing spiritualism he chided its practitioners with similar failings.

He once remarked: 'It's not death I'm afraid of, it's doctors.' Enlarging this view he now said: 'It's the way one dies which can be hell. Death holds no torments. But for God's sake choose a decent way to die.'[24]

23   ibid., 121.
24   Talk with Vincent Brome, September 1981.

Death coming closer every year did not dismay Priestley and he ended his book on a note of qualified optimism. Referring to the Wall – a symbol of division between life and death – he wrote: 'I hope some readers will climb up and at least try a peep over it. I hope even more fervently that at least a few readers with me all the way will go in search of a far wider view and a sunlit horizon – simply by walking through the wall.'[25]

Priestley was a life-enhancing man who had run the whole gamut of experience. He saw now that time was running out and he faced the prospect of leaving life with the greatest reluctance, but the luck was on his side. There were many more years to come.

Early in November he at last went into the private block of Warneford Hospital, Leamington Spa for the recommended operation. 'It is not a major operation, though I cannot pretend I am looking forward to it.'[26]

Any reader familiar with the pain, discomfort and indignity of an operation for piles will appreciate the euphemism 'not a major operation'.

Discharging himself from hospital, Priestley was home again by 20 November but unable to sit up at a typewriter. Determined not to become a 'fat, lazy old codger', 'a demanding and unproductive 200 lb parasite', he discussed with Jacquetta the possibility of a trip to New Zealand. 'Being the kind of bragging male bully who can suddenly look innocent, helpless, appealing, I was fussed over and implored to take it easy.' Still not his old self there was the danger of cracking up in mid-journey and the certainty of feeling 'seedy' some of the time. Displaying considerable bravura Priestley brushed aside all hazards and set out on a 26,000-mile journey carefully avoiding doctors, treatments and tonics, supported when he felt downright ill by the indomitable Jacquetta. She herself was now sixty-two but possessed of 'survival instincts', a rugged constitution and an adaptive capacity to new and strange cultures unmatched in Priestley's experience. She also remained a striking and beautiful woman whose regal presence sometimes solved problems by reason of sheer personality. For a sick man Priestley survived the 13,000 miles with comparative equanimity and the visit began well when they met 'a broad-shouldered, enthusiastic chap about 40 who introduced himself as Derek Morris from the Ministry of Foreign Affairs'. Priestley commented: 'I was pleased

25  *Over the Long High Wall*, J. B. Priestley, 142.
26  Priestley to Mary Priestley, 10 November 1972.

to observe that he was quite unlike anybody I have ever met from our own Foreign Office which banished enthusiasm about the time of Lord Palmerston.'[27] The otherwise infallible Mr Morris had booked their room in an hotel undergoing reconstruction and there was hammering all day 'as if [we] had moved into a gigantic blacksmith's'.

Within no time they were on the road heading towards Wellington and one beautiful landscape after another culminated in a view from high above Lake Taupo which was in Priestley's two words 'a wonder'. 'The lake was calm, still and seemed to cover everything with a delicate blue haze . . . Not a sound reached us . . . This was a lake out of another and better world. Romantic beauty had arrived at last.' Reluctantly they pushed on from Wellington with Jacquetta continuously protesting at the violation of the countryside by industry. Priestley sat dozing in one car after another, half aware of the entrancing scenery and reflecting on what he would say at the next TV interview or lecture. Exposure to the media on one occasion led to a report in a local newspaper which began: 'He came in slowly and hesitantly, a bit like a sleepy old bulldog, early disturbed. He was dressed informally – baggy, grey slacks, black carpet slippers, badly stained, unpressed jacket, stringy tie.'

Priestley had abandoned press cutting agencies forty years before, 'but a friend sent [him] the cutting and he commented: "Only the first three words [were] accurate."'

Overwhelmed by commitments he asked to escape on his own one day and visited Mount Possession to stay with an old sheep-farmer. There came a high moment of pantheist communication with the farmer and the land. The sheep-farmer complained that the young were overtaking him since he could no longer climb as fast as these youngsters. Priestley replied that he too was being overtaken by young writers and could not produce books as snappily alive as theirs. Thousands of feet up on the mountainside with cloud shadows chasing the brilliant sunshine they condoled with one another, and then fell silent, absorbed back into the beauty of the countryside and their shared sense of being overtaken by the young.[28]

The book he eventually wrote had elements of the pot-boiler since the trip had been arranged and sponsored by the New Zealand

27  *A Visit to New Zealand*, J. B. Priestley, 6.
28  Interview with Rupert Withers, 20 September 1985.

Government, but he did not pull his punches. 'There are dull people everywhere . . . and for my part I prefer amiable and cheerful dullards not uncommon in New Zealand, to aggressive, chip-on-the-shoulder types not uncommon in Australia . . . Possibly some visitors may react against a certain complacency carried like a badge by some middle-income New Zealanders.'[29] This offended Australians as much as New Zealanders.

His last paragraph drove home his general impression: 'Even if all goes wrong, if New Zealand turns into just another place with too many dull-eyed people, too much computerised technology and high-pressure advertising and salesmanship and not sufficient critical intelligence, too many pills and mental homes and too few life-enhancing values, I shall still remember with affection my visit, the people and scenes it brought me.'[30] One New Zealander commented: 'Limeys never learn.'[31]

Back in England August brought some good dramatic news. The National Theatre was to revive *Eden End*, a new musical of *The Good Companions* promised to replenish the coffers of The Good Companions Trust and *An Inspector Calls* had a successful launch at the Mermaid with a possible transfer to the West End. Despite all this he remained gloomy about his finances. By the end of the year what he described as 'appalling inflation' meant that he had spent every penny of his earnings and when the tax bill arrived he was forced to sell occasional pictures and dig into the last of his savings. Where he ought to be spending his last years in peace it was all fuss and worry 'even though Jacquetta was far from being a fusser and worrier' and did her splendid best.[32]

In September he recapitulated his belief that what happened after death 'probably depended on the particular person's breadth and depth, so to speak, of consciousness'. By October he was in danger of becoming a great-grandfather with Mary's son Peter expecting a child. 'It's just about right that I should soon be a great-grandfather because that's about what I feel like – ancient but not ill yet and still keeping some of my wits.'[33]

It was in 1973 that his penultimate book of any consequence, *The English*, appeared, a book full of contradictions about a race he had once seen in much simpler terms. Since the English vary from dour

29  *A Visit to New Zealand*, J. B. Priestley, 141.
30  ibid., 152.
31  Interview with John Burrows, 10 January 1986.
32  Priestley to Mary Priestley, 30 August 1973.
33  Priestley to Mary Priestley, 29 September 1973.

northerners and robust Yorkshiremen to genteel Home County residents and snobbish southerners, all subdivided by class, profession and sex, any generalisation becomes suspect but undismayed Priestley plunged into the first chapter.

> I suggest that in the English psyche the barrier between consciousness and the unconscious is not fixed, high and strong and indeed is not really complete so that the conscious and unconscious often merge as if they were two English counties, sharing irregular misty boundaries. We can put it another way . . . and declare that the English depend more upon instinct and intuition than other West Europeans do. They are not unreasonable but they are hardly ever rational and almost always they suspect the closed-in creatures of pure rationality: they prefer the open-ended. It is essentially English not to allow the intellect to go its own way and decide everything; it must submit to some shaping and colouring by the instinctive and the intuitive. All this does not make them better or worse than other Europeans but, as so many foreign observers have testified, it does make them different.[34]

If you are a sociologist or psychologist you will riddle this statement with inadequacies, but if you are a creative writer you will embrace it as a version of artistic truth and such a description would have delighted Priestley.

Audacity characterises every other page of *The English* with statements like: 'There are good reasons why Englishness creates a climate in which true humour can flower.' No less difficult to defend was the claim: 'The larger if hazy outlook of Englishness brings its humorists tolerance and a smiling acceptance of all manner of people.'[35]

In *Rain upon Godshill* he had been even more explicit. Because they were his own people, naturally he preferred them to all others, he said, but even within such an unexamined generalisation that included certain types he actively detested. The ordinary folk remained in his view the nicest in the world and no other race were 'more fundamentally decent and kind'.[36] It was a large claim and but for the fact that he had deeply encountered a multiplicity of peoples in scores of countries such sentiments would have smacked of Little England chauvinism but he had an array of evidence which

34  *The English*, J. B. Priestley, 12.
35  ibid., 176.
36  *Rain upon Godshill*, J. B. Priestley, 211–12.

he readily produced with the skill of an advocate convinced of his case.

Donald MacRae had the last word:

> If to me as a Scot Mr Priestley has been one of my great mentors about England it is because he is so aware of its diversity and pluralism, the range of its tones, the divisions of its life. No man can comprehend – far less communicate – the full detail of any modern or complex society. Who in our time has done more through his art in this way than Mr Priestley?[37]

In September 1973 a great reconciliation took place in Bradford. A running feud between Priestley and his home town had fluctuated over the years, hard-line Bradfordians identifying the cosmopolitan Londoner as a renegade from their culture. Not that he had neglected the city. Many a time he made a 'definitely last appearance' at one function or another which did not stop the selection committee denying him the freedom of the city. In 1964 he had ceremonially opened the new buildings of his old school of Belle Vue, and later was to propose a toast to the school. Now on 8 September 1973, as *The Times* put it, 'all was forgiven'. In a packed council chamber, with purple robes flashing, the mayor paid tribute to Priestley and an inscribed casket was presented. 'It'll be the last thing I'll pawn,' he commented amid bursts of high good humour. He was now at last a Freeman of the City of Bradford. 'I owe far more to this city than it owes me,' he commented. Moreover, with his plays revived enthusiastically in the West End of London and this new affinity with his home town he felt 'that time had come full circle . . . We people in the Industrial West Riding pretend to be grumpy and tough, but really we are easy and warm-hearted, perhaps a little soft.'[38] There followed the announcement that none other than David Hockney had been commissioned to make a drawing of Priestley which would hang in the city hall and be the first Hockney work the council had seen fit to buy. Priestley returned the gesture by presenting two of his paintings of the Yorkshire Dales and a set of specially bound copies of some of his works. As he went into the Lord Mayor's private banquet he winked at the *Times* reporter and blew a kiss to his family. The *Times* reporter said: 'I bet he gave them hell.'

37 *The World of J. B. Priestley*, ed. Donald MacRae, ch. VII.
38 *The Times*, 9 September 1973.

# 34

# The Last Years
## 1978–84

There were so many luncheons, dinners, interviews and reassessments on his eightieth birthday that the celebrations left him completely exhausted. A splendid buffet lunch at Albany for the family included several grandchildren and it continued far into the afternoon. Among the many toasts drunk one was in expectation of the day when he reached his ninetieth birthday and began yet another book.

The image which appeared on the television screen in a glittering show of recollection, revealed a deepening of all its characteristic features. The chin had disappeared in jowls, the bags under the eyes were heavy, the eyebrows bushing over the eyes and the whole sculptured mass no longer completely surrendered to the powerful line of the nose.

Yet another dinner provided by his publisher Heinemann at the Savoy brought together an array of literary and public figures. It did not run altogether smoothly. Sir Charles Snow in the chair had drunk too much, his speech was, in English understatement, ineffective, and he kept jumping up and down for one reason or another. Jack sat brooding over the scene acutely aware that some of the speeches had a fulsome ring which did not appeal to a man who had always disliked false praise. Moreover, a single phrase kept recurring in Snow's ramblings, a phrase which, according to Diana Collins, he rather fancied: "'Jack was a whisper of the conscience of England." We all sat there in an absolute agony of embarrassment and of course nobody could stop poor old Snow. Eventually he sat down, Jack got up and I don't think I ever admired him more. He thanked the speakers and then said, "And now, ladies and gentlemen, if you will accompany me after dinner I will walk on the water." Everyone relaxed and laughed.'[1]

Priestley professed to have no illusions himself about his standing in the public eye. He complained that the newspapers characteristi-

1 Diana Collins to the author, July 1986.

cally overlooked him when they listed people who had attended distinguished dinners. 'Invariably my name was missing.' He told the story of encountering one day in Fleet Street Richard Church who talked enthusiastically about a collection of famous broadcasts he had been asked to edit and reeled off a number of names which Jack received in total silence. 'I saw the colour drain out of his face suddenly. It had just occurred to him that he had forgotten me.'[2]

Coming away from another eightieth-birthday luncheon at the Wellcombe Hotel, Stratford, Jack Lambert drew a vivid picture of a fantastically youthful Priestley almost dancing from step to step, 'looking like something out of *The Good Companions*'. Mrs Lambert reaffirmed that picture. 'Jack had a great capacity for laughter and *joie de vivre*.'

The period surrounding his birthday saw the revival of several plays with *Dangerous Corner*, *Time and the Conways* and *I Have Been Here Before*, all receiving productions in various parts of the country.

His birthday was also a suitable occasion for a revival of a book which had clung to him all his life, earned over a million pounds, re-echoed in forty different languages and made his name a household word for reasons which he still found embarrassing. A new musical of *The Good Companions* with music by André Previn opened in Manchester and transferred to London early in July. 'Wish it success,' he wrote to his daughter, 'because The Good Companions Trust has a one per cent share in this ambitious enterprise.'[3] Relations between Angela, Mary and himself had momentarily turned sour. He wrote to Mary: 'I don't think you and Angela are in some way leprous, and I fancy there may be just a touch of guilt on your part here. You have both written rather rude things to me but in fact I didn't really mind and quite understood why you felt like letting off steam.' He offered to pay for seats at *The Good Companions* if they would book them but 'You will probably retort that it is my company and not free seats you would like . . . I can only reply that just now while I still have the strength to cope and – just remember I really am an old man – I have a hell of a lot to attend to and hate going to London.'[4]

The family of his daughter Sylvia spent Christmas 1974 with Jack and Jacquetta at Kissing Tree and he wrote: 'The only difficulty is

2 Interview with J. W. Lambert, 1 July 1986.
3 Priestley to Mary Priestley, 5 May 1974.
4 ibid.

that I am now a little deaf and they are all whisperers and mutterers so that half the time I didn't know what was being said.'[5]

By January he was mourning the imminent demise of *The Good Companions* musical which had run for six months. He now regretted that he had ever had his bowel operation, the discomfort of which made the New Year a dreary scene.[6]

Now at eighty he rose later, lingered over breakfast, dictated replies to selected letters and at certain times of the day still he sat down at his desk with cotton wool in his ears, tapping away with diminishing results. Frequently he turned over first one idea, then another, but the words no longer flowed on paper with ease. Always ready to share, discuss, analyse, Jacquetta remained a powerful presence in his life even when at night they retired to their separate beds, and she continued to give him the reassurance he occasionally needed.

Priestley's presence has overwhelmed Jacquetta's in this book but she had fulfilled a career no less distinguished in its different field than his, and for the last twenty-five years merged with him as a writer in her own right. Many classically written and thoughtful books had been torn from her typewriter, the Apollonian compliment to his highly subjective work. *A Land, Man on Earth, Man and the Sun*, the *UNESCO History of Mankind*, vol. I, part I, *The Dawn of the Gods, Providence Island, Fables* and above all, from the perspective of this biography, *A Quest of Love*. They were all books to be reckoned with.

From time to time, looking out on his beautiful garden at Kissing Tree Priestley reflected that the world about him had changed out of all recognition. Queen Victoria's all-embracing empire, into the heart of which he had been born, no longer existed. The class system once rigid enough to be equivalent to a caste system had become more mobile, sexual mores had ceased to be completely hypocritical and admitted quasi-libertarian attitudes, social security once non-existent underpinned the unemployed in a manner which would have been luxurious to their equivalent of the 1930s. Ordinary men and women who years before walked or bicycled to work now possessed motor-cars. The telephone, a sorcerer's accomplice in the late nineteenth century for the chosen few, reached into thousands of relatively humble homes. The black people of the empire had turned the tables on the white and now represented a

5 Priestley to Mary Priestley, 28 December 1974.
6 Priestley to Mary Priestley, 17 January 1975.

high percentage of his home town Bradford. Abstract art and literature no longer traced their origins to any traditional roots. The trade unions, once a persecuted minority, threatened to rival parliamentary power. But behind all the revolutionary changes the same intractable problems remained insoluble. Unemployment had never swelled its ranks with such success, psychiatric disturbance involved 10 per cent of the population, divorce ended every third marriage and the horrors of Admass had come no nearer producing happiness – whatever that might be – for thousands of people who continued to complain of all-pervading *angst*.

Priestley now spoke frankly about the details of encroaching age:

> Tendency to delay putting on trousers because one foot is standing on braces. Odd recent behaviour of pipes scattering sparks and hot ashes on carpets and lapels of coats. Going upstairs for something and forgetting on the way what on earth it was. Remembering in detail the face, voice, name, habits of a man met in 1909 but no clues to the man who called last week and is coming again this afternoon . . . Growing horror of stag parties whether pompous or drunken and sharp preference for feminine company, though not in large groups.[7]

He had a renewed 'heart-warming love' of scenery, sky, sunsets, gathering storm clouds and 'those palest and clearest blues that belong to the Kingdom of Heaven'. He held what he called 'constant dialogues with death'. He still claimed to fear doctors more than death. Their sole aim was to keep him alive 'at the expense of all dignity and decency'.[8] There remained something which he had never known before: 'the blessed feeling coming through occasionally like some snatch of a heavenly song, the blessed feeling of *conscious* love. What a prize for fumbling and bewildered old age.'[9] The identity of the prize must be clear to the reader.

Sometimes together, sometimes apart they walked the hedge-bound lanes after lunch, he wearing a beret, using a walking-stick, she elegantly clad in country clothes with a man's stride. What a striking pair they made. Sometimes of a summer evening they sat on the terrace sipping Martinis remembering those heady days when love burned fiercely and satisfactions were scattered in secret

---

7  *Outcries and Asides*, J. B. Priestley, 93–4.
8  ibid., 94.
9  ibid., 95.

places and peace and serenity such as they now had seemed an impossibility. Thirty long years ago it had all begun and now for twenty-five a deeply satisfying relationship had created a third 'entity' in which they merged.

Always enjoying country living it is part of the multiple paradoxes completing the phenomenon known as Jack Priestley that his novels and plays were never set in rural England. Yet he remained the quintessential Englishman. Since his teens he had never properly lived in the north of England but his work drew on the rich life of his birthplace and gave it a vitality of its own. His roots were not regional but national and his commitment to England so powerful that in all the multifarious expeditions which carried him to the remotest parts of the world he still returned to England with relief.

> I have travelled often and sometimes travelled far, and I have never been sorry to see the magical white cliffs again. In those boat trains from Southampton I have stared out of the window with tears in my eyes, not because the chop on my plate was half-raw and the vegetables uneatable . . . but because I was seeing once again the misty trees and the gold-and-white scribble of the buttercups and daisies in the passing meadows. Nobody has praised more enthusiastically than I have the diamond light of the Arizona Desert, but it never catches at my heart as a certain light in England does.

He looked out now on a fine morning in June on just such a light when every leaf and blossom near the house was sharply vivid and melted away into green tenderness . . . This light was newly poignant because he knew that one morning soon he would not be there to see it. For the moment it remained 'heart-breakingly beautiful, turning earth and air into music'.[10]

Unlike so many wealthy writers Priestley never contemplated spending his later years in Greece, the South of France or some forgotten fishing village in the Mediterranean. 'It's too classical and cut-and-dried. Too many damned olives.'[11] Born to a mixture of working- and lower-middle-class roots he migrated to the artistic classes. The rapport remained. It was an Englishman speaking in his work with inside knowledge about his own kind, enlivened by ironic overtones and undertones. Not a man given to bland celebra-

10  *Rain upon Godshill*, J. B. Priestley, 211–12.
11  *J. B. Priestley*, Susan Cooper, 158.

tion of the virtues of the land which bore him, he could still occasionally surrender to some splendid reaffirmations of his faith.

There were no major works in 1974–6. *Outcries and Asides* reprinted many earlier essays and was respectfully reviewed. *The Carfitt Crisis and Two Other Stories* brought together some earlier works and Priestley complained that the critics missed their main point. The *Observer* wrote: 'All three stories read like productions by Mr Priestley's little finger, an instrument that carries such disdainful professionalism exercised over so many decades that criticism is confounded.'

*The Carfitt Crisis* sandwiched a short horror story between two romantic novellas originally conceived in dramatic form. Writing to his old friend Charles Pick, managing director of Heinemann, Priestley said: 'If any reader chooses to see these two novellas as an old writer's toys I shan't take offence even though the ideas that can be discovered in them are serious ideas important to us in the present age . . . this has encouraged me to make an experiment in my manner of narration . . . deliberately avoiding all but the barest description and refusing to offer the usual accounts with which so many novels are overloaded.'

The energy and drive required for full-scale plays and novels had dwindled away. 'I told Jacquetta some time ago that I believed in bad years and good years and that this was going to be a bad one. I am a superstitious man, I'm afraid.'

By January of the following year he was disappointed at the reception of the reissue of *The Image Men* in one volume, but meditated a new novel based on that watershed year in his life, 1913. This he never completed. 'The trouble is that now in my 83rd year I don't enjoy writing any longer having written so much. Yet I can't afford to sit down and do nothing because although money keeps coming in, especially from old plays . . . produced abroad, income tax is so hellishly high and ferocious – I can't save a penny.'[12]

The year 1977 brought the crowning public recognition of someone who had outlived most men of his own generation and crowded so many experiences into his life it seemed beyond the possibility of adequate representation. He was awarded the Order of Merit by the Queen. As everyone knows, the OM confers no title and its recipient is not enrobed in purple with a royal laying on of hands. It is an order in the personal gift of the sovereign, never

12   Priestley to Mary Priestley, 18 January 1977.

awarded to mere politicians and unencumbered by political consultation. Membership is restricted to '24 subjects of the crown whom the Queen considers to have given meritorious service in the Armed Services or towards the advancement of arts, literature and science'.

Twenty-one members arrived that day for the service of thanksgiving in the glittering splendour of Henry VIII's Chapel Royal in St James's Palace. It was an intimate family occasion in a chapel which had been the cradle of English church music for centuries. 'A row of the cleverest old faces in the United Kingdom sat opposite the Queen, the Duke of Edinburgh and Queen Elizabeth, the Queen Mother . . . The music composed by such holders of the Order as Elgar, Vaughan Williams and Benjamin Britten was sung beautifully by the six gentlemen and ten children of the Chapel Royal, worthy descendants of the itinerant chapels of singers of the medieval kings.'[13] The Duke of Edinburgh read the lesson from Ecclesiasticus including the passage which strongly approves of praising famous men.

Sitting in the midst of it all Priestley dourly reflected – famous for what? – remembering how many famous men in his day qualified for infamy. Pleased though he was to be given an honour freed from the usual corruptions he remained uneasy amongst all the pomp and ceremony. 'Anyway,' he commented to Jacquetta, 'they always wait until you're too old to appreciate it.'

When the Savile Club decided to give a special dinner to celebrate the award the question arose, did etiquette permit the display of decorations if wearing mere dinner jackets? It seems that the palace graciously granted the concession which produced a throaty chuckle from the honoured guest.

One among the distinguished guests in the Savile Club's ballroom was Sir Ralph Richardson and his presence led to an awkward moment. Priestley surveyed the rich, candle-lit scene of the Savile ballroom with a mixture of pleasure, irritation and sadness. Called upon unexpectedly to speak, Sir Ralph Richardson was for once at a loss to find the right words and suddenly remembered an episode from earlier days.[14] Arriving at Billingham Manor one day on his motor bike he found that the butler had surveyed his slightly dishevelled appearance with distaste. Richardson was to discuss a play with Priestley who greeted him with 'reasonable warmth'.

13 *The Times*, 18 November 1977.
14 Interview with Sir Ralph Richardson, 9 October 1981.

They were not as yet the close friends they later became and an interval elapsed in which Richardson was 'dying for a drink'. Priestley at last sent the butler to the cellar for a bottle of wine and he returned, placing the bottle on the table. Taking it up Priestley glanced at the label and suddenly exploded, 'You've given him the best claret.'

The story aroused gusts of laughter among Savilians but Jack received it with a half grin which conveyed a mixture of irritation and embarrassment.

Sir Ralph Richardson summed up: 'We have had many distinguished members of the Savile Club but never one who wrote so many books, plays, dabbled in so many arts and made such an impact on millions of people creating – even in the middle of the war – a rapport rarely achieved on such a scale by any other figure since Dickens.'

In the same year came a much lesser ceremony which Priestley regarded with pleasure. He proposed the toast at the centenary celebrations of his old school Belle Vue.

Journalism once a major source of income had fallen away seriously and one foray into the *Sunday Times* ended with a touch of humiliation. Harry Evans asked him to contribute a weekly feature but as the weeks advanced the material was systematically cut until at last it drifted into nothingness.[15]

*Instead of the Trees*, published in 1977, was important among the last books as a significant contribution to autobiography. The quotation on the frontispiece anticipated his death. It was his old and favourite quotation: Edgar, in *King Lear*:

> Men must endure
> Their going hence, even as their coming hither;
> Ripeness is all.

The title of the book was not, as he explained, 'a bit of whimsy'. The two earlier volumes of autobiography had been carefully planned from a certain milieu. The first volume was written in the desert of Arizona, appropriately named *Midnight on the Desert*; the second emerged from his study in the Isle of Wight looking out on Godshill and was entitled *Rain upon Godshill*.

A third, planned volume was to have been set in the giant redwood trees of California, 'tranquil ancients to which I had taken

15  Interview with Jack Lambert, 1 July 1986.

a great fancy'. The Second World War intervened and the years dragged away until at eighty-two he revived the project. By then he had long abandoned the romantic notion of returning to California and 'finding a lodging somewhere near the giant trees' and thus arose the title *Instead of the Trees*.

It was a loosely connected series of essays one moment nostalgic about the past and the next ferociously contemporary. 'Bitter? . . . Certainly I am bitter if only because I am old and *I have had enough of it*. I have paid my whack and now we who are really old – all of us frustrated grandfathers – should at least be let off and not badgered, bullied and mulcted right to the edge of the grave.'[16]

For years he had raged – quite rightly – about the iniquities of income tax on authors whose earnings could be mountainous one year and nothing the next. *Instead of the Trees* reorchestrated the complaint into a whole symphony.

Describing himself as – no hero – he believed that he was half brave half cowardly and perhaps the victim of haunting apprehension because he could not escape the penalties of a heightened imagination. 'What I do know is that time and again I have been horribly frightened and then at a magical stroke terror has vanished and a calm curiosity has taken its place.' Still involved in Jungian theory he explained this experience somewhat hazily: 'Isn't it just possible that at these desperate times without any willing on my part, my ego was taken over by the kind of self the system was telling us to achieve? Do I owe my sudden deliverance not to any Immortal Observer hard to justify but simply to some desultory reading of Jung or this Gurdjieff–Ouspensky System?'[17]

His view of the English had changed dramatically from that expressed in *The English*. England had produced its share of very clever men and women but 'its general level is marked by stupidity. I may be prejudiced here but it does seem to me that there are more stupid people here, some of them in high places, than there are in most Western European countries . . . If we are half ruined now, as we appear to be, I feel it is entirely our own fault.'[18] Rambling, relaxed, *Instead of the Trees* drifted from subject to subject with endearing inconsequentiality. Immensely readable it fell short of the total frankness it implied.

At eighty-four, he said, he lived a life in contradiction to the

16  *Instead of the Trees*, J. B. Priestley, 33.
17  ibid., 53.
18  ibid., 81.

bearded oracle who sat beside the fire in his dressing-gown making gnomic utterances. He described a daily routine which was now relaxed but still very active. He came down to breakfast at nine, glanced at *The Times*, dictated a few letters and returned upstairs to shave and dress at ten thirty a.m. Shortly afterwards he began work downstairs facing the wall as usual and typing – stiffly – until about twelve fifty p.m. His afternoon walk was much shorter than of old and he reflected dourly that too many cars had taken the place of the walkers he once encountered. Reading, thinking and more work occupied the time until tea. Work began again roughly between five thirty and six thirty p.m. 'Only an hour, but an hour of actual writing and not thinking about writing.' At six thirty p.m. he took a shower and changed into different clothes neither more nor less elegant. 'Bed about 11.30 p.m. Read until about one o'clock sometimes later.'[19]

Recapitulation of a schedule gives no account of the tremendous willpower now required to cope not only with the details of ordinary living but to 'keep going' from nine in the morning till midnight. 'I use enough willpower to command an army corps. Is there no fun along the way? Yes, of course; but I wish there was more – and much less effort.'[20]

Recollection included a search for the mistakes he had made in his life, the greatest of which he believed was 'to spend too much time – writing!' He could have followed Jacquetta's example, 'enjoying natural history', or developed his piano-playing beyond amateur strumming, or come to some accommodation with philosophy. Once he had been absorbed in philosophy but the arrival of the 'linguistic fellows' turned him off and he had avoided modern philosophy ever since. 'This is a disgraceful record and if I am now a dissatisfied grumpy old man it serves me right.'

There was a last nostalgic visit to Brookhill in June of 1977. The West Wight, their favourite part of the island, had been overrun and was beginning to resemble Blackpool. Empty, deserted Brookhill looked forlorn but they deliberately ate a picnic on one of its terraces and 'remembered the many happy times we had there with music and all . . . We felt rather sad.'[21]

A visitor in the spring of 1980 approached Kissing Tree unheralded through a blaze of daffodils to hear coming softly on the

19   ibid., 30.
20   ibid.
21   Priestley to Mary Priestley, 20 June 1977.

scented air Brahms's Violin Concerto. Before Priestley became aware, the visitor saw the burly figure on the terrace, his big head sunk forward over his considerable stomach, a Buddhistic figure, half asleep in another world where music transcended commonplace experience. His library of discs reconciled him to many of the ills of ageing. Someone later recalled the Buddhistic image to Priestley who replied with a grin: 'My thoughts were far removed from Buddha – I was thinking of a beautiful young American girl I knew years ago I nearly had an affair with.'[22]

There remained occasions when the beauty of his surroundings, the music and the capacity to reflect half asleep, half awake, took him into deep waters where he continued to grapple with such age-old unanswerable questions as why are we here? Sometimes Jacquetta accompanied him on these wordless occasions and sitting together on the terrace simply to be in each other's company was deeply satisfying. Their lives were shared in a different way now but they continued to make love until Jack was eighty-three. Moreover, new satisfactions replaced old and vanished ones. Photographs show them laughing together on a summer's day among the blossoms on the terrace of Kissing Tree and whatever happiness may mean, it permeates such pictures.

Periodically the well-ordered rhythms of Kissing Tree House were broken into by the arrival of his daughters and their children. Barbara and Sylvia, born of his first marriage to Pat, each had three children, Mary and Rachel, born of his marriage to Jane, had – respectively – three and six, his stepdaughter Angela two and Jacquetta's son by her first marriage, Nicholas, two. Gathered together with ten great-grandchildren, the family constituted a Priestley dynasty but it is doubtful whether Priestley often encountered such a splendid display.

Jacquetta Priestley struggled to recollect an example of the inevitable quarrels which bedevil most marriages and could recollect only one which approximated to a row. She had been lecturing on an Hellenic Swan Tour in the Aegean and returned to find Jack waiting for her in a black hired car, looking very disgruntled. Almost immediately he burst out: 'I've just turned down a C.H. this morning.' His guilt at doing so before consulting her made him bad-tempered. Everything went wrong that day. The car broke down, the lunch was terrible, and they were very late returning home. Within a few hours they were laughing about it all.

22   Interviewee who wishes to remain anonymous.

In January of 1979 he wrote to Mary: 'I am not ill but I do not feel particularly well at any time. I shall probably feel better if I do a little work especially as I have done none lately.'[23]

Shortly afterwards a very strange missive arrived among his ordinary post. Mary had at last changed her name by deed poll to Priestley and she sent him the bill.[24]

In his middle eighties Priestley's insomnia grew worse and there were nights from which he emerged grey and haggard hardly having slept at all. Nightmares interwove with dreaming and one day he told Barbara, 'I think I'm almost manic depressive.' He was troubled by a number of allergies like eczema and hay fever. Where, for years, Jacquetta had tended to be the serious one asking what is the meaning behind it all and Jack the jokey one, dominating the conversation with laughter, now he talked far less and sometimes fell into silences. On one occasion Nancy Mitford came to lunch and he remained so gloomy and withdrawn, his daughters had to redouble their efforts to keep her entertained.

In February of 1984 he experienced a series of gastric attacks which his doctor first thought was gastric 'flu, but the illness developed symptoms characteristic of partial blockage of the bowel and an operation became necessary.[25] His favourite Edward VII Hospital was full and Jacquetta decided that he must have the best possible surgeon ('Mr Todd who had treated his hernia') and tests were carried out in the London Clinic.[26] The tests confirmed a blockage but 'Mr Todd still hoped that it was only a kink or polyp as Jack was in such good general health.'[27]

It was in fact cancer of the bowel. Immediately before the operation Barbara said to Jacquetta, 'I'm so glad you're here to look after him because he is so dear to me.'[28] Whatever differences the family may have had they closed ranks round him in the last years. According to his daughter Barbara it was Jacquetta who willed Jack through the operation. He had 'talked a lot about death' for some time and now he barely survived a major operation. A period of intensive care became necessary. Where before he had seen himself on his deathbed with his family gathered all round him, now the weather was good and he began to enjoy his convalescence,

23  Priestley to Mary Priestley, 13 January 1979.
24  Interview with Mary Priestley, 9 October 1985.
25  Priestley to Mary Priestley, 22 October 1979.
26  Jacquetta Priestley to Dr Charles Lack, 29 April 1984.
27  ibid.
28  Interview with Barbara Wykeham, 15 April 1985.

477

walking about the garden.

A subtler erosion of his defences came when encroaching deafness made it impossible to detect a certain pitch in music and he no longer listened to his records. The great solace of music had been taken from him.

Chronic insomnia persisted and the nightmares came back again. When he walked now he kept within sight of the house and when he talked his words came slower and sometimes he reached out for one that was not there. 'When you die,' he said to Barbara one day, 'you see all the people you have known all over again.'

'Even those you don't like?' she said and he pondered the question without answering.[29]

Talking of life and death to Jacquetta one day he admitted that he 'didn't believe in anything any more'. An author researching a book went to see him in his last year and Jacquetta showed him in, saying: 'It's not one of his good days.' She left the room and almost at once Priestley went to sleep.[30]

Diana Collins remembers that his deafness made him difficult to talk to and he would now retreat into silences. On one occasion Jacquetta had to spend the night at Cambridge and Mrs Collins stayed with him for a day and night, because Jacquetta did not like to leave him alone. 'One afternoon when Jacquetta was upstairs he got out of his chair,' Diana Collins said, 'turned to knock out his pipe and began to fall. Fortunately I caught him just in time . . . He told me that day he was depressed because he could not write any more. "I am a creative man or nothing," he said.'

There came the evening when he did not enjoy his dinner and went to bed 'not feeling well'. Until now he had managed to continue walking up and down the stairs but on the Friday morning he decided to stay in bed.

The doctor was called, pneumonia diagnosed and penicillin prescribed but he did not respond to treatment and his breathing became difficult.

Barbara was one of a few last witnesses. She had telephoned every day and arrived at Kissing Tree with Sylvia on Sunday but it was not until Monday that she realised how ill he had become. A day nurse was already in attendance and Jacquetta now arranged for a night nurse. In the intervals between the two, Jacquetta, Barbara and Sylvia took turns to sit with him 'and he was never alone for a

29  ibid.
30  Interviewee who wishes to remain anonymous, 8 November 1985.

minute'.[31] By Tuesday morning he could no longer talk easily and he simply lay in bed clasping Barbara's hand fondly. She realised that he was saying goodbye and was very distressed. That evening Miss Pudduck (who had been with them since 1937) sat with him for half an hour while Sylvia, Jacquetta and Barbara had dinner. Afterwards they took it in turns to be with him until the doctor and night nurse arrived. By then his hands had become cold, he could not see very well and only just registered when the electric light was switched on.

Sylvia recorded the last moments: 'I took over from Barbara . . . My turn was quiet except that I remember him pointing up to the ceiling as if looking at something beyond it – not towards the electric lights which were elsewhere. Some time later he put his hand over his eyes and said with great difficulty "I can't see." Jacquetta came in to take over and his breathing was by then very laboured.' They each held a hand and presently Jacquetta said, 'His hand has gone cold, hasn't it?' and Sylvia stroked it and agreed. Jacquetta kissed him and said, 'Goodbye, my love!' 'The nurse checked his pulse and asked us to return again later.'[32]

On 14 August Barbara was half asleep in her room at twelve thirty when Sylvia and Jacquetta came in to say it was all over. He had died peacefully with no pain. It was very quiet. In the early hours they heard the owls hooting. A voice familiar to millions of people who had never known him was silent at last.

There was a memorial service in Westminster Abbey. Over 100 distinguished friends gathered in the abbey to pay tribute to someone whose life had deeply intertwined with theirs. The address was given by Diana Collins, Sir Denis Forman read the lesson from Ecclesiastes, Charles Pick read an extract from *Margin Released*, Peggy Ashcroft from *What Happened to Falstaff?* Among them sat Jacquetta, the central figure. Bach's Sonata for Flute in B Minor flowed round the chamber and then Blake's 'Jerusalem' swelled out to the thunder of the organ. Like *Johnson Over Jordan* Priestley remained half in life as well as death because the power of his presence was so vital in the memories of those close to him that temporarily he was among them again.

31  Barbara Wykeham to the author, 9 October 1986.
32  Sylvia Goaman to the author, 14 October 1986.

# Epilogue

Priestley's prodigality and unpredictability made him extremely difficult to place as a writer. His publisher spoke of him as the 'gasfire Dickens' but he preferred to work in the tradition of Fielding and Smollett, creating picaresque works 'crammed with characters bordering on caricature', as Anthony Burgess wrote. At the outset he admired the work of Hugh Walpole and there are those who believe that he has not advanced the novel beyond Walpole's range. 'I remember J. B. Priestley denying to me', Burgess commented, 'that he was a genius but claiming that he had "a hell of a lot of talent". He was not being just to himself. Talent is a small fiddling capacity for producing the conventional and the well-shaped. It rarely means volcanic ebullience. Priestley was volcanic, fertile, often careless but never dull.'[1]

As essayist, novelist, playwright and journalist he remained derivative as much from writers like Wells, as from men of his own generation. He dared to step out of the study into the market-place and if he never fully accustomed himself to the sneers and brickbats, he was highly skilled at retaliation.

The world he created in his works was fundamentally a warm world full of belief in simple values and its strength lies in the 'gusto for the physicality of life – pies with a dark crust, and real ale'. It was a world enjoyed by the middlebrow reader who could respond to those values but such simplifications underestimate Priestley. *The Good Companions* rose above its sentimentality and created a fairy-tale myth, which realised the frustrated fantasies of millions. It was obligatory in the myth that his nice characters should finally reap some form of reward and the nasty be suitable for reformation. As a result academics warned students in English departments about his work and either patronised or derided him, but Priestley's diatribe against Dr Leavis was a splendid reprisal. Concern for the human condition and compassion for the average man permeated his work.

1   *Observer*, 19 August 1984.

As a secular preacher and broadcaster he appealed to his audience to respect the higher forms of common sense and warned against the comfortable delusions of outdated traditions. His unsystematic socialism included a touch of the Old Tory and he could crustily dismiss the shortcomings of pop singers with swingeing invective. An implacable enemy of Admass, his relations with political parties were always uneasy because his independence of mind, nonconformist values and romanticism made compromise difficult. His humanism was presented with something approaching heartiness. Decency ranked high in his moral values and he shrank from such extreme notions as wickedness.

There were so many Priestleys. One, the warm, sane, highly talented human being, left the world a richer place than he found it. Another, the gloomy, cantankerous grumbler, outraged many a stranger encountered on the wing. His bluntness was part of his sincerity, and he could be very provocative. If he made fun of people, mimicking them unmercifully on occasion, it was never black humour with malicious intent. Underneath all the many selves there persisted a shy, kind, compassionate man whose good intentions were frequently distorted by the interventions of everyday living.

Not in the strict meaning of the word an intellectual, Priestley was complicated in a different and rewarding way. If he overdid the powers of Jung's creative unconscious he certainly dwelt for long periods in that twilit world of the imagination where he encountered subtleties far beyond the range of *The Good Companions*. His claim that he did not give a hang about literary style was flatly contradicted in advanced middle age by the following: 'As I write this I have behind me a quarter of a century's work in the theatre, and there are few tricks of the trade I do not know. With what result? I have to plan and plot far more carefully than I did twenty years ago: I write at about half the speed. I have to rewrite whole scenes where once I might not have changed a hundred words in a complete script: and even then I commit blunders and fall into traps I would once have avoided with ease.' In all his dialogue his aim was to build up from ordinary speech to what he called 'heightened realism'.

As a novelist he could be a superb entertainer and his verbal exuberance was interlaced with telling social comment. His philosophising lacked originality and there were those who felt he elevated a number of statements above their true philosophic value. He sometimes drew on the miseries of life and the darker places of

481

physical reality to redeem many a work from superficiality. His love of England and the English shone through what one writer described as his 'crusty prose and crotchets'.

It was his capacity to evoke time and place as an immediate experience alive on the pages, drawing the reader into the fantastic wonders of Death Valley, or the wastes of Peru, or the dingy alleys of Angel Pavement, which made alien places a reality to those who had never visited them. This power over places was brilliantly realised by Proust in Balbec, Joyce in Dublin and Balzac in Paris but since their day such realism has become unfashionable. Priestley vividly evoked the social scene and skilfully interweaved the lives of his many-sided but uncomplicated characters. He gave thousands of readers the shock of recognition. There were things they knew about themselves and the human condition of which they were unaware. Priestley brought their hidden intuitions to the surface and the experience gave great pleasure. Some of the novels were self-indulgent, needed cutting and lost their grip but nobody would deny his narrative gift.

In his element with Yorkshire men and women he ranged across the social classes, deliberately isolating the upper classes. (How Evelyn Waugh berated him.) Certainly a rare excursion into upper-class ambience produced some nasty caricatures in *Black-out in Gretley*. Country life did not interest him in his novels and no agricultural worker interrupts his smooth-flowing narrative. His dialogue in plays and novels was not innovative because his 'social realism' wanted to mirror dialect as closely as possible.

He remained an eloquent prophet of the divide between north and south and suffered total scorn from some Bradfordians for running away from his roots. As Donald MacRae has said: 'Priestley is open to surprise and therefore he sees further and more clearly than most into the jungle of English social arrangements and expression. He does not take England for granted.'[2] Nor did he make the poor and the lower classes part of a timeless order. 'He takes neither England nor the English as something given but within his limitations he instead proclaims their life and their diversity.'

Perhaps artistic deception is practised. Industrial pollution, unemployment, deprivation are dwelt upon but not to the exclusion of the wonderful brotherhood of Yorkshire people whose life

2  *The World of J. B. Priestley*, ed. Donald MacRae, ch. VIII.

we are unlucky enough to have missed. Recollection of youth endows Bradford with its own glamour even when seen through the eyes of a young and very insecure youth.

The London of *Angel Pavement* has a reality no less vivid. 'We often think the seediness of England was discovered by Mr Graham Greene. Mr Priestley was there before him. He is not melodramatic but just clear and accurate. *Angel Pavement* is about the long decline of the 1920s and 30s. It is still a reality changed but not abolished. It is a London most of us do not know.'[3]

People are more important than places – a cliché heavily under-written by Priestley. He enjoyed creating his characters with gusto. Oakroyd, Jollifant, Golspie, Linden, Saltana came alive and lived with him for long periods. They are not done in depth. They do not search their souls in introspective monologues. They remain living, laughing, emotional human beings who mediate some of the great events of human experience through Priestley's sensibility.

Priestley's books are still read today. Only last year, 1987, *The Good Companions* was reprinted once more. If there are limitations in the world they inhabit and the thoughts they engender that is necessary to any representation of average human beings and their lives.

The plays are another matter. Critics have invoked every theoretical device to decide whether he was a better playwright than novelist without much success. Individual plays and novels tower above others thus confusing the scene. Theatrically he took risks, he married the unmarriageable, he experimented with what were then fashionable theories of time, which invited disaster. He could fall over into sentimentality and sometimes his dialogue which set out to heighten common speech merely reported it, but he remained a very effective playwright who reflected life in multi-faceted detail and entertained millions throughout the world. Priestley lifted the commonplace thriller above its limited range, produced one classic broad comedy, and several other plays which are alive in repertoire. At least three of his plays were revived in the West End of London in 1986–7.

His reputation in the theatre was capricious and he learnt to roll with the punches but he could never quite face the fact that there are no longer any fixed criteria of dramatic judgement and always assumed that his own evaluations fulfilled that ideal. Late in life he sometimes claimed not to read reviews only to be discovered

3   ibid.

furtively investigating them one Sunday morning. If the costs of production had not been so prohibitive he might have continued writing plays but whether any further development was within his range we do not know. Undoubtedly another broad comedy like *When We Are Married* would have wide audiences but some of the more serious plays are period pieces in the light of the modern theatre. Such period pieces are becoming popular again. The dreary desert of dramatic experiment for experiment's sake has thrown up few genuinely original plays. Some of Priestley's have a perennial life: *Dangerous Corner*, *Time and the Conways*, *An Inspector Calls* and *When We Are Married*, continue to be produced somewhere in the world at irregular intervals. There remains the glittering display of *A Severed Head*.

His *Literature and Western Man* was breathtakingly ambitious, permeated with his personality and a successful bridge between the middlebrow reader and writer. As we have seen, many another author would have considered its 650 pages a feat sufficient to establish his reputation. His three socio-historical volumes were not academic history but something of a *tour de force*. As for *English Journey* its footsteps were retraced by Beryl Bainbridge on television, but the presence of his powerful personality was missing. The book brings back the quintessential Jack Priestley: Priestley the Englishman.

Priestley's *English Journey* has been compared to Cobbett's *Rural Rides*, but their styles, preferences and temperaments remain different. Both are full of the gamy personality and gossipy diversions of their authors but Cobbett, as Donald MacRae has pointed out, is a radical conservative which flatly contradicts Priestley's conservative radicalism. Priestley's confrontation with industrial pollution, unemployment and their consequences is unrelenting. He derives much more from Orwell's *Road to Wigan Pier* and Bakke's *The Unemployed Man* only to redeem their bleak dismay with his unfailing touch of optimistic pessimism. 'I still believe what is wrong can be put right,' he wrote in *Thoughts in the Wilderness* in 1957.

There remains a little-known play of Priestley's, *Summer Day's Dream*, which brings him right back into the contemporary scene. Written in 1949 it was set in 1975 and its prophecies were premature but alarmingly prescient. Dream-like in conception the play married past and present to a nightmare future. Atom war has devastated England and the scattered handful of surviving people are reduced to primitive attempts at farming, bartering, and self-created diversions. Technically unsophisticated, in 1949 Priestley did not realise that such a picture was romantic but a midsummer dream gave him artistic licence. World power is divided between Russia and America who compete peacefully for the redevelopment of material progress. In the light of modern technical knowledge the play travesties the realities of atom war but it is a morality tale breaking the bonds of verisimilitude. An American administrator, a Russian female bureaucrat and an Indian scientist arrive at a crumbling mansion on the South Downs where the simple back to nature movement is gathering pace. Instead of imposing efficiency and production targets the three accidental intruders are drawn into the deeply satisfying rhythms of the natural life, but their sense of loyalty to their ideology drags them away again. They have failed to galvanise the oafish peasants back to civilised living but leave uneasily aware of a mysterious harmony which they themselves lack.

Nothing could be further from what we now know will be the consequences of an atom war but it crystallised one strand in Priestley's philosophy which resurrected the time-worn belief in escape from Admass horrors back to simpler forms of living. Derivative from Rousseau, idealists have fought over the years to justify their belief in resurrecting a past way of life. Such resurrection would mean dismantling the modern state, and anarchy and chaos would seem to be too high a price to pay. If this clashed with his periodic intervention in political life here and now he had a great gift for accommodating opposites when it suited his purposes. Sexual loyalty could surrender to deviation, children become a mixed blessing, socialism riddled with self-assertion, good manners a prerequisite of rudeness, generosity inhibited by meanness, vanity qualified by self-laceration and a deep sense of another dimension in life vaguely derisory to the solid, down-to-earth, pipe-smoking Yorkshireman.

There remained the brooding Priestley eternally mulling over the meaning of life who did not originate new interpretations but underwent psychological struggles in his search for new insights. His career demonstrated a new thread of mobility in the classes from working and lower middle to middle-class professional which remained an unrealised dream in general but was supremely epitomised in his own life. So many phases in his development were representative of unfolding English history between the years 1894 and 1984.

Where in all this was simple, old, down-to-earth, Jolly Jack

Priestley? Priestley answered the question brusquely in *Thoughts in the Wilderness*: 'There never was a Jolly Jack.' When Desmond Flower, once managing director of Cassell, met Priestley's publisher Cass Canfield in New York, Canfield said: 'I hope you don't mind. We've got Jack Priestley coming. Some people simply cannot stand him.' When Mary Merrington spoke to me of her love affair with the same man she said he was an enchanting companion.

If the bluff Yorkshireman frequently broke into the assembled company of his many selves and sent them flying in confusion, it was certainly the solid pipe-smoking writer who remained one basis of all the rest. There was another. Consider Priestley through the eyes of his favourite analyst Jung, who believed that two of the most important components of his model of the psyche were the Persona and the Shadow. According to Jung, 'the Persona is a compromise between the individual and society as to what a man should appear to be'. Pouring psychic energy into the Persona some people come to believe that the projected image is the real self and in consequence lose contact with the actual self – Self-As-It-Is. Whereas the Persona deliberately externalises itself the Shadow is the sum of those characteristics we wish to conceal, not only from the world but also from ourselves. Possessing considerable manipulative power the Shadow can project itself on to other people while the Self rejects responsibility for its behaviour. Despite the sense of jargon pretentiously overwhelming what could be spelt out in simpler terms, some of this could be applied to Priestley. He was adept at trying out different Personas and it could be said that the warm, shy, sensitive Priestley did get overwhelmed. As for the Shadow – yes – there were aspects which he wished to conceal from the public, but it is doubtful whether he concealed them from himself.

When I set out to explore the tumultuous hinterland stretching for miles in every direction which was the life of Jack Priestley, I entered some very rough country. There were many compensations. In the beginning I had reservations about some aspects of the man and his work. In the final analysis I came to admire many aspects of both. Finishing my book, all professional preoccupations with objectivity vanished. I experienced a sense of loss.

# Appendix
## Royalties of English Plays, 1956–7

| | | | | | |
|---|---|---|---|---|---|
| December | 1955 | £143 18s 9d | January | 1957 | £64 0s 8d |
| | | 632 7s 2d | | | 431 0s 4d |
| January | 1956 | 51 6s 11d | February | 1957 | 363 3s 3d |
| | | 169 5s 3d | | | 17 9s 1d |
| February | 1956 | 513 4s 0d | March | 1957 | 69 1s 3d |
| | | 266 9s 7d | | | 347 5s 6d |
| March | 1956 | 487 12s 4d | April | 1957 | 1,272 4s 11d |
| | | 110 11s 5d | | | 24 2s 2d |
| April | 1956 | 871 10s 11d | May | 1957 | 21 3s 6d |
| | | | | | 424 1s 10d |
| May | 1956 | 140 16s 8d | June | 1957 | 390 1s 2d |
| | | 682 16s 7d | | | |
| June | 1956 | 162 6s 6d | July | 1957 | 745 9s 11d |
| | | 364 17s 11d | | | |
| July | 1956 | 28 16s 10d | August | 1957 | 321 7s 1d |
| | | 245 12s 11d | | | |
| August | 1956 | 160 9s 1d | September | 1957 | 549 8s 4d |
| | | 355 12s 11d | | | |
| September | 1956 | 597 4s 6d | October | 1957 | 859 13s 7d |
| | | 209 9s 9d | | | |
| October | 1956 | 499 4s 1d | November | 1957 | 596 7s 2d |
| | | 173 19s 10d | December | 1957 | 810 15s 2d |
| November | 1956 | 231 4s 7d | | | |
| December | 1956 | 252 19s 1d | | | |
| | | 47 16s 9d | | | |

Source: A. D. Peters Ltd. (Literary Agents)
Correspondence files relating to J. B. Priestley: accounts 1956–7

487

# Select
# Bibliography

## Works by J. B. Priestley

*The Chapman of Rhymes*, Alexander Moring Ltd, 1918.
*Brief Diversions*, Bowes & Bowes Ltd, 1922.
*Papers from Lilliput*, Bowes & Bowes Ltd, 1922.
*I For One*, John Lane, The Bodley Head Ltd, 1923.
*Figures in Modern Literature*, John Lane, The Bodley Head Ltd, 1924.
*The English Comic Characters*, John Lane, The Bodley Head Ltd, 1925.
*George Meredith*, Macmillan & Co. Ltd, 1926 (*English Men of Letters* Series edited by J. C. Squire).
*Essays of To-day and Yesterday, J. B. Priestley*, George Harrap & Co. Ltd, 1926.
*Talking, One of a Series of Essays Entitled: These Diversions*, Jarrolds Publishers, 1926.
*Adam in Moonshine*, William Heinemann Ltd, 1927.
*Open House, A Book of Essays*, William Heinemann Ltd, 1927.
*Thomas Love Peacock*, Macmillan & Co. Ltd, 1927.
*Benighted*, William Heinemann Ltd, 1927.
*The English Novel*, Ernest Benn Ltd, 1927.
*Apes and Angels, A Book of Essays*, Methuen & Co. Ltd, 1928.
*Farthing Hall*, by Hugh Walpole and J. B. Priestley, Macmillan & Co. Ltd, 1929.
*English Humour*, Longmans Green & Co. Ltd, 1929.
*The Good Companions*, William Heinemann Ltd, 1929.
*The Balconinny and Other Essays*, Methuen & Co. Ltd, 1929.
*The Town Major of Miraucourt*, William Heinemann Ltd, 1930.
*Angel Pavement*, William Heinemann Ltd, 1930.
*Dangerous Corner, A Play in Three Acts*, William Heinemann Ltd, 1932.
*Faraway*, William Heinemann Ltd, 1932.
*Self-Selected Essays*, William Heinemann Ltd, 1932.
*Wonder Hero*, William Heinemann Ltd, 1933.
*The Roundabout, A Comedy in Three Acts*, William Heinemann Ltd, 1933.

*I'll Tell You Everything*, by J. B. Priestley and Gerald Bullett, The Macmillan Company, 1932.

*Laburnum Grove, An Immoral Comedy in Three Acts*, William Heinemann Ltd, 1934.

*English Journey, Being a Rambling but Truthful Account of What One Man Saw and Heard and Felt and Thought During a Journey Through England During the Autumn of the Year 1933*, William Heinemann Ltd in association with Victor Gollancz Ltd, 1934.

*Eden End, A Play in Three Acts*, William Heinemann Ltd, 1934.

*Cornelius, A Business Affair in Three Transactions*, William Heinemann Ltd, 1935.

*The Good Companions, A Play in Two Acts by J. B. Priestley and Edward Knoblock (from the novel by J. B. Priestley)*, Samuel French Ltd, 1935.

*Three Plays and a Preface*, William Heinemann Ltd, 1935.

*Charles Dickens*, Thomas Nelson, 1936.

*Bees on the Boat Deck, A Comedy in Two Acts*, William Heinemann Ltd, 1936.

*They Walk in the City, The Lovers in the Stone Forest*, William Heinemann Ltd, 1936.

*Midnight on the Desert, A Chapter of Autobiography*, William Heinemann Ltd, 1937.

*Time and the Conways, A Play in Three Acts*, William Heinemann Ltd, 1937.

*Mystery at Greenfingers, A Comedy of Detection*, Samuel French Ltd, 1937.

*I Have Been Here Before, A Play in Three Acts*, William Heinemann Ltd, 1937.

*People at Sea, A Play in Three Acts*, William Heinemann Ltd, 1937.

*The Doomsday Men, An Adventure*, William Heinemann Ltd, 1938.

*When We Are Married, A Yorkshire Farcical Comedy*, William Heinemann Ltd, 1938.

*Johnson Over Jordan, The Play and All About It (an Essay)*, William Heinemann Ltd, 1939.

*Rain upon Godshill, A Further Chapter of Autobiography*, William Heinemann Ltd, 1939.

*Let the People Sing*, William Heinemann Ltd, 1939.

*Postscripts*, William Heinemann Ltd, 1940.

*Out of the People*, William Collins Ltd in association with William Heinemann Ltd, 1941.

*Black-out in Gretley, A story of – and for – Wartime*, William Heinemann Ltd, 1942.

*Britain at War*, Harper & Brothers Inc., 1942.

*Daylight on Saturday, A Novel about an Aircraft Factory*, William Heinemann Ltd, 1943.

*British Women Go To War*, 49 Colour Photographs by P. G. Hennell, William Collins Ltd, 1943.

*Manpower, The Story of Britain's Mobilisation for War*, His Majesty's Stationery Office, 1944.

*Desert Highway, A Play in Two Acts and an Interlude*, William Heinemann Ltd, 1944.

*They Came to a City*, Samuel French Ltd, 1944.

*Three Men in New Suits*, William Heinemann Ltd, 1945.

'Letter to a Returning Serviceman', Home & Van Thal Ltd, 1945.

*Russian Journey*, Writers Group of the Society for Cultural Relations with the USSR, 1946.

*Bright Day*, William Heinemann Ltd, 1946.

*Ever Since Paradise, An Entertainment Chiefly Referring to Love and Marriage*, With Music by Dennis Arundell, Samuel French Ltd, 1946.

*The Secret Dream*, Turnstile Press Ltd, 1946.

*The Arts Under Socialism, Being a Lecture Given to the Fabian Society*, Turnstile Press Ltd, 1947.

*Theatre Outlook*, Nicholson & Watson Ltd, 1947.

*An Inspector Calls, A Play in Three Acts*, William Heinemann Ltd, 1947.

*Music at Night, A Play*, Samuel French Ltd, 1947.

*The Long Mirror, A Play in Three Acts*, Samuel French Ltd, 1947.

*The Rose & Crown, A Play in One Act*, Samuel French Ltd, 1947.

*The Linden Tree, A Play in Two Acts and Four Scenes*, William Heinemann Ltd, 1948.

*The Golden Fleece, A Comedy in Three Acts*, Samuel French Ltd, 1948.

*The Olympians, An Opera in Three Acts*, Libretto by J. B. Priestley, Music by Arthur Bliss, Novello & Co. Ltd, 1949.

*Home Is Tomorrow, A Play in Two Acts*, William Heinemann Ltd, 1949.

*Delight*, William Heinemann Ltd, 1949.

*Bright Shadow, A Play of Detection in Three Acts*, Samuel French Ltd, 1950.

*Summer Day's Dream, A Play in Two Acts*, Samuel French Ltd, 1950.

*Festival at Farbridge*, William Heinemann Ltd, 1951.

*Dragon's Mouth, A Dramatic Quartet in Two Parts*, by Jacquetta Hawkes and J. B. Priestley, William Heinemann Ltd, 1952.

*Treasure on Pelican, A Play in Three Acts*, Evans Brothers Ltd, 1953.

*The Magicians*, William Heinemann Ltd, 1954.

*Low Notes on a High Level, A Frolic*, William Heinemann Ltd, 1954.

*Journey Down a Rainbow*, by J. B. Priestley and Jacquetta Hawkes, Heinemann/Cresset, 1955.

*The Writer in a Changing Society*, Hand and Flower Press Ltd, 1956.

*All About Ourselves and Other Essays*, chosen and introduced by Eric Gillett, William Heinemann Ltd, 1956.

*The Scandalous Affair of Mr Kettle and Mrs Moon, A Comedy in Three Acts*, Samuel French Ltd, 1956.

*The Art of the Dramatist, A Lecture Together with Appendices and Discursive Notes*, William Heinemann Ltd, 1957.

*Thoughts in the Wilderness*, William Heinemann Ltd, 1957.

*The Glass Cage, A Play in Two Acts*, Samuel French Ltd, 1958.

*Literature and Western Man*, William Heinemann Ltd, 1960.

*Saturn Over the Water, An Account of His Adventures in London, South America and Australia by Tim Bedford, Painter; Edited – with Some Preliminary and Concluding Remarks – by Henry Sulgrave; and Here Presented to the Reading Public*, William Heinemann Ltd, 1961.

*Charles Dickens, A Pictorial Biography*, Thames & Hudson Ltd, 1961.

*The Shapes of Sleep, A Tropical Tale*, William Heinemann Ltd, 1962.

*Margin Released, A Writer's Reminiscences and Reflections*, William Heinemann Ltd, 1962.

*A Severed Head, A Play in Three Acts*, by Iris Murdoch and J. B. Priestley, Chatto & Windus Ltd, 1964.

*Sir Michael and Sir George, A Tale of COSMA and DISCUS and the New Elizabethans*, William Heinemann Ltd, 1964.

*LOST EMPIRES, Being Richard Herncastle's Account of His Life on the Variety Stage from November 1913 to August 1914 together with a Prologue and Epilogue*, William Heinemann Ltd, 1965.

*Man and Time*, Aldus Books Ltd in association with W. H. Allen Ltd, 1964.

*The Moments*, William Heinemann Ltd, 1966.

*The World of J. B. Priestley*, chosen and introduced by Donald G. MacRae, 1967.

*Out of Town*, Vol. One of *The Image Men*, William Heinemann Ltd, 1968.

*Trumpets Over the Sea*, William Heinemann Ltd, 1968.

*London End*, Vol. Two of *The Image Men*, William Heinemann Ltd, 1968.

*All England Listened, The Wartime Broadcasts*, Chilmark Ltd, 1968.

*Essays of Five Decades*, William Heinemann Ltd, 1969.

*The Prince of Pleasure*, William Heinemann Ltd, 1969.

*Time and the Conways, and Other Plays*, Penguin Books Ltd, 1969.

*When We Are Married, and Other Plays*, Penguin Books Ltd, 1969.

*Charles Dickens and His World*, Thames & Hudson Ltd, 1969.

*The Edwardians*, William Heinemann Ltd, 1970.

*Snoggle, A Story for Anybody Between 9 and 90*, William Heinemann Ltd, 1971.

*Victoria's Heyday*, William Heinemann Ltd, 1972.

*Over the Long High Wall*, William Heinemann Ltd, 1972.

*The English*, William Heinemann Ltd, 1973.

*A Visit to New Zealand*, William Heinemann Ltd, 1974.
*Outcries and Asides*, William Heinemann Ltd, 1974.
*The Carfitt Crisis*, William Heinemann Ltd, 1975.
*Particular Pleasures*, William Heinemann Ltd, 1975.
*English Humour*, William Heinemann Ltd, 1976.
*Instead of the Trees*, William Heinemann Ltd, 1977.
*The Works of J. B. Priestley*, intended to be a definitive collected edition, began publication in 1931 and five volumes appeared before 1940. Another volume was published in 1947 and then the whole project lapsed. A twenty-six volume edition of Priestley's works was issued by Heron Books Ltd, in 1968–9.

## Periodical Studies

'J. B. Priestley, Author of *The Good Companions*', *Wilson Library Bulletin*, February 1930.
'J. B. Priestley, Servant of the Comic Spirit', Dorothea Lawrence Mann, *Bookmark*, May 1931.
'J. B. Priestley, A Yorkshireman at Large', F. L. Stevens, *Everyman*, 27 August 1931.
'Mr Priestley's Novels', Edward Shanks, *London Mercury*, July 1932.
'The Case of Mr J. B. Priestley', Vernon Fane, *Sphere*, 8 August 1936.
'J. B. Priestley, All-Round Man of Letters', John T. Frederick, *English Journal*, May 1938.
'The Men Who Speak for Britain', *London Calling* 43, 4 July 1940.
'Priestley on the Russian Stage', Simon Drieden, *Theatre World*, October 1945.
'Profile of J. B. Priestley', Peter Noble, *Theatre*, Spring 1946.
'J. B. Priestley', *Writers of Today*, edited by Denys Val Baker, Sidgwick & Jackson Ltd, 1946.
'The Futility of Mr Priestley', Michael Foot, *Tribune*, 16 January 1949.
'J. B. Priestley – The Butt of the Intellectuals', S. K. Hudson, *School Librarian*, March 1950.
'Peace and Mr Priestley', Ivor Montagu, *Labour Monthly*, June 1950.
'Contemporary British Dramatists – J. B. Priestley', *Drama*, Winter 1952.
'Bradford Enchanted', J. C. Trewin', *Dramatists of Today*, 1953.
'Magnificent Grumbler', David Millwood, *Books & Bookmen*, October 1955.
'The Priestley I Know', Richard Church, *TV Monthly*, February 1956.
'Anything Wrong with Priestley?', Evelyn Waugh, *Spectator*, 13 September 1957.
'I Won't Go With The Sentimental Three', Henry Fairlie, *Daily Mail*, 6 March 1958.

'I've Had Enough of This Do-Gooder Priestley Hamming It Up', *Daily Mail*, 13 March 1958.
'Lunch with J. B. Priestley', John Braine, *Encounter*, 1958.
'Storytelling Plus Ideas, J. B. Priestley discusses his books with the Editor', *Books & Bookmen*, July 1961.
'Priestley Celebrates 40 Years as a Writer', John Pearson, *Sunday Times*, 23 September 1967.
'J. B. Priestley, Man of Letters', A. E. Day, *Library Review*, Summer 1969.
'John Boynton Priestley', Makers of the Twentieth Century, *Sunday Times Magazine*, 31 August 1969.
'Big Daddy', Michael Billington, *Guardian*, 24 August 1973.
'Priestley and the Art of the Dramatist', David Wright, *Drama*, Spring 1974.
'J. B. Priestley At Eighty Chuffs But Works On', *New York Times*, 6 April 1974.

## Celebrations of Birthdays

'Priestley on the Brink of Seventy', *Sunday Telegraph*, 6 September 1964.
'Jack's All Right', Jacquetta Hawkes, *TV Times,* 11 September 1964.
'Birthday Letter', Kingsley Martin, *New Statesman*, 11 September 1964.
'J. B. Priestley at Seventy', Gareth Lloyd Evans, *Manchester Guardian*, 12 September 1964.
'The Disappearing All-Rounder', *The Times* (Fourth Leader), 14 September 1964.
'That's J. B. Priestley For You', *Sunday Times Magazine*, 7 September 1969.
'The 75th Birthday of the Glowering Pudding', Anne Chisholm, *Radio Times*, 11 September 1969.
'A Birthday Letter', Paul Johnson, *New Statesman*, 11 September 1969.
'Priestley: One Hell of a Lot of Talent . . . A Birthday Portrait', *The Listener*, 12 September 1974.
'Union Jack', David Hughes, *Guardian*, 14 September 1974.
'A Time for Celebration', *Sunday Times*, 8 September 1974.

## Interviews

'The Best of Good Companions: My Husband, by His Wife: J. B. Priestley', *Daily Express*, October 1934.

'Mrs Priestley As Told to Winifred Loraine: We Are Such Good Companions', *Daily Mail*, 9 November 1938.
'A Day Off with J. B. Priestley', *Weekly Illustrated*, 1 September 1934.

## Books concerning J. B. Priestley

R. Acland, *How It Can Be Done*, 1943.
J. Agate, *Ego*, vols 1–9, 1935–48.
J. Atkins, *The Last of the Sages*, 1981.
D. Barker, *A Man of Principle*, 1963.
A. Bliss, *As I Remember*, 1970.
J. Braine, *J. B. Priestley*, 1978.
A. Briggs, *The History of Broadcasting in the United Kingdom* (4 vols), 1961–79.
L. Browne, *J. B. Priestley*, 1957.
C. Chaplin, *My Autobiography*, 1969.
R. Clark, *Bertrand Russell*, 1975.
L. John Collins, *Faith Under Fire*, 1966.
S. Cooper, *J. B. Priestley, Portrait of an Author*, 1970.
B. Crick, *George Orwell*, 1980.
A. E. Day, *A Bibliography of Priestley*, 1980.
B. Dean, *Autobiography* (2 vols), 1970–3.
A. Dent, *Preludes and Studies*, 1942.
M. Drabble, *Arnold Bennett*, 1975.
C. Driver, *The Disarmers*, 1964.
G. L. Evans, *J. B. Priestley – the Dramatist*, 1964.
J. Forsyth, *Tyrone Guthrie*, 1976.
J. Gielgud, *An Actor and His Time*, 1979.
G. Greene, *Stamboul Train*, 1947.
T. Guthrie, *Astonish Us*, 1977.
T. Guthrie, *Life in the Theatre*, 1960.
S. Haffner, *Profiles*, 1954.
R. Hart-Davis, *Hugh Walpole*, 1963.
J. J. Hawkes, *A Land*, 1951.
J. J. Hawkes, *Dragon's Mouth*, 1952.
R. Hayman, *John Gielgud*, 1971.
D. Hughes, *J. B. Priestley, an Informal Study of His Work*, 1958.
C. G. Jung, *Collected Letters* (2 vols), 1973–6.
J. Lehmann, *Coming to London*, 1957.
C. Mackenzie, *My Life*, 1960–70.
D. MacRae (ed.), *The World of J. B. Priestley*, 1967.
H. V. Marrot, *Life and Letters of John Galsworthy*, 1935.
K. Martin, *Autobiography*, 1968.

G. Orwell, *Collected Essays*, 1966.
C. H. Rolph, *Life and Letters of Kingsley Martin*, 1973.
E. Sprigge, *Sybil Thorndike*, 1971.
C. Sykes, *Evelyn Waugh*, 1975.
V. Woolf, *Diaries* (4 vols), 1915–1935.
K. Young, *J. B. Priestley*, 1977.


'J. B. Priestley: An Exhibition of Manuscripts and Books (Austin, Texas)', Humanities Research Center, the University of Texas.

# Index